MATISSE IN THE 1930s

MATISSE IN THE 1930s

PHILADELPHIA MUSEUM OF ART | MUSÉE DE L'ORANGERIE | RMN–GRAND PALAIS
IN ASSOCIATION WITH
YALE UNIVERSITY PRESS, NEW HAVEN AND LONDON

EXHIBITION ORGANIZATION

Published on the occasion of the exhibition *Matisse in the 1930s* at the Philadelphia Museum of Art, October 20, 2022–January 29, 2023, and *Matisse: Cahiers d'art – Le tournant des années 1930* at the Musée de l'Orangerie, Paris, February 28–May 29, 2023, and the Musée Matisse Nice, June 23–September 24, 2023.

This exhibition was organized jointly by the Philadelphia Museum of Art, the Établissement Public du Musée d'Orsay et du Musée de l'Orangerie – Valéry-Giscard-d'Estaing, Paris, and the Musée Matisse Nice.

CURATORS

Matthew Affron
Muriel and Philip Berman Curator of Modern Art, Philadelphia Museum of Art

Cécile Debray
President, Musée National Picasso–Paris

Claudine Grammont
Director, Musée Matisse Nice

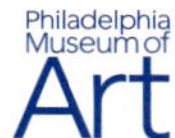

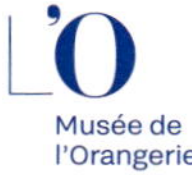

MUSÉEMATISSE

PHILADELPHIA MUSEUM OF ART

Timothy Rub
Director Emeritus

Alphonso Atkins Jr.
Miller Worley Deputy Director for Diversity, Equity, Inclusion, and Access

Karleen Gardner
Kathleen C. Sherrerd Deputy Director for Learning and Engagement

Katie Reilly
Deputy Director for Digital Resources and Content Strategy

Jessica Sharpe
Deputy Director for Visitor Experience

Hyunsoo Woo
Pappas-Sarbanes Deputy Director for Collections and Exhibitions

Jennifer Thompson
Gloria and Jack Drosdick Curator of European Painting and Sculpture

Yana Balson
Director of Exhibition Planning

Kara Furman
Associate Registrar for Exhibitions

Emily Rice
Collections Assistant

Jonathan Peterson
Director of Development

EXHIBITION DESIGN – PHILADELPHIA

Jack Schlechter
Park Family Director of Exhibition Design

Jillian Matthews
Exhibition Designer

Luis Bravo
Director of Graphic Design

Andrew Slavinskas
Lighting Designer

MUSÉE DE L'ORANGERIE

Établissement Public du Musée d'Orsay et du Musée de l'Orangerie – Valéry-Giscard-d'Estaing, Paris

Christophe Leribault
President, Musées d'Orsay et de l'Orangerie

Claire Bernardi
Director, Musée de l'Orangerie

Pierre-Emmanuel Lecerf
General Administrator

Virginie Donzeaud
Deputy General Administrator

Nathalie Vaguer-Verdier
Deputy Director, Musée de l'Orangerie

Clémence Maillard
Director of Exhibitions

Maud Ramier
Exhibition Manager

Guillaume Blanc
Director of Audiences

Sophie Bauer
Interim Director of Performing Arts and Public Programs

Hélène Charbonnier
Director of Digital

Amélie Hardivillier
Director of Communication

Guillaume Roux
Director of Development and International Relations

EXHIBITION DESIGN – PARIS

Sylvie Jodar
Exhibition Designer

Tania Hagemeister
Graphic Designer

Thomas Eschbach
Registrar for the works of the Musée de l'Orangerie

MUSÉE MATISSE NICE

The Musée Matisse is a municipal institution of the city of Nice. It is sponsored by the State and holds the "Musée de France" title, according to the terms of the January 4, 2022, law. The city of Nice is represented by its current mayor, Christian Estrosi.

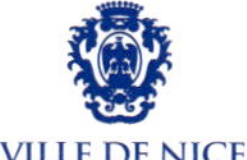

Claudine Grammont
Director

Aymeric Jeudy
Deputy Director

Laurent Magnaud
Director of Administration and Finance
With the help of Patricia Nunzi

Florence Perez
Director of Collections

Alix Agret
Head of Documentation for the Collections and of the Library

Laurence Schlosser
Head of Publishing, Images, and Photo Library

Sylvie Garet
Head of Public Outreach

Christine Grillo, Maria Mascalchi, Edwige Rzepa, and Laurence Vautron
Visitor Experience Associates

Anthony Danet
Building Manager

ACKNOWLEDGMENTS

We wish to express our deep gratitude to the heads of public and private institutions who, through the generous loans of exceptional pieces from their collections, were vital contributors in making this exhibition possible:

Austria
Vienna
Albertina

Canada
Toronto
Art Gallery of Ontario

Denmark
Copenhagen
Statens Museum for Kunst

France
Bordeaux
Musée des Beaux-Arts

Issy-les-Moulineaux
Archives Henri Matisse

Le Cateau-Cambrésis
Musée Départemental Matisse

Lyon
Musée des Beaux-Arts

Paris
Bibliothèque Nationale de France
Daniel Malingue, Malingue S.A., Paris
Musée d'Art Moderne
Musée National d'Art Moderne–Centre National d'Art et de Culture Georges-Pompidou
Musée National Picasso–Paris
Musée du Quai Branly–Jacques-Chirac

Villeneuve-d'Ascq
LaM, Lille Métropole Musée d'Art Moderne, d'Art Contemporain et d'Art Brut

Switzerland
Basel
Kunstmuseum

United Kingdom
London
David and Ezra Nahmad Collection
Tate

United States of America
Baltimore
Baltimore Museum of Art

Cambridge (MA)
Harvard Art Museums/Fogg Museum

Chicago
The Art Institute of Chicago
Newberry Library

Cincinnati
Cincinnati Art Museum

Cleveland
Cleveland Museum of Art

New York
The Metropolitan Museum of Art
The Morgan Library & Museum
The Museum of Modern Art
The Pierre and Tana Matisse Foundation

Oberlin (OH)
Allen Memorial Art Museum, Oberlin College

Philadelphia
Barnes Foundation Archives
Kislak Center for Special Collections, Rare Books and Manuscripts, University of Pennsylvania Libraries
Special Collections Research Center, Temple University Libraries

Saint Louis
Saint Louis Art Museum

San Francisco
San Francisco Museum of Modern Art

Toledo (OH)
Toledo Museum of Art

Washington
Hirshhorn Museum and Sculpture Garden, Smithsonian Institution
National Gallery of Art

Private Collections
The Lewis Collection
The William Rubin Collection

We also extend our thanks to all private lenders who wish to remain anonymous.

In Philadelphia, the exhibition was made possible by the Annenberg Foundation Fund for Major Exhibitions, The Women's Committee of the Philadelphia Museum of Art, the Gloria and Jack Drosdick Fund for Special Exhibitions, the Harriet and Ronald Lassin Fund for Special Exhibitions, the Jill and Sheldon Bonovitz Fund for Exhibitions, the Robert Lehman Foundation, Leslie Miller and Richard Worley, Katie and Tony Schaeffer, and Robbi and Bruce Toll.

Support for the accompanying publication was provided by The Davenport Family Foundation and The Gladys Krieble Delmas Foundation.

We wish to express our gratitude to all those who have made this exhibition and this catalogue possible:
Nicholas Acquavella, Beatrice Affron, Staffan Ahrenberg, Laura Albans, Jonathan Astoul, Sylvie Aubenas, Colin B. Bailey, Maria Balshaw CBE, Andaleeb Banta, Sophie Barthélémy, Gunhild Bauer, Michael and Frances Baylson, Christopher Bedford, Carola Bell, Peter Bell, Neal Benezra, Raphaële Bianchi, John Bidwell, Paula Binari, Mikkel Bogh, Raphaël Bouvier, Hubert Braun, Victoria Caetana, Carla Caputo, Alessandra Carnielli, Delphine Cazus, Mélina Champernaud, Jean-Marc Chatelain, Cyril Chazal, Céline Chicha-Castex, Melissa Chiu, Thom Collins, Harry Cooper, Leslie Cozzi, Emily Cushman, Sophie Daynes-Diallo, Sébastien Delot, Patrice Deparpe, Andria Derstine, Caitlin Draayer, Laurence Dubaut, Constance Dumont, Sonja Eiböck, Laurence Engel, Mélissa Etave, Valérie Eyéné, Jennifer Farrell, Kaywin Feldman, Paul Ferloni, Sylvie Ferreira, Gwenaëlle Fossard, Claire Garnier, Victoire Gineste, Gaëtane Girard, Eric Gleason, Lily Goldberg, Alison de Lima Greene, Daniel Greene, William M. Griswold, Meghan Gross, Jodi Hauptman, Josef Helfenstein, Karoline Helmer Petersen Hvalsøe, Fabrice Hergott, Saïda Herida, Christopher Higgins, Alison Hinderliter, Colleen Hollister, Joachim Homann, Jessica Hong, Nathalie Houzé, Suzanne Karsten, Emmanuel Kasarhérou, Gisela Kirpicsenko, Cameron Kitchin, Jeanne-Bathilde Lacourt, Sarah Lagrevol, Abby Lang, Brigitte Leal-Rodenas, Laurent Le Bon, Antoine Lebouteiller, Sophie Le Flamanc, Adam M. Levine, Jen Levy, Marie Liard-Dexet, Sarah Ligner, Olivier Lorquin, Glenn Lowry, Lisa MacDougall, Georges Matisse, Amanda McKnight, Mitchell Merling, Christof Metzger, Gretchen Shie Miller, Delphine Minotti, Antoine Monnier, Mary Morton, Lori Mott, Jacqueline Munck, Hannah Murray, Asma Naeem, David and Colette Nahmad, Romy Peires, Lili Perre, Caitlin Perry-Vogelhut, Emilia Philippot, Giselle Piqué, Brandi Pomfret, Juliette Pozzo, Grégoire Prangé, Carmen Prokopiak, Sarah Puech, Sean Quimby, Mark Ramirez, Sylvie Ramond, Anne Reeve, Jonathan Rendell, Louise Respaud-Bouny, Xavier Rey, Janet Rhodes, Laura Ritter, Brigitte Robin-Loiseau, William Robinson, James Rondeau, Sophia Rosenfeld, Katy Rothkopf, Klaus Albrecht Schröder, David Seguin, Marianna Shreve Simpson, Margery N. Sly, Lucille Stiger, Andrew Strauss, Jeanne Sudour, Martha Tedeschi, Anne Théry, Gary Tinterow, Giulia Trabaldo Togna, Elisa Urbanelli, Stéphanie Verdavaine, Aurélie Verdier, Heinz Widauer, Thomas Wierzbinski, and Elizabeth Wyckoff.

The Philadelphia Museum of Art wishes to extend warm thanks to the many staff members who have been instrumental in making the exhibition and catalogue such a success:
Cindy Albertson, Nicole Allen White, Justyna Badach, Peter Barberie, Marcia Birbilis, Dilys Blum, Miriam Cady, Tara Contractor, Tammi Coxe, Rachel Crouch, Joy Deibert, Gretchen Dykstra, Christopher Ferguson, Nancy Finn, Elizabeth Freeburg, Dave Gallagher, Shakeera Grays, Emma Gunuey, Kristina Haugland, Sharon Hildebrand, Rosalie Hooper, Jonathan Hoppe, Joseph Hu, Margaret Huang, Anastasia Hughes-Peng, Mary-Jean Huntley, Jane Joe, Deric Johnson, Deborah Johnston, Hanna Karraby, Hannah Kauffman, Stephen Keever, Wynne Kettell, Norman Keyes, Kyoko Kinoshita, Ann Kirschner, Jeanine Kline, Jane Lawson-Bell, Shivon Love, Sally Malenka, Louis Marchesano, Melissa Meighan, Lisa Morra, Lindsey Nevin, Caroline New, James Paris, William Petersen, Thomas Primeau, Nisa Qazi, Natalia Quinteros, Kristen Regina, Sara Reiter, Erika Remmy, Christophina Richards, Genevieve Richardson, Nicole Stribling, Albert Suh, Mark Tucker, Alexa Vallejo, Kate Virdone, Tim Tiebout, Morgan Webb, and Andrew Wurst.

For the Musée de l'Orangerie venue, the curator wishes to address special thanks to Alice Marsal for her help throughout the project.

This exhibition would not have been possible without the invaluable support and participation of many at the Musées d'Orsay et de l'Orangerie: Agnès Abastado, Mélinée Audiard, Saskia Bakhuys, Stéphane Bayard, Tommaso Benelli, Stéphanie Busquet, Cécile Castagnola, Renaud Cesson, Augustin Chaunu, Sophie Crépy, Silvia Cristini, Apolline Defrémont, Coralie Deschamps, Murielle Desdoigts, Sophie Eloy, Thomas Eschbach, Agnès Faravel, Didier Frémond, Delphine Frison, Laureen Grant, Alexandre Grey, Marion Guillaud, Laurence Imbert, Clio Jalabert, Éric Jouvenaux, Camille Kenarlikdjian, Gabrielle Lacombe, Sandrine Lambert, Aude Lambotin, Morgane Lanoue, Gisèle Lassey, Cyrille Lebrun, Anne Le Floch, Ludovic Le Goff, Fanny Livet, Steeve Lowinsky, Pierre Malachin, Perrine Marx, Frédérique Matagne, Céline Migot, Clotilde Monroe, Bénédicte Oisel, Isolde Pludermacher, Rémy Rappart, Scarlett Reliquet, Bruno Roman, Rachel Scrivo, Jacqueline Tayeb, and Catherine Tudoret.

Christian Estrosi and Claudine Grammont give thanks to the teams of the city of Nice and the Métropole de Nice Côte d'Azur for their immense creativity and unfailing involvement throughout the whole project.

Their gratitude goes particularly to Robert Roux, Deputy Mayor for Culture, Councillor of the Métropole, for the support he has shown throughout the completion of this endeavor.

Claudine Grammont and the museum team would also like to thank Thomas Aillagon, Deputy Director General for Culture and Heritage; Laure Nesa, Director of Administration and Finances; and Hélène Jacquart, Director of Art Museums Coordination, as well as all their colleagues.

Claudine Grammont extends her warmest thanks to the technical team of the Art Museums Coordination Department and its manager, Yannick Mocquais.

The Musée Matisse Nice and its director also wish to thank the Insurance and Risk Management Department and Jean-François Blanchet; the Communications Department and Nathalie Bolot; and the Press Service and Élodie Ching.

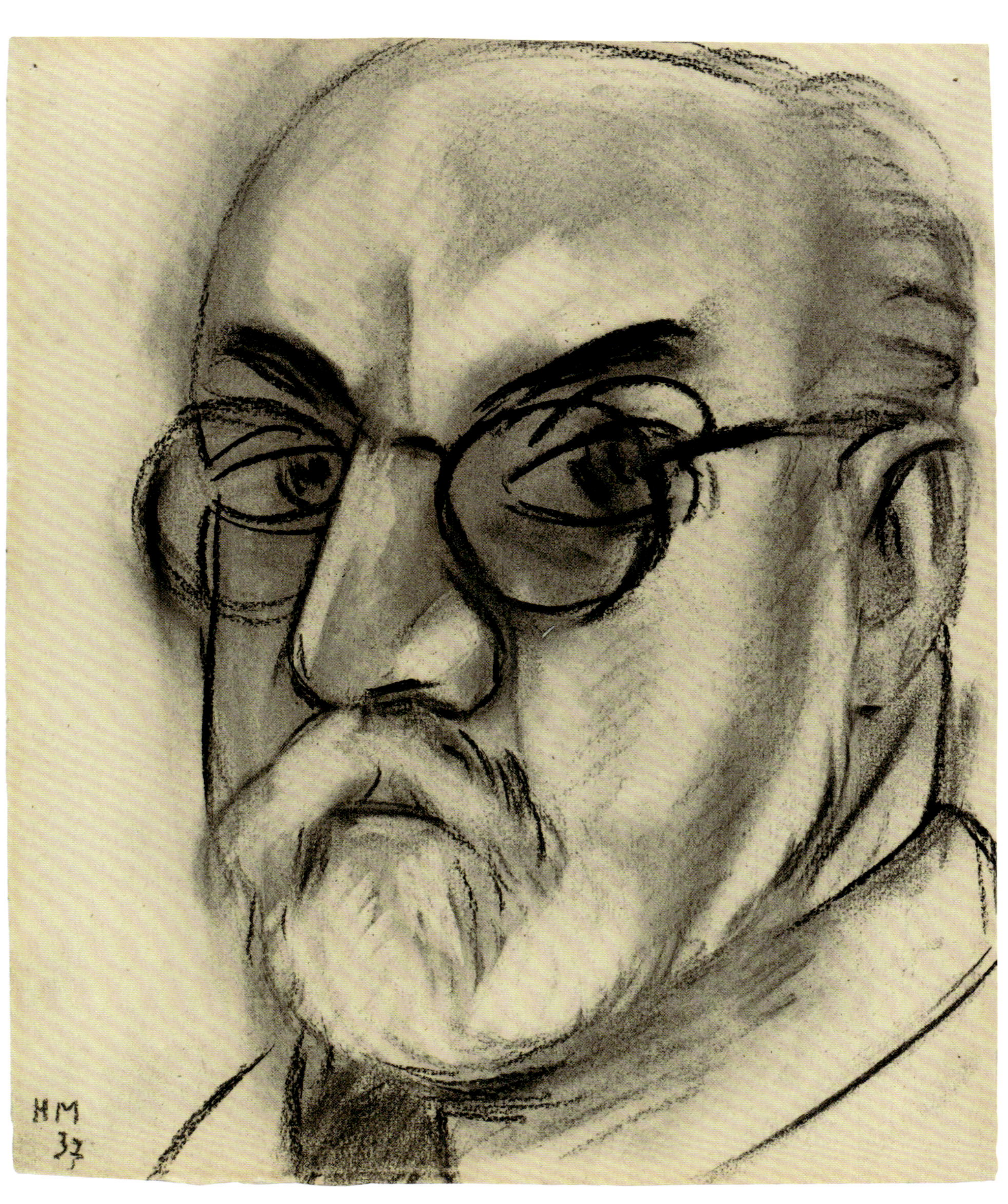

1
Self-Portrait, 1937
Charcoal and stump on laid paper,
13 ⅜ × 11 ¼ in. (34 × 28.5 cm)
National Gallery of Art, Washington

FOREWORD

In 1928 the inaugural exhibition celebrating the opening of the new home of the Philadelphia Museum of Art on the Benjamin Franklin Parkway included a still life by Matisse. Two decades later the museum mounted the exhibition *Henri Matisse*. Curated by Henry Clifford in collaboration with the artist, it included some 270 works in a variety of media and was the second large-scale, comprehensive survey of his art to be presented in this country. Since then Matisse's work has reappeared, alongside that of other pathbreaking modern artists, in a number of exhibitions organized by the museum, including *Henri Matisse and Modern Art on the French Riviera* in 2008–9, *Cézanne and Beyond* in 2009, and *Gauguin, Cézanne, Matisse: Visions of Arcadia* in 2012.

Matisse in the 1930s exemplifies our ongoing commitment to the study of Matisse and is the first in-depth presentation of his work at the Philadelphia Museum of Art since the 1948 retrospective. It is also substantially different, focusing on a pivotal period, one that began in the fall of 1930 with a commission from the collector Albert C. Barnes, who offered Matisse the opportunity to decorate the lunettes of his foundation's main hall with a mural. This project opened a remarkably productive chapter in Matisse's career. The evolution of his work over the course of this decade is the subject of this exhibition, which traces the challenges he embraced to move his artistic practice in a new direction.

In light of its early recognition of Matisse, and with the Barnes Foundation now located nearby, the Philadelphia Museum of Art is a fitting first venue for this exhibition. The project has benefited from a close collaboration with two other institutions: the Musée de l'Orangerie in Paris and the Musée Matisse in Nice. We warmly thank our colleagues for their partnership in the planning and realization of the exhibition and this catalogue. While the French versions of the show direct a tighter focus on the decade of the 1930s, in particular the role the influential journal *Cahiers d'art* played in the reception of Matisse's work during these years, the Philadelphia presentation includes works from the 1920s and 1940s that provide a framework for understanding the innovations of the 1930s and after.

An exhibition such as this relies on the good will of lenders (listed on p. 5) willing to part with major works of art for an extended period, for which we are very grateful. The project was also made possible by the generous funders of the Philadelphia exhibition. We thank the Annenberg Foundation Fund for Major Exhibitions, The Davenport Family Foundation, The Women's Committee of the Philadelphia Museum of Art, the Gloria and Jack Drosdick Fund for Special Exhibitions, the Harriet and Ronald Lassin Fund for Special Exhibitions, the Jill and Sheldon Bonovitz Fund for Exhibitions, the Robert Lehman Foundation, Leslie Miller and Richard Worley, Katie and Tony Schaeffer, Robbi and Bruce Toll, and The Gladys Krieble Delmas Foundation for their crucial support.

We hope that visitors to the exhibition and readers of this catalogue will come away with a new understanding and appreciation of an artist who remains one of the titans of modern art.

TIMOTHY RUB
DIRECTOR EMERITUS, PHILADELPHIA MUSEUM OF ART

NOTE TO THE READER

Unless otherwise specified in the captions for the works reproduced in this volume, paintings, sculptures, and works on paper are by Henri Matisse, and photographs are by Henri Matisse, his family members, and his friends. Works of art that are not displayed in the exhibition are indicated by the use of (fig.) following the image number.

List of abbreviations:
AHM – Archives Henri Matisse, Issy-les-Moulineaux
CDA – Cahiers d'art
MNAM–CP – Musée National d'Art Moderne–Centre Pompidou, Paris
MoMA – The Museum of Modern Art, New York
PMGA – Pierre Matisse Gallery Archives, New York

AUTHORS

MATTHEW AFFRON
Muriel and Philip Berman Curator of Modern Art, Department of European Painting and Sculpture, Philadelphia Museum of Art

ALIX AGRET
Art historian and Research Associate, Musée Matisse Nice

JULIET BELLOW
Associate Professor of Art History, American University, Washington, DC

ÉRIC DE CHASSEY
Director, Institut National d'Histoire de l'Art; Professor, ENS-Lyon

CÉCILE DEBRAY
President, Musée National Picasso–Paris

CÉCILE GIRARDEAU
Curator, Musée de l'Orangerie, Paris

CLAUDINE GRAMMONT
Director, Musée Matisse Nice

AYMERIC JEUDY
Deputy Director, Musée Matisse Nice

CHARA KOLOKYTHA
Teaching Fellow, Athens School of Fine Arts (ASFA)

ALICE MARSAL
Associate Curator, Musée de l'Orangerie, Paris

ELLEN MCBREEN
Professor and Chair, History of Art Department, Wheaton College, Norton (MA)

DENISE MURRELL
Associate Curator, Nineteenth and Twentieth Century Art, Metropolitan Museum of Art, New York

LAURENCE SCHLOSSER
Art historian and Head of Publishing, Musée Matisse Nice

ANNE THÉRY
Archives Henri Matisse, Issy-les-Moulineaux

CONTENTS

ESSAYS

CAHIERS D'ART

WORKS

CHRONOLOGY

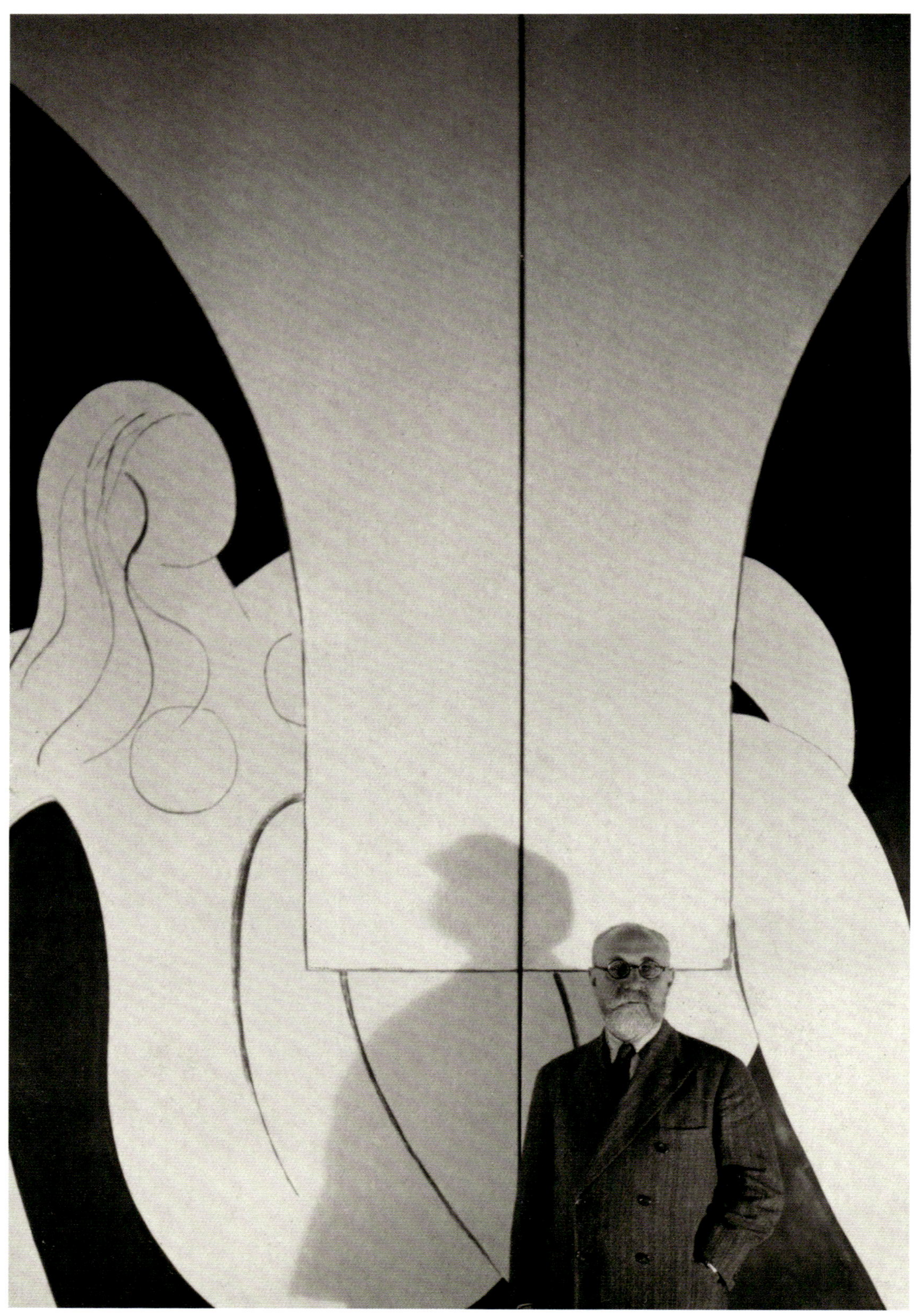

2 (fig.)
Henri Matisse, Nice, April 1933.
Photograph by Wolfgang Vennemann
Pierre Matisse Gallery Archives,
The Morgan Library & Museum,
New York

MATISSE IN THE 1930s

Henri Matisse began his sixtieth year on December 31, 1929, not at his apartment in Nice but thousands of miles away in Merion, a township in the suburbs of Philadelphia. He was visiting a patron, the American collector Albert C. Barnes, who had just commissioned from him a large mural composition on the theme of the dance for the main hall in his foundation [103]. This auspicious commission would validate Matisse's oeuvre on the international scene. It would also denote a career high-water mark, as well as a fresh point of departure that permitted him to resume his hand-to-hand battle with easel painting after fifteen years of making tranquil, intimate pictures of models posed in decorative interiors.

These were the stakes, and also the paradox, of this key turning point. Matisse's work had by this time clearly found its public, was beloved by collectors worldwide, and was handled by dealers in Europe and the United States at well-established market values. Matisse's institutional recognition had also led to an invitation to sit on the jury of the prestigious Carnegie Prize in 1930; retrospectives of his work in Berlin in 1930, and in Paris, Basel, and New York in 1931; and the publication of monographs with essays by some of the most well-recognized authors of the time. Matisse played his public role. He traveled across the United States and was received by the Rockefellers in New York, appeared on the cover of *Time* magazine, and posed with the German filmmaker F. W. Murnau in Tahiti. But a different reality was hidden behind the public image.

Matisse had succeeded in completing only a few canvases since 1928, and only through much labor and effort. The *need* to paint had gradually slipped away. Meanwhile, some French observers now saw this once-dominant artist as having become problematic, even second rank. The high-quality Post-Impressionism of his early years in Nice had cut him off from the Paris avant-garde, from which he had voluntarily separated himself by withdrawing to Nice in the first place. The retrospective mood around Matisse at age sixty tended to frame his work as approaching its end—the final link in the chain of a bygone Impressionism. And rather than being thrilled by his public consecration, Matisse was feeling the weight of his years and feared that he was indeed nearing the end of his artistic path. During the preparation of his retrospective at the Galeries Georges Petit in 1931, he told his dealer Étienne Bignou that he dreaded "a first-class burial" and wanted "no flowers or wreaths."[1]

The Barnes commission offered a way out of this impasse. Having endured months of artistic crisis, Matisse found the strength to resist the weight of the past, and of his age and renown, and threw himself into Barnes's challenging mural project. This major architectural decoration on the subject of the dance, whose two completed versions would be displayed on both sides of the Atlantic, one in Merion and the other in Paris (the latter after World War II), restored social and ideological import to his oeuvre while steering clear of the realism of the propaganda art of the day: "That is where the great problem is, at present," Matisse noted to the Marxist critic Alexander Romm in 1934.[2] Matisse used the making of *The Dance* to lay new foundations for his art, to reformulate and radicalize his formal creative process, and to reinsert his art into the reigning intellectual and artistic trends of the decade.

Exhibitions on Matisse abound, but none of those touching on specific moments in the artist's career have investigated the 1930s. To enumerate the most significant examples of the last half century: *Henri Matisse 1904–1917*[3] dealt with the avant-garde Fauve years and their immediate aftermath; the traveling exhibition *Matisse in Morocco: The Paintings*

1 Henri Matisse–Étienne Bignou, quoted in Pierre Schneider, *Matisse*, trans. Michael Taylor and Bridget Strevens Romer (New York: Rizzoli, 1984), 655n48.

2 "Letters to Alexander Romm, 1934," in *Matisse on Art*, ed. and trans. Jack Flam, rev. ed. (Berkeley: University of California Press, 2015), 116.

3 Musée National d'Art Moderne–Centre Pompidou, Paris, February 25–June 21, 1993.

and Drawings, 1912–1913[4] and *Le Maroc de Matisse* (Matisse's Morocco)[5] specifically addressed the works the artist produced in North Africa; while *Matisse: Radical Invention, 1911–1917* in Chicago and New York[6] focused on his crucial, highly experimental phase before and during World War I. The vast exhibition titled *Henri Matisse: The Early Years in Nice, 1916–1930* examined the so-called first Nice period of the 1920s.[7] Two large exhibitions devoted to Matisse's work employing cut paper, *Henri Matisse: Paper Cut-Outs*[8] and *Henri Matisse: The Cut-Outs*,[9] did not so much explore a period but rather a technique to which the artist devoted himself nearly entirely beginning in 1947.

The present exhibition was organized by three institutions in three cities that are emblematic of the 1930s moment in Matisse's career: the Philadelphia Museum of Art, where the artist has been a continuous presence since 1928, the year of the institution's founding in its present incarnation at the terminus of the city's Benjamin Franklin Parkway, and only a short distance from the current location of the Barnes Foundation, with its version of Matisse's *The Dance*; the Musée de l'Orangerie in Paris, with its roots in the collection of Paul Guillaume, one of Matisse's dealers, whose personal holdings, when put on public display at the onset of the 1930s, helped spark a renewal of interest in the artist's radical pre-World War I work; and finally the Musée Matisse in Nice, the city that inspired Matisse, and where he lived and worked from 1917 onward.

In both its Paris and Nice presentations, the exhibition looks at Matisse in the 1930s through the lens of *Cahiers d'art*, the prominent French art journal that played a decisive role in positioning the artist within contemporary discourse and in the perception of the public throughout this period. It is worth noting that it was the journal's continuous, abundant publication of Matisse's work in reproduction, perhaps more than the myriad texts by critics appearing within its pages, that made *Cahiers d'art* a major access point for Matisse and established him as a defining artist of the time. Such was certainly the case, for example, with issue 5–6 in 1931, devoted solely to Matisse. It coincided with both the Galeries Georges Petit exhibition in Paris and, through its English-language edition, the show at the Museum of Modern Art in New York. Christian Zervos, the publisher of *Cahiers d'art*, began his opening article in the issue with a paradox: "We know Matisse much less than we admire him."[10] *Cahiers d'art* would endeavor not only to make Matisse known, but to restore the artistic relevance he had gradually lost over the course of the 1920s. To mark the salience of *Cahiers d'art* as an iconographic resource, a sixteen-page section in this volume provides a selection of its covers and interior pages devoted to Matisse.[11]

Philadelphia's version of the exhibition, rather than contextualizing Matisse through a focus on the concerns of *Cahiers d'art* during this time, as the Paris and Nice presentations do, offers a broad, chronological survey of the 1930s and the years that bookend the decade. It includes both well-known and rarely seen paintings (in both easel and larger decorative formats), sculptures, drawings, prints, and illustrated books, as well as documentary photographs and short films. A prelude titled "Interiors and Odalisques" opens the exhibition, surveying the Nice period of 1917–30, when Matisse painted the interiors where he lived and worked as self-contained worlds suffused with the unvarying, crystalline light of the Riviera and the energy of vibrantly decorated objects and furnishings, including from regions of the Islamic world he had visited years before. Key works such as *The Three Sisters* 66 and *Woman with a Veil* 72 provide an opportunity to examine Matisse's manner of synthesizing decorative design, fashion, and the sensuality of the female figure into a modern aesthetic idiom, an effort much debated both in its day and in recent years. The second section traces the parallel genesis and development of two commissions—the Barnes mural and the concurrent project for an edition of poems by the influential Symbolist writer Stéphane Mallarmé, Matisse's first major endeavor in the realm of the illustrated book—and shows how the artist used these projects to pull himself through his moment of great questioning, and toward a reinvigoration of his art.

4 National Gallery of Art, Washington, March 18–June 3, 1990; Museum of Modern Art [MoMA], New York, June 24–September 4, 1990; Pushkin Museum of Fine Arts, Moscow, September 28–November 20, 1990; Hermitage Museum, Leningrad, December 15, 1990–February 15, 1991.

5 Institut du Monde Arabe, Paris, October 19, 1999–January 30, 2000.

6 Art Institute of Chicago, March 20–June 20, 2010; MoMA, July 18–October 11, 2010.

7 National Gallery of Art, Washington, November 2, 1986–March 29, 1987.

8 National Gallery of Art, Washington, September 10–October 24, 1977; Detroit Institute of Arts, November 23, 1977–January 8, 1978; Saint Louis Art Museum, January 29–March 12, 1978.

9 Tate Modern, London, April 17–September 7, 2014; MoMA, New York, October 12, 2014–February 10, 2015.

10 Christian Zervos, "Henri-Matisse: Notes on the Formation and Development of His Work," *Cahiers d'art*, nos. 5–6 (1931), as quoted in *Matisse: A Retrospective*, ed. Jack Flam (New York: Hugh Lauter Levin Associates, 1988), 269.

11 See pages 92–107 in this volume.

The exhibition's third section, "Artist and Model," relates how Matisse returned to easel painting in 1935 with new methods developed in the course of executing the Barnes mural. He began using photography to systematically document the cumulative process of building his motifs and to test his own reactions as he went along. And he instituted a practice of employing precolored cut papers to plan his compositions, which led him away from the illusion of modeling and deep space and toward a style of flat tones and bold shapes. The highly experimental painting *Large Reclining Nude* [110] exemplifies this moment of reinvention. Matisse's intense focus over a two-year period on the unclothed model in the studio shows the significance this motif held for him. The artist believed that the beauty and erotic power of the model were indispensable for focusing his imagination and artistic energy. But he also believed that the process of representing any observed subject involved its profound transformation through an act of artistic imagination. We can see this process revealed in the photographs recording the many states of the *Large Reclining Nude* [111].

Though Matisse never received another commission for a decorative mural for a specific architectural setting, he did engage in further experiments in a decorative and architectural mode. The exhibition's "Painted Decorations" gallery highlights Matisse's work in the genre of painted tapestry cartoons, the largest of which, *Nymph in the Forest (Verdure)* [116], occupied the artist's attention for more than eight years, becoming a true artistic touchstone for him. The section that follows presents an abundant and inventive corpus of pictures from 1936 through the end of the decade. In this series, Matisse posed models in fine dresses and embroidered blouses and arranged the women's forms in counterpoint to the sinuous lines of the tropical plants that filled his spacious, luminous studios in the manner of a winter garden. A vibrating, at times hesitating, tension between line and color and compositional clarity and ornamental overflow validated the regained vitality in his painting.

A penultimate section takes Matisse out of the studio to explore his collaboration with the Ballet Russe de Monte-Carlo on a production titled *Rouge et noir* (Red and black) in 1937–39. Matisse cowrote the scenario, designed the costumes and the stage curtain, and laid out a backdrop in three immense vaults directly echoing the main gallery of the Barnes Foundation. The dancers moved in bodysuits with flame-like designs against this three-arched backdrop. Little known today, *Rouge et noir* is important as a marker of *The Dance*'s continuing hold on Matisse's artistic imagination at the end of the decade.

The exhibition concludes with an epilogue that evokes a major turning point in Matisse's life and career. The artist underwent a risky operation for abdominal cancer in January 1941. Afterward, he spoke of embarking on a second artistic life, but he painted little at first and focused instead on a major effort in drawing, resulting in a corpus of 158 images divided into seventeen suites depicting two of his favorite motifs: models in the studio, and fruit and floral still lifes. Two complete suites of *Themes and Variations* [158 | 159] are included in the final gallery (together with a small selection of contemporaneous paintings on the same subjects), representing Matisse's reflections on the discoveries of artistic form and method he had made in the 1930s.

The present publication gathers a group of essays by art historians on various aspects of Matisse's work in the 1930s. Chara Kolokytha tracks milestones in the evolution of *Cahiers d'art* and its principal orientations, spelling out the prominence that Zervos gave to Matisse between 1926 and 1949 and surveying in detail the main issues and articles devoted to the artist. Éric de Chassey presents a thorough study of the four retrospective exhibitions of 1930–31—in Berlin, Paris, Basel, and New York—and shows how they constituted a type of reception, not to say historiography, with the European exhibitions positioning Matisse as an heir to Impressionism while the New York show presented him as a pioneer of Modernism. In her text, Cécile Debray elucidates how *Cahiers d'art* gave Matisse not only tremendous visibility in reactivating the Matisse/Picasso dichotomy, but also a real, and reinvigorating, artistic rivalry in the 1930s. Two essays take up the question of the artist's studio. Ellen McBreen considers the singular position of Lydia Delectorskaya, showing how a young Russian émigré came to be an essential partner—above and beyond the fictive role she played as a model—in the creation of Matisse's work. Claudine Grammont examines transformations in the studio space and its setup, as other actors took on roles and the strategy of photographing works at different stages became an essential component of Matisse's creative process. Matthew Affron surveys the artistic, social, and political context for mural art at the time *The Dance* was made and shows how Matisse took on those contemporary concerns.

Major Matisse works and themes are the topics of the more tightly focused studies in this volume. Denise Murrell considers the artist's visits to Harlem and the question of Black modernity, while Juliet Bellow traces the genesis, in the midst of the leftist Popular Front movement, of Matisse's abstract decor for the ballet *Rouge et noir*, which premiered in May 1939, and interprets it politically. Cécile Girardeau presents the collection of Paul Guillaume and the dealer's relationship to Matisse; Alix Agret comments on both the painting *Woman with a Veil* and Matisse's around-the-world travels; Matthew Affron examines the collecting and display of Matisse in Philadelphia, and also presents the artist's 1941–42 *Themes and Variations*; Aymeric Jeudy surveys the role of the Pierre Matisse Gallery in New York, and examines Matisse's *Large Reclining Nude*; Claudine Grammont analyzes *Nymph in the Forest (Verdure)*; Ellen McBreen investigates the question of clothing in *Woman in Blue* 134; and Alice Marsal elucidates the emergence in Matisse's work of the theme of the Romanian blouse. Finally, Anne Théry closes this volume with a new, in-depth chronology of the period, based on the artist's archives.

Undertaken in a spirit of friendship as well as collaboration, this collective French and American project could not have been realized without the involvement of a great many participants and partners: the authors who contributed to this catalogue, the teams at our respective institutions, Georges Matisse and Anne Théry at the Archives Henri Matisse, Issy-les-Moulineaux, the teams at the Cahiers d'Art gallery and at the current *Cahiers d'art* journal, directed by Staffan Ahrenberg, and our many generous lenders. To all of them we express our deep gratitude.

MATTHEW AFFRON | CÉCILE DEBRAY | CLAUDINE GRAMMONT

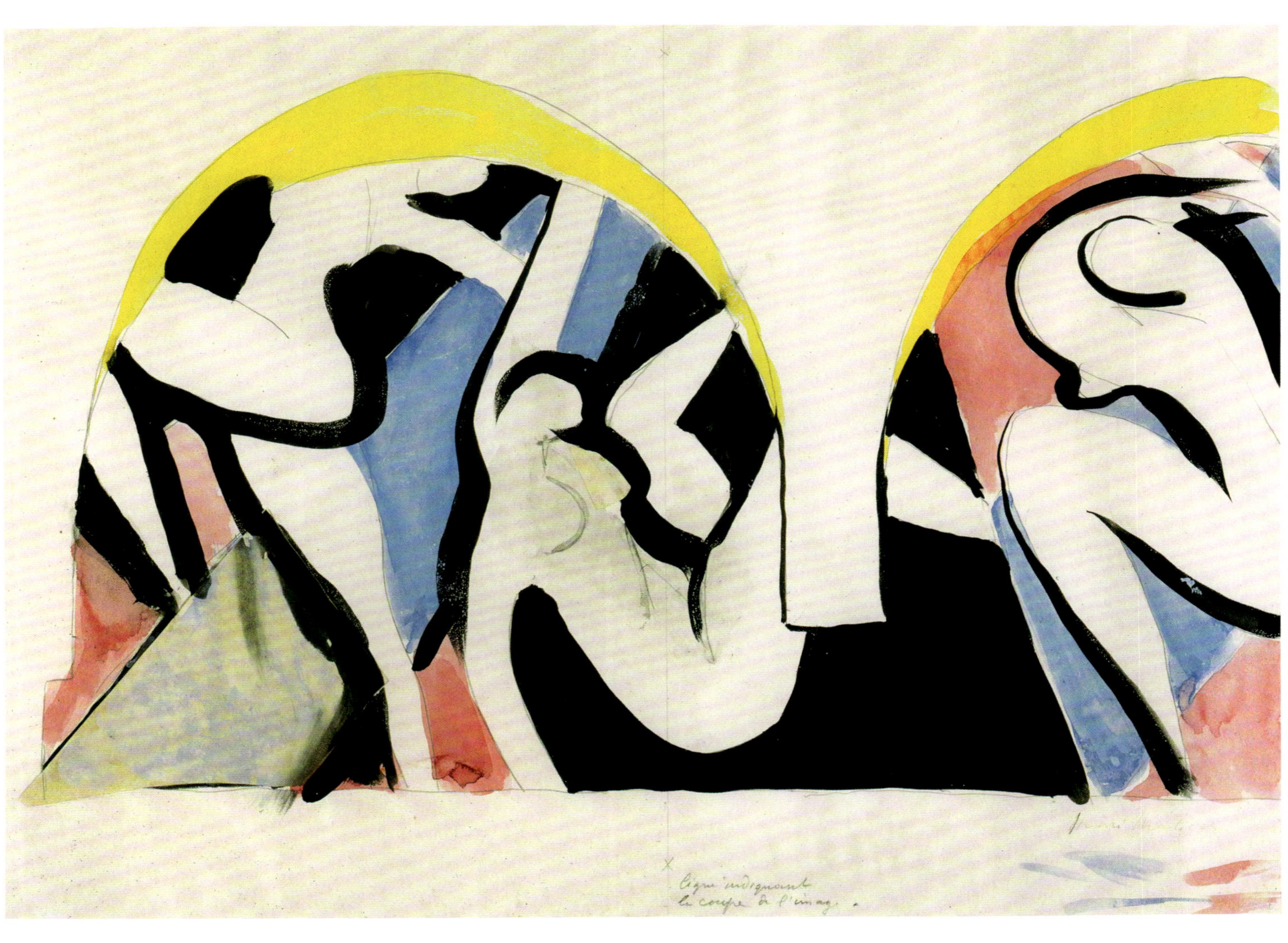

3
The Dance, created for *Vogue*,
June 1938
Watercolor on paper, 20 ⅞ × 29 ⅛ in.
(28.5 × 49 cm)
Musée Matisse Nice

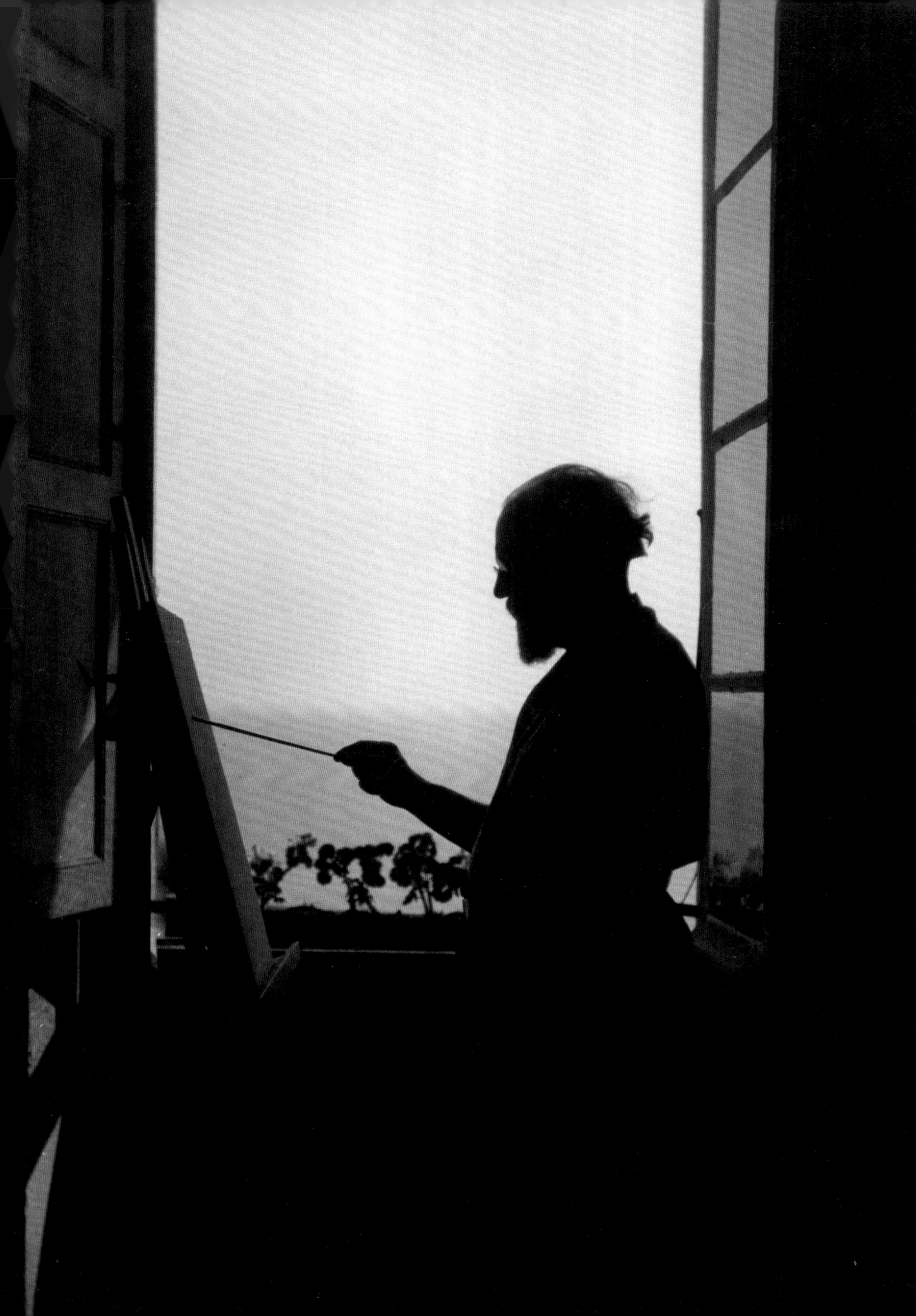

ESSAYS

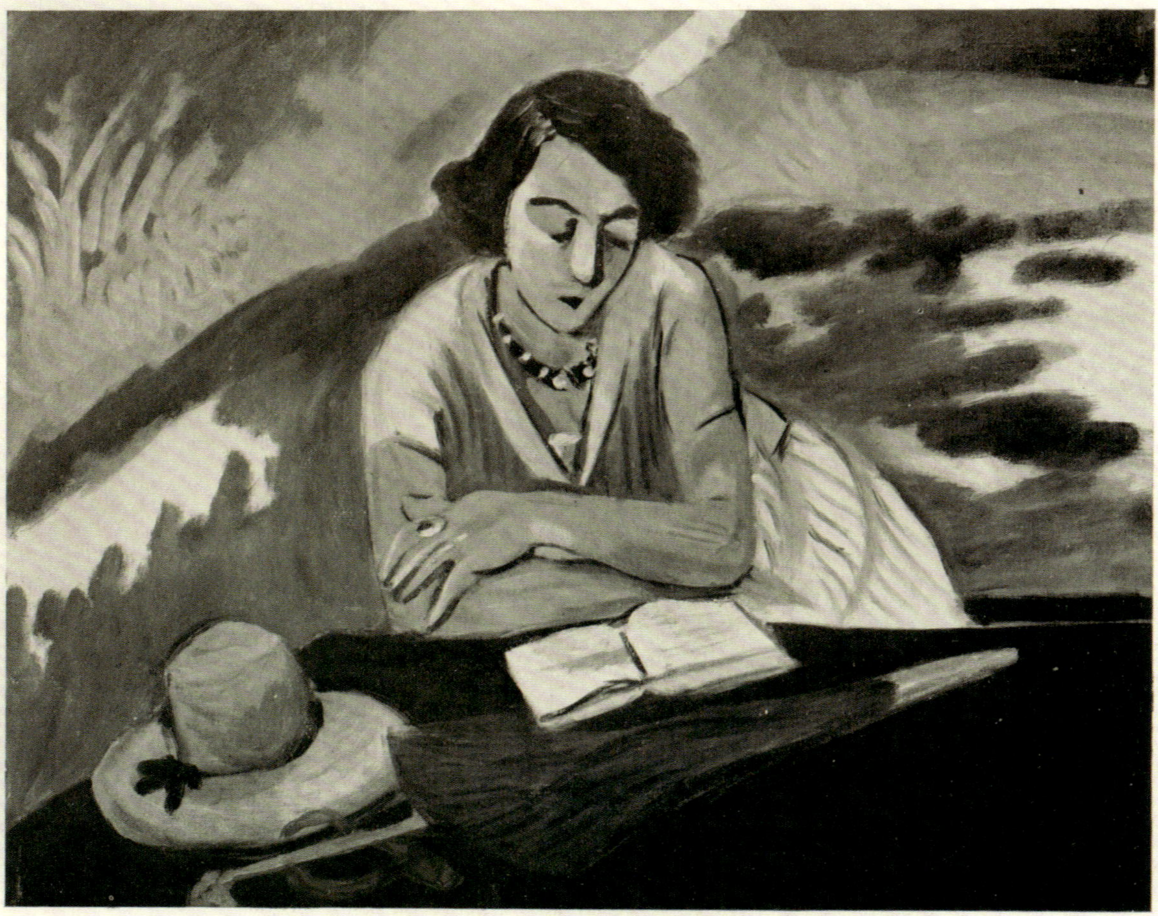

FIG. 1. — LISEUSE, PLEIN AIR, 1920. TATE GALLERY, LONDRES.

NOTES SUR LA FORMATION ET LE DÉVELOPPEMENT DE L'ŒUVRE DE HENRI-MATISSE

PAR CHRISTIAN ZERVOS

Nous connaissons Matisse beaucoup moins que nous ne l'admirons. Sans doute, nous nous accordons à reconnaître qu'il montre toujours un rare souci de perfection, qu'il se fait un devoir de reprendre sans cesse un accord qui le satisfait mal ; nous reconnaissons que son dessin est achevé, harmonieux et pur. Mais ce n'est là, en somme, qu'une appréciation presque extérieure de son œuvre dont on ne comprend l'importance et la valeur que si on la connaît dans son ensemble. Il faut suivre cette œuvre pas à pas, en considérer les étapes successives et l'évolution organique, pour comprendre à quel point elle est une dans son extrême richesse et pour en saisir l'extraordinaire fraîcheur, l'étincelante jeunesse et les audaces toujours renouvelées. On peut dire que la plupart des hardiesses qui sollicitent notre intérêt dans la peinture contemporaine, Matisse en a donné de magnifiques exemples.

Il ne peut être question d'étudier ici en détail les recherches de Matisse. Un volume n'y suffirait pas, tant son effort est multiple et varié. Nous voudrions seulement marquer à grands traits les principales

9

Previous page
4 (fig.)
Henri Matisse, Place Charles-Félix, Nice, c. 1927
Archives Henri Matisse, Issy-les-Moulineaux

Above
5 (fig.)
Cahiers d'art, 1931, nos. 5–6, p. 9
Éditions Cahiers d'Art, Paris

CHARA KOLOKYTHA

MATISSE, ZERVOS, AND *CAHIERS D'ART*

Matisse's densely textured lithograph *Young Girl with Brown Curls* (1924)—quite likely portraying Henriette Darricarrère, the artist's favorite model throughout the 1920s—became the cover image of the inaugural issue of *Cahiers d'art* 55. The journal was launched in January 1926 by Christian Zervos, a Greek émigré originating from Argostoli on the Ionian island of Kefalonia, but raised entirely in Alexandria, Egypt. Having moved to Paris around 1911 to pursue studies in law and philosophy, Zervos had already left a notable editorial and literary mark in the intellectual circles of the Greek diaspora, yet he was armed with determination, as the correspondence of his youth reveals, to pave a new way forward.[1] The first issue of *Cahiers d'art* encapsulates the aesthetic agenda of the Parisian publishing house of Albert Morancé, under whose auspices the journal was published in its first year of existence—namely, a concern for painting and lithography (Morancé's great passions), along with architecture, interior design, and applied and industrial arts, all topics of vital interest in Morancé's periodicals edited by Zervos (*Les Arts de la maison* [Home arts], *L'Art d'aujourd'hui* [Art today]) and Jean Badovici (*L'Architecture vivante* [Living architecture]) in the early 1920s. The latter had introduced Zervos to Morancé, who appointed him subeditor of the above-mentioned journals. Matisse's lithograph had originally been published in 1924 by Morancé in one of a special series of *L'Art d'aujourd'hui* print portfolios,[2] coinciding with the artist's renewed passion for printmaking—he produced about fifty prints from 1922 to 1925—that motivated his collaboration with Morancé.[3]

Though initially materially and aesthetically dependent on the directives of Morancé, including his stock images, *Cahiers d'art* soon gained its independence and established its authority as an institution of the Parisian art scene. Matisse's presence in the pages of the journal is typified by an emphasis on the graphic aspects of his art and the vindication of their antidecorative conception. Though the journal's black-and-white reproductions fail to do justice to his talent as a colorist, they accurately justify the paeans to his virtuosity as a designer in the articles that accompany them, mainly penned by Zervos. Discussing Matisse's lithographs, Zervos claimed in 1926, "is discussing his drawing, and explaining his drawing is analyzing his painting, which is always built on the solid foundation of drawing."[4] The journal did, however, publish a number of articles on Matisse's pure painting signed by Sylvain Bonmariage, Gabriel J. Gros, and Tériade.[5] In the late 1930s, the latter pushed the printing technology of his time to its limits in order to accurately print and faithfully reproduce Matisse's work in the journal *Verve* (1937–60), which became a rival publication to *Cahiers d'art* from December 1937.

Zervos's journal was published as a "monthly bulletin of art news," a subtitle that accompanied its first three issues. These featured covers by Matisse (lithography), Pablo Picasso (painting), and Henri Laurens (sculpture), summing up its thematic and aesthetic predilections. In due course, it introduced—possibly influenced by the cover design of the purist *L'Esprit nouveau*—imageless solid color surfaces on a neutral background that eventually became its signature covers 58 | 60 | 62. Zervos had already encountered Matisse's art prior to his profound

1 Zervos's activities in Paris between 1911 and 1923, when he started collaborating with Morancé, have tended to be reduced to his studies at the Sorbonne and the publication of his thesis on the neo-Platonist philosopher Michel Psellos in 1919. What is less well known is that Zervos quit law school to follow an academic route that focused on his native culture, and that he produced two further dissertations: one, completed around 1913, questions the influence that Greek philosophy (in particular Plato) and Christianity exerted over the communist doctrines of Epiphanius; the other completed prior to 1913, considers the views of various philosophers on the notion of union between man and God.

2 *L'Art d'aujourd'hui* print portfolio, Spring/Summer 1924.

3 See *Christian Zervos and "Cahiers d'art": The Archaic Turn*, exh. cat. (Athens: Benaki Museum, 2019).

4 Christian Zervos, "Lithographies de Henri Matisse," *Cahiers d'art* [*CDA*], no. 1 (1926): 7 (author's translation).

5 Sylvain Bonmariage, "Henri Matisse et la peinture pure," *CDA*, no. 9 (1926): 239–41; G. J. Gros, "Henri Matisse," *CDA*, nos. 7–8 (1927): 268–74; É. Tériade, "L'actualité de Matisse," *CDA*, no. 7 (1929): 285–98.

contact with Picasso. The latter nevertheless became the ultimate protagonist in *Cahiers d'art*, with ninety-five of the approximately fifteen hundred articles published over its thirty-four years of existence dedicated to his artistic production, in addition to which Zervos edited the complete catalogue of Picasso's work between 1932 and 1978, a project posthumously completed in thirty-three volumes.

There are twenty-five articles dedicated to Matisse's work in *Cahiers d'art*, in addition to dozens of references to his contributions to the development of modern art and his connection to various pictorial traditions. Following Matisse's exhibition at the Museum of Modern Art (MoMA) in New York in 1951–52, and Alfred H. Barr Jr.'s important study *Matisse: His Art and His Public* (1951), the artist refused that same year to grant Zervos permission to engage, rather belatedly, in a catalogue listing his works, claiming that he had "very firm commitments for the publication of the complete catalogue of his work."[6]

Ahead of its hard-won independence—hindered by its material hardship—from the publisher Morancé, the journal had proclaimed itself an international avant-garde publication, a subtitle that nonetheless appeared only in the last seven issues of 1926. *Cahiers d'art* hardly fit the profile of an avant-garde art journal, with its didactic tone addressing Zervos's concern for Picasso's stylistic development and the aesthetic cultivation of the younger generation of Parisian artists. A critical aspect of its mission was to elucidate the ambiguities that plagued contemporary art through exhaustive surveys of modern art and comprehensive analyses of the household names of Parisian Modernism. Serving the needs of artists and art enthusiasts was the journal's declared vocation. Consecutive subscriptions were taken out by official institutions and bookstores across and outside Europe. Unpaid, intellectually independent contributions turned out to be a prerequisite for the journal's subsistence, especially during its long periods of financial strain, which rendered it more polemical and isolated from standard periodical networks of the time. The journal progressively gained an art historical focus, its art-news reports moving into the supplement *Feuilles volantes* (Loose leafs) from 1927–28, "the modern man's journal," mirroring its founder's aspiration—according to a 1930 statement—to raise in *Cahiers d'art* fundamental questions of broad art historical interest.[7] In collaboration with the German dealer Alfred Flechtheim and his then assistant Curt Valentin, Zervos envisaged a German edition of *Feuilles volantes* under the title *Neue Kunsthefte* (New art books), a project that failed to materialize. To fill the gap left by the premature discontinuation of its supplement, Zervos launched in 1933 the monthly *14 rue Dragon: Lettres, arts, philosophie, documents, spectacles, actualités* (1933–34), which suffered the same fate as its predecessor, disappearing about a year later.[8]

Aside from producing the review, Cahiers d'Art additionally operated as a publishing house and turned part of its offices into an art gallery in 1934. In 1926 it had launched the book series *Les Maîtres de la peinture contemporaine* (Masters of contemporary painting), which published illustrated volumes devoted to single artists. The first of the series was dedicated to Picasso. Fernand Léger, Henri Rousseau, and Raoul Dufy followed, and two volumes on Paul Klee and Wassily Kandinsky were published in collaboration with Flechtheim.[9] In 1927 a small album with engravings by contemporary artists was made available exclusively to *Cahiers d'art* subscribers. It was printed in fifty copies and included seven etchings by Matisse, Picasso, Dufy, Henri Laurens, Léopold Lévy, Jean Lurçat, and Maurice de Vlaminck—"the current stars" of the contemporary art market, judging by their remarkable commercial successes at the time.[10] Zervos became dependent on works offered by artists in return for his support. Matisse's drawing *Seated Nude* was auctioned, together with fifty works by artist-friends of the journal, in 1933 at the Hôtel Drouot, raising 80,000 francs for the benefit of the "young mother-journal aided by its elder sons."[11]

The *Cahiers d'art* journal that is published today[12] still has a strong connection to the history of Cubism, even if the original publication emerged in a period that strove to measure its effect and influence the course of contemporary art after Cubism. From 1926, the Cubist

6 In 1946, Matisse had entrusted the publication of the catalogue of his work to his daughter, Marguerite Duthuit. See Claudine Grammont, ed., *Tout Matisse* (Paris: Robert Laffont, 2018), 149–50. "Incidentally, I learn that . . . you are in the process of publishing some sort of catalogue of my work. This information surprises me greatly as I suppose that if this were correct, I would have been the first to be informed by you. However, in order to avoid misunderstanding on this topic, I would point out to you that I cannot authorize you to publish a collection of this kind because I have very firm commitments for the publication of the complete catalogue of my work." Henri Matisse [HM]–Christian Zervos, March 14, 1952, Archives Galerie Cahiers d'Art, Paris (author's translation).

7 "Aux amis des *Cahiers d'art*," *CDA*, no. 10 (1930): n.p.

8 A third short-lived project was *L'Usage de la parole* (1939–40), edited by Georges Hugnet, a small bimonthly literary journal that was launched in 1939 by Zervos and only ran for three issues.

9 Christian Zervos, *Picasso: Œuvres 1920–1926* (1926), forty heliotypes and two color plates; Zervos, *Rousseau* (1928), one hundred heliotypes; Tériade, *Fernand Léger* (1928), seven watercolors and engravings; and Zervos, *Raoul Dufy* (1928), ninety-six heliotypes.

10 Malcolm Gee, *Dealers, Critics, and Collectors of Modern Painting: Aspects of the Parisian Art Market between 1910 and 1930* (London: Garland, 1981), 1:245–54 and 2:227. See also Christopher Green, *Cubism and Its Enemies: Modern Movements and Reaction in French Art, 1916–1928* (New Haven: Yale University Press, 1987), 136.

11 See *CDA*, nos. 1–2 (1933). However, Matisse's drawing presumably belonged to Flechtheim and was handed out to cover part of his debt to Zervos.

12 The original journal folded in 1960 but was revived in 2012 under the editorship of the Swedish art collector and film producer Staffan Ahrenberg.

dealer Léonce Rosenberg exerted pressure on Zervos to avoid references to Fauvism and Impressionism in his journal, yet articles on the pure painting of Matisse, the Impressionist Auguste Renoir, and the Fauvists Othon Friesz and Dufy recurred in its pages.[13] In 1929, to coincide with the twenty-fifth anniversary of the birth of Fauvism, Georges Duthuit, an art historian and Matisse's son-in-law since 1923, was invited to author a series of articles dealing with the movement and its multifaceted approach to painting.[14] The survey presented unpublished material and previously unknown Fauvist works from the collections of Albert C. Barnes, Robert Ellissen, and Leo Stein (Matisse), and Ambroise Vollard (André Derain and Vlaminck).[15] Duthuit ascribed to Matisse's coloration process a philosophical dimension by comparing it to Henri Bergson's concept of duration, and approached Fauvism through the prism of art history, philosophy, and psychology.[16] The movement was treated as a historical style, just as Cubism had been a few years earlier, with Tériade declaring the "need for a new Fauvism" and interpreting the movement in terms of "youth" as reflecting the impulsiveness of young artists and a necessary step in the evolution of a mature style.[17] It was in effect the perpetual urge for renewal and inquisitiveness that rendered the work of Picasso and Matisse emblematic of this highly valued, everlasting painterly youth.

Cahiers d'art published a special issue on Matisse in 1931 on the occasion of an exhibition at the Galeries Georges Petit 60, and an English version was published in New York.[18] In Paris, the anticipation of an official announcement of the creation of a state museum of contemporary art in the early 1930s was accompanied by long debates over the artists and styles having a claim to the institution. According to the responses to the 1925 survey of *L'Art vivant*, Matisse was among the top ten artists deserving a place in the new museum. His 1931 New York retrospective exhibition at MoMA was definitely a high point in his career, given that foreign approval tacitly guaranteed state recognition.[19] It is worth noting that Picasso's first museum retrospective was held about a year later, at the Kunsthaus Zürich, and coincided with the publication of the first volume of Zervos's catalogue raisonné on the artist. The special *Cahiers d'art* issue on Matisse featured a full-page advertisement of his forthcoming illustrations for Stéphane Mallarmé's *Poésies* published by Albert Skira, which ensured the artist's collaboration a couple of years later on *Minotaure* (1933–39), Skira's journal that provided competition for *Cahiers d'art*. Zervos's lengthy survey presented the origins and development of Matisse's work and included a thorough outline of his artistic career. The issue's content was trilingual and included studies by Will Grohmann and Curt Glaser in German; Roger Fry and Henry McBride in English; and Paul Fierens, Karel Asplund, Giovanni Scheiwiller, Georges Salles, and Pierre Guéguen in French 61. Most articles were concerned with putting right certain misreadings of the artist's work. Discussing the female body in Matisse's art, Fierens maintained that, unlike Gustave Courbet, Renoir, and Derain, Matisse was not a painter of nudes—his figures were firmly fused with the background motifs that surrounded them, his subject matter being treated as a harmonious ensemble in Cézannesque ways. McBride discussed Matisse's success in North America, and Scheiwiller defended the artist against the label of "decorator" and the unfair criticism leveled at his art.

In 1934, the same year that the creation of two museums of modern and contemporary art in Paris—the Musée National d'Art Moderne and the Musée d'Art Moderne de Paris—was officially announced, Zervos opened the Cahiers d'Art gallery in rooms on the ground floor of the journal's offices.[20] The capital invested in the project was significant, particularly given Zervos's tenuous financial position.[21] He declared its noncommercial character, however, and a not-for-profit mission to serve the interests of the younger generation. The list of the journal's protégés nevertheless became progressively shorter in the 1930s, with Zervos putting his faith in the stylistic development of a significantly narrower group of relatively successful young artists active in Paris, such as Hans Arp, André Masson, and Joan Miró. Both the gallery and the journal adopted the tried-and-true strategy of promoting less successful artists by presenting them side by side with established names on the Parisian art scene.

13 Léonce Rosenberg–Zervos, July 10, 1926, letter 336, quoted in Christian Derouet, ed., *Fernand Léger: Une correspondance poste restante*, Cahiers du MNAM, Hors-Série/Archives (Paris: Centre Pompidou, 1997), 216.

14 Georges Duthuit, "Le fauvisme (I)," *CDA*, no. 5 (1929): 177–92; "Le fauvisme (II)," *CDA*, no. 6 (1929): 258–68; "Le fauvisme," *CDA*, no. 10 (1929): 429–35; "Le fauvisme (IV)," *CDA*, no. 3 (1930): 129–32; "Le fauvisme (fin)," *CDA*, no. 2 (1931): 78–82.

15 Works by Matisse in these collections include: *The Joy of Life* (1905–6; Barnes), *The Idol* (1906; Ellissen), *Woman with a Hat* (1905; Stein), and *Study for The Joy of Life* (1905; Stein).

16 Duthuit, "Le fauvisme (IV)," 130, and "Le fauvisme (fin)," 79. See also Georges Duthuit, *Les Fauves* (Geneva: Les Trois Collines, 1949); and Rémi Labrusse, ed., *Les Fauves: Braque, Derain, Van Dongen, Dufy, Friesz, Manguin, Marquet, Matisse, Puy, Vlaminck* (Paris: Michalon, 2006).

17 Tériade, "Documentaire sur la jeune peinture I: Considérations liminaires," *CDA*, nos. 8–9 (1929): 360; É. Tériade, "Besoin d'un nouveau fauvisme II: Réalisme subjectif ou peinture d'imagination," *Comœdia*, September 8, 1927.

18 *Henri Matisse* (New York: E. Weyhe, 1931).

19 See Jean-Paul Morel, *Pour un musée français d'art moderne: Une enquête de "L'Art vivant" en 1925* (Paris: RMN, 1996).

20 Wassily Kandinsky–Will Grohmann, cited in Christian Derouet, ed., *"Cahiers d'art": Musée Zervos à Vézelay* (Paris: Hazan, 2006), 82.

21 On the financial conditions under which the gallery operated, see Chara Kolokytha, "Christian Zervos, les galeries Cahiers d'art et M.A.I," in *Les Artistes et leurs galeries: Paris-Berlin*, vol. 2, *Berlin*, ed. Denise Vernerey and Hélène Ivanoff (Mont-Saint-Aignan: PURH, 2020), 281–99.

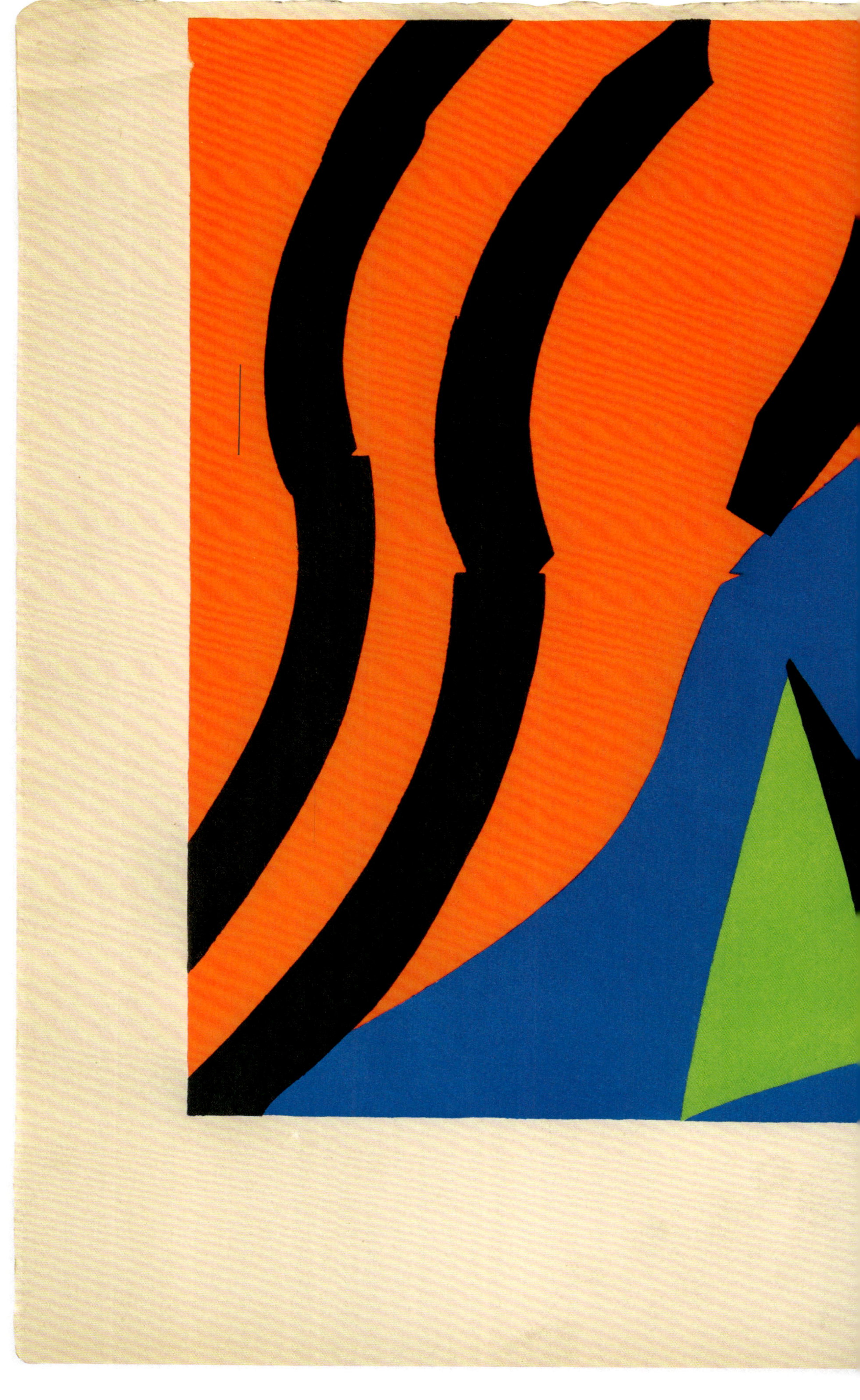

6 (fig.)
Henri Matisse, front and back cover design for the special issue of *Cahiers d'Art*, 1936, nos. 3–5
Gouache-painted paper cut-outs, 15 9/16 × 22 7/16 in. (39.5 × 57 cm)
Éditions Cahiers d'Art, Paris

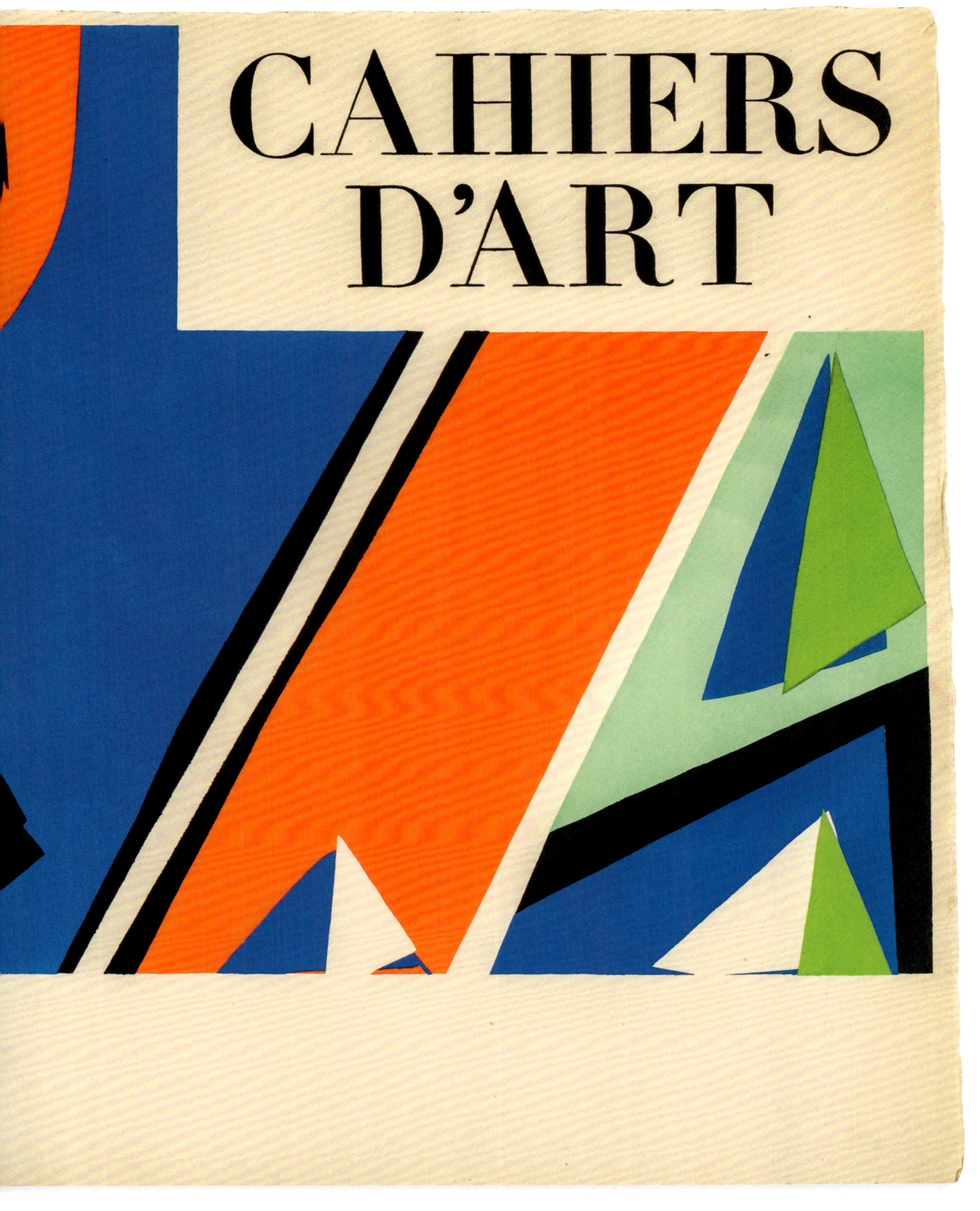
CAHIERS
D'ART

In light of institutional recognition, Zervos began to look with favor on the interplay between the ancients and the moderns. His avid interest in "primitive" imagery was part of the same rationale that encouraged the modern formal reinvention of the art of the distant past and saw innate spiritual links with primeval image-makers. An album of interpretive engravings after the old masters by Arp, André Beaudin, Francisco Borès, Georges Braque, Dufy, Max Ernst, Kandinsky, Klee, Laurens, Léger, Lurçat, Louis Marcoussis, Masson, Matisse, Miró, and Picasso, available only to subscribers, was advertised in 1934 as part of the journal's efforts to promote exchanges with the art of the past, although it better addressed the museological concerns of its time associated with aspects of continuity and tradition in French art pending the opening of the two museums.

Throughout the 1930s, Zervos's critical stance was defined by developments on the political front, his reconciliation with the Surrealist movement, his publications' increasingly archaeological bent, and his growing interest in collaborations with high-ranking institutions in France and abroad. The decorative triptych mural *The Dance* that Matisse produced for the Barnes Foundation in Merion, Pennsylvania, between 1930 and 1933, was a turning point in his career, with the introduction of cut-outs **103**. Surprisingly, Matisse participated in the 1935 exhibition of the Temps Présent group, headed by André Lhote, in the Galerie Charpentier, which brought together artists concerned with technical revolution, classicism, and politics (Yves Alix, Jean Bazaine, Robert Delaunay, André Favory, Édouard Goerg, Marcel Gromaire, and Lhote). The show was negatively received as lacking soul due to its emphasis on the material and technical aspects of painting.[22] Zervos published the special issue "Dessins de Matisse" in 1936 in an effort to defend the artist once again and inspire a renewed appreciation of his drawing technique. He also brought out a deluxe edition in a print run of 150 copies, which included a special cover and an original print by Matisse **6**. Strongly influenced by his recent contact with Surrealism, Zervos penned the text "Automatisme et espace illusoire" (Automatism and illusory space) **63**, which associated Matisse's technical quality and spiritual energy with the Surrealist practice of automatism. Zervos absurdly employed a terminology—delirium, automatism, dream, imagination, drawing as action, etc.—that was quintessential to Surrealist writing and sought to emancipate Matisse's art from associations with realism, mathematics, and purely technical preoccupations. The Surrealist overtone of the volume was sealed by a poem dedicated to the artist by Tristan Tzara, whom Matisse greatly admired.[23]

The formalist appropriation of Surrealist jargon by Zervos did not go unnoticed by Matisse, who was somewhat unhappy with the Surrealist reading of his drawings. In the first issue of *Verve*, in 1937, the artist published a series of lithograph-drawings comparable to the set in *Cahiers d'art* and titled the accompanying text "Divagations" (Wanderings), addressing his critique to the Surrealist misappropriation—in the same vein as Zervos—of famous quotes by renowned masters of the past. He stated with irony that "Ingres affirmed that drawing is the probity of art, though one might wonder whether these words, constantly repeated by pompous ignoramuses, are to be linked with those contained in Leonardo da Vinci's manuscript recommending that lines of composition be sought in the fissures of old walls or indicating coarse tricks for giving expression to the likeness of young girls."[24]

Leonardo's words epitomized the intentions of Dada and Surrealism, Jean Cassou had earlier affirmed in a volume dedicated to the history of contemporary art, while Matisse's reference has to be understood in terms of both André Breton's appropriation of the Renaissance artist's saying in "Le message automatique" (The automatic message) a few years earlier and Zervos's audacious attempt to pair his drawing with the Surrealist technique of automatism in 1936.[25] Zervos returned to the discussion of Matisse's charcoal drawings in 1939 in a lengthy article that was accompanied by a specialist study of Leonardo's drawings by Kenneth Clark.[26]

Ingres's dictum was indeed frequently quoted in a broad range of discussions about painting, including in Georges Rouault's response to a 1935 survey launched by Zervos on the "parasitic" role of young artists in relation to their elders. Rouault's article was illustrated

22 M[ichel] F[lorissone], "Exposition du Temps présent," *L'Art et les artistes*, no. 29 (February 1935): 177–78.

23 Tristan Tzara, "À Henri-Matisse," *CDA*, nos. 3–5 (1936): 76. See also André Lhote, "Dessins de Matisse (*Cahiers d'art*)," *Nouvelle Revue française*, no. 284 (May 1937): 811–12. Matisse later produced illustrations for Tzara's poems: *Midis gagnés* (Paris: Denoël, 1939) and *Le Signe de la vie* (Paris: Bordas, 1946.

24 Henri Matisse, "Divagations," *Verve* 1, no. 1 (December 1937): 80–84, translation given in *Matisse on Art*, ed. and trans. Jack Flam, rev. ed. (Berkeley: University of California Press, 1995), 126.

25 Jean Cassou, "Le dadaïsme et le surréalisme," in *Histoire de l'art contemporain: La peinture*, ed. René Huyghe and Germain Bazin (New York: Arno, 1968 [1936]), 337; André Breton, "Le message automatique," *Minotaure*, nos. 3–4 (1933): 56.

26 Christian Zervos, "Dessins récents de Henri-Matisse," *CDA*, nos. 1–4 (1939): 5–6; Kenneth Clark, "Dessins de Léonard de Vinci, 1513–1515," *CDA*, nos. 1–4 (1939): 41–46. See also David Lomas, "Painting is Dead – Long Live Painting! Notes on Dalí and Leonardo," in *The Dalí Renaissance: New Perspectives on His Life and Art after 1940*, ed. Michael Taylor (Philadelphia: Philadelphia Museum of Art, 2008), 153–89. In 1938, Zervos dedicated a generous part of his book on the history of contemporary art to Matisse as a leading figure of Fauvism. See Zervos, *Histoire de l'art contemporain* (Paris: Cahiers d'Art, 1938).

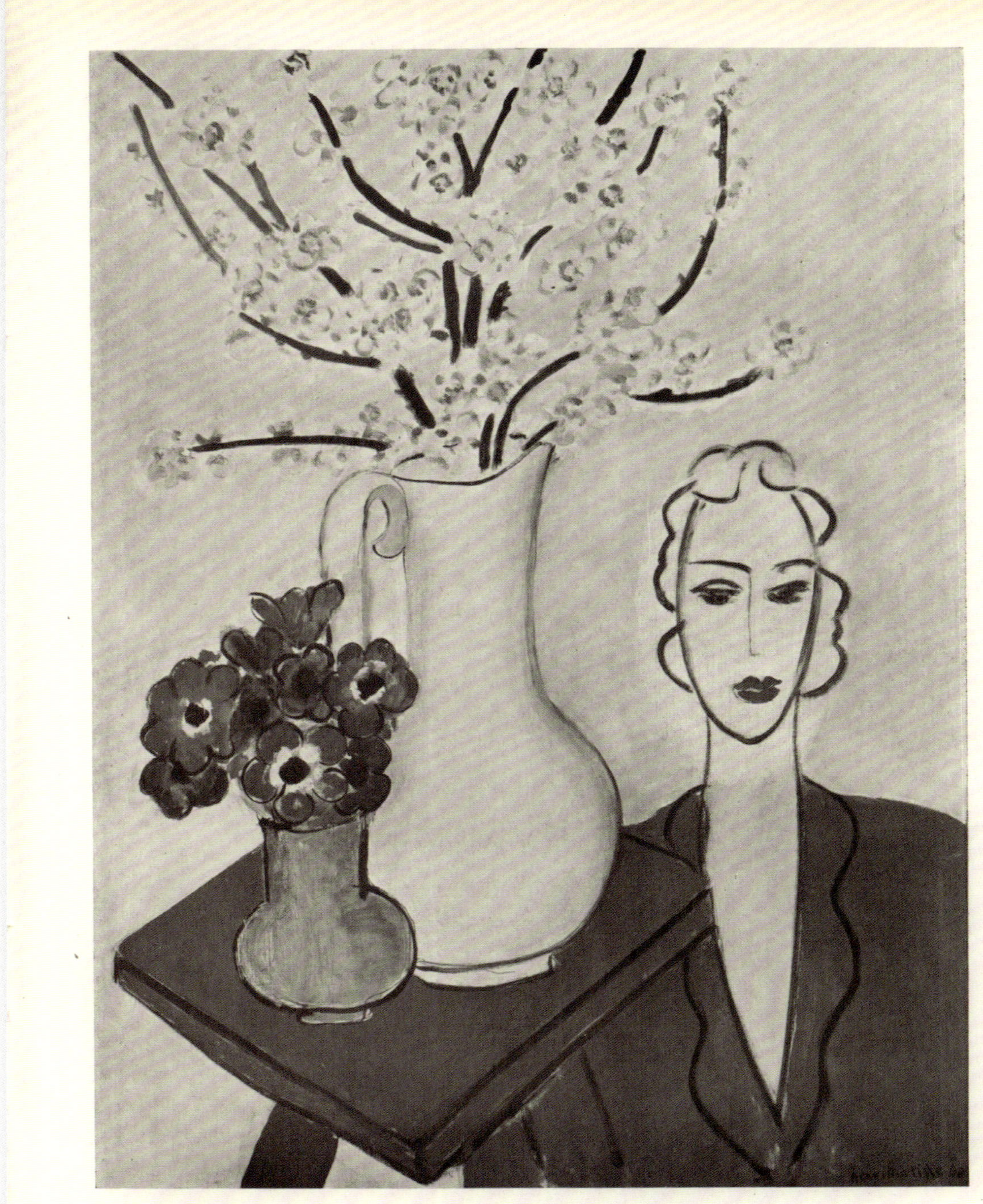

HENRI-MATISSE. FEMME AU CORSAGE ROUGE ET VASES AVEC FLEURS. 1940. HUILE SUR TOILE. 81 X 60 CM.

127

7 (fig.)
Cahiers d'Art, 1940–44,
p. 127
Éditions Cahiers d'Art,
Paris

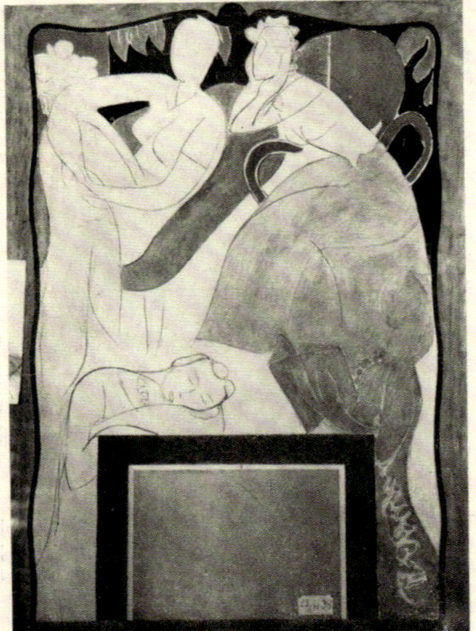

HENRI-MATISSE. DÉCORATION. ÉTAT DU 23-XI-38.

éloquent pour qu'on puisse dire qu'elles expriment plus de rapports significatifs que ne le font toutes les tentatives similaires de notre siècle.

C'est un fait remarquable que la tendance qui se manifeste chez les meilleurs de nos peintres en faveur de l'art mural se fortifie tous les jours, qu'ils en demandent l'extension, qu'ils le considèrent comme satisfaisant pleinement aux besoins plastiques de l'artiste. Dès lors il devient nécessaire de lui faire une place bien déterminée.

Mais cette expression de l'art pourra-t-elle trouver son essor, dépassera-t-elle jamais les limites si étroites dans lesquelles elle fut enfermée ? Cette appréhension subsiste très forte chez de bons esprits restés sous l'impression des attaques dirigées contre l'art individuel par les prôneurs d'un art collectif, attaques où il ne s'agissait de rien moins pour l'artiste que d'abdiquer toutes les conditions qui décident de sa valeur, pour subir les goûts des masses.

Certes ils n'ignorent point que l'esprit vivant de la multitude est un stimulant de l'art. Ils reconnaissent que la question des rapports entre l'artiste appuyé sur son instinct et les problèmes sociaux qui influent de toutes parts sur lui et le poussent

168

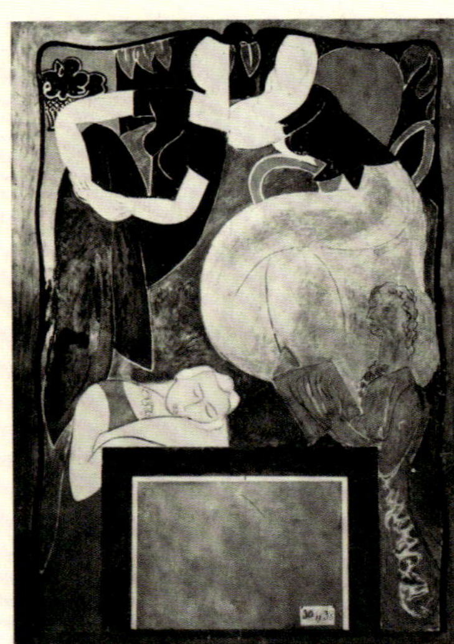

HENRI-MATISSE. DÉCORATION. ÉTAT DU 30-XI-38.

Autant que faire se peut l'artiste doit rester en contact avec les masses, seulement il ne lui faut pas demeurer en deçà mais aller au-delà de leurs désirs. Ce n'est pour lui que continuer ce qui fut aux grandes époques de l'art : se laisser pénétrer par le courant populaire pour le soutenir en retour de toute son autorité et le féconder dans l'œuvre. A l'intérieur de ces limites peut s'exercer librement l'influence de la multitude.

Je souhaiterais que ces notes pussent susciter quelque effort général où l'on prît en réelle considération d'une part les besoins profonds de l'artiste, d'autre part l'influence des masses sans que celle-ci soit jamais partie prépondérante de l'œuvre d'art.

Je souhaiterais également que les tentatives de Matisse et de Picasso ne restassent pas des tentatives isolées, sans espoir, persuadé que la peinture murale pourra trouver de notre temps emploi et faveur et rentrer dans le domaine de l'art d'où elle était à tort sortie.

CHRISTIAN ZERVOS.

171

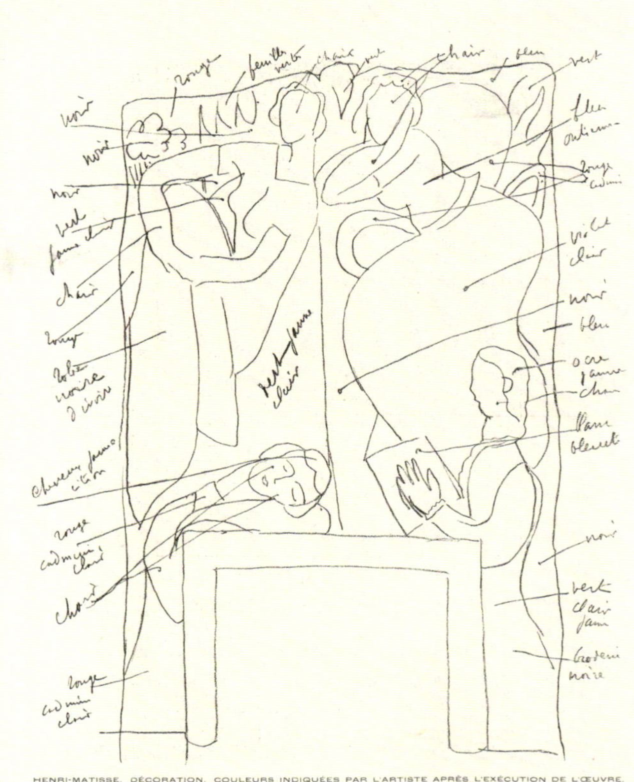

HENRI-MATISSE. DÉCORATION. COULEURS INDIQUÉES PAR L'ARTISTE APRÈS L'EXÉCUTION DE L'ŒUVRE.

172

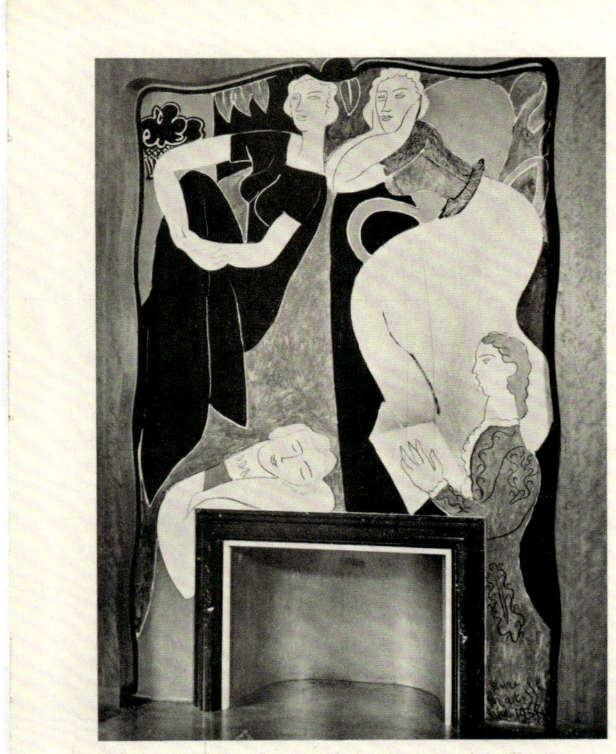

HENRI-MATISSE. DÉCORATION POUR M. NELSON ROCKEFELLER. ÉTAT DÉFINITIF.

173

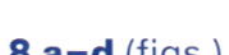

8 a–d (figs.)
In-progress photographs of
The Song and color instructions,
Cahiers d'art, 1939,
nos. 5–10, pp. 168, 171–73
Éditions Cahiers d'Art, Paris

with five reproductions of Matisse's recent works: a photograph, two drawn studies presenting the installation of *The Dance* in the Barnes Foundation, and full-page reproductions of the four stages of the decoration in its two versions, the one then in Nice and the second in Pennsylvania, the ingeniousness of which served as an example of painstaking work and profound research for the younger generation to follow.[27] In 1939, Zervos returned to Matisse's decorative work publishing his "Réflexions sur l'art mural" (Thoughts on mural art) with references to and illustrations of Matisse's *Song* 42 and its planned companion, *Music* 48. Before the Barnes mural, in the context of the renovation of his New York apartment, Nelson A. Rockefeller had commissioned Matisse and Léger to produce two overmantel paintings for the fireplaces of his New York apartment, which was under renovation. Matisse received full-scale drawings of the mantel space, and in 1938 he completed the *Song* mural in Paris. *Cahiers d'art* published photographs taken by Matisse documenting the stages of the execution of these works, which highlighted the difficulties the artist faced in tying the composition together without altering its geometrical structure. Due to its black-and-white reproduction, a full textual description was used to detail the rich coloration of *The Song*, bringing to the fore once again the journal's weak spot in the presentation of Matisse's painting 8. Matisse, through his decorations, and Picasso, through *Guernica* (1937; Museo Nacional Centro de Arte Reina Sofía, Madrid), had created "without going beyond the limits of time and place, forms that have become a common property for the human spirit."[28]

In 1940, Zervos's wife, Yvonne, registered the gallery M.A.I. (Meubles – Architectures – Installations), which opened with the group exhibition *Art représentatif de notre temps* (Art representative of our time) including works by Arp, Alexander Calder, Salvador Dalí, Ernst, Alberto Giacometti, Julio González, Juan Gris, Jean Hélion, Klee, Wifredo Lam, Laurens, Léger, Masson, Matisse, Miró, Piet Mondrian, Picasso, and Yves Tanguy. The show assembled two generations of Parisian painters that, in Zervos's opinion, bore the scepters of contemporary art in succession. The gallery held a number of solo exhibitions but closed its doors for good a few months later. The journal published two double issues in 1940 before suspending its publication for the duration of the German occupation. It came back in 1944 with the 1940–44 volume, which, according to Zervos, contained "degenerate art" produced during the occupation.[29] The volume was anathema to Le Corbusier and Vlaminck, who had been openly accused of collaboration. Picasso's new friend and well-known partner on the art market Martin Fabiani came to Zervos's aid, furnishing twenty-one photographs of works produced under oppressive conditions during the occupation. The material catered to Zervos's aspiration to give a full account of the creative resistance in occupied France, as he disclosed in a letter to Matisse.[30] The volume reproduced thirty-one paintings and drawings made by Matisse between 1940 and 1944, including his *Tulips and Oysters on a Black Background* (1943; Musée Picasso, Paris) from Picasso's collection.[31]

The 1945–46 volume of *Cahiers d'art* presented the ensuing year thirty-one pages with full-page reproductions of Matisse's charcoal drawings produced between 1942 and 1946, complemented by a 1944 photograph of the artist in his Vence studio, captured while he was painting a female sitter, Mme Lucienne, and an illustration for René Char's poem "Le requin et la mouette"(The shark and the seagull).[32] Zervos grew interested in retrieving artworks looted during the war and became involved in reinstating the ownership of a work by Matisse belonging to Alphonse Kann, which appears to have been sold by the notorious dealer Paul Petrides during the occupation.[33] In addition, the 1945–46 volume published an open call for information about the fate of ten missing artworks, nine by Picasso and one by Matisse 7, emphasizing the fact that their publication in the journal would make it impossible to sell them.[34]

Though it was first published as a periodical operating on the margins of and at odds with officialdom, *Cahiers d'art* subsequently became an established institution and a highly influential advocate for contemporary art, pursuing collaborations with high-ranking institutions

27 It is pertinent to note that Barnes forbade color reproduction of the works in his collection. Christian Zervos, "Enquête," *CDA*, nos. 1–4 (1935): 5–18. On the Barnes mural see John Klein, *Matisse and Decoration* (New Haven: Yale University Press, 2018), 66–67; and John O'Brian, *Ruthless Hedonism: The American Reception of Matisse* (Chicago: University of Chicago Press, 1999), 70–79.

28 Christian Zervos, "2 décorations de Henri-Matisse: Réflexions sur l'art mural," *CDA*, nos. 5–10 (1939): 165–78.

29 César Domela–Zervos, February 12, 1945, cited in *Lettres et manuscrits, dessins et gravures: Archives Zervos et divers*, sale catalogue, Drouot-Richelieu, November 12–13, 1998. I am grateful to Christian Derouet for drawing my attention to this source.

30 Zervos–HM, December 23, 1944, Archives Henri Matisse, Issy-les-Moulineaux. I am thankful to Christian Derouet for communicating the content of the letter to me. Matisse had collaborated with Fabiani for the publication of Henri Matisse, *Dessins: Thèmes et variations*, preceded by "Matisse-en-France" by Louis Aragon ([Paris]: Martin Fabiani, 1943).

31 See *CDA* 1940–44 (1944): 123–46. Swapping artworks was a common practice between the two artists from the beginning of the century. HM–Picasso, June 12, 1944: "Do you know that there is a still life for you in Martin Fabiani's trunk?. . . It represents oysters, a flower on a yellow-brown table, and all that on a black checkered background. It should be exchanged for one of your works. I had told Pellequer that a beautiful rooster would please me, but I thought that if there wasn't one, you couldn't make one for me. A canvas of your choice would suffice," cited in *Matisse–Picasso*, ed. Elizabeth Cowling, Anne Baldassari, and John Elderfield, exh. cat. (London: Tate, 2002), 383 (author's translation).

32 Christian Zervos, "Peines d'esprit et joies de Matisse," *CDA* 1945–46 (1946): 162–96. René Char, "Le requin et la mouette," *CDA* 1945–46 (1946): 76–77.

33 On the Kann affair, see Fonds Cahiers d'Art CAPROV 7, Bibliothèque Kandinsky, Centre Pompidou, Paris.

34 Anon., "Les tableaux de Picasso et celui d'Henri Matisse," *CDA* 1945–46 (1946): 428. Matisse's work was reproduced in the previous issue; see *CDA* 1940–44 (1944): 127.

in France and North America. Matisse often failed to agree with Zervos's intellectual position, given the latter's idiosyncratic way of thinking and frequent use of confrontational rhetoric. Zervos's unfair criticism of Pierre Bonnard, for example, in an article published in 1947, prompted a reaction from Matisse. The dispute was motivated by the special issue "Couleur de Bonnard" (Bonnard's color) published by *Verve* the previous year and Zervos's failure—after his persistent attempts—to guarantee the display of Bonnard's works in his 1947 exhibition of contemporary art at the Palais des Papes in Avignon 9, a fact that renders his dispute with Bonnard invalid. Zervos's article, which coincided with the artist's passing in January, was titled with the provocative question "Is Pierre Bonnard a Great Painter?" In it, Zervos accused the Nabi artist of lacking the strength to react against Impressionism, as Matisse and the Cubists had done, reducing his imagination to mediocre originality.[35] Matisse's reaction is often referenced: in addition to his letter of complaint to the journal in defense of Bonnard in 1948, he confidently wrote across the first page of the article in response to the question of its title, "Yes! I maintain that Bonnard is a great artist for our time, and, naturally, for posterity."[36]

Zervos's rage-driven texts from the postwar years—fueled by his ideological conflicts and personal ambitions—inevitably influenced the reliability of his criticism.[37] At the culmination of his dispute with the French Communist Party in 1949, his commentary on the Matisse exhibition at the Musée National d'Art Moderne[38] further damaged his relationship with the artist. In this analysis, he utterly devalued the conception of Matisse's paper cut-outs, claiming that they were the result of the artist's "insomnia converted to a pleasant distraction," and calling them totally negligible "pastimes [that] are no good for his glory but enough for his amusement" and a "bad neighbor" to his paintings. Zervos would have preferred an exhibition of Matisse's lesser-known paintings from the somber period 1939–48, insisting that his paper cut-outs had nothing in common with the Cubist papiers collés, the "plastic drama" of which was absent from Matisse's new creations.[39] Tériade, on the other hand, had zealously accepted the challenge to generously reproduce Matisse's cut-outs in *Verve* and his artist's books throughout the period in question. Following the artist's refusal to grant permission to Zervos to publish a catalogue of his works two years earlier, in October 1954, about a month before the artist's death, Zervos made a passing reference to Matisse's cut-outs, withdrawing his earlier position with the proclamation that they confirmed the artist's "refined and safe taste."[40] The journal published three annual issues up to 1960, when it ceased to exist. The gallery extended its activities under the direction of Zervos until his death in 1970, together with the publishing house Cahiers d'Art, which served as a link between contemporary artists and their ancestors, seeking, through a Eurocentric approach, to popularize their formal and spiritual bonds.

35 Christian Zervos, "Pierre Bonnard est-il un grand peintre?," *CDA*, no. 22 (1947): 1–6.

36 Christian Derouet, ed., *"Cahiers d'art": Musée Zervos à Vézelay* (Paris: Hazan, 2006), 98. See also Albert Kostenevitch, *Bonnard et les Nabis* (New York: Parkstone International, 2012), 7.

37 See Chara Kolokytha, "Picasso vs. Fougeron: *Cahiers d'art* and Quarrels over Realism in France (1932–1949)," in *European Avant-Garde and Modernism Studies*, vol. 6, *Realism of the Avant-Garde*, ed. David Ayers et al. (Berlin and Boston: De Gruyter, 2020), 375–90; and Kolokytha, "Christian Zervos critique d'art: Partis pris, polémiques et débats," in *Critique(s) d'art: Nouveaux corpus, nouvelles méthodes*, ed. Marie Gispert and Catherine Méneux, 2019, 257–72, https://hicsa.univ-paris1.fr/documents/pdf/PublicationsLigne/Actes%20Critiques%20art%20Meneux%20Gispert_2019/14_KOLOKYTHA.pdf.

38 *Henri Matisse, œuvres récentes, 1947–1948*, Musée National d'Art Moderne, Paris, June–September 1949.

39 Christian Zervos, "À propos de l'exposition Matisse au musée d'Art moderne de Paris," *CDA*, no. 1 (1949): 159–70.

40 Christian Zervos, "Jeune peinture et critique: À propos du Xe Salon de mai," *CDA*, no. 1 (1954): 5.

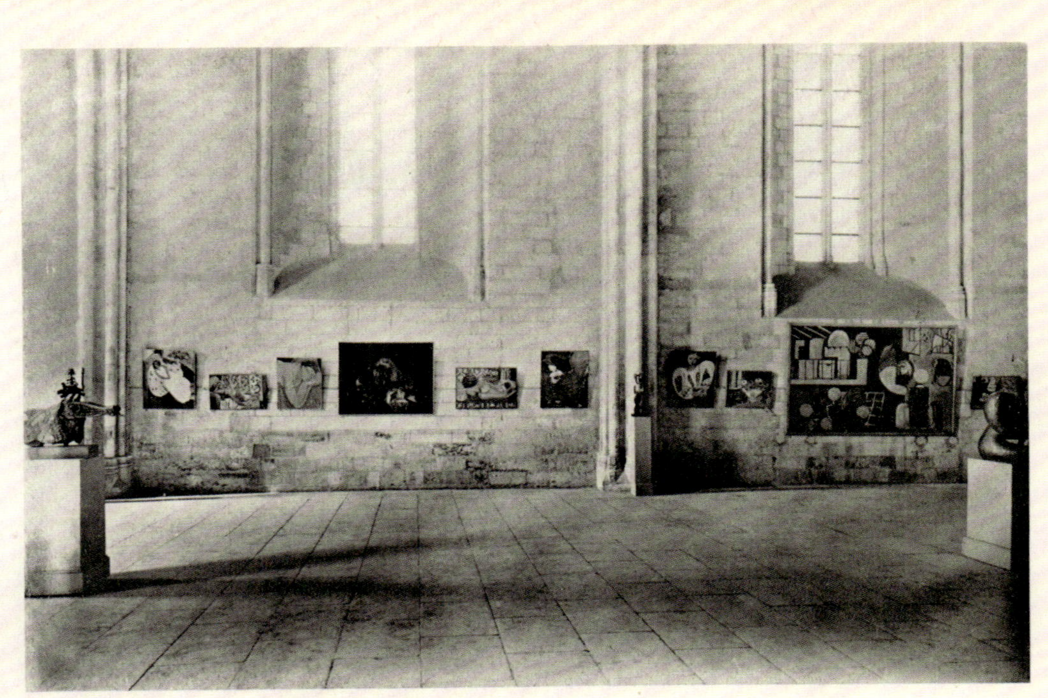

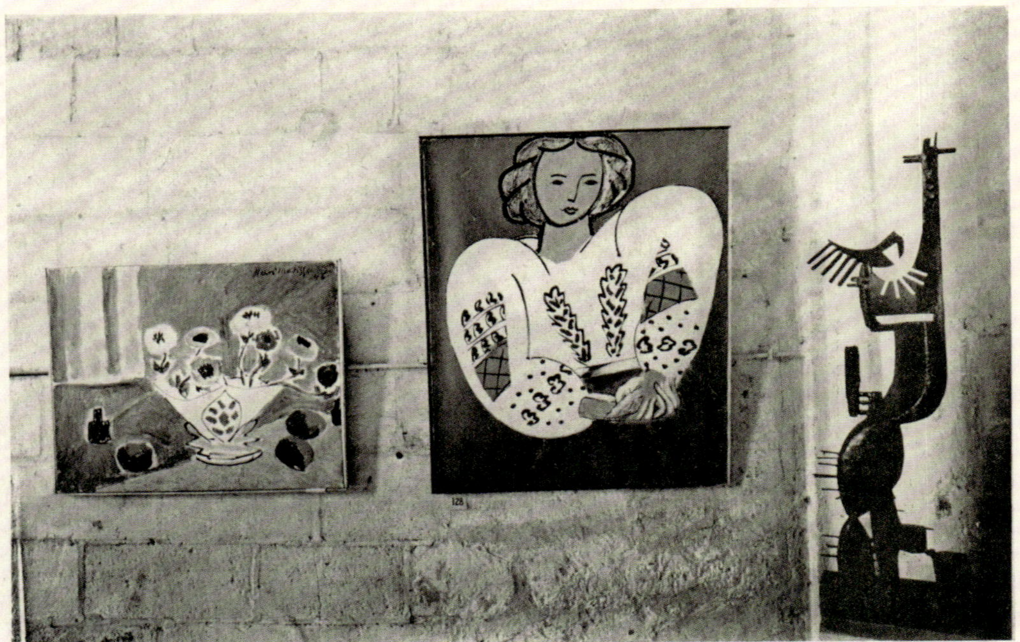

En haut : Peintures de Henri-Matisse. En bas : Peintures de Henri-Matisse, sculpture en fer de Gonzalez.

318

9 (fig.)
Cahiers d'art, 1947, p. 318

10–18, pp. 30, 35–38
Front covers of the catalogues and views of the 1930–31 *Henri-Matisse* exhibitions
Archives Henri Matisse, Issy-les-Moulineaux

10 (fig.)
Galeries Georges Petit, Paris, 1931

11 (fig.)
The Museum of Modern Art, New York, 1931

12 (fig.)
Galerien Thannhauser, Berlin, 1930

13 (fig.)
Kunsthalle Basel, 1931

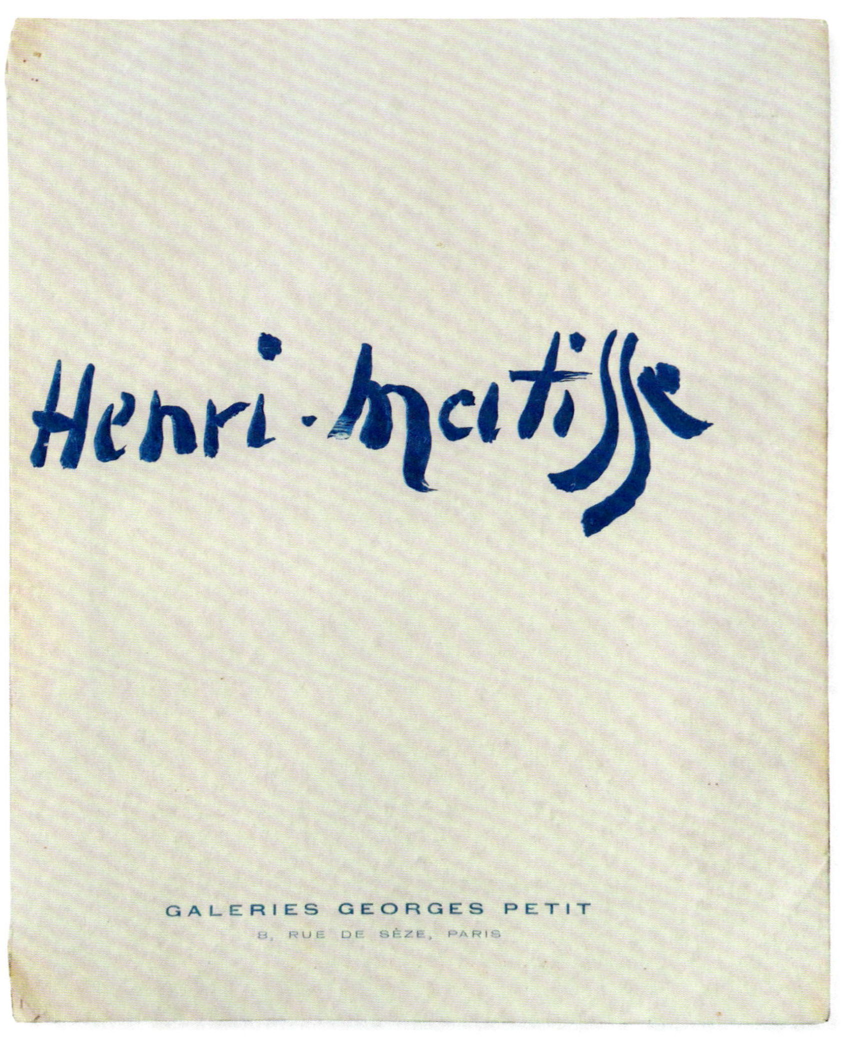

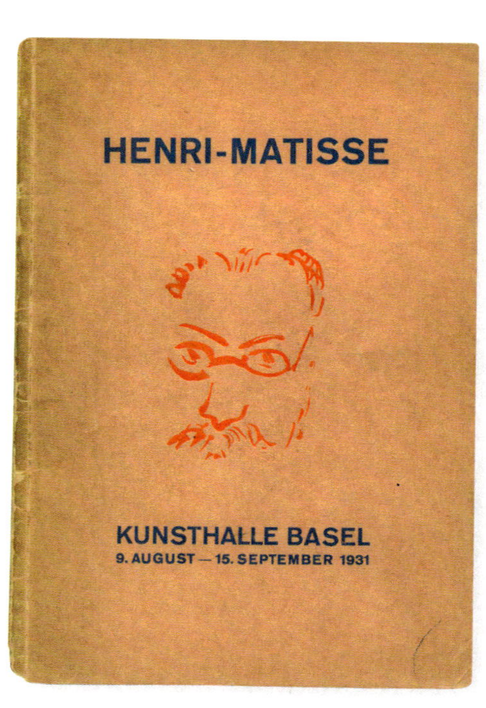

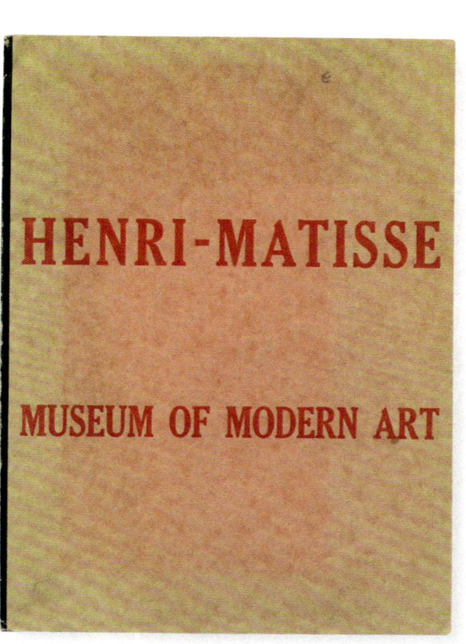

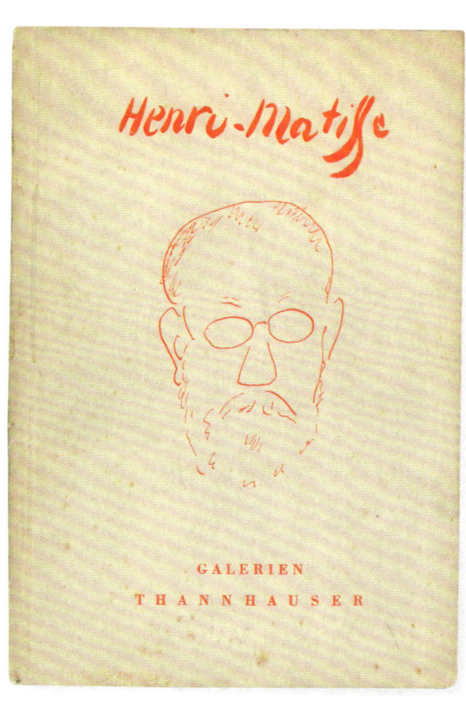

ÉRIC DE CHASSEY

A CRISIS AND FOUR EXHIBITIONS

In 1930, Matisse turned sixty. It was a time of crisis for him, in part occasioned by economic conditions that had reduced purchases by the American collectors who were his most important clients in the 1920s.[1] But, more significantly, he had to acknowledge that the sources that had nourished him for some fifteen years, an era known as the "Nice period," had dried up. His productivity slowed markedly in 1928, and in November 1929 he was forced to admit, "in front of the canvas, I have no ideas whatever."[2] His recovery from this crisis is often attributed to his trips to Tahiti and the United States in 1930, as well as to Albert C. Barnes's commission for a large mural, a major decorative project that gave rise to three versions of the composition *The Dance*. The years 1930–31 also marked the first large exhibitions of Matisse's work that were retrospective in nature (presenting works produced throughout his career rather than just those of a single period). These shows were organized at the Thannhauser Gallery in Berlin, the Galeries Georges Petit in Paris, the Kunsthalle in Basel, and the Museum of Modern Art (MoMA) in New York. There were thus two commercial galleries and two nonprofit institutions sponsoring the exhibitions, although this distinction was not absolute. The galleries displayed many works that were not for sale, while the museums in Basel and New York were "not averse to potential sales."[3]

These exhibitions were organized in honor of the artist's sixtieth birthday, although Matisse "thought it was completely pointless to speak of his age."[4] There had been several previous efforts to arrange a retrospective of his oeuvre, but these had been very limited in scope.[5] The 1930–31 shows were complemented by an exhibition dedicated entirely to his sculptures—*Sculpture by Henri Matisse*—held at the Brummer Gallery in New York from January 5 through February 7, 1931, and which included forty-six pieces. The exhibitions were accompanied by publications that covered the artist's full career in a fairly balanced manner, avoiding focusing too heavily on his most recent output.[6] A special number of *Cahiers d'art* in three languages (French, German, and English) was published just in time for the opening of the Paris exhibition. Its reproductions gave little space to Matisse's Nice period, although works from this era dominated the gallery's walls.

Looking at an artist's entire oeuvre is an occasion for an overall assessment of his work. Historically, such exhibitions have often been an artist's opportunity for a fresh departure. But, the 1930–31 exhibitions have seldom been factored into considerations of the history of Matisse's work; it was thought that, except for the Paris show, they had not been overseen directly by the artist and were instead organized by his children Marguerite and Pierre. However, documentation shows that Matisse was actively involved to the extent that his residence in Nice, his travels (he was in the United States and Tahiti while the exhibition was hanging in Berlin), and his work on *The Dance* (beginning in January 1931) allowed. The selection of works to be displayed was made under his supervision, and his choices reflected the desire to appeal to two constituencies. He was attentive to the expectations of local audiences, particularly

This essay could not have been written without the assistance and guidance of the following individuals over a period of almost thirty years: Georges Matisse, Anne Théry, and Wanda de Guébriant (†) in the Archives Henri Matisse, Issy-les-Moulineaux; Colin B. Bailey and Polly Cancro at the Morgan Library & Museum in New York; Rona Roob (†) at the archives of the Museum of Modern Art in New York; Elena Filipovic and Giulia Ficco at the Kunsthalle in Basel; all the teams in the library of the INHA; and Yve-Alain Bois, Victor Claass, Anne Consigny, Dominique Fourcade, Claudine Grammont, Marine Kisiel, Emeline Mouasseh, France Nerlich, and Juliette Trey. I hope they will recognize this work as an expression of my gratitude.

1 On the collectors of Matisse in the 1920s, see Margrit Hahnloser-Ingold, "Collecting Matisses of the 1920s in the 1920s," in *Henri Matisse: The Early Years in Nice (1916–1930)* (Washington: National Gallery of Art/ New York: Abrams, 1986), 235–74.

2 Henri Matisse [HM]–Marguerite Duthuit [MD], November 21, 1929, quoted in Hilary Spurling, *Matisse the Master: A Life of Henri Matisse; The Conquest of Colour, 1909–1954* (New York: Alfred A. Knopf, 2005), 301. On the artistic crisis and its resolution, see Yve-Alain Bois, "Matisse's Awakening," in *Matisse in the Barnes Foundation*, ed. Bois (Philadelphia: Barnes Foundation/ London: Thames & Hudson, 2015), 1:90–169.

3 The catalogue of the exhibition in Basel used asterisks to indicate which works were for sale. The correspondence between Alfred H. Barr Jr., director of MoMA, and Pierre Matisse demonstrates that certain works were indeed for sale and that this was a customary practice.

4 MD–Thannhauser Gallery, undated draft (late 1929–early 1930, before January 2, 1930), Archives Henri Matisse, Issy-les-Moulineaux [AHM].

5 In 1926, Paul Guillaume organized the exhibition of three major paintings executed between 1913 and 1916 in Paris. In 1927, Pierre Matisse organized an exhibition of nineteen pictures covering the period 1890–1926 for the Valentine Gallery in New York. Some of these were also displayed in the 1930–31 exhibitions.

6 Aside from *Cahiers d'art*, these include Florent Fels, *Henri-Matisse* (Paris: Chroniques du Jour, 1929), which was produced in an English version in 1930 with a text by Roger Fry, a German version with a text by Gotthard Jedlicka, as well as a special number "Pour ou contre Henri-Matisse" in *Chroniques du jour* (April 1931).

the interests of potential buyers, hoping to recapture his clientele in Germany and Switzerland and catering to the taste of collectors in France and the United States. He also considered the opinions of art critics, intent on reorienting the critical perception of his work.

Many works were withdrawn or substituted from one exhibition to the next. This approach allowed all periods to be represented and defined a revelatory core of work that the artist considered to be characteristic of his full career. There was clearly a fine-tuning of the selection process. The varying choices reflected the preferences of the different organizers, but also corresponded to the artist's decision to distance himself from his output of the early 1920s. He wanted to return to his basic principles, to works that represented the most satisfying aspects of his artistic practice in years past. These works could point the way to methodologies that might have been abandoned over time, but which now offered the most fertile ground for his future development. These exhibitions were not solely responsible for unleashing this potential, but they clearly played an important role in helping Matisse to chart new paths in the 1930s.

HISTORIC PRECEDENTS Retrospective exhibitions are now commonplace, but they were the exception in the early twentieth century (French museums reserved them for deceased artists). These shows became "a central means through which the art market positions, contextualises and circulates value, in dialectical tension with the institutional production of legitimating distinction or edification," to summarize the analysis of João Ribas.[7] Like the organizers of his exhibitions, Matisse was aware that solo retrospectives had played a major role in the popular perception of the featured artist's work. Such shows also influenced young artists, who discovered earlier painters and drew inspiration from the creations of their predecessors—and these rediscoveries served in turn to revive popular taste for artists who had fallen out of favor.[8] Matisse and the organizers must have hoped that their initiatives would have the same effect, at a time when the aura and mystique surrounding Matisse had faded as his work seemed in danger of being eclipsed by competition from artists deemed more innovative and inspiring, including Pablo Picasso, the Surrealists, and the international abstract painters. These perceptions affected critics, collectors, and young artists to varying degrees.[9]

There were historic precedents to these shows in the monographic exhibitions of the Impressionist and Post-Impressionist painters that the Durand-Ruel and Georges Petit galleries mounted in the 1880s. Martha Ward has shown that during this era these shows were "a refuge for aesthetic appreciation, remote from the mercenary commerce of the art market, the polemics that cleaved art criticism, and the 'public's' taste for the sensational."[10] Matisse had himself been profoundly impressed by his visit to the retrospective of Paul Cézanne's work organized by Ambroise Vollard in 1895. As a young artist who was not fully aware of the latest trends in contemporary art, he had been "surprised by the extraordinary qualities . . . found in those canvases, but at the same time a little bit shocked by the deformations or malformations, which were unexpected at that time."[11] Some fifty years later, he recalled how the show was arranged: "All the Cézannes were on the wall—there were several ranks of them, not one had a frame—as many as could fit between floor and ceiling and, sometimes, if [Vollard] could show one on an easel, he did."[12]

This same gallery—Galerie Vollard—offered Matisse his first solo show in 1904, and the artist later benefited from his first retrospective at the Galerie Bernheim-Jeune in February 1910. This included sixty-five paintings and twenty-six drawings dating between 1893 and 1910; only ten paintings were officially for sale. The show elicited very negative commentary from critics: one of the most outspoken—Jacques Rivière for *Nouvelle Revue française*—concluded with a condemnation of the very notion of a retrospective in the case of Matisse: "For him, a canvas is not an image of reality but rather a plastic supposition to be rendered in as much isolation as possible, without precedent or analogy."[13] In 1930, the artist's situation was completely different: he was incontestably one of the best-selling and most respected

7 João Ribas, "Notes towards a History of the Solo Exhibition," *Afterall*, no. 38 (Spring 2015): 15.

8 Robert Jensen observed that "after 1900, the retrospective was widely and self-consciously employed as a weapon to redress the exclusions of the past, to rewrite history, to construct a canonical history of . . . great male artists that lives on today." Jensen, *Marketing Modernism in Fin-de-Siècle Europe* (Princeton: Princeton University Press, 1994), 111–12. See also Maia W. Gahtan and Donatella Pegazzano, eds., *Monographic Exhibitions and the History of Art* (New York: Routledge, 2018).

9 On the mimetic rivalry between Matisse and Picasso, see especially Yve-Alain Bois, *Matisse and Picasso* (Paris: Flammarion, 1999) and Elizabeth Cowling, Anne Baldassari, and John Elderfield, eds., *Matisse–Picasso*, exh. cat. (London: Tate, 2002). Matisse took an interest in Surrealism from a distance and established a relationship with André Masson in November 1931. His son Pierre saw the abstract artists as distinct rivals at the same time as an exhibition in the Galeries Petit was underway: "It's not yet the time this year, nor will it be soon, for abstract painting to dominate the art market. I foresee a backlash that will be no small matter for some of them." Pierre Matisse [PM]–HM and Amélie Matisse [AM], March 25, 1931, Pierre Matisse Gallery Archives, Department of Literary and Historical Manuscripts, The Morgan Library & Museum, New York [PMGA], MA 5020, box 195, letter 173.

10 Martha Ward, "Impressionist Installations and Private Exhibitions," *Art Bulletin* 73, no. 4 (December 1991): 599–622.

11 Henri Matisse and Pierre Courthion, *Chatting with Henri Matisse: The Lost 1941 Interview*, ed. Serge Guilbaut (Los Angeles: Getty Research Institute, 2013), 62.

12 Matisse and Courthion, *Chatting with Henri Matisse*, 61. Regarding the delayed impact of Cézanne on Matisse, see Yve-Alain Bois, "Cézanne and Matisse: From Apprenticeship to Creative Misreading," in *Cézanne and Beyond*, ed. Joseph J. Rishel and Katherine Sachs, exh. cat. (Philadelphia: Philadelphia Museum of Art, 2009), 103–20.

13 Jacques Rivière, "Une exposition de Henri Matisse," *Nouvelle Revue française*, no. 16 (April 1910), quoted by Isabelle Monod-Fontaine and Claude Laugier in *Henri Matisse 1904–1917*, ed. Dominique Fourcade and Monod-Fontaine, exh. cat. (Paris: Centre Pompidou, 1993), 93.

artists of his time, even if his status was less secure than it might seem. It was potentially useful to provide Matisse with new frames of reference, for reasons that were more critic-oriented than market-driven (although these concerns are always mixed when artistic creation takes place in the context of a capitalist society).

BERLIN The idea for a series of exhibitions did not come from the artist. The Thannhauser Gallery (in German, Galerie Thannhauser) clearly took the initiative.[14] Up until this point, the Thannhausers, father and son, had sold Matisse's works only on the secondary market, but their galleries in Munich (the Moderne Galerie, opened in 1909), Lucerne, and Berlin (which took over from the Munich gallery in 1927 under the name Galerien Thannhauser, in the plural) were among the most important venues for avant-garde art in Germany, with undeniable commercial success. The documentation currently available does not reveal whether Justin Thannhauser, who managed the Berlin gallery, had prior discussions with Matisse. They had become acquainted when he was a young man, during an extended stay in Paris in 1911.[15] It is clear, however, that Thannhauser proposed that the Galerie Bernheim-Jeune take on the exhibition,[16] much to the annoyance of the artist, who felt ignored and canceled the plans for Berlin: "This is a beginning that makes me fear for the future of our relationship, and I prefer not to start it."[17] The situation was finally resolved, and Marguerite received Siegfried Rosengart, a cousin of Justin Thannhauser and manager of the recently independent gallery in Lucerne, a few months later in Paris. She showed Rosengart her father's paintings and discussed the selection of works to be exhibited in Berlin.[18]

The exhibition lasted from February 15 to March 22, 1930.[19] It included eighty-four or eighty-six paintings (two that are visible in photographs of the exhibition seem to have been omitted from the catalogue), fifty-four drawings, 104 prints, and twenty sculptures created between 1894 and 1929. Most of the paintings were not for sale ("unless however it involved a museum"[20] for those that belonged to the artist), in contrast to most of the sculptures and graphic works. A small illustrated catalogue was printed for the occasion 12, with a short generalized introductory text by Hans Purrmann, Matisse's student and friend, who had been one of the painter's greatest enthusiasts in Germany since his Fauve period.[21]

PARIS The retrospectives that followed, of varying sizes and scopes, presented the same four categories of artwork, an illustrated catalogue with a brief introductory text, and a combination of works both for and not for sale. The first of these subsequent shows was organized by the Galeries Georges Petit in Paris. This was clearly an effort to recapitulate the Berlin show and had been planned since the summer of 1929 by the Galerie Bernheim-Jeune. Matisse, who had been under contract with this gallery from 1909 until 1926 (except for commissions and works of very large format), had affiliated with the dealer Étienne Bignou in early 1930. Bignou took over the Galeries Petit and made use of its very extensive space (large enough for an additional small exhibition to be hung at the same time as the Matisse exhibition).[22] From the project's outset, the intention was to display more works than had been shown in Berlin and to make the choice "together" with the artist.[23] To this end, Matisse made contacts during one of his trips to the United States in December 1930.[24] Marguerite and Pierre were also enlisted to help, she in Paris, and he primarily in New York, where he had established himself as a dealer in 1924.[25] Pierre's involvement clearly demonstrated how the exhibition was influenced by the desire to establish Matisse's critical and historical standing as well as by commercial interests. The obsession with "quality," a term that appears frequently in correspondence, expresses the convergence of these two concerns.

The exhibition opened on June 16, 1931, with a reception attended by the artist. According to press reports, also present were his colleagues Constantin Brancusi, Charles Despiau, Marie Laurencin, Fernand Léger, Picasso, and the couturière Elsa Schiaparelli, American and international critics, and French and American collectors, with the latter attending the

14 Claude Bernheim de Villers–HM, August 16, 1929, AHM.

15 Megan Fontanella, "Guidée par l'audace artistique: La collection Thannhauser," in *Chefs-d'œuvre du Guggenheim: De Manet à Picasso, la collection Thannhauser*, ed. Fontanella, exh. cat. (Paris: Hazan, 2019), 30.

16 Bernheim de Villers–HM, August 16, 1929, AHM.

17 HM–Mr. Thannhauser, Berlin, draft [September] 1929, AHM. See also HM–Galerie Bernheim-Jeune, draft, August 26, 1929, AHM.

18 Justin Thannhauser–MD, December 12, 1929, AHM.

19 The gallery initially requested an extension set on March 20 and then two additional days to allow time for several directors of German, Danish, and Austrian museums to visit the exhibition, Siegfried Rosengart–MD, March 3, 1930; MD–Thannhauser Gallery, draft, March 9, 1930; and Thannhauser Gallery–MD, March 10, 1930, AHM.

20 MD–Thannhauser Gallery, draft, January 16, 1930, AHM.

21 The list of exhibited works and the reproductions very rarely provide dates for the works, which has the effect of obscuring differences, even though they follow a general chronological order. This fault was corrected in the catalogues of the three other exhibitions in the series, with many approximations in the Paris and Basel catalogues. For the diffusion of Matisse's works in Germany and Purrmann's role, see especially Peter Kropmanns, ed., *Inspiration Matisse*, exh. cat. (Munich: Prestel, 2019).

22 An exhibition of watercolors by Jean-Jacques Haffner was also presented between June 16 and 30: Pierre Sanchez, *Les Expositions de la galerie Georges Petit (1881–1934): Répertoire des artistes et liste de leurs œuvres* (Dijon: L'Échelle de Jacob, 2011), 3: 131.

23 "If it is convenient for you, we would be delighted to be able to show the Parisian audience, in late June 1930, an exhibition whose selection of works we would make together." Bernheim de Villers–HM, August 16, 1929, AHM.

24 Claudine Grammont, "New York," in *Tout Matisse*, ed. Grammont (Paris: Robert Laffont, 2018), 602. Reading this veritable bible of all things Matisse, which is reliable because it is so rigorously vetted, but also speculative when necessary, is now indispensable for anyone wishing to write about the artist.

25 See p. 158 in this volume.

glamorous dinner that capped the event.[26] Until it closed on July 25, the show displayed 140 paintings (several not in the catalogue), six pastels, one bronze, and uncatalogued drawings and engravings. The wealthiest attendees could purchase (or be gifted) the large and sumptuous catalogue, replete with numerous meticulous reproductions but lacking any explanatory text 10.

BASEL Plans for the exhibition in Basel were shaped at the same time as those for the show in Berlin; it is not possible to determine if they were made independently.[27] The process was initiated by Wilhelm Barth, director of the Kunsthalle since 1909, which he had made a citadel of the European avant-garde. He communicated through Thannhauser, and later, in the spring of 1930, he negotiated with Marguerite, who was once again representing her father's interests.[28] Barth postponed his exhibition to follow the Paris show, careful to address an issue raised by art history, since the challenge was to "extend the scope of the exhibition to include prior periods so as to be able to provide a general overview of Mr. Matisse's work."[29] Marguerite assisted in convincing hesitant collectors and participated actively in selecting works.[30] Barth, aided by his collaborator Charles Egger, who met the artist in Paris, began with the list from the Paris exhibition but also placed particular emphasis on Swiss and German collections. On his own initiative, he added requests for major paintings still in Matisse's possession, such as *The Painter and His Model* (1916–17; Musée National d'Art Moderne–Centre Pompidou [MNAM–CP], Paris).[31]

The exhibition, displayed from August 9 to September 15, 1931, presented 111 paintings, twenty-eight drawings, thirty-four lithographs, and sixteen bronzes; only the prints and sculptures and seven of the paintings were for sale (according to the catalogue). The small catalogue offered a selection of reproductions that was well balanced geographically and chronologically (aside from the fact that no post-1925 works were included) 13. It was introduced by a brief poem in honor of Matisse, written by Egger in German, and by a selection of the artist's statements drawn from his article "Notes d'un peintre" of 1908 and from recent publications in French. Max Sulzbachner printed lithographic posters reproducing a drawing sent by Matisse representing a stylized image of a woman wearing a caftan.[32]

NEW YORK Alfred H. Barr Jr., a young art historian, opened MoMA in November 1929 with the support of several billionaires. He was determined to make it "the world's greatest museum of modern art."[33] Barr did not begin to shape the plans for a Matisse exhibition until the summer of 1931. The museum's first solo show, it replaced a scheduled Picasso retrospective, planned for June 1931, which did not come to fruition for a variety of reasons.[34] It is difficult to be sure exactly when Barr actually began to work on the project. The first concrete steps toward choosing works occurred when he traveled to Paris and saw the show at the Petit gallery. Its list of works, as well as those featured in Basel, formed the basis of his selection.[35] However, he varied the range considerably, limiting the section dedicated to paintings from the artist's Nice period and making additions from the period he would later describe as "experimental" (1913–17).[36] Working closely with Pierre, and meeting the artist on at least one occasion, Barr returned to Paris when the Petit exhibition closed to see paintings he considered important but that had not been included (such as *The Moroccans*, 1915–16; MoMA).[37] He insisted, "We must redouble our efforts to increase the quality. To do this I am omitting many American owned pictures. Of those which we have on our European list, I do not feel that the *Manila Shawl*, ~~the *Little Girl Reading* from Grenoble,~~ *Baronne Gourgaud*, and the Ellissen *Idol* are of essential interest."[38] These comments clearly incentivized the artist, involving him more deeply and leading him to suggest the addition of several other works.[39]

The exhibition was held from November 3 through December 6, 1931. It was, by far, the tightest of the four shows, with seventy-eight paintings, one pastel, thirty-eight drawings (Barr had given equal attention to selecting these, wishing them to supplement the show in

26 Names cited in Helen Appleton Read, "Matisse, Accepted at Last," *Brooklyn Eagle Magazine*, July 26–31, 1931.

27 "As to the wishes of the Basel museum, we had initially refused them following our conversation. But today we received an urgent appeal to intervene. Knowing your point of view, we immediately refused once again, which we are letting you know so you will be aware." Thannhauser Gallery–MD, March 3, 1930, AHM.

28 Wilhelm Barth–MD, March 27, 1930, AHM.

29 Charles Egger–MD, April 5, 1930, AHM.

30 Egger–MD, July 11, 1931, AHM.

31 Egger–MD, July 3, 1931, AHM.

32 Egger–MD, July 28, 1931, AHM.

33 Alfred H. Barr, *A New Art Museum* (New York: Museum of Modern Art, 1929), n.p.

34 Rona Roob, "From the Archives: Matisse and the Museum," *MoMA*, no. 13 (Fall 1992), 24n1.

35 A typed list of paintings displayed by Petit, with annotations doubtless in Barr's hand (or that of his wife, who accompanied him to Paris), is in the archives of the Pierre Matisse Gallery (PMGA, MA 5020, box 81, file 02). The AHM have a copy of the Basel exhibition catalogue with Barr's handwritten notes commenting on various paintings, indicating that he must have gone to Switzerland.

36 This classification by period appeared in the exhibition catalogue in 1931 and was revived in Barr's very detailed 1951 monograph on Matisse, Alfred H. Barr, *Matisse: His Art and His Public* (New York: Museum of Modern Art, 1951).

37 Alfred H. Barr–MD, June 30, 1931, AHM. This painting was shown in New York in 1927 in an exhibition organized by Pierre at the Valentine Gallery. It is astonishing that Barr had not seen it; it was, after all, Barr who wrote in 1926 that Picasso "may have a less enduring influence" than Matisse (Alfred H. Barr, "Plastic Values," *Saturday Review of Literature*, July 24, 1926, quoted in Sybil Gordon Kantor, *Alfred H. Barr Jr. and the Intellectual Origins of the Museum of Modern Art* [Cambridge, MA: MIT Press, 2002], 99).

38 Barr–PM, July 8, 1931, PMGA, MA 5020, box 81, file 02.

39 "We have found a painting from 1902, reproduced in the *Cahiers d'art*, page 244, which my father would like to have included in the New York show. It is a very simple but powerful work which would add to the exhibition." PM–Barr, duplicate, August 2, 1931, with a copy sent to Pierre Matisse, PMGA, MA 5020, box 81, file 02.

14 (fig.)
Galerien Thannhauser,
Berlin, 1930

15 (fig.)
Galeries Georges Petit,
Paris, 1931

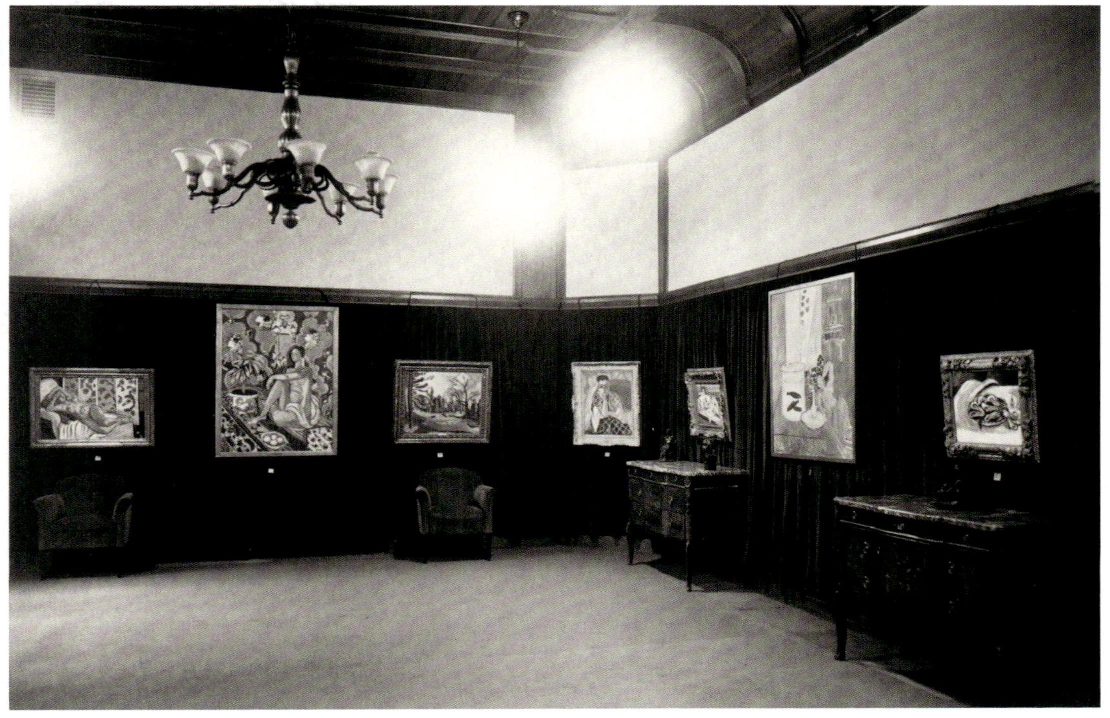

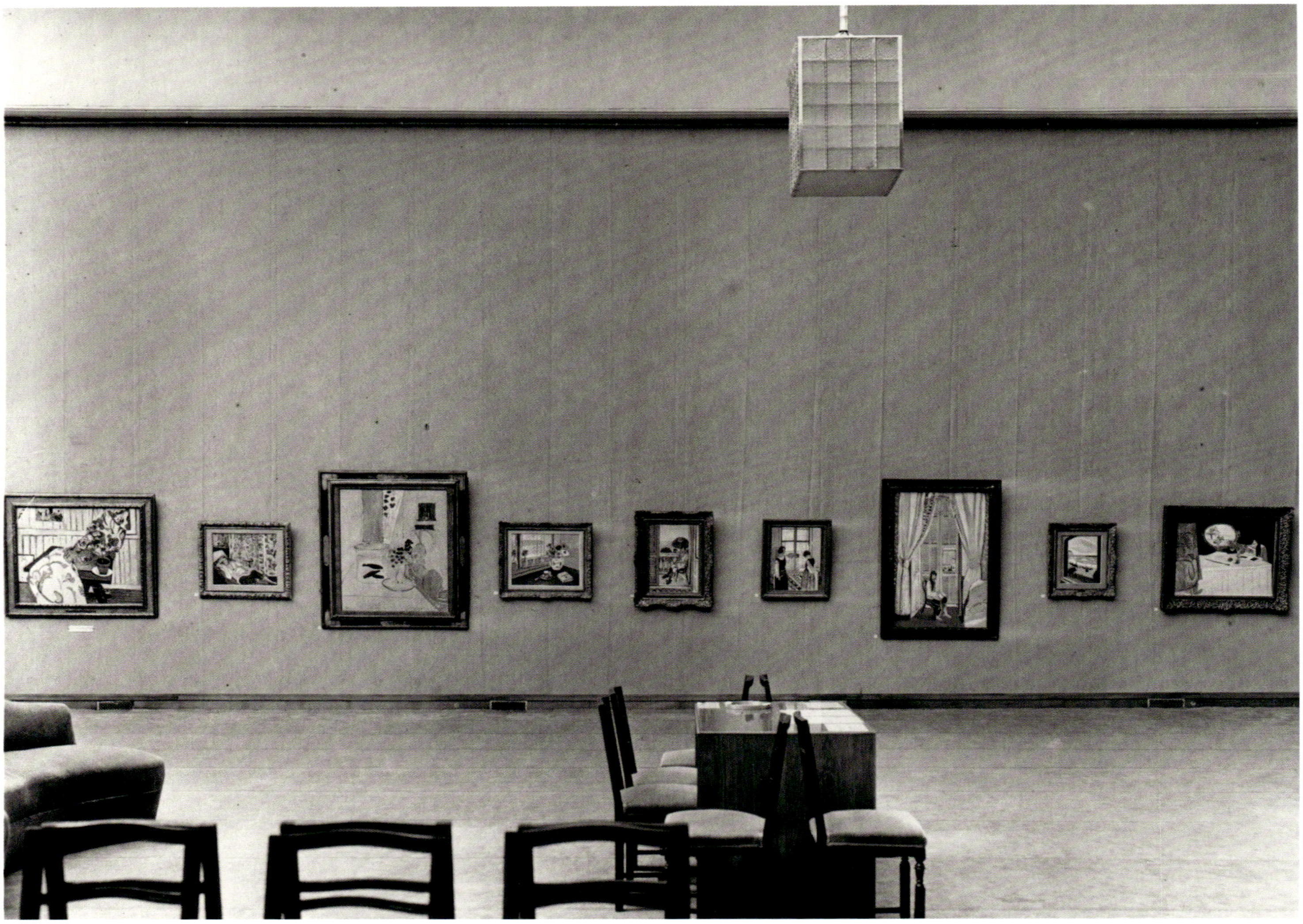

16 (fig.)
Kunsthalle Basel,
1931

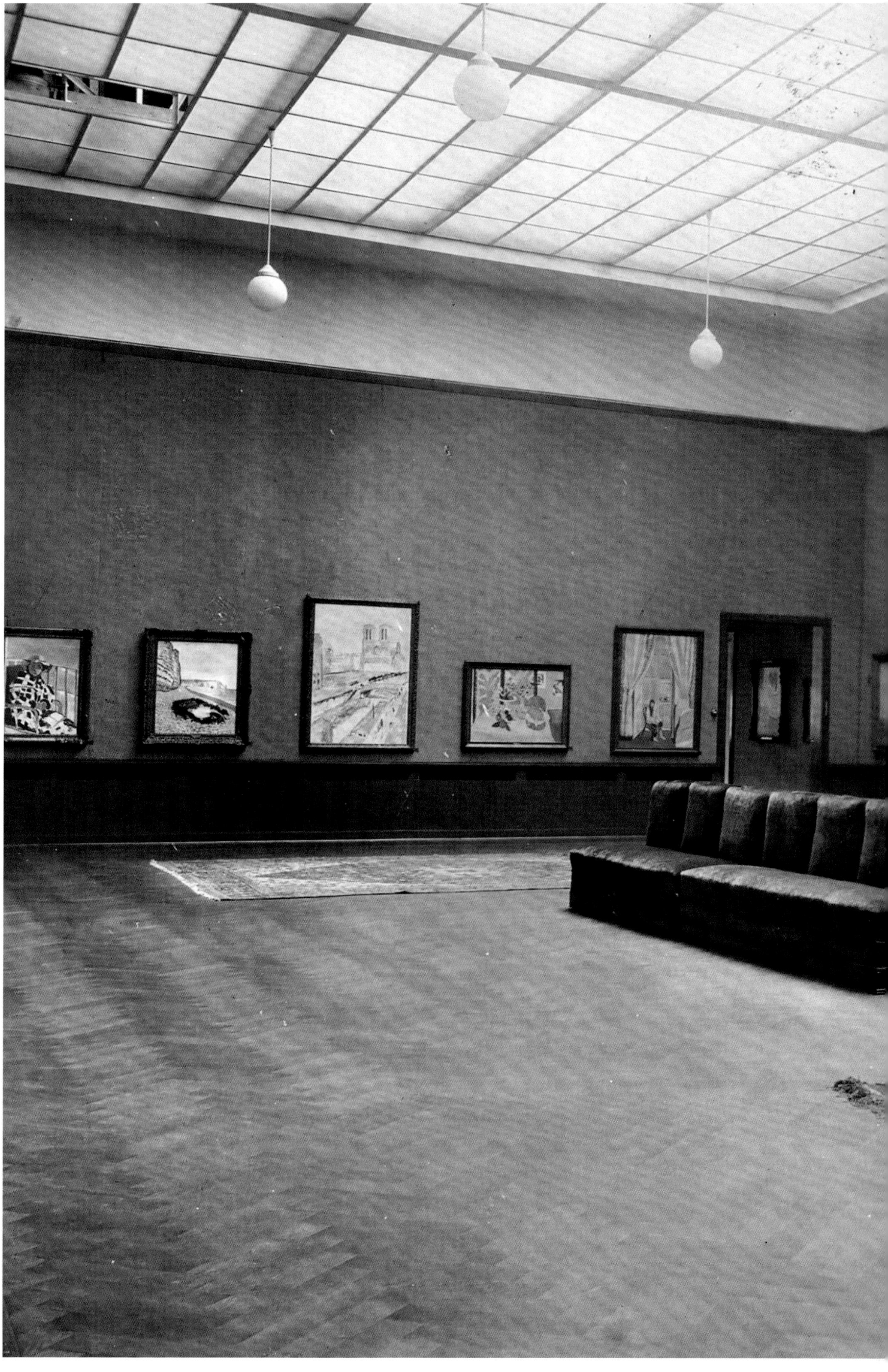

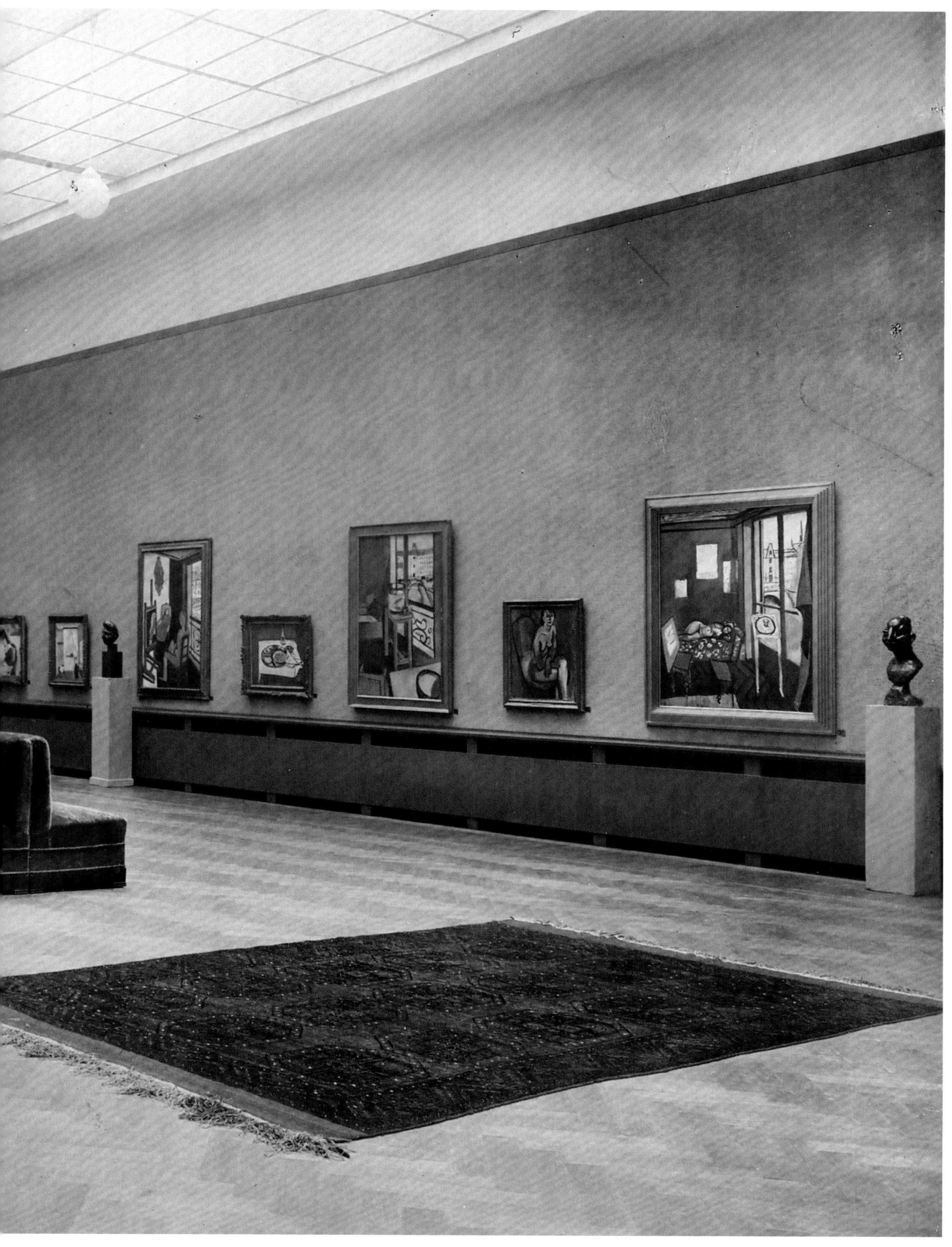

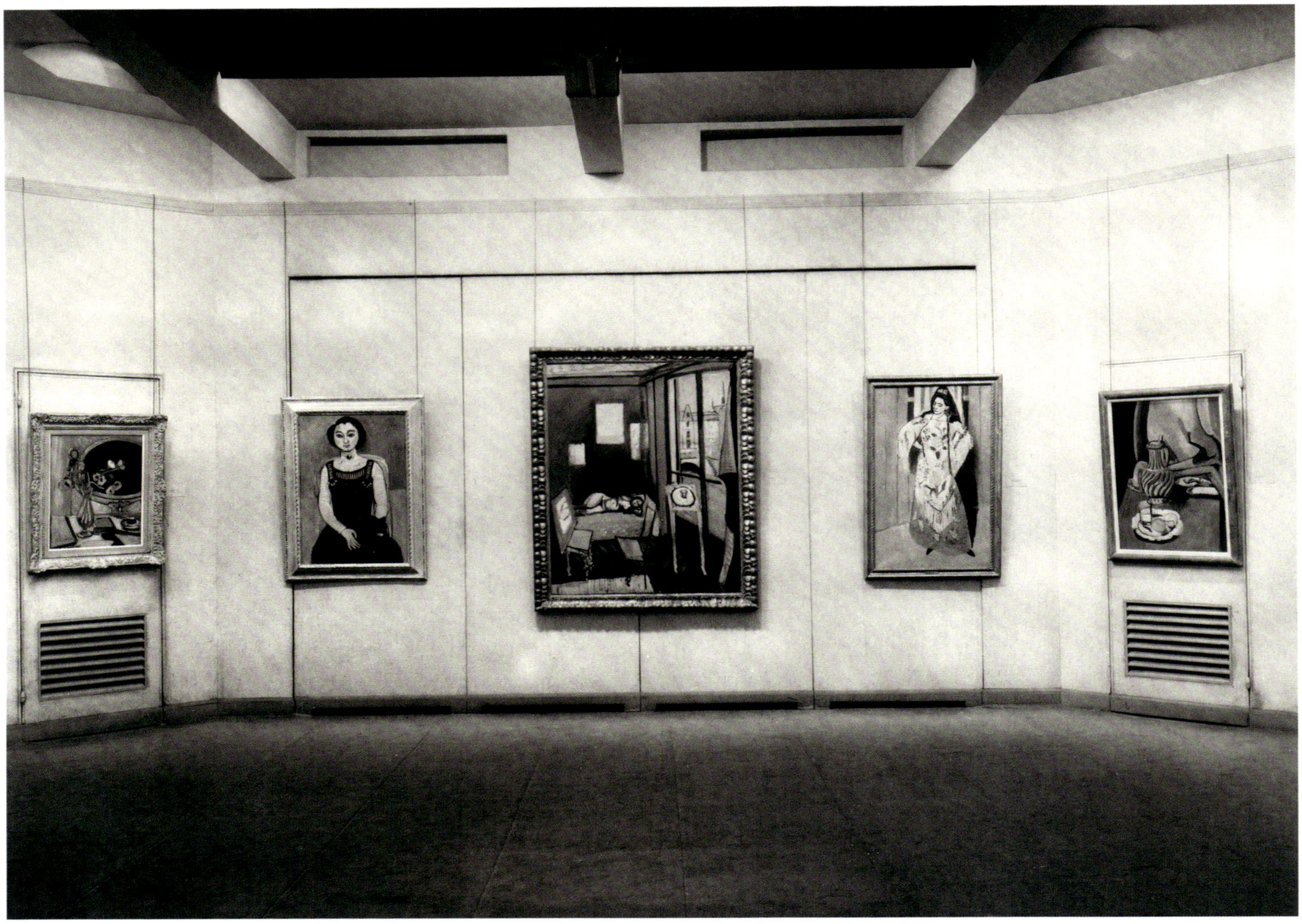

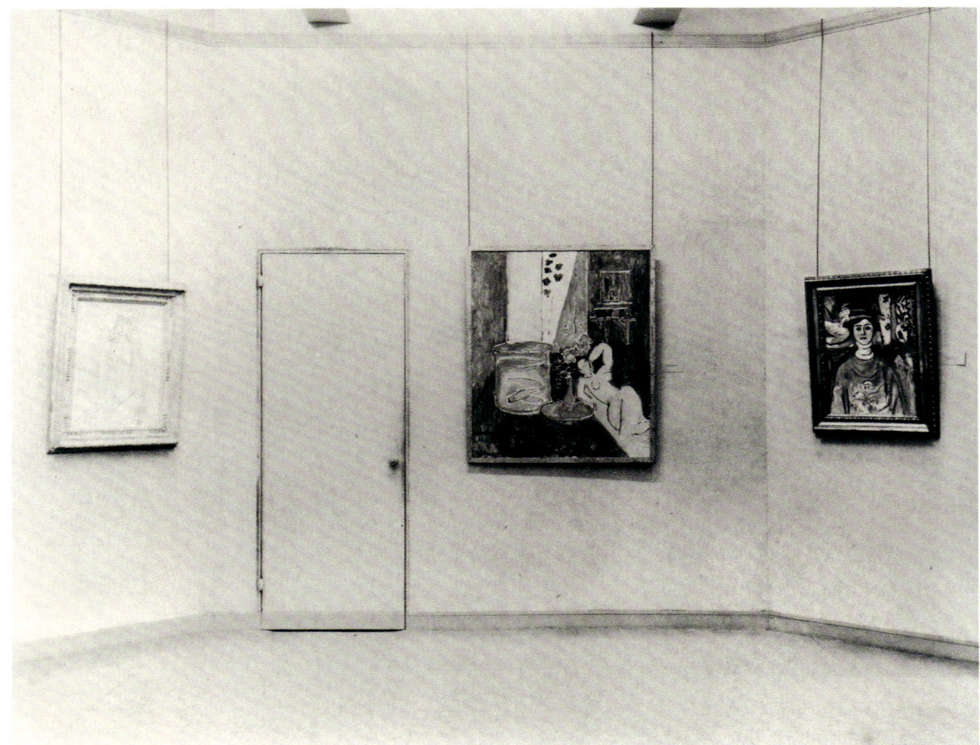

17, 18 (figs.)
The Museum of Modern Art,
New York, 1931

the absence of various large compositions that were unavailable), thirty-five prints, and nine bronzes.[40] The exhibition was accompanied by a catalogue that resembled a school notebook rather than a luxury volume 11. But Barr's lengthy introduction undoubtedly constituted the first genuine history of Matisse's work. It divided his oeuvre into seven periods, with systematic verification of dates and chronology that was missing from earlier accounts. "Notes d'un peintre" from 1908, which Barr had spotted in the Basel exhibition catalogue, was also included, translated into English and published in full.

NEUTRALITY MoMA's exhibition was incontestably scholarly—similar to those organized by museums today, although somewhat more subdued and with "interpretive materials" limited to technical labels placed beside the works. There were not, however, as many differences in its installation compared with those in Berlin, Paris, and Basel as have been suggested by the art historians who have studied the matter so far, even if, in the case of exhibitions—where appearances may embody thoughts—minimal differences can have major consequences. The four shows were in fact hung according to similar principles.

The Thannhauser Gallery in Berlin included a room draped with heavy curtains that served as a backdrop for the paintings, and smaller, paneled rooms, but, as in the other locations, its main gallery had a monochrome background from floor to ceiling (it was rather dark, as seen in photographs). The decor had been designed in a Modernist style when the gallery first opened three years earlier 14. The Galeries Georges Petit was entirely redesigned by the architect André Lurçat during the winter of 1930–31, a few months after Bernheim and Bignou took over the premises. Lurçat had "skillfully replaced time-worn [red] hangings by light-colored, pale canvas and unstained wood,"[41] and its exhibition rooms were no longer paneled 15. In Basel, there was a vestibule whose "white walls generally were hung with rather decorative studies, designs for compositions, etc., but it also lent itself to drawings and engravings." The walls of the "rooms as such . . . [were] covered in a neutral tone with a heavy cloth that . . . retained its natural linen color, a yellowish deep gray" 16.[42] At MoMA, the rooms were hung from floor to ceiling with monk's cloth, a smooth undyed cotton fabric that was pale gray 17.[43]

All these locations adopted—almost entirely—the principle of chromatic neutrality, which had been embraced by the Neo-Impressionists in the late 1880s. MoMA radicalized the principle even further by eliminating all furnishings, in contrast to the three other venues (there were even rugs in Basel). This feature distinguished the gallery space from places where life's daily activities were carried out, although it was not yet strictly speaking a "white cube."[44] As Kristina Wilson noted, the museum's location was within a commercial building (the Heckscher Building, built in 1921), where it remained until it relocated in 1932. The structure's decor was Neoclassical up to the museum entrance, so visitors were admitted into a palatial setting that was somewhat at odds with the principle of neutrality.[45]

With a few minor exceptions, the approach to hanging the works conformed to the convention of installing paintings in a single row (centered at eye level in Paris and New York, a little lower in Berlin, and aligned along the bottom in Basel). They were regularly spaced, making room here and there for sculptures, and paintings were separated from graphic works. This presentation was gradually accepted as standard practice for contemporary art. It was based on practices advocated in the late nineteenth century by James Abbott McNeill Whistler, the Impressionists, and the Neo-Impressionists. As Martha Ward has observed, this display technique highlighted "the autonomy of the work . . . the separation of the painting from its environment and its exclusive claim on the viewer's attention."[46] Nevertheless, none of the 1930–31 exhibitions fully adopted Paul Signac's directive of 1895: "The usual exhibition of paintings will be one that, with the exclusion of all colorful objects (catalogues, hangings, flowers, frames, even ladies' hats), allows the colors of the canvases to sing triumphantly in their inviolate harmonies."[47] Matisse's paintings usually had elaborate gilded frames, and these were not replaced by more neutral frames, even at MoMA, which normally did so.

40 A selection of about half the works shown in New York was presented at the Rhode Island School of Design in Providence, December 14–28, 1931. A plan for a stop in California was abandoned.

41 Seymour de Ricci, "Henri Matisse Honored at Dinner Opening Exhibition of His Works," *New York Herald*, June 17, 1931.

42 Barth–MD, October 3, 1930, AHM. The walls did however have paneling on their lower portions.

43 Mary Anne Staniszewski, *The Power of Display: A History of Exhibition Installations at the Museum of Modern Art* (Cambridge, MA: MIT Press, 1998), 61–62.

44 See Brian O'Doherty, *Inside the White Cube: The Ideology of the Gallery Space* (Berkeley: University of California Press, 1999); Walter Grasskamp, "Die weiße Ausstellungswand: Zur Vorgeschichte des 'white cube,'" in *Weiß*, ed. Wolfgang Ullrich and Juliane Vogel (Frankfurt: Fischer, 2003), 29–63.

45 Kristina Wilson, *The Modern Eye: Stieglitz, MoMA, and the Art of the Exhibition (1925–1934)* (New Haven: Yale University Press, 2009), 130–44.

46 Ward, "Impressionist Installations," 619.

47 P.S. [Paul Signac], "Catalogue de l'exposition des XX," *Art et critique*, February 1, 1890, quoted in Ward, "Impressionist Installations," 620n73.

Pictures were no longer hung above each other (except in the small rooms of the Galeries Petit), so such frames were no longer needed to perform the function they had served since the Renaissance—assuring that "the eye's gaze is captured and not at all distracted elsewhere, being besieged by other nearby objects, mingling with the things depicted, confusing the sight," as advocated by Nicolas Poussin.[48] Traditional frames thus became an implicit acknowledgment that a work's final destination was the home of a private collector rather than a museum's walls. Such frames made no effort to "escape the laws of the market," although at that time Matisse "was suffocating . . . from the constraints of easel painting," according to Yve-Alain Bois.[49]

THE AESTHETIC PRINCIPLE None of these hanging methods followed a chronological order. Strictly speaking, the function of these shows was not retrospective: they did not attempt to follow the artist's evolution step-by-step, or show his development as a historical narrative. The rationale for hanging was an aesthetic choice, emphasizing the continuity of the artist's themes and preoccupations beyond mere formal variations. These displays harkened back to the tradition of symmetrical hanging, where a rhythmic frieze was based on the presentation of two similarly sized paintings on either side of a much larger canvas with which they shared thematic or formal similarities (these echoes might be in terms of composition or predominant color palette, for example).[50] This approach did not come exclusively from the exhibition organizers, whose preoccupations were primarily commercial in the case of the gallery shows and curatorial for the museum exhibitions, nor was it merely an adaptation to the space available.

The hanging of the exhibition in Berlin was initially supervised by Justin Thannhauser, who had reserved the main gallery for "French painters of the nineteenth century: Cézanne, Van Gogh, Renoir, Monet, etc. and . . . had piled up the Matisse works in other spaces, some of which were corridors." Marguerite, who was on site for at least three days, started over and, with Purrmann's help, managed to achieve a result that she described as "rich and handsome—light—French" in a letter to her mother.[51] The Galeries Georges Petit stressed in its communications that "the hanging of the pictures will be arranged by Monsieur Henri Matisse himself."[52] Although the artist's actual degree of involvement is a matter of conjecture, it is clear that he at least approved what was proposed and that Pierre, who had returned to Paris for the occasion, was roped in as well. Matisse was involved in the Basel show only peripherally. Rather than going to Switzerland, he chose to visit Italy in September 1931 to see Giotto's frescoes in Padua again. The Basel exhibition was once again overseen by Marguerite, who made a special trip three days before the opening reception.[53] Barr was intensively involved in the early stages of the New York exhibition's hanging, fine-tuning the number of works selected to the space available.[54] This was in part because the Matisse family—perhaps reacting to what had been done in Paris—requested that "the exhibition should not be crowded."[55] Also, Pierre apparently intervened, although he had "almost nothing to change," as he reported to his father in a lengthy account of the exhibition.[56]

Leaving aside the issue of the quality of the works selected and their arrangement (which I will address shortly), the major difference in the hanging of the exhibitions lay in the spacing of the pictures. The New York show clearly stands out from this perspective. The pictures in the Berlin, Paris, and Basel exhibitions were between 11 13⁄16 and 19 11⁄16 inches (30 and 50 cm) apart, even less in the small room in the Galeries Petit, where they were hung in two rows. The spacing in New York was about a meter. The museum's main gallery, which measured about 52 feet 6 inches by 19 feet 8 inches (16 × 6 meters), presented twenty-one paintings, while that of the Thannhauser Gallery, measuring 2 feet 10 5⁄8 inches by 32 feet 9 11⁄16 inches (8.5 × 10 meters), accommodated twenty-three. The vast main hall of the Galeries Petit, approximately 82 feet by 49 feet 2 ½ inches (25 × 15 meters), had no fewer than forty-nine. Visitors in Berlin and Paris were thus assailed by a mass of visual information that was overwhelming in its sheer

48 Nicolas Poussin–Paul Fréart de Chantelou, April 28, 1639, quoted by Jean-Claude Lebensztejn, "À partir du cadre," in *Le Cadre et le socle dans l'art du XXe siècle*, ed. Daniel Abadie and Serge Lemoine (Dijon: Université de Bourgogne/Paris: Centre Pompidou, 1987), 6.

49 Yve-Alain Bois, "Exposition: Esthétique de la distraction, espace de démonstration," *Cahiers du MNAM*, no. 29 (Fall 1989): 62, 64.

50 In preparing this essay, I constructed a 3D maquette of the hangings in Berlin, Paris, and New York with color images of the paintings, which helped me to make a more intuitive assessment of the rationale that guided the choices related to the hanging, if not the selection. These reconstructions were based, particularly for Paris, on initial identification work performed by Dominique Fourcade, who generously shared it with me when I was working closely with him in the preparation of the 1993 exhibition *Henri Matisse (1904–1917)* at the MNAM–CP, Paris.

51 MD–AM, February 17, 1930, AHM.

52 Press release (in English) announcing the exhibition in the Galeries Georges Petit (scrapbook of the exhibition, AHM).

53 Egger–MD, July 28, 1931, AHM.

54 "After calculating our gallery space carefully I find that we have room (and this includes three large pictures) for about 26 size 100 cm. About 51 size 75 to 50 cm. And about five size 30 cm. In other words about 82 paintings in all. I should prefer to limit this to 75." Barr–PM, July 8, 1931, PMGA, MA 5020, box 81, file 02.

55 Barr–PM, July 8, 1931, PMGA, MA 5020, box 81, file 02.

56 PM–HM and AM, November 12, 1931, PMGA, MA 5020, box 81, file 02.

abundance—only viewers who were already familiar with the works or had come to explore a possible purchase could effectively distinguish among the artworks presented. In New York, on the other hand, individualized appreciation was entirely feasible—a viewer could concentrate on each work individually while discerning links with paintings hung nearby or at a greater distance. As John O'Brian has shown, with a few approximations in the analysis of the hanging, this approach demonstrated Barr's particular care for the "audience" that he wished to develop for his new museum and more generally persuade of the merits of contemporary art.[57]

If we focus on the core works (nineteen paintings and one sculpture) that were presented in all four exhibitions, we realize how the significance attributed to them varied from one show to the other. The guidelines for hanging changed very little. For example, *Goldfish and Sculpture* (1912; MoMA, owned by Purrmann at the time) was flanked in a similar way by two smaller canvases: in Berlin by a nude (*Reclining Nude*, 1928; Barnes Foundation, Philadelphia) and a still life (*Oysters*, 1925; Kunstmuseum, Bern) whose compositions were complementary in their dominant color palettes and measurements, despite the differences in their subject matter; in Paris by an odalisque (*Odalisque in Red Trousers*, 1924–25; Musée de l'Orangerie, Paris) and an interior (*Still Life, "Pascal's Pensées,"* 1924; private collection) that had the same characteristics; and in New York by a standing nude (*Antoinette*, 1919; private collection) and a female portrait bust (*The Girl with Green Eyes*, 1908; San Francisco Museum of Modern Art). But the effect was quite different due to the expanses of neutral wall separating them (although a very awkward door interrupted the serenity of the display at MoMA 18). There are numerous other examples, including the *Decorative Figure on an Ornamental Ground* (1925–26; MNAM–CP) and *Ballet Dancer Seated on a Stool* (1927; Baltimore Museum of Art).[58]

The New York show was also distinguished by the space allocated to pictures of large and very large format. Such paintings were few in Berlin, where there were only eleven large paintings (measuring at least 3 feet 3 inches [a meter] on a side, to follow Barr's criteria, with the largest measuring about 4 feet 11 inches [1.5 meters]). There were very few in Paris (twenty-four did not exceed 5 feet 1 inch [1.55 meters] in height). In Basel there were twenty-three (including the monumental *Bathers with a Turtle*, 1907–8, now in the Saint Louis Art Museum, but which belonged to the Museum Folkwang in Essen at the time), and twenty-one in New York (where *Bathers with a Turtle* was joined by two other monumental paintings, *The Moroccans* and *Nasturtiums with the Painting "Dance I,"* 1912, Metropolitan Museum of Art, New York). Incontrovertibly, the variety of formats and the presence of monumental canvases alleviated the impression of monotony (very evident in Paris) and contributed to a perception of the artist's tendency toward "monumentality" while emphasizing the limited market potential for such large works (for the time being: this sentiment would change after the war with the emergence of Abstract Expressionism).

SELECTION The effect of saturation or, in contrast, what could be called the effect of abstraction (or the autonomy of the works) is further accentuated by the selections made from various periods of Matisse's career. All the exhibitions presented paintings that included the full chronological range, but the eras were represented in varying proportions. Works painted in Nice after 1917 constituted almost two-thirds of the paintings shown in Berlin and Paris, and a little over half the works displayed in Basel and New York. The differing proportions are even more apparent when we consider how the paintings were hung in the main galleries of each exhibition, the locations that were most likely to attract visitors. With the exception of four paintings, the walls of the main room of the Thannhauser Gallery were completely filled with works from the artist's years in Nice. They represented two-thirds of the pictures presented in the main room of the Galeries Petit, but only one-third of those displayed in MoMA's main gallery.[59] Furthermore, in the case of MoMA, with a single exception, they were pictures that were atypical of Matisse's work in that period: the only odalisque presented was the architectural *Decorative Figure on an Ornamental Ground*.

57 John O'Brian, *Ruthless Hedonism: The American Reception of Matisse* (Chicago: Chicago University Press, 1999), 99ff.

58 None of these core works was visible in a single sightline in the Basel exhibition (AHM), which shows only a portion of the main gallery cleared of the partition walls used in other exhibitions during the same period (see https://www.kunsthallebasel.ch/wp-content/uploads/Ausstellungstext_Exposed_Exhibitions_EN.pdf, last accessed January 30, 2022).

59 In views of the Basel exhibition, there are works from the 1910s and the 1920s, as well as a painting dated 1906.

Barr did not entirely neglect the years in Nice, but, by concentrating on paintings executed after 1926, he limited them, instead displaying works from his favorite period, the years 1913–17. These works were marked by an "austere form," a "restrained palette," and "experimentation with 'abstract' design."[60] Barr relegated to the exhibition's margins—the side rooms—the few examples that he apparently felt obliged to include (such as *White Plumes*, 1919; now in the Minneapolis Institute of Arts, which at the time belonged to Stephen C. Clark, one of MoMA's trustees, along with many other paintings of the Nice period).[61] Whereas in Paris, Matisse appeared as a painter of profusion and fragmented color, in New York he was a painter of flat color zones and simplified shapes of pure hues, often structured by a visible drawing, including most of the Nice canvases that Barr presented. It is easy to understand how the exhibitions evoked such varying reactions: they differed in both interpretation and in the way the works were selected and displayed.

Several worthwhile subjects merit further study. These include the commercial success (or lack thereof) of the exhibitions, particularly those where it was an implicit objective, despite claims to the contrary (and by "commercial" we should also understand sales by museums); the impressive attendance figures boasted by every organizer; and critical reaction to the shows. I will not try to address them here, much as I would like to. Suffice it to say that the general sentiment of the written reviews did not vary much from one venue to the next, although a kind of inversion came into play. Conservative critics applauded the Berlin and Paris exhibitions, while those more closely associated with the avant-garde disparaged them. In New York, the opposite was the case. In Europe, Matisse was viewed, for better or worse, as an artist who was fully an heir of Impressionism (the German critic Carl Einstein began an article with a definitive sentence: "Matisse seems to be the last of the significant Post-Impressionists; his work is still bathed in the erstwhile happiness of the prewar era"),[62] and even of the painting of the eighteenth century (an English critic, as a form of compliment, called him the "Gainsborough of French art").[63] In the United States, he was known as the "world's most important Modernist."[64]

LESSONS It is difficult to determine the effect of these retrospectives on Matisse himself. His son Pierre compared his impression of the exhibitions in New York and Paris: "The critics, with [Henry] McBride at their head, write that the exhibition is better than the one in Paris, and that the selection and presentation of the paintings is also superior.[65] They were delighted that the art is better understood and appreciated in New York than in Paris with an exhibition that served him well without overwhelming him. That is absolutely true! Viewing this exhibition, one experiences an impact much greater than in Paris where they made the error of showing too many paintings—and most of all—I now regret I was not insistent enough—did not display Guillaume's large paintings [*The Lilac Branch*, *Bathers by a River* 20, and *The Piano Lesson*, which were shown in Paris in 1926, without great success] in the large gallery. It is clear that we did not heed all the different voices."[66] The artist simply responded, "I appreciate what you have told me about the conditions of the exhibition in Paris. But you know that for Guillaume's pictures it was difficult. And we said we would keep them for another time."[67]

It was to be expected that Matisse would prefer to emphasize recent pictures, since it was obviously the work he felt closest to. All the exhibitions allotted a certain amount of space to the paintings done in the period 1927–29; these were often not very nice-looking, but, in the case of Paris (and unlike Berlin), they represented only a tiny percentage of the whole. Most of the canvases from Nice (and from Étretat) dated from the years 1920–23. This was no doubt because the Parisian dealers, as well as Bernheim and Bignou, and Paul Rosenberg and Paul Guillaume, had accumulated inventories of these works that they wanted to sell. It is difficult to avoid the thought that Matisse was dismayed when contemplating the large assortment of odalisques and still lifes in Paris that were stylistically close to Impressionist works. He must have felt that he had allowed himself to fall into a comfortable torpor

60 Alfred H. Barr, "Introduction," in *Henri-Matisse: Retrospective Exhibition*, ed. Barr, exh. cat. (New York: Museum of Modern Art, 1931), 18.

61 When Clark wished to donate this painting to the museum a few years later, Barr declined, saying—very unjustly—that the painting resembled a "cheesecake" (O'Brian, *Ruthless Hedonism*, 116).

62 Carl Einstein, "Henri Matisse," *Die Weltkunst* 5, no. 24 (June 14, 1931) (reprinted in Carl Einstein, *Werke*, vol. 3, *1929–1940*, ed. Marion Schmid and Liliane Meffre [Berlin: Medusa, 1985], 203–8). Published on the occasion of the Paris exhibition, but several days before it opened, this lengthy article was not a review of the show. Matisse, who did not speak German, almost certainly was unaware of its contents.

63 "Art in Paris: The Henri Matisse Exhibition," *The Times* (London), June 18, 1931, press cutting AHM.

64 Ralph Flint, "Matisse Exhibit Opens Season at Modern Museum," *Art News* (November 7, 1931): 5.

65 See Henry McBride, "The Museum of Modern Art Gives a Matisse Exhibition with Special Success," *New York Times*, November 7, 1931.

66 PM–HM and AM, November 12, 1931, PMGA, MA 5020, box 195, letter 179.

67 HM–PM, November 29, 1931, PMGA, MA 5020, box 195, letter 183.

for years on end. It is one thing to see pictures individually in a studio, and the first Nice period had its share of significant pieces and complex compositions. But because they functioned based on an alliance between saturation (which Einstein described as an "amalgamate of impressions")[68] and lightness, they required a degree of focused concentration that was impossible in Paris.[69]

This was apparently the most important lesson that Matisse learned from the four exhibitions: he wanted to be an artist who opened a path rather than closed it, a pioneer rather than an inheritor. He needed to reenter history; he had intuitively grasped that "history is not a repetition of the same thing" (to quote Einstein one last time).[70] Beginning in 1934–35, with the completion of *The Dance*, he returned to familiar themes, but transformed the role of repetition in his creative process. He made it a vital and programmatic principle, even an experimental one (in the drawings collected under the title *Thèmes et variations* in 1943, for example),[71] or he developed each painting in successive stages (which were systematically documented in photographs beginning in 1935). In any case, Matisse never returned to the Impressionist space of the paintings of the Nice period. Instead, he applied to their themes the lessons learned from the experimental period as broadly defined (1907–17). These included the tension between line and color, even at the risk of dissociating the two. This was a conflict that would only be reconciled through his gouache cut-outs. Later exhibitions never devoted as much space to the Nice period, with the exception of *Henri Matisse: The Early Years in Nice (1916–1930)*, organized at the National Gallery of Art in Washington in 1986. The last general retrospective to date (*Matisse comme un roman* [Like a novel], 2020–21; MNAM–CP) once again relegated the Nice period to the smallest portion of works shown, another indication of the lasting influence of the 1930–31 exhibitions. Nearly a hundred years later, those exhibitions still influence the way we perceive "Matisse"—not as an individual who lived his life, but in terms of what distinguishes his oeuvre, of what entitles him to be recognized as a "great artist."

68 Einstein, "Henri Matisse," 206.

69 When I created maquettes of the hangings in Berlin and Paris, I found it impossible, confronted with the accumulation of paintings of the Nice period, to distinguish their salient features; this was not the case for the pictures of other periods. It is now time for an exhibition to again focus on this period and cast a discerning eye on the works of those years.

70 Einstein, "Henri Matisse," 208.

71 See p. 215 in this volume.

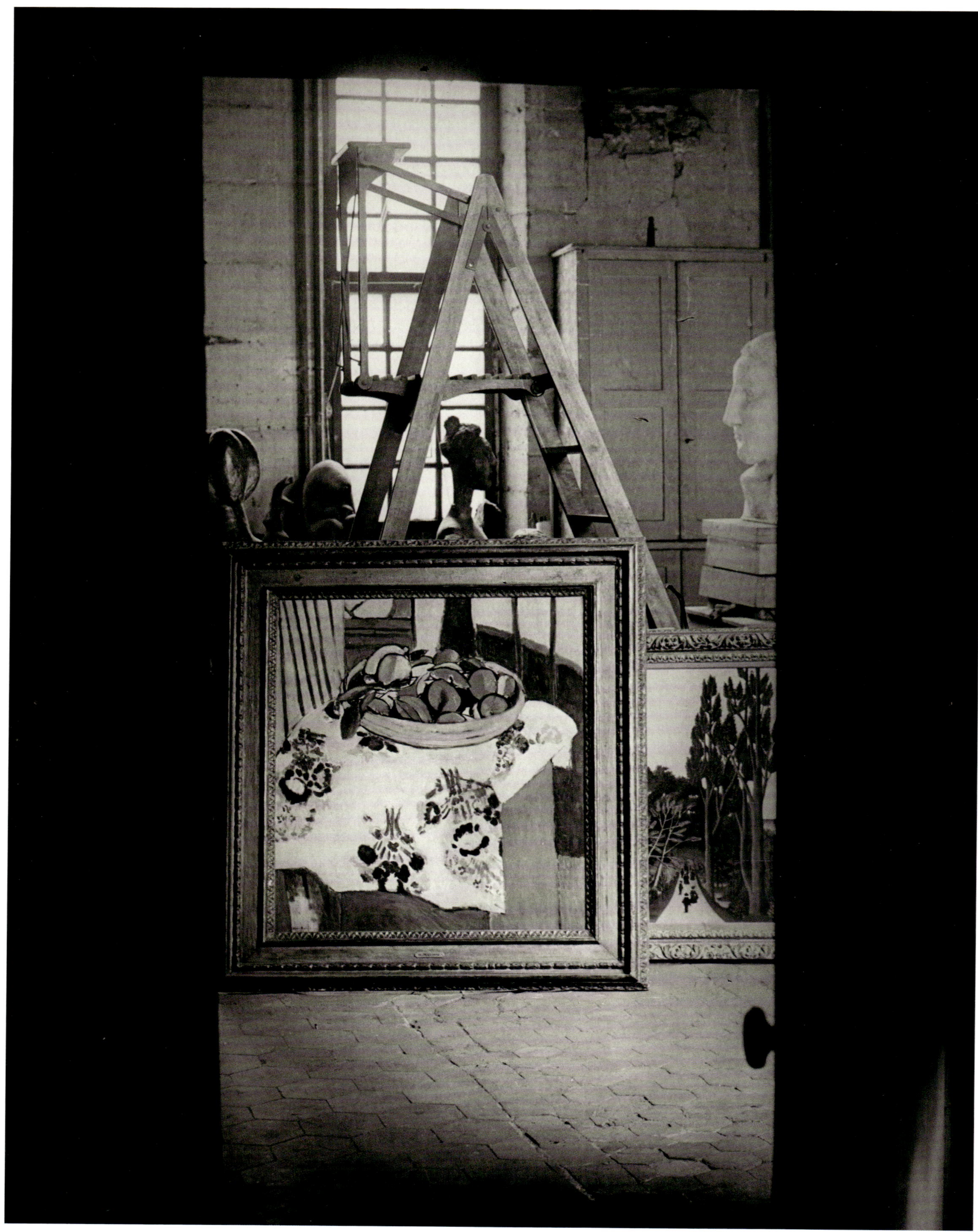

19 (fig.)
Still Life with Oranges
by Henri Matisse in Picasso's
Grands Augustins Studio, 1943.
Photograph by Brassaï
Musée National Picasso–Paris

CÉCILE DEBRAY

MATISSE/PICASSO

THE DUO'S REVIVAL IN THE *CAHIERS D'ART*

The Matisse/Picasso duo lent an original and specific structure to the French modern art scene during the first half of the twentieth century—North Pole versus South Pole, as Matisse liked to describe it. The effective, lasting, and profound relationship between the two artists and their respective oeuvres has been interpreted, through a dialectical approach, in binary, opposing terms, based on the French classical, academic tradition of "schools," notably in the arts, dating all the way back to the Quarrel of the Ancients and the Moderns: Poussinists/Rubenists, Pierre Mignard/Charles Le Brun, André Félibien/Roger de Piles, down to the opposition Delacroix/Ingres, and even Manet/Cabanel.

This pictorial contest was launched at Leo and Gertrude Stein's salon on the Rue de Fleurus, in particular over Matisse's *Blue Nude* (1907; Baltimore Museum of Art) and Picasso's *Nude with Towel* (1907; private collection) and studies for *Les Demoiselles d'Avignon* (1907; Museum of Modern Art [MoMA], New York). The competition was simplified and fantasized by the critics and Parisian coteries in the years 1908–10 as a battle between Matissists and Picassoists, between Fauves and Cubists, with the crowning event in 1918 and the *Matisse–Picasso* exhibition at the Galerie Paul Guillaume, an evocation of the "two sides to avant-garde painting" at a time when this moment was being irremediably swept away by World War I.[1]

However, the resumption of dialogue and interactions between the two painters at the turn of the 1930s clearly marked Matisse's return as a player in Modernism, following his withdrawal to Nice. The crisis that his painting was then facing seems oddly enough to have been ahead of the curve, coming before the crisis about to shake European society and the economy following the stock market crash of 1929. Among the multiple factors behind this competitive revival, including for Matisse a period of self-doubt, a change of gallery, a trip to the United States, a commission for the mural decoration *The Dance* 103, and provocations from Picasso, the young *Cahiers d'art* in particular would appear to have inspired this dialogue and brought this bipolarity back into the spotlight.

Sensitive to Modernist architecture as influenced by the Bauhaus, and attracted in both intellectual and aesthetic terms to abstraction, from Cycladic art to Cubism and Mondrian, the young art historian Christian Zervos met Matisse in 1924 while working on a special issue of *L'Art d'aujourd'hui* (Art today), a publication on which he acted as a subeditor under Albert Morancé.[2] He made Picasso's acquaintance shortly afterward, in 1926, when establishing his own journal, *Cahiers d'art*, around which he brought together young writers and art critics such as Georges Duthuit, Matisse's son-in-law, Tériade, a compatriot, Jean Cassou, Faure, Sigfried Giedion, Will Grohmann, Georges Hugnet, and Georges-Henri Rivière. That same year, Zervos placed his new journal under the aegis of the two painters. The cover of the inaugural issue of *Cahiers d'art* reproduced a lithograph by Matisse, headlining Zervos's article on the artist's lithographs inside 55 | 56;[3] the cover of the second issue, opening with Faure's article "Peinture d'aujourd'hui" (Painting of today), showed a painting by Picasso.[4]

1 Roger Bissière, in *L'Opinion*, with reference to the *Matisse–Picasso* exhibition at the Galerie Paul Guillaume (January 23–February 15, 1918).

2 See Christian Derouet, ed., *Zervos et "Cahiers d'art"* (Paris: Centre Pompidou, 2011).

3 *Cahiers d'art* [*CDA*], no. 1 (1926).

4 *CDA*, no. 2 (1926). The illustration on the cover of the third issue is a photograph of a sculpture by Henri Laurens. The covers of subsequent issues offer a single typographical composition for the title in a range of different colors.

The journal was characterized by a wealth of luxurious iconography, at the very moment when Aby Warburg was developing his iconographical method; the images—whether reproductions of works or photographs taken in the studio or at exhibitions—broke away from their purely illustrative function to claim an autonomous role often in parallel to the text. Quite a few images of Matisse's latest works found their way into issues of *Cahiers d'art* bereft of any commentary, like a powerful, enigmatic presence, allowing readers to make of them what they would. The issue of images was precisely the stumbling block in the relationship between Matisse and the magazine, and it worked to Picasso's advantage. Zervos was convinced of the two artists' status as the dominant figures in modern art, while also persuaded of the need to show the radical works of the prewar period, which were little known at that time.[5] The heroic paintings of the early days, those collected by the Steins, had been scattered abroad (to the Russian Sergei Shchukin in Germany, the Norwegian Walther Halvorsen, and so on), and Picasso's Cubist works were confiscated and sold off cheaply with the sequestration of the Galerie Kahnweiler. Thus, together with his project to highlight the modernity of Matisse by placing him alongside Picasso, Georges Braque, Alexander Calder, Wassily Kandinsky, Paul Klee, Henri Laurens, Fernand Léger, Joan Miró, and Piet Mondrian, as well as Le Corbusier and the Bauhaus, Zervos sought to bring together a wide-ranging and comprehensive art library and to undertake the catalogue raisonné of Matisse's work in addition to Picasso's, in order to better understand how their contributions fitted into this bigger picture. In the fifth issue, of June 1926, Zervos authored and published the article "Œuvres récentes de Picasso" (Recent works by Picasso) and then, in the seventh issue, dated September of that year, Georges Duthuit responded with the article "Œuvres récentes de Henri-Matisse."

In 1929, Picasso agreed to assign to Zervos the task of publishing the catalogue raisonné of his paintings and drawings, volume 1 of which came out in 1932.[6] Zervos kept and managed Picasso's image library in his Parisian offices on the Rue du Dragon, and the painter gradually became the journal's tutelary figure. Matisse, on the other hand, was reluctant to release any images of his works beyond his family circle, and in 1946 he commissioned his son-in-law, Georges Duthuit, and his daughter, Marguerite, to draw up the catalogue raisonné of his paintings for the Swiss publisher Albert Skira, but nothing ever came of it.

This mistrust and doubt came to define Matisse's apparent position in the late 1920s. His large painting from 1925–26, *Decorative Figure on an Ornamental Background* (Musée National d'Art Moderne–Centre Pompidou [MNAM–CP], Paris), shown at the Salon des Tuileries in 1926, came across as a sign of change, a return to stylization breaking with the naturalism of his odalisques painted in Nice. Tériade, in his review, saw the work as marking the return of the prewar Matisse: "A movingly youthful Matisse, a canvas offering sovereign proof of art. Beyond a shadow of doubt, the sharpest and most captivating of the paintings at this Salon. When we look at this painting, we no longer fear old age, since the mind can remain so eternally young."[7] While *Cahiers d'art* was reporting on the artist's current output—his lithographs, his etchings of nudes, his odalisques, and his work submitted to the Salon des Tuileries—interest in the works of 1910–20 was boosted by the exhibition mounted by Paul Guillaume centering on two recent acquisitions: the two large sophisticated and revolutionary paintings *The Piano Lesson* (MoMA), from 1916, and *Bathers by a River* 20, from 1909–17.[8] Full-page reproductions in the magazine were accompanied by an essay by Sylvain Bonmariage, who recounts a story told by Jean Metzinger of Matisse declaring in front of a Picasso painting, "Now that's what I call Cubism . . . by which I mean a huge step toward pure technique," and then reportedly adding, "This is where we are all heading."[9] The two masterpieces were thus associated with Cubism and imperceptibly linked to the Matisse/Picasso duo. Yve-Alain Bois has shown how inspirational these paintings were for Picasso in strengthening his desire to renew a pictorial dialogue with Matisse, even if it meant really going after him and provoking him.[10] Thus, Picasso's paintings *Seated Woman* (1927; MoMA), *Figure and Profile* (1928; Musée Picasso, Paris), and especially *Painter and Model* 21 literally quote compositional elements

5 The following were among those reproduced in *CDA*: *Bathers by a River* (1909–17) and *The Piano Lesson* (1916), no. 9 (1926); *The Three Sisters* (1917), no. 1 (1927); *Boy with Butterfly Net* (1907) and *Portrait of Marguerite* (1906–7), no. 4 (1928); *Le Luxe I* (1907) and *The Green Stripe* (1905–6), no. 10 (1929); *Still Life with Goldfish* (1916), *Bowl of Oranges* (1914) and *Still Life with Ivy* (1916), no. 3 (1930).

6 To keep his readers happy while awaiting publication of the following volumes, Zervos published special "Picasso" issues of *CDA* in 1932, 1936, 1937, and 1938; he published volume 2 of the catalogue raisonné on Picasso's Cubist period in 1942 and carried on up until his death. Altogether he published thirty-three volumes.

7 É. Tériade, "Propos sur le salon des Tuileries," *CDA*, no. 5 (1926): 110.

8 See p. 115 in this volume.

9 Sylvain Bonmariage, "Henri Matisse et la peinture pure," *CDA*, no. 9 (1926): 239–41.

10 Yve-Alain Bois recalls how Picasso showed his *Odalisque* (1925), clearly an ironic reference to Matisse's odalisques, in June 1926 at Paul Rosenberg's gallery. Paul Guillaume promptly purchased the work and renamed it *Woman with Tambourine*; Zervos, in his catalogue raisonné, gives it the title *Reclining Dancer with Tambourine* (Z, V, 415). Had Matisse by then completed his own *Odalisque with a Tambourine*, which was given a full-page reproduction in *CDA* of September 1926 and displayed at the Salon d'Automne (November 5–December 19, 1926)? Or did he paint it as a riposte to Picasso? See Yve-Alain Bois, "À la fin des années vingt: Le décor," in Bois, *Matisse et Picasso* (Paris: Flammarion, 1999), 33–55.

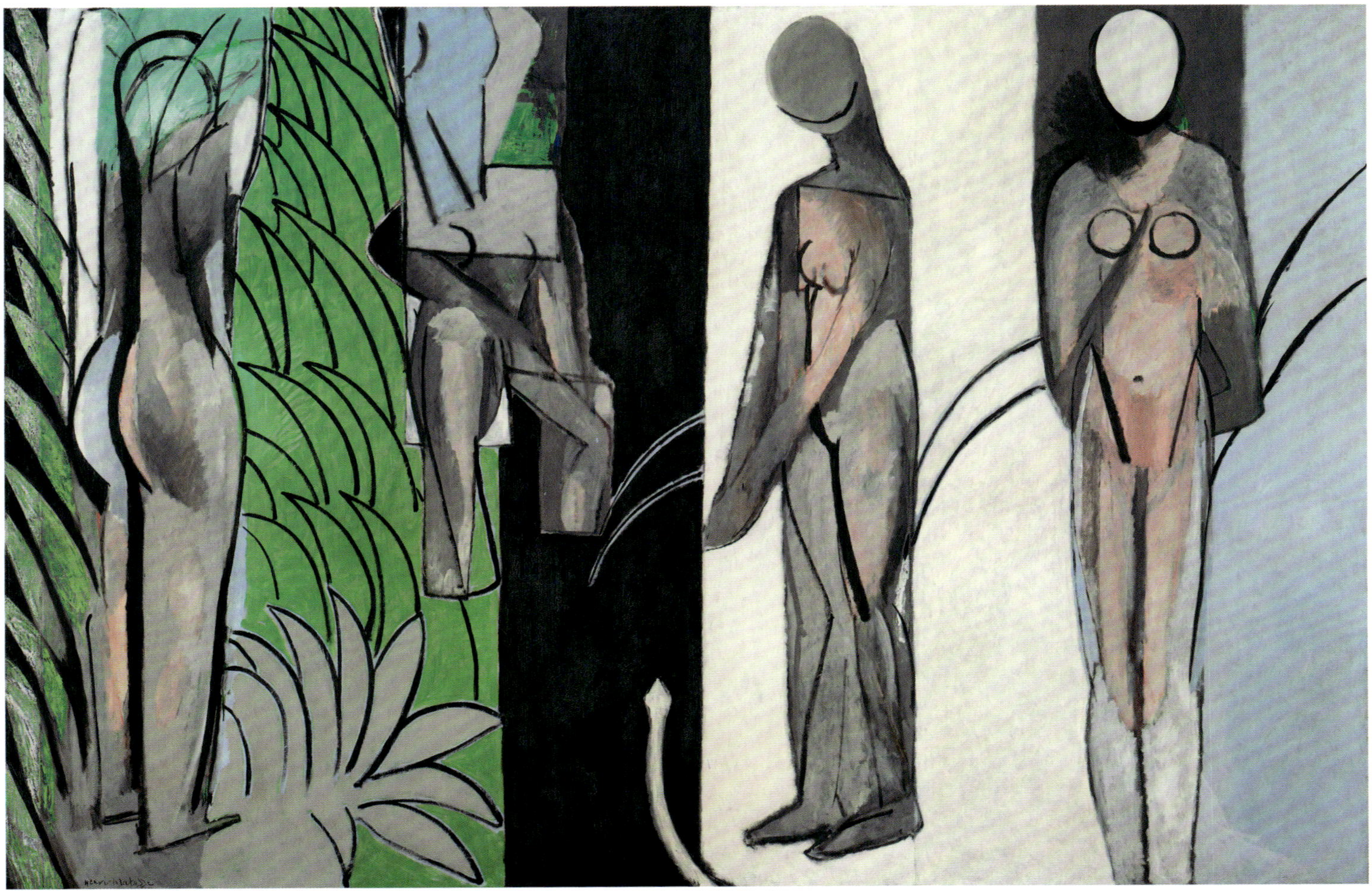

20 (fig.)
Bathers by a River,
1909–17
Oil on canvas,
8 ft. 6 ½ in. × 12 ft. 10 3⁄16 in.
(260 × 392 cm)
The Art Institute of Chicago

21 (fig.)
Pablo Picasso,
Painter and Model,
1928
Oil on canvas,
51 ⅛ × 64 ¼ in.
(129.8 × 163 cm)
The Museum of Modern Art,
New York

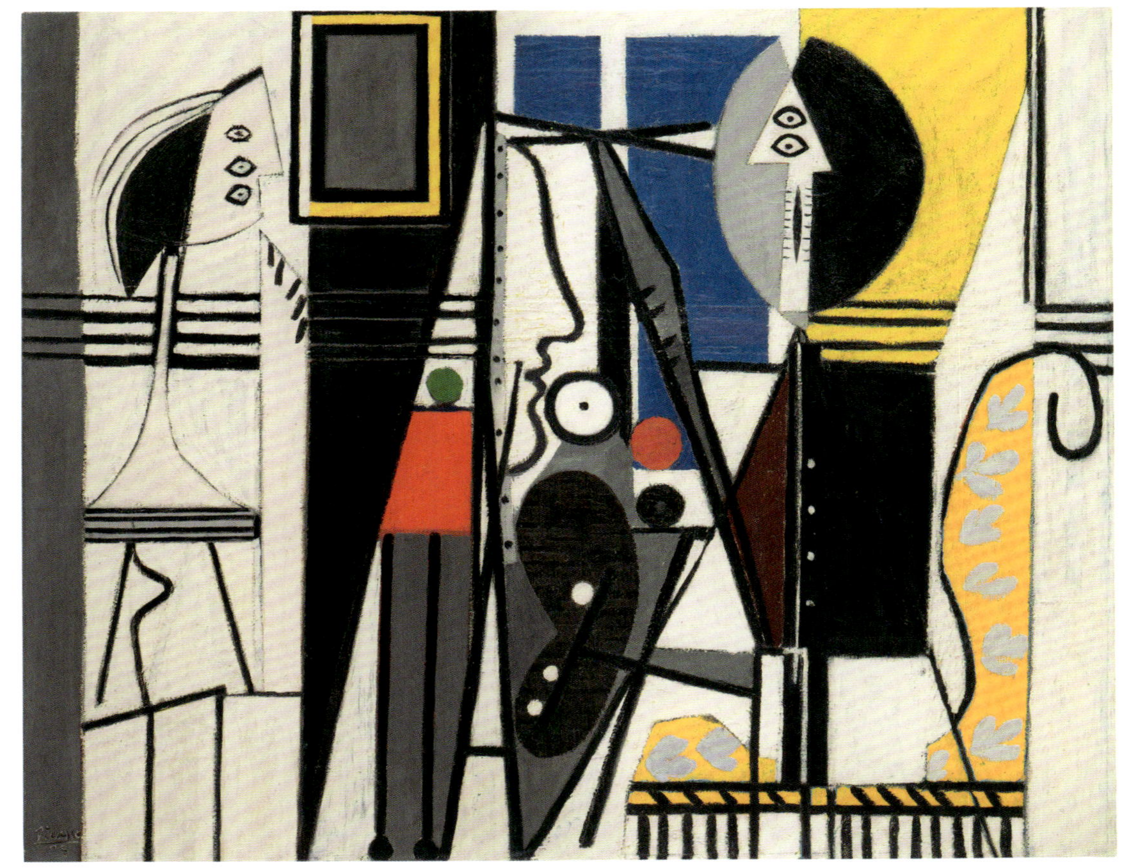

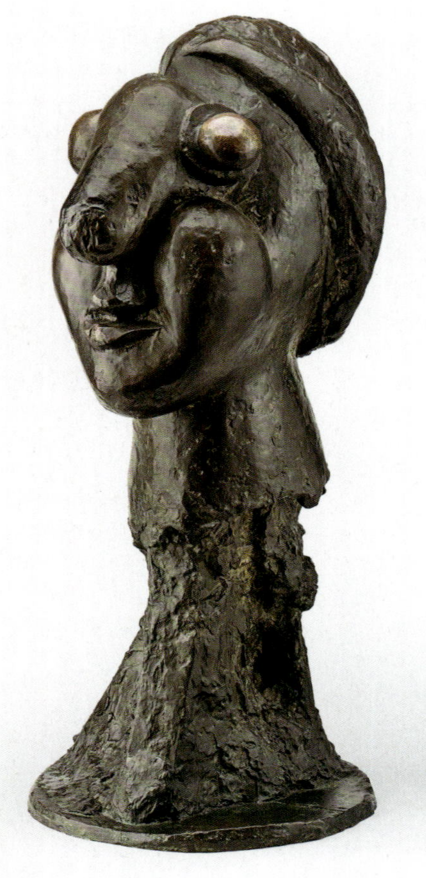

22

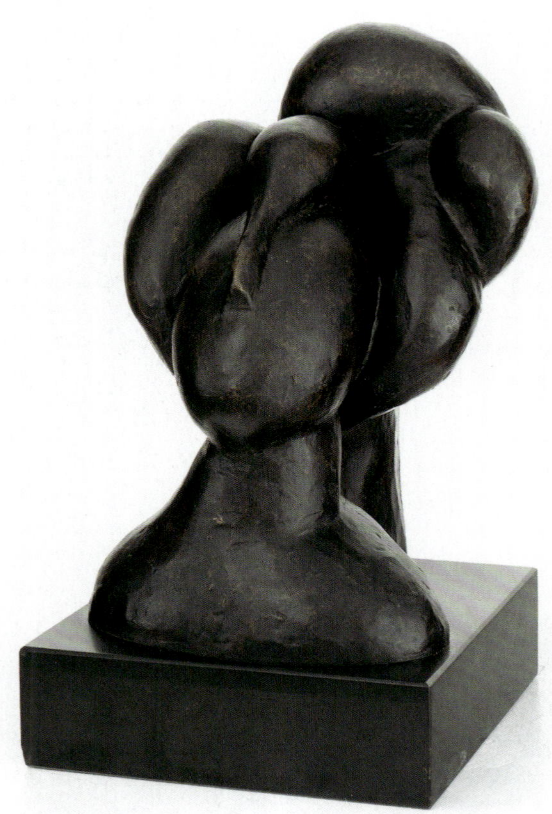

23

22
Pablo Picasso,
Head of a Woman, 1931
Bronze,
33 ⅞ × 12 ⅝ × 19 ⅛ in.
(86 × 32 × 48.5 cm)
Musée National Picasso–Paris

23
Henri Matisse, *Tiari*,
1930 (cast 1951)
Bronze,
8 1/16 × 5 ⅞ × 7 5/16 in.
(20.4 × 15 × 18.5 cm)
Musée d'Orsay, Paris,
held at the Musée Matisse
Nice, 1978

24
Pablo Picasso,
Metamorphosis II, 1928
Plaster, 9 ½ × 7 1/16 × 4 ⅜ in.
(24 × 18 × 11 cm)
Musée National Picasso–Paris

25 (fig.)
Pablo Picasso,
Head of a Woman, 1931
Bronze, 28 ⅛ × 16 ⅛ × 13 in.
(71.5 × 41 × 33 cm)
Musée National Picasso–Paris

26
Venus in a Shell I, 1930
Bronze, 12 3/16 × 6 13/16 × 7 ⅞ in.
(31 × 17.3 × 20 cm)
Musée d'Orsay, Paris,
held at the Musée Matisse
Nice, 1978

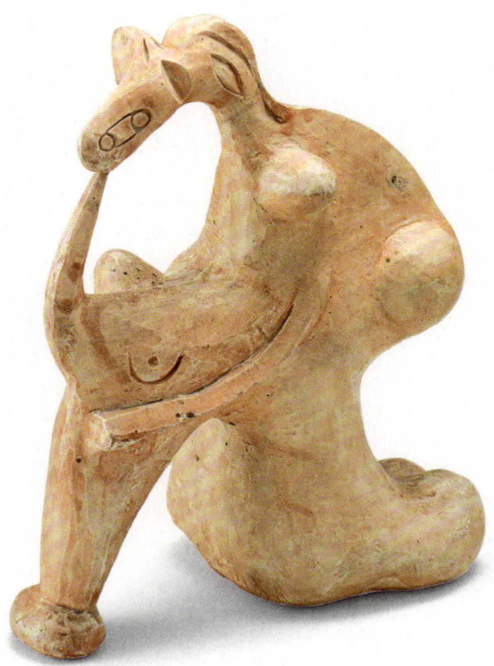

24

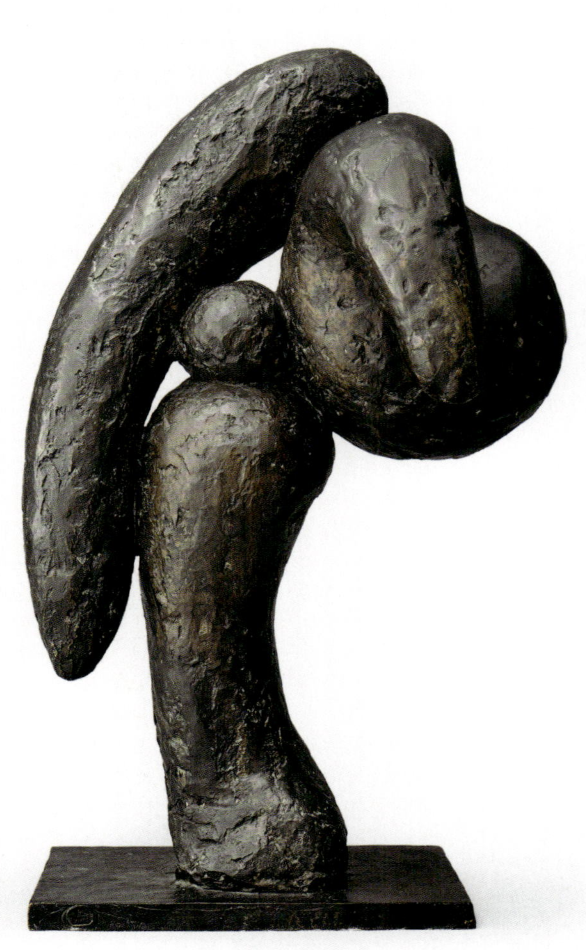

25

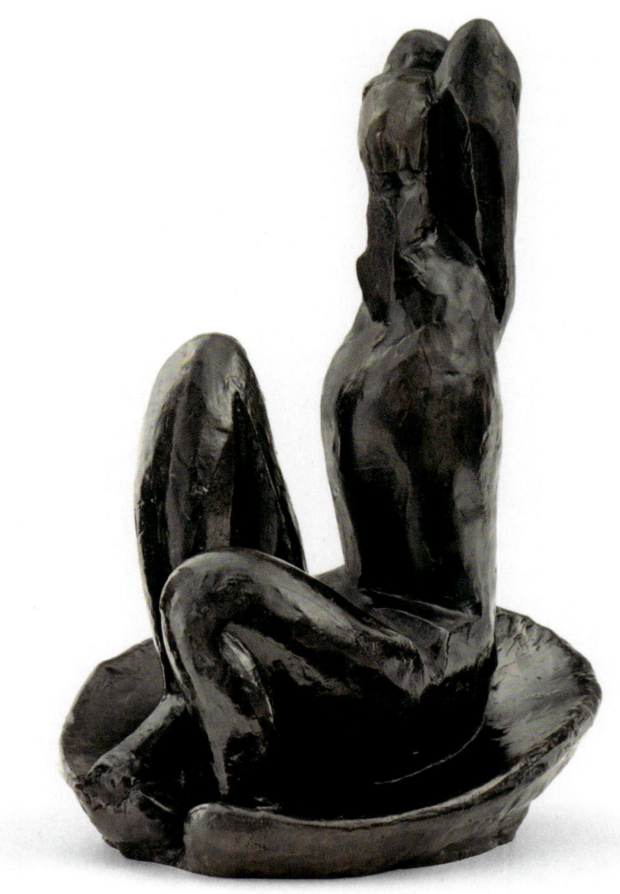

26

and motifs from *The Piano Lesson* and *Bathers by a River*—colored vertical strips, foliage motifs, the window rail and frame, stylized silhouettes of the faces and figures, and so on.

Paradoxically, at the very moment when he was inspiring Picasso to make this demanding, synthetic reinterpretation of Cubism, Matisse was making slow progress with his own painting and not producing very much. He was viewed as the aging painter of the odalisques, the man André Breton described as "a discouraging and discouraged old lion."[11] Picasso's recent Matisse-inspired paintings were exhibited at the Galerie Rosenberg, overshadowing Matisse's small Nice paintings hung nearby on the perpendicular wall.[12] The 1929 canvas *The Yellow Hat* (private collection), with its irresolute drawing constructed entirely on a yellow-purple contrast, graphically illustrates this doubt-ridden phase. Disturbed himself by this revival of his prewar works, Matisse seemed to be groping his way back to the formal issues of Cubism, painting *Woman with a Veil* 72, in which the figure's face and clothing appear subject to a kind of analytical decomposition. The two works were illustrated in *Cahiers d'art*, with no real commentary, to accompany Tériade's article "L'actualité de Matisse" (Matisse today).[13]

Matisse wrote to his daughter, Marguerite, on November 21, 1929: "I have sat down several times to do some [painting], but in front of the canvas, I am at a loss for ideas." Finding himself at a crossroads, he set off on his great voyage to the other side of the world, to Tahiti and New York,[14] at the very moment when the trend toward retrospective celebration of his work was intensifying: Georges Duthuit published a serialization of his book on Fauvism in *Cahiers d'art*;[15] Marguerite and Pierre Loeb prepared a minor exhibition of his prewar sculptures at the Galerie Pierre Loeb;[16] his first retrospective at the Galeries Georges Petit took place in 1931. Matisse himself revised the paintings of his youth, including *The Joy of Life* (1905–6; Barnes Foundation, Philadelphia), at the foundation of the collector Albert C. Barnes, who commissioned from him a large mural decoration for the foundation, the famous *Dance*, produced between 1931 and 1933.

Since Matisse is on record as wanting to steer clear of the "bandit lying in ambush,"[17] which is how he described Picasso, clearly the head-to-head revival was engineered by *Cahiers d'art*, with Picasso's forceful backing. Zervos's article "Sculptures des peintres d'aujourd'hui" (Sculptures by today's painters) 59 showcases Matisse's practice, with ten of his works reproduced alongside Picasso's.[18] Then, in his review of the Matisse exhibition at the Galerie Pierre Loeb, he re-endorses the duo: "Thus Matisse and Picasso attach considerable importance to sculpture. For them it is no mere leisure activity. It is even more than a kind of control that effectively disciplines the mind, represses or orders its immediate movements. It enables these artists to do things not allowed under the laws of painting."[19]

The fact is that the two artists both made a powerful return to sculpture around the same time, in the years 1927–30. Back home from Tahiti, Matisse modeled *Tiari* 23, *Venus in a Shell* 26 | 83, and then *Back IV* 82 in 1930–31; meanwhile, Picasso abandoned *Monument to Apollinaire* for *Metamorphosis II* 24—a reworking of his models for the initial sculpture project. Zervos devoted a full-length article to *Monument to Apollinaire* in 1929. However, what seems to have crystallized a genuine dialogue was Skira's concomitant commission in 1930, at the suggestion of Tériade, a frequent contributor to *Cahiers d'art*,[20] for illustrations of Ovid's *Metamorphoses* by Picasso and Stéphane Mallarmé's *Poésies* by Matisse.

While his painting was at a dead-end, Matisse had not stopped drawing, and since 1927–28 he had distanced himself from the painted output of his Nice years through the absence of modeling in his drawings. This aspect is not mentioned explicitly in the *Cahiers d'art* articles, but the works were widely reproduced and viewed, not least by Picasso.[21]

Yve-Alain Bois has drawn attention to the entanglements between the pair's works from 1930 onward: plainly Picasso's *Acrobats* series (1929; MNAM–CP, and 1930; Musée Picasso, Paris) borrows from Matisse's *Dance* of 1910 (State Hermitage Museum, St. Petersburg). Conversely, when, as part of his *Dance* project for Barnes, Matisse started making sketches of dancers and acrobats, they bore some striking similarities to the series of paintings on

11 André Breton, "Le surréalisme et la peinture," *La Révolution surréaliste*, no. 6 (March 1, 1926): 31.

12 *Picasso, Braque, Derain, Matisse, Léger, Laurencin*, Galerie Paul Rosenberg, Paris, April–May 1929.

13 É. Tériade, "L'actualité de Matisse," *CDA*, no. 7 (1929): 285–98.

14 See p. 137 in this volume.

15 Georges Duthuit, "Le fauvisme (I)," *CDA*, no. 5 (1929): 177–86; "Le fauvisme (II)," *CDA*, no. 6 (1929): 258–68; "Le fauvisme," *CDA*, no. 10 (1929): 429–34.

16 *Exposition de peintures et de sculptures de Henri Matisse*, Galerie Pierre Loeb, Paris, June 12–end of July 1930; in August of 1929, Matisse terminated his contract with Bernheim-Jeune, his dealer since 1909.

17 Henri Matisse [HM]–Marguerite Duthuit, June 13, 1926: "I haven't seen Picasso in years. . . . I have no inclination to see Picasso again, he is a bandit lying in ambush," cited by Rémi Labrusse, "Esthétique décorative et expérience critique: Matisse, Byzance et la notion d'Orient," PhD diss., University of Paris 1–Panthéon-Sorbonne, 1996, 2:556–57.

18 Christian Zervos, "Sculptures des peintres d'aujourd'hui," *CDA*, no. 7 (1928): 277–81.

19 *Exposition de peintures et de sculptures de Henri Matisse*, Galerie Pierre Loeb, Paris, 1930. Zervos published a review in *CDA*, no. 5 (1930): 275.

20 Tériade arrived in France in 1915; as a young critic, he learned his trade at *CDA*; as artistic director of *Minotaure*, a lavish journal created by Skira, he founded in 1937 *Verve*, which defended Matisse's work.

21 The first issue of *CDA*, in 1926, included an article by Zervos, "Lithographies de Henri Matisse." In addition to reproductions of the drawings and etchings spread over the issues that followed, Zervos, who attached real importance to drawing and to the work as process, devoted a dossier to Matisse's drawings in 1936, "Automatisme et espace illusoire," *CDA*, nos. 3–5. In 1939, he published a dossier on Matisse's charcoal drawings, "Dessins récents de Henri-Matisse," *CDA*, nos. 1–4.

the same theme then being produced by Picasso.[22] In November 1932, Picasso painted *Beach Game and Rescue* (private collection), in which the planes of color and the syncopated rhythm of the figures seem to foreshadow Matisse's *The Dance*; Picasso may well have seen the "Mallarmé" drawings at the Galerie Pierre Colle in February 1933 (February 3–10) and also the in-process photographs of *The Dance* in the journal *Beaux-Arts*.[23] *Cahiers d'art* printed photographs of the mural at Barnes's foundation and the four successive states of the first decoration 62—the composition made on the basis of incorrect measurements and kept at the artist's studio—and also those of the second in 1935.[24]

While generally reluctant to accept commissions, Picasso was spurred on by a spirit of emulation, producing in a single extended campaign, between September 13 and October 25, 1930, all fifteen etchings of the *Metamorphoses*; barely three months later, *Cahiers d'art* devoted an illustrated study to this forthcoming book 27 | 29 | 31.[25] The aggregative structure of Ovid's text, the lack of a clear plotline, and its accumulation of erotic and violent tales, make it an anticlassical poem that the artist fluently portrays, as if under the spell of some kind of automatic speed writing in which John Flaxman-like Neoclassical lines are subverted and duplicated in order to suggest movement.[26] While Picasso seems to plagiarize Matisse's odalisques in a few engravings, such as his *Three Nude Women* (1931),[27] in Matisse's drawings we find a resurgence of the same motif of the struggle of love or combat. Picasso would amplify and dramatize a violent and archaic approach to myth through the Vollard Suite (March–May 1933), based on the Minotaur theme, to which Matisse was by no means indifferent. The suite's scenes of horrific violence—the death of Marat, the wounding of a horse, the evisceration of a woman, a rape—seem to resonate with the pre-fascist political climate of 1934 and other works such as André Masson's *Massacres*, a certain return to the reading of de Sade's texts in the circle of Georges Bataille, Antonin Artaud's theater of cruelty, and the journal *Documents*.[28] Matisse focused on the "struggle of love" theme—*Nymph and Faun*—while experiencing greater difficulty in infusing his scenes with the carnal and dynamic violence of Picasso's compositions 112–14. Thus, in Matisse's painting *Nymph in the Forest (Verdure)* the two figures in a clinch are blurred, appearing almost as a pentimento 116. The drawings of wrestling he did for James Joyce's *Ulysses*,[29] *Calypso* and *Polyphemus* 28 | 32, although more dynamic, more expansive, are his answer to the line drawings of wrestling found in Picasso's *Metamorphoses*.

While artists were casting around for language to reflect the crisis and tension of the 1930s, the conservative, sometimes even reactionary critics, caught up in the climate of xenophobia, reiterated their claim of a North–South divide, whereby Picasso was ever the violent, barbaric foreigner perverting the moderate, classical genius of Matisse the Frenchman. Faure, regretting Matisse's Modernist change of direction, delivered a civilizational interpretation: "Only Picasso on the one hand, and Matisse on the other, represented the two poles of aesthetics at loggerheads, the one seeking in colorful sensation a kind of concrete alchemy capable of extracting from form the full chromatic richness that it contains, the other calling upon his linear arabesques to take him to abstract constructions. . . . On the one hand, a Westerner come to the end of the long European inquiry. On the other hand, an Oriental desensualized by the Semitic genius and having reached the end of the Asiatic reverie."[30] Waldemar George associated Picasso with "a modern neurosis, a thirst for mystery, an obscure escapist desire peculiar to godless eras," and defined Matisse as "the flower of French painting."[31] This was a political reading. Meanwhile, in Alexander Romm's book on Matisse, the Russian writer takes a Marxist line in order to stress how Matisse, with his harmonious and decorative art, has nothing to say about the contemporary world, unlike Picasso, who "identifies with the tempestuous rhythms and dissonances of the time, with its cacophony, with its ugliness."[32] This remained a minority view; it was close not only to the sympathies of Surrealist circles but also to the extremely pro-Picasso *Cahiers d'art*, which advanced a more formalist interpretation.

22 Matisse drew from it a series of ten lithographs that clearly show the influence of Picasso's *Acrobats* on *The Dance* (Rodin's influence can also be seen in it).

23 "*La Danse* d'Henri Matisse à Pittsburg [*sic*]," comprising a large reproduction of *The Dance* by Louis Gillet, *Beaux-Arts* (May 1933): 1.

24 *CDA*, nos. 1–4 (1935): this issue is devoted to the art of the day with interviews of artists (but not Matisse). In addition to reproductions of *The Dance*, there are plates of four paintings by Matisse: Figure 1933–1934 (*The White Dress*), Figure 1933 (*Nude in a Robe*), *Interior with Dog*, 1934, and *The Yellow Dress*, along with a lithograph for Joyce's *Ulysses*, 1935.

25 Christian Zervos, "*Les Métamorphoses* d'Ovide illustrées par Picasso," *CDA*, no. 10 (1930), with seven illustrations.

26 See Lisa Florman, *Myth and Metamorphosis: Picasso's Classical Prints of the 1930s* (Cambridge, MA: MIT Press, 2001).

27 See Bois, *Matisse et Picasso*, fig. 45.

28 Laurie Monahan, "A Knife Halfway into Dreams: André Masson 'Massacres' and Surrealism of the 1930's," PhD diss., Harvard University, 1997, 141–56.

29 In 1934 the American publisher George Macy gave commissions for illustrations to Picasso for Aristophanes's *Lysistrata* (published in the fall of 1934 with six etchings and thirty-four lithographs); and to Matisse for Joyce's *Ulysses* (published in 1935 with six soft ground etchings).

30 Élie Faure, "L'agonie de la peinture," *L'Amour de l'art* (June 1, 1931): 235–36.

31 Waldemar George, "Les cinquante ans de Picasso et la mort de la nature morte," *Formes*, no. 14 (April 1931): 56.

32 Alexander Romm, *Henri-Matisse* (Moscow, 1935; English trans., Moscow, 1937) 69–70, cited in *Matisse–Picasso*, ed. Elizabeth Cowling, Anne Baldassari, and John Elderfield, exh. cat. (London: Tate, 2002), 386.

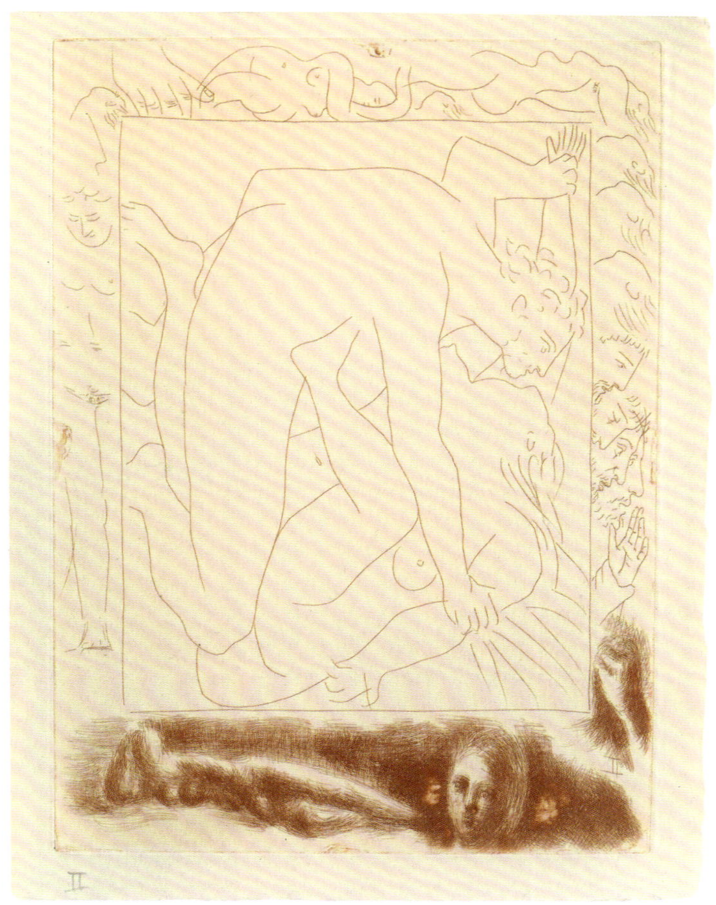
27

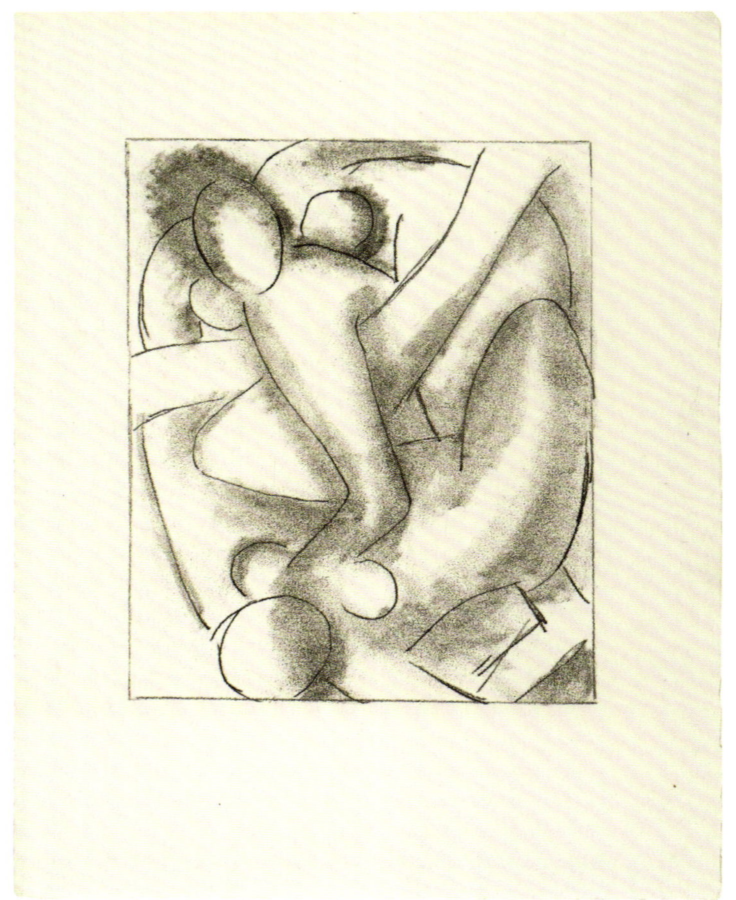
28

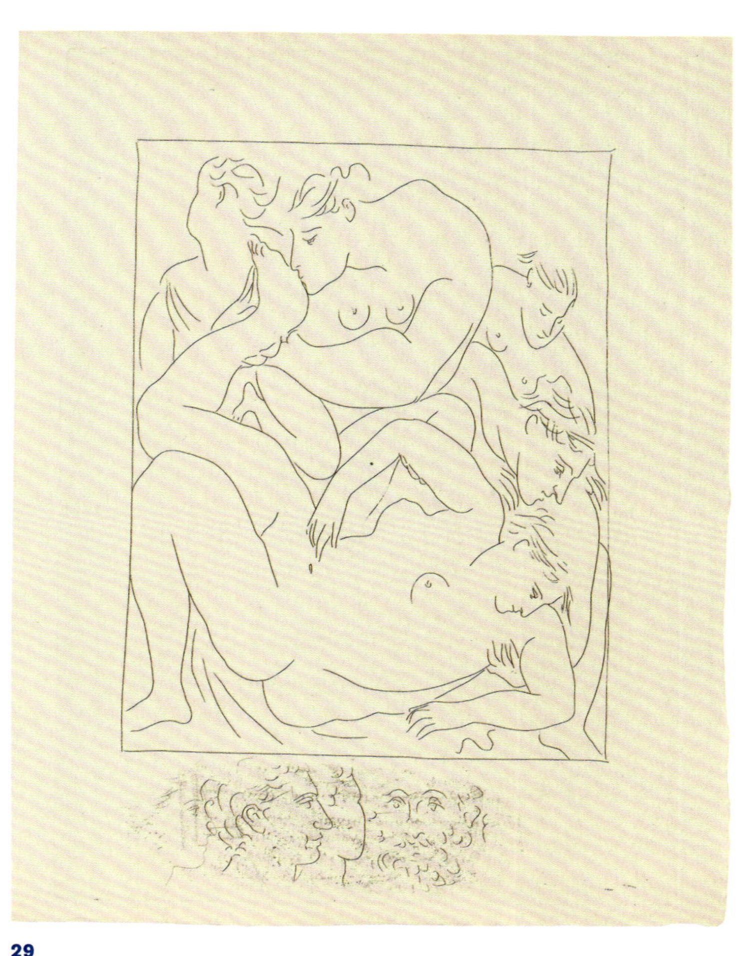
29

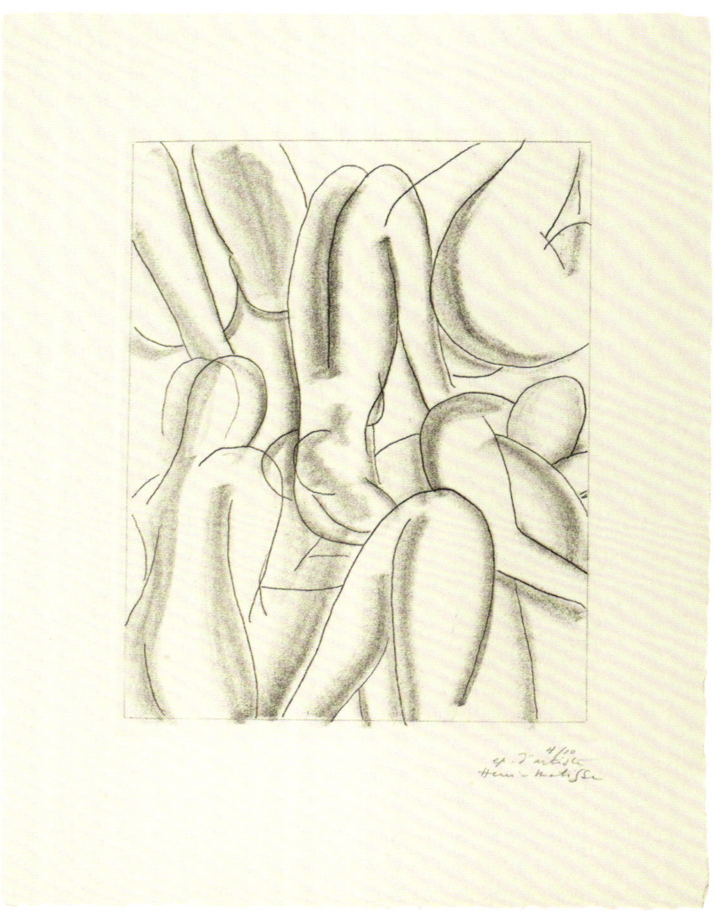
30

Pablo Picasso,
illustrations for Ovid's *Metamorphoses*, 1930
Etchings
Musée National Picasso–Paris

27
Struggle between Tereus and His Sister-in-Law Philomela, 2nd plate
13 3/8 × 10 1/4 in.
(33.9 × 25.9 cm)

29
Eurydice Stung by a Serpent, 2nd plate
13 1/4 × 10 1/4 in.
(33.7 × 26 cm)

31
The Combat of Perseus and Phineus for Andromeda
12 3/4 × 9 13/16 in.
(32.3 × 25 cm)

Henri Matisse,
illustrations for James Joyce's *Ulysses*, 1934
Soft ground etchings
The Pierre and Tana Matisse Foundation, New York

28
Calypso
11 5/8 × 9 1/16 in.
(29.6 × 23 cm)

30
Circe
11 1/8 × 8 9/16 in.
(28.3 × 21.8 cm)

32
Polyphemus
11 3/16 × 8 7/8 in.
(28.4 × 22.5 cm)

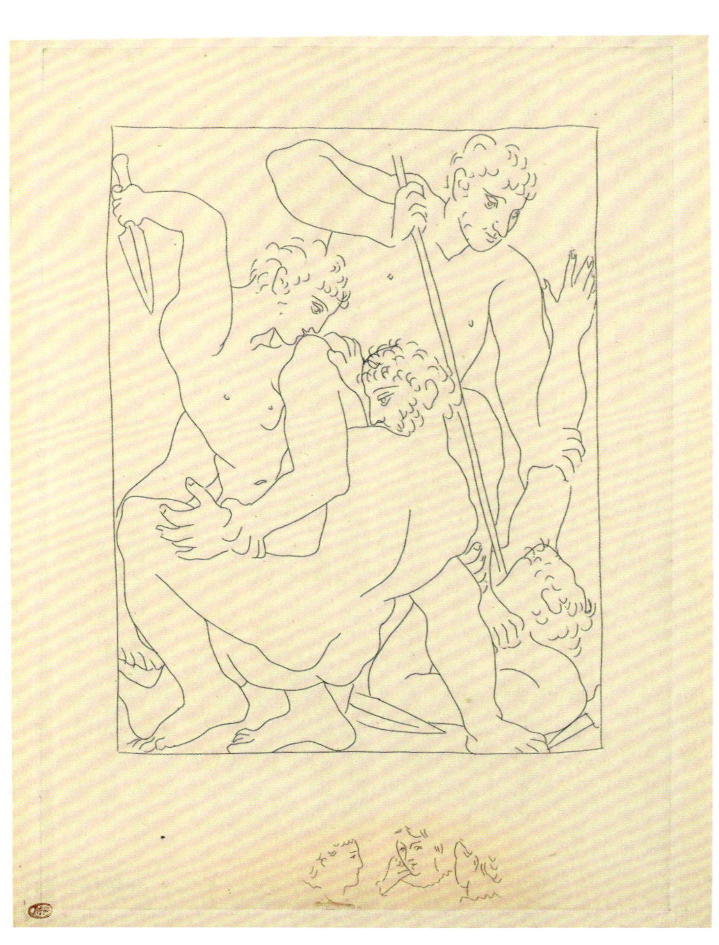

31

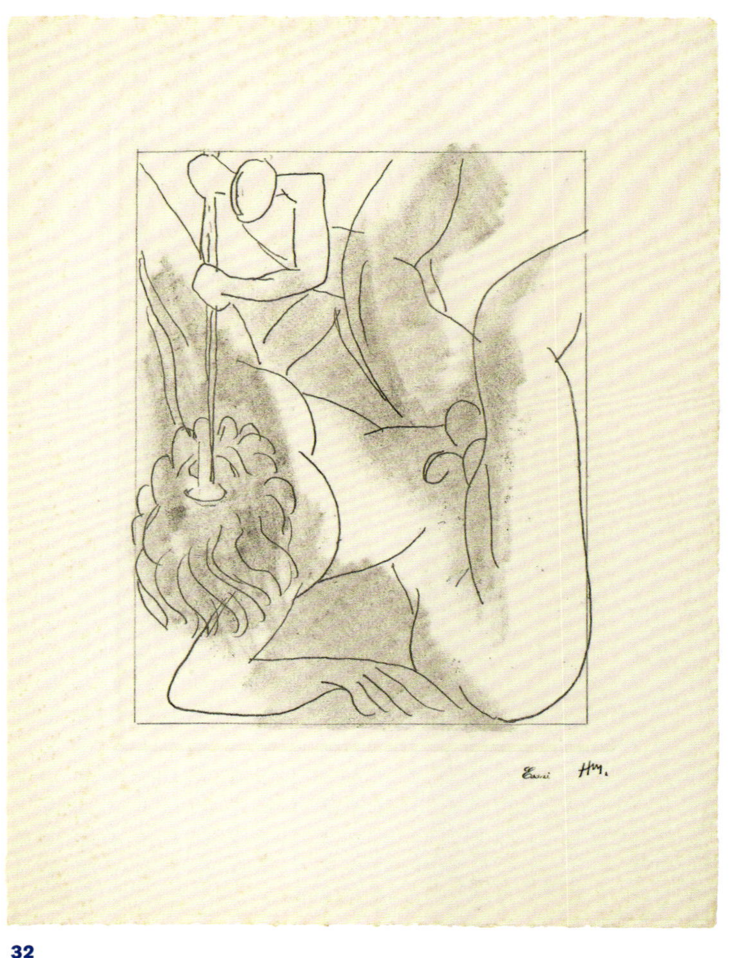

32

During the spring of 1936, through successive exhibitions at the Galerie Paul Rosenberg of recent works by Picasso (March 3–31) and Matisse (May 2–20), in which the latter asserted a new abstract style, the right-wing critics continued to deplore Picasso's harmful influence: "To convey the malaise one feels before Picasso's teratology, in front of his evil inventions, I spoke of an 'atmosphere of crime.' And now we are shown a fresh attack by an artist against himself. Such an attitude that we tolerated coming from Picasso, a specifically Spanish painter, we find hard to stomach coming from a French painter."[33]

The two artists certainly had drawn closer together. In 1934 they began to see each other again in the art galleries, during Paul Guillaume's memorial service at the Musée d'Ethnographie on December 7, 1934, but also at each other's studios; Matisse called on Picasso on June 1, 1937, the day his exhibition opened at Rosenberg's, and again on June 25 and July 3, 1937.[34] He recaptured his creative momentum in painting, buoyed by the experience of the genesis of *The Dance*, by his use of gouache paper cut-outs in the making of his paintings, and through the experimentation of his drawing, enabling a more stylized, abstract approach. He was doubtless also enchanted all over again by his romantic encounter with Lydia Delectorskaya.[35] The cross-connections and interchanges between the paintings of Picasso and Matisse become more frequent. Picasso's *Nude in a Garden, August 4, 1934* (Musée Picasso, Paris) directly influences Matisse's *The Dream* 33, while there is something very Picassoesque about the assurance and frontality of the figure in the latter's *Seated Pink Nude* 123. Matisse's series of nude drawings from the autumn of 1935, remarkable for the spatial ambiguity of their composition, for the play of mirrors, and for the proliferation of decorative motifs, was published in a special issue of *Cahiers d'art* devoted to the artist's latest drawings 63.[36] At a time when Picasso did no painting for several months in 1936 while undergoing a crisis both personal (his studio was placed under seal during his divorce proceedings) and political, Matisse was doing a great deal, again exploring the question of the relationship of his line drawing to color; and he introduced a disjunction between the two in the recent paintings that were exhibited at Paul Rosenberg's in June 1937.[37] Zervos was fascinated by these works and drew a comparison with older Picasso paintings; and he reproduced, facing each other on a two-page spread, Matisse's *Romanian Blouse* 139 and Picasso's *Seated Woman* (Fondation Beyeler, Basel) from 1930, with its similar chromatic range.[38] *Cahiers d'art* also published in 1936, in the special issue "Picasso 1930–1935," poems by Picasso with a facsimile of "J'ai vu sortir ce soir..." (I saw go out tonight), along with texts by Paul Éluard, Breton, Zervos, Hugnet, and reproductions of sculptures from Boisgeloup, the Normandy castle owned by Picasso.

Under the Popular Front, the two painters saw more of each other, lending their support to the young Spanish Republic and attending to the preparations for the Exposition Internationale of 1937. In July 1936, Matisse and Picasso participated in the exhibition preparations for Louis Aragon under the auspices of the Maison de la Culture at the Théâtre de l'Alhambra in Paris: Matisse loaned *The Moroccans* 43, while Picasso designed the stage curtain for *Le 14 Juillet*, an antifascist play by Romain Rolland. It was again the Zervoses, particularly Yvonne, who brought them together on the honorary committee for the fringe exhibition they mounted at the Jeu de Paume in July 1937, alongside the main official event *Les Maîtres de l'art indépendant (1895–1937)* (Masters of independent art), arranged by Raymond Escholier and held at the Petit Palais. Matisse visited the Spanish Pavilion at the Exposition Internationale on August 9, 1937, to see Picasso's great painting *Guernica* (1937; Museo Nacional Centro de Arte Reina Sofía, Madrid). *Cahiers d'art* supported Picasso's commitment to the Spanish Republican Front, and also devoted special issues to *Guernica*.[39] There can be no doubt that Matisse's approach to mural decoration for *The Dance* served to fuel the creative process behind this major achromatic history painting treated like a frieze. Zervos returned to this aspect quite late, in 1939, in his article "2 décorations de Henri-Matisse: Réflexions sur l'art mural"[40] (2 Decorations by Henri-Matisse: Thoughts on mural art). The year 1937 also saw the start of the series of exhibitions revolving around the stigmatization by the Nazis of

33 Claude Roger-Marx, "Œuvres récentes d'Henri Matisse," *Le Jour* (May 9, 1936).

34 Diary, Archives Henri Matisse, Issy-les-Moulineaux.

35 See p. 57 in this volume.

36 Christian Zervos, "Automatisme et espace illusoire." For all of Matisse's dislike of this notion of automatism, borrowed from psychoanalysis, in vogue in those days from a Surrealist standpoint, he nonetheless developed the concept extensively, notably at the time of his *Themes and Variations* project in 1940–41. See p. 215 in this volume.

37 *Œuvres récentes de Henri-Matisse*, Galerie Paul Rosenberg, Paris, June 1–29, 1937. Rosenberg opened his gallery at 21 rue de La Boétie in 1914; he was the art dealer for Picasso, Braque, and Léger. Matisse broke off from Bernheim-Jeune in 1929. Prior to signing the first contract with Matisse in 1936, Rosenberg mounted an exhibit at his gallery showing his recent output, including *Large Reclining Nude* and *Nymph in the Forest (Verdure)*; two other exhibitions were held in 1937 and 1938; being Picasso's dealer as well, he appears to have stimulated the pair's competitive streak. Matisse renewed his contract in 1939; in May 1940, Rosenberg had to flee France for the United States; his possessions, which included some thirty works by Matisse, were confiscated by the Germans.

38 *CDA*, nos. 6–7 (1937): 61–62.

39 Paul Éluard, "La victoire de Guernica" / Rêve et mensonge de Franco / 14 gravures par Pablo Picasso, *CDA*, nos. 1–3 (1937); "Aidez l'Espagne," special issue with a reproduction of Picasso's *Guernica* and some preparatory drawings, *CDA*, nos. 4–5 (1937).

40 *CDA*, nos. 5–10 (1939): 165–78.

"degenerate art" in Germany, in which the works of Picasso and Matisse featured prominently, having moreover been taken down from the walls of museums in Germany, confiscated, and put up for auction in Lucerne, Switzerland, on June 30, 1939. *Cahiers d'art* ceased publication during the war years; the Zervoses withdrew to Vézelay and joined the Resistance.[41]

Across the Atlantic, Alfred H. Barr Jr., the director of the new MoMA in New York, inspired by Zervos's Modernist and formalist vision, mounted the 1939 retrospective *Picasso: Forty Years of His Art*, which constituted a critical panorama of the artist's oeuvre, including *Les Demoiselles d'Avignon*, acquired by the museum earlier that year; *Still Life with Chair Caning* (1912; Musée Picasso, Paris), shown as the first collage; and the large manifesto painting *Guernica*. It was not until 1951 that the response came, with the retrospective *Matisse: His Art and His Public*, devised with the help of the artist's son Pierre Matisse, again in tune with what Zervos was doing.

Taking part in 1949 in the controversy around Andrei Zhdanov, who had had the backing of the French Communist Party, which advocated for a modern art that was necessarily figurative and even academic in its form, Zervos reaffirmed his journal's aesthetic stance, with a reassertion of the two artists' innovative genius: "Neither Matisse nor Picasso have ever claimed to astonish or fill with wonder. It was not from the high ground of authority that they transformed art; it was because they had been brought to that place by an inner necessity. Both of them have always stepped forward honestly in the face of incalculable difficulties, for our age has truly placed before them some very complex issues arising from the great antiquity of our culture, and from the infinite number of its discoveries."[42]

This is the complexity that *Cahiers d'art* invoked with reference to the works of Matisse, Picasso, and other modern artists, through forays—by means of image and text—into the realms of non-Western art, prehistoric artifacts, modern architecture, poetry, reflections on wall art and the purpose of decoration, and the sensitive and rare iconography of drawing and illustration.

41 See "Pablo Picasso et *Cahiers d'art* (1935–1944)," in Derouet, *Zervos et "Cahiers d'art,"* 2.

42 *CDA*, no. 1 (1949); in the next issue, Zervos published numerous black-and-white reproductions of recent works by Matisse and Picasso.

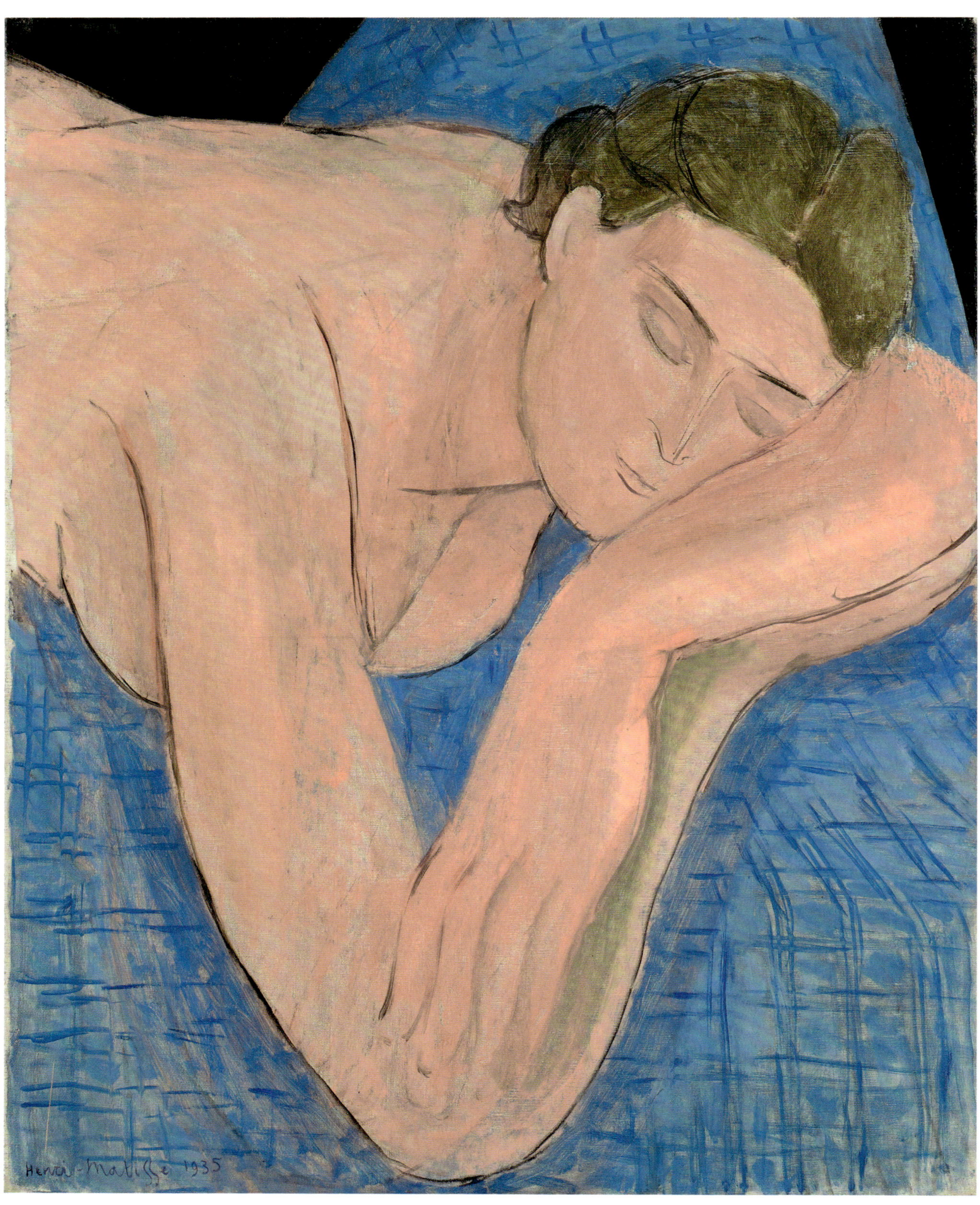

33
The Dream, 1935
Oil on canvas, 31 7/8 × 25 9/16 in.
(81 × 65 cm)
Musée National d'Art Moderne–
Centre Pompidou, Paris

ELLEN MCBREEN

LYDIA DELECTORSKAYA
AND THE MAKING OF MATISSE

The labels that frequently follow Lydia Delectorskaya's name are model, secretary, or Henri Matisse's last muse. In 1935, "the Russian who looks after my wife" was how Matisse described her, with a vagueness visually paralleled in a photograph of Delectorskaya standing dutifully between her employers, an immigrant caretaker to a then mostly bedridden Amélie Matisse 36.[1] Delectorskaya would become Matisse's principal model between 1935 and 1939 while also working as his indispensable studio assistant. Over their twenty-two-year creative partnership, she also helped manage the "petite enterprise," or creative firm, of Matisse's art. But in this 1934 photograph, she is in the presence of more powerful women who also made critical contributions to Matisse's art, including his Baltimore patron Etta Cone, conjured in charcoal portraits. As domestic help, Delectorskaya was not intended to be a focus. She wears a boxy white uniform, a sign for what she was meant, if eventually failed, to be: an inconspicuous "necessity." Delectorskaya used that word to describe herself when later recalling the family's puzzled perception of her as "a specimen of that famous 'Slavic soul' [*âme slave*]."[2] Her keen sense of how she would be regarded by others—as an outsider, a schemer, a usurper, and even, in her own words, a "dirty emigrant," helped to reappropriate the stereotypes thrust upon her.[3] She deployed them again, to fend off questions about private conversations she had with Matisse: "You don't understand, I wasn't an interlocutor: I was an employee, a foreigner, stateless. . . . Me, the emigrant who knows nothing, who knew nothing at all."[4]

Delectorskaya arrived in France in 1928 from Manchuria, where she had been taken to the Russian colony of Harbin by an aunt who looked after her when she was orphaned at twelve, having lost both parents to epidemics of typhus and cholera that swept through her native Siberia. Delectorskaya was, by her own account, desperate ("in a state of extreme destitution," "I was starving and so I was looking")[5] when she knocked on Matisse's door in October 1932. Anti-immigrant regulations in France prevented her from holding a job for wages, and so like many young women she turned to what were for her demoralizing intimacy industries exploiting youth and beauty: modeling, working as a film extra, dancing in casinos.[6] Initially Delectorskaya was hired as a studio assistant to help Matisse with the Barnes *Dance* mural for about six months. It was Amélie Matisse who proposed to her husband that she return ("What about your Russian?") the following year as her live-in nurse and paid companion.[7] Caretaking was a calling; "I'm basically a stretcher-bearer: first aid is written on my heart," she told Matisse's biographer Hilary Spurling.[8] Her father had been a respected pediatrician in Tomsk, Siberia, and she had intended to follow in his footsteps. Although she qualified for medical school in France, tuition was out of reach, so instead she fell into a disastrous marriage at age nineteen that lasted about a year. Despite the socioeconomic standing of her once-comfortable, educated family, Delectorskaya found herself in Nice, borrowing money from the Matisses to open a tearoom, a scheme hatched with a ne'er-do-well Russian-exile boyfriend who promptly blew the entire loan gambling. In an effort to pay off her debt,

1 Henri Matisse [HM]–Simon Bussy, cited in Hilary Spurling, *Matisse the Master: A Life of Henri Matisse; The Conquest of Colour, 1909–1954* (New York: Alfred A. Knopf, 2005), 355n58, where she dates the letter to April 28, 1935. Thanks to Spurling, we now have a much fuller sense of Delectorskaya's exceptional life and the many roles she played in Matisse's art.

2 As Delectorskaya recalled of those early days: "... I was a 'necessity' in his household. It seemed he was especially puzzled at the presence, in their very French family, of a specimen of that famous 'âme slave.'" Lydia Delectorskaya, *L'Apparente Facilité: Henri Matisse: Peintures de 1935–1939* (Paris: A Adrien Maeght, 1986), 15 (author's translation).

3 Delectorskaya used "sale émigrée" in the context of a story about her donating Matisse drawings to Moscow. Gonzague Saint Bris and Vladimir Fédorovski, *Les Égéries russes* (Paris: J.-C. Lattès, 1994), 323.

4 Both quotes are from "Entretien de Lydia Delectorskaya par Xavier Girard," 1992, unpublished typescript, p. 98 and p. 252, Centre de Documentation, Musée Matisse, Nice (author's translation). Elsewhere in this interview (p. 262), Delectorskaya describes having been raised as a "sort of ward of the state." A series of Soviet decrees in late 1921 deprived Russians abroad of their citizenship, rendering them stateless. I am grateful to Claudine Grammont, director of the Musée Matisse and Les Héritiers Matisse, for making this unpublished material available to me.

5 Saint Bris and Fédorovski, *Les Égéries russes*, 292; "Entretien de Delectorskaya," 62.

6 Delectorskaya: "... I belonged to the category of emigrants who, according to French law, had no right to paid work, except for some temporary or occasional jobs such as being an extra in a movie, a model, a babysitter, etc." Quoted in Saint Bris and Fédorovski, *Les Égéries russes*, 292 (author's translation).

7 It was Delectorskaya who remembered Amélie Matisse using this nameless phrase to describe her, "Entretien de Delectorskaya," 67.

8 Spurling, *Matisse the Master*, 364.

Delectorskaya signed up for a four-day endurance marathon, dancing with men at the Casino in Nice for a chance at a bonus awarded to the last-standing woman who survived the spectacle of subjugation. The Matisses apparently sent a car to rescue her from bodily collapse.[9]

Delectorskaya later returned the succor many times over, diligently caring for both the physical and mental health of Amélie Matisse, and then, until his death in 1954, for Matisse's as well. Thirty-eight years after his death, she could name all of Matisse's doctors, the cures she used to calm his anxiety-driven insomnia, and the duration and convalescence of his annual bouts of bronchitis.[10] Owing to her efforts, Matisse was able (in her words) to "preserve his artistic essence until his last day." [11] To friends and confidants, Matisse readily confirmed that his body's well-being was "thanks to Lydia's kind care." [12]

It is perhaps why her 1996 book *Henri Matisse: Contre vents et marées* (Against all odds) begins by swiftly dismantling two misrepresentations about the artist: the first, that after his 1941 operation he could almost no longer paint; and the second, that he turned to cut-outs and the Vence chapel project because of physical limitations. Little wonder she was motivated to settle that score, considering how intensely she labored to manage a protected space where an elderly Matisse could work. He may have had trouble walking from time to time, "But easel painting doesn't require the use of your legs." [13] The primary limbs he needed were arms, of course, but even well before 1941, she was acting as one for Matisse. Matisse's *main-d'œuvre* (labor force) was mostly women, but Delectorskaya was his "right-hand man."

The multiple, sometimes conflicting, identities she negotiated—both the ones she claimed and those projected onto her—are distinct from the fictional roles she played as a model. But they do provide other points of entry to understand how a young Russian immigrant woman in the 1930s was transformed in and by Matisse's art. Looking more closely at her non-caretaking studio labors offers ways to read works for which she was the primary subject. Modeling for Matisse immortalized her, and that process, we should be clear, largely belonged to the artist. But how Delectorskaya chose to represent herself, in navigating exile and ethnic Otherness, a liminal class position, and demeaning expectations about her sexual availability is foundational to how Matisse depicted her. Delectorskaya is present in the studio for some of his most compelling work in the immediate years after 1935, but the romantic clichés of the muse and the selfless nurse-secretary has clouded over her material contributions. The less-than-illuminating truth that Matisse was inspired by her exceptional beauty has minimized a fuller sense of her serious vocation. And moralizing assumptions about her as the mistress who destroyed his marriage singles out a supposed sexual relationship from a whole series of more complex and consequential ways these two beings interacted.[14]

It is not by chance that Delectorskaya's arms are a focus in multiple works from the 1930s. *The Blue Eyes* 34, for example, the very first painting for which she modeled, originated with a pose that Matisse discovered her in at his wife's bedside. "Don't move!" he reportedly told her, fixing her in an arrangement that would spark a sequence of exceptionally rich images, all variations on Delectorskaya's head framed by crossed arms over the back of a chair.[15] Intentionally reminding us of the uneasy class position she would come to occupy—intimately a part of the family but also not—she wrote that its lack of "decorum" was "a somewhat inappropriate pose for an employee." [16] When modified for *The Dream* 33, Matisse removed her from the prosaic details of domesticity, replacing the upholstered chair with a radiating spotlight of blue-checked textile, the same motif that enriches the rose tones of her flesh in his most ambitious nude painting that year, *Large Reclining Nude* 110.[17] In *The Dream*, her upper body floats in from the left as it seems to hover above a heavenly blue canopy. Photographs of different states in its elaboration show Matisse working out the placement and contours of her resting arms, key to the impression of her figure lifting away from the support. Delectorskaya tells us "he cursed" over the "descent" of those arms, in typically tense work sessions, with a mood quite unlike the one in the painting, of stillness and peace.[18] In this fiction, he cocoons a just recently precarious day laborer with the luxury of deep slumber. It is one of many representations

9 Spurling, *Matisse the Master*, 346–47.

10 "Entretien de Delectorskaya," 238 (on doctors), 88–89 (insomnia), 236 (bronchitis).

11 Lydia Delectorskaya, *Henri Matisse: Contre vents et marées; peintures et livres illustrés de 1939 à 1943* (Paris: Irus et Vincent Hansma, 1996), 546 (author's translation).

12 HM–André Rouveyre, February 5, 1943, in Delectorskaya, *Henri Matisse*, 464 (author's translation).

13 Delectorskaya, *Henri Matisse*, 11 (author's translation).

14 Spurling proposes that it was the more serious betrayal of their working alliance, not adultery, that prompted Amélie Matisse to leave her husband in 1939. Supporting Delectorskaya's denials—"there was no question of adultery"—Spurling points out that other members of Matisse's inner circle refused to endorse the prurient assumptions about their relationship. As Delectorskaya later told Spurling: "I realized what people would say about a young beauty and a rich old man, but I wasn't interested in protecting my reputation." Spurling, *Matisse the Master*, 384 and 388.

15 For a discussion and reproductions of works where she appears in this same pose, see Isabelle Monod-Fontaine, "La pose de Lydia," in *Lydia D.: Lydia Delectorskaya, muse et modèle de Matisse*, ed. Dominique Szymusiak et al., exh. cat (Paris: Réunion des Musées Nationaux, 2010), 82–101.

16 Delectorskaya, *L'Apparente Facilité*, 16 (author's translation).

17 Photographs of earlier states indicate that the blue textile was initially more clearly draped over a couch, with Delectorskaya's weight on its arm. For images, see Delectorskaya, *L'Apparente Facilité*, 45–46.

18 "Entretien de Lydia Delectorskaya," 260 (author's translation).

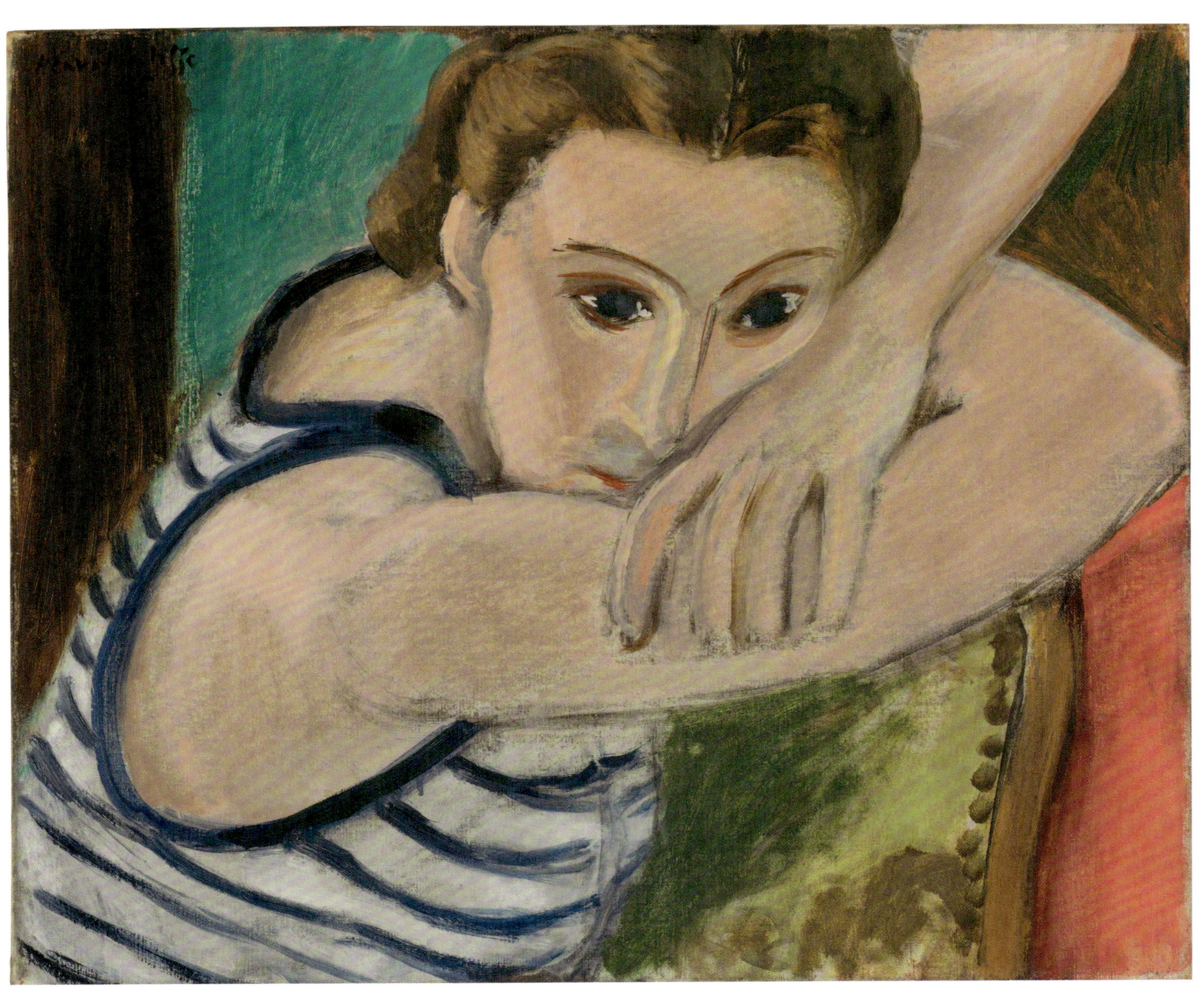

34 (fig.)
The Blue Eyes, 1935
Oil on canvas, 15 × 18 in.
(38.1 × 45.7 cm)
Baltimore Museum of Art

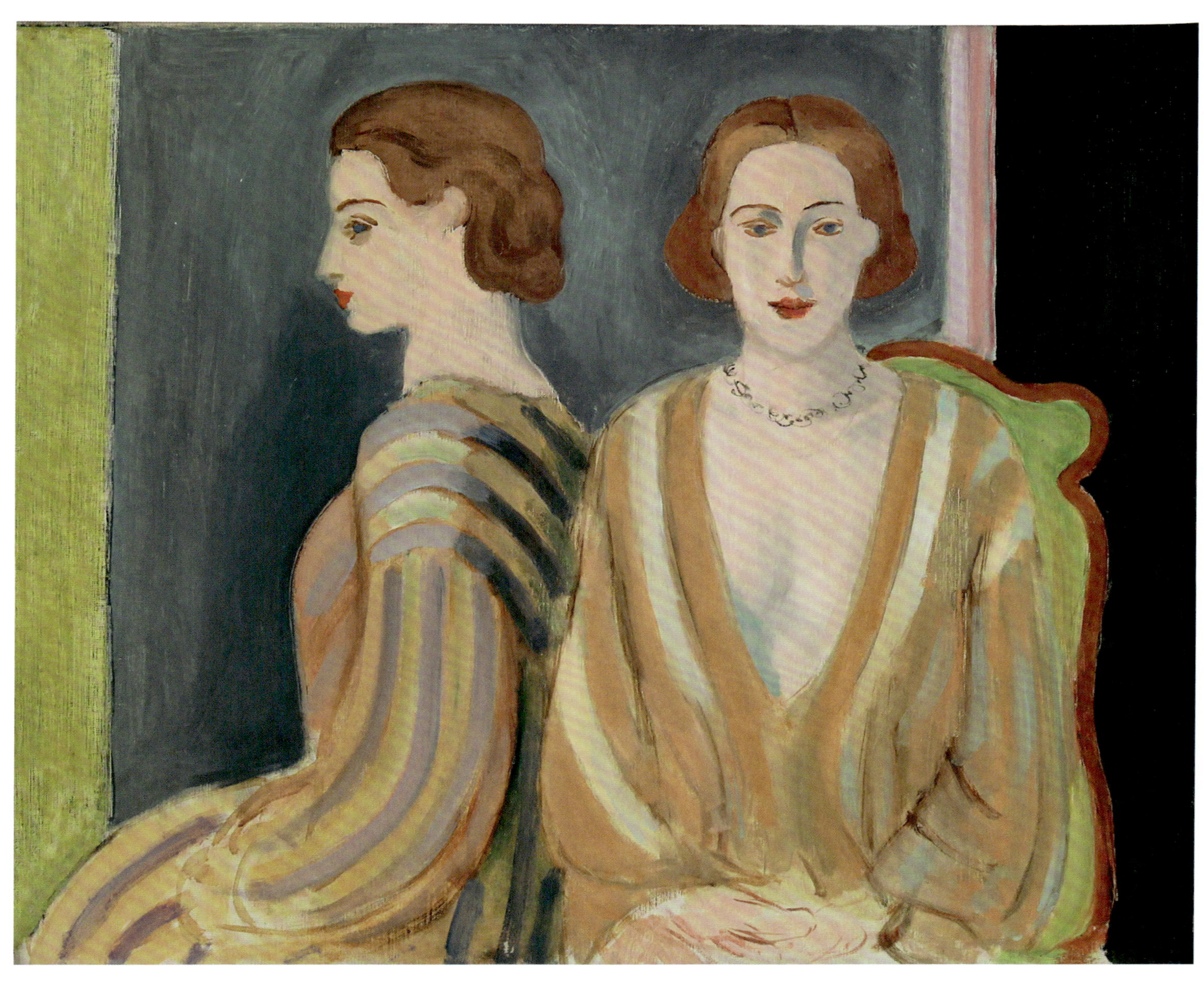

35
The Reflection, 1935
Oil on canvas, 18 ¼ × 21 ⅞ in.
(46.3 × 55.5 cm)
The William Rubin Collection

where her body emits a weightlessness, an imaginative deliverance from gravity and the frictions of everyday life. In her many retellings of her origin narrative as Matisse's model, she insisted that she was not his type, that she had no intention of returning to a métier that with other artists before Matisse had been "true drudgery."[19] But with Matisse, she wrote, "Gradually, I began to adapt and feel less 'shackled.'"[20] *The Dream* transforms the body of an actual "stateless" person into a fiction of infinitely expanding space.

By the summer of 1935, it seems that Delectorskaya had retired her domestic servant smock. During a family vacation to Beauvezer, she typed correspondence, babysat the grandson, and continued her work for Amélie Matisse; she also enjoyed a few moments of relaxation, which were recorded in a group of exceptional family photographs. Matisse and Delectorskaya took two shots of each other, each seated against a view of the nearby mountains 177 | 178. In his, she is reading (an article about Matisse, illustrated by one of his sculptures). In hers, part of her own body enters the frame, and, in the intimacy of this moment, she manages to dismantle the normally "grim" look of *Patron*. Among the published photographs of Matisse, this one is relatively rare for its air of joviality. While these images may seem like a minor interruption to the imbalance of power embedded in their art worker–artist relationship, in this to-and-fro we find a model of the mutual regard necessary to the process of making Matisse.

Their partnership began this way, as a back-and-forth work routine in the rented garage space/studio on Rue Désiré-Niel in Nice. She helped him with the cut-paper technique used for the *Dance* mural, placing pins along charcoal lines Matisse had drawn on the paper so that he could follow with his scissors. She then pinned paper of another color (using the "palette" of prepared painted sheets) to form the negative of those cut shapes, replacing the excess that had fallen. In essence, she helped to build the negative from the positive sketches by Matisse, which he would then adjust and correct. While she managed her pieces of this evolving puzzle, Matisse walked the dog or went rifle shooting at a local fair, the only things that helped to ease his gnawing anxieties about the enormity of the project. Delectorskaya recalled the intensity of his eagerness to continue work, quietly agonizing while she finished her part ("I felt at my back his impatience to continue, since as long as I wasn't done, he could not continue.")[21]

By 1935, Delectorskaya was working on easel painting, posing for canvases like *Large Reclining Nude* and *The Reflection* 35, but helping on the other side of the easel, too—wiping away sections with turpentine and once again teeing Matisse up for a future round of production. A photograph taken in October captures a carefully staged version of that process 38. Remarkably chic in her overalls, her workaday outfit is offset by a pair of elegant heels. As she later recalled: "I always wore an apron, to make it perfectly clear that I was doing a job."[22] Delectorskaya lifts her arm to make visible the performative gesture of her hand, wiping paint away from a rendering of her left leg as she steadies a bottle of turpentine on her real one. Directly behind the easel we see another long-term project Delectorskaya had a hand in, the *Window at Tahiti II* tapestry cartoons 119. A later photograph shows her laboring away on the curtain section which appears on the left side of *Tahiti II* 37. On the wall next to her are four works for which she modeled, including an earlier state of the painting *Blue Blouse* (begun January 1936; Kusntmuseum, Bern) for which Delectorskaya posed in a blue taffeta bodice of her creation.[23] The white organdy jabot she wears recalls the ruff collar of European aristocracy: a conspicuous sign of status, of dependence on the labor of others, but for her, a fantasy cut out of whole cloth. This painting's fictions belie the realities of the photograph in which it appears, a document of the subtle yet incomplete story of her "indispensable" studio contributions.[24] *Tahiti* was an especially meaningful project through which the intensity of their give-and-take working relationship was mediated. No wonder Matisse gave it central staging in other images depicting her, like *The Green Blouse* 120 and *Sketch: Standing Nude and Painter* (1936; private collection), where Matisse lightly paints himself painting Delectorskaya using "her" medium of turpentine.[25] In a series of pen-and-ink drawings from 1935–37, one of which

19 Delectorskaya, *L'Apparente Facilité*, 15 (author's translation).

20 Delectorskaya, *L'Apparente Facilité*, 16 (author's translation).

21 "Entretien de Delectorskaya," 65 (author's translation).

22 Spurling, *Matisse the Master*, 390.

23 The final version of *Blue Blouse* (1936) is reproduced in Delectorskaya, *L'Apparente Facilité*, 109.

24 Girard asked Delectorskaya why it was important to Matisse that she and other family members devoted themselves to artistic work, and she responded: "Maybe he thought that if I explored painting myself, I would better understand it, and I would be more useful to him. Because he was very possessive. He knew how to convince you that you were indispensable to him." "Entretien de Delectorskaya," 64 (author's translation).

25 For both a reading of the latter work, and a close analysis of the studio photographs, I am indebted to Camran Julian Mani, whose dissertation "'To Reinvent the Inventions': The Modernisms of Henri Matisse, 1930–1948" is forthcoming.

also hangs on the wall beside her in the photograph, *Window at Tahiti II* will signal the duration of their collaboration, beyond the transactional limitations embedded in the act of posing.

Delectorskaya selected this same pair of photographs to be shown side by side in her book *L'Apparente Facilité.*[26] In them, she touches Matisse's work directly, signaling a kind of power that her acolyte-witness voice often mutes in the accompanying text, where she tempers her confidence with modesty and discretion, often to the point of self-effacement.[27] With her interviewer Xavier Girard, for example, she stakes out responsibility for the much-transformed tree motifs in *Nymph in the Forest (Verdure)* 116: "I was in charge of erasing them. And so the cleaned sections not yet repainted by Matisse, which form beams of light; those are due to me."[28] But when he asks her about cleaning Matisse's brushes, she connects this mundane task to her scraping off areas of the canvases as he painted: "Yes, that was my role, the palette and brushes. And yes, most importantly, he suffered from shoulder pain very quickly. Since erasing hurt him, I was the one who cleaned up the corrections."[29] Significantly, she shifts focus from studio responsibilities back to her care of Matisse's body (in this case, his neuritis), deemed a more "appropriate" role for a woman, perhaps, but which was also continuous with her work on his paintings. Just months earlier Matisse asked her to tear up notes she was keeping of his remarks, since, as he told her: "You haven't understood a thing." He proposed post-session dictation instead. Delectorskaya reappropriated that negative assessment, too, selecting it as the ironic title of her essay in *L'Apparente Facilité*.

How could an artist as exacting as Matisse trust her with this level of intervention into his creations? Delectorskaya may have publicly rejected the role of "interlocutor," but in the dialogue of making she was part of a constant conversation. Her sensitivity and comprehension were essential to tasks for which she either anticipated the next stage in his process or surmised the intentions of his last one. In addition to her erasing oil paintings, for example, she also applied fixative to charcoal drawings.[30] More can be said (and hopefully will be) about her other hands-on contributions in later years, to both the cut-outs and to the Vence chapel, among other projects.[31]

In 1941, Matisse wrote to André Rouveyre about a demoralizing day when he was "tout chaviré" (very upset) and "désemparé" (distraught): "It was impossible for me to continue my idea, and Lydia spent her afternoon, the end of her afternoon—since she had to walk up to Cimiez—*erasing the entire canvas* which is now completely clean. I plan on restarting tomorrow."[32] That same year, he made an ink drawing in a similar spirit of tribute which he called *L.D. at Work*, where Delectorskaya with her bottle of spirits is laying hands on Matisse's work again, this time on an earlier state of *Still Life with Magnolia*.[33] He rarely referred to her "at work" or mentioned her proper name in titles. But we know Matisse regarded her as a partner in the enterprise, given that, from 1939 to 1951, she received five percent of the sales of his works, after which their agreement (at her request) shifted to a flat bonus that doubled her monthly salary.[34]

One of Matisse's most audaciously creative accomplishments with Delectorskaya as model was a series of pen-and-ink drawings of 1935–37 depicting her sinuous body, nude or dressed, adorned by an extravagance of decorative patterns. They seem to epitomize the pleasure and privileges of the male artist's gaze. The nude, after all, is a genre where the agency of an often anonymous model is assumed to be circumscribed or even emptied out by the artist, who recreates a voyeuristic experience from a dominant position of power 124–27. But it is in some of these drawings where a fuller range of Delectorskaya's existence can be read as central to the conception of the work itself. As an indication of Matisse's belief in the drawings' centrality to his production, thirty-five of them appeared in a special 1936 issue of *Cahiers d'art* laid out like a richly orchestrated cinematic narrative. It begins with three 1930 drawings made in Tahiti 87–89, followed by sheets that depict the reactivation of those memories, through textiles ("pareos brought back from Tahiti, but made in Toulouse" according to Delectorskaya) and the *Window at Tahiti II* cartoon, providing one of many frames within a frame in this group's layered mise en abyme.[35] In the nesting of one illusion inside another,

26 The book was first published in French in 1986; an English translation, *With Apparent Ease*, was published by the same publisher, Adrien Maeght, in 1988.

27 Additional photographs of her at work in the studio appear in Delectorskaya, *L'Apparente Facilité*, 13 and 142.

28 "Entretien de Delectorskaya," 280 (author's translation).

29 "Entretien de Delectorskaya," 65 (author's translation). In *L'Apparente Facilité*, 28, Delectorskaya again connects her work on canvases to physical caretaking, explaining how "[Matisse] had me do it when he was affected by neuritis in his right shoulder and wanted to spare it in order to be able to paint" (author's translation).

30 For charcoal drawings see Annelies Nelck, *L'Olivier du rêve: Matisse à Vence, témoignage* (Nice: Presses d'Imprimix, 1999), 85.

31 Examples include her overseeing of ceramic firing at Aubagne in 1950, and her contribution on tracing and mounting the cut-outs with Gloria de Herrera at the Parisian art suppliers and restorers Lefebvre-Foinet.

32 HM–Rouveyre, October 6, 1941, cited in Delectorskaya, *Henri Matisse*, 188 (author's translation).

33 As John Klein suggests about this drawing: "Sometimes Matisse seemed to use her image as a surrogate for himself, acting the part of the artist. . . ." Klein, *Matisse Portraits* (New Haven: Yale University Press), 245.

34 In 1955, Delectorskaya typed up a description of their agreement, which is reproduced in Szymusiak et al., *Lydia D.*, 213.

35 "Entretien de Delectorskaya," 151.

36 (fig.)
Henri Matisse, Lydia Delectorskaya, and Amélie Matisse in the studio, Place Charles-Félix, Nice, 1934
Archives Henri Matisse, Issy-les-Moulineaux

37 (fig.)
Lydia Delectorskaya working on *Window at Tahiti II*, Place Charles-Félix, Nice, 1936
Archives Henri Matisse, Issy-les-Moulineaux

38 (fig.)
Lydia Delectorskaya in front of *Large Reclining Nude*, Place Charles-Félix, Nice, October 1935.
Photograph by Hélène Adant
Bibliothèque Kandinsky, Musée National d'Art Moderne–Centre Pompidou, Paris

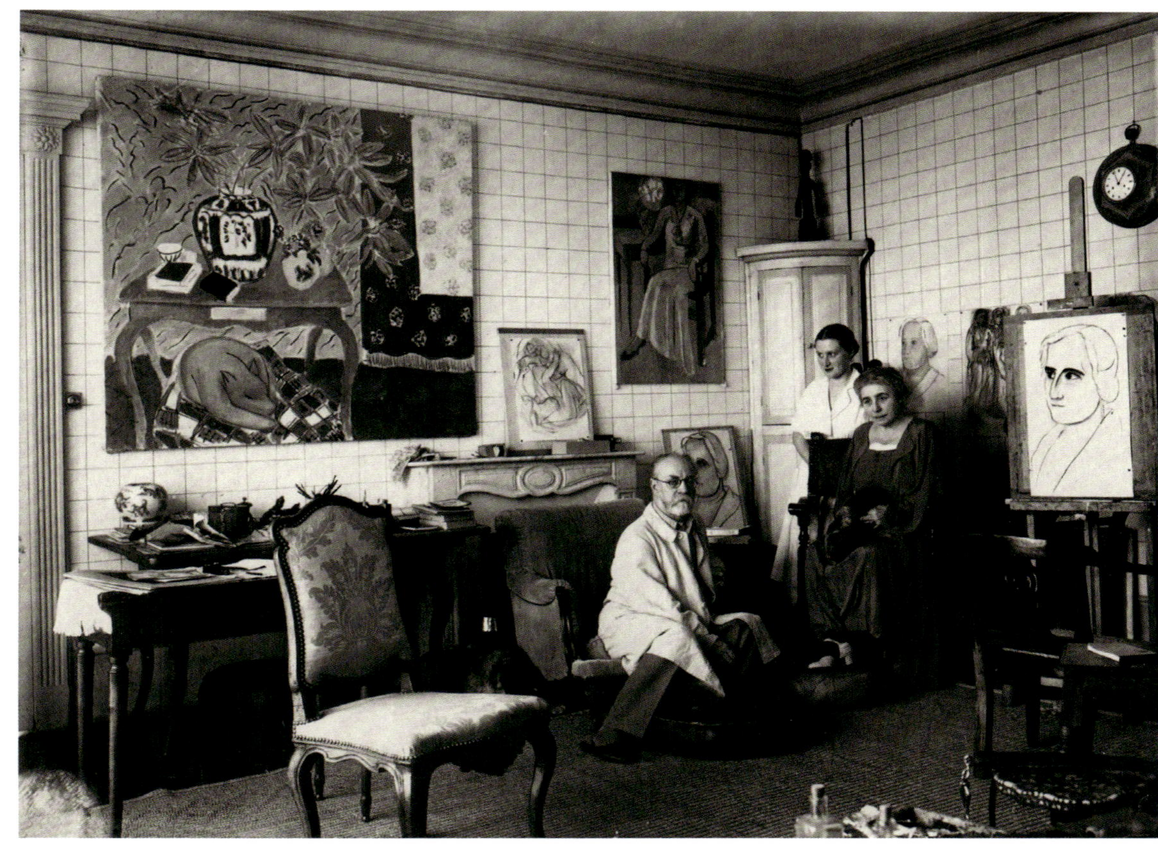

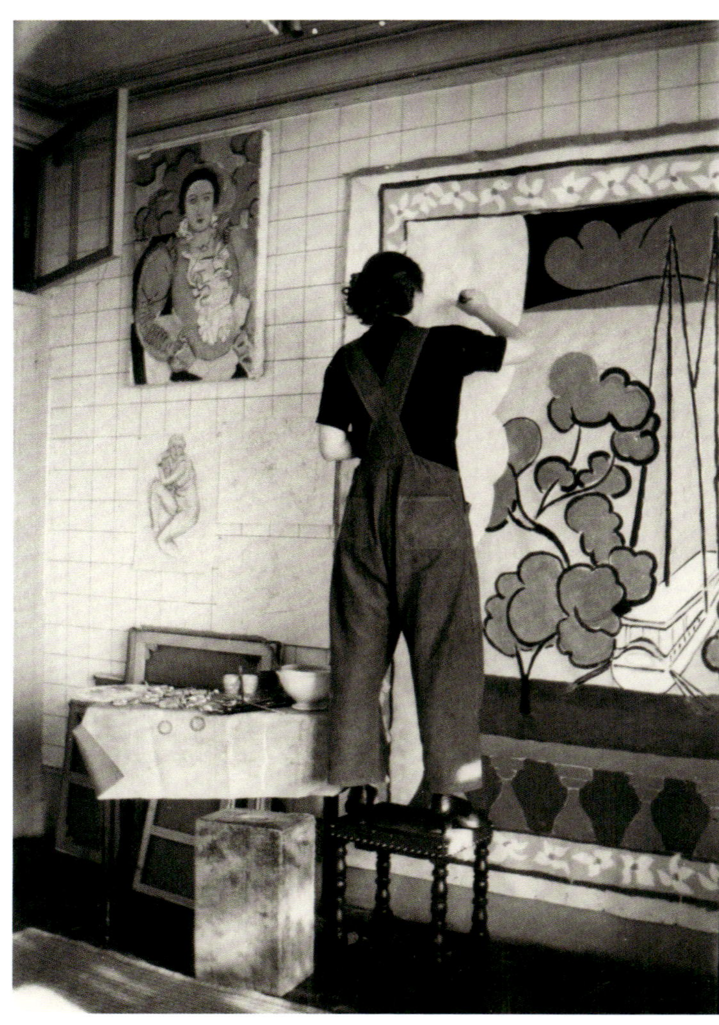

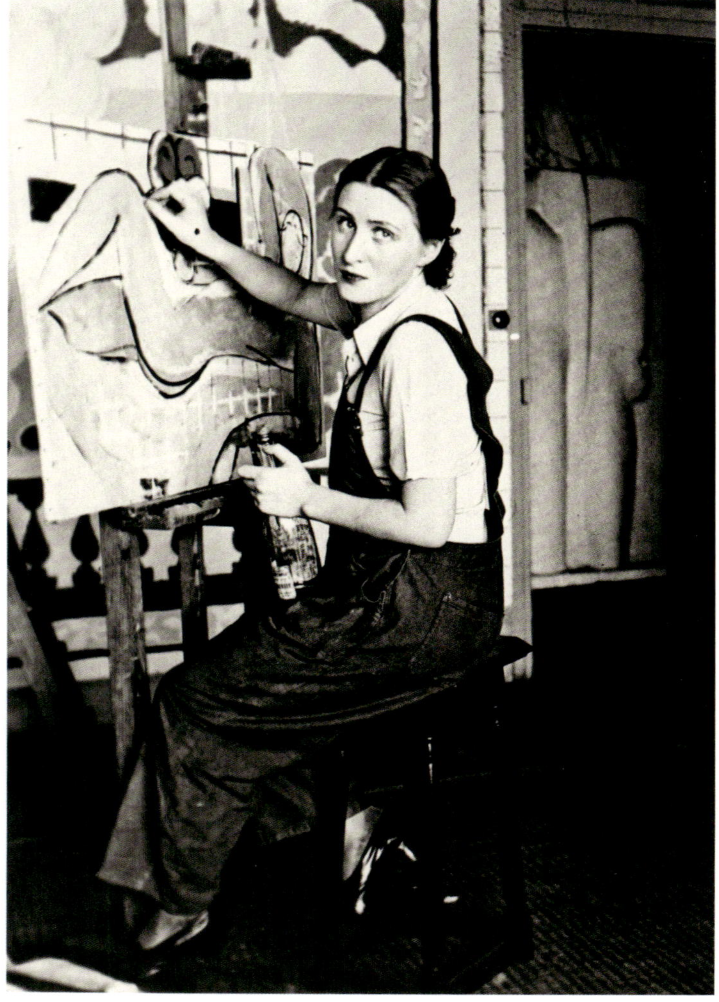

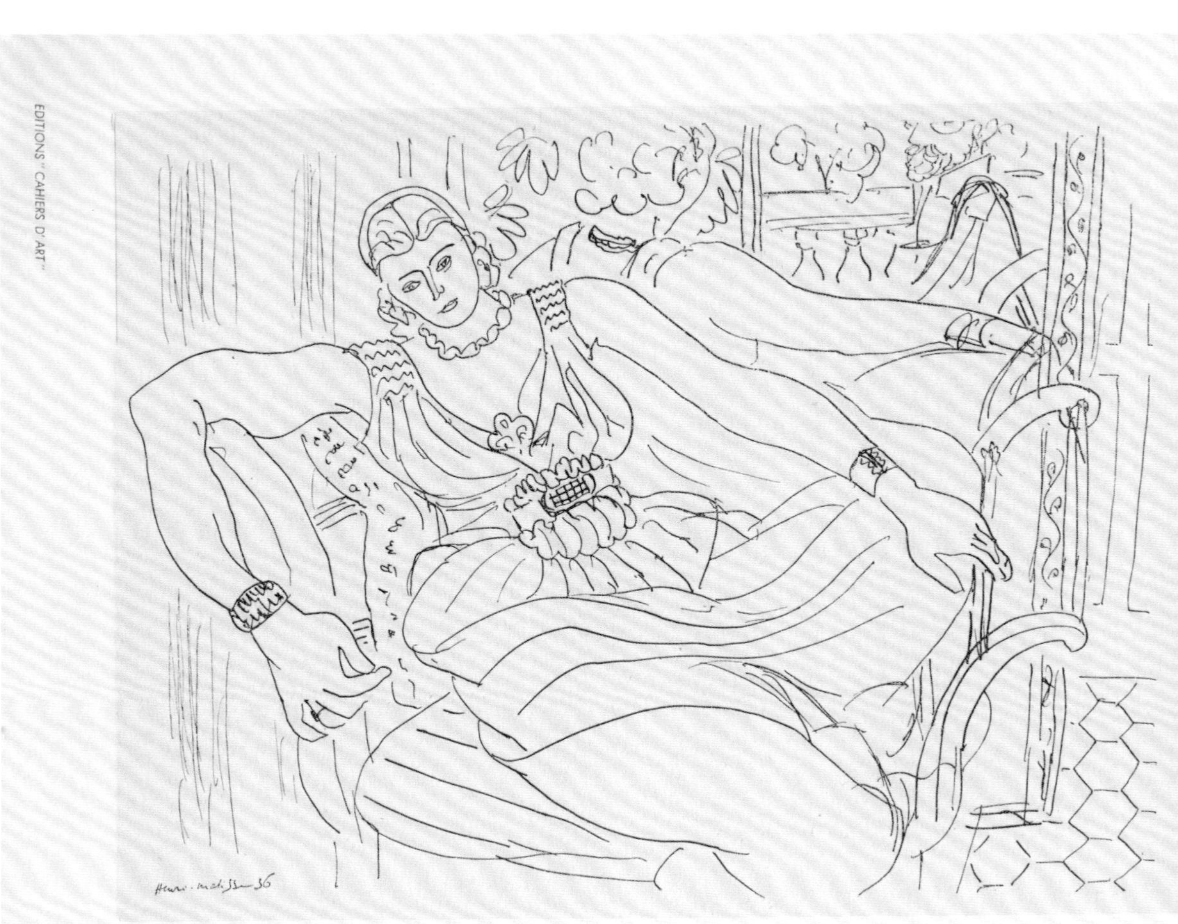
EDITIONS "CAHIERS D'ART"
109

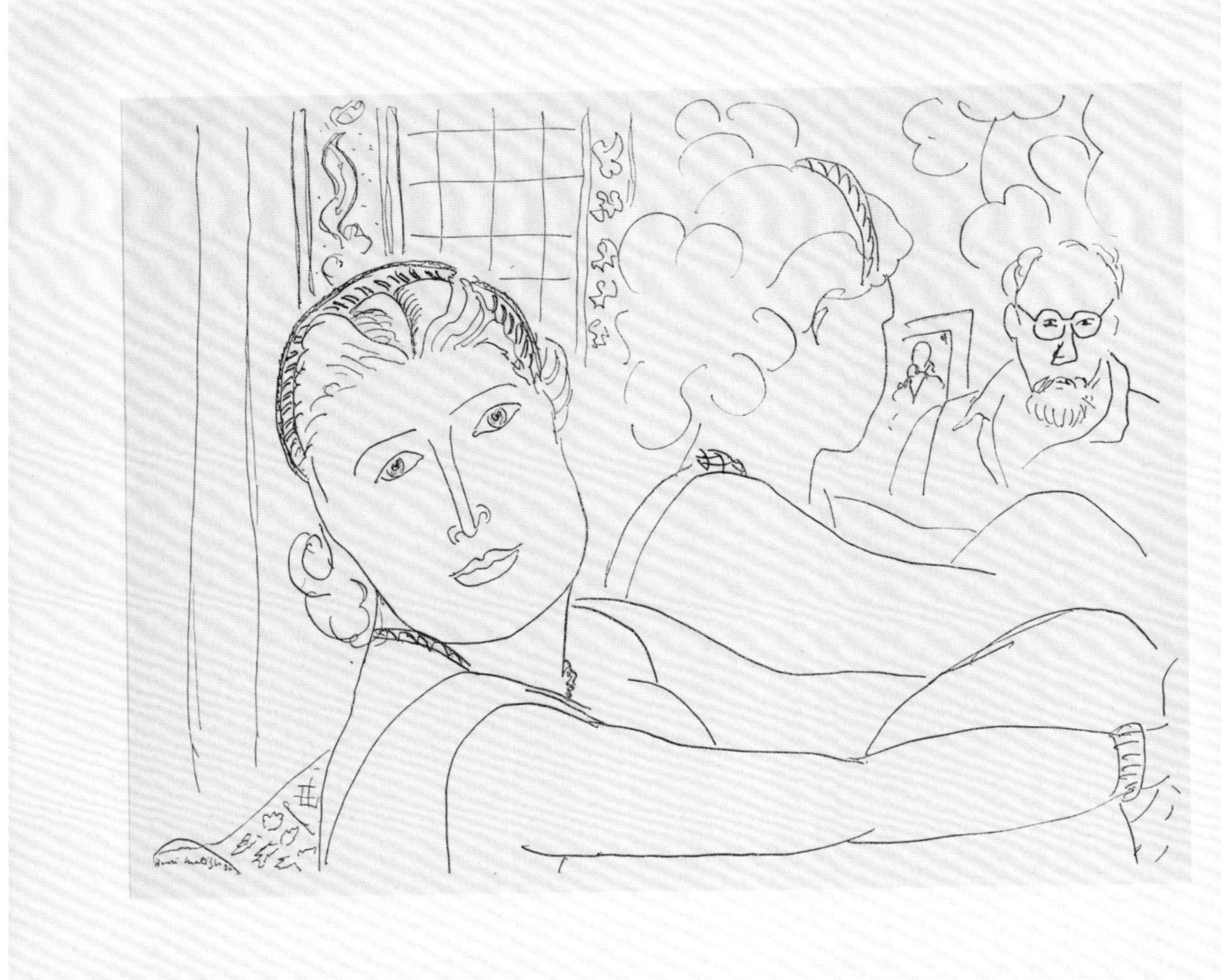

39, **40**
Cahiers d'art, 1936,
nos. 3–5, pp. 109, 110
Éditions Cahiers d'Art, Paris

41
Nude Seated on a Banquette in front of a Mirror, 1937
Ink on paper, 15 ¼ × 11 in. (38.8 × 28 cm)
Musée National d'Art Moderne–Centre Pompidou, Paris

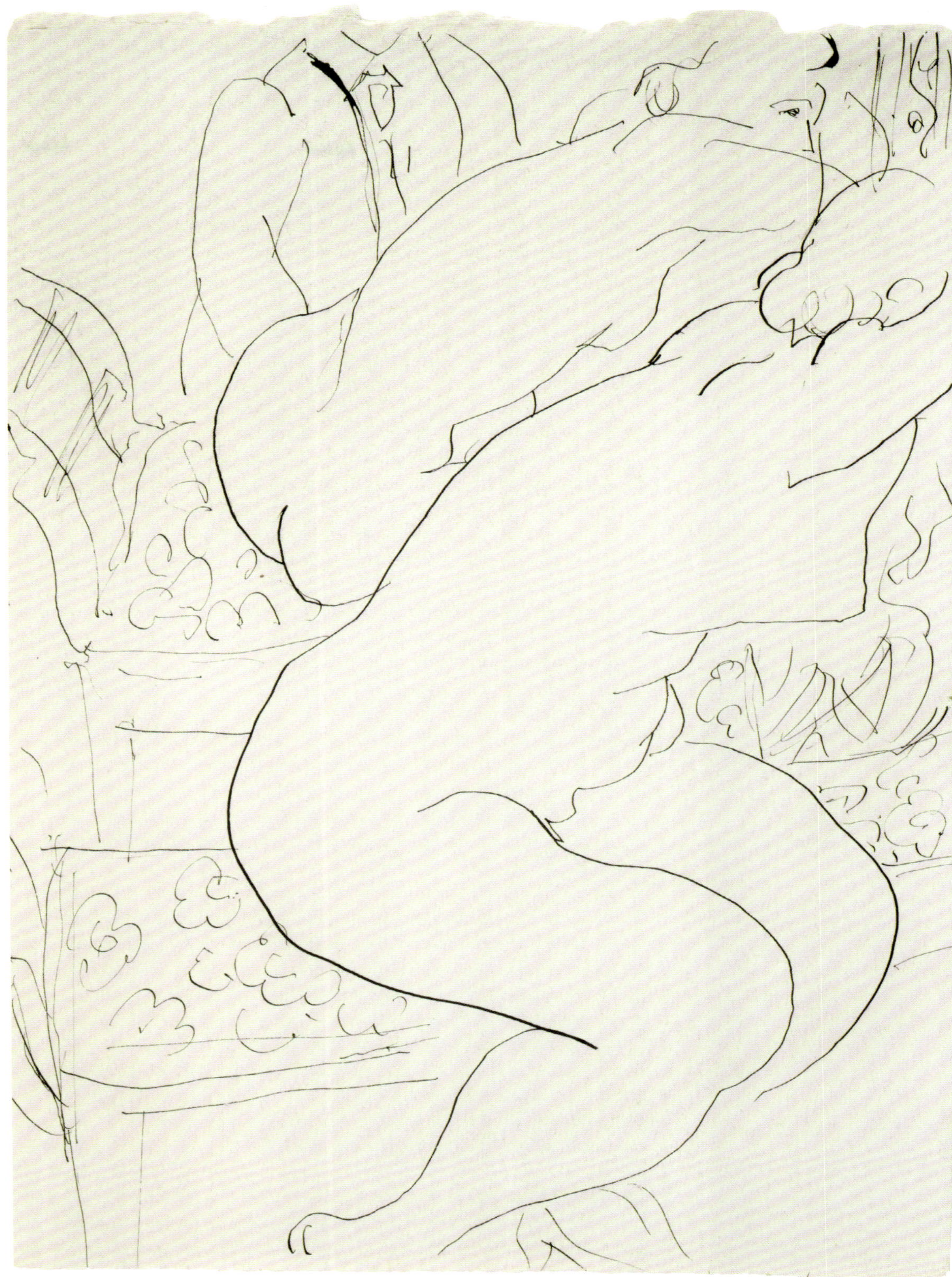

which also includes mirrors, art on studio walls, and Matisse drawing himself drawing, several back-and-forth exchanges are blurred: reality and reflection, ornament and anatomy, the art of textile and the art of drawing. Richly decorated fabrics embellish the white flesh of a nude Delectorskaya, scattered beneath her sprawling limbs like so many sheets of paper, not unlike the partial views of one of the drawings in progress, with Matisse's hand entering the frame in a gesture parallel to hers. Another blurring, aided by disorienting mirrors, is the distinction between an omniscient artist and his surveyed model. While *vanitas* motifs have so often been employed to suggest authorial control, the spectral reflections of Matisse read less as dominance than as fantasies of bodily eclipse.[36] The mirror doubles the partial fragments of Delectorskaya, but also gives us the possibility to imagine what she sees. In one sheet, Matisse appears in the mirror as a beady-eyed parodic afterthought, rising up from behind her presence, the top of his head pushed out of view 39. With an arm span of gigantesque proportions, space is engulfed by her body bedecked in a gown of garnet velour gathered by a golden buckle that she confected herself.[37] Matisse seems driven to distraction by fabric folds, leaving out coordinates for the scene's left side, where we search in vain for the rest of a mirror frame that should be there. Spatial dislocation makes Matisse's relative position to his model unclear: is he standing by an open door to a real balcony at the back of the room, or closer still, in the fictional balcony depicted at bottom of the hanging *Window at Tahiti II*? In the next sheet of the *Cahiers* layout, the space between Matisse and Delectorskaya collapses into the world of *Tahiti* 40. Both look out at the viewer, but only by way of looking intently at each other first. Matisse is entirely suspended inside *Tahiti's* floral frame, while Delectorskaya's head and its reflection doubles down on her meditative regard of him and the work she had a hand in creating.

When writing about these drawings, Maurice Merleau-Ponty observed that "painters have often liked to draw themselves in the act of painting (they still do—witness Matisse's drawing), adding to what they saw then, what things saw of them."[38] Christian Zervos, too, in his introduction to this *Cahiers d'art* issue, also focused on Matisse's self-reflexive observations, his making of himself into a spectator within an "illusory space."[39] While neither is especially concerned with the model as among the "things" that saw Matisse, Delectorskaya is integral to the diffusion of space in these drawings, expanded by a shared, immersive process of seeing and being seen.

What other period viewers saw more immediately, however, was their heightened eroticism, which raised complications during a 1936 exhibition at the Leicester Galleries in London. Matisse, normally reticent about erotic content, was well aware that their "innocent yet indiscreet nudity . . . surely precludes hanging them in a respectable home."[40] His daughter Marguerite Duthuit had to negotiate the installation, reporting back to her parents that no other gallery would have accepted them.[41] In a grateful note to Clive Bell, thanking him for a review that refuted the persistent idea of enchanting superficiality ("Matisse has both seen and felt what he has rendered"), the painter told the English critic Bell that hidden behind the "apparent ease" were his many "painful efforts."[42] Delectorskaya later adopted this notion as both book title (*L'Apparente Facilité*) and leitmotif in her many analyses of Matisse. What is also hidden, or *sublimated* in these images—to borrow a word Matisse used about the voluptuousness of his nudes—is labor. And not just his.

Modeling was a form of labor distinct from other corporeal demands on Delectorskaya's time and energy. In the early days before their percentage agreement, Matisse insisted on paying her separately for these sessions. Time was a precious commodity. The mirrors, Zervos noted, create the illusion of "arrested space" which also comes with an extended pause, granting both artist and model liberty from a regimented workday where every hour was counted.[43] In that pause, there is also an expansion of the studio's geographical reach. Describing one of the drawing's Tahitian allusions, John Klein poetically notes how "[t]he journey in the studio calls on points from within the self to halfway around the world."[44]

36 John Klein has thoroughly examined Matisse's use of the mirror with Delectorskaya, "as a means to expand the sense of space and to reinforce the intimacy of his relationship with the model," beginning with the destroyed *Nu rose crevette*. Klein, "Artiste, modèle, miroir, plume: Dessins 1935–1937," in Szymusiak et al., *Lydia D.*, 102–13.

37 For Delectorskaya's reproduction of the drawing, along with an explanation of her creation of the outfit, see Delectorskaya, *Henri Matisse*, 232.

38 Yve-Alain Bois suggests Maurice Merleau-Ponty is referring to the 1936 *Cahiers d'art* issue in Maurice Merleau-Ponty, *L'Œil et l'esprit* (Paris: Gallimard, 1967), 34. The passage is discussed by Bois, "On Matisse: The Blinding," *October*, no. 68 (Spring 1994): 75n48.

39 Christian Zervos, "Automatisme et espace illusoire," *Cahiers d'art* 11, nos. 3–5 (1936): 69–75. Reprinted in English translation by Richard Howard as "Automatism and Illusory Space" in *Henri Matisse: Drawings 1936; A Facsimile Edition* (New York: George Braziller), n.p.

40 HM–Bussy, February 27, 1936, INHA, Paris. My thanks to Anne Théry for sharing this letter, and to Matthew Affron for help in translating it.

41 Marguerite Duthuit–HM and Amélie Matisse, February 3, 1936, Archives Henri Matisse, Issy-les-Moulineaux.

42 Clive Bell, "Black and White," *New Statesman and Nation*, February 15, 1936, 226–27. HM–Clive Bell, cited in Richard Shone, "Matisse in England and Two English Sitters," *Burlington Magazine* 135, no. 1084 (1993): 482 (author's translation).

43 "Often he projects his figures in a mirror to create alongside what we might call real space, an arrested space, since it is merely the reflection of the other one." Zervos, "Automatism and Illusory Space."

44 Klein, "Artiste, modèle, miroir, plume," 113.

But, in reality, Delectorskaya would not have been able to travel to Tahiti. As a Russian exile, the movements of her body were restricted by regulations. In order for her to flee Paris at the onset of war, Matisse needed to ask the director of the École des Beaux-Arts to help grant "approval" so that she could return to the Midi.[45] During the occupation, the Germans allowed her to stay on with Matisse, so long as she did not attend meetings with other immigrants. Matisse refused the offer of World War II exile to the United States for several reasons, but chiefly because she could not accompany him.[46]

What we see in his many representations of Delectorskaya is a distillation, in both audacious line and deft play with value, of Matisse's many desires and his need for proximity to her. But we might also think of ways in which images of her unselfconscious, almost complete absorption potentially narrate her imagined pleasures, her state of becoming "unshackled" and finding respite from the "void" of exile. Being involved in the making of Matisse's art, she often suggested, gave her dignity and purpose, a reason and means to survive.[47] A "stateless" refugee, alienated in and by her historical moment, she channeled her copious energies into laying a claim for space in Matisse's art, and in making a conspicuous home for herself there.

45 "Entretien de Delectorskaya," 311.

46 Matisse made this clear to Pierre Matisse, in responding to his news of an offer from Mills College in California, 1940. John Russell, *Matisse: Father and Son* (New York: Abrams, 1999), 196.

47 As she told Girard: "I had nothing: I had left my husband, I found myself alone, I had no attachments in life ... without insisting or explaining, I simply became useful. . . . I devoted myself entirely." "Entretien de Delectorskaya," 63 (author's translation).

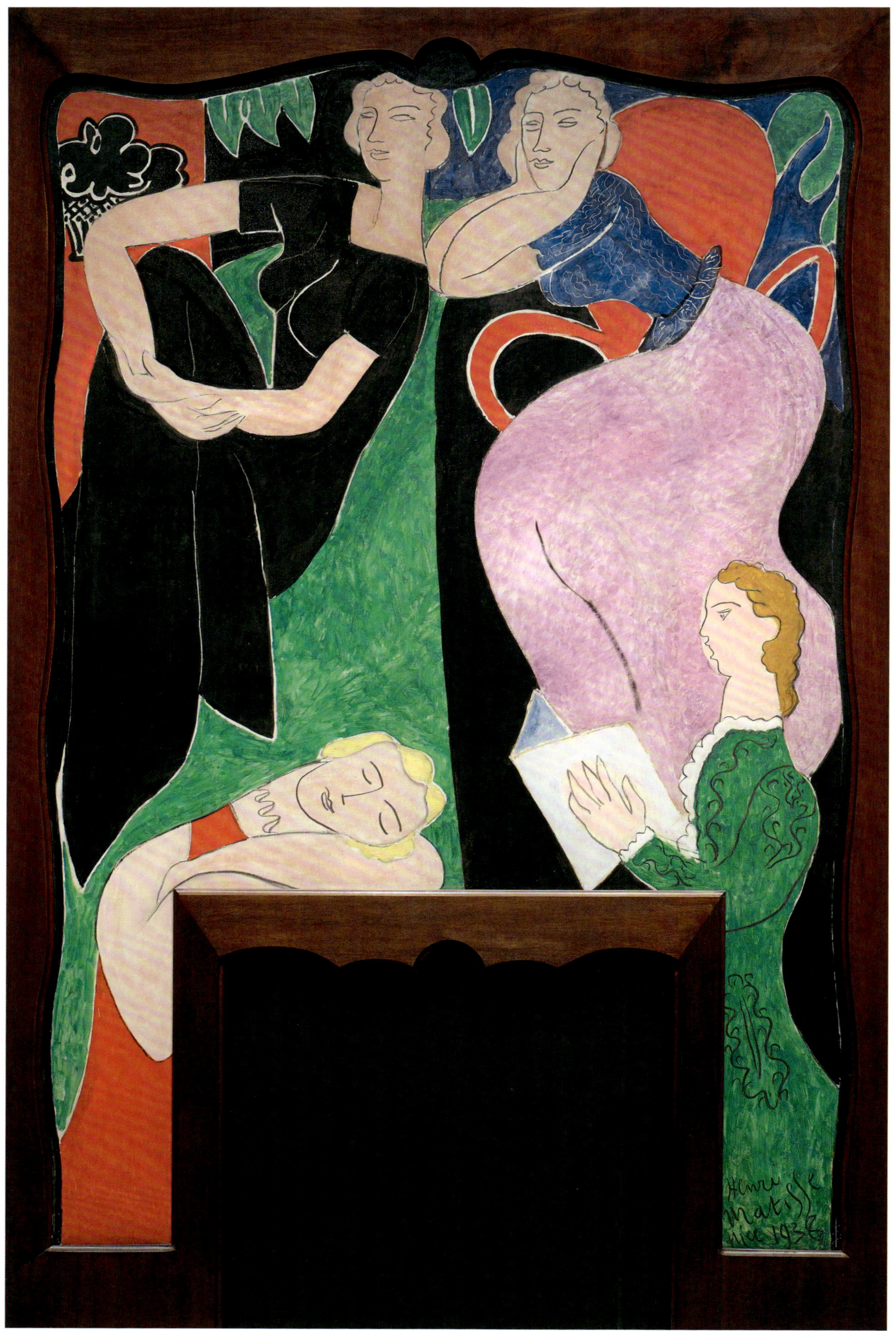

42
The Song, 1938
Oil on canvas,
9 ft. 3 in. × 6 ft. 1⁄16 in.
(282 × 183 cm)
The Lewis Collection

MATTHEW AFFRON

MATISSE'S MURAL ART

At the end of 1939, the journal *Cahiers d'art* published a dossier on two ornamental paintings by Henri Matisse. *The Song*, executed in the previous year, depicted a musical performance in which a woman sings from a songbook for three female companions 42. The work had an unusual format owing to its function as an overmantel for the living room in the New York apartment of Nelson A. Rockefeller. Matisse had made the second picture, a large square canvas titled *Music* 48, as a companion piece for the same interior (though Rockefeller never acquired it). It showed two models, one with a guitar in her lap, dressed in costumes of contrasting yellow and blue and seated under a continuous frieze of large philodendron leaves in a conservatory-like interior. *Cahiers d'art* published in-process photographs of both works to document Matisse's working method 8 | 47.

Interleaved with all these images was a set of reflections on the politics of mural art by Christian Zervos, the art critic and editor of *Cahiers d'art*. In effect, Zervos was attempting to have the last word in a debate about mural painting as an art for the masses that had emerged with considerable force in the era of the Popular Front, France's left-wing government of 1936–38. His own position was that mural painting represented the best vehicle for artists to work for a wide public while maintaining their creative freedom.[1] Zervos mentioned only two artists as harbingers of this hoped-for mural renaissance: Henri Matisse and Pablo Picasso. These were unsurprising choices given that the pairing of those two major figures was already a commonplace in art criticism and a leitmotif in *Cahiers d'art*. Zervos's example from Picasso was, inevitably, *Guernica* (1937; Museo Nacional Centro de Arte Reina Sofía, Madrid), the mural-sized canvas for the Spanish Pavilion of the 1937 Paris Exposition Internationale that depicted one of the horrors of the ongoing Spanish civil war. Unusually for Picasso, this work fused unmistakable propaganda value with abstruse Cubist-Surrealist style. Its intention was to move the multitude of visitors to the fair to sympathy for the Republican cause. There was an equally inevitable example on the Matisse side of the ledger: *The Dance* 103, the monumental decoration for the main gallery of the Barnes Foundation, then located in Merion, a suburb of Philadelphia, which Zervos mentioned along with both *The Song* and *Music*. For Zervos, the fact that Matisse had made all of them on behalf of private art collectors and for spaces that were either private or semipublic—not to mention situated on far-off American shores—in no way diminished their significance for his argument. Neither did their resolutely aesthetic subject matter. That aspect of Zervos's argument raises two questions for this essay: How did Matisse's approach to mural art develop in the 1930s? And how should we situate the artist and his work in relation to broader debates on the mural question in this period?

The idea of the decorative picture was the central, constantly evolving basis of Matisse's oeuvre from the start. His basic operating premise was as follows: whether a picture takes the form of a still life, a landscape, or the human figure, it is fundamentally through the harmony of flat, ornamental color and design that it affects the viewer. A corollary was that paintings grow in expressive intensity to the extent that they emphasize the harmonious

1 Christian Zervos, "2 décorations de Henri-Matisse: Réflexions sur l'art mural," *Cahiers d'art* [CDA], nos. 5–10 (1939): 165–78. As Alfred H. Barr Jr. explained, the hyphen was widely adopted to distinguish Henri Matisse from another painter with the same surname (see Alfred H. Barr, *Henri-Matisse: Retrospective Exhibition* [New York: Museum of Modern Art, 1931], 9).

organization of color, drawing, and surface design over literal representation, naturalistic detail, and conventional perspective. Matisse drew his concept of decorativeness as the engine of artistic expression from a range of sources in art theory, including academic theory, nineteenth-century decorative arts manuals, and Modernist theoretical texts; his study of artworks in both the European and Islamic tradition; and his own discoveries as a painter and sometime maker of decorated objects. He defended the idea in what became one of the well-known passages in "Notes d'un peintre" (Notes of a painter), his influential, first theoretical statement on art, published in 1908: "The entire arrangement of my picture is expressive: the place occupied by the figures, the empty spaces around them, the proportions, all of that has its share. Composition is the art of arranging in a decorative manner the diverse elements at the painter's command to express his feelings."[2]

By the 1910s, Matisse had also applied this decorative aesthetic in a new type of large-scale, experimental easel painting. Major examples include two large canvases commissioned by the Russian collector Sergei Shchukin to adorn the staircase in his Moscow residence, *Dance II* and *Music* (1909–10; State Hermitage Museum, St. Petersburg), as well as the four so-called "symphonic interiors" of 1911 (also for Shchukin), *The Pink Studio* (Pushkin Museum of Fine Arts, Moscow), *The Painter's Family* (State Hermitage Museum, St. Petersburg), *Interior with Eggplants* (Musée de Grenoble), and *The Red Studio* (Museum of Modern Art [MoMA], New York). Or consider *The Moroccans*, which Matisse executed in 1915–16 43. Nominally, this is a street scene viewed from a café terrace, with an architectural zone featuring the dome of a shrine at the upper left, a still-life area featuring melons and their leaves at lower left, and a section with turbaned figures at lower right. As Matisse worked through the states of the composition on the large, horizonal canvas, he transposed the vista he had sketched in Tangier to a more poetic, cryptic totality. The final composition is remarkable for its generalization of forms, intensification of colors, flattening of spatial relationships to emphasize surface relations, and use of large areas of dense black both to provide expressive force in contrast to the vivid colors and to bridge the disparate parts of the motif. In the words of a Danish author who visited Matisse in his studio and who wrote the first near-contemporary description, "the result was a decorative, synthetic style of great beauty and simplicity."[3]

Matisse's application of his decorative sensibility did not, however, follow a straight or predictable path. A shift of direction came in December 1917, when Matisse went to the city of Nice to paint. For the next dozen years, he generally painted in an intimate manner, as exemplified by many pictures set in interiors that he rendered as little worlds infused with the vibrant patterns of objects and furnishings and the brilliance of the Mediterranean sun 44. Matisse defended his new approach as a logical move toward a more complete mode of expression.[4] Some critics, however, when confronted with Matisse's latest style based on tonal modeling and traditional perspective, found themselves ready to write his epitaph—if not as an artist, then as a prime mover in the avant-garde art scene.[5] As the 1920s wore on, Matisse internalized the criticism and faced a creative block.

The opportunity to work in the format of mural decoration finally offered a path forward. The turning point was the commission from Albert C. Barnes for a painted decoration for the main hall at his foundation, a building designed by the French-born Philadelphia architect Paul Cret. Matisse designed his mural to fit a high and irregularly shaped band of wall some forty-five feet across, directly under a triple-vaulted ceiling and over a trio of tall French doors that led to a garden. He selected a theme from his earlier days that he associated with the expression of joy, exuberance, and renewal: a circle of dancing nymphs.[6] This chain of dancers had been at the center of *The Joy of Life* (1905–6), his first large-scale arcadian composition, which Barnes had acquired in 1923. Matisse had also drawn on the same image in *Dance II* for Shchukin.

But to realize his motif on the scale of a mural for Barnes, Matisse needed to develop a new way of working. In early 1931, he set up three rectangular canvases in a rented automobile

2 Henri Matisse, "Notes of a Painter, 1908," in *Matisse on Art*, ed. and trans. Jack Flam, rev. ed. (Berkeley: University of California Press, 2015), 40. On Matisse's use of the decorative as an artistic paradigm, see Rémi Labrusse, *Matisse: La condition de l'image* (Paris: Gallimard, 1999); Joseph Masheck, *The Carpet Paradigm: Integral Flatness from Decorative to Fine Art* (New York: Edgewise, 2010), 63–85; and John Klein, *Matisse and Decoration* (New Haven: Yale University Press, 2018), 21–35.

3 Alex Salto, "Henri Matisse" (1918), quoted in Stephanie D'Alessandro and John Elderfield, *Henri Matisse: Radical Invention, 1913–1917* (Chicago: Art Institute of Chicago, 2010), 295.

4 "Interview with Ragnar Hoppe, 1919," in Flam, Matisse on Art, 75.

5 André Levinson, "Henri Matisse at Sixty" (1930), in *Matisse: A Retrospective*, ed. Jack Flam (New York: Hugh Lauter Levin Associates, 1988), 240.

6 "Interview with Georges Charbonnier, 1950," in Flam, *Matisse on Art*, 189. On *The Dance*, see Jack Flam, *Matisse: "The Dance"* (Washington, DC: National Gallery of Art, 1993); and Karen K. Butler, "The Dance," in *Matisse in the Barnes Foundation*, ed. Yve-Alain Bois (Philadelphia: Barnes Foundation / London: Thames & Hudson, 2015), 3:21–62.

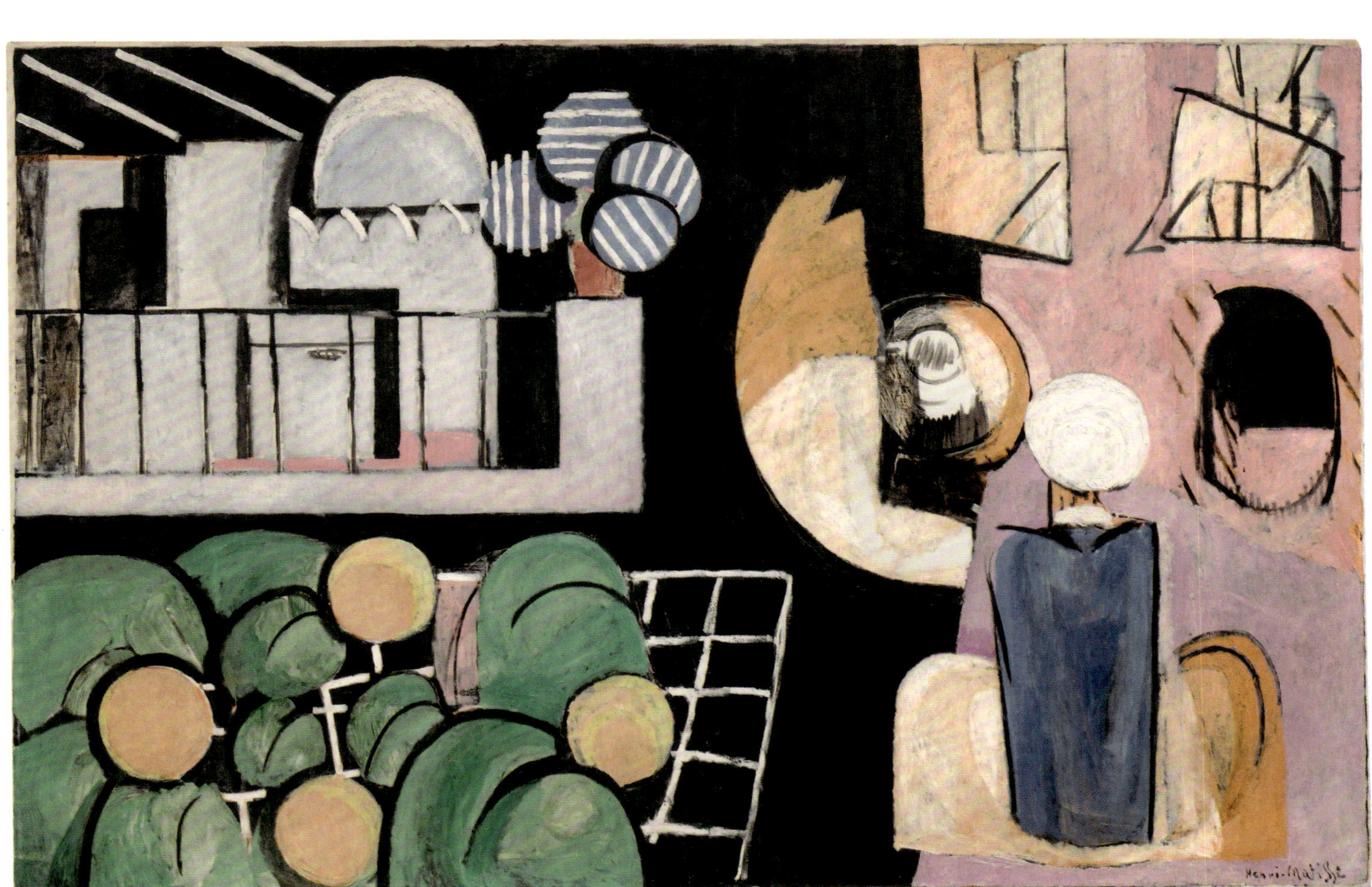

43 (fig.)
The Moroccans, late 1915–fall 1916
Oil on canvas, 71 3/8 in. × 9 ft. 2 in. (181.3 × 279.4 cm)
The Museum of Modern Art, New York

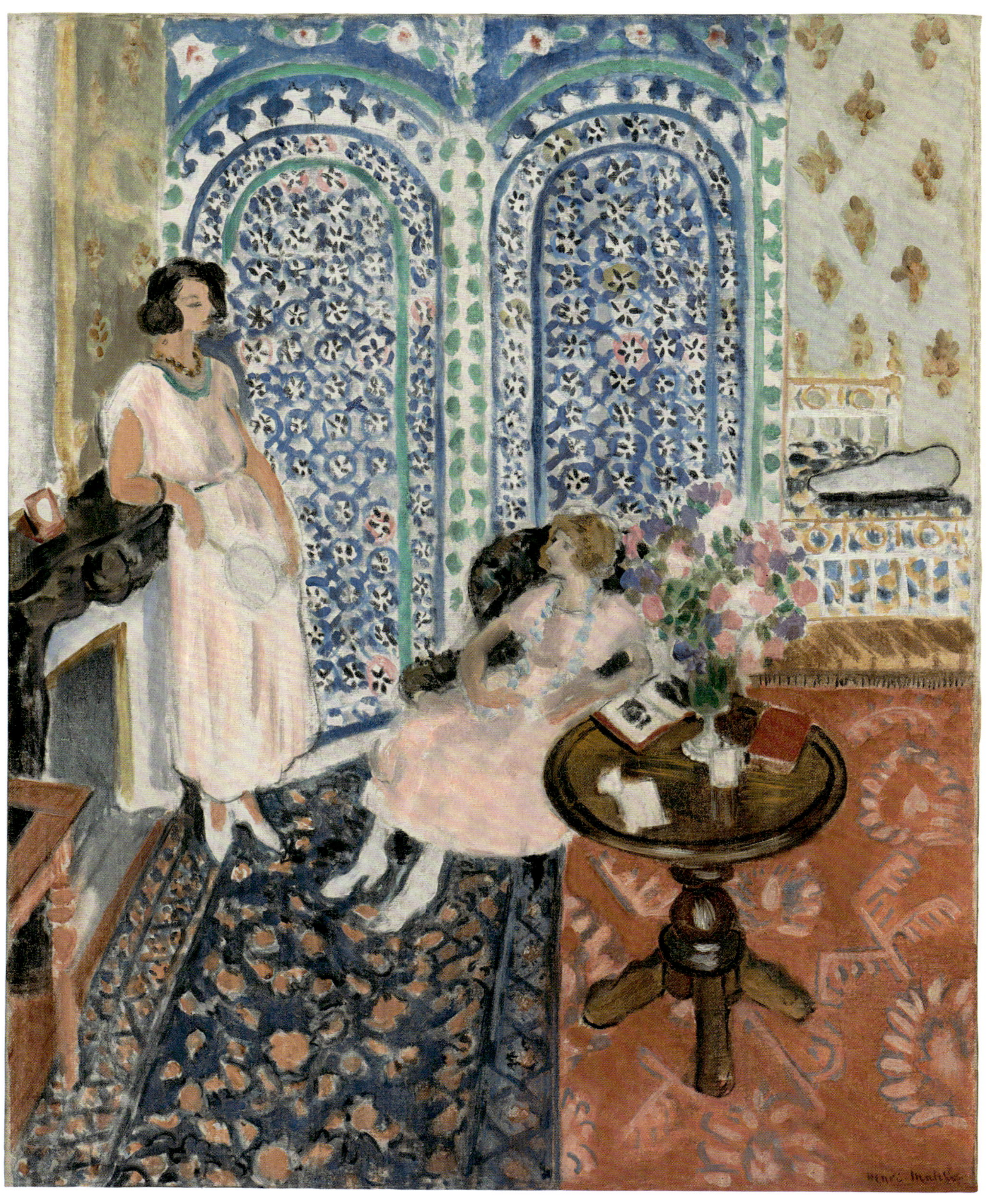

44
The Moorish Screen, 1921
Oil on canvas, 36 3/16 × 29 1/4 in.
(91.9 × 74.3 cm)
Philadelphia Museum of Art

garage not far from his Nice studio and began planning. There the artist found a practical method to accomodate successive compositional adjustments without having to constantly repaint his immense image: cutting out pieces of colored paper with scissors and, with the assistance of a model, first Lisette Löwengard and then Lydia Delectorskaya, setting them in place using pins. This working technique produced, in turn, new expressive effects. Articulating the picture like a jigsaw puzzle led Matisse away from the illusion of modeling and deep space, as in the Nice period, and toward bold, flat shapes and unshaded colors without visible brushwork **49 | 50**. The nearly continuous circular formation of dancing nymphs in the earlier paintings turned into a wavelike movement of bodies leaping and tumbling across the expanse of the linked lunettes. Matisse chose his colors—pearl gray for the giant figures against bands of brilliant pink, blue, and black—to infuse the shadowy wall surface with luminosity, to bond the picture with ambient architectural conditions such as the hardness of the building's limestone, and to harmonize with the strong backlighting that flooded through the glazed French doors directly below **46 | 103**. In early 1932, with the project now well along, Matisse discovered that an error in measurement had thrown off the dimensions of his panels, and some months later he was forced to start a new version of the composition. A housepainter was hired to assist with the ultimate application of paint, and Matisse then accompanied his three canvases to Merion, where he oversaw their installation at the foundation in May 1933.

The most complete explanation Matisse offered about what the Barnes mural implied for his evolving understanding of mural art came in a set of letters in 1934 to Alexander Romm, a Soviet art critic who was preparing a monograph on Matisse. In his first letter, Matisse compared the 1909–10 *Dance* commissioned by Shchukin, a work that his interlocutor would have known well, and the Barnes mural, photographs of which Matisse provided. Matisse stressed that, despite the analogous subject matter, the underlying principles were in fact quite distinct. The Shchukin panel retained the logic of the mobile easel picture despite its decorative function, meaning that it had been designed without reference to its specific destination. In contrast, the Barnes *Dance*, although having been executed on canvas supports and wooden stretchers, counted as architectural painting: immovable and site-specific from the start.

A comment that Romm sent back—to the effect that the "human element" seemed much less pronounced in the Barnes mural—led Matisse to further thoughts on the way in which architectural decoration addresses the spectator: "In architectural painting, which is the case in Merion, it seems to me that the human element must always be tempered, if not excluded. I, who let myself always be guided by my instinct (so much so that it manages to overcome my reason), had to avoid it, for it led me away from my architectural problem each time it appeared on my canvas." Matisse was suggesting that different formats set up different standpoints for the viewer. The easel picture, as he put it to Romm, is a closed world, isolated from its milieu by means of a frame; it demands scrutiny in close proximity and with focused concentration, and it communicates through feeling and emotion on an individual level. Things are reversed with architectural painting. The picture's purpose is to animate a place. Matisse spoke of his painted decoration as functioning, in its placement over the three doors, like a pediment on a cathedral porch. This analogy served to underline the total integration of the image with its setting as an issue of paramount importance. "I will even add," Matisse remarked in one of the letters to Romm, "that by the action of my lines and my painted surfaces I have raised the arches of the vault, which were very oppressive and gave a crushing feeling."[7]

Matisse was by no means done with *The Dance*. After returning from Merion, he transferred the mismeasured panels onto a fresh set of canvases and executed a new, completed version, now known as the *Paris Dance Mural*. He also began thinking about exhibiting it in Paris (which did not happen); produced a reproductive aquatint **99**; and enlisted his son Pierre Matisse, the New York art dealer, in further publicizing the project in the United States. Moreover, Matisse was certainly not done with projects in decorative formats. It is worth

7 "Letters to Alexander Romm, 1934," in Flam, *Matisse on Art*, 115–16. On Matisse's concept of architectural painting, see Yve-Alain Bois, "Matisse's Awakening," in Bois, *Matisse in the Barnes Foundation*, 1:141–42.

noting that, just as with the dealer contracts he had signed with the Galerie Bernheim-Jeune starting in 1909, the three-year agreement he struck with the dealer Paul Rosenberg in 1936 put decorative works in a category apart and gave Matisse the right to receive such commissions directly from patrons.[8]

The year before, in 1935, Marie Cuttoli, a Parisian decorative arts entrepreneur and dealer in modern art, had approached Matisse with a proposal for a tapestry commission. Cuttoli was already engaged in a campaign to revitalize the art and industry of French tapestry by assuming the role of *marchand-mercier*, or producer-merchant. Her innovation was to promote, in the context of a traditional craft, an alliance between modern design and the sensibility of the most adventuresome of Modernist painters of her time.[9] Cuttoli asked Matisse to make a cartoon after one of the etchings he had done in 1931–32 for an illustrated edition of the *Poésies* of Stéphane Mallarmé. This had been Matisse's first major foray into the genre of the artist's book, completed concurrently with the Barnes mural. The etching depicted a view through a window onto the harbor of Papeete, the capital of Tahiti, which Matisse had sketched and photographed in 1930; he had paired it in the Mallarmé volume with "Les Fenêtres" (The windows), a poem about escape to a land of ideal beauty. Matisse transposed his motif, with the addition of an internal border of tropical gardenia blossoms, into a cartoon in oil on a canvas nearly eight feet tall, titled *Papeete, Tahiti* 118. In mid-November he sent the cartoon off to Beauvais with written instructions that telegraphed his worries about depending on the weavers to faithfully transcribe the cartoon's light brushwork and variety of tones.[10] Sure enough, Matisse came away disappointed from a first inspection of the tapestry on the loom. In response, he made *Window at Tahiti II* 119, a second cartoon, switching his medium from oil to gouache for a flatter, more clear-cut effect—that he finally deemed appropriate to stained glass instead of tapestry.[11] The collaboration with Cuttoli was already at an end. Only the tapestry after the first cartoon was ever produced.[12]

This apparent setback nevertheless opened a rich vein of pictorial experimentation in works of hybrid format that were as close in spirit to full-scale mural sketches and tapestry cartoons as they were to conventional easel pictures.[13] From a cluster of studies of the erotic-pastoral subject of a faun serenading a recumbent nymph in a wooded landscape—a bucolic theme with deep roots in Matisse's art—came a pair of drawings that stood out for their unusual combination of pictorial medium and support (charcoal on primed canvas) and their extraordinary dimensions (approximately five feet in both length and breadth). They projected a mural effect by virtue of both their scale and their use of monochrome grisaille—a technique often associated with the decorative arts. In one version, *Nymph and Faun*, Matisse applied a relatively crisp, firm line to offset the whiteness of the primed support 112. He would rework *Nymph and Faun*, its sibling, over a much more extended period, using the stump and the eraser to yield an image with an even more irradiated, ethereal style. The nymph-and-faun theme culminated in a painting on a canvas of even larger dimensions that Matisse conceived as a painted variation on the historical genre of verdure tapestry, which is characterized by landscape scenes, sometimes populated by mythological or historical figures, and includes interior borders embellished with plant forms. Matisse's *Nymph in the Forest (Verdure)* 116 is remarkable for its sketch-like effect and its bright, unmixed palette. He intended it as a parallel expression of the motif that he had already achieved in the grisaille of charcoal; the later composition is painted in a triad of yellow, green, and blue for the landscape, and the body of the nymph, who reclines in the lower left corner, is in eye-catching mauve.[14]

Nymph in the Forest (Verdure) was complete enough to be included along with the two *Tahiti* cartoons and recent easel pictures in a 1936 exhibition at Paul Rosenberg's gallery 45. But Matisse refused to release his painted verdure tapestry to Cuttoli as a functioning cartoon, explaining to her in a letter that it needed further work.[15] In the end, he was most galvanized by the idea, a venerable one in the history of cartoons by artists, that they are to be appreciated in their own right for the way they test out, resolve, and even surpass the essential pictorial

8 The Rosenberg contract is transcribed in John O'Brian, *Ruthless Hedonism: The American Reception of Matisse* (Chicago: University of Chicago Press, 1999), 51.

9 Marie Cuttoli, "La tapisserie" (1937), in *Marie Cuttoli: Myrbor et l'invention de la tapisserie moderne*, Dominique Paulvé, ed. Dominique Paulvé, exh. cat. (Paris: Norma, 2010), n.p.

10 Matisse's diary, November 15, 1935, Archives Henri Matisse, Issy-les-Moulineaux [AHM]. I thank Anne Théry for guiding me to sources in the Matisse archive. See also: Henri Matisse [HM]–Cuttoli, November 21, 1935, quoted in Paulvé, *Marie Cuttoli*, 64.

11 HM–Marguerite Duthuit, March 6, 1936, AHM.

12 Klein, *Matisse and Decoration*, 75–81.

13 This was a continuation of the older, academic procedure of the cartoon but used in a new way to radicalize his art. See Dominique Fourcade, "'Je crois qu'en dessin j'ai pu dire quelque chose,'" in *Henri Matisse: Dessins et sculpture*, ed. Fourcade and Isabelle Monod-Fontaine, exh. cat. (Paris: Musée National d'Art Moderne, 1975), 19–12; and Pierre Schneider, *Matisse*, trans. Michael Taylor and Bridget Strevens Romer (New York: Rizzoli, 1984), 98.

14 HM–Lydia Delectorskaya, February 4, 1936, quoted in Delectorskaya, *With Apparent Ease . . . Henri Matisse: Paintings from 1935–1939*, trans. Olga Tourkoff (Paris: Adrien Maeght, 1988), 115.

15 HM–Cuttoli, July 2, 1936, https://www.auctionzip.com/auction-lot/Henri-Matisse-refusing-a-commission-for-a-tapestr_F0D4AB99B2/, accessed September 1, 2021.

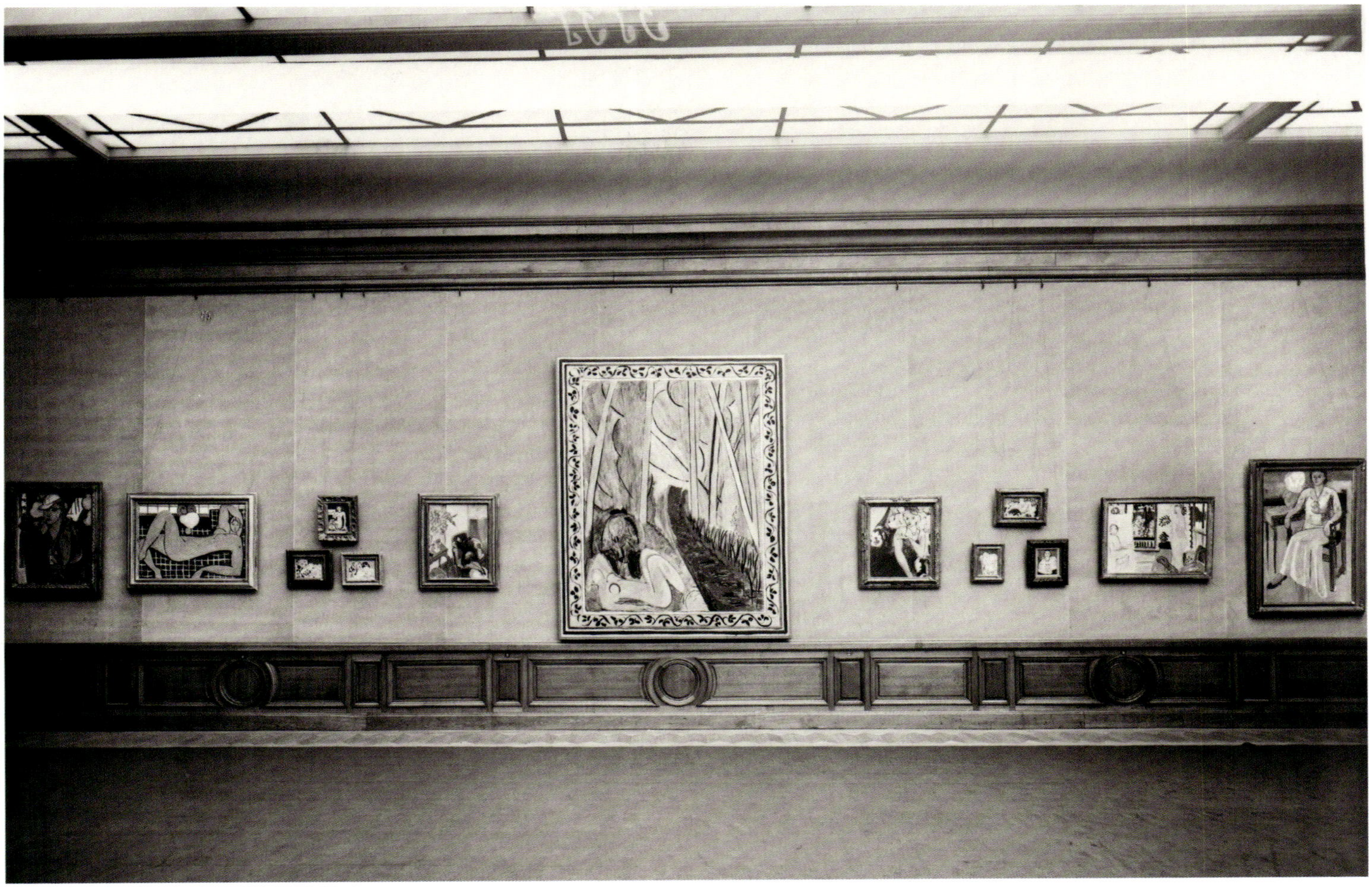

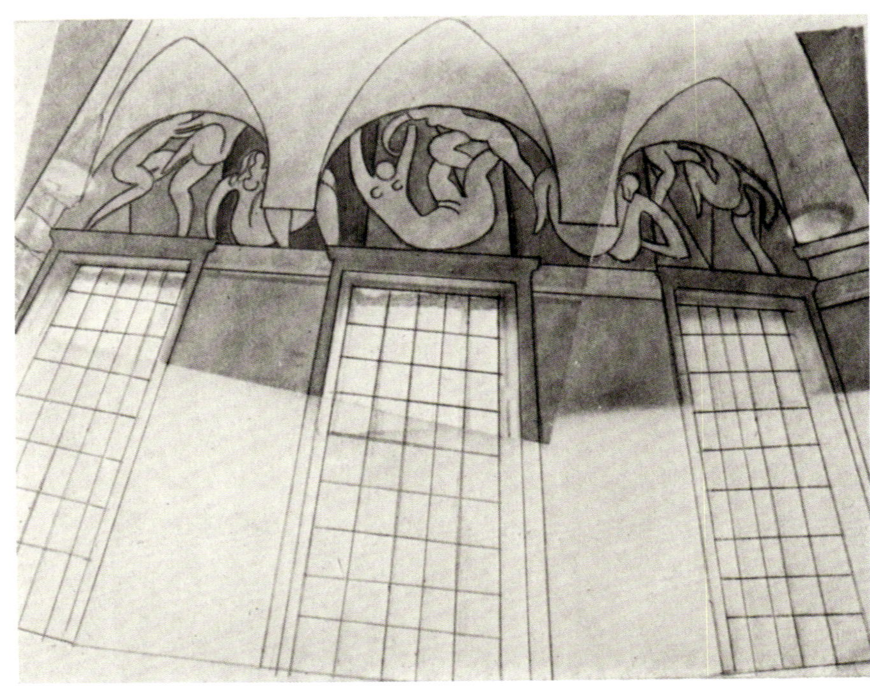

45 (fig.)
View of the *Exposition d'œuvres récentes de Henri-Matisse* at the Galerie Rosenberg, 1936
Musée National d'Art Moderne–Centre Pompidou, Paris

46
Study for Matisse's decoration at the Barnes Foundation, Merion, *Cahiers d'art*, 1935, nos. 1–4, p. 14
Éditions Cahiers d'Art, Paris

16 Roseline Bacou, introduction to *Cartons d'artistes du XVe au XIXe siècle* (Paris: Éditions des Musées Nationaux, 1974), 7–8.

17 "Union pour l'art," *L'Architecture d'aujourd'hui* 7, no. 6 (June 1936): 79. See also Pascal Ory, *La Belle Illusion: Culture et politique sous le signe du Front Populaire, 1934–1938* (Paris: Plon, 1994), 236.

18 [Amédée] Ozenfant, "L'art mural," *CDA*, nos. 9–10 (1934): 274 (author's translation). On French artists and the mural debate, see Romy Golan, *Muralnomad: The Paradox of Wall Painting; Europe 1927–1957* (New Haven: Yale University Press, 2009), 51–58.

19 [Amédée] Ozenfant, "Mur d'abord," in *Édition catalogue critique du Salon de l'art mural*, ed. J[ean]-M[arc] Campagne (Paris: Association de l'Art Mural, 1935), 1.

challenges that artists face.[16] So, after the exhibition at Paul Rosenberg's, the three painted tapestry cartoons went back to the studio, where Matisse used them as objects for his own contemplation, or as aesthetic lodestones. Their significance for his life in the studio was confirmed by further paintings depicting artist's models in that space, where the cartoons are visible, in bits and pieces, as elements of the decor.

Meanwhile, beyond the sanctum of the studio, interest in the future of mural art, as well as new directions in the fine and decorative arts under the aegis of architecture, was rising in the Paris art world, along with questions about their social impact. Matisse took part in various ways. For example, in 1936, a new association called Union pour l'Art made the case for bringing together innovators in the domains of painting, sculpture, the functional and decorative arts, and architecture in a spirit of solidarity. Through its collective exhibitions, the group intended to demonstrate a modern synthesis of the arts and architecture. The list of founding members at its constitutive assembly, held at the Grand Palais, a hub of artistic activity in Paris, was a who's who of eminent names. Not only did Matisse allow himself to be enlisted; at that initial meeting, he was elected unanimously to the interim board as a vice-president (representing painting) alongside Aristide Maillol (sculpture) and Le Corbusier (architecture). But the group proved ephemeral; nothing was heard from it after that highly symbolic first meeting. The reasons for this failure remain unknown, but the simplest answer is that another association was already in place with much the same personnel, a parallel remit, a membership and organizational structure that was less elitist, and a considerably stronger sense of the social and political moment.[17]

L'Art Mural had been instigated by a circle of young artist-organizers with the backing of a committee of more senior and prominent avant-garde painters. One of those leading lights, the painter and writer Amédée Ozenfant, signed the group's founding statement, which appeared in the final issue of *Cahiers d'art* for 1934. (Zervos certainly reread it in 1939 while preparing his "Réflexions." [Thoughts]) Like a manifesto, that declaration began by naming a crisis. A vital point of contact between art and society at large had been lost, noted Ozenfant, to the vast detriment of both: "An art which aspires to nothing more than aesthetic pleasure (a costly pleasure), even of a very high class, and we have plenty of it—can no longer attract many 'customers.'"[18] The premise of L'Art Mural would be to bring together, like guild artisans or skilled workers, painters, sculptors, architects, and artisans in stained glass, mosaic, and tapestry. A shared emphasis on the craft of mural art would provide a common purpose; on top of that, the solid know-how of construction was something, Ozenfant claimed, that ordinary people understood, appreciated, and demanded.[19] These principles connected L'Art Mural to the progressive interclass politics of the Popular Front, whose cultural arm, known as the Maison de la Culture, it joined in mid-1936.

To fathom how Matisse's thinking might have aligned with such ideas, we must collect and collate bits and pieces of commentary from a broad span of time. Two main points emerge. First, while Matisse was a strong defender of the post-Romantic image of the artist as an autonomous individual motivated by originality and genius, a concept of "collective art" did matter to him, though he used the term with varied meanings in different contexts. For one thing, Matisse thought it was the collective project of each generation of artists to enrich through its individual accomplishments the principles that it inherited from preceding generations. But Matisse also deployed the phrase "collective art" when speaking of activities that happen when the artist moves outside the solitude of the studio to work as part of a team. That connotation is illuminated by a story told by the painter André Masson, who lived not far from Matisse and was an eyewitness to the creation of the Barnes *Dance*. Masson and Matisse were conversing with the writer André Gide in the studio. Masson described a current project of his own—the design of costumes and sets for a new production of the Ballet Russe de Monte-Carlo dance troupe—as interesting to him precisely because it put him in a situation of collective creative effort. After a remark from Gide that Matisse read as putting down the work of the painter-decorator, Matisse countered by turning to his own mural and making a statement about mural art as a collective art, but with a final turn of phrase that was meant to needle Gide, who was then a Communist fellow traveler: "Do not assume that we painters are opposed to working collectively. For example, for no money, only some bread and cheese, I would be ready to make all the frescoes you like! But beware: do not force me to paint hammers and sickles all day long!"[20]

As that barbed comment indicates, Matisse was adamant that art be kept out of contemporary politics as much as possible. He believed that artists should be completely free to serve their own programs; the idea of the politically engaged artist was anathema to him. In 1933 a member of the New York press asked Matisse about his reaction to the controversy surrounding Diego Rivera, the prominent Mexican muralist, and the commission for a lobby mural at the Radio Corporation of America (RCA) building, the tower at the center of the grand commercial development known as Rockefeller Center, then under construction in midtown Manhattan. Rivera's transformation of the assigned theme, involving the progress of humanity, into a face-off between US capitalism and Soviet communism led to his dismissal from the project and the destruction of the partly completed mural. As it happens, the Rockefellers, prominent art collectors and patrons of New York's MoMA, which had mounted a major Matisse retrospective in 1931, had also approached Matisse (and Picasso as well), about this project at an early stage. Picasso had not replied, and Matisse had demurred, saying that the bustling RCA lobby seemed ill suited to the reflective appreciation his work needed.[21] When questioned about the Rivera affair after his installation of *The Dance* in Merion, Matisse answered with an improvised maxim: "Politics are temporary; they pass. Art lives on forever." He then proceeded to repudiate the very concept of propagandistic art: "It is not necessary for the artist to associate himself with the class struggle or for him to seek to interpret it."[22] Matisse would make similar comments over the years, including this reply to a question about the connections between art, society, and politics in which he referred to the example of one of his own idols: "Delacroix made some paintings in 1848. Revolutions can sometimes be of use. Nevertheless, one must stand absolutely apart from politics. One may hold liberal ideas, but the time we have for self-expression is precious and we must not waste it."[23] Such statements have been cited, with justification, as illustrations of Matisse's apoliticism as a painter. When it came to making or viewing art, he insisted on the paramount importance of individual instinct and experience over social institutions and relationships.

Nevertheless, Matisse was able to align himself with the Popular Front cultural agenda. While its political program rested on principles of antifascism and social reform in favor of workers, its watchwords in terms of cultural politics were "defense of culture," signifying that intellectual and artistic freedom and innovation were considered essential to the protection of France's democratic traditions.[24] Matisse's views on politics and art did not stand in the way of his engaging with that idea on the basis of civic conscience or ethical conviction. Indeed, he took part in activities of the Popular Front's cultural arm alongside other artists. In July 1936, to celebrate the recent victory of its coalition in national elections and to mark the Bastille Day celebration, the Popular Front government commissioned through the Maison de la Culture a revival of *Le 14 Juillet*, a turn-of-the-century drama of the French Revolution by Romain Rolland, at the Alhambra music hall, situated in the vicinity of the Place de la République in Paris. An exhibition was set up in the lobby by a group representing the painting section of the Maison de la Culture. Matisse loaned the 1915–16 *Moroccans*, the large-scale foray into a decorative aesthetic mentioned above, from his own collection.[25] He also signed his name to open letters and manifestos sent by the Maison de la Culture, such as a message of solidarity with the Spanish Republic in 1936. Then in 1938, at Picasso's instigation, he donated a picture to a gallery exhibition of works by one hundred prominent artists to benefit Spanish children.[26] During the same summer he also took part in the third edition of the Salon de l'Art Mural, once again sending his *Moroccans*. In his review of this exhibition, the critic Waldemar

20 André Masson, *Entretiens avec Georges Charbonnier* (Paris: René Julliard, 1958), 162 (author's translation). For a digest of Matisse's use of the term "collective art," see Henri Matisse, *Écrits et propos sur l'art*, ed. Dominique Fourcade (Paris: Hermann, 2014), 120n78.

21 Alfred H. Barr, *Matisse: His Art and His Public* (New York: Museum of Modern Art, 1951), 220–21; see also Leah Dickerman, "Leftist Circuits," in *Diego Rivera: Murals for the Museum of Modern Art*, exh. cat. (New York: Museum of Modern Art, 2011), 47n99.

22 "Matisse Speaks," *Art News* 31, no. 36 (June 3, 1933): 8.

23 Yves Bridault, "J'ai passé un mauvais quart d'heure avec Matisse" (1952), quoted in Flam, *Matisse on Art*, 275n8 (author's translation).

24 Ory, *La Belle Illusion*, 119.

25 Boris Taslitzky, "Le Front Populaire et les intellectuels: Témoignage," *La Nouvelle Critique*, no. 70 (December 1955): 15; Édouard Pignon, *La Quête de la réalité* (Paris: Denoël, 1966), 61–63. Matisse's name appeared on the roster of a committee for the celebration of Rolland's seventieth birthday in 1936; see "Hommage à Romain Rolland," *Commune* 3, no. 31 (March 1936): 790.

26 "Aide aux combattants de l'ordre républicain!," *L'Humanité* (August 1, 1936): 7; George Besson, "Pour les enfants espagnols," *Ce soir* 2, no. 497 (July 13, 1938): 2.

George defended its presence in an exhibition that was ostensibly devoted to works executed using mural techniques. "One may ask oneself if the *Moroccan Landscape* by Matisse should be considered a mural painting. Rendered in large, flat areas, it does hold and adhere to the wall. Is that not the case with all work by the painter of the *Joy of Life*?"[27]

Still, Matisse was not among those who received mural commissions for the 1937 Paris Exposition Internationale, subtitled "Arts et Techniques dans la Vie Moderne" (Arts and Technology in Modern Life), the event that finally put the idea of murals as a collective, social art form to the test. Acting on a policy of supporting innovative modern art—a mark of its cultural progressivism—the state set aside numerous high-profile mural projects for prominent avant-garde artists, many of them affiliated with the Maison de la Culture.[28] Matisse, on the other hand, was approached by Raymond Escholier, the curator of the Petit Palais in Paris and author of a 1937 monograph on Matisse, with a proposal. The *Paris Dance Mural* would be acquired by the city (using funds from the budget of the exposition), with the understanding that it was to be displayed in Paris's new museum of modern art in the east wing of the Palais de Tokyo, one of the exposition's new constructions. The sale was approved in early 1937, but circumstances prevented the installation of the work in that location for forty years.[29]

In his 1939 "Réflexions," Zervos positioned *The Song*, as well as its intended companion piece, *Music*, as carrying forward the exemplary achievement of Matisse's Barnes mural at the decade's onset 47 | 48.[30] Indeed, Matisse's initial idea for *The Song*, a scene with nymphs, would have connected it directly to the Barnes mural, but he ended up painting a scene in the setting of his own studio, where the women were models and the theme was music. The languorous poses taken by those elegant figures signified voluptuous states of feeling; Matisse arranged the composition with an arabesque line and organized relations of color, pictorial elements that he believed could produce an emotional power and purity analogous to that of music.[31] Still, the Rockefeller overmantel was like the Barnes mural in combining Matisse's decorative sensibility with the functional purpose of embellishing an architectural setting, in this case the oval living room designed by Wallace K. Harrison, Nelson Rockefeller's architect, in collaboration with the interior designer Jean-Michel Frank. Matisse responded with an ornamental composition made to fit the allotted location of a floor-to-ceiling space some nine feet tall set into the room's cherrywood paneling. The mural's graceful opposing curves suited the room's architectural treatment.

Zervos closed his essay with the hope that Matisse's 1930s mural work also be a harbinger of greater things to come. However, as far as Matisse was concerned, that aftermath would play out in ways the critic could not have predicted. In the ensuing years, Matisse indeed grew ever more convinced that architectural decoration was his ultimate calling and destiny. He said as much in a 1942 conversation with the writer Louis Aragon: "Perhaps after all I believe, without knowing it, in a future life... in some paradise where I shall paint frescoes."[32] What is more, he declined to renew his dealer contract in 1946, explaining to Paul Rosenberg that he intended to focus on decorative projects—he specified tapestries, frescoes, and so forth—and expected to make easel pictures only very sparingly.[33] Also, by that time Matisse was on the verge of another consequential move. Colored paper cut-outs, once a convenient tool for composing the Barnes *Dance*, now became his primary medium. Matisse valued cut-outs for their expressive purity and directness: contour, color, and surface brought forth by the single action of the scissors. By 1948 cut-paper compositions were covering the walls of his bedroom and studio. In the final years of his life, the artist would produce large-scale decorations using that method.[34]

During this period, when a novel form of wall-bound decoration so thoroughly occupied Matisse's thoughts, the artist was sometimes asked questions that echoed 1930s-era discussions of art's social impact. In 1951, for instance, a journalist queried him: "Do you believe in art for the people? In a state-controlled art? Or rather in the liberty of the individual?" Matisse responded by casting the premise of the question in terms of the avant-gardist

27 Matisse's diary, May 19, 1938, AHM; Waldemar George, "Le IIIe Salon de l'art mural," *Beaux-Arts*, no. 286 (June 24, 1938): 11 (author's translation).

28 Ory, *La Belle Illusion*, 280–90.

29 Jacqueline Munck, "*La Danse de Paris*," in *Autour d'un chef-d'œuvre de Matisse: Les trois versions de "La Danse Barnes" (1930–1933)*, exh. cat. (Paris: Paris-Musées / Réunion des Musées Nationaux, 1993), 154–57.

30 After Rockefeller chose not to acquire *Music*, it was displayed in the French Pavilion at the 1939 New York World's Fair and subsequently sold by Pierre Matisse to the Albright Art Gallery. Object intake form, n.d.; located in RCA1940:13 document file, Albright-Knox Art Gallery, Buffalo, New York. I thank Natalie McGrath for providing this information.

31 "The Role and Modalities of Color" (1945) and "Interview with André Verdet" (1952), in Flam, *Matisse on Art*, 155, 210. On the *Song* project, see Klein, *Matisse and Decoration*, 84–88.

32 Flam, *Matisse on Art*, 150.

33 HM–Paul Rosenberg, June 2, 1946, Italian translation quoted in Claude Duthuit et al., *Matisse: "La révélation m'est venue de l'Orient"* (Florence: Artificio, 1997), 246.

34 Jodi Hauptman, "Inventing a New Operation," in *Henri Matisse: The Cutouts*, ed. Karl Buchberg et al., exh. cat. (New York: Museum of Modern Art, 2014), 17–23.

dialectic of innovation versus tradition. “Art for the people? Certainly, if by the people you mean youthful spirits that are not stuck in traditional art.”[35] Matisse’s attitude was epitomized by the Chapelle du Rosaire, a chapel for the Dominican nuns in Vence, a municipality west of Nice (1948–51). Matisse designed the building and all its decorations, including twenty-three stained-glass windows after cartoons in cut paper, seven ceramic tile compositions, and designs for furnishings and priestly vestments, with the help of four advisers and collaborators: the young Dominican novice Louis-Bertrand Rayssiguier; Marie-Alain Couturier, the Dominican friar and co-leader of L’Art Sacré (the Sacred Art movement), which spearheaded the decoration of Catholic churches by renowned modern artists; Sister Jacques-Marie, a former nurse and model for Matisse who had taken the veil; and Matisse’s longtime assistant and muse Lydia Delectorskaya. The Vence chapel, a total environment, summarized both Matisse’s decorative aesthetic and his thinking on the possibilities of public art.[36]

35 André Léjard, “Propos de Henri Matisse” (1951), excerpted in Matisse, *Écrits et propos sur l’art*, 120n78 (author’s translation).

36 See Éric de Chassey, “Chapelle de Vence,” in *Tout Matisse*, ed. Claudine Grammont (Paris: Robert Laffont, 2018), 168; see also Klein, *Matisse and Decoration*, 159–93.

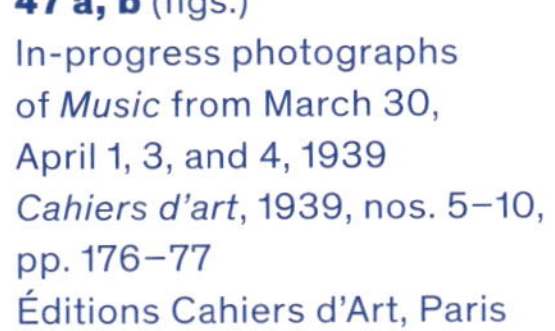

47 a, b (figs.)
In-progress photographs of *Music* from March 30, April 1, 3, and 4, 1939
Cahiers d’art, 1939, nos. 5–10, pp. 176–77
Éditions Cahiers d’Art, Paris

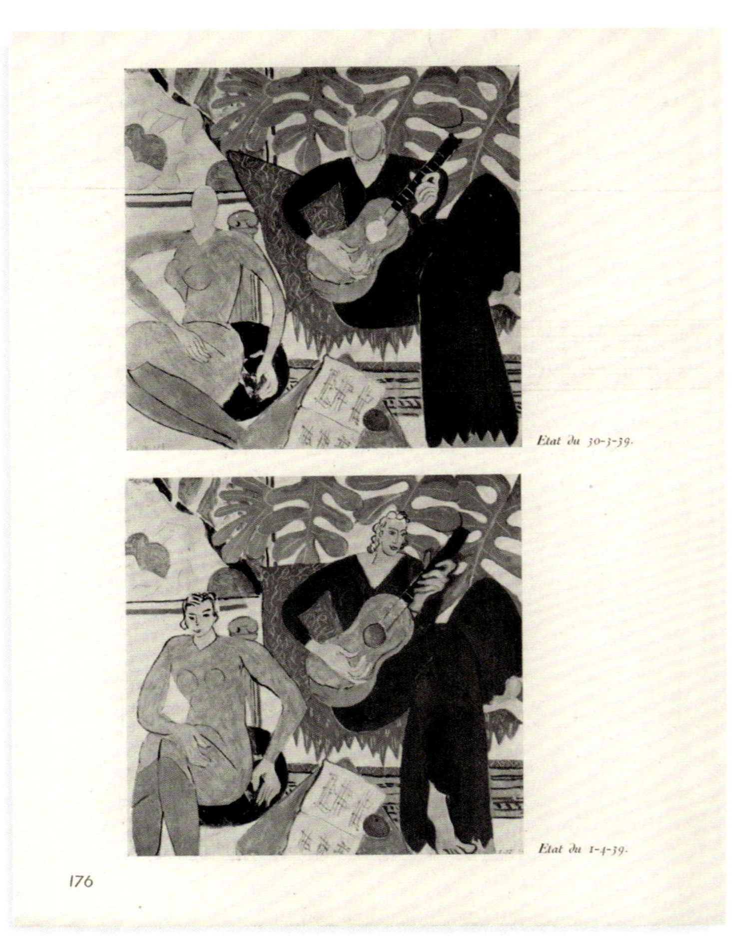

Etat du 30-3-39.

Etat du 1-4-39.

176

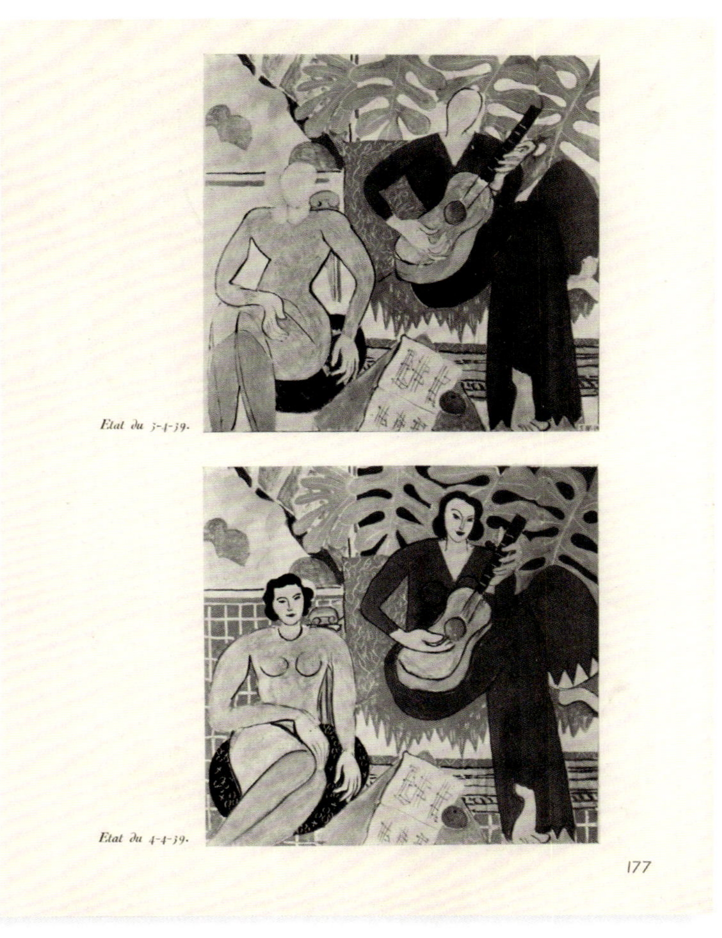

Etat du 3-4-39.

Etat du 4-4-39.

177

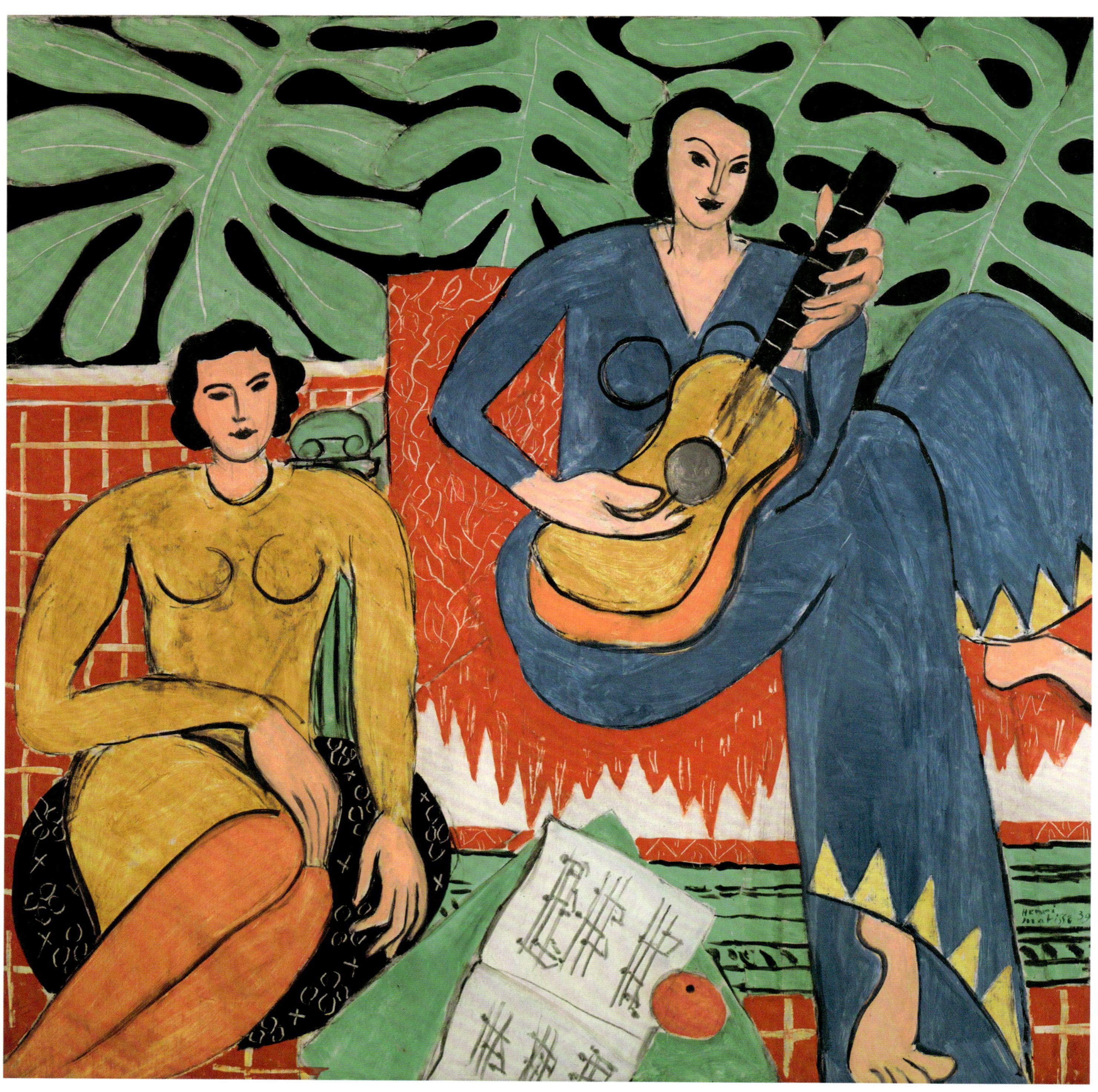

48 (fig.)
Music, 1939
Oil on canvas, 45 ⅜ × 45 ⅜ in.
(115.25 × 115.25 cm)
Collection Albright-Knox
Art Gallery, Buffalo

CLAUDINE GRAMMONT

MATISSE'S STUDIO
IN THE MAKING OF HIS WORK

It is an established fact that Albert C. Barnes's commissioning of *The Dance* 103 marked a watershed, "an awakening," to quote the title of Yve-Alain Bois's important essay devoted to this foundational event so decisive for the artist in the years that followed.[1] As he sees it, this was when, through creating the three versions of *The Dance* at a time when he was also working on his illustrations to Stéphane Mallarmé's *Poésies*, Matisse reconnected with the pre-1914 years, to the Matisse of the experimental period, finally leaving behind the persona of the odalisque painter and returning to that of his younger years, with all the concomitant promises of renewal. This then opened up the possibility of a return to disorder,[2] or at least to its prerequisite, namely a resumption of risk-taking and the questioning of painting and its methodologies. So, there was a before *The Dance* and an after. Before, it was the retreat to Nice away from the bustle of Paris, and a painting habit that came naturally, supported by the ever-increasing demands from art lovers addicted to these interior scenes, windows, and odalisques that had become the artist's trademark output during the postwar period and that had brought him international fame. But, around 1925, he was assailed by doubt, and the onset of a growing distaste for this painting treadmill, until one day in 1928 he wrote to his wife, Amélie: "You will see that there is something new. It's going to get me away from the odalisques."[3] There followed a couple of critical years during which he almost gave up painting altogether, until finally in 1930 he decided to head out to sea—the high seas, to be precise—embarking for Oceania and Tahiti on a long voyage lasting more than six months, via the United States, and back. Out went the painter's messy studio; in came vast panoramas, the brutal modernity of New York skyscrapers, the vastness and clear horizons recalled from the westerns he loved to watch at the movie theater, and the enchantment of the South Seas.[4] Plunging into those crystal-clear waters elicited an awakening of the senses, wonderment at the splendor, but also, on a more physical level, the emergence of new sensations, and in particular—this was of crucial importance—a perception of weightlessness that restored the body in its entirety, so that no longer was just the organ of sight the concern of the painter. The Barnes commission for a large mural decoration was thus the catalyst that allowed him to channel this wonderfully reinvigorating and rejuvenating flow of sensations and held out the possibility of getting back to hand-to-hand combat with painting.[5] The watershed before-and-after moment began there and then, in full awareness of the groundswell he had begun experiencing and all the effort the mural would surely involve. It took no small amount of courage to turn his back on fifteen years and more of painterly habits. Matisse's comfortable routine in the studio was based on his increasingly sophisticated vision within the immutable setting of the four walls and the model, which posed the metaphorical terms of the camera obscura and hence of painting as a projection outside of the studio. This daily grind had numbed his senses.[6] The subject matter of *The Dance* took him back to what had been one of the major advances of the prewar period: an approach to painting as a performative act and no longer as a projection of the retinal image onto the two-dimensional surface of the canvas.

1 Yve-Alain Bois, "Matisse's Awakening," in *Matisse in the Barnes Foundation*, ed. Bois (Philadelphia: Barnes Foundation / London: Thames & Hudson, 2015), 1:90–169.

2 In contradiction to the values of the "Return to order" that characterized the work of the postwar period. See Claudine Grammont, "Retour à l'ordre," in *Tout Matisse*, ed. Grammont (Paris: Robert Laffont, 2018), 757–75.

3 Henri Matisse [HM]–Amélie Matisse [AM] on the subject of *Still Life with Green Buffet*, July 7, 1928, cited in Hilary Spurling, *Matisse, le maître*, vol. 2, *1909–1954* (Paris: Seuil, 2009), 315.

4 See p. 137 in this volume.

5 On the genesis of the work, see Jack Flam, "Histoire et métamorphose d'un projet," in *Autour d'un chef-d'œuvre de Matisse: Les trois versions de "La Danse Barnes" (1930–1933)*, exh. cat. (Paris: Paris-Musées / Réunion des Musées Nationaux, 1993), 23–91.

6 "When the means of expression have become so refined; so attenuated that their power of expression wears thin, it is necessary to return to the essential principles that made the human language," Henri Matisse to Tériade in "Constance du fauvisme," *Minotaure* 2, no. 9 (1936), reprinted in *Matisse on Art*, ed. and trans. Jack Flam, rev. ed. (Berkeley: University of California Press, 2015), 122.

In order to consider here the after, I would like to examine, rather than the actual works per se, the background to their creation. Matisse always attached great importance to the ritual of painting, to his limbering-up exercises, and each major turning point in his artistic career coincides with both a change of address and a new modus operandi. The making of *The Dance* marks a stage that would radically transform the organization of his studio, and likewise its space. In this regard, it can be posited that the 1930s represent a complete paradigm shift that would have enormous repercussions on his later work. While up to that point Matisse had operated as somewhat of an heir to the romantic notion of the heroic, solitary artist, this period marks the switch henceforward to a collective model for the making of a work. At the same time, the commission for *The Dance* would lead to an expansion of his working environment, and this continued with the move in 1938 to the apartment in the former Excelsior Régina Palace hotel, on the upper part of Cimiez, at a time when an ever-greater symbiosis was taking place between the artist and his studio.

For a long time, until Matisse left for Nice in December 1917, the running of his studio relied to a great extent upon Amélie, who with her "exceptional dedication, worked to leave him free to devote all his time to his painting."[7] At their home in Issy-les-Moulineaux, the studio and family were a single unit. Marguerite, their eldest child, who was then twenty years old, described herself as a "studio kid"[8] good at preparing her father's canvases and various implements. The move to Nice altered this arrangement. Thereafter, Matisse spent most of the year in the South of France and brought his models to an anonymous room, bereft of personal effects, that he rented at the hotel. It was not until 1921 that he rented a two-room, fourth-floor apartment on the Place Charles-Félix, with a view to setting up a studio there. He was then able to live in his work space, on the job, although his family life did not get back to normal until 1928. From Paris, Amélie and Marguerite performed his secretarial work, in particular taking delivery of the works exhibited almost every year at the Galerie Bernheim-Jeune.[9] Based on an exclusive contract, Matisse's commercial relationship with the gallery on Rue Richepanse, while contributing immensely to keeping him in the public eye, also ensured the circulation of his works, their framing, and the taking of photographs when they were added to the inventory: in this way, 791 paintings and drawings by Matisse passed through the gallery.[10] Although the commercial relationship extended beyond the official end of the contractual term in 1926,[11] notably through the Galeries Georges Petit, with which Josse and Gaston Bernheim were associated, Matisse could no longer rely on the dealer's integrated system.[12] While business was already brisk in the 1920s thanks to the action of the Galerie Bernheim-Jeune and its branches, the pace of his exhibitions picked up even more over the following decade, as did their scale.[13] It all began with the series of four major retrospectives in 1930–31 to mark the artist's sixtieth birthday, in Berlin, Paris, Basel, and New York,[14] which monopolized a large number of paintings, drawings, and sculptures and thus required a complex arrangement of loans and a range of different types of publications. From the Rue César-Franck in Paris, where she settled in 1929 following her marriage to Georges Duthuit, Marguerite saw to her father's affairs, under his supervision. Based in New York since 1924, Pierre Matisse, who opened his own gallery there in 1931, managed operations in the United States, where the market was growing considerably. It was notably Pierre who, along with Alfred H. Barr Jr., was in charge of mounting the 1931 exhibition at the Museum of Modern Art (Pierre also mounted the 1931 exhibition at the Galeries Georges Petit). Without enjoying sole agency for his father's work, Pierre now represented it on American soil.[15] As the circulation of Matisse's works gathered speed on the market and through exhibitions, the volume of publications likewise increased. Thus, in 1929 alone, and at a time when he had virtually given up painting altogether, Matisse engraved around a hundred plates on copper or zinc, their purity of line a sign of things to come with the illustrations for the *Poésies* of Mallarmé. Marguerite, who was supervising the print runs in Paris, wrote to him, demonstrating both her degree of involvement and her very sound judgment: "The trial runs coming off the press

7 Charles Camoin, in Raymond Escholier, *Matisse, ce vivant* (Paris: Fayard, 1956), 104.

8 Marguerite Duthuit-Matisse and Claude Duthuit with Françoise Garnaud, *Henri Matisse: Catalogue raisonné de l'œuvre gravé* (Paris: C. Duthuit, 1983), 1:xi.

9 From 1935 on, Delectorskaya also took over in Nice, becoming both his secretary and his model, while Marguerite continued that assignment in Paris; see p. 57 in this volume.

10 Guy-Patrice and Michel Dauberville, *Henri Matisse chez Bernheim-Jeune* (Paris: Bernheim-Jeune, 1995).

11 Between 1922 and 1925, Matisse also worked with Georges Bernheim and Walther Halvorsen. A joint sales agreement for these years covers half of the artist's output: HM–Bernheim and Halvorsen, draft, March 25, 1922, Archives Henri Matisse, Issy-les-Moulineaux [AHM].

12 He may possibly have wished at that time to gain more independence and look after his own affairs directly.

13 The count is twenty-one exhibitions during the 1930s, fifteen for the previous decade.

14 See p. 31 in this volume.

15 It was he who organized his father's visits between 1930 and 1933, and again he, and Étienne Bignou, who obtained the American loans for the 1931 retrospective in Paris. He supervised the installation of *The Dance* in Merion and was behind the subsequent commissions, most notably the one for *The Song*. See also p. 158 in this volume.

were amazing and incredibly full of life. You have made strides, and it seems to me that you use the needle and copper like a pencil and paper; it is a good thing that the medium and the technique no longer bother you, and it really shows."[16] In the field of sculpture, the 1931 exhibitions at the Thannhauser Gallery in Berlin, then those at Pierre Loeb's gallery in Paris and the Brummer Gallery in New York—the last two devoted exclusively to this medium—spawned a salvo of bronzes cast at Valsuani's, including the most recent works, such as *Henriette II* from 1927, and *Henriette III* and *Large Seated Nude* from 1929 79–81.[17] Here again, the artist being only very rarely in Paris, someone was needed to monitor operations at the foundry, a task that was entrusted to his son Jean, now a sculptor. So, for a long time after moving out of the house at Issy, the Matisse studio remained a family business, with everyone pulling their weight.[18] In the editorial field, art publications, whether linked to exhibitions or unconnected, called for images of works both old and new in ever-increasing numbers. The monographs published in 1929 and 1930 by Éditions des Chroniques du Jour each included some thirty reproductions of paintings and drawings,[19] and it was a similar story with the American Henry McBride's publication of 1930 (25 plates),[20] followed in 1933 by Barnes's large tome (151 reproductions).[21] On top of that, the catalogues of exhibitions were more often richly illustrated, especially those accompanying the monographic exhibitions of 1931. It was on that occasion that *Cahiers d'art* brought out a special issue, in French and English, comprising ninety-seven images of the artist's works (the most richly illustrated album of its day). Christian Zervos thus showed his determination to represent Matisse's work in his journal, the very same year that the first volume of Picasso's catalogue raisonné was published.[22] Did he have similar plans for Matisse? There is no evidence to suggest so.[23] But the parsimony with which the artist supplied him with the images relating to the articles for *Cahiers d'art* shows that he was chary and disinclined to provide Zervos with even the slightest access to documentation over which he intended to remain in control.

On the other hand, the question of the catalogue raisonné, and hence the reproduction of his works and the dissemination thereof, especially where his main rival was concerned, definitely had an impact on his studio operations and the importance of photography as a documentary. Generally speaking, from early on in his career, Matisse behaved with the utmost caution regarding the reproduction of his work, as he was fully aware of what was at stake.[24] During the 1930s, he endeavored to meet the growing demand for reproductions. No longer able to rely solely on the Bernheim-Jeune negatives, he began to work with several photographers, principally Marc Vaux and Georges Lemare in Paris, and Matossian in Nice, who would shoot the paintings and drawings.[25] Sometimes he took pictures of his works himself, or his son Pierre might. In addition to fulfilling requests for images for the abovementioned publications, and those for the specialist art press, he used these pictures for self-promotion to his collectors, in Europe and in the United States, with a helping hand from Pierre. Matisse thus had a fairly exhaustive library of photographs of his paintings, which he continued to update for his personal use. The studio operation was made to adapt to a radical transformation in the way the works would circulate.

Given the success of his work on the art market, and with the rivalry with Picasso still as fierce as ever, Matisse was forced to make this adjustment in order to keep pace with modernity, despite deliberately staying away from the capital. The commissions of the 1930s would further hasten this trend, leading Matisse, at age sixty, to overhaul his creative process. In this regard, the commission from Barnes for a decoration in the hall of his foundation in Merion, Pennsylvania, over forty-five feet long, was an initial challenge that the painter, in his quest for renewal, took on without realizing what he was getting himself into, underestimating the difficulty of the task ahead.[26] The very scale of the composition to be produced, thousands of miles away from its destination site, and the site itself, complex in terms of its position within the building's architecture, established the basic parameters of the problem. Immediately upon his return to Nice in mid-January 1931, he rented a vast garage space on Rue Désiré-Niel,

16 Marguerite Duthuit [MD]–HM, December 4, 1929, AHM.

17 Claude Duthuit with Wanda de Guébriant, *Henri Matisse: Catalogue raisonné de l'œuvre sculpté* (Paris: C. Duthuit, 1997).

18 The 1939 separation from Amélie momentarily upset this routine without entirely calling it into question.

19 Monographs in three languages, by Florent Fels in French (1929), Roger Fry in English (1930), and Gotthard Jedlicka in German (1930).

20 Henry McBride, *Matisse* (New York: Alfred A. Knopf, 1930).

21 Albert C. Barnes, *The Art of Henri Matisse* (New York: Scribner's Sons, 1933).

22 According to Jeffrey Weiss, the grid-like visual structure of Zervos's catalogue raisonné had a major impact on the oeuvre itself as well as on Matisse's method of taking photographs of intermediate stages, which was first implemented in 1935. See Weiss, "The Matisse Grid," in *The Repeating Image: Multiples in French Painting from David to Matisse*, ed. Eik Kahng, exh. cat. (Baltimore: Walters Art Museum, 2007), 173–93.

23 In the early 1950s, Matisse refused Zervos permission to draw up a catalogue raisonné of his oeuvre. See p. 20 in this volume.

24 See Claudine Grammont, "'Peindre solide'. Henri Matisse et l'œuvre reproductible," in *Matisse comme un roman*, ed. Aurélie Verdier, exh. cat. (Paris: Centre Pompidou, 2020), 240–47.

25 The diaries for this period contain numerous notes relating to these systematic photo shoots of the paintings. My thanks to Anne Théry for sharing these transcriptions, which are key to understanding this procedure.

26 HM–AM, December 26, 1930, from Merion: "I think it won't be too difficult for me, because my feeling is that my sabbatical year did me a power of good in terms of clear-mindedness." AHM.

27 "One day, armed with a piece of charcoal on the end of a long bamboo cane, I started drawing the whole thing in one go. It was like a rhythm inside me was carrying me along." HM–Gaston Diehl, reproduced in Matisse, *Écrits et propos sur l'art*, 151.

28 HM–MD, February–March 1931 and April 8, 1931, AHM.

29 Masson saw Matisse on a regular basis in February and March of 1933. He recalls his modus operandi, "impressive and innovative too," and describes "these cut-outs constantly in motion because it was from their reciprocal relationships that the entire form of the composition was to come into being." André Masson, *Le Rebelle du surréalisme: Écrits*, ed. Françoise Levaillant (Paris: Hermann, 1976), 91.

30 Explaining his work method in a letter to Alexander Romm dated October 1934, he makes a reference to the Shchukin panels: "What seems essential to me was the surface quantity of colors. It seems that these colors, applied by no matter what medium, fresco, gouache, watercolor, colored material would give the spirit of my composition." Cited in Flam, *Matisse on Art*, 118.

31 Henri Matisse, in George Besson, "Pictorial Photography: A Series of Interviews," *Camera Work*, no. 24 (October 1908): 13–22.

32 Cited in Pierre Schneider, *Matisse* (Paris: Flammarion, 1984), 98.

33 "I have, in order to get away from the individuality of the artist..., copied photographs while striving to produce the closest possible likeness." HM–Louis Aragon, February 10, 1942, reproduced in Louis Aragon, *Henri Matisse, roman* (Paris: Gallimard, 1971), 1:135.

where the proportions, the lighting, and even the appearance of the walls were practically identical to those of the hall of the Barnes Foundation. Working at full scale was unavoidable because Matisse realized that he would not be able to scale up from an enlarged sketch: he needed to experience the space physically in order for the dance to develop to the rhythm of his own body. He therefore sketched his composition in one go on three sixteen-foot canvases, and, so as to obtain a more sweeping gesture, he armed himself with a long bamboo cane onto which he fastened his charcoal 53.[27] This alla prima work, which he started several times over, caused him to have "his round dance" photographed prior to being erased by the next version: "I may need to remember," he wrote his daughter. "The photos," he continued, "showed me that my mind was making a single canvas across the entire width."[28] It was by following this same principle of a very large surface treated as a single whole that he addressed the issue of how to color it. Working directly on the canvas was out of the question, because it meant too much hard work. So he got a housepainter called Goyo to prepare large sheets of pink, blue, gray, and black paper, which a female assistant would then pin up following the composition as drawn on the canvas, and these he cut along the outlines so as to obtain the desired proportions between filled and empty spaces, the figures and the background. In this way an extraordinary mosaic of mobile paper figures kept changing day to day, and then month to month, until, like Sisyphus, he had to start all over again, upon discovering in February 1932 the mistake in the initial measurements. The handful of eyewitnesses were staggered by the titanic struggle that the undertaking had become. André Masson, at the time caught up with difficulties of his own in producing his ballet *Les Présages* (Omens) for the Ballet Russe de Monte-Carlo, was struck by the unstable nature of this painting, which had turned into some protean creature undergoing constant transformation.[29] The photographs revealed the work's excessiveness, which had to do not so much with its sheer size as with this transitory dimension of something in a perpetual state of becoming and whose deeper meaning lay in this dynamic incompleteness 49 | 50. The mural progressed in this manner throughout 1932, up until the final stage when, late in March 1933, Goyo transferred the composition onto the canvases and set about painting the entire thing on the basis of the predefined flat tints.

So this commission brought about several new developments that were crucial for the running of the studio. To begin with, it was no longer just Matisse creating his work; several others now had a hand in it: assistants, Lisette Löwengard and/or Lydia Delectorskaya, pinned the papers painted in gouache in position following the artist's instructions; Goyo did the painting; and a photographer took snapshots as required. Hence the work came into being through a collective effort in which the artist was no longer painting, but devising his painting, working out in purely plastic terms how to proceed. In the case of the wall decoration, this meant focusing on the spatial quality of color, its ability to construct a space.[30] Photography had an "objective charm" that played a key role here.[31] On several occasions, Matisse recalled how he exploited this by copying photographic images in order to "see things untrammeled by feeling,"[32] or to "get away from the artist's individuality."[33] The work from the black-and-white photographic states of the *Dances* would therefore tie in with his desire to temper, if not exclude, the "human element," which he felt was getting in the way of the painting's architectural dimension. What the artist meant by this "human element to be tempered" was its representation through the figure, but also the projection of one's own subjectivity through gesture or nuance.

Not only did the making of *The Dance* revitalize Matisse's painting work—although it did not really get going again until 1935, and never reached the production levels of the 1920s—it also reinstated the artist-designer. All his efforts, in the years that followed, and as his physical strength waned, tended toward optimizing his ability to design in such a way that the actual execution remained as faithful as possible to the idea. Most of the commissions that came after the Barnes mural were further opportunities to rise to this challenge and come up

49 a, b
Paris "Dance" Mural, Early State, October–December 1931
Barnes Foundation Archives, Philadelphia

50
Merion "Dance" Mural, State XVII, December 5, 1932
Barnes Foundation Archives, Philadelphia

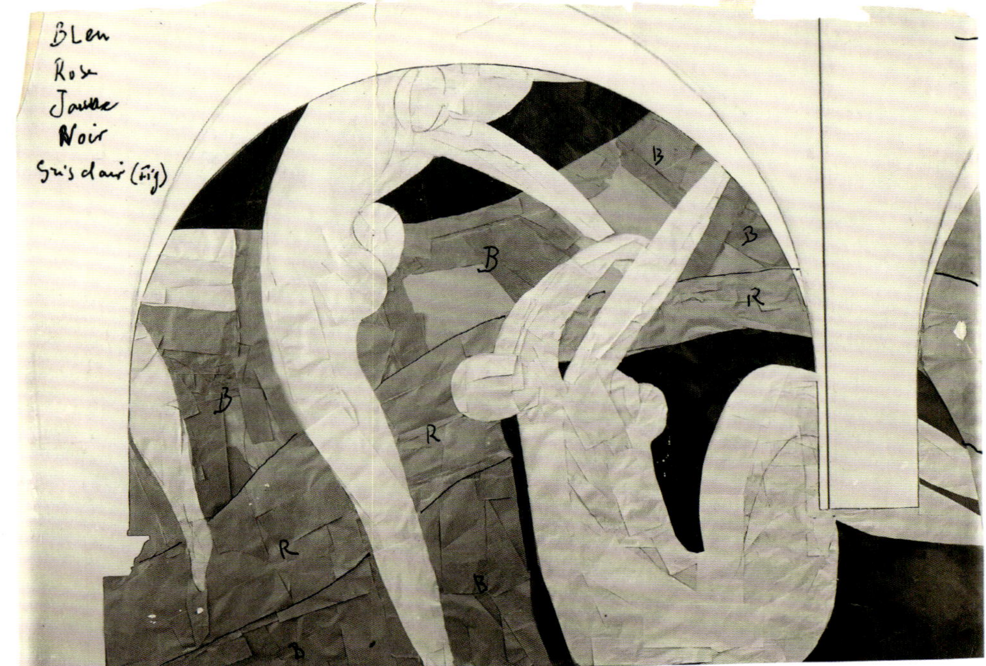

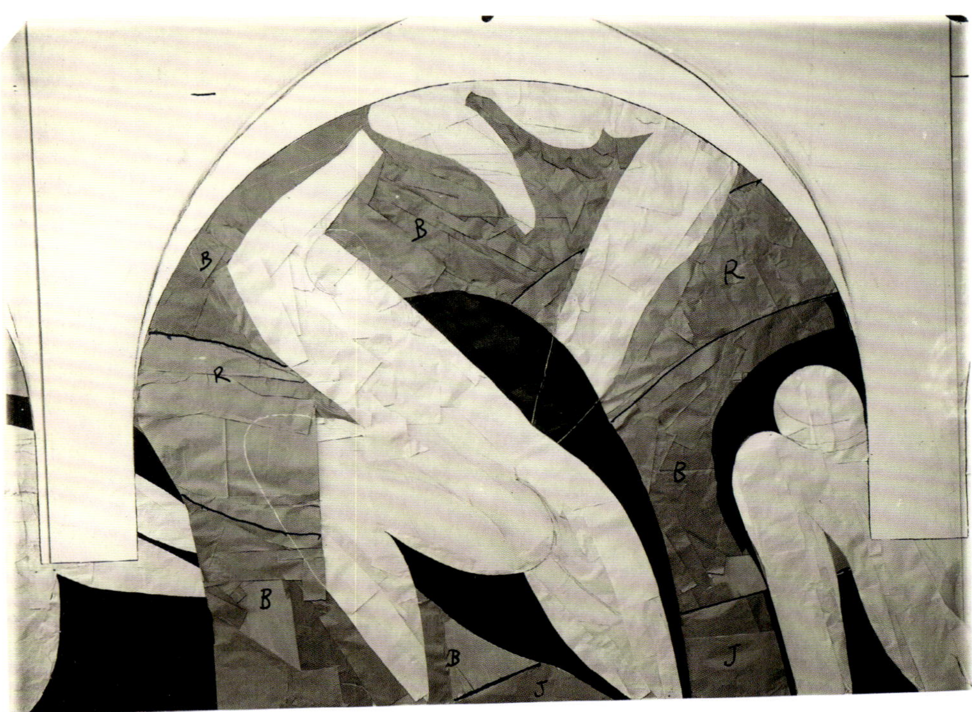

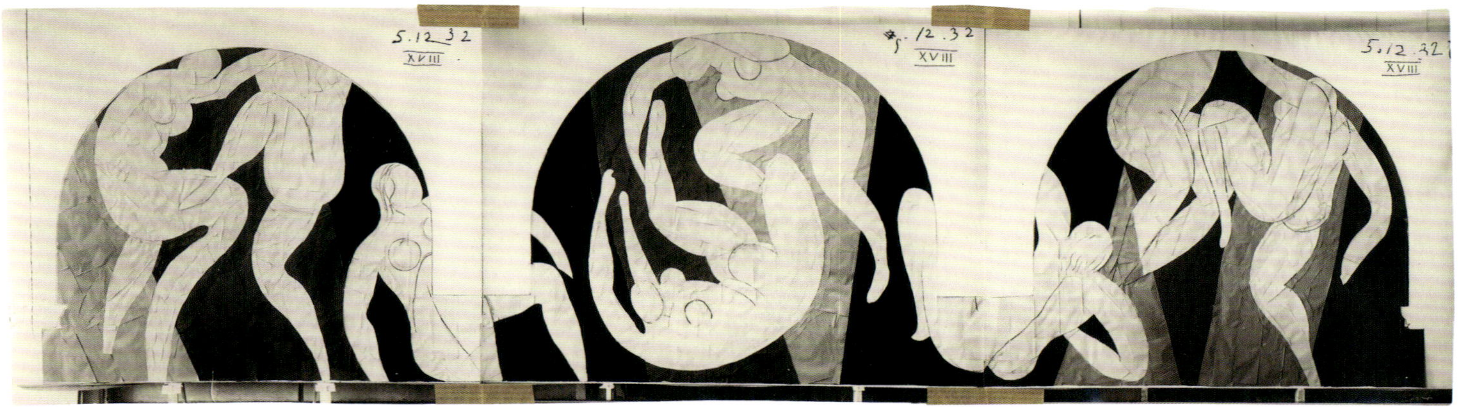

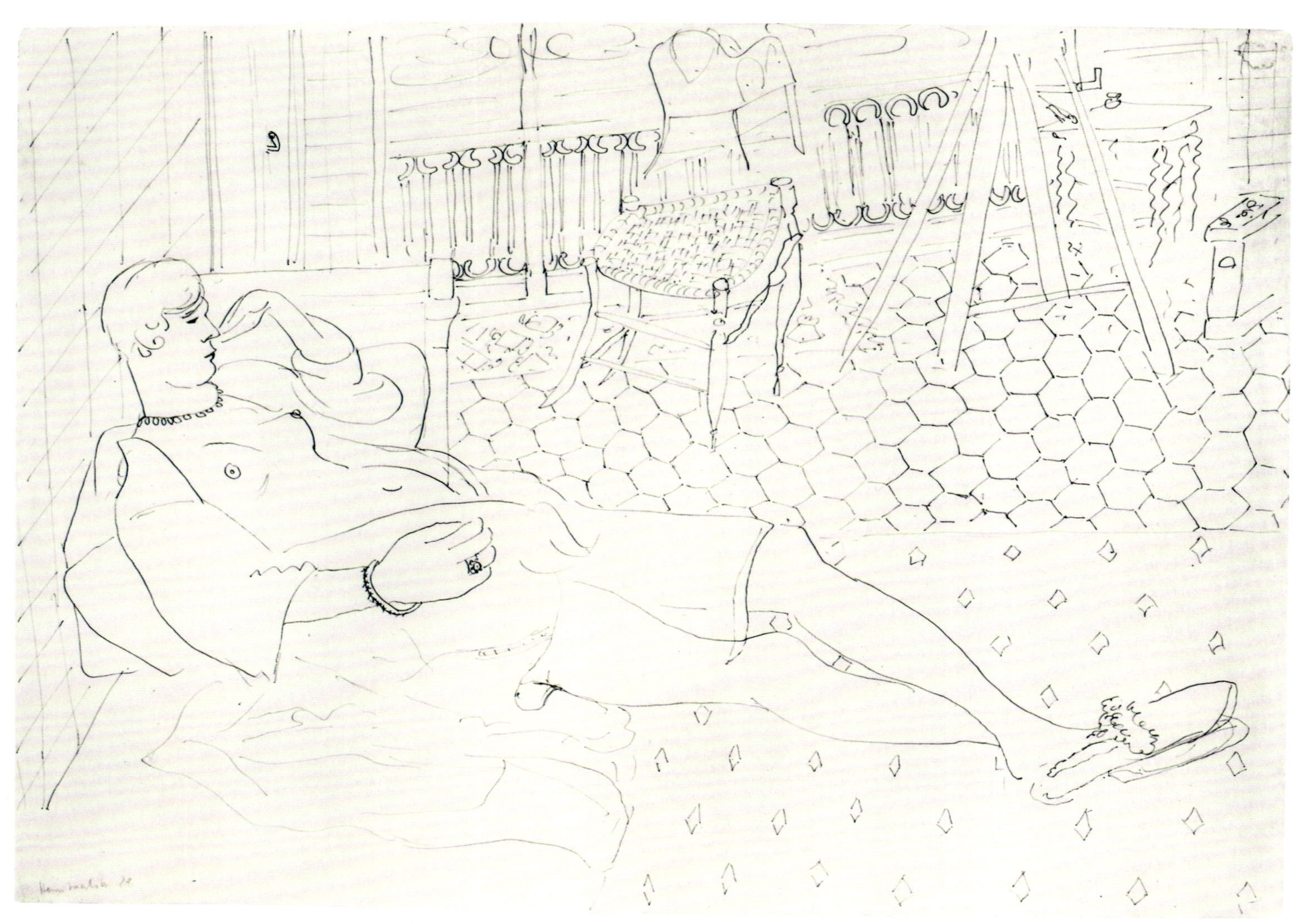

51 (fig.)
Reclining Woman Wearing a Robe, 1928
Pen and India ink on paper, 19 × 26 in. (48 × 68 cm)
Private collection

with appropriate technical solutions. More generally, the practice of painting felt the effects of this evolution, particularly in what he called his "experimental pictures" (*tableaux d'expérience*), such as *Interior with Dog* (1934; Baltimore Museum of Art), *Large Reclining Nude* 110, and *Nymph in the Forest (Verdure)* 116. While designing *The Dance* had led him to a radical simplification of his means and methods, by eschewing texture in favor of flat tints, here texture was reasserting itself and integrating the painter's thinking from one stage to the next. Process photography, which he began to use more systematically beginning in 1935 for paintings evolving over a long period of time, went hand in hand with this transformational thinking, and there followed, as it developed, material that was actually feeding off its transient state.[34] So much so, in fact, that he came to regret not being able to devote himself exclusively to paintings of this type. In 1935, shortly after the visit from his friend Pierre Bonnard, Matisse wrote to his son Pierre: "He told me that my decorations have certainly raised my level—but the canvases have to be made—it would suit me better if the material circumstances let me leave them pretty much as a work in progress" 111.[35]

Alongside this transformation of the process of making the work, these years saw a trend toward a greater symbiosis between the artist and his studio. In his painting practice, the atelier had been a major theme of the prewar period, always a potential self-portrait, inasmuch as it was a metaphorical projection of his inner psyche.[36] From the "Oriental" refinement of *The Pink Studio* (1911; Pushkin State Museum, Moscow) to the almost Jansenist austerity of the *Quai Saint-Michel* series between 1914 and 1917, the studio made its presence felt as a mental repository. That is, until its eradication between 1917 and 1921, making way for the perfectly artificial neutrality of the hotel bedroom in Nice. Until, again, he decided to rent an apartment on the fourth floor, in a very attractive building in the Ponchettes neighborhood of Nice, with lovely high ceilings and large windows facing south onto the Baie des Anges, and east onto the Cours Saleya. Matisse organized the place as a theatrical space filled to the rafters with various props he had picked up somewhere or had sent down from Paris—exotic furniture, hangings, dresses, screens used as scenery for his odalisques—and had his model sit in a small, raised, purpose-built alcove 52.[37] But he did not really make himself at home there until April 1928,[38] when on the fifth story of the same building he had two apartments merged into one and reconfigured. This marked a return to the work-from-home setup he had enjoyed at Issy before 1914, for the apartment had two bedrooms (one for Mme Matisse, one for her husband), a large kitchen, various other rooms, and two studios. One studio had a large bay window looking out over the sea; the other had corner windows, easily discernible by their trompe-l'oeil walls made by a local artisan, one with a faux-tile grid, the other in imitation marble. It was in this double studio that most of the paintings of the period were painted, altogether around seventy paintings (not that many), until the couple left it for the Régina in June 1938. In this renovated apartment tailored to their needs, the stage props and costumes were swapped for more up-to-date versions. With the exception of the *Persian Dress* series in 1936 136, the Oriental-flavored bric-a-brac made way for new dresses, coats, and hats in keeping with the latest fashions, while the Romanian blouse, then very much in vogue on the French Riviera, arrived on the scene. Although it is featured just twice in the paintings, the large bay window in the studio with the mock tiling introduced a crucial element that would substantially alter the painting space. Just as New York and its skyscrapers had given Matisse a feeling of newfound freedom by opening up his mental space, the bay window looking out across a width of more than thirteen feet of blue vastness gave the painter a similar feeling of boundlessness. Furthermore, this was no longer a vertical window, but a bay window opening lengthways. The viewing height, with no more palm trees in the middle distance, meant that on this floor the artist found himself immersed in an immaterial transparency, further accentuated when standing against the light. This same transparency, to which the representation of the goldfish bowl alludes, was dear to Matisse for thematizing the meditative, sublimated space of his inner reverie as a state of suspended consciousness. The extraordinary

34 Matisse claimed priority as the original inventor of this procedure. In a letter to Barnes, he hints that word of this method might have gotten to Picasso who was reportedly doing the same thing with his copper plates: HM–Albert Barnes, undated letter (February–March 1933), reproduced in Bois, *Matisse in the Barnes Foundation*, 3:258.

35 HM–Pierre Matisse [PM], January 21, 1935, Pierre Matisse Gallery Archives, The Morgan Library & Museum, New York [PMGA].

36 See notably Claudine Grammont, "Atelier," in Grammont, *Tout Matisse*, 51–59.

37 We are only referring here to the studios in the South of France, since Matisse was no longer painting in Paris, except during the summer of 1936, on the Boulevard du Montparnasse, and in 1939 in the studio at the Villa Alésia loaned by the artist Mary Callery.

38 Lease of April 5, 1928 between Henri Matisse and Mme Veuve François Veran, AHM. (He had already settled into the fifth floor in 1924: lease of October 1, 1924 between Henri Matisse and M. le comte César Caïs de Pierlas.)

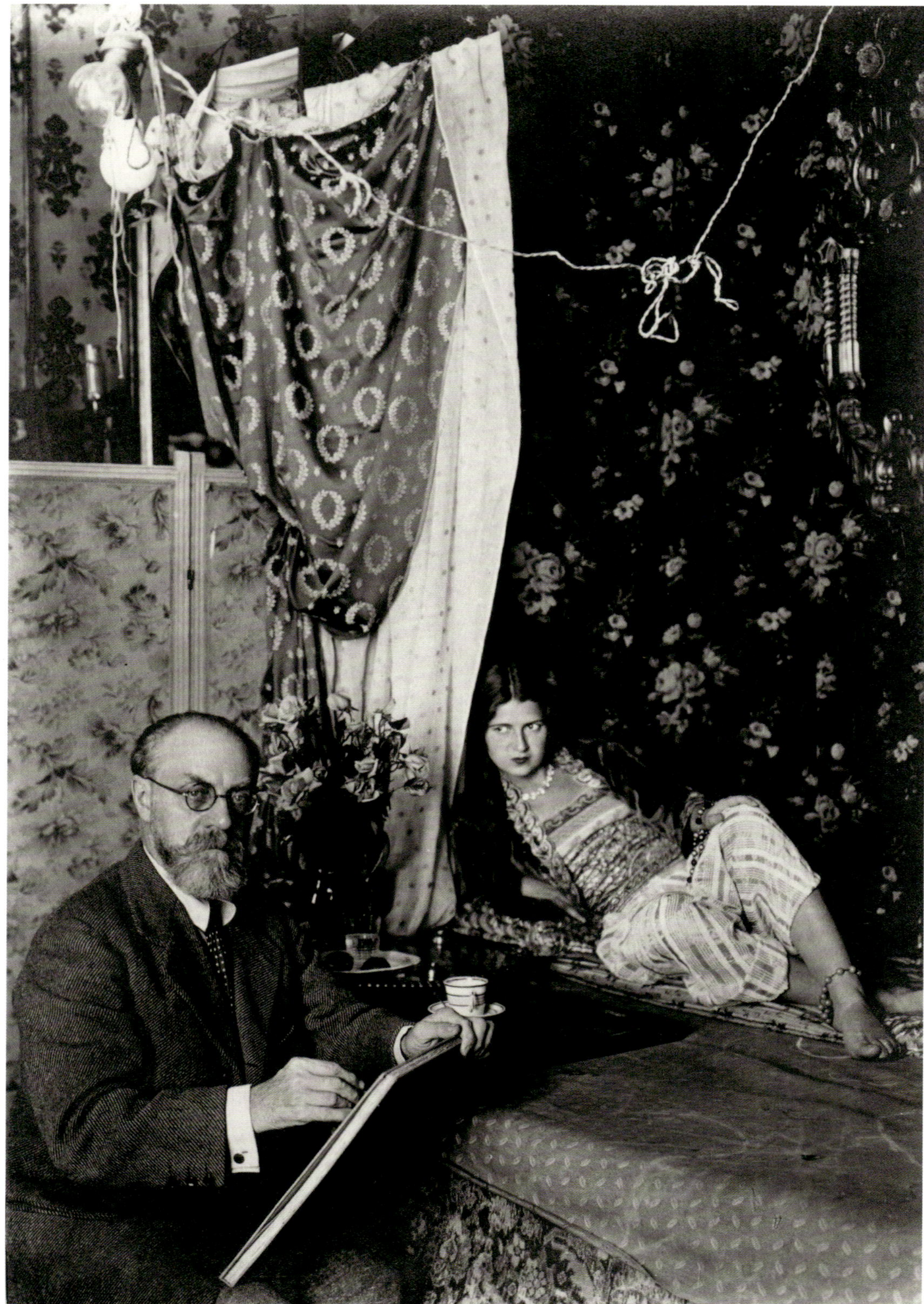

52 (fig.)
Henri Matisse with his model Zita, c. 1928
Archives Henri Matisse, Issy-les-Moulineaux

53 (fig.)
Agnes Mitchell Sattler, *Henri Matisse Working on "The Dance" in the Rue Désiré-Niel Studio*, April 16, 1932
Film still
Archives Henri Matisse, Issy-les-Moulineaux

54 (fig.)
Henri Matisse working on *Nymph in the Forest (Verdure)*; on the wall to the left, the canvas and collage *Still Life with a Seashell on Black Marble*, studio in the Régina, Nice, summer 1941.
Photograph by Varian Fry
Archives Henri Matisse, Issy-les-Moulineaux

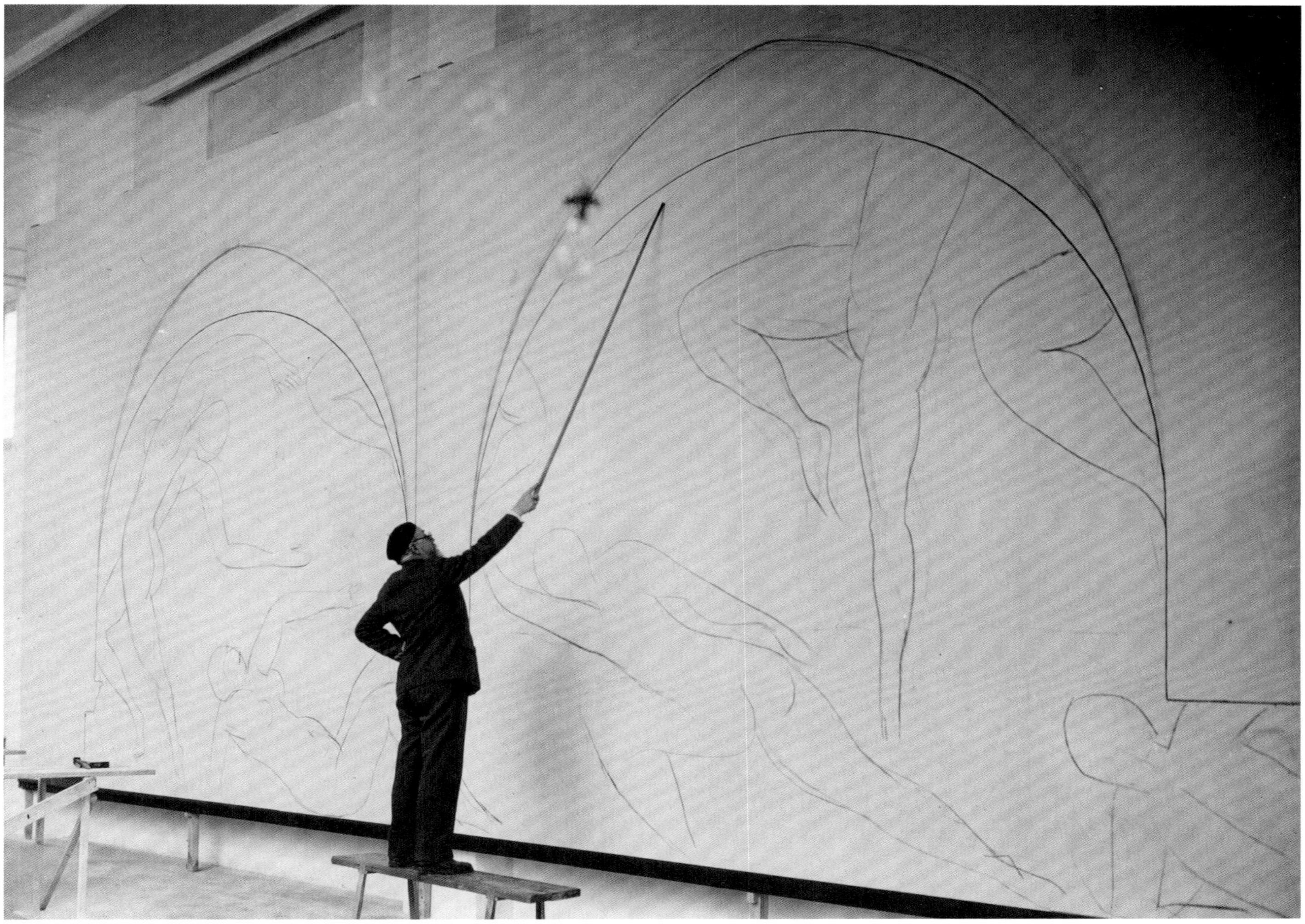

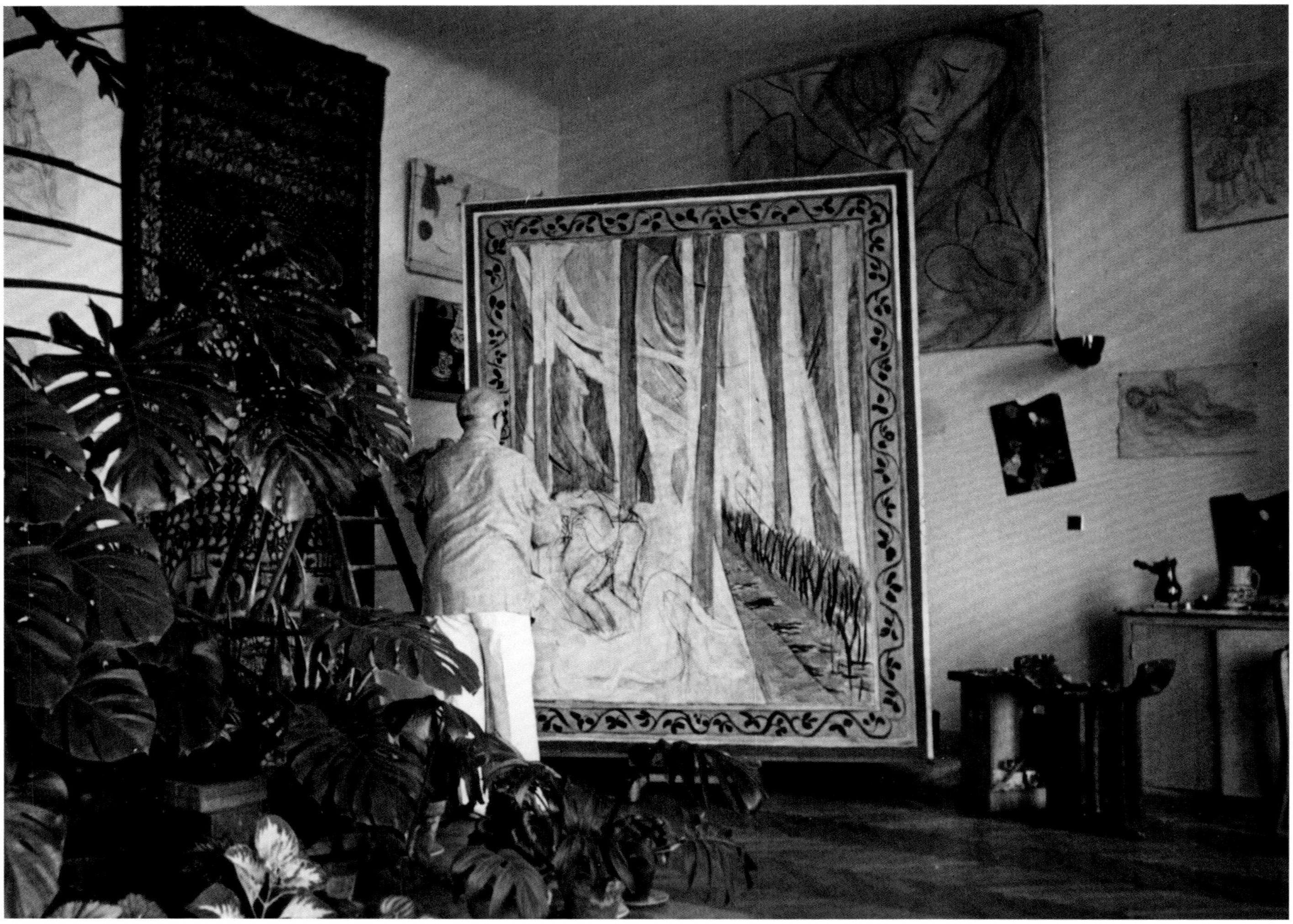

39 Cited in Tériade, "Visite à Henri Matisse," *L'Intransigeant*, January 14 and 22, 1929, reproduced in Flam, *Matisse on Art*, 86.

40 It was well enough known for *National Geographic* to report on it in its December 1938 issue.

41 "Entretien de Lydia Delectorskaya par Xavier Girard," 1992, unpublished typescript, Centre de Documentation, Musée Matisse, Nice, 122.

42 The lease was terminated on October 1, 1938: lease termination, AHM.

43 HM–PM, November 2, 1938, PMGA.

series of drawings of 1928–29 51 provides a clearer insight into this radical change of perspective: anticipating the famous series of 1936 39 | 40 | 63b | 124–29, reprinted in *Cahiers d'art*, the artist represents the model in the studio. The numerous shorthand forms and distortions of the body and the space produce the odd impression that the line runs through the room and permeates its every corner, searching and frisking it, looking for all kinds of sensations. This totalizing space is a far cry indeed from the staged decorum of the cramped theater of the odalisques, which set the figure against a backdrop. As Matisse confided in a January 1929 interview with Tériade, just a few months after moving house: "My purpose is to render my emotion. This state of mind is created by the objects that surround me and that react in me: from the horizon to myself, myself included."[39] So this was an all-encompassing vision that physically enlisted the artist as part of an active, multisensory world view. And from the perpetual dialogue with everything around him—familiar objects, models—and in this continually renewed day-to-day exchange, he would draw out the material for what then amounted to a meditative transport. Which is why he favored anything that could sustain and suggest a sensation, or enrich it with distant echoes. Back home from the Pacific, which had created a vast pool of new impressions, the studio gradually began to resemble a winter garden—the title given to a 1937 picture that launched a whole series of paintings and drawings with two female figures. The most obvious clue to this transformation is the philodendron, a proliferating plant with unmistakable leaves, featured in many paintings and drawings of the period. Its thick, sinuous leaves follow meandering paths that find an echo in the model's voluptuous curves. The highpoint of this tropicalizing of the Matissian interior, before the gouache cut-outs came along, was *Music* 48: from one stage to the next in the making of this painting, the exuberance of the philodendron leaves encroaches on the space, while the figures blossom in the very process of becoming vegetalized. Such profusion, stirred by the memory of Oceania, is in tune with the spatial quality of the colors, which by then had recaptured the expansiveness that Matisse had attained in certain works prior to 1914. This luxuriant atmosphere, a metaphor for his creative aftermath (in the original sense of a second crop), was joined by smells and sounds as well. This was in fact the moment when the first birds of a collection eventually numbering several hundred arrived at the studio:[40] they included tropical species whose songs took him back to memories of Polynesia better than any picture could.

In January 1938, Matisse was given the opportunity of a lifetime: the piecemeal sale of the Régina in the upper part of Cimiez. One of the first buyers, he purchased a vast area of over 4,300 square feet on the fourth floor. "He wanted to be high up," recalled Delectorskaya. "On the third floor he still had the landscape getting in the way, and on the fifth he said that he was already cut off from the outside world, floating above it all, but the third was still in touch with everyday life."[41] The refurbishment took several months, so he and Amélie did not move in until November, having terminated the Place Charles-Félix lease in October.[42] The apartment's rooms were arranged on either side of a sixty-foot-long central corridor: on the south side were the bedrooms, a large room in which he installed his bird cages, and a 650-square-foot studio; on the north side, another studio with a marble floor, and the domestic quarters, kitchens, storerooms, and so on. The ceilings were over thirteen feet high, enabling him to work with much larger dimensions overall. In addition, there were the numerous windows, openings onto the outside world, including the large bow window in the south studio. "We really love our apartment," he wrote to Pierre, "it's a whole new country. It is light, bright, and warm."[43] Omnipresent on the Cours Saleya, the sea was now relegated into the distance, where it no longer affected the light. The extra spaciousness perfectly suited Matisse's desire to work in larger formats and apply himself to painting with something more monumental and decorative in mind. Instead of the Cours Saleya wallpaper decorations, he now had blank walls on which he could spread out his works in configurations that changed over the course of the creative process. And the new apartment was big enough for him to set out various items from his own collection: antiques like the large kouros statue brought down from

Issy-les-Moulineaux or the Greek torso (now in the Musée Matisse, Nice), primitive art objects such as the Pende mask hung opposite the archaic Greek cast in the lobby, the Kuba helmet mask acquired in 1937, and the embroidered raffias from the Congo with their geometric patterns reproduced in *Cahiers d'art* in 1927 57,[44] and the Chinese panel that was his sixtieth birthday present from Amélie. There was also a change of furniture: the Moroccan furniture, tables, and armchairs virtually disappeared, making way for newcomers such as the African stool, the green marble table,[45] and the Marcel Breuer steel chaise longue adorned with a zebra skin, a rare Modernist touch among such an assortment. Every item, picture, piece of furniture, object, or plant kept in the studio was a deliberate choice, and was moved around from place to place as the inspiration took him.[46] Of all Matisse's studios, this was surely the one where the symbiosis between the artist and his work environment reached its peak and was most operative. In the section of the large studio converted into a winter garden, the now enormous philodendron sat enthroned 54, its creeping tentacles circulating from one pot to another. Right next to it was the aviary, from which a variety of birdsong added luxuriance, all other exotic flourishes having been cast aside. The studio's process of becoming plantlike, starting from this emblematic houseplant, marked the new beginning of the 1930s, a metaphor for the creative aftermath and for the expansive quality of the space. Even when the war put an end to this little Matissian paradise, the artist, although weakened by illness following his operation in 1941, continued to make his—now boundless—imaginary world proliferate directly on the studio wall, to the point where, as with the gouache cut-outs, the wall became an integral part of the work.

44 For an overview of Matisse's collection of primitive art, see Hélène Ivanoff, "Collection personnelle: Arts primitifs," in Grammont, *Tout Matisse*, 188–90.

45 This was a slab of sea-green marble which he had had recut and set on a wooden table. See "Entretien de Lydia Delectorskaya," 245.

46 Numerous photo-reportages show how these objects would migrate from one room to another.

Discussing
Matisse's lithographs
is discussing his drawing,
and explaining
his drawing is analyzing
his painting,
which is always built
on the solid foundation
of drawing.

CHRISTIAN ZERVOS
CAHIERS D'ART, 1926, NO. 1

PEINTURE — SCULPTURE
GRAVURE ET ESTAMPE
LES RÉALISATIONS ARCHITECTONIQUES LES PLUS RÉCENTES
L'ARCHITECTURE ET L'AMÉNAGEMENT INTÉRIEURS — LES ARTS APPLIQUÉS ET INDUSTRIELS
CHRONIQUE DES EXPOSITIONS — A TRAVERS ATELIERS ET GALERIES
LES VENTES — NOTICES

Sommaire de Janvier 1926

ÉLIE FAURE
PEINTURE D'AUJOURD'HUI

MATISSE
LITHOGRAPHIES

VLAMINCK
PEINTURES

LA MAISON D'AUJOURD'HUI

PIERRE CHAREAU
ANDRADA
LE CORBUSIER
ARCHITECTURE INTÉRIEURE

LA CHRONIQUE DES EXPOSITIONS ET DES BEAUX LIVRES

Prix : 3 fr. 50

CAHIERS D'ART

BULLETIN MENSUEL D'ACTUALITÉ ARTISTIQUE PUBLIÉ SOUS LA DIRECTION DE CHRISTIAN ZERVOS

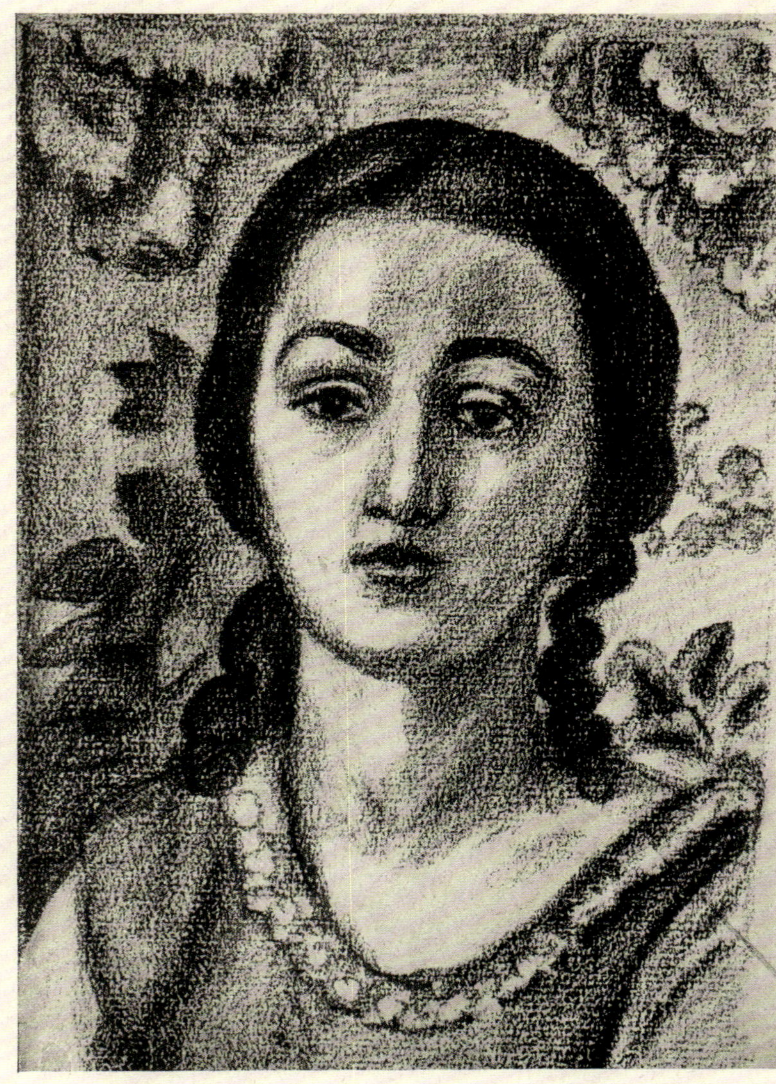

Henri Matisse (Lithographie)

N° 1

SE VEND AUX ÉDITIONS
ALBERT MORANCÉ
A PARIS (VI^{E} ARRONDT^{T})
30 & 32, RUE DE FLEURUS

55
Cahiers d'art, 1926, no. 1, front cover

LITHOGRAPHIES
DE HENRI MATISSE

Parler des lithographies de Matisse, c'est parler de son dessin, et expliquer son dessin, c'est analyser sa peinture. Celle-ci est toujours construite sur le solide fondement du dessin. C'est le dessin qui fait la matière dense de ses toiles, c'est lui qui a mené Matisse au moyen de certaines exagérations, nécessaires pour recréer un élément du beau, à ces solides constructions intimement alliées avec l'éclat et la netteté du coloris, les tons ardents.

Mainte particularité des toiles de Matisse se retrouve dans ses dessins. Ainsi, on y constate cette apparence d'improvisation qui communique à son œuvre un air de grande liberté. En réalité, ce sont des inspirations préparées de longue main. Pour créer, le hasard a lu dans la réflexion et dans l'expérience de l'artiste.

Dans ses dessins, pas plus que dans ses peintures, Matisse ne cherche jamais à mettre les objets en saillie, de manière que l'œil puisse tourner autour. Qualité qui lui a valu de la part des médiocres l'épithète de décorateur. Matisse semble écouter leurs bons conseils. Mais il est convaincu que sa manière de voir est juste, que c'est d'un talent ordinaire que de faire consister le mérite pictural à détacher les objets du fond, et que Titien, ce merveilleux coloriste, avait constamment négligé cette formule.

Que ce soit dans ses dessins ou dans ses peintures, Matisse se contente de sujets quelconques de la vie. On a dit que les esprits extraordinaires tiennent grand compte des choses communes et familières, et les esprits communs n'aiment et ne cherchent que les choses extraordinaires. Chez les premiers, en effet, il y a assez d'idéal pour nous transporter du monde de la nature où tout est vrai, à celui de l'imagination où tout est beau, parce que vraisemblable. Ainsi pour Matisse. Sachant que la beauté pure n'existe pas en image, il a fait avec des objets ordinaires ces beautés de second ordre qui sont joie pour les yeux, consolation pour le cœur et apaisement pour l'esprit.

Cependant, si bien soudés que soient dans l'œuvre de Matisse l'élément graphique et l'élément pictural, il n'en reste pas moins vrai que, pour étudier son talent graphique, il faut surtout consulter ses dessins. C'est que, chez les grands coloristes, la peinture, au risque de perdre son prestige, exige une exécution rapide. Et cette promptitude d'exécution ne saurait s'accorder avec une étude approfondie de la forme. C'est dans les dessins, les gravures sur bois, les lithographies que l'on se rend vraiment compte du talent de Matisse pour créer des formes avec des moyens presque transparents et aériens. Après maintes déformations, après s'être aventuré en des dissymétries audacieuses, après avoir essayé des modèles anguleux ou carrés, il est arrivé à cette expérience, toute personnelle, qui lui a fait retrouver l'art de modeler rond, et sans que les contours extérieurs se creusent. Il a découvert aujourd'hui par lui-même la belle forme et le moyen de faire une œuvre d'une telle limpidité d'armature qu'on la dirait naturelle.

Cependant, les esprits qui confondent les « moyens » d'un effort avec son but et qui préfèrent ces moyens parce qu'ils imposent à l'artiste de se singulariser, proclament la supériorité de son œuvre de jadis. On distingue mal cette supériorité. Guidé par ses instincts, Matisse a su, au moment nécessaire, courir le risque de briser la forme pour la reconstruire. Alors, il nous laissa voir de quoi son œuvre était faite, quels en étaient les éléments. Il les laissa voir, parce qu'il s'était hasardé à le savoir lui-même. Toutes les fois qu'il descendait dans les profondeurs de sa pensée, il s'éloignait pour se regarder.

Son expérience terminée ou presque, tout en étudiant la structure et la travaillant de partout, il n'en laisse pas voir l'organisme. Il n'y a que les esprits incertains pour aimer les exagérations en elles-mêmes et s'épuiser en conceptions singulières. Un grand peintre, comme un grand poète, doit suivre la nature qui travaille toujours du dedans au dehors.

Les dessins de Matisse se présentent sous deux aspects. D'abord le dessin poussé en tous ses détails; Matisse y fait une large place à l'accessoire, bien que cet accessoire soit intimement lié à l'essentiel. Dans ces dessins, il y a comme une servitude à la grâce. Ils imposent en outre des limites à notre esprit. Celles que l'artiste a voulu lui dicter.

Matisse semble avoir cherché, toutes proportions gardées, de nous donner dans ces dessins en noir et blanc, l'équivalent de ses toiles. Cela est d'autant plus difficile que chez Matisse, la couleur n'est pas

7

un moyen sans valeur intrinsèque. Elle est, au contraire, une fin; elle a une personnalité et elle impose *sa* lumière. Aussi le lyrisme du dessin n'étant plus soutenu et exalté par les éblouissements du coloris perd-il de son acuité et de sa signification.

Au lieu que dans une figure circonscrite par un simple trait le dessin garde toute sa poésie, nous suggère autant de formes que nous sommes capables d'en imaginer, le crayon semble conduire en même temps tous les détails et les abstraire.

Dans cette espèce d'abstraction sensuelle, la pureté du contour a le même éclat que dans un dessin très poussé, la même beauté et montre la même maîtrise, mais de plus elle implique davantage de nuances et de finesses, de nerf et de plénitude, et les grands plans débarrassés de l'accessoire acquièrent une puissance qui amplifie et enveloppe les figures.

Il faut dire aussi que le trait d'une allure coulante et heureuse éveille davantage l'idée du rythme. De plus, parce qu'il n'a rien coûté à l'artiste, il nous semble tout à fait libre ; les lignes paraissent lancées par l'instinct avec une hardiesse et une désinvolture qui nous plaisent.

On ne doit pas non plus oublier que tous les dieux reposent en nous, et que nous nous attachons à tout ce qui les éveille. Les choses évoquées par le trait ressuscitent en nous des mobiles ignorés, nous permettent de rassembler quelques uns des éléments épars d'un bout à l'autre de l'étendue mentale de chacun de nous. Et cela nous enchante, car il nous plaît toujours d'imaginer que l'artiste a pensé nos idées et de rencontrer en son œuvre la pensée qui lui vient de nous. L'esprit est ainsi fait qu'il aime réaliser avec des suggestions une image décisive, selon ses désirs.

Mais, des distinctions que nous venons d'établir, il faut se défier. Elles valent ce que valent les affirmations du jugement toujours errant et divers. Ce qu'il faut surtout retenir des dessins de Matisse, c'est le drame intérieur que suppose chacun d'eux. Drame d'agitations, de fécondes inquiétudes, de longs errements, de pensées et de décisions alternantes.

On suit l'artiste créant et défaisant continuellement dans ses pensées et dans ses sensations, épuisant toute possibilité d'expérience, retirant de la peinture ses ressources implicites, exerçant sa faculté analogique entre toutes les formes.

Dans la mémoire de chacun demeurent ces images variées qui nous laissent deviner par quels sursauts de pensée, par quelles inductions, après quelles immenses minutes de doute, de scrupules, d'objections froides, de surveillance de soi-même, se sont montrées à Matisse ses œuvres futures.

Merveilleuse destinée que celle de l'artiste placé devant le spectacle de sa propre diversité.

CHRISTIAN ZERVOS.

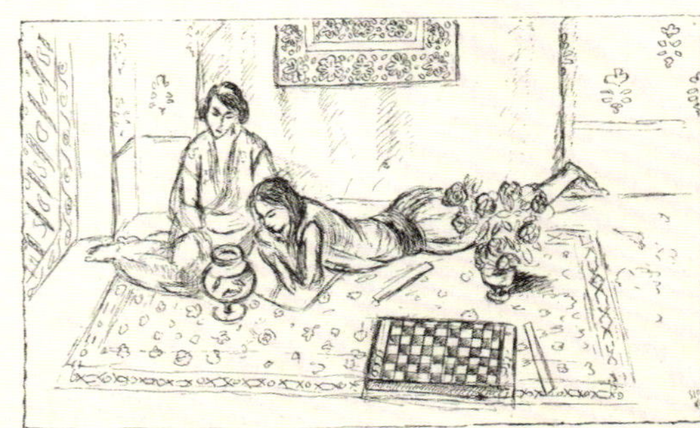

Matisse, dessin

8

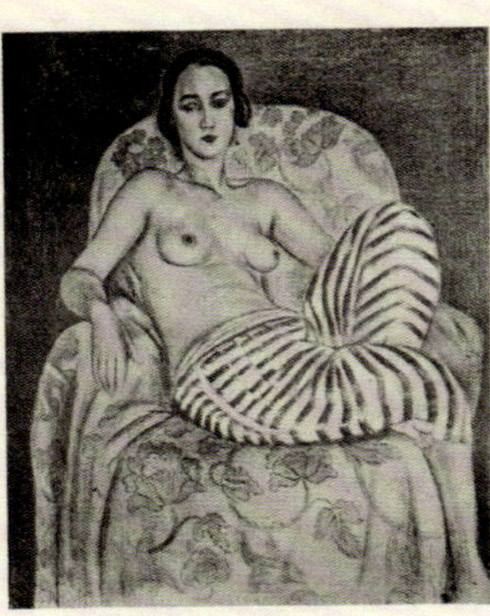

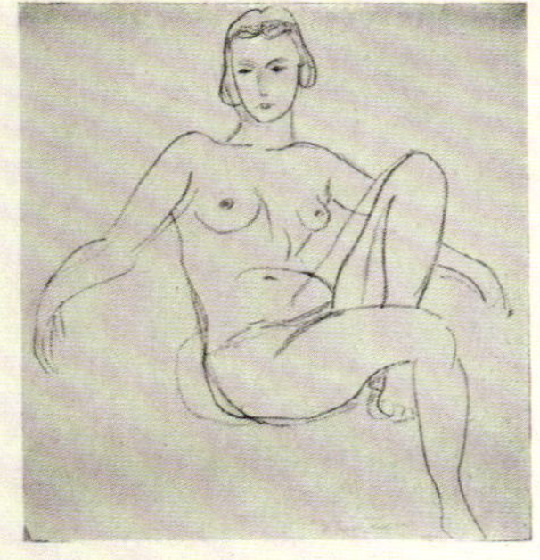

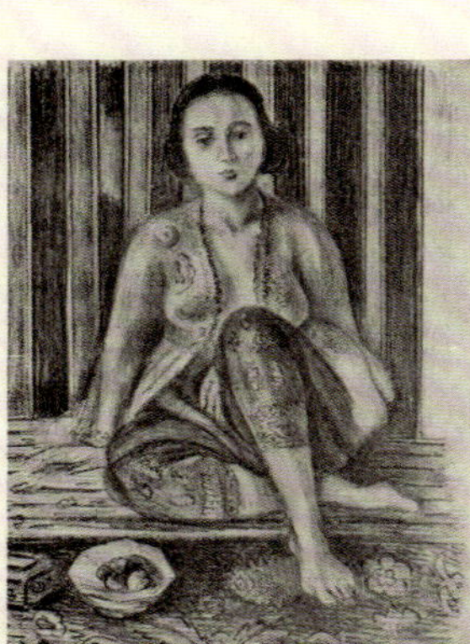

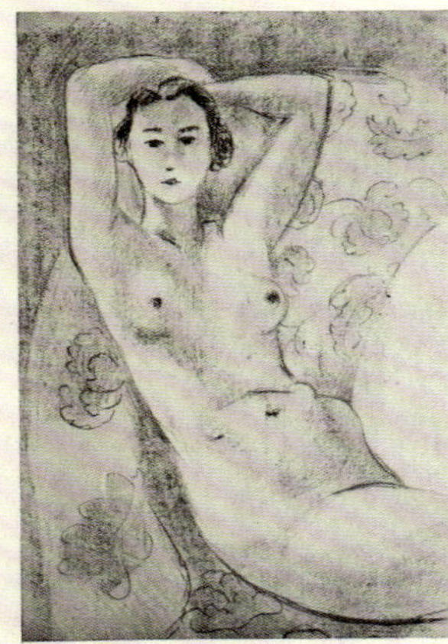

HENRI MATISSE (Lithographies)

56 a–c
Christian Zervos, "Lithographies de Henri Matisse," *Cahiers d'art*, 1926, no. 1, pp. 7–9

57
Christian Zervos, "L'art nègre," *Cahiers d'art*, 1927, nos. 7–8, p. 229 (illustration: garment fragment, Kuba, from Matisse's collection)

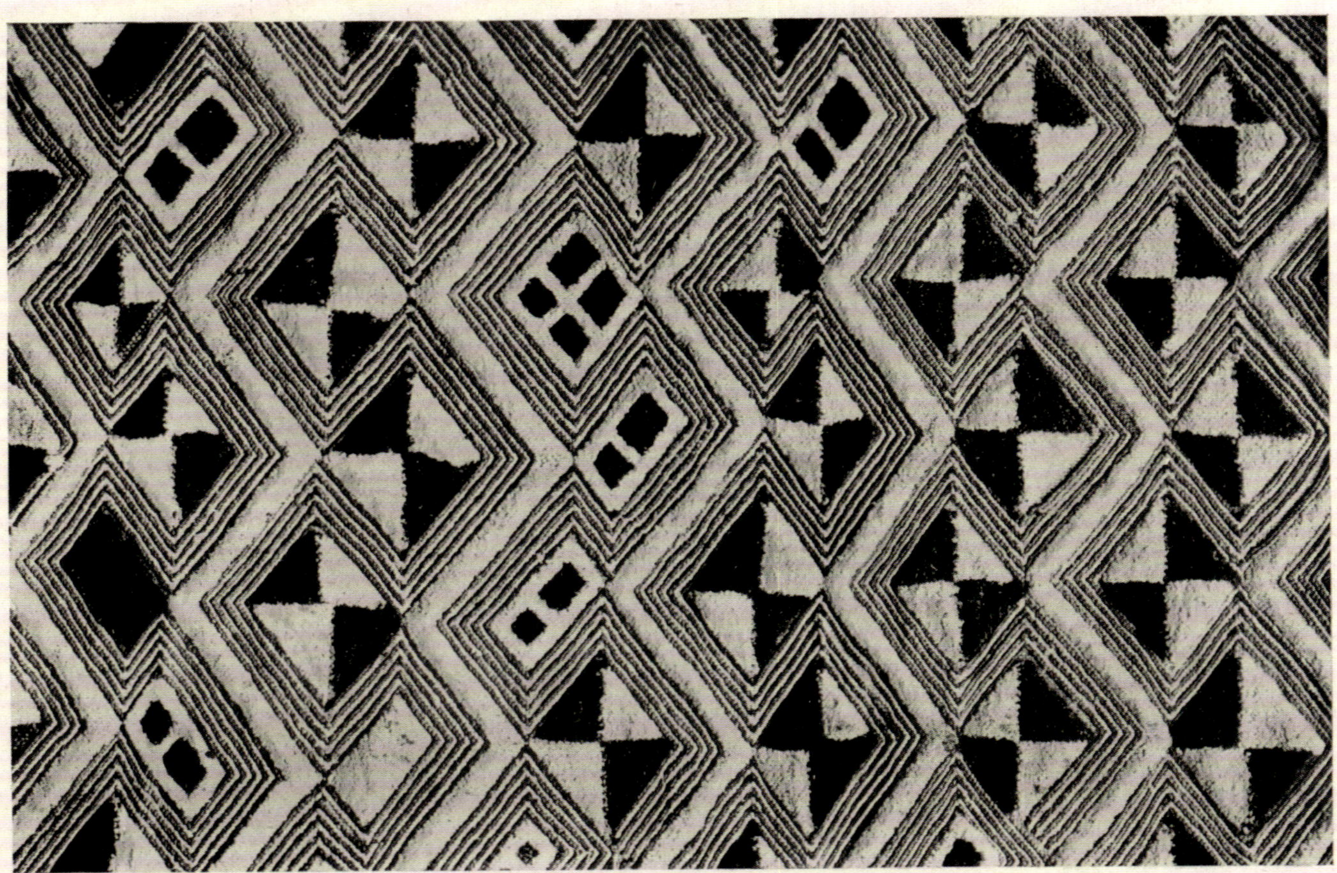

Coll. Henri Matisse.

L'ART NÈGRE

Il y a vingt ans, l'aspiration des jeunes artistes d'introduire dans la peinture ce qui manquait à l'œuvre des aînés, fit naître en leur âme une ardente passion de poursuivre tout ce qui était instinct, idée initiale, curiosité, en un mot, tout ce qui était susceptible d'élargir le domaine de la peinture.

Ce développement des valeurs picturales acquises, les jeunes peintres le cherchèrent rarement dans les grandes œuvres des civilisations reconnues. Ils donnèrent surtout en pâture à leur cœur et à leur esprit, assoiffés d'instinct, les créations de peuplades primitives.

Certains d'entre ces peintres, par l'acte d'imagination, surent se reporter dans un monde différent du nôtre, tout différent des tendances que nous avons aimées et souvent admises par la force de l'habitude. Ils regardèrent les œuvres des races simples, non pas historiquement, mais en cherchant d'y découvrir ce qu'il y avait en elles de correspondances avec notre idéal.

Dans leur effort de saisir tous les élans du cœur, dans leur belle croyance en l'éternelle poésie qui, à un moment ou à un autre, chez une race ou chez une autre, remplit l'homme de plus d'exaltation que n'en contient généralement la vie quotidienne, les jeunes peintres s'étaient senti de la prédilection pour l'art de certaines tribus africaines. La poésie venue du Congo, de la Côte d'Ivoire, du Dahomey, du Gabon, avec un tissu, un objet utilitaire, un masque ou une sculpture, mit en éveil la sensibilité des peintres qu'avait assoupie le trop grand attachement aux expériences d'ordre matériel. Dans les formes et dans les expressions réalisées par les nègres, les jeunes peintres avaient puisé le désir de possibilités insoupçonnées jusqu'alors, la recherche d'expressions, de volumes, de tons, qui allaient considérablement augmenter notre patrimoine pictural. Mais les travaux des nègres nous apportèrent surtout cette fraîcheur, ces promesses incertaines de la poésie, qui font vibrer l'âme de mille passions, mille et mille suggestions.

CAHIERS D'ART

REVUE D'ART PARAISSANT DIX FOIS PAR AN - DIRECTEUR : CHRISTIAN ZERVOS
PEINTURE-SCULPTURE-ARCHITECTURE-MUSIQUE-MISE EN SCÈNE-DISQUES-CINÉMA

4

1928

TROISIÈME ANNÉE

FERNAND LÉGER PAR E. TÉRIADE — JACQUES LIPCHITZ PAR V. HUIDOBRO — IDÉALISME ET NATURALISME DANS LA PEINTURE MODERNE PAR CHRISTIAN ZERVOS — AVENIR DE LA MUSIQUE AUTOMATIQUE PAR JACQUES BRILLOUIN — ILLUSTRATIONS DE CHAGALL PAR RENÉ SCHWOB — ART PRÉCOLOMBIEN PAR TRISTAN TZARA — PEINTURES DE SIMA PAR G. RIBEMONT-DESSAIGNES — L'EFFORT PLASTIQUE D'ANDRÉ LURCAT PAR CHR. ZERVOS

10 francs

ÉDITIONS « CAHIERS D'ART » 40, RUE BONAPARTE, 40 PARIS VIe ARROND^{T}

58 a, b
Cahiers d'art, 1928, no. 4,
front cover and Christian Zervos,
"Idéalisme et naturalisme
dans la peinture moderne," p. 159

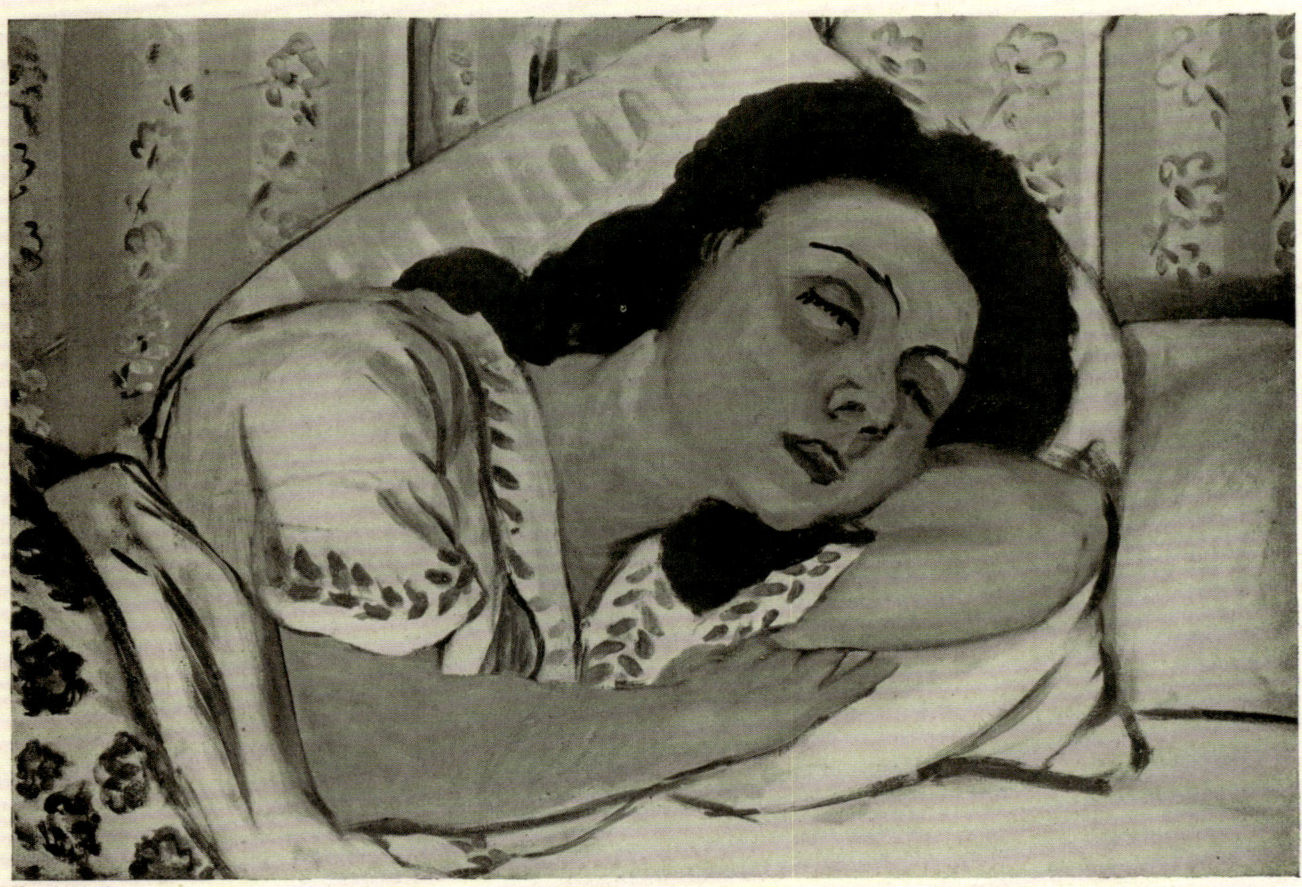
Henri Matisse.

IDÉALISME ET NATURALISME DANS LA PEINTURE MODERNE

IV. — Henri Matisse

Nous disposons aujourd'hui d'un pouvoir d'illusion sans limites. C'est ainsi que nous aimons regarder un tableau comme un paysage démesuré pris dans le cadre d'une fenêtre. Même, dans une nature morte, notre esprit se plaît à découvrir toutes les perspectives de son inquiétude.

C'est le bonheur imparti à certains êtres doués d'une sensibilité, disons orphique, de pouvoir épouser, au moyen de leurs perceptions, la variété du mouvement universel qui imprime à toutes choses non seulement un mouvement incessant dans l'espace mais aussi un incessant changement de qualité. Les perceptions sensibles qui transmettent les affections du cœur à l'âme, sont chez eux très diverses et peuvent susciter en leur esprit d'innombrables représentations. La chose leur est d'autant plus facile qu'ils sont à même d'envisager les originaux en même temps que leurs copies qui constituent le monde phénoménal. D'où la nécessité pour le vrai peintre de se rendre attentif à l'image des objets.

Je sais bien que tout le monde ne l'entend pas ainsi. En réaction contre l'imitation par trop étroite des réalités qui environnent le peintre, certains esprits se montrent hostiles à toute représentation du réel, alors même que l'apparence de l'objet figuré revêt la distinction et la grandeur de la sensibilité humaine. Ils considèrent comme une grave erreur le fait d'emprunter ses modèles ailleurs que dans les profondeurs de l'âme.

Cette abdication des artistes me paraît fort excusable. Il est hors de doute qu'un esprit élevé doit, dans la limite du possible, rester étranger au monde de la réalité, se tenir écarté des apparences extérieures, s'en évader pour se contempler dans son âme. Mais, le peintre ne saurait s'empêcher de regarder les objets avec une curiosité facile à expliquer. Car, s'il

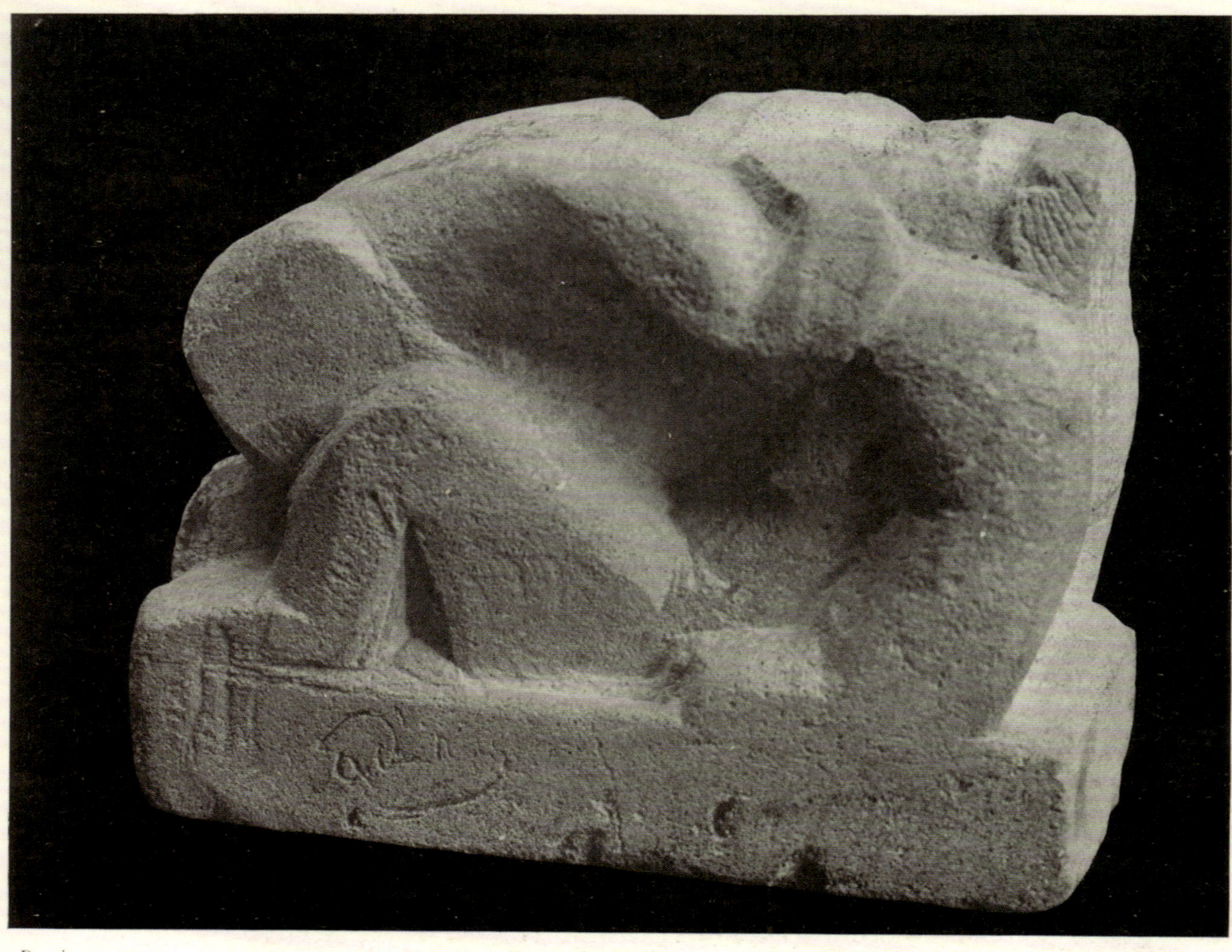

Derain.

SCULPTURES DES PEINTRES D'AUJOURD'HUI

Les œuvres sculptées des peintres contemporains que nous publions dans ce fascicule, témoignent que l'art est une aventure séduisante de l'esprit pour expliquer l'univers et lui rendre l'hommage qui lui est dû. L'artiste s'attache passionnément à pénétrer les multiples vérités des aspects naturels, afin de saisir ce qu'il s'y trouve de constant. Il se permet l'espoir de surprendre dans la mobilité du monde visible l'essentiel, qui est la raison d'être de chacun des aspects de l'univers.

Séduit par cette hasardeuse entreprise il cherche à augmenter les possibilités qui lui permettront d'élever son œuvre jusqu'à la hauteur de l'art et d'en justifier l'existence. Pour y parvenir il se doit de reprendre les idées que la nécessité du changement fait abandonner chaque fois aux générations qui se succèdent.

Ainsi, en dépit de la solidarité certaine du genre humain dans le rêve et dans l'illusion, solidarité qui relie une génération à l'autre, chacune de celles-ci se distingue de la précédente par sa capacité d'invention qui lui fait nécessairement oublier les résultats acquis pour s'essayer à l'éternelle expérience.

A ce point de vue l'effort artistique de nos jours est incontestablement très important. Un pareil besoin de renouvellement s'explique surtout par le désir de retrouver les sources mêmes de l'art. D'où notre croyance qu'il n'est pas un art primitif, en quelque lieu qu'il se soit développé, qui ne mérite un regard d'admiration ou d'examen attentif. Croyance qui justifie la curiosité de notre génération pour tous les arts qui semblent renfermer les sources mêmes de l'émotion, et son anxieux appel à toutes les inquiétudes dont le pouvoir irrésistible a sommé les formes d'apparaître.

Toutefois, cette recherche des sources mêmes de l'art ne fait pas oublier à l'artiste que pour y

59 (fig.)
Christian Zervos, "Sculptures des peintres d'aujourd'hui," *Cahiers d'art*, 1928, no. 7, p. 277

CAHIERS D'ART

REVUE D'ART PARAISSANT DIX FOIS PAR AN - DIRECTEUR : CHRISTIAN ZERVOS
PEINTURE, SCULPTURE, ARCHITECTURE, ART ANCIEN, ETHNOGRAPHIE, CINÉMA

5·6

6e ANNÉE 1931

L'ŒUVRE DE

HENRI MATISSE

ÉTUDIÉE PAR

CHRISTIAN ZERVOS
PAUL FIERENS
PIERRE GUÉGUEN
Dr CURT GLASER
WILL GROHMANN
GEORGES SALLES
ROGER FRY
HENRY McBRIDE
KAREL ASPLUND
G. SCHEIWILLER

ÉDITION ORIGINALE

EDITIONS «CAHIERS D'ART» 14, RUE DU DRAGON, PARIS (VIe ARRONDISSEMENT)

60
Cahiers d'art, 1931, nos. 5–6, front cover

61 a–d
Cahiers d'art, 1931, nos. 5–6
Paul Fierens,
"Matisse et le corps féminin," p. 35
Pierre Guéguen,
"Poésie d'Henri-Matisse," p. 41
Henry McBride,
"Matisse in America," p. 71
Woman with a Hat, p. 95

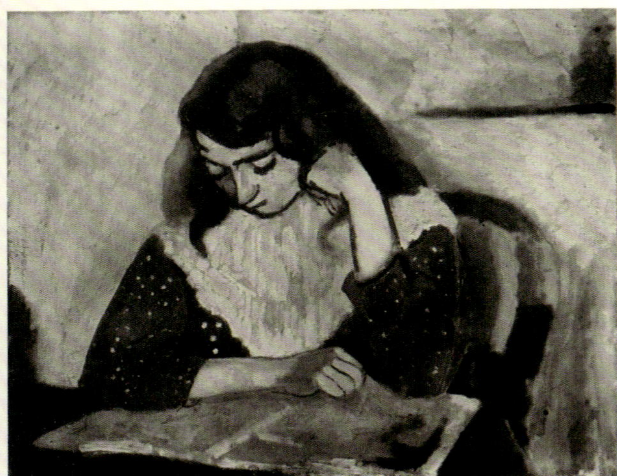

FIG. 25. — FILLETTE LISANT, 1905. MUSÉE DE GRENOBLE. LEGS MARCEL SEMBAT.

MATISSE ET LE CORPS FÉMININ

PAR PAUL FIERENS

Puisqu'il est difficile aujourd'hui de parler peinture sans soulever quelque *problème*, puisqu'aussi bien Matisse en a déplacé quelques-uns, demandons-nous ce qu'est devenue la figure au centre de son esthétique. La figure, la féminine, nue ou drapée, est bien demeurée, quoi qu'en puissent dire les *humanistes*, partie intégrante de sa conception de l'univers, de la peinture. Mais elle a perdu son autonomie en conservant sa primauté. Il n'y a point, chez Matisse, comme chez tant d'autres, différence d'esprit, de consistance, de technique même, entre le motif principal et ce qui l'entoure, lui sert de fond, de repoussoir. Il n'y a point un sujet et une atmosphère ; il y a fusion des deux éléments, intégration de l'accompagnement dans la mélodie. Une baigneuse de Courbet ou de Renoir se silhouette sur un paysage, un ciel, un mur, elle en reçoit peut-être une influence, mais elle s'en détache bien ; un nu de Derain se tient par lui-même. Une odalisque de Matisse n'existe pas sans le décor qui l'environne. Elle fait corps avec l'ambiance picturale. Elle est, si j'ose dire, *picturalisée* complètement.

Renoir est un peintre de nus, le plus admirable sans doute et le plus complet de l'école française. Matisse a peint beaucoup de nus mais n'est pas un *peintre de nus*. M'entendez-vous? Cézanne, le premier, je pense, a traité la figure et même le portrait comme une autre nature morte. Matisse a traité tout en fonction du tout, qui est une harmonie de lignes et de tons, un équilibre de masses et de couleurs, ou mieux de masses colorées. La chair n'a point, à ses yeux, le privilège d'absorber et de concentrer

35

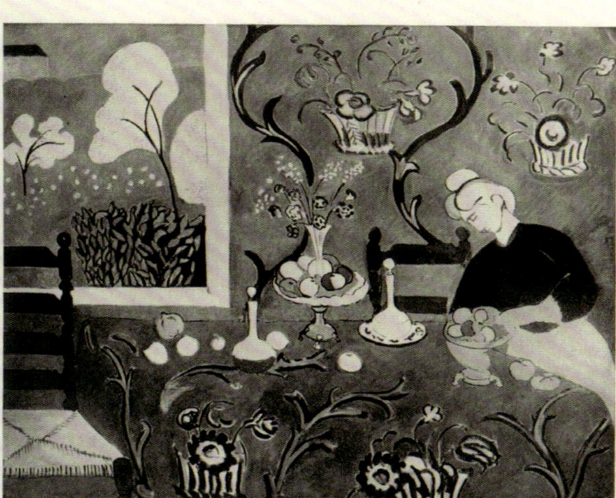

FIG. 31. — LA DESSERTE, 1909. CAMAIEU FOND ROUGE. MUSÉE D'ART MODERNE, MOSCOU.

POÉSIE D'HENRI-MATISSE

PAR PIERRE GUÉGUEN

Je ne connaissais de lui que quelques tableaux et je ne les avais pas revus depuis dix ans peut-être lorsqu'on me demanda à brûle-pourpoint : « Quel livre moderne s'accorderait le mieux avec des illustrations de Matisse? »

Si peu qu'on les mérite, on reçoit néanmoins des grâces, sans quoi on repêcherait trop de noyés à Javel, sur certaine petite plage de sable orange où ils ont tout juste la place de venir dire, un à un, en langue exsangue, leur nausée. N'ai-je pas traduit sans broncher, en 1916, devant un téléphone de minuit, pour le sous-Tigre (je veux dire M. Mandel) les télégrammes qui constituaient le Message du Président Wilson... alors que je ne savais pas l'américain? Sans guère mieux savoir le matisse, je pus pourtant satisfaire le subtil Odysséen qui m'interrogeait. D'un invisible lambris de mémoire partit je ne sais quel résidu irisé, quelle miette de couleur éclatante, quelle bouffée d'une mousseline de joie, cependant qu'à un autre coin se levait une jeunesse de pivoines et retentissait une aubépine de rires. Les deux printaniers météores se croisèrent : aussitôt je répondis au sphinx : « Je ne vois qu'un livre, *A l'ombre des jeunes filles en fleur.* »

Maintenant que je viens d'enchanter longuement mes yeux devant de si nombreux Matisse, dans le limpide silence des salons de M. Paul Guillaume, en cette Avenue du Bois, le seul endroit de France, disait Stendhal, où l'on pût vivre en paix à la campagne (que n'eût-il dit devant la campagne renforcée des cimaises !), ou à Vaucresson, chez M. Stein, frère de la poétesse Gertrude Stein, l'amateur de la première heure, qui a cueilli à point les œuvres « fauves » et même pré-fauves ; à présent que Matisse

41

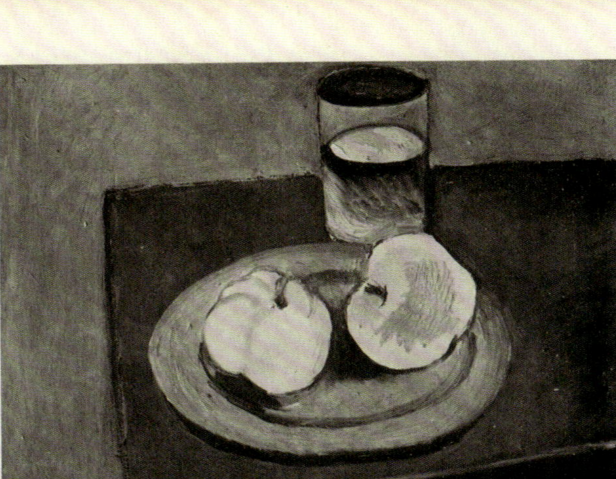

FIG. 59. — NATURE MORTE AUX POMMES VERTES, 1916. COLL. PAUL GUILLAUME.

MATISSE IN AMERICA

BY HENRY McBRIDE

Matisse has been famous in America for twenty years or more. He began by being famous with the young people who saw in him a prophet who might get them out of the impasse into which, in New York, art had been pushed in the early decade of this century. This "impasse" is simply another word for the National Academy of those days. This institution was largely controlled by several individuals whose names are still mentioned whenever bigotry comes under discussion but who are seldom mentioned in any other connection. These official martinets controlled all the politics of the situation. They awarded honours, decided commissions for public work and refused all non-conformists the opportunity to expose. The academy was the sole avenue to success for the American painter. There was not then an Independent Society nor were there dealers who had the courage for experimental painting. It is difficult to realize in this period of emancipation how restricted and enchained the American painters of 1890-1910 were. One was more or less obliged to be a copyist to live.

Into all this stuffiness the advent of Matisse was, as James Stephens has it, "like a breath of fresh air in a scap factory". The puzzled young artists who had spent years in acquiring manners that might be acceptable to their elders suddenly saw that their elders had nothing to do with the affair and that any manner was all right that gave them a chance to use their own eyes and their own experiences. They probably thought, deep down in their hearts, that Matisse himself was thumbing his nose at officialdom, but — very well — that of all gestures, at the moment, seemed the most superb and the most completely à propos. In the first excitement of worshipping a cult that was to bring them, too,

71

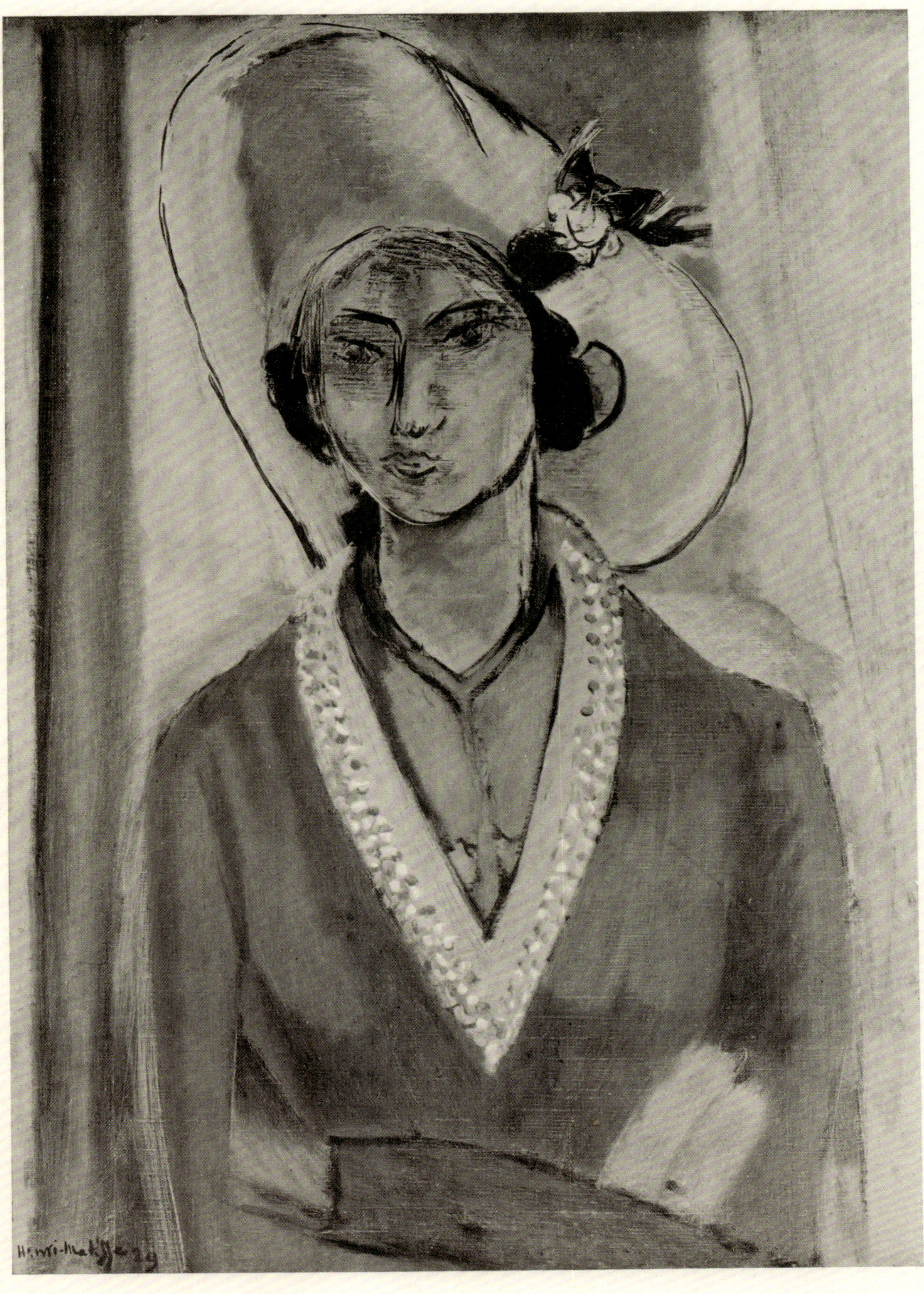

FIG. 96. — FEMME AU CHAPEAU, 1929.

CAHIERS D'ART

REVUE D'ART PARAISSANT DIX FOIS PAR AN - DIRECTEUR : CHRISTIAN ZERVOS
PEINTURE, SCULPTURE, ARCHITECTURE, ART ANCIEN, ETHNOGRAPHIE, CINÉMA

1-4

10e ANNÉE 1935

Ce numéro se propose de montrer que l'art d'aujourd'hui est plus vivant que jamais.

FRANCE FRANCS 40

ÉDITIONS "CAHIERS D'ART" 14, RUE DU DRAGON, 14, PARIS VI[E] ARRONDISSEMENT

62 a, b
Cahiers d'art, 1935, nos. 1–4,
front cover and p. 10

Première décoration

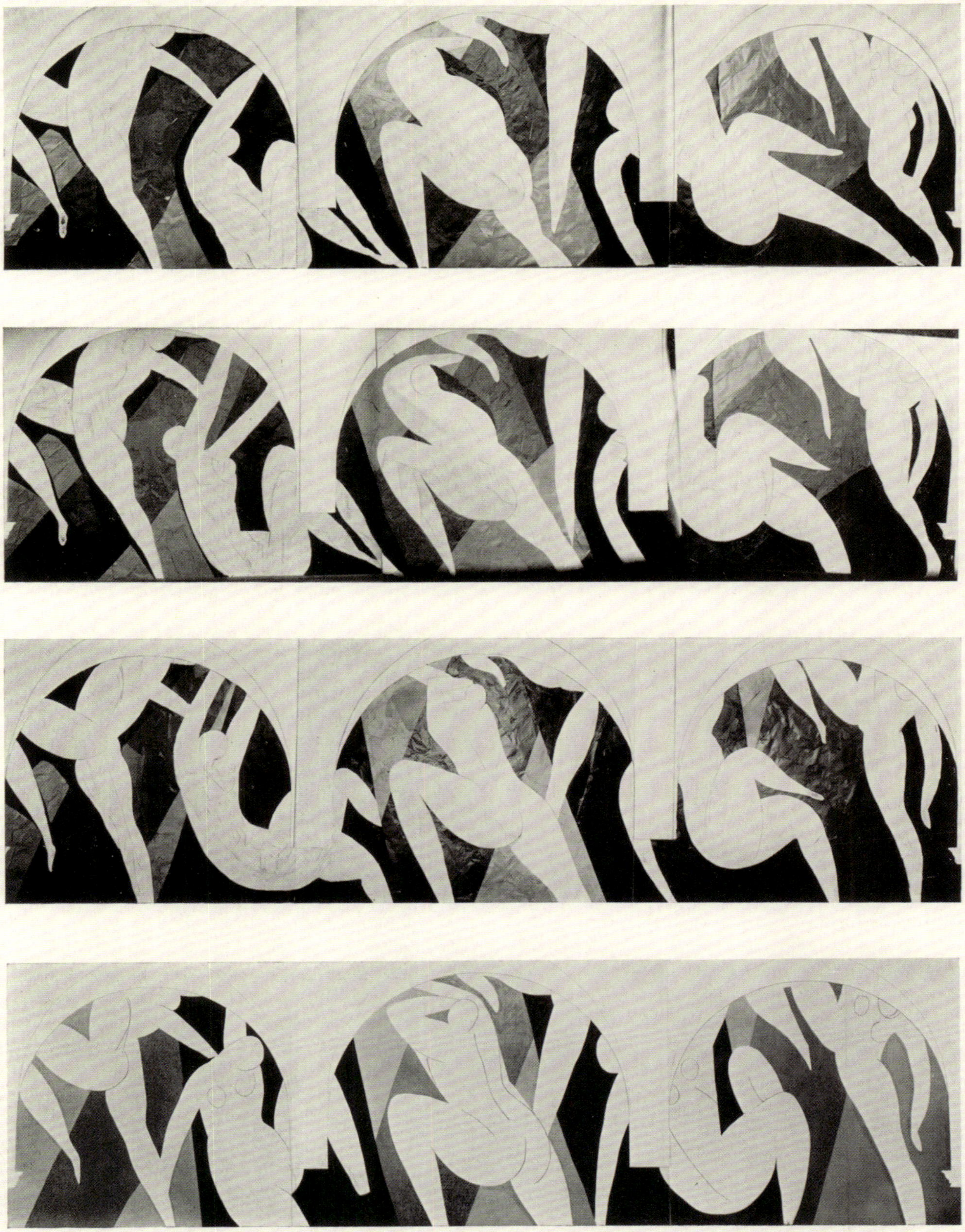

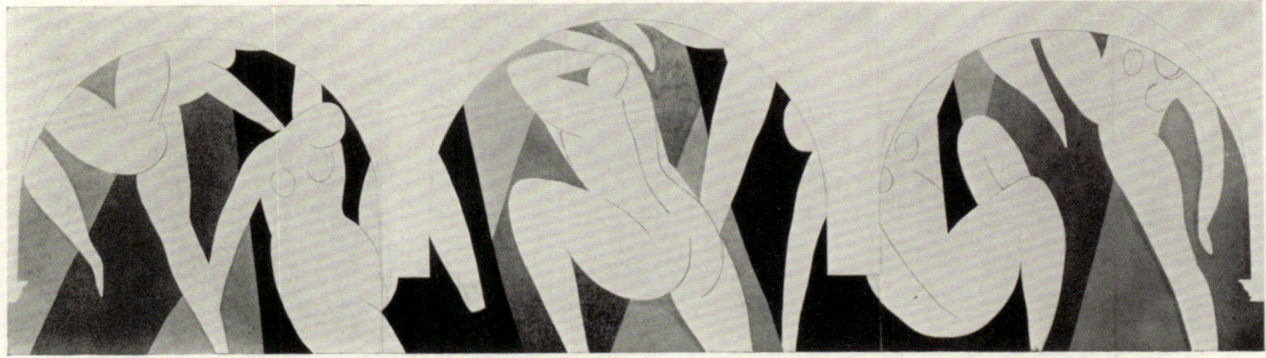

Henri-Matisse. Quatre états. Cette décoration se trouve chez l'artiste, à Nice.

AUTOMATISME ET ESPACE ILLUSOIRE

On n'a pas assez dit le rôle de Matisse dans la préparation esthétique d'aujourd'hui; par là cependant, autant que par ses qualités, son œuvre prend une importance considérable et modifie la première idée que nous nous étions faite de nos préoccupations les plus actuelles.

N'allons plus croire que nous avons découvert une certaine action de la pensée sans délibération. Qui proclame de nos jours le rêve, qui invoque le songe, qui prêche l'automatisme et s'élève contre les commandements, ne doit pas oublier que déjà Matisse a cherché de donner à son esprit la plus grande liberté.

Faut-il rappeler que, dès la période fauve, Matisse a œuvré en dehors du prévisible, avant que l'artiste ait pleinement pensé son action ? N'était-ce pas un art libérateur où l'on trouvait tout le ramassé et le vif du mouvement de l'âme, non encore réglé et contenu ?

Toutefois une remarque s'offre d'elle-même à l'esprit, qui l'aide à mieux saisir les tendances présentes.

Il importe d'abord de reconnaître le rôle de l'imagination arrachant et entraînant les images du fond de la nuit. Entendez l'inspiration comme un pouvoir contemplatif lié à des perceptions sibyllines, indéterminées, évanescentes. L'état de délire qu'elle implique est par lui-même séduisant. Il transporte dans l'oubli, allège les conséquences, dispense de toute précision, invente des raisons à ce point charmeresses, bien que spécieuses, se pare de tant de libertés, presse par tant de nouveautés, qu'il est difficile de lui tenir tête. Peut-on lui reprocher de favoriser l'indétermination, quand il nous offre tant d'avantages dont on ne voit pas tout de suite les ombres ?

L'émotion renvoyée de perception à perception, envahit l'artiste au point que le besoin de la témoigner s'empare de lui. Ce qui fait dire qu'un certain délire conduit les arts.

Il faut toutefois considérer que si les images de l'inspiration, autant qu'on en peut parler, sont *données,* elles le sont seulement d'après l'impression. Or, il va de soi que l'impression exclut le contrôle. Qui dit délire invoque le contraire de la précaution et de l'ordre. Bien entendu la rêverie oisive procure à l'artiste, comme nous venons de le dire, plus de joie que l'action; mieux encore, elle lui fait apparaître le monde du rêve comme nettement supérieur à celui où l'ordre sert d'appui.

Mais il est certain que celui qui veut écrire son rêve se doit d'être éveillé. Il ne peut pas grand chose en dehors de l'ordre inflexible qui lui donne assiette et fermeté. Toutes les fois qu'il n'y a pas concordance entre l'inspiration et l'ordre, les inventions paraissent peut-être émouvantes, mais sans rien qui puisse en fixer la beauté. La différence entre l'imaginatif et le peintre, c'est que le pouvoir d'exécution est chez ce dernier aussi puissant et aussi multiple que son imagination et ses rêves. Il y a un étrange abîme entre les discours que nous tiennent les images de l'inspiration et ceux que nous leur prêtons dans nos œuvres; un intervalle inconcevable entre l'impression ou l'invention et leur expression achevée.

63 a, b
Christian Zervos, "Automatisme et espace illusoire," *Cahiers d'art*, 1936, nos. 3–5, pp. 69, 90

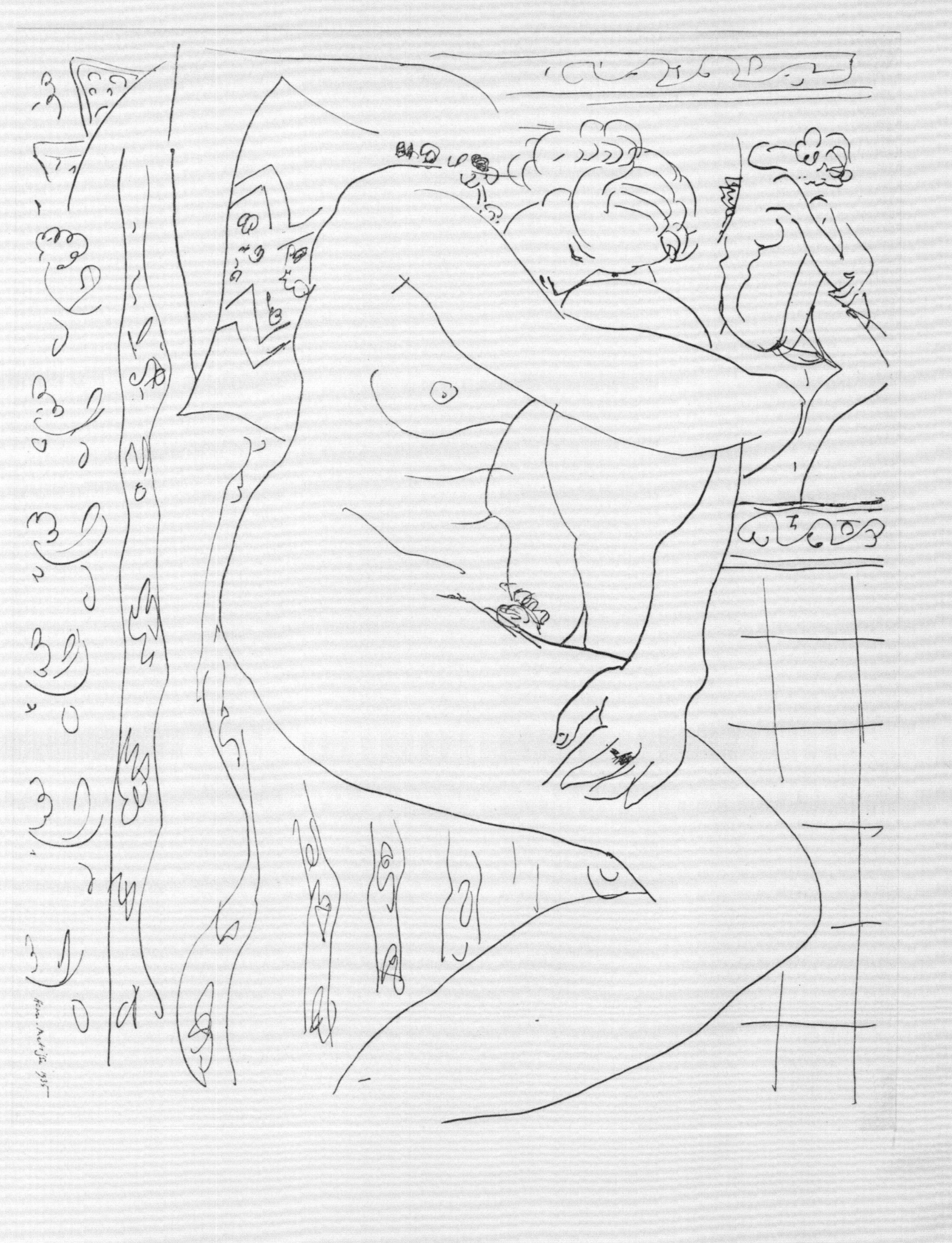

cahiers d'art

HENRI-MATISSE. DESSINS AU FUSAIN.

GEORGES DUTHUIT. KENNETH CLARK. ROGER CAILLOIS. GEORGES BATAILLE
JOHN PIPER. BRAQUE. LAURENS. LÉGER. MASSON. MIRÓ. PICASSO

N° 1-4 1939 FRS 75

64 a–d
Cahiers d'art, 1939, nos. 1–4, front cover and Christian Zervos, "Dessins récents de Henri-Matisse," pp. 6, 17, 24

DESSINS RÉCENTS
DE
HENRI-MATISSE

Le dessin est une action complète. L'investigation n'est pas son rôle unique. Il se propose des fins plus hautes. Dans l'aventure d'une image qui part, indéterminée, des profondeurs du peintre, pour se diriger par la voie de la perception, vers la réalisation de sa forme plastique, le dessin constitue l'étape première de cette réalisation.

Il n'est pas de genre de dessin qui ne soit apte à serrer du plus près l'image des choses avant qu'elle soit engagée dans la technique picturale, et de qui l'on ne puisse obtenir un riche contenu avec des ressources d'expression très réduites.

Ses moyens sont tout par eux-mêmes; c'est que le dessin ne profite pas, comme la peinture du secours d'autres éléments, il n'est pas accompagné de facteurs qui le corrigent et lui donnent son vrai sens, il lui est impossible d'agir indirectement. Aussi lui faut-il apporter une bonne part de ce qu'apporte la peinture et y joindre sa propre part. Alors que dans le tableau la couleur a de nombreuses possibilités pour s'exprimer, le dessin ne dispose que de moyens fort limités pour affirmer sa présence, non pas à l'arrière-plan, comme un rappel, comme une invitation ou comme une sorte d'accompagnement fragile, mais en première place.

N'est-ce pas encore un des traits essentiels du dessin que son pouvoir de surprendre la lumière dans ses effets les plus divers ? Quoi qu'il veuille représenter c'est la lumière qui l'aide, le guide et le soutient. Il ne voit les choses qu'à travers la lumière, ou plutôt, ne voit qu'elle. Pas un trait qui ne s'y fonde et ne devienne partie de cette source.

Le voilà le rôle du dessin, du moins tel que nous le trouvons à présent chez Matisse dont l'esprit se diversifie et s'affine tous les jours. Dans ses derniers dessins le peintre a passé du choix passionné pour le trait pur au crayon ou à la plume, à un choix différent, non moins passionné, pour le fusain. L'art qu'il apportait dans ses dessins au trait pour suggérer les dehors du monde, nous le retrouvons ici délicat, précis, musical, avec en plus la sensuelle densité de la matière du fusain. Car, si particulier qu'apparaisse l'aspect de chacun de ces genres de dessin, tous deux doivent leur beauté aux mêmes lois fondamentales de la personnalité, aux profondes attaches entre l'homme et l'œuvre, qui donnent à celle-ci sa garantie et son authenticité.

Ces dessins sensationnels qui enserrent les objets dans leurs signes vibrants, chauds et riches de lumière nous sont une occasion de rappeler, en y insistant même, le dessin de Matisse où la puissance de la vision et la virtuosité de la main créent des sensations et des techniques parmi les plus parfaites que propose l'art de notre temps.

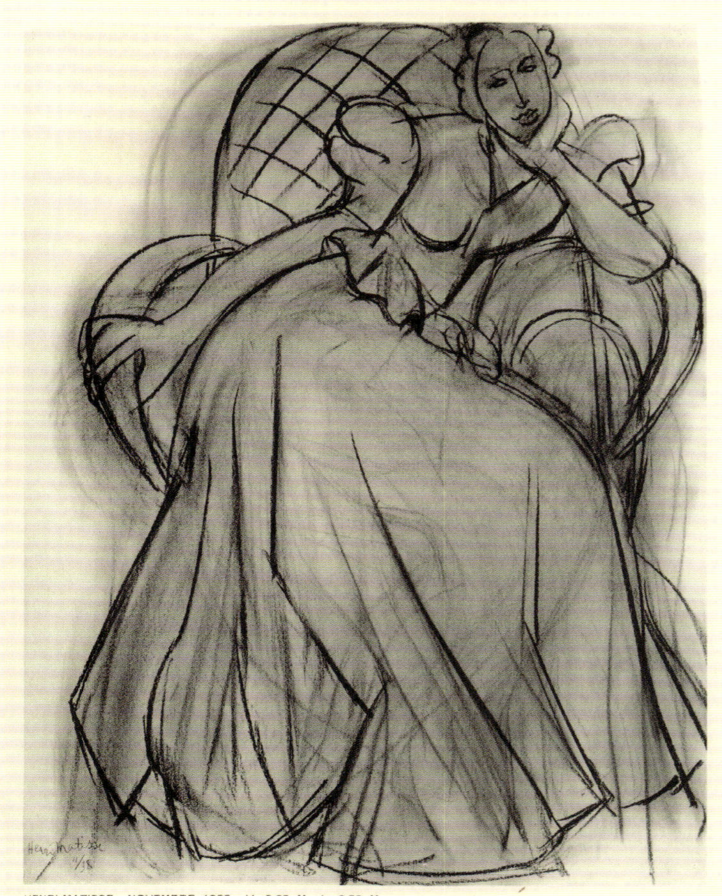

HENRI-MATISSE. NOVEMBRE 1938. H. 0.65 M. L. 0.50 M.

17

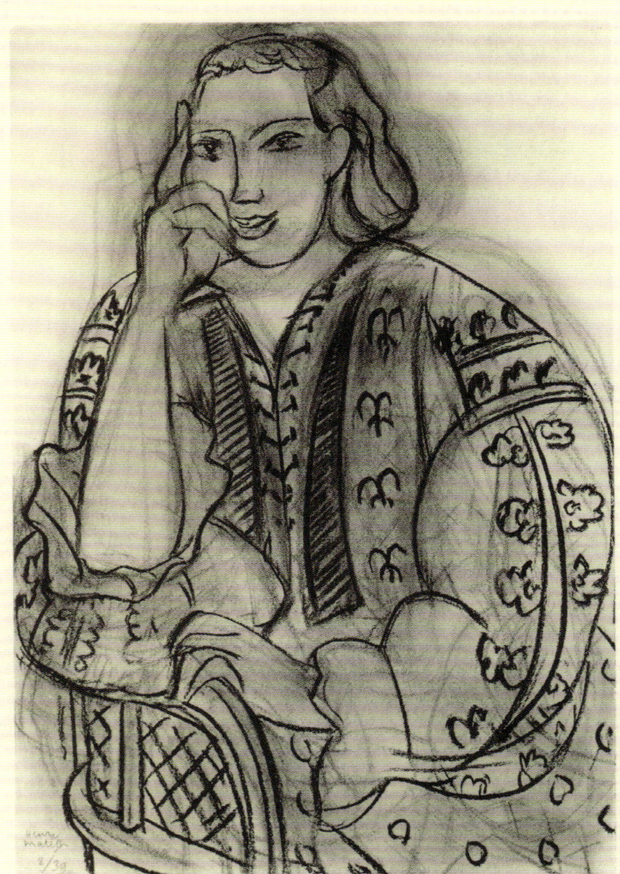

HENRI-MATISSE. FÉVRIER 1939. H. 0.56 M. L. 0.49 M.

24

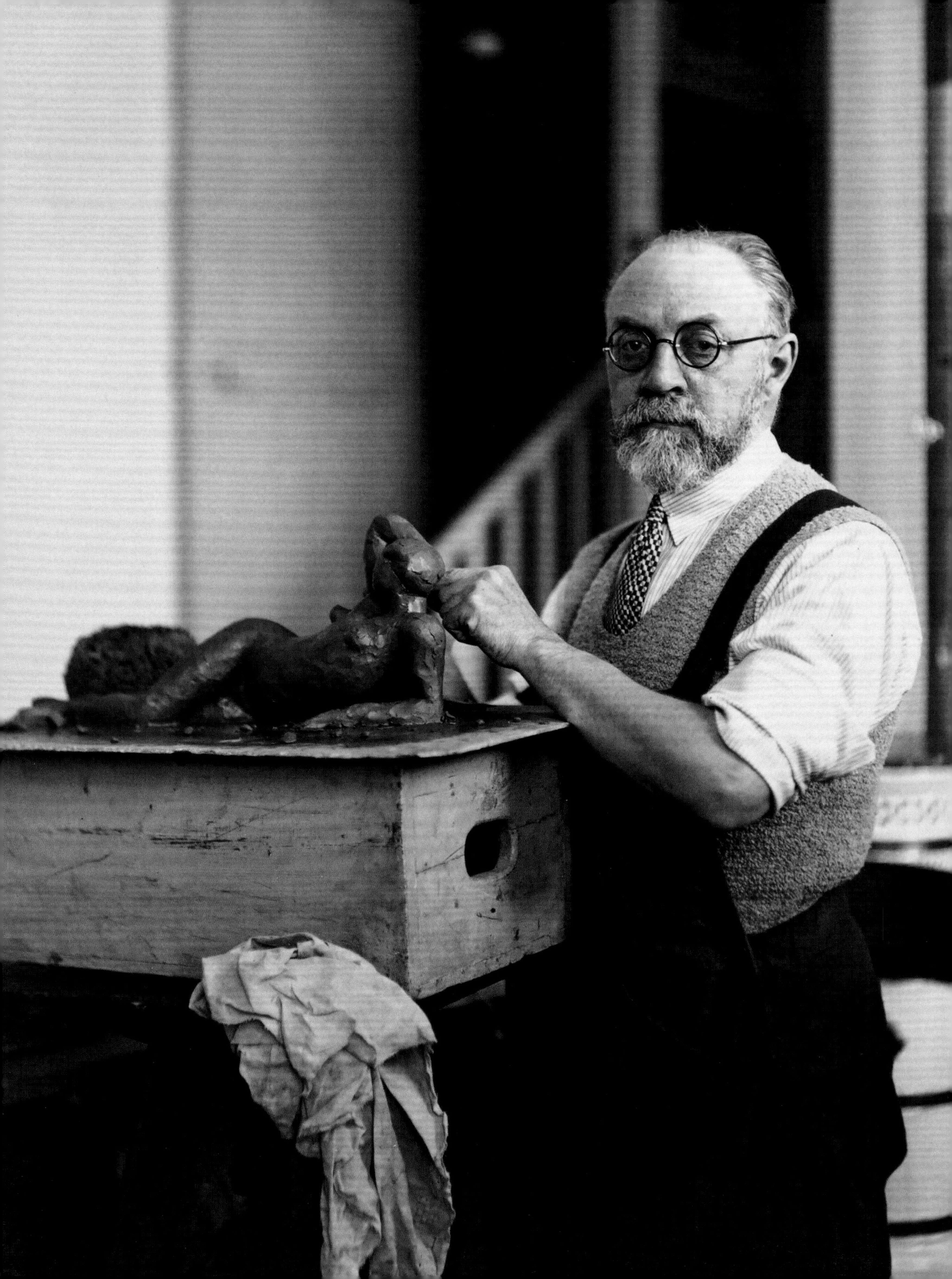

WORKS

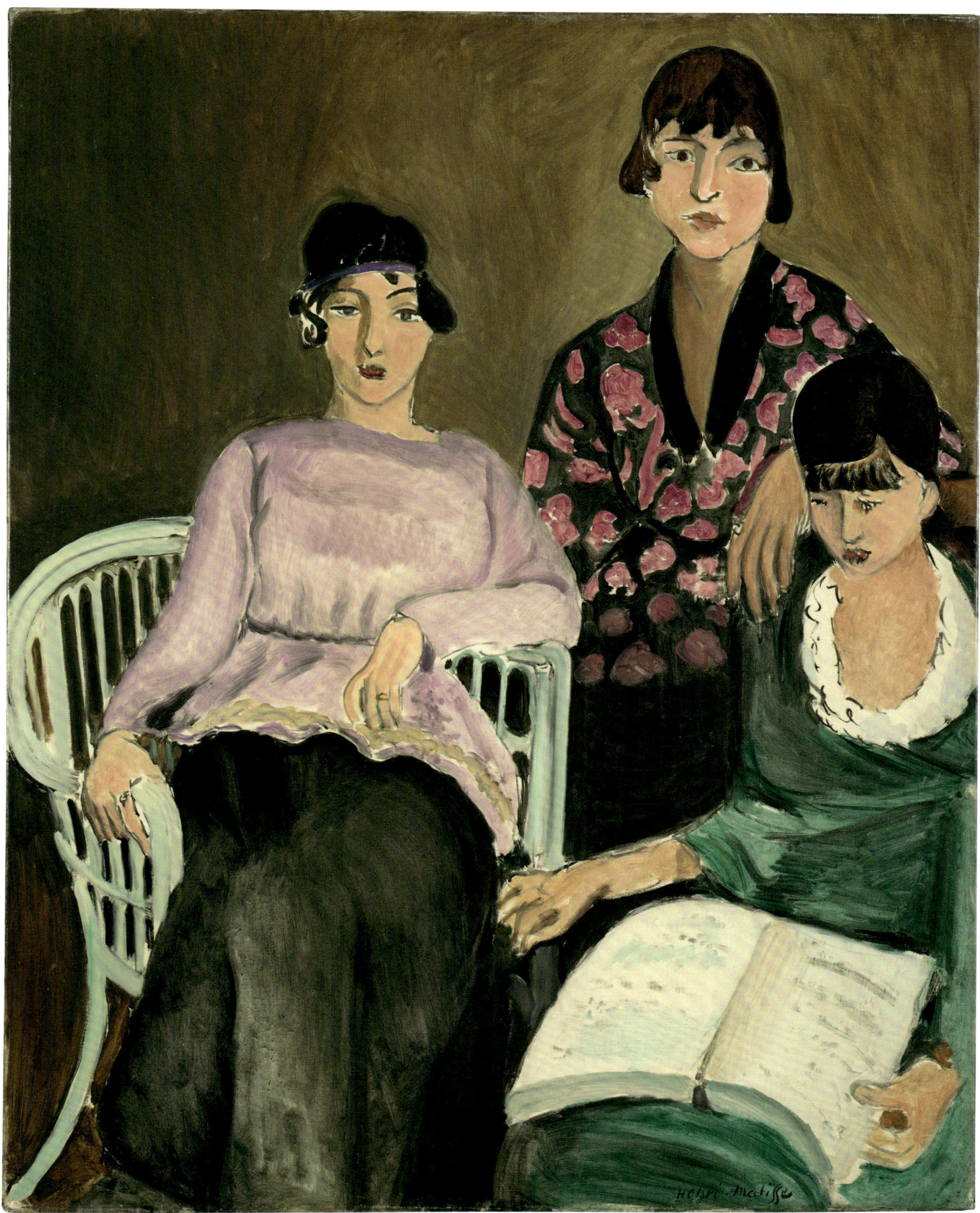

Previous page
65 (fig.)
Henri Matisse working on a sculpture [*Reclining Nude III*], c. 1929.
Photograph by Marc Lenoir
Archives Henri Matisse, Issy-les-Moulineaux

Above
66
The Three Sisters, 1917
Oil on canvas, 36 ¼ × 28 ¾ in. (92 × 73 cm)
Musée de l'Orangerie, Paris

THE THREE SISTERS

The art dealer and collector Paul Guillaume purchased this painting 66, now at the Musée de l'Orangerie, as part of the Walter-Guillaume Collection on May 7, 1926, at the Auguste Pellerin auction held at the Hôtel Drouot in Paris.[1] This was one of the major items in the private collection of Guillaume and figured prominently in his successive residences. The work was displayed over the sitting-room fireplace in his mansion on the Avenue de Messine in the eighth arrondissement of Paris, as can be seen from Tériade's illustrated reportage published in *Cahiers d'art* in 1927.[2] It is seen resting on the mantelpiece alongside works by Auguste Renoir on the right, André Derain's large-format *Harlequin and Pierrot* (c.1924; Musée de l'Orangerie, Paris) on the left, and non-Western sculptures (from Africa, Oceania, and Asia). The picture was also highlighted in the selection from Guillaume's personal collection exhibited two years later, in 1929, at the Galerie Bernheim-Jeune. The work belongs to a watershed moment in Matisse's output, around 1916–17, when he began experimenting with double or triple portraits, repeatedly employing the model Lorette. At that time the figure was one possible way for him to overcome a tendency toward abstraction.

The three female models in contemporary dress stand out against a gray-brown background. Two of the young women are looking in our direction, while the third appears engrossed in her reading. The painter here strikes a perfect balance between seemingly irreconcilable elements: the variety of poses, the clashing colors, the juxtaposition of multiple perspectives, the influences of different pictorial traditions—from the Japanese to the Byzantine—as well as a nod to Manet. It stands as one of the artist's masterpieces from this period and may be compared to the trio in the Barnes Foundation in Philadelphia, in which, in one of the paintings, we again find the motif of the three "sisters," this time wearing exotic costumes foreshadowing the odalisques of the 1920s (*Three Sisters with Grey Background*, 1917), or to another trio in modern dress (*Three Sisters and "The Rose Marble Table,"* 1917), also at the Barnes, that is very similar to the Musée de l'Orangerie version. This is one of the very few works that Guillaume purchased at public auction, doubtless remembering the canvases sold to Albert C. Barnes. The painting was also reproduced in issues 5 and 6 of *Cahiers d'art* in 1931, in an advertising insert for Guillaume's business.

CÉCILE GIRARDEAU

1 A wealthy industrialist, Auguste Pellerin owned several of the painter's pictures, including *The Three Sisters,* which he acquired through the Galerie Bernheim-Jeune. The Pellerin auction catalogue mentions the works under the title *Group of Three Girls* (no. 66).

2 E. Tériade, "Nos enquêtes: Entretien avec Paul Guillaume," *Feuilles volantes* [supplement to *Cahiers d'art*], no. 1 (1927): 1–2.

67
Arabesque, 1924
Transfer lithograph,
19 1/8 × 12 11/16 in. (48.6 × 32.2 cm)
The Museum of Modern Art,
New York

68
Odalisque with a Tambourine,
1925–26
Oil on canvas, 29 1/4 × 21 7/8 in.
(74.3 × 55.6 cm)
The Museum of Modern Art,
New York

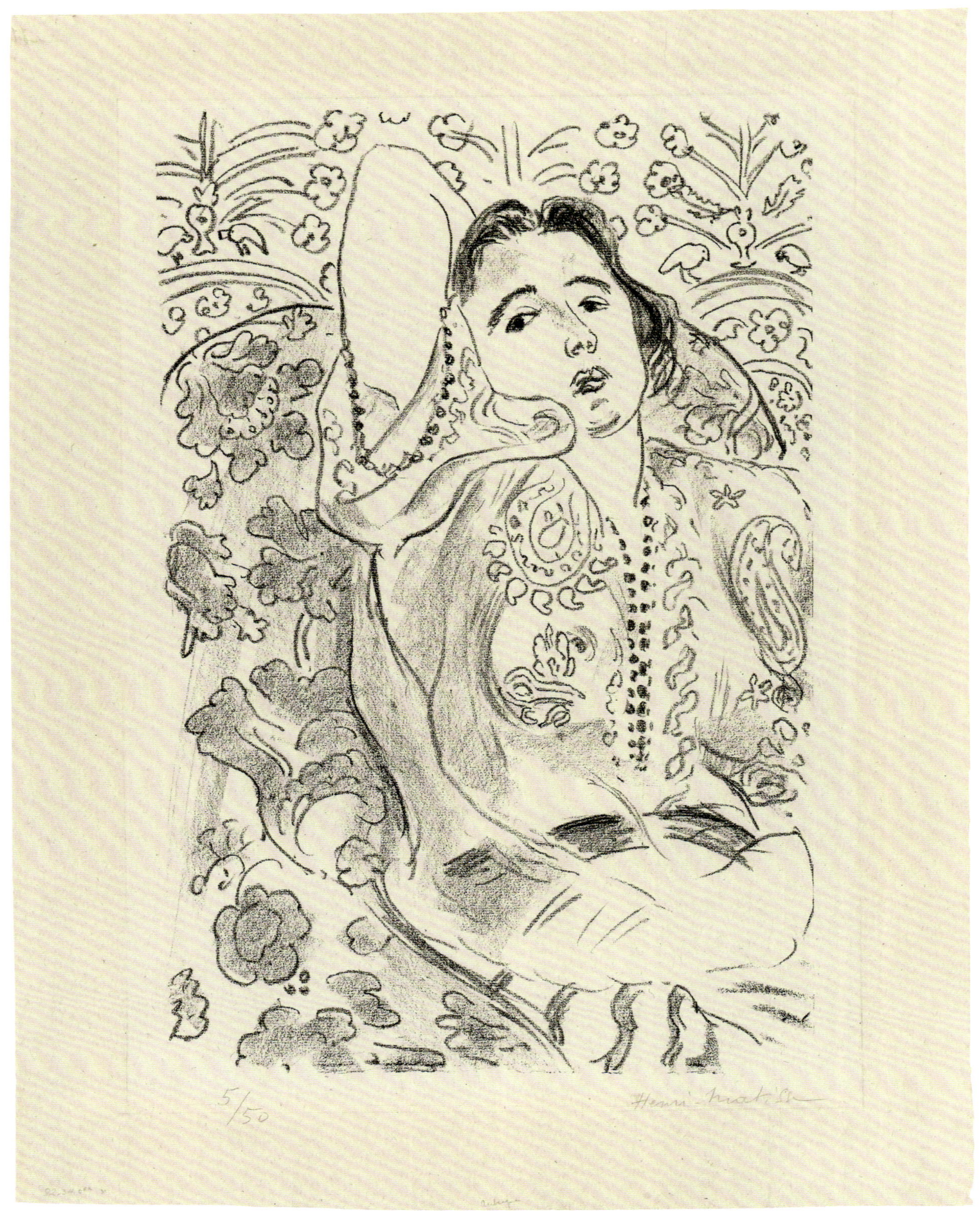

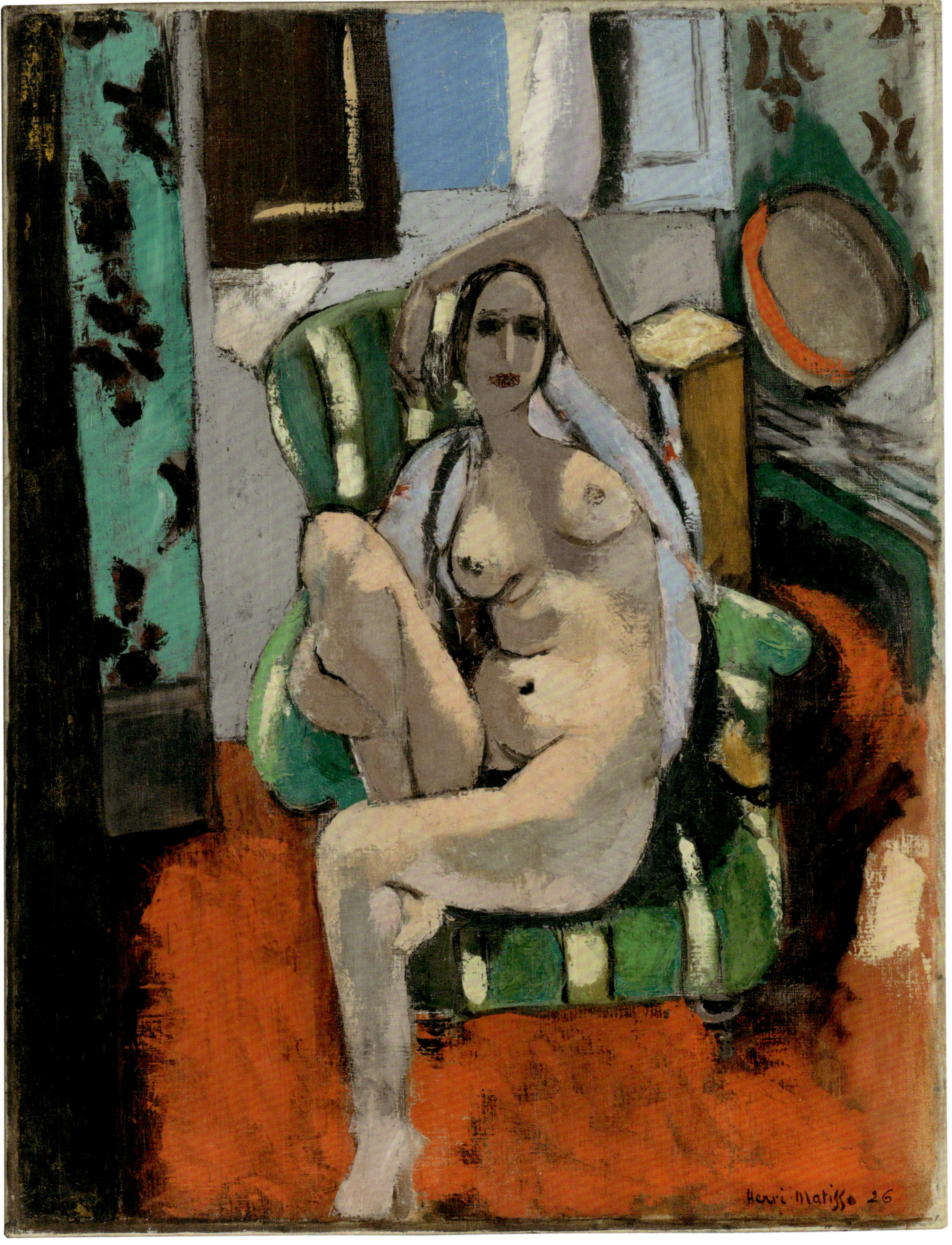
Henri Matisse 26

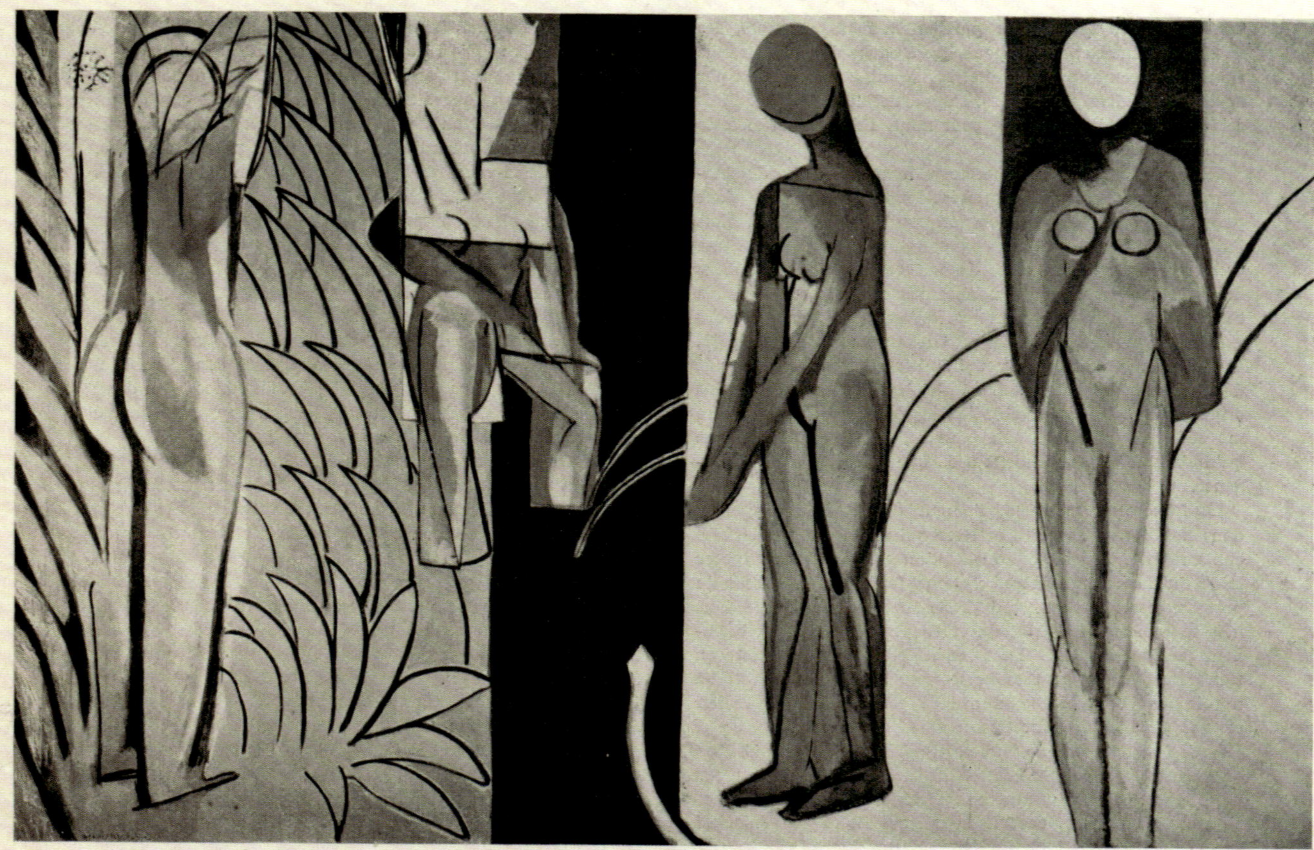

Henri Matisse, “ Jeunes Filles au bain ” exposé à la galerie Paul Guillaume, époque fauve, terminé en 1918.

HENRI MATISSE ET LA PEINTURE PURE

Mon vieux camarade Metzinger se rappelle peut-être aussi bien que moi le jour mémorable où Henri Matisse s'attarda pour la première fois devant une toile de Picasso. C'était, je crois, en 1909 et la phrase célèbre du père Degas s'était déjà vulgarisée, que les écrivains expliquent la peinture sans la comprendre. Abandonnant à Gleizes et à Metzinger la critique, je me contentais de tâcher de comprendre la peinture sans éprouver le besoin de l'expliquer aux autres. Pourtant j'eus bien l'impression qu'il y avait brusquement quelque chose de changé dans le monde de ce jour, de cette minute où Henri Matisse, se retournant vers Metzinger et moi-même nous dit, cherchant un mot pour définir sa pensée, précise dans l'esprit, mais vague encore dans le mot qui devait l'exprimer : « Ça, c'est du cubisme... je veux dire par là un pas immense vers la technique pure ».

Et Matisse ajouta : « Nous y viendrons tous. »

A vrai dire, Matisse y venait déjà. Depuis il y est revenu, mais par un autre chemin.

A cette époque, son art prestigieux versait à nos jeunes cervelles l'un des vins les plus puissants que notre ivresse ait bu. Nous étions envoûtés par le charme. Mais j'avoue qu'à cette époque où l'œuvre du Maître se traduisait surtout par des recherches touchant aux couleurs, unités magnifiques obtenues par la confusion des nuances les plus diverses, rapports mystérieux entre les valeurs les plus imprévues, je fus l'un des premiers à admirer sans réserve, en lui, le dessinateur. Sans doute le trait de Matisse n'avait pas l'acuité de celui de Toulouse-Lautrec ni la force définitive de celui de Rodin, mais j'y voyais je ne sais quel charme de langueur subtile, je ne sais quelle exactitude vibrante, pleine de séduction et de paresse. Lautrec, c'est le mouvement lui-même, indiscontinu. Matisse c'est un temps défini

239

69 (fig.)
Sylvain Bonmariage,
“Henri Matisse et la peinture pure,” *Cahiers d'art*, 1926, no. 9, p. 239
Éditions Cahiers d'Art, Paris

PAUL GUILLAUME AND MATISSE

An influential figure in the Parisian market for modern and African and Oceanic art from 1914 to 1934, Paul Guillaume had shown an early interest in Matisse during the years of World War I. While he never became the artist's official dealer (not for lack of trying), up to a hundred works by the artist reportedly passed through his hands at one time or another.

From 1917 to 1926 the contract renewed between Matisse and the Galerie Bernheim-Jeune covered only half of the artist's output, and Guillaume jumped at this opportunity to showcase the painter's pictures in his gallery and enter the market for his works. For the opening of his new space on the Rue Saint-Honoré in the eighth arrondissement of Paris early in 1918, he pulled off a masterstroke: the first-ever exhibition placing the two giants Matisse and Picasso in confrontation.[1] This "[boxing] match," as Matisse called it,[2] was orchestrated skillfully and expeditiously, much to Matisse's initial annoyance, for he had no desire to hold any large-scale event featuring his painting during the war. But in the end he sent Guillaume a telegram saying: "HOLD YOUR EXHIBITION GOOD LUCK – MATISSE."[3] The catalogue for the exhibition was prefaced by the poet Guillaume Apollinaire, and there was an extensive poster campaign all over Paris and newsreels helping to immortalize three of the paintings displayed in the show, one of them being Matisse's *Studio, Quai Saint-Michel* (1916; Phillips Collection, Washington).[4]

Feted in the *Feuilles volantes* (Loose leafs) supplement of *Cahiers d'art* in 1927 with a report on his private collection, Guillaume is presented as a dealer-cum-collector and a connoisseur. The article, by Tériade, describes paintings by Matisse as being "spontaneous as sketches, but filled with eternity,"[5] and as placed alongside works by Pablo Picasso, Paul Cézanne, André Derain, and non-Western sculptures in his apartment located in a mansion on Avenue de Messine.

Guillaume had already seen the latest activity at his gallery draw the journal's attention at the time of his purchase of two major works from Matisse. From October 1 to 14, 1926, he displayed *The Piano Lesson* (1916; Modern Museum of Art, New York), and *Bathers by a River* 20 | 69. The event enabled a Parisian audience to rediscover the Matisse of the bold, synthetic large-format compositions at a time when—during his Nice period—he was focusing mostly on odalisques. Described in *Cahiers d'art* as a dealer "doubling as a highly enlightened art lover," Guillaume was, according to the art critic, doing "a significant propaganda service for French art by exposing two Matisses to the publicity of an exhibition."[6]

Guillaume also extended this promotional activity outside of France, notably acting as a go-between for the purchase of several canvases by Matisse when Albert C. Barnes was building his collection in the United States in the mid-1920s. He had a hand in the acquisition of some of the masterpieces at Barnes's foundation in Merion, just outside Philadelphia, such as *The Joy of Life* (1905–6), *The Seated Riffian* (1912), and *The Music Lesson* (1917).

The artist and the dealer also shared an interest in non-Western art. Thus the album *Sculptures nègres*, published in 1917, and with forewords by Apollinaire and Guillaume, includes a photograph of a work in Matisse's personal holdings, presented under the caption *Idole de la région de Bobo-Dioulasso (Soudan)* (Idol from the Bobo-Dioulasso Region [Sudan]).

The ten works by Matisse currently held in the Walter-Guillaume Collection at the Musée de l'Orangerie belong for the most part to the artist's Nice period and are not necessarily representative of what defined the dealer's taste for Matisse. He is thought to have had up to twenty-five Matisses in his private collection.[7]

CÉCILE GIRARDEAU

1 The exhibition ran from January 23 to February 15, 1918.

2 "I have received the catalogue for the Guillaume, which I call the Carpentier Joe Janette match [*sic*]," Henri Matisse [HM]–Amélie Matisse, January 26, 1918, quoted by Anne Baldassari, "Exposer Matisse et Picasso. Note historique," in *Matisse–Picasso*, ed. Elizabeth Cowling, Anne Baldassari, and John Elderfield, exh. cat. (London: Tate, 2002), 361–65 (364).

3 HM–Paul Guillaume, telegram, January 20, 1918, Documentation du Musée de l'Orangerie, Paris, Fonds Alain Bouret, DOCOR 2011.0.63.1068.

4 Pathé-Gaumont newsreel archives, 1918, inv. 1805GJ 00004.

5 E. Tériade, "Nos enquêtes: Entretien avec Paul Guillaume," *Feuilles volantes* [supplement to *Cahiers d'art*], no. 1 (1927): 1–2.

6 Sylvain Bonmariage, "Henri Matisse et la peinture pure," *Cahiers d'art*, no. 9 (1926): 239–41.

7 Guillaume–HM, February 17, 1931, in which he declares ownership of twenty-five works by the artist including three sculptures, cited in Claudine Grammont, ed., *Tout Matisse* (Paris: Robert Laffont, 2018), 405.

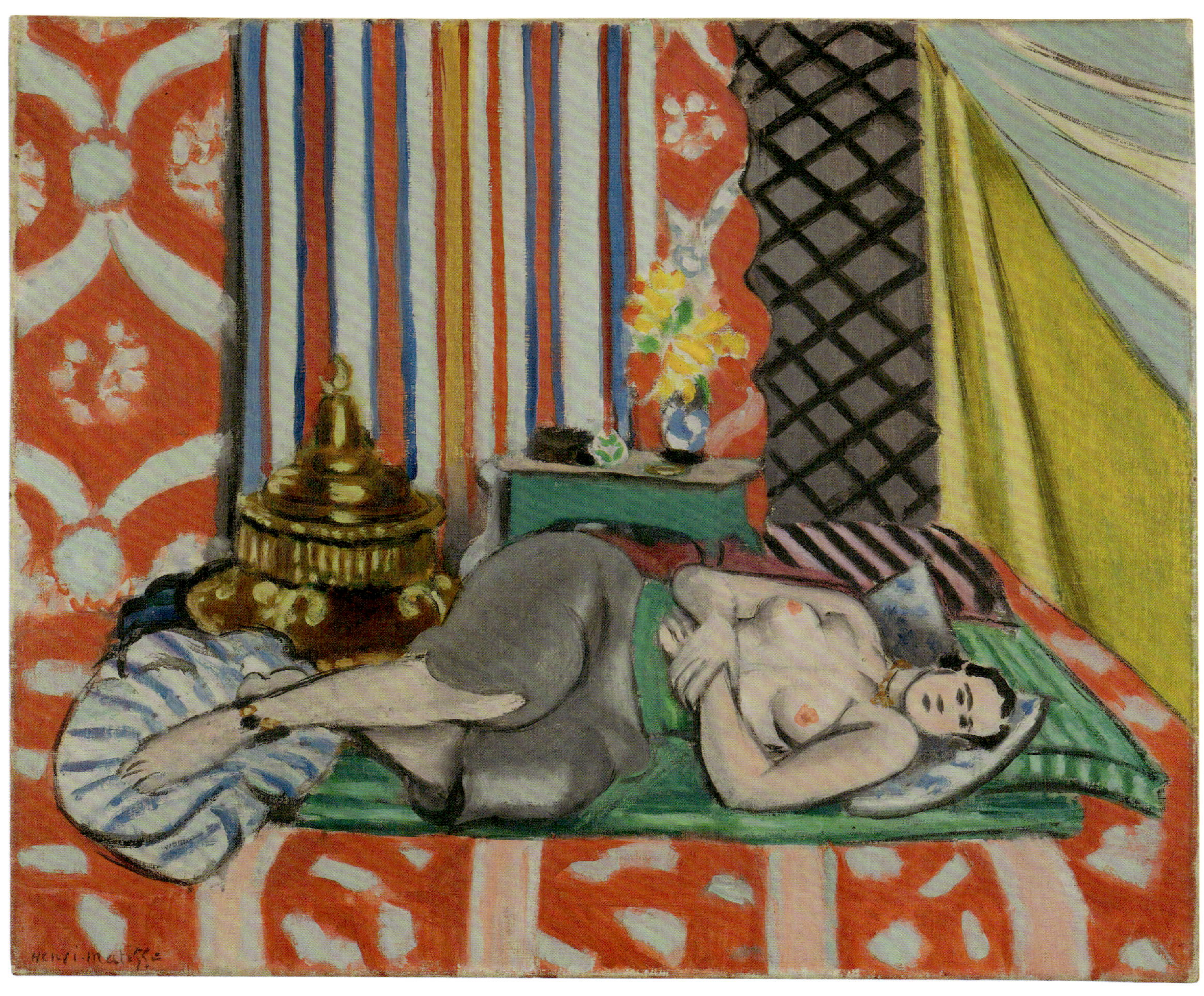

70
Odalisque in Gray Pantaloons,
1926–27
Oil on canvas, 21 ¼ × 25 ⁹⁄₁₆ in.
(54 × 65 cm)
Musée de l'Orangerie, Paris

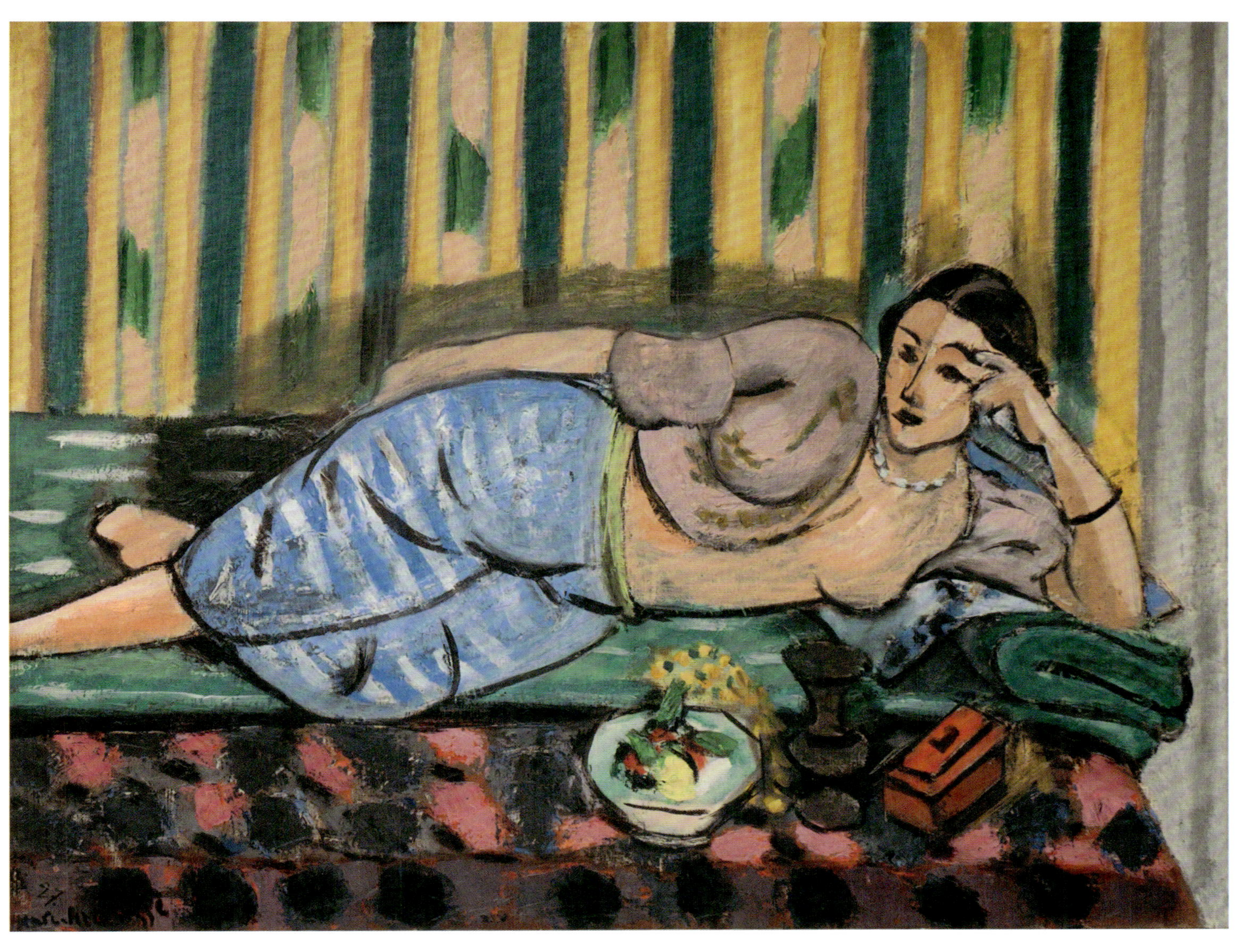

71
Odalisque with Red Box,
1927
Oil on canvas, 20 ⅛ × 25 ⅝ in.
(50 × 65 cm)
Musée Matisse Nice

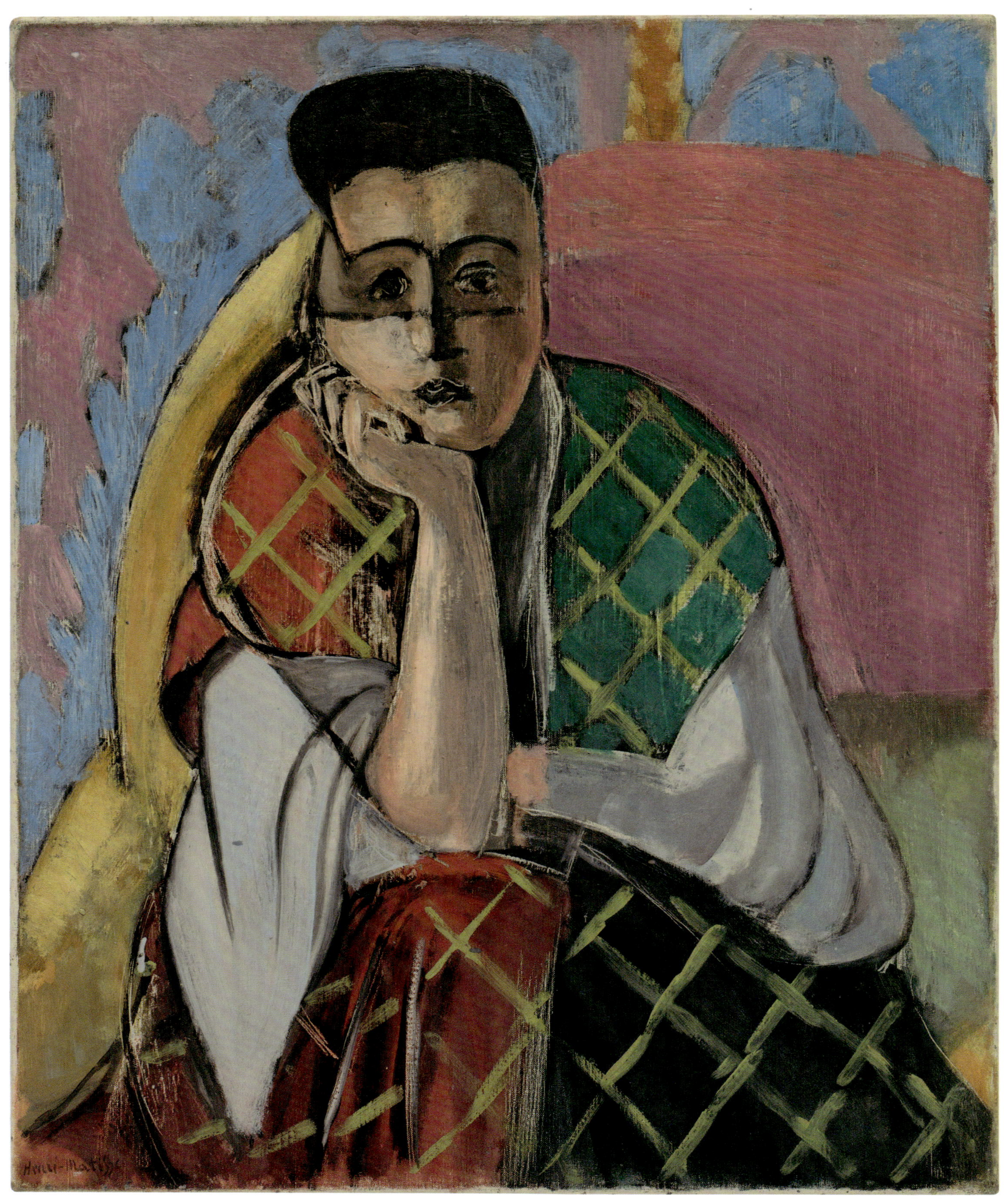

72
Woman with a Veil, 1927
Oil on canvas, 24 ¼ × 19 ¾ in.
(61.6 × 50.2 cm)
The Museum of Modern Art,
New York

WOMAN WITH A VEIL

The final picture Matisse painted of the model Henriette Darricarrère, during the winter of 1926, *Woman with a Veil* is a transitional work infused with the melancholy gaze—at once penetrating and vacant—of this woman who sat for him for the best part of seven years 72. The dilated pupil effaces the white of her right eye, thereby piercing the surface of what resembles a mask more than a face. This semi-abstract stylization evinces the inspiration that Matisse drew from the iconography of non-Western art as he shook off the Western mimetic tradition. Some of the objects in his collection of African art, begun in 1906, have been compared to the schematization he inflicts upon Darricarrère's features here.[1]

The helmet of her hair, her veil turned into an element of geometrization (a far cry from its usual orientalizing function), her asymmetrical chin, the excrescence of her right cheek—distorted as if she had a dislocated jaw—and the accentuation of the bridge of the nose and of the single line her delineating eyebrows at once harden and simplify her features. From this severe countenance comes a feeling of unreality. It is with this same hardness that he carves and breaks Darricarrère's head into pieces in 1929 in the third version of her sculpted portrait 80. Composed of roughly hewn volumes fitted together, the face mutates into an object.

Despite the richness of the colors all around her and the toile de Jouy vibrating in the background of *Woman with a Veil*, Darricarrère seems absent, stripped of a corporeality concealed by four pieces of checked fabric that weigh her down more than they clothe her. Everything, down to the stump of her wrist, placed at the edge of the bluish gray of a puffed-up sleeve, points to an overall principle of whittling away the body, which is swallowed up by the invasive yellow criss-cross pattern on her garment. The voluptuous curves of her nudity have either disappeared or migrated to the curves of the monumental armchair encasing her. Some see in this fading the sign of her exhaustion after some trying modeling sessions, but also her sadness caused by the certainty that with this work a friendship is coming to an end.

Of the nudity exalted in the serialized exotic fantasies of Darricarrère from the 1920s, only the flesh of her forearm remains. The sensuality of the odalisque painting so intensely linked to her slender, athletic litheness has been erased, suppressed by a return to the formal research of the 1910s and the dialogue with Cubism that Matisse had abandoned upon arriving in Nice. Evidence of this is his use of the scraping technique employed for the *Portrait of Mme Matisse* (1913; State Hermitage Museum, St. Petersburg) and the *Portrait of Yvonne Landsberg* (1914; Philadelphia Museum of Art). With the tip of his brush, he incises the pictorial material so as to highlight the contour of the sitter's fingers, mouth, arm, and the folds of her clothing, but also to inject a little life into the portrait.

As a double farewell both to the woman and to the pictorial style of the Nice period, this work, described by Louis Aragon as "just as tragic as the Mona Lisa,"[2] announces the crisis that would paralyze Matisse in the early 1930s.

ALIX AGRET

1 Suzanne Preston Blier, "Portraiture and Masking," in *Matisse in the Studio*, ed. Ellen McBreen and Helen Burnham, exh. cat. (Boston: MFA Publications, 2017), 111.

2 Louis Aragon, *Henri Matisse, roman* (1971; repr., Paris: Gallimard, 1998), 550.

THE YELLOW DRESS

The Yellow Dress is a crisis painting 73. It embodies in Matisse's work the transition from the first period in Nice (1917–29) to the watershed of the 1930s. The extended date next to the artist's signature, 1929–31, betrays the unresolved issues and doubts that were plaguing him during this period.

In the winter of 1930, Matisse left Nice for New York, and crossed the United States on his way to Tahiti. On his return, in the summer of 1930, he determinedly revisited *The Yellow Dress*, but it was during another voyage to the United States that he apparently found a solution: "I could feel what I needed to do, that is to say the weakness of my painting's construction and where I could take it from there."[1] A study of the set of preparatory drawings, fourteen of which are held at the Baltimore Museum of Art, sheds light on this long process.

The Yellow Dress is in keeping with the interiors of the first Nice period thanks to the decorative and colorful profusion of the background: the pattern of the floor tiles, the lavender hanging causing the walls and curtains to vibrate, the windows and shutters adding horizontal and vertical striping to the space. But unlike the odalisques, who often get lost in the scenery, here the model, sitting in the center of the composition, fully frontal, erect and hieratic, strikes us with her almost sculptural monumentality. The seating disappears completely under the puffy skirt of the sumptuous yellow and shimmering green taffeta dress, to the point where the sitter appears to be levitating.[2] The wide brim of the matching hat, painted like a halo around the face, recalls Byzantine icons and adds to the work's mystical dimension.

As he did for *The Yellow Hat* and *Woman with a Madras Hat* 84, Matisse used as his model Lisette Löwengard, a young girl he spotted in 1928 at an antique dealer's shop in the Masséna district of Nice 167. In a 1989 interview looking back on the five years she spent with the Matisses, Löwengard recalled the artist's tastes in fashion: "Matisse fell in love with those dresses in which he took obvious pleasure in painting me, but also in photographing me."[3] The article is illustrated with a photograph of the model wearing the famous yellow dress, in the same pose as in the painting. This photo is reminiscent of the "tableau vivant" that Matisse staged to welcome Etta Cone, the buyer of the painting, upon her visit to his studio during the summer of 1933.[4]

LAURENCE SCHLOSSER

1 Henri Matisse, interview with Tériade, *L'Intransigeant*, October 19, 20, and 27, 1930, reproduced in Henri Matisse, *Écrits et propos sur l'art*, ed. Dominique Fourcade (Paris: Hermann, 1989), 101.

2 Yve-Alain Bois, ed., *Matisse in the Barnes Foundation* (Philadelphia: Barnes Foundation / London: Thames & Hudson, 2015), 1:112.

3 C. de Pesloüan, "Matisse photographe," *Madame Figaro*, November 25, 1989.

4 See the letter from Etta Cone to Fred Cone, July 22, 1933, Cone Papers, Baltimore Museum of Art Archives.

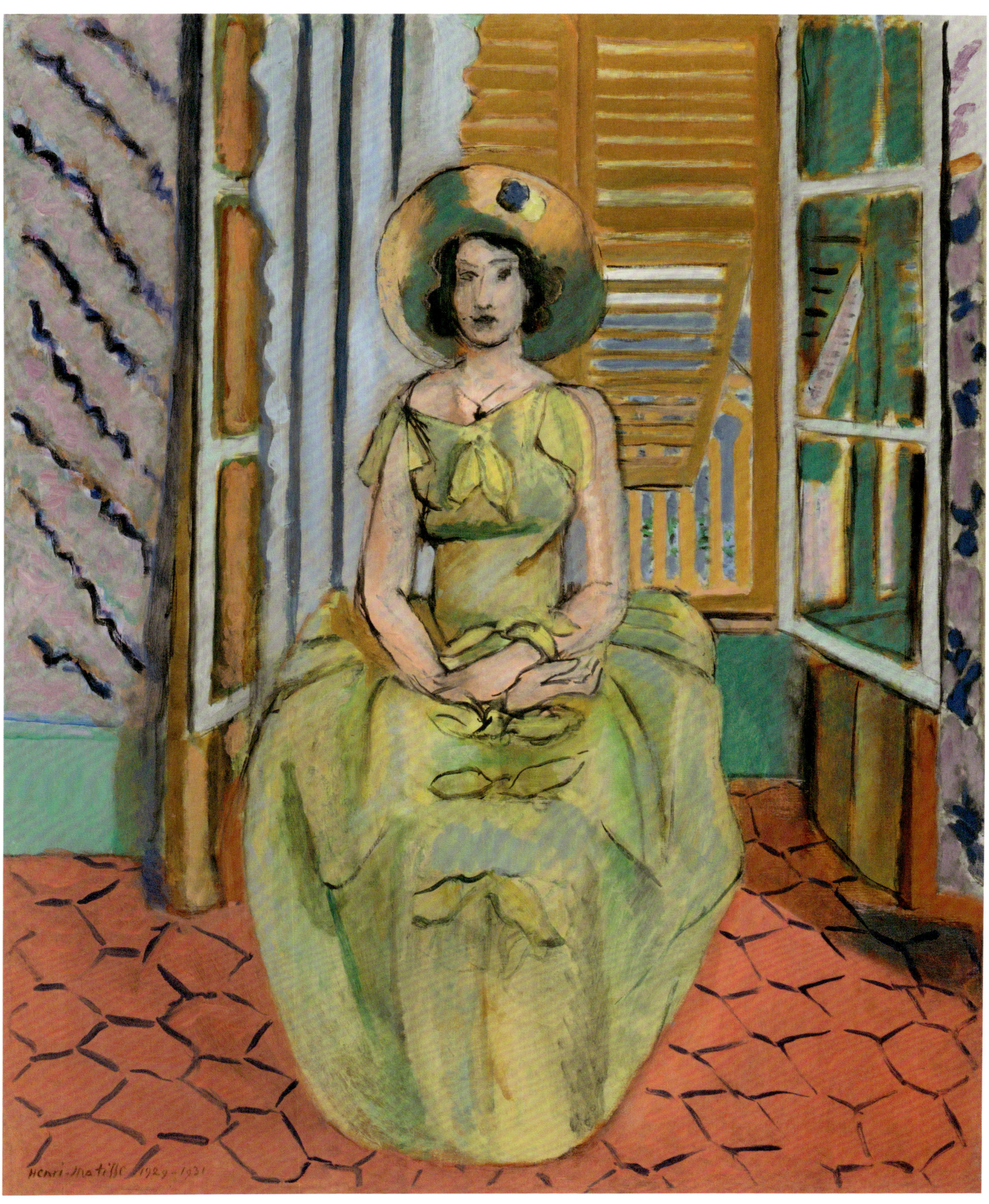

73
The Yellow Dress, 1929–31
Oil on canvas,
39 9/16 × 32 1/8 in.
(100.5 × 81.6 cm)
Baltimore Museum of Art

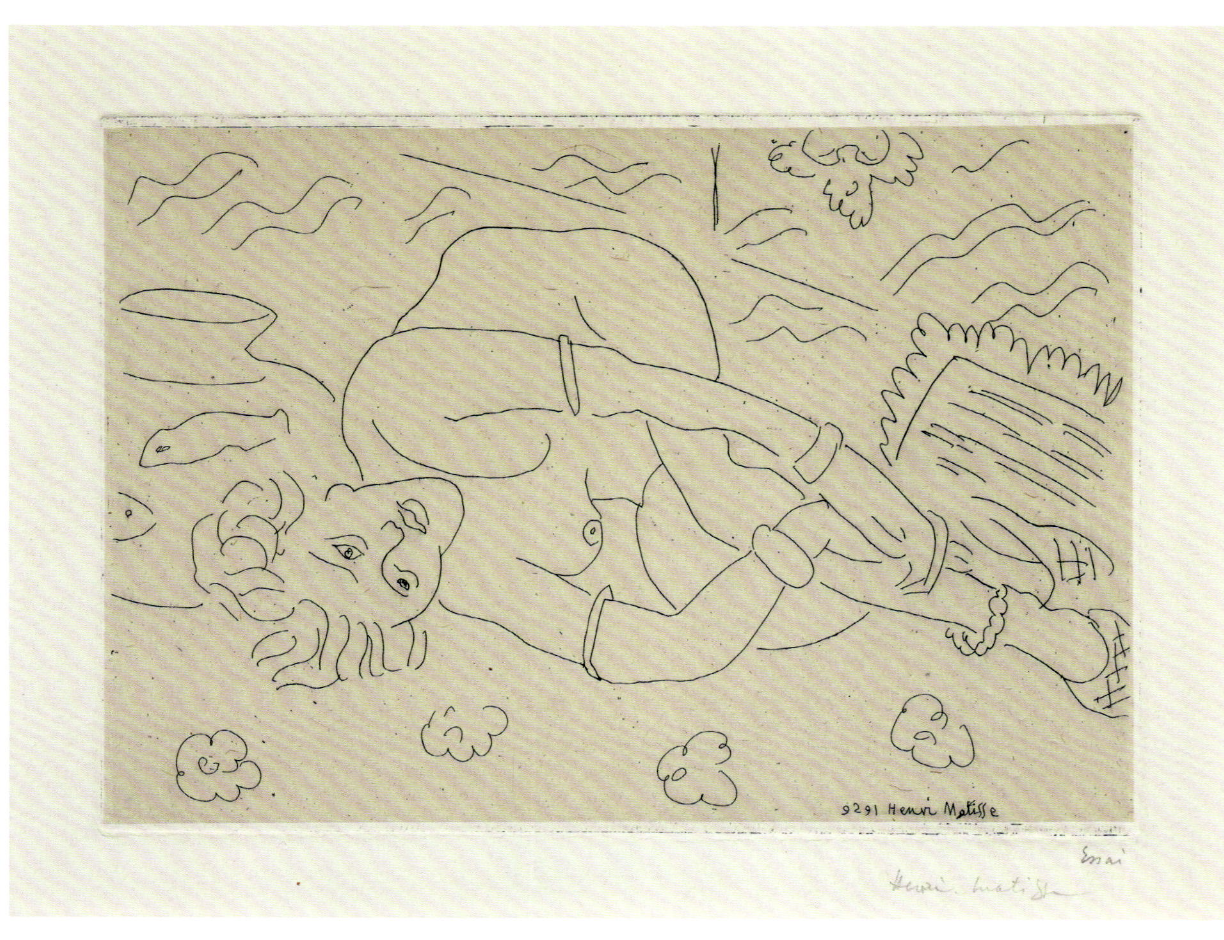

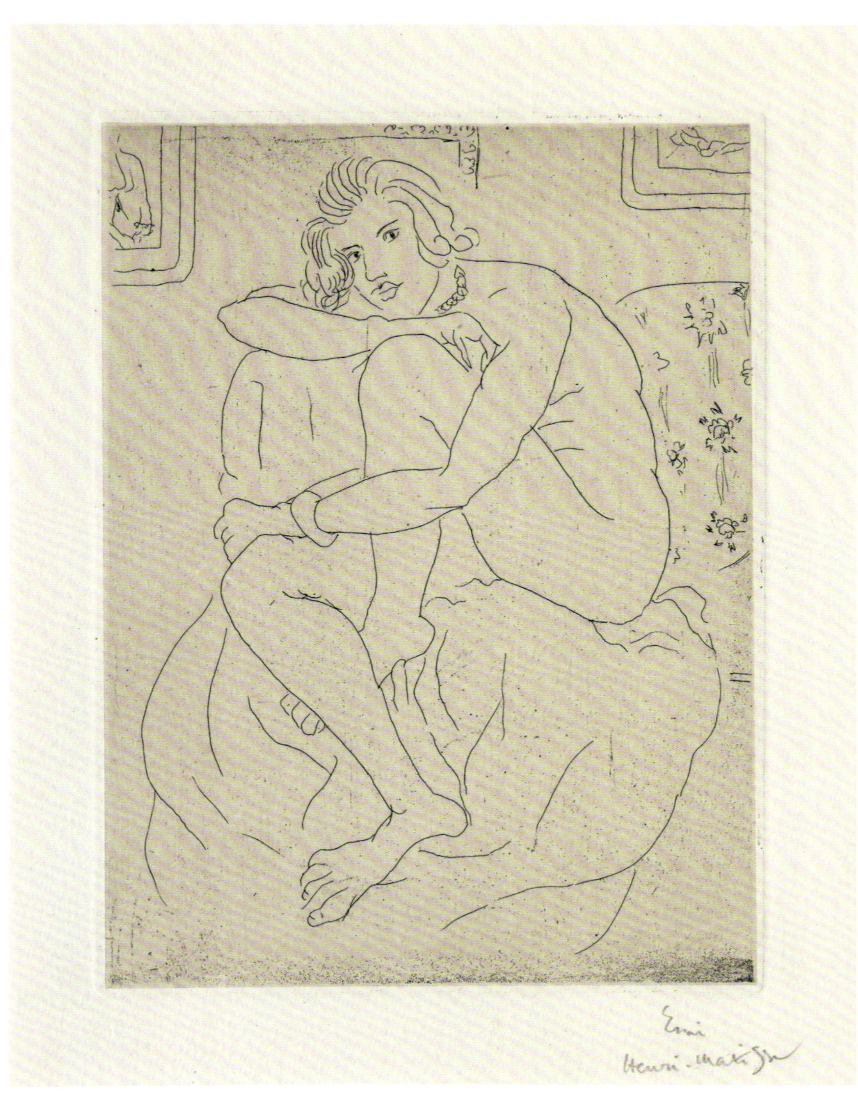

74
Study for Upside-Down Nude, 1929
Etching printed chine collé, 6 ⅝ × 9 ½ in. (16.8 × 24 cm)
Musée Matisse Nice

75
Seated Nude, Hands on Knees, 1929
Etching printed chine collé, 8 ¹⁄₁₆ × 6 in. (20.4 × 15.3 cm)
Musée Matisse Nice

76
Nude Seated in the Studio, 1929
Etching printed chine collé, 8 ⅛ × 6 in. (20.6 × 15.2 cm)
The Metropolitan Museum of Art, New York

77
Figure with Face Partly Missing, Seated in an Interior, 1929
Etching printed chine collé, 5 ⅝ × 8 ⁹⁄₁₆ in. (14.3 × 21.7 cm)
Musée Départemental Matisse, Le Cateau-Cambrésis

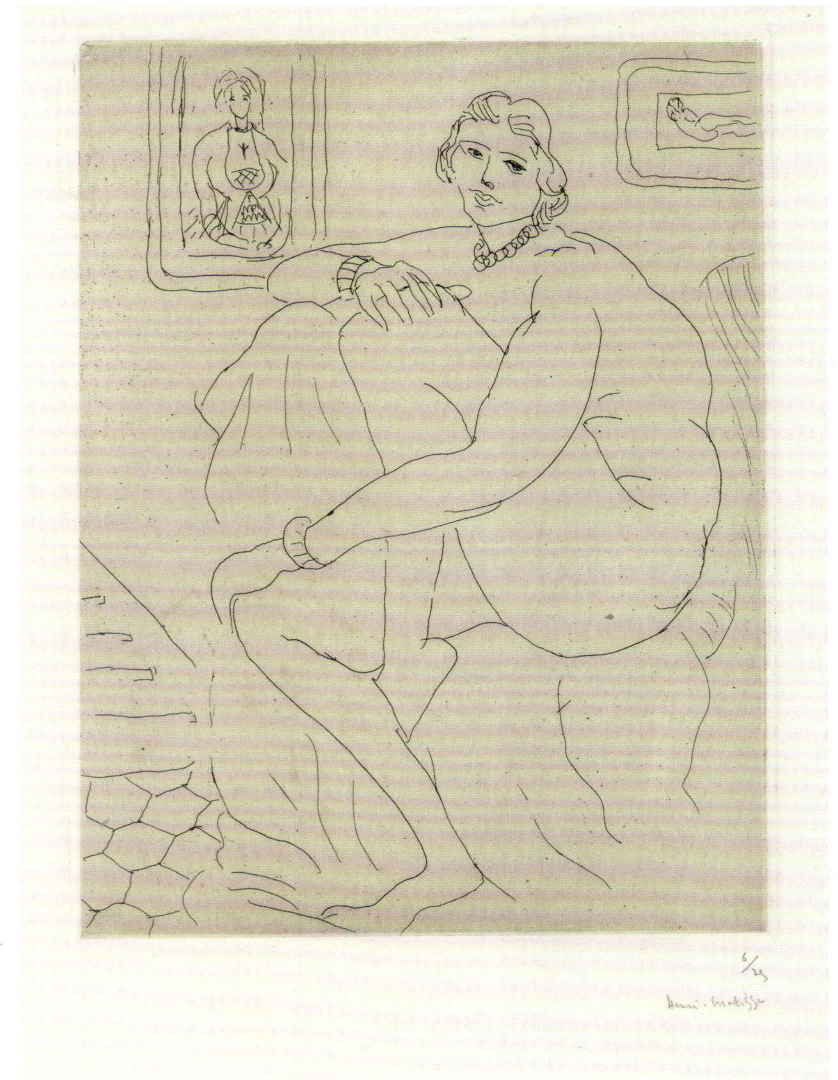

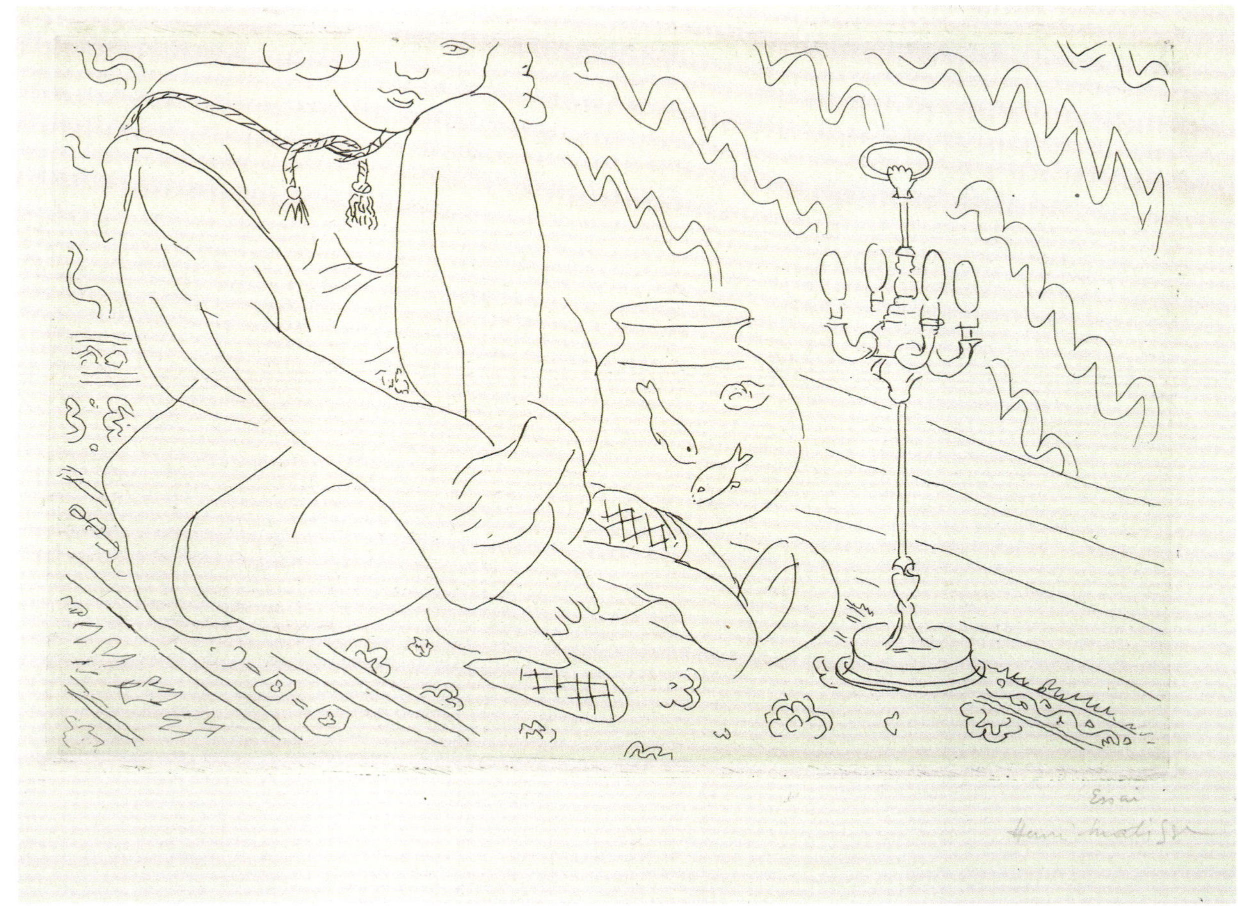

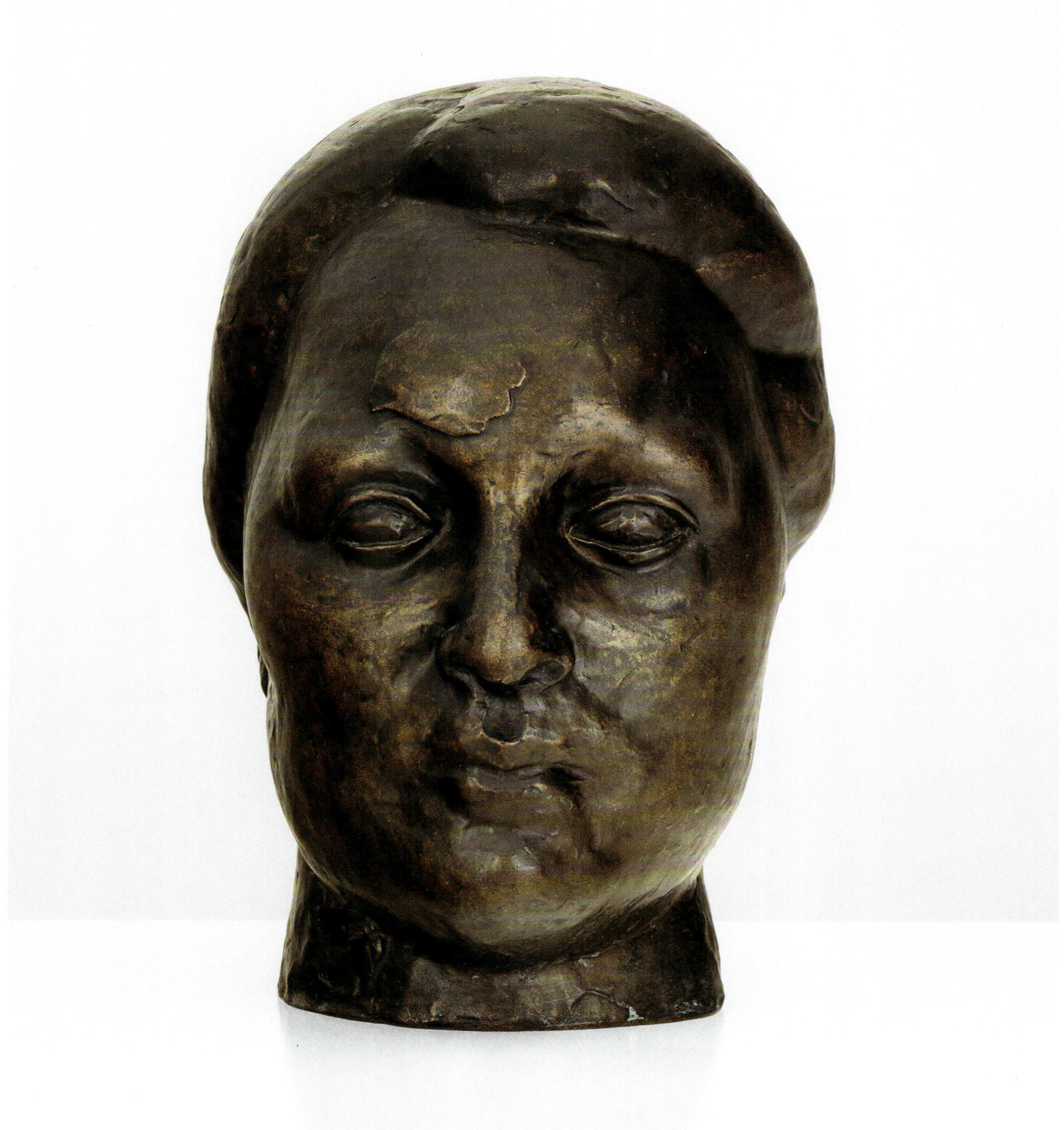

78
Henriette I, 1925
Bronze, 11 3/16 × 7 1/16 × 9 1/16 in.
(28.4 × 18 × 23 cm)
Musée d'Orsay, Paris, held at the Musée Matisse Nice, 1978

HENRIETTE I, II, III

These three portraits of Henriette Darricarrère, each sculpted two years apart, illustrate the process of metamorphosis set up by Matisse for several series of sculptures (the five *Jeannettes* and the four *Backs*) but used in his pictorial practice as well.[1] The photographs of his paintings taken at different stages, according to a procedure he put in place in the 1930s, reveal the sometimes radical transformations made to the composition as the work progressed 111.

The first version of *Henriette* (1925 78)—executed directly after Darricarrère and, unlike the other two, cast in bronze after the artist's death—is the one bearing the closest physical resemblance to the model. The following two versions were done from memory, taking as their starting point a cast of the previous sculpture along with several study drawings. Matisse was also thoroughly imbued with the objects laid out in his studio, as attested by several photographs taken around 1926 of the artist sculpting 164. Of particular note are the correspondences with his African Baoulé and Gelede masks.

With *Henriette II*, also known as *Stout Head* (1927 79),[2] Matisse performs a definite stylization and abstraction of the features: the swelling of the face is exaggerated, the appearance of the bulging eyes is amplified by heavily rimmed eyelids, and the hair is treated as a succession of ovoid masses. "*Henriette I* is still a representation of the head, whereas *Henriette II* is no more than a 'head' sign," Pierre Schneider observed.[3] The perfectly smooth surface, possibly reminiscent of Aristide Maillol's manner or Jacques Lipchitz's portrait of *Gertrude Stein* (1920; Musée National d'Art Moderne–Centre Pompidou, Paris), is quite unusual for Matisse, who liked to leave traces of the modeling in the material. It was in fact by taking issue with this overly smooth material that he sculpted *Henriette III* (1929 80). The face, especially the jaw and cheeks, is recarved, with the knife marks left visible, restoring an expressiveness that seemed to have disappeared from *Henriette II*. The eyebrows, now two protruding arches joined at the nose, make the expression almost stern. The base, having become an integral part of the work, emphasizes its objectality.

Through such formal about-turns allowing him to extricate himself from the individuality of the sitter, Matisse was doubtless seeking to transcribe his own subjectivity: "The essential expression of a work depends almost entirely on the projection of the artist's feeling; after his model and not her organic exactness."[4]

LAURENCE SCHLOSSER

1 This connection, in Matisse's work, between painting and sculpture is also put forward in a review of the *Sculptures de Matisse* exhibition at the Galerie Pierre (Paris, June–July 1930) published in *Cahiers d'art*, no. 5 (1930): 275: "Matisse's sculptural research goes further than his sculpture and shows us the deepest workings of his mind. It is moreover essential to his pictorial work."

2 Alfred H. Barr, *Matisse: His Art and His Public* (New York: Museum of Modern Art, 1951), 217.

3 Pierre Schneider, *Matisse*, rev. ed. (Paris: Flammarion, 2020), 587.

4 Henri Matisse, foreword to *Portraits* (Monte-Carlo: André Sauret, 1954), reproduced in *Matisse, Écrits et propos sur l'art*, ed. Dominique Fourcade (Paris: Hermann, 1989), 177.

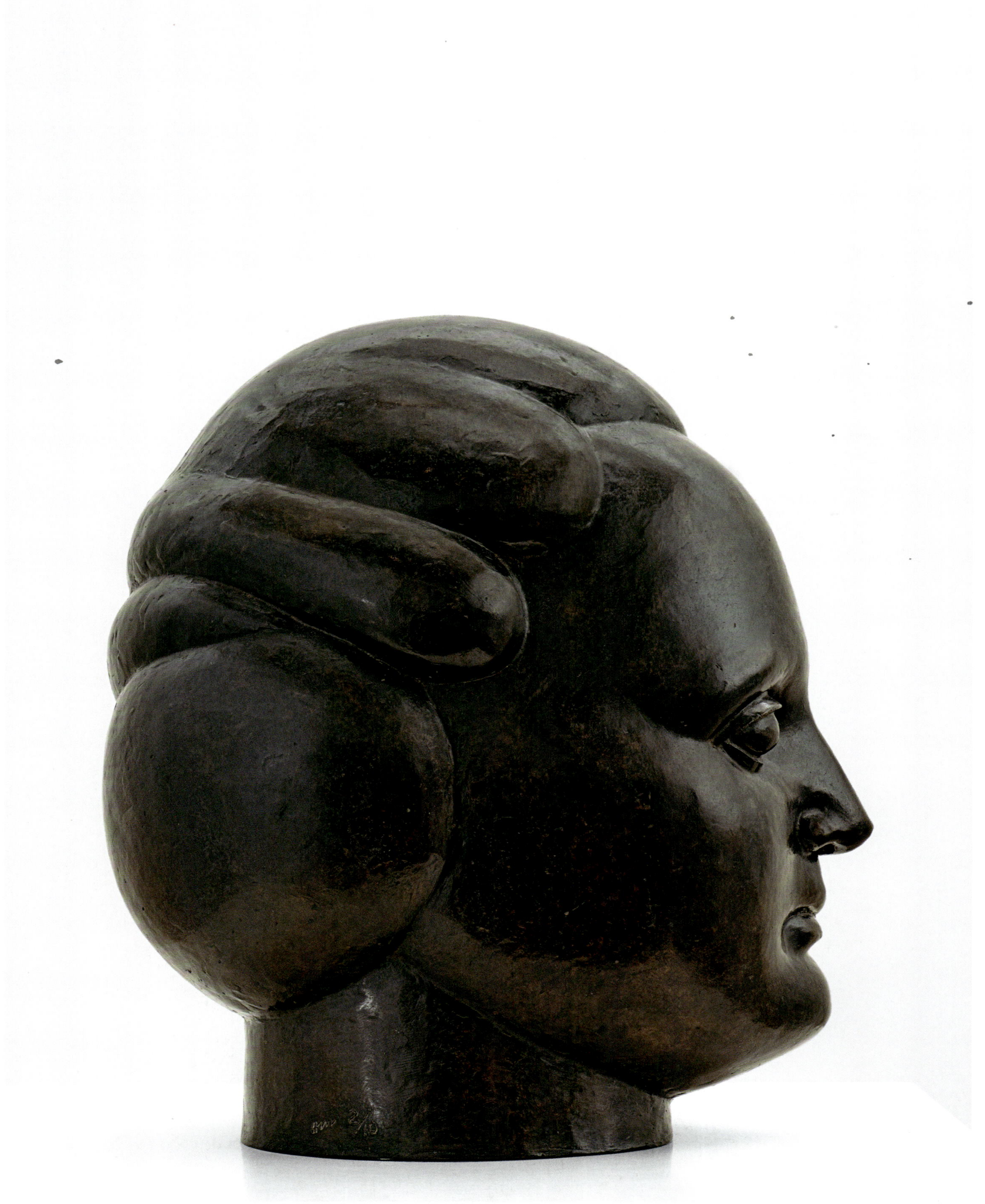

79
Henriette II, 1927
Bronze, 12 ⅝ × 8 11⁄16 × 10 ⅝ in.
(32 × 22 × 27 cm)
Musée d'Orsay, Paris, held at the
Musée Matisse Nice, 1978

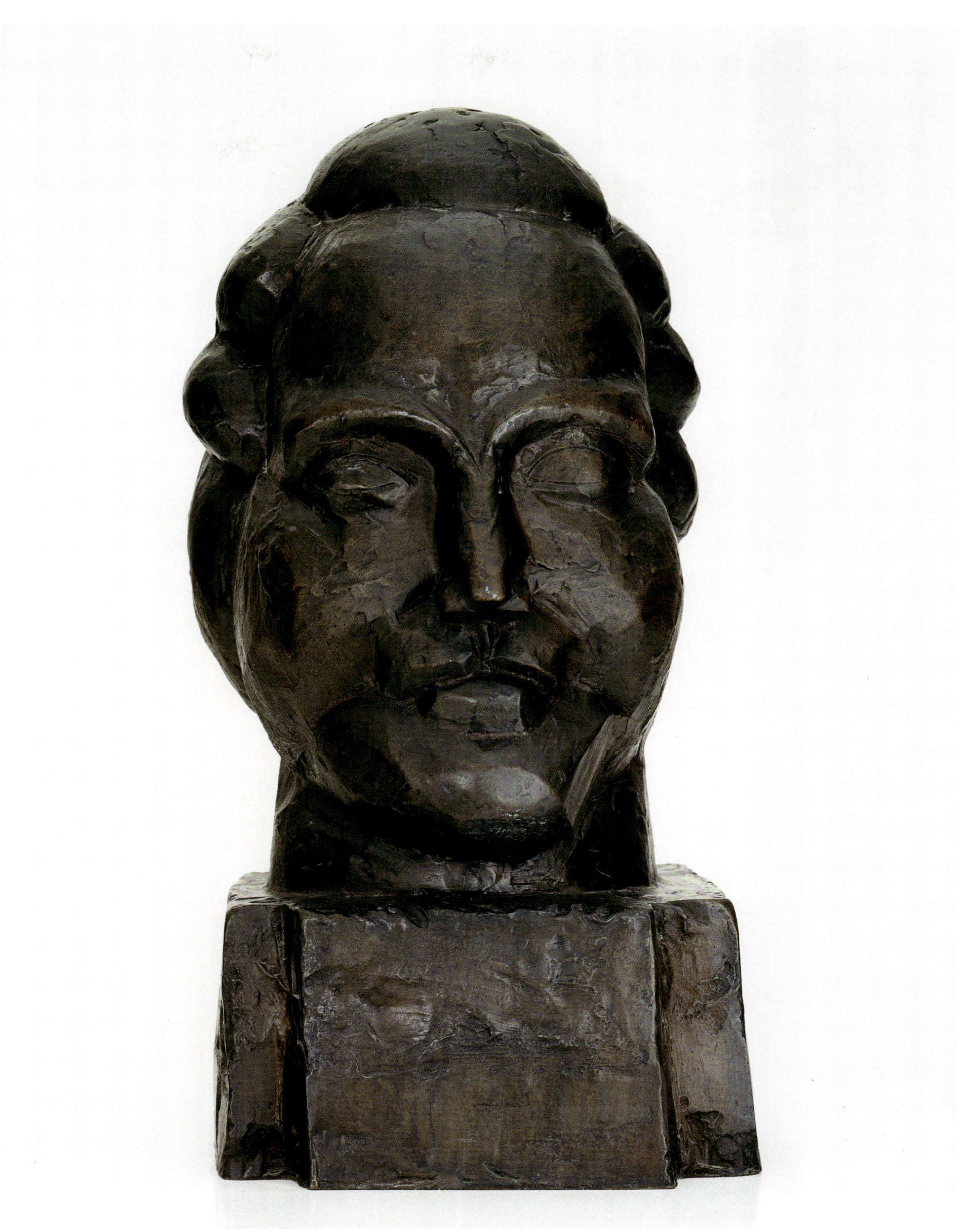

80
Henriette III, 1929
Bronze, 15 ¾ × 8 11/16 × 9 ¼ in.
(40 × 22 × 23.5 cm)
Musée d'Orsay, Paris, held at the
Musée Matisse Nice, 1978

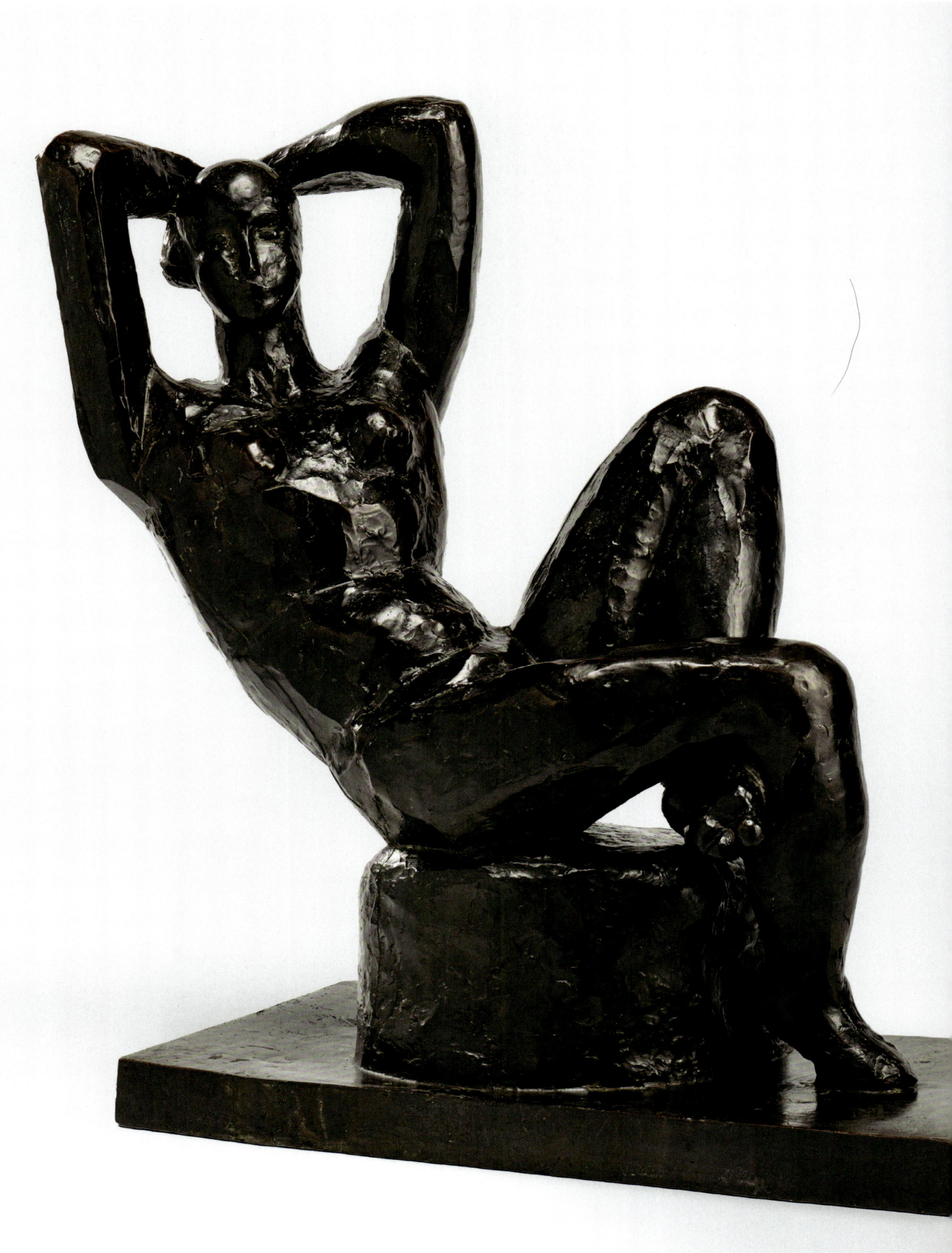

81
Large Seated Nude, 1922–29
Bronze, 31 × 33 × 14 in.
(78.7 × 83.8 × 35.6 cm)
Philadelphia Museum of Art

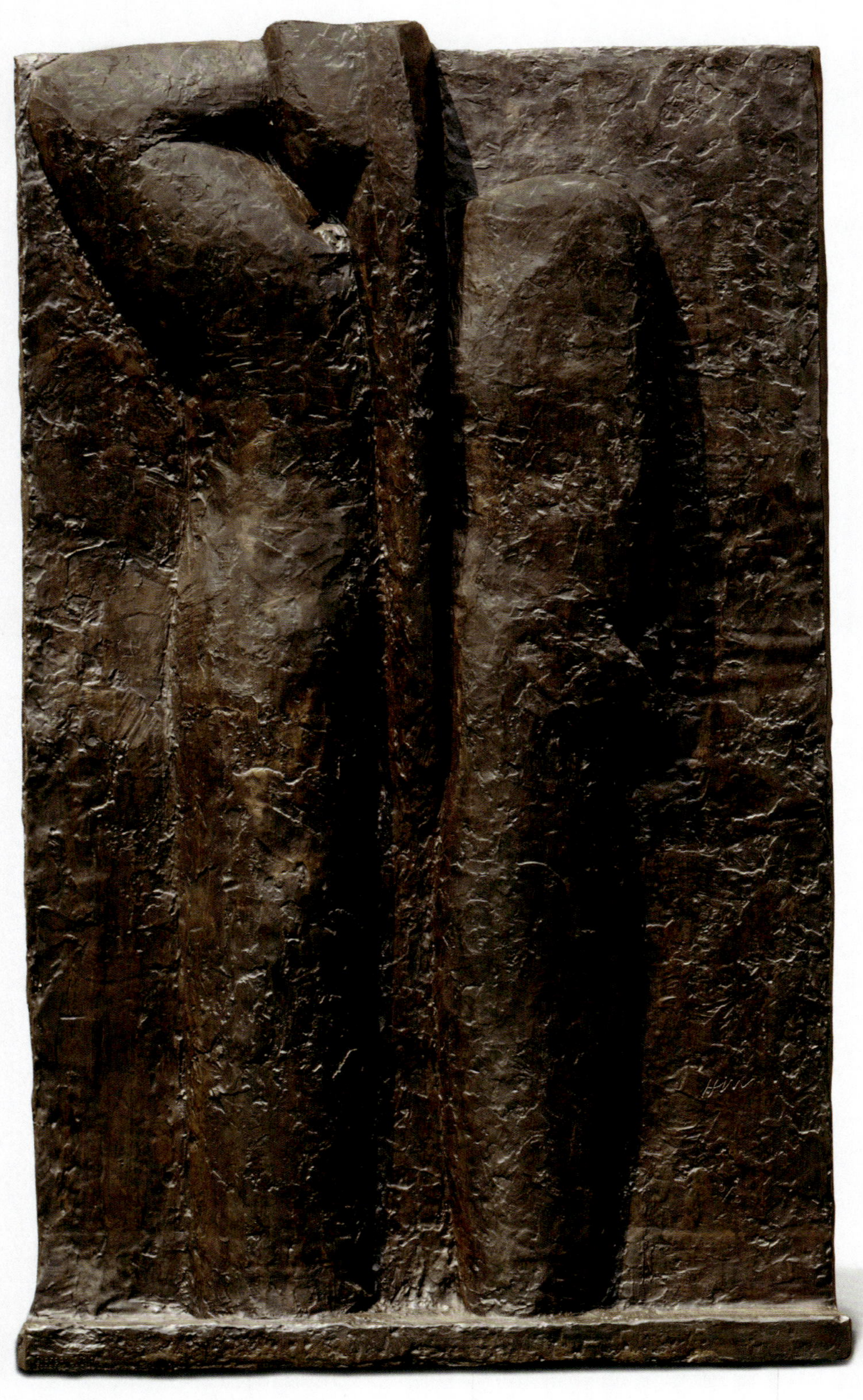

82
Back IV, 1930–31 (cast 1959–60)
Bronze, 6 ft. 2 ⅜ in. × 45 in. × 6 ¼ in.
(188.9 × 114.3 × 15.9 cm)
Hirshhorn Museum and Sculpture Garden, Smithsonian Institution, Washington, DC

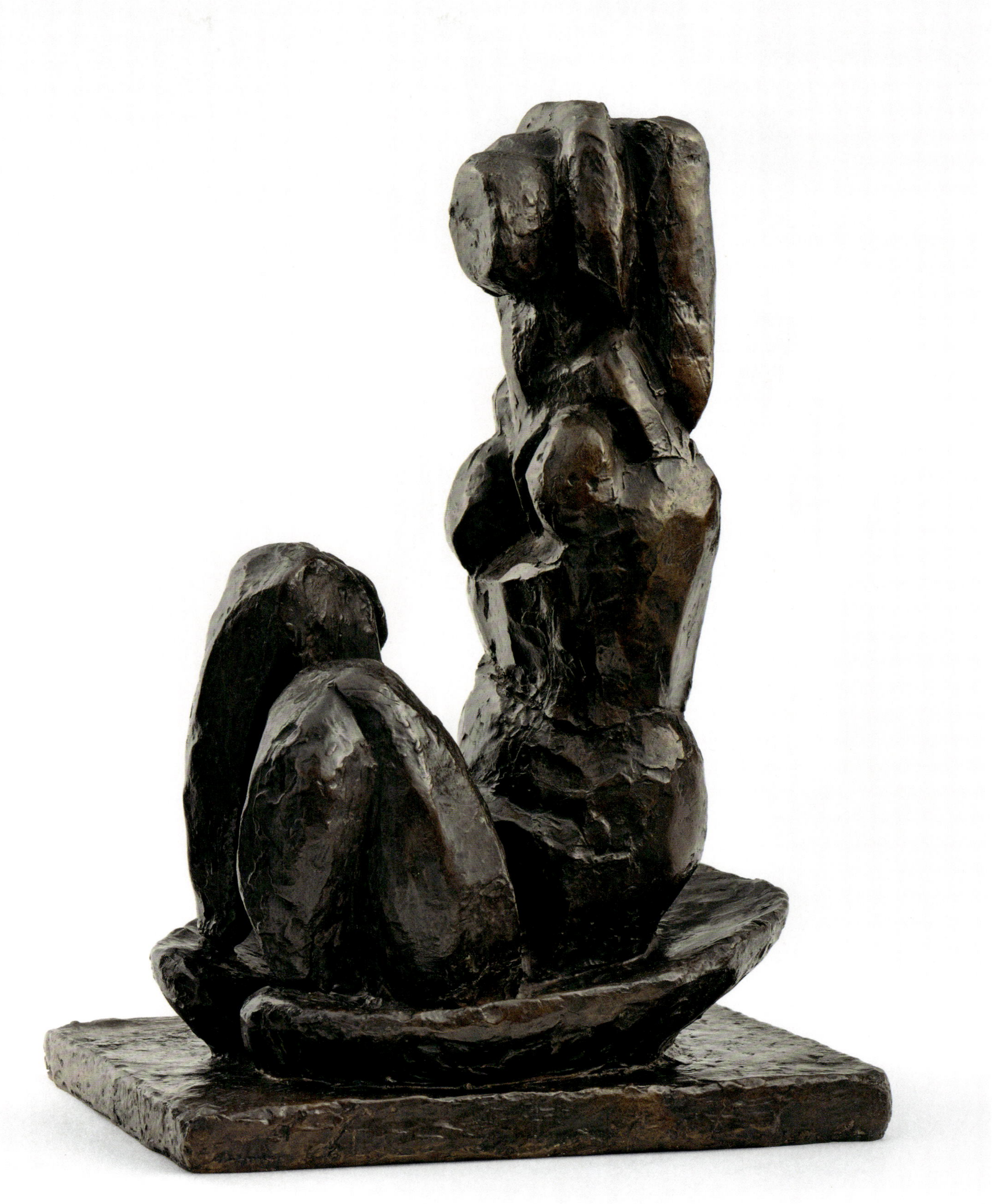

83
Venus in a Shell II, 1932 (cast 1958)
Bronze, 13 × 6 ¹¹⁄₁₆ × 9 ¹⁄₁₆ in.
(33 × 17 × 23 cm)
Musée d'Orsay, Paris, held at the
Musée Matisse Nice, 1978

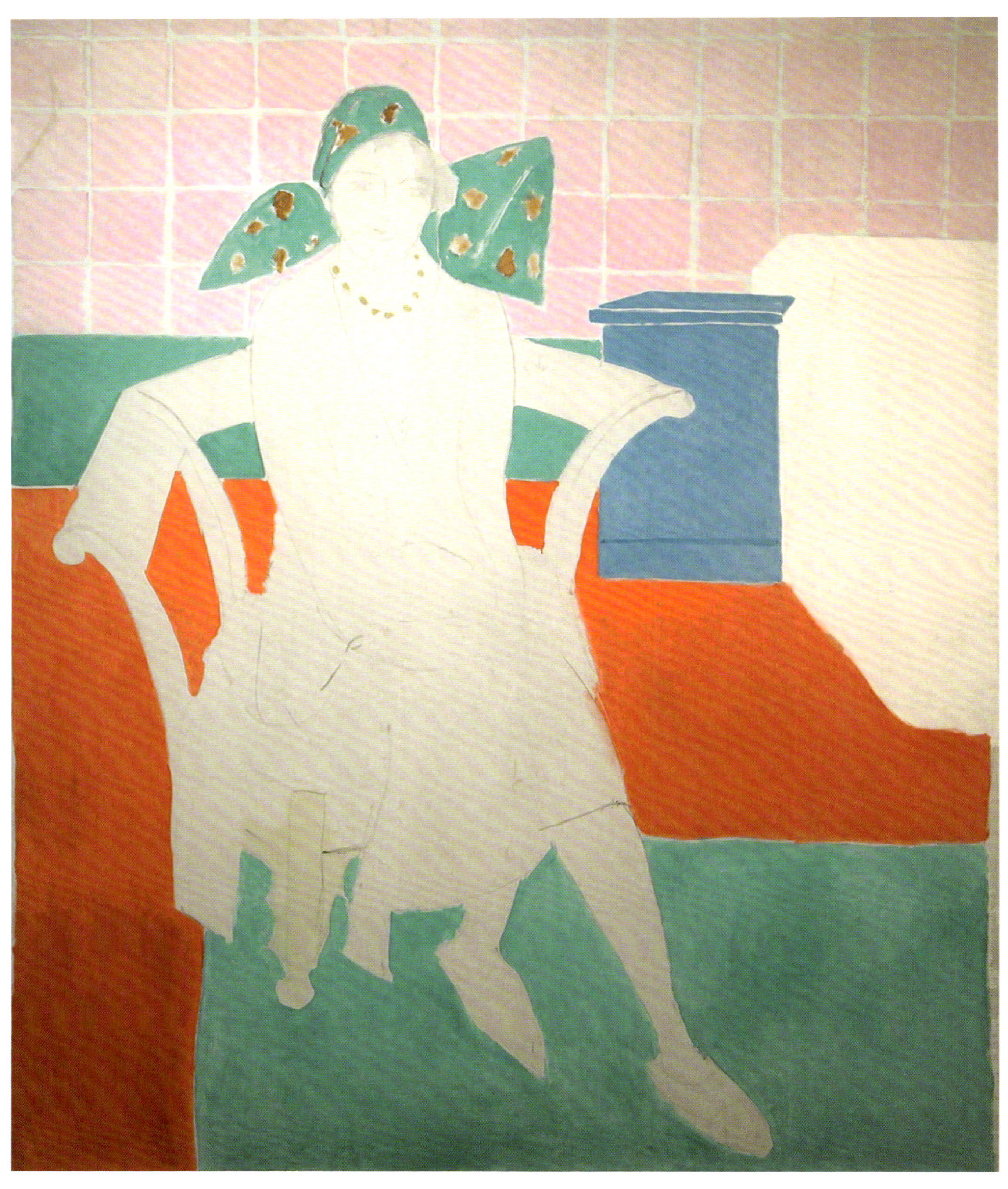

84 (fig.)
Woman with a Madras Hat, 1929
Oil on canvas,
70 1/8 × 59 13/16 in. (180 × 152 cm)
Private collection

MATISSE AND INTERNATIONAL BLACK MODERNITY

AN EVOLVING AESTHETIC

On February 26, 1930, Matisse boarded the ocean liner *Île de France* to begin the first of four trips to the United States he would make in the 1930s. Upon arrival in New York, he wrote to his wife, Amélie, of being "bewitched"[1] by the city and claimed, "If I were thirty years old, this is where I would work."[2]

Matisse's visits to New York's museums and appearances at art patrons' lavish events were detailed in the American press. But his visits to Harlem, a rapidly expanding African American neighborhood in northern Manhattan, received almost no mention, except in his copious letters to his family. Recent research has revealed Matisse's interest in Harlem and his brief stay in the French Caribbean as a possible impetus for the transformation of his visual language in representations of the Black presence in transatlantic artistic circles in the years that followed.

This transformation is apparent in a decrease of Orientalism in his portrayals of models, dancers, and other sitters of color. Motivated by his travels to North Africa, Orientalism had been an episodic feature of his work in the decade 1910–20: seen, for example, in two portraits of the North African woman Fatma in 1912–13 and his two known portrayals of the Martiniquaise model Aïcha Goblet in 1916–17.

His unfinished *Woman with a Madras Hat*, 1929 84, can be seen as a transitional work—while a tentative reprise of his powerful and iconic *Red Madras with a Headdress* (1907; Barnes Foundation, Philadelphia), it also marks a decisive shift of his attention to Americas-inspired subject matter informed by his transatlantic travel in the early 1930s.

A defining component of this shift was Matisse's synthesis of his expanding appreciation for African American jazz and his attention to the styling and color tonalities of French Caribbean attire. These new aesthetic influences, combined with his career-long passion for both modern fashion and traditional costuming, imbued his depictions of African diasporic models with a cosmopolitan elegance increasingly free of past ethnic tropes.

Matisse's interest in and collection of jazz recordings is chronicled in family correspondence. In 1926 his son Pierre wrote to Matisse from New York, "I have in my suitcase a stack of 'Black records' that you will have to give me your opinion about. I looked for them in a store in Haarlem [*sic*], the Black town, where one can find some superb ones."[3] During his own visit to New York in 1930, Matisse wrote to Amélie, "I went to see an amazing Black play. Serious Black. It's the story of the Old Testament told from the perspective of a Black man. Very well acted, very good stage design. Amazing."[4]

It is perhaps as a visitor to such events, and to iconic Harlem jazz clubs like Connie's Inn, that Matisse had his most direct encounter with the aesthetics of African American modernity. The club's mainly Black musicians and dancers performed for an all-white audience, replicating the racist social structures of the 1930s, an era of legally mandated racial segregation in the United States.

In contrast, Paris clubs such as the Caribbean Bal Nègre in Montmartre and the nearby Bricktop, owned by an African American expatriate, attracted an interracial clientele with their blend of jazz and Caribbean music. Still, the era's white creative elites defined themselves as a Modernist avant-garde in part through their simultaneous, and problematic, embrace of primitivism and exoticism along with the creative output of Black musicians, writers, and artists.[5]

Though it is unclear whether Matisse visited the Paris dance clubs, archival correspondence reveals some of his thoughts about his brief visit to Fort-de-France, Martinique, and Pointe-à-Pitre, Guadeloupe, on July 15 and 16, 1930, en route from the Tahitian city of Papeete to New York. In at least one lengthy letter to his wife,

1 Henri Matisse [HM]–Amélie Matisse [AM], March 5, 1930, Archives Henri Matisse, Issy-les-Moulineaux [AHM], cited and translated in Hilary Spurling, *Matisse the Master: A Life of Henri Matisse; The Conquest of Colour, 1909–1954* (New York: Alfred A. Knopf, 2005), 305–6.

2 HM–AM, March 10, 1930, AHM (author's translation).

3 Pierre Matisse–HM, March 24, 1926, Pierre Matisse Gallery Archives, The Morgan Library & Museum, New York. The transcription was provided to me by email in November 2012 by Wanda de Guébriant, AHM (author's translation).

4 HM–AM, March 7, 1930, AHM (author's translation). It has not been possible to establish the name of the referenced play. The art historian Carrie Pilto thought it might have been *Green Pastures*, which featured an all-Black cast in a plot similar to what Matisse describes and won the 1930 Pulitzer Prize. But that play was on Broadway, while the play Matisse attended was performed—according to Spurling, *Matisse the Master*, 305—in Harlem.

5 Petrine Archer-Straw, *Negrophilia: Avant-Garde Paris and Black Culture in the 1920s* (New York: Thames & Hudson, 2000), 159–61.

6 HM–AM, July 16, 1930, AHM, 2–3 (transcription from the artist's handwriting and English translation by Marie-Isabelle Pinet and Denise Murrell). With thanks to Anne Théry of the AHM for emailing scans of the letter to me.

7 Anne Théry, AHM, notes in emails to me dated August 18 and September 13, 2021, that the term "chapeau créole" appears in 1937 files of Marguerite Duthuit for the loan of this work to a Petit Palais exhibition.

8 Images of these drawings provided by Anne Théry, AHM.

he described the "very beautiful landscapes, with a tropical aspect such as illustrations in travel books make one dream of," as well as encounters with residents: "Few beautiful Black men and women, all decked out in short dresses. . . . Only 2 or 3 clothed in the traditional dress with a train over the arm. A lady of about 50 years old, a black embroidered silk dress with rather discreet old gold designs. Very beautiful, very dignified."[6]

Matisse notes this blend of tradition and modernity, also on display in New York jazz clubs, with a clarity that appears to inform much of his subsequent work. While in the 1930s he evokes African diasporic motifs in depictions of European models, in the 1940s he achieves a deeper resolution in sustained work with Black models.

The painting *Woman with a Scarf* (Pola Museum of Art, Hakone) is dated 1936, several years after his travel in the Americas. The seated young woman wears a "creole hat" styled with a rolled border and bow-like extensions resonant of traditional French Caribbean madras plaid headwraps; yet the black and gold tonalities and flattened squares reflect contemporary international fashion.[7] Matisse depicted the same Russian model, Hélène Mercier-Galitzine, wearing the "creole hat" in a related series of drawings in 1937.[8]

His 1939 *The Gandoura (Seated Figure and Greek Torso)* 85 features the traditional flowing white robe and headwrap of North African tradition. But the indeterminate detailing of the garment constitutes a clear break with the orientalizing embellishment of his portrayals of Fatma and Aïcha two decades earlier.

In the 1940s Matisse produced a plethora of paintings and drawings after Black models with whom he worked on an extended basis over several years. His numerous drawings and book illustrations, often titled *The Martiniquaise*, portrayed the Haitian dancer Carmen Lahens as an embodiment of both decorative traditional style and sleek modern elegance. The Belgian Congolese journalist Elvira Van Hyfte sat for several of Matisse's final easel paintings, including *Woman in White* (1946; Des Moines Art Center), which reprises the stylized modernity of the 1936 *Woman with a Scarf*, but now presents a Black woman as the personification of modern elegance, with none of the earlier visual markers of race and ethnicity.

In the final years of his life, Matisse evoked the African American dancers Katherine Dunham and Josephine Baker in monumental paper cut-out paintings, including *Creole Dancer* (1950; Musée Matisse Nice).

With these late works, Matisse completes the transformation of his visual vocabulary for depictions of the international African diaspora, now informed less by formulaic past tropes of racialized identity than by the blend of tradition and modernity he had observed during his 1930s visits to Harlem and the French Caribbean.

DENISE MURRELL

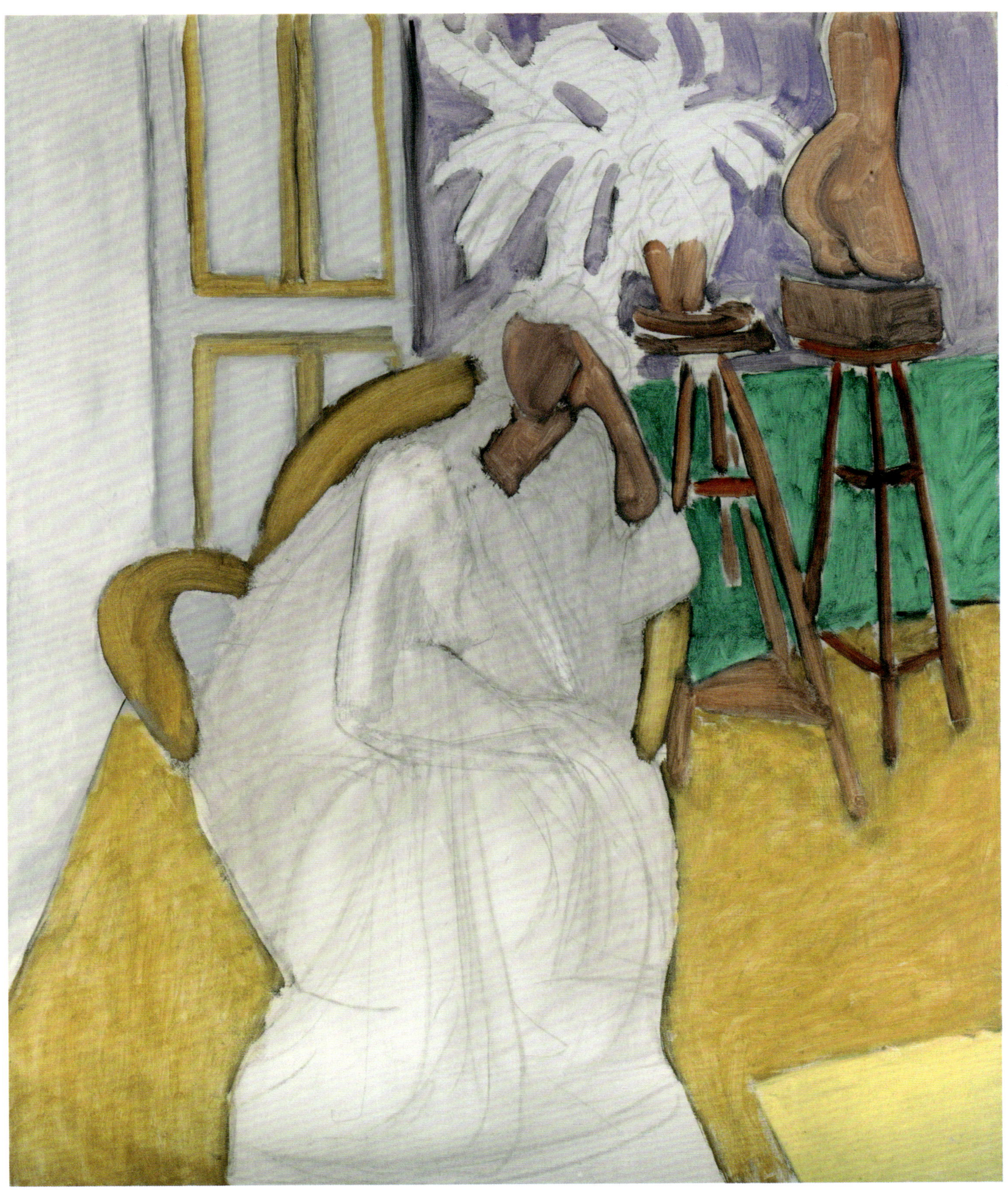

85
The Gandoura (Seated Figure and Greek Torso), January 1939
Oil on canvas, 25 9⁄16 × 21 ¼ in. (65 × 54 cm)
David and Ezra Nahmad Collection

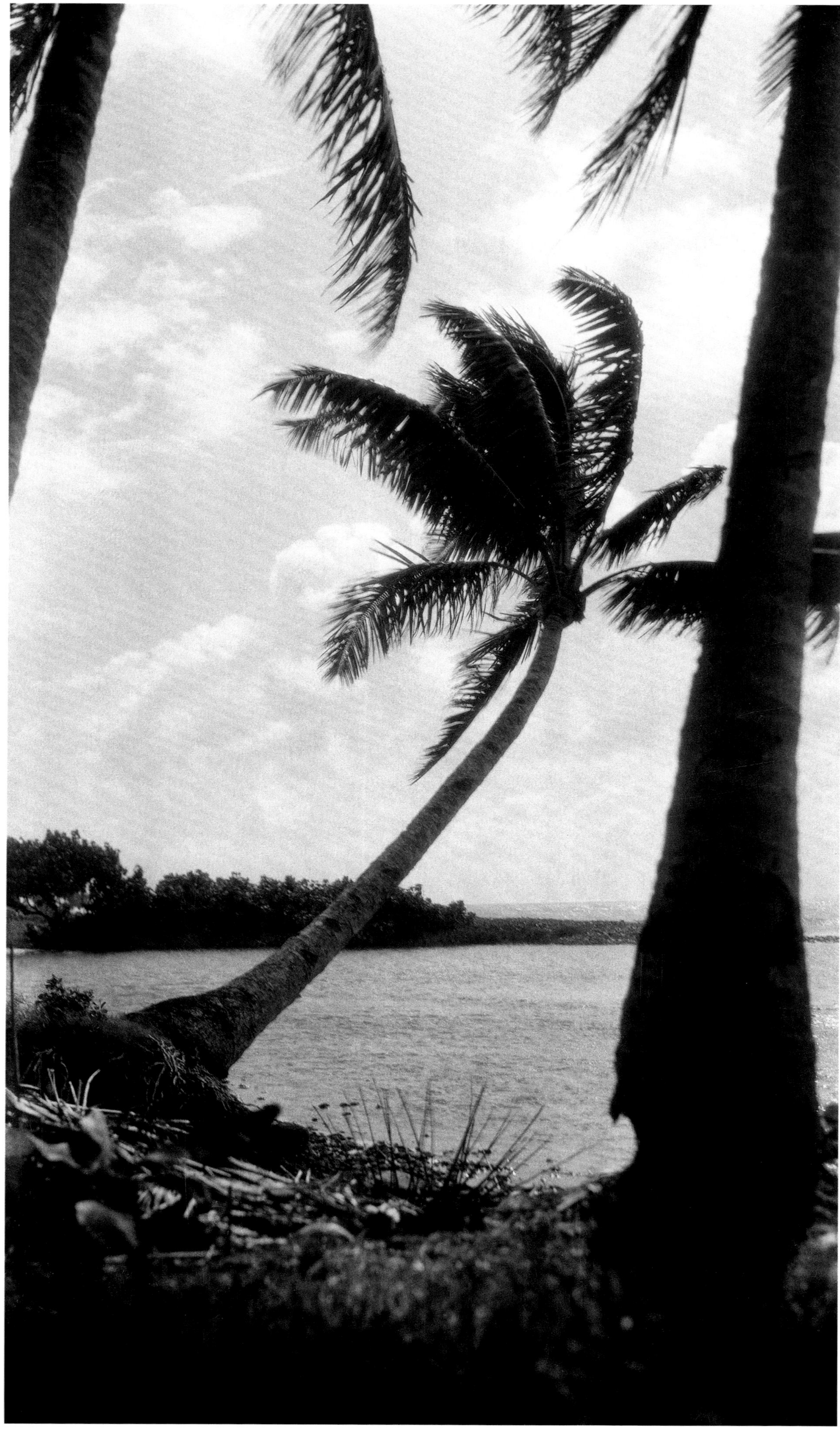

MATISSE'S WORLD TOUR

"The obsession with Tahiti has not left him," wrote Louis Aragon of Matisse's time there from March 29 to June 15, 1930.[1] This statement is seemingly belied by the ambivalence the painter always showed with regard to that sojourn. He often played down its importance, merely recalling the laziness and artistic bemusement he felt there, but the trip nevertheless marked a turning point in his practice and a return to the experimental work of his Fauvist and post-Fauvist years. This great journey of his life—he considered Algeria (1906), Spain (1910), Russia (1911), and Morocco (1912, 1913) to have been nothing more than study trips—is probably the only real vacation he ever took.

Vacationing notably included bathing. With the help of diving goggles, he engaged in a careful study of the refraction of light on and in water, full of the joy of contemplating the "film" of underwater life. He noted how a harpoon fisherman moves "like slow-motion pictures" and looks like "a large piece of seaweed gently floating in the water"[2]—themes and motifs that would reappear in his later work.

With the exception of a few reinvigorating days in the atolls of the Tuamotu Archipelago, this trip was the continuation of a crisis that had paralyzed him since 1929 and prevented him from painting. At the age of sixty, he had reached a dead end with easel painting and odalisques, and had grown dissatisfied. In Tahiti, he produced little (just one rough sketch: *Landscape in Tahiti*, 1930; private collection) but wanted to preserve traces of what he had experienced. He was not yet out of the country when he was already trying to remember it, insisting that his letters must not be mislaid. He devised a set of mnemonics through his letters, photographs, and drawings to record the sensations, colors, and shapes that would *impress* his future work. Like a photographer working "in the future perfect, . . . later to discover what he has seen, once the picture has been developed," he would "live the present of his experience as the past of a future."[3]

Matisse took some fifty photographs in Tahiti, all of which he thought bad. However, they avoided the stereotypes (Tahitian women in a state of undress) of photographers like Lucien Gauthier, an album of whose he possessed. The films of Robert Flaherty and W. S. Van Dyke, the works of Pierre Loti, Robert Louis Stevenson, and Marc Chadourne, and the purchase in 1899 of Paul Gauguin's *Young Tahitian Boy with a Tiaré Flower* meant that he arrived with readymade images, reassuring filters of an otherness already held in check by the policies of the French colonizer. In Papeete he "recognized" rather than discovered and was not without prejudices toward the people of Tahiti.[4] But his exoticizing lay elsewhere, in the way he would intertwine tropical fauna and flora and decorative elements in the gouache cut-outs and the way he would reproduce with plants and birds a miniature paradise in his studios.

Technical considerations—he was annoyed by the postcard format and the black and white of his Kodak camera, and would take the same picture several times over, being "unsure of the pose"—show that his photos were about more than mere tourism.[5] In addition to ordinary memories (his cabin during the filming of the F. W. Murnau film *Tabu*, the Buick in which he traveled around the island), he focused mostly on nature (the tangle of plant life filling the picture), light effects (the shadows of palm trees), the plasticity of clouds, the layering of planes (water, earth, sky), and the repeated verticality of the coconut trees.[6] Apart from Pauline Schyle, who acted as his guide

1 Louis Aragon, *Henri Matisse, roman* (1971; repr., Paris: Gallimard, 1998), 259.

2 Henri Matisse [HM]–Amélie Matisse, May 27, 1930, Archives Henri Matisse, Issy-les-Moulineaux [AHM].

3 Jean-François Chevrier, *Proust et la photographie / La Résurrection de Venise* (Paris: L'Arachnéen, 2009), 51.

4 John Klein, "Matisse after Tahiti: The Domestication of Exotic Memory," *Zeitschrift für Kunstgeschichte* 60, no. 1 (1997): 75.

5 HM–Marguerite Duthuit, May 10, 1930, AHM.

6 He spent a week with the filmmaker to observe the shooting in Tautira Bay and saw the film three times.

86 (fig.)
Tahiti, 1930
Inscription (verso): "Coconut tree about which I wrote to you"
Archives Henri Matisse, Issy-les-Moulineaux

(and kept him supplied until his death with dried bananas, pandanus hats, and vanilla pods, proof that he was expecting from the Pacific a renewal of the senses), and a family in front of a cabin that he described as "a Gauguin from life," the few Tahitians he photographed disappear into the luxuriant vegetation. His annotations on the backs of these pictures signal his attention to barely visible details and a memory of sensory experiences such as the "sharp green note" of a bunch of bananas or the "biting fresh wind." [7]

Picking up where the photographs left off, drawing enabled him to approach and isolate elements such as the tiaré flower, the trunk of a banyan tree, breadfruit trees, or the jagged outline of a shell. We note the sensuality and the speed of line drawing with which Matisse sought to capture this living matter, this blossoming of typical Polynesian organisms. A proliferation of materials and impressions that many reminiscences, whether literal (*Tiari*, Mallarmé's *Poésies*, *Papeete, Tahiti*, and *Window at Tahiti II* 23 | 118 | 119) or transposed (gouache cut-outs), or sometimes fragmentary (*Tahiti II* as a backdrop for paintings in 1936), would now perpetually bring back to life 117. The publication in 1936, in issues 3–5 of *Cahiers d'art*, of drawings reflecting this time (the hotel rocking chair, views with schooner and dugout canoe 89) confirmed that Tahiti was now part of his inner landscape.

ALIX AGRET

7 Cited by Dominique Szymusiak, ed., *Matisse et l'Océanie: Voyage à Tahiti*, exh. cat. (Le Cateau-Cambrésis: Musée Matisse, 1998), 168, 147.

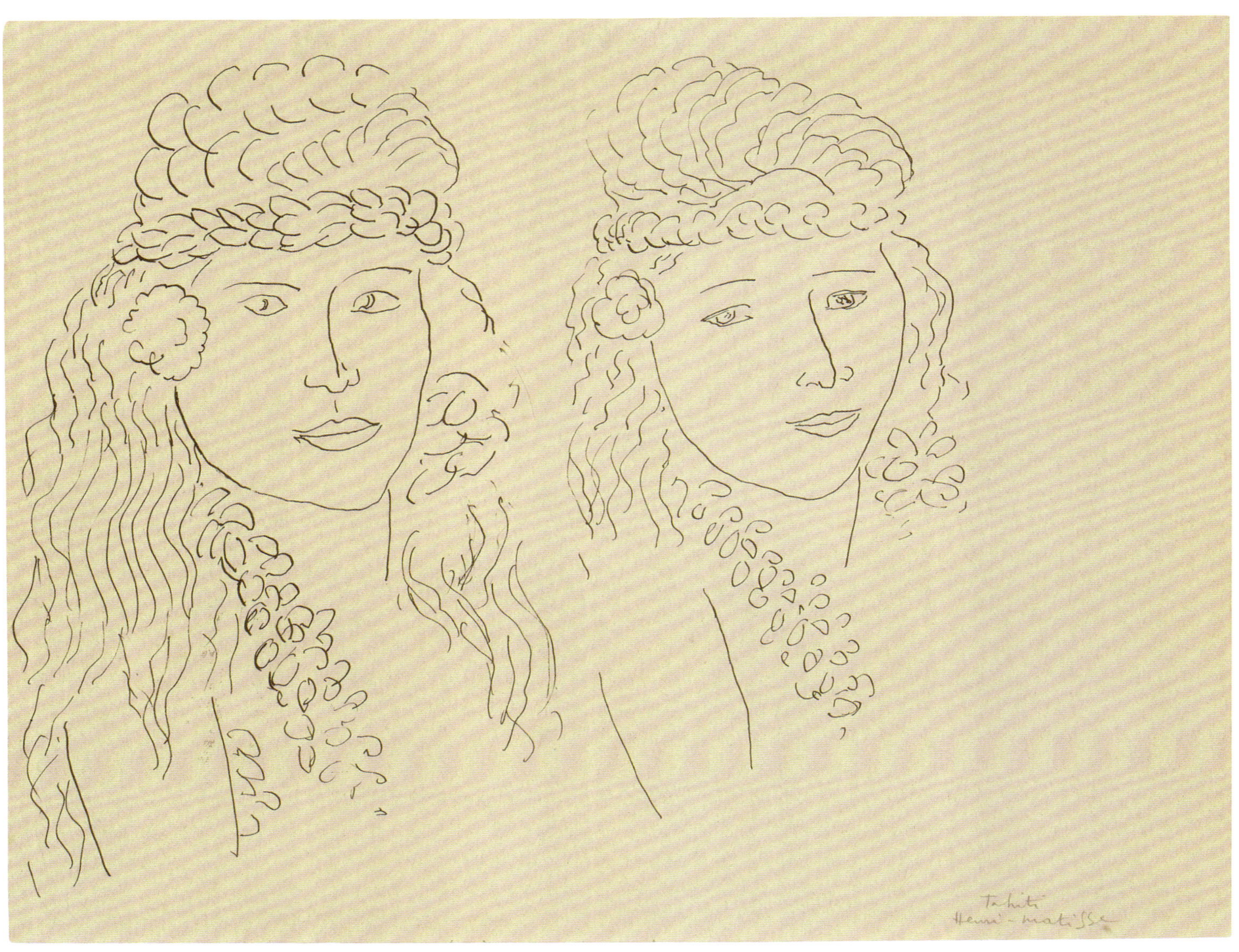

87
Tahitian Women, 1930
Pencil and ink on paper,
9 ½ × 13 in. (24 × 33 cm)
Musée du Quai Branly–
Jacques Chirac, Paris

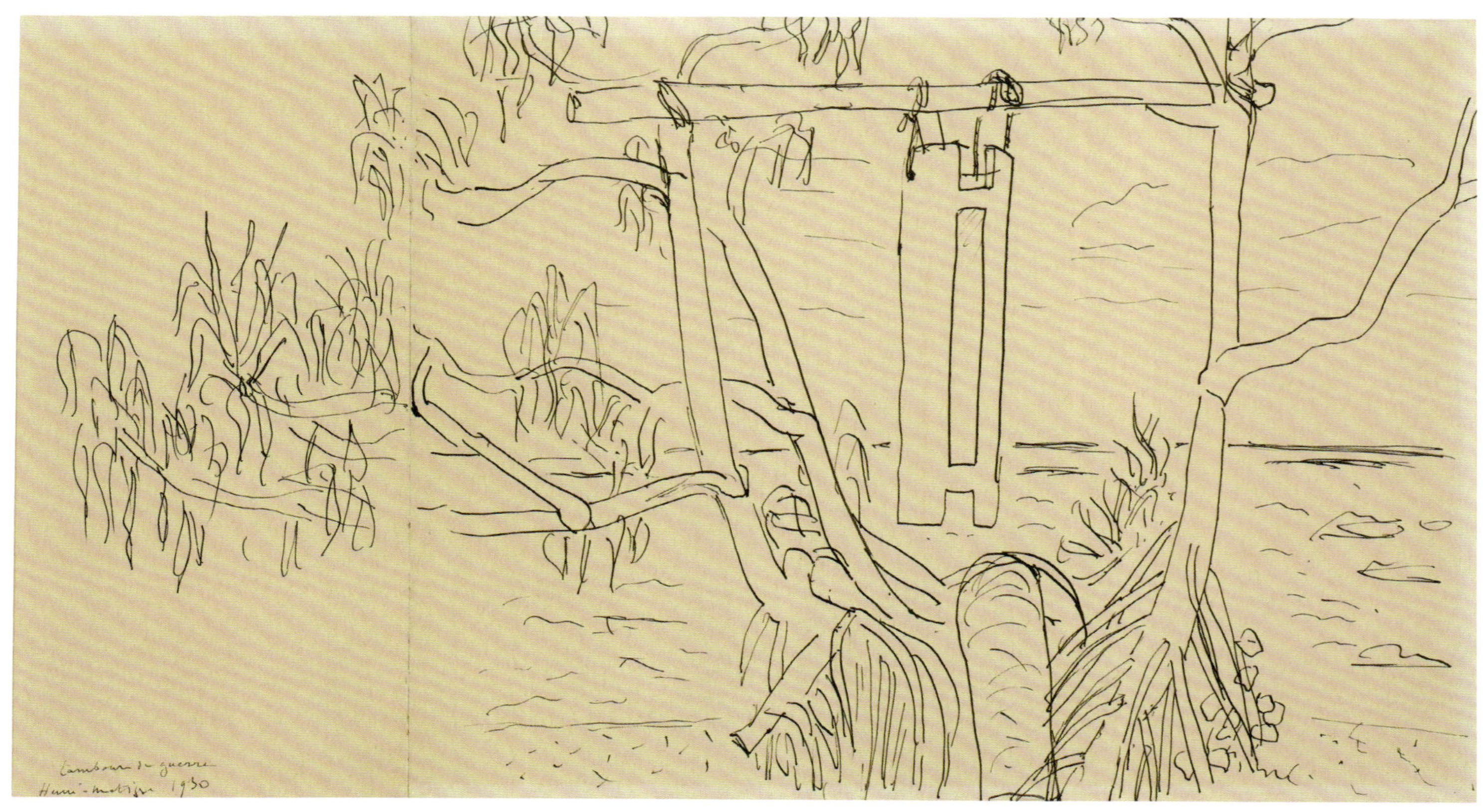

88
War Drum, 1930
India ink on sketchbook paper (recto),
9 ⅞ × 25 ⅝ in. (25 × 65 cm)
Musée du Quai Branly–
Jacques Chirac, Paris

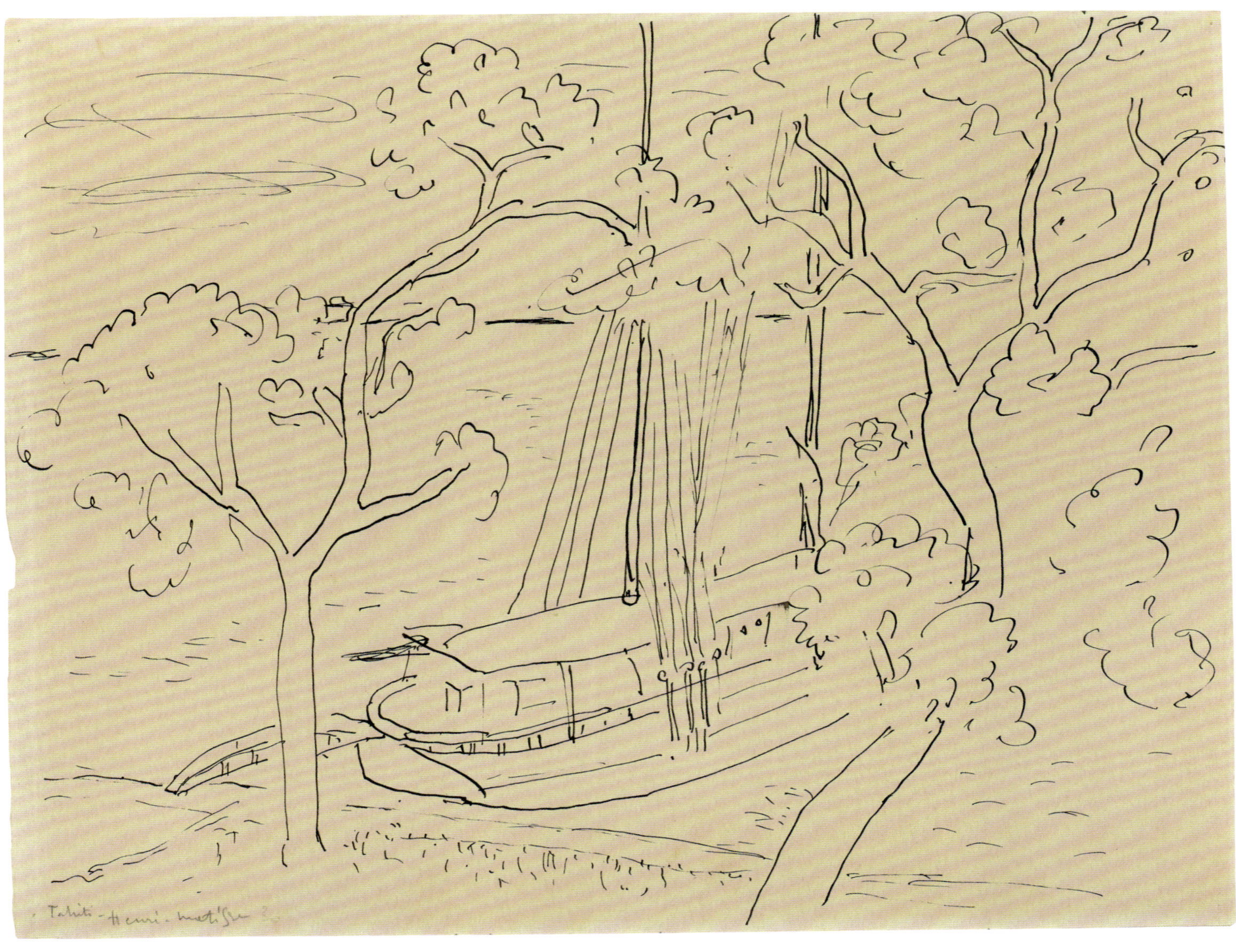

89
Tahitian Landscape,
April–May 1930
Pen and India ink on wove paper,
9 ⅞ × 12 ¾ in. (25.1 × 32.4 cm)
Musée Matisse Nice

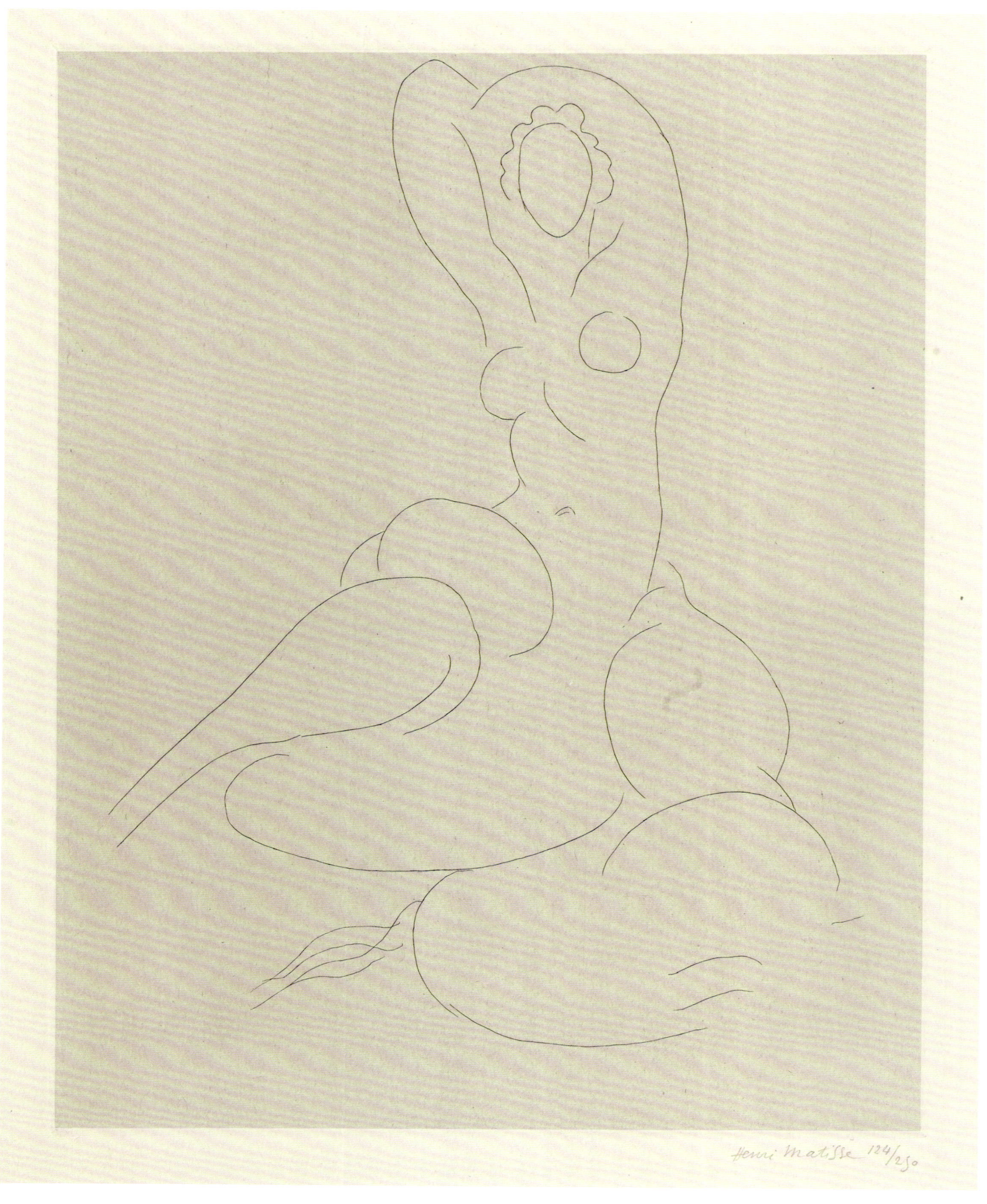

90
Nude for Cleveland, 1932
Etching printed chine collé,
14 7/16 × 11 5/16 in. (36.7 × 28.7 cm)
The Metropolitan Museum
of Art, New York

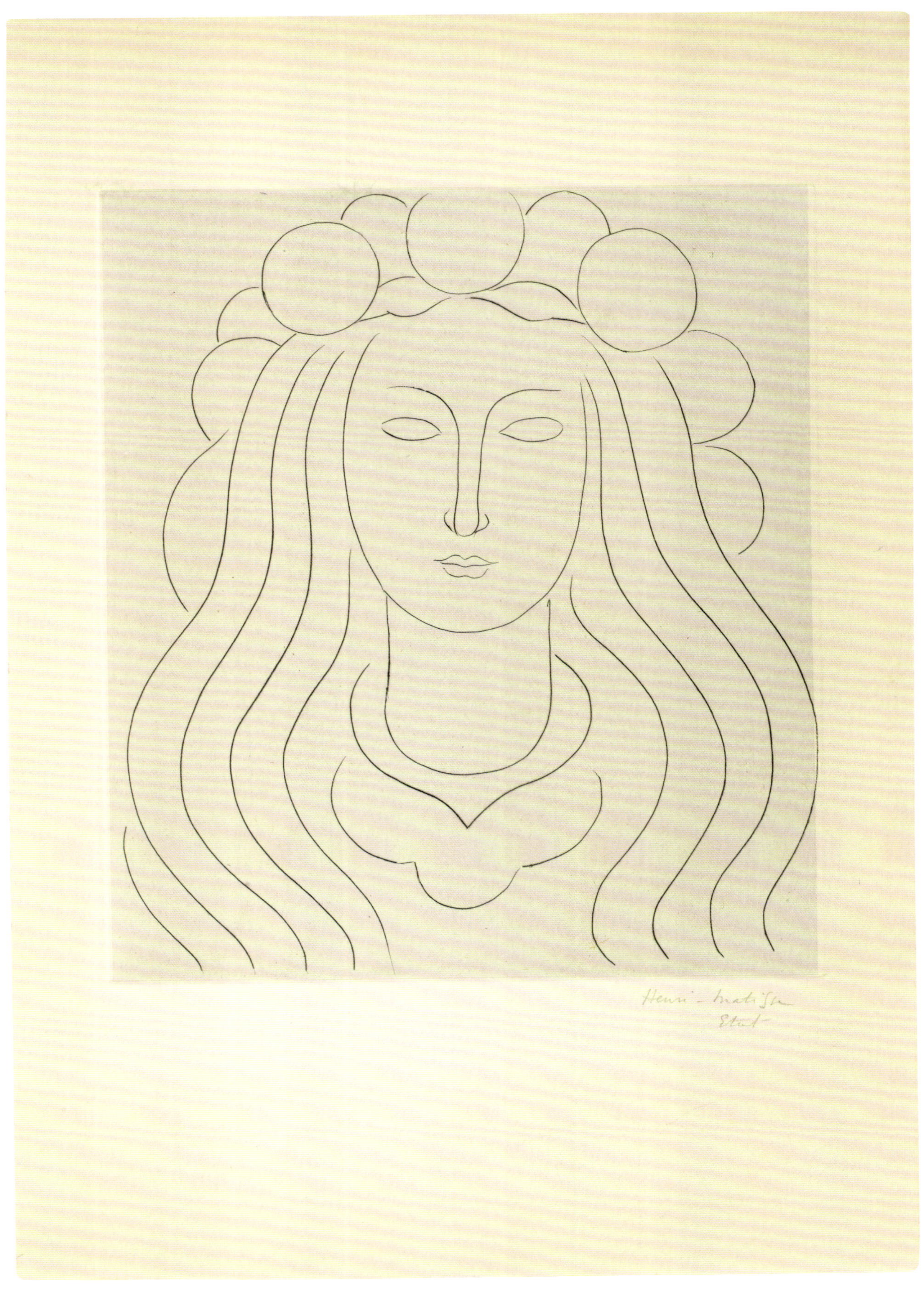

91
Fairy in a Luminous Hat—
Remembrance of Mallarmé, 1933
Drypoint printed chine collé,
14 7/16 × 12 5/8 in. (36.6 × 32 cm)
The Pierre and Tana Matisse
Foundation, New York

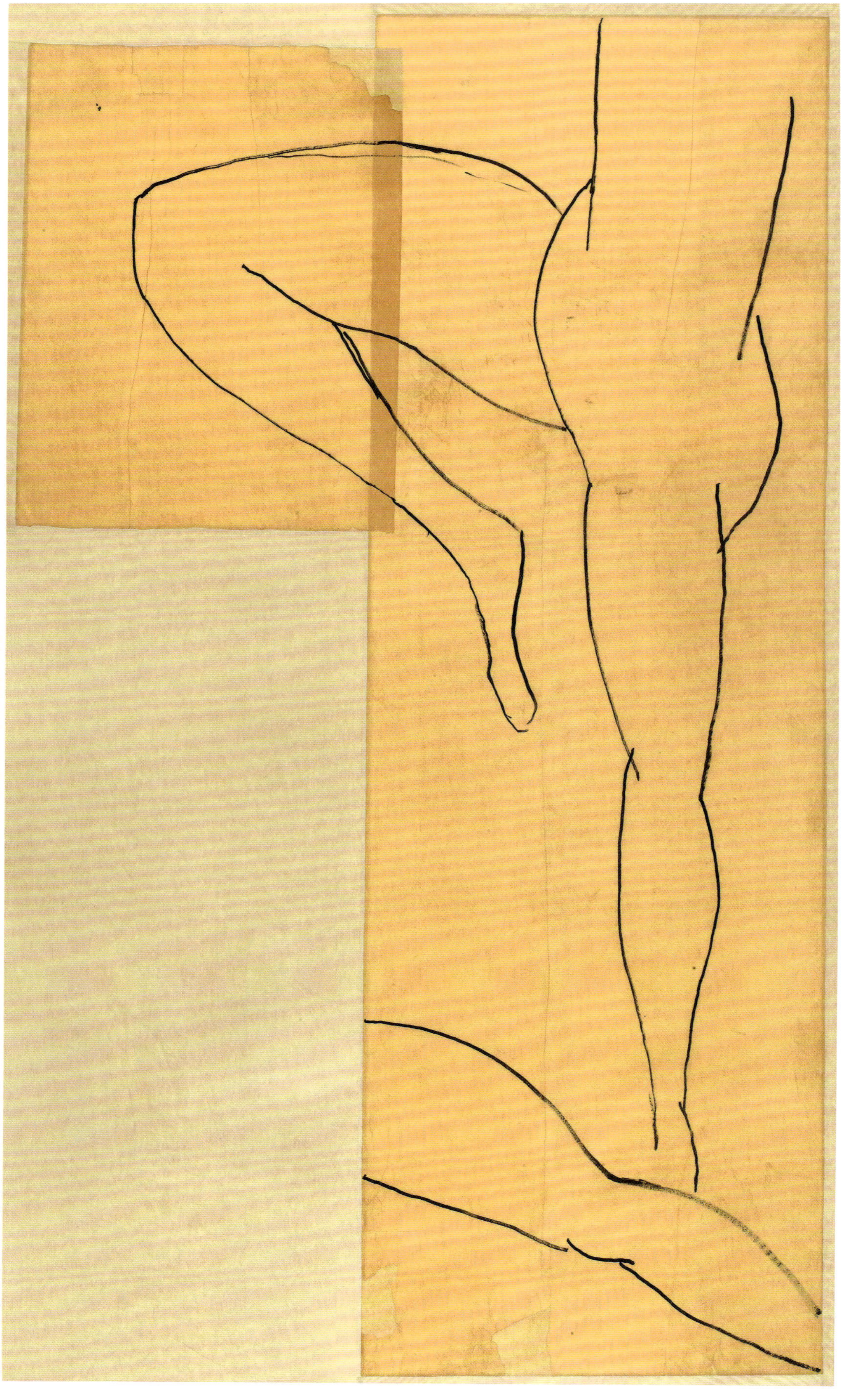

92
The Dance, First Version—
Sketch at the Scale of
the Central Figure, 1930–31
India ink and brush on two
sheets of transparent paper,
10 ft. 11 7/8 in. × 6 ft. 4 9/16 in.
(335 × 194.5 cm)
Musée d'Orsay, Paris,
held at the Musée Matisse
Nice, 1988

MATISSE AND PHILADELPHIA

The earliest recorded exhibition in Philadelphia of works by Matisse took place in a Center City art gallery in 1916.[1] But the story of the artist's recognition and patronage in Philadelphia effectively begins with Albert C. Barnes, the region's most celebrated collector of modern art.[2] Barnes was introduced to Matisse's work by Leo Stein in Paris, from whom he purchased two of the artist's Fauve-period paintings in 1912. Still, it was not until early 1923 that the Philadelphia public had its first glimpse of Barnes's collection, in an exhibition hosted by the Pennsylvania Academy of the Fine Arts that included five paintings by Matisse.[3] By this date Barnes had already received his charter from the Commonwealth of Pennsylvania for a foundation to promote education in and appreciation of the fine arts and had hired Paul Cret, a French-born professor of architecture at the University of Pennsylvania, to design its quarters in a modern Renaissance style. The Barnes Foundation was inaugurated in the suburb of Merion in 1925.

When Matisse visited Merion for the first time in September 1930, Barnes immediately offered him a commission for a mural decoration in the lunettes of the foundation's main hall 103. This encounter would prove to be a turning point for both artist and patron. Matisse came away favorably impressed by Barnes's method of displaying old master and modern paintings in juxtaposition. "This bringing together helps students understand a lot of things that the academies don't teach," he remarked soon after.[4] More importantly, the process of executing *The Dance* would be catalytic, propelling Matisse in fresh directions after a long dry spell in his work. By the time *The Dance* was installed, in 1933, Barnes held forty-seven paintings by the artist, and he would continue to acquire his work through the 1940s. But the mural essentially set the seal on the foundation's presentation of Matisse as the foremost living exponent of the French art tradition.[5]

The story of Matisse in Philadelphia is, however, a tale of not one but two institutions. The Philadelphia Museum of Art came of age in the spring of 1928, when it opened its current building located at the northwest end of the Benjamin Franklin Parkway. Matisse figured prominently in the institution's display of works by living artists alongside its wide-ranging historical holdings, first thanks to loans from its network of supporters and eventually through their donations. In 1947, the museum mounted an exhibition of some 200 nineteenth- and twentieth-century paintings, drawings, and prints from Philadelphia collections; ultimately, the eight paintings by Matisse featured in this exhibition came as gifts or bequests from the collectors Samuel and Vera White, William and Lisa Norris Elkins, R. Sturgis Ingersoll, Henry P. McIlhenny, and Bernice M. McIlhenny.[6] A vast Matisse retrospective followed in 1948. Organized by Henry Clifford, the museum's curator of paintings, this exhibition comprised 271 paintings, sculptures, prints, drawings, and illustrated books, including a large body of works selected and loaned by the artist himself. Barnes, who rejected standard museum displays as incompatible with a proper appreciation of works of art and used his foundation as a laboratory for a strict and idiosyncratic formalist mode of display, not only refused to lend, but publicly denounced the event. The museum nevertheless promoted its retrospective as both the definitive account of Matisse's work and—though loans also came from France, Switzerland, and Japan—a validation of the role of US collectors in the recognition and patronage of Matisse.[7]

MATTHEW AFFRON

1 *Philadelphia's First Exhibition of Advanced Modern Art*, McClees Galleries, Philadelphia, May 17–June 15, 1916. The checklist mentions two paintings by Matisse: *The Leather Hat* (1915) and *Fruits* (nos. 11 and 12). This was a version of an April 1916 exhibition at the Bourgeois Galleries in New York.

2 See Claudine Grammont, "Matisse in the Laboratory of Dr. Barnes: How and Why Barnes Collected Matisse" (trans. Paul Micio), and Karen K. Butler, "Henri Matisse According to Dr. Barnes," in *Matisse in the Barnes Foundation*, ed. Yve-Alain Bois (Philadelphia: Barnes Foundation / London: Thames & Hudson, 2015), 1:28–59, 170–99.

3 *Contemporary European Painting and Sculpture*, Pennsylvania Academy of the Fine Arts, Philadelphia, April 11–May 9, 1923. Works by Matisse on the checklist: *Woman Reclining* (1921); *The Joy of Life* (1905–6); *Flower Piece* (1906–7); *Three Sisters and "The Rose Marble Table"* (1917); and *Standing Nude near Window* (1919–20; cats. 17 19, 21, 44, and 61).

4 "Statement to Tériade: On Travel, 1930," in *Matisse on Art*, ed. and trans. Jack Flam (Berkeley: University of California Press, 2015), 92.

5 See the commentary on the artist's classification in art history in Albert C. Barnes and Violette de Mazia, *The Art of Henri-Matisse* (New York: Charles Scribner's Sons, 1933), 210–11.

6 "Masterpieces of Philadelphia Private Collections," *Philadelphia Museum Bulletin* 42, no. 214 (May 1947): 75–76.

7 Fiske Kimball, "Matisse: Recognition, Patronage, Collecting," *Philadelphia Museum Bulletin* 43, no. 217 (March 1948): 47. On this exhibition see John Elderfield, "Drawings at an Exhibition," in *Matisse*, ed. Caroline Turner and Roger Benjamin, exh. cat. (South Brisbane, Australia: Queensland Art Gallery, 1995), 53–69; John O'Brian, *Ruthless Hedonism: The American Reception of Matisse* (Chicago: University of Chicago Press, 1999), 125–49; and Éric de Chassey, *La Violence décorative: Matisse dans l'art américain* (Nîmes: Jacqueline Chambon, 1998), 87–95.

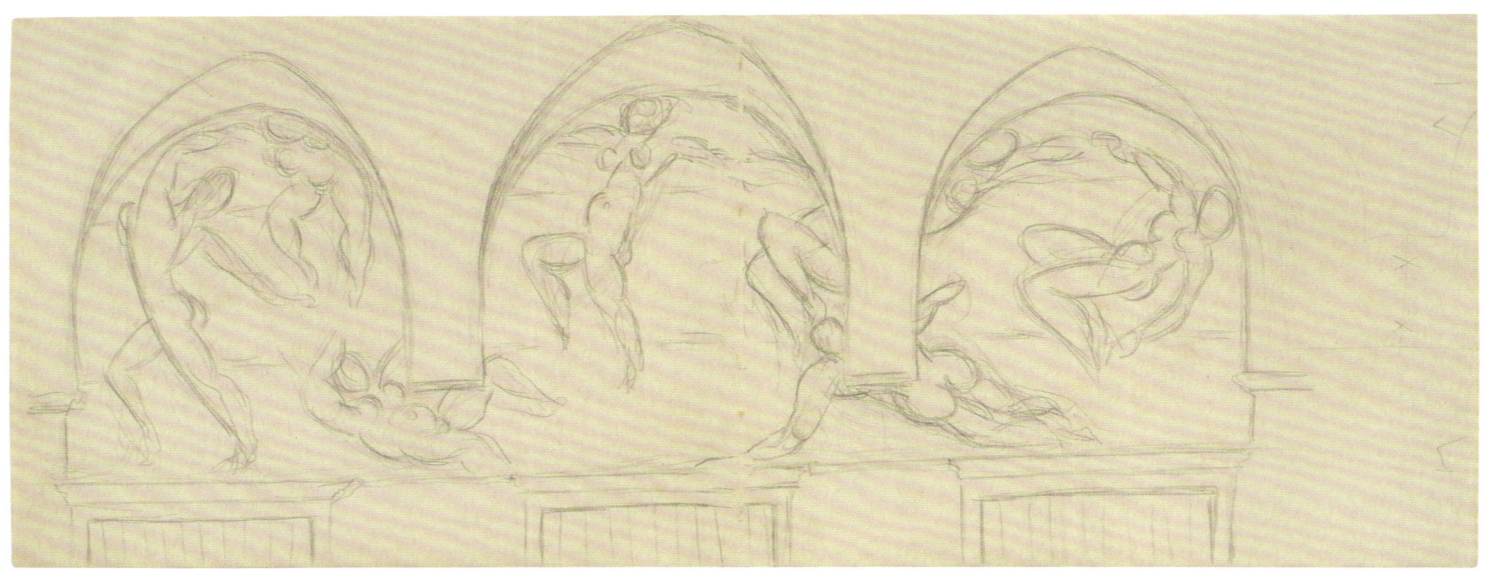

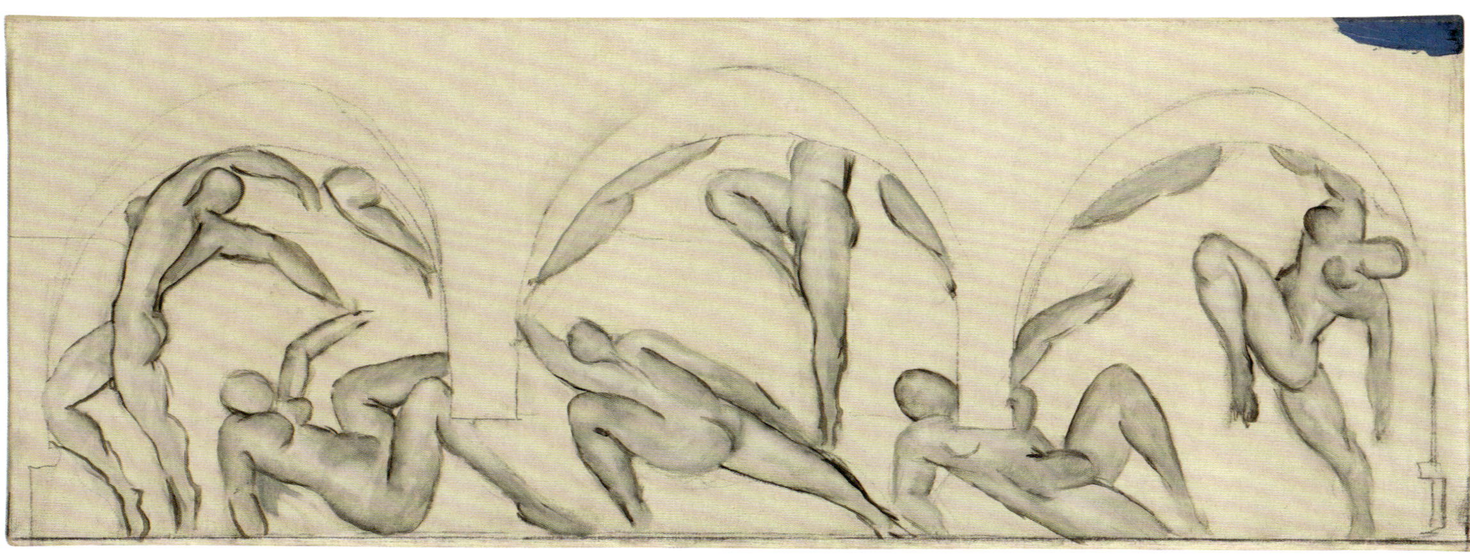

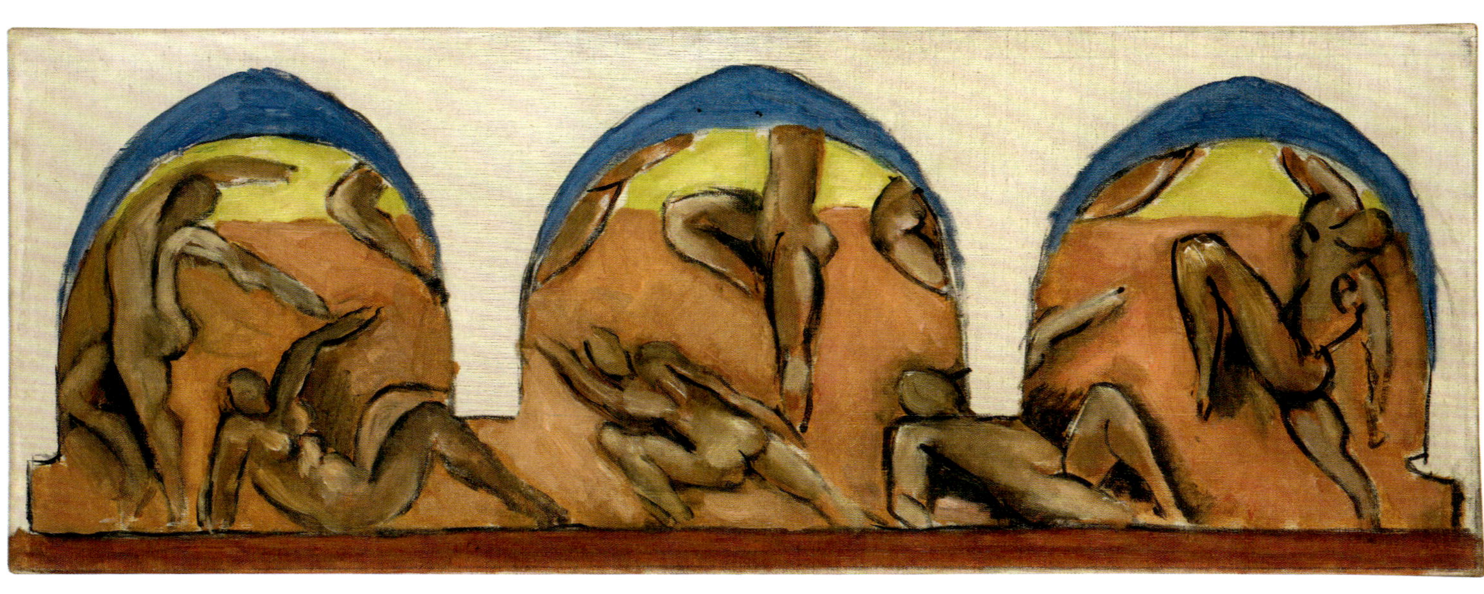

93
The Dance, First Version—Compositional Study, 1930–31
Graphite and pencil on paper, 10 × 26 1/16 in. (25.4 × 66.2 cm)
Musée Matisse Nice

94
The Dance, Gray Harmony, 1930–31
Oil on canvas, 13 × 34 9/16 in. (33 × 87.8 cm)
Musée Matisse Nice

95
The Dance, Ochre Harmony, 1930–31
Oil on canvas, 13 × 34 9/16 in. (33 × 87.8 cm)
Musée Matisse Nice

96 (fig.)
Henri Matisse working on *The Dance*, c. 1931
Archives Henri Matisse, Issy-les-Moulineaux

97
The Dance, Blue Harmony, 1930–31
Oil on canvas, 13 × 34 9/16 in. (33 × 87.8 cm)
Musée Matisse Nice

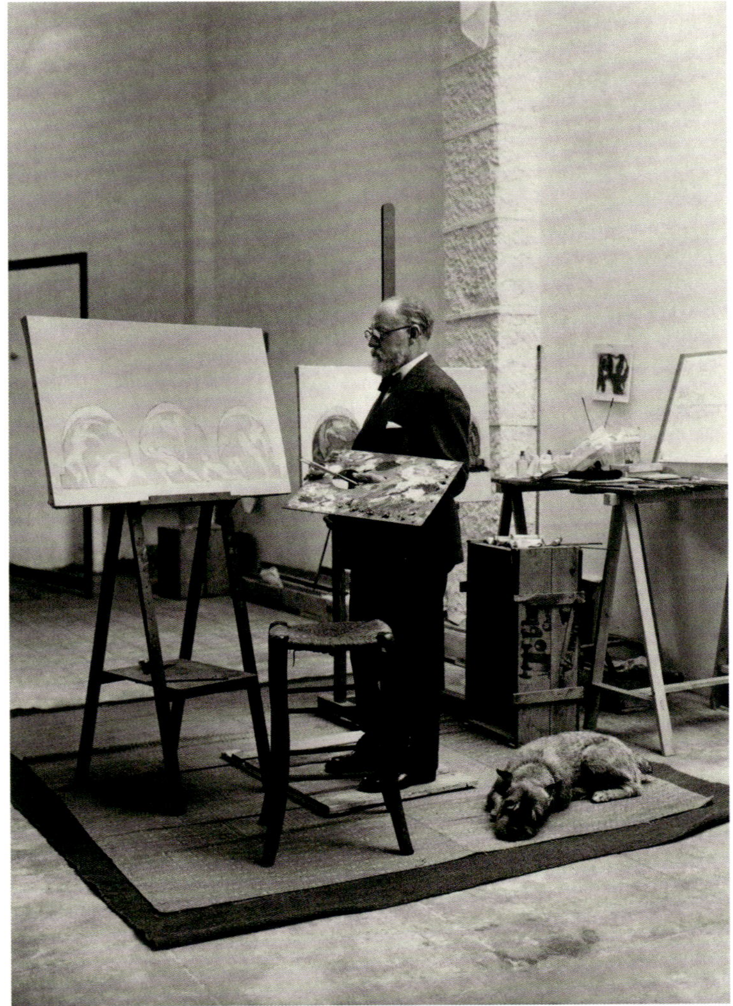

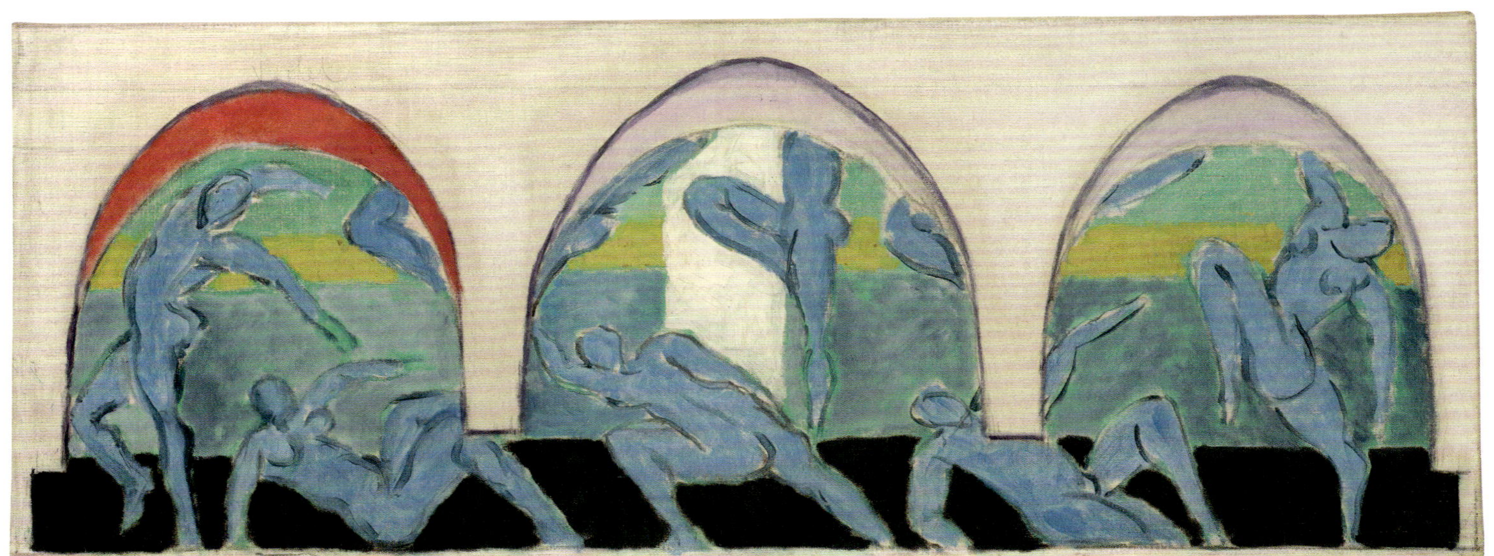

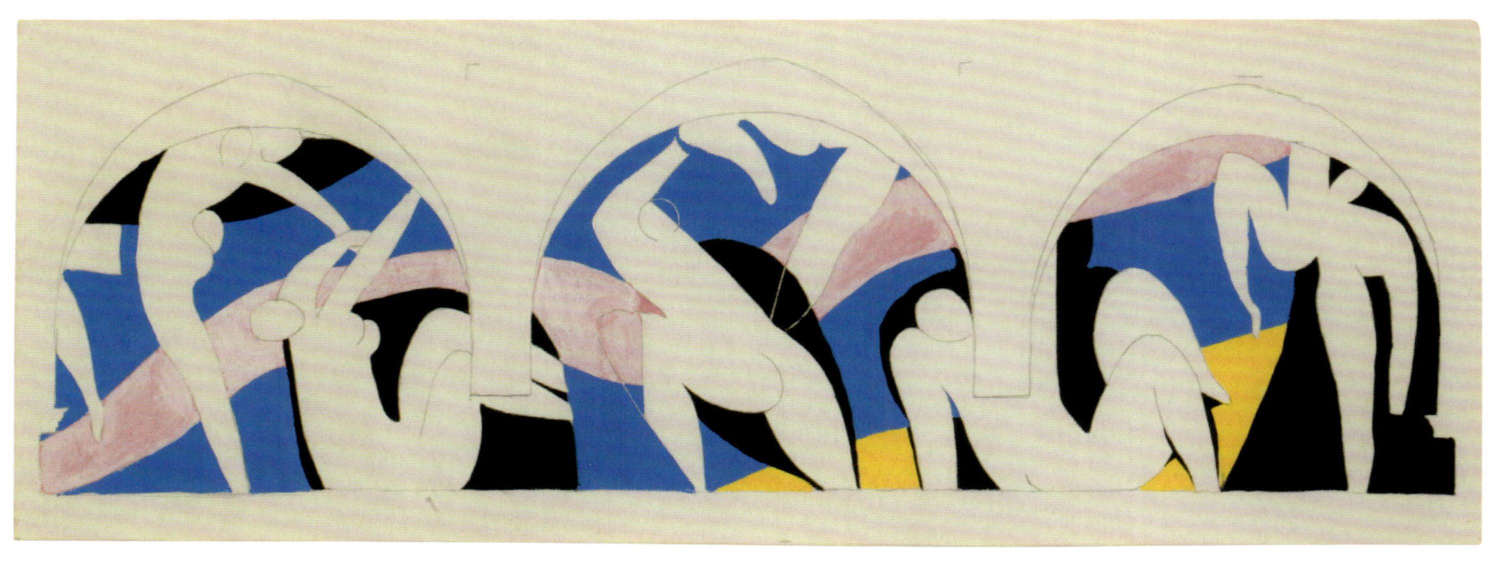

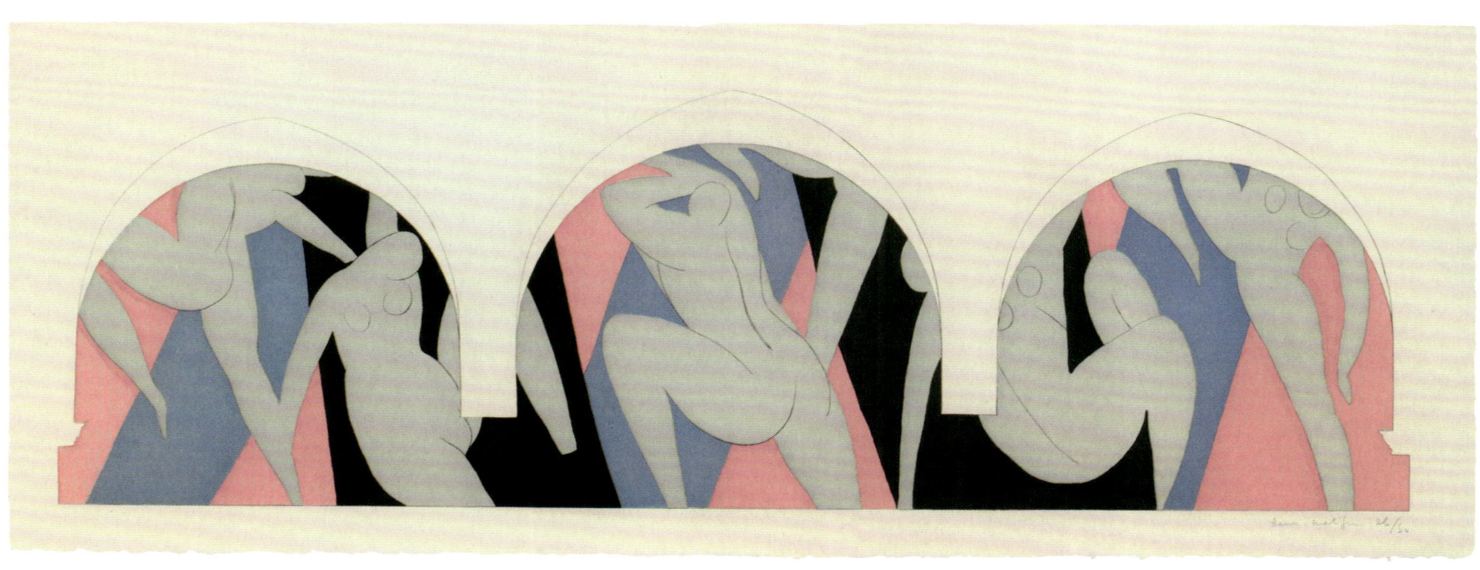

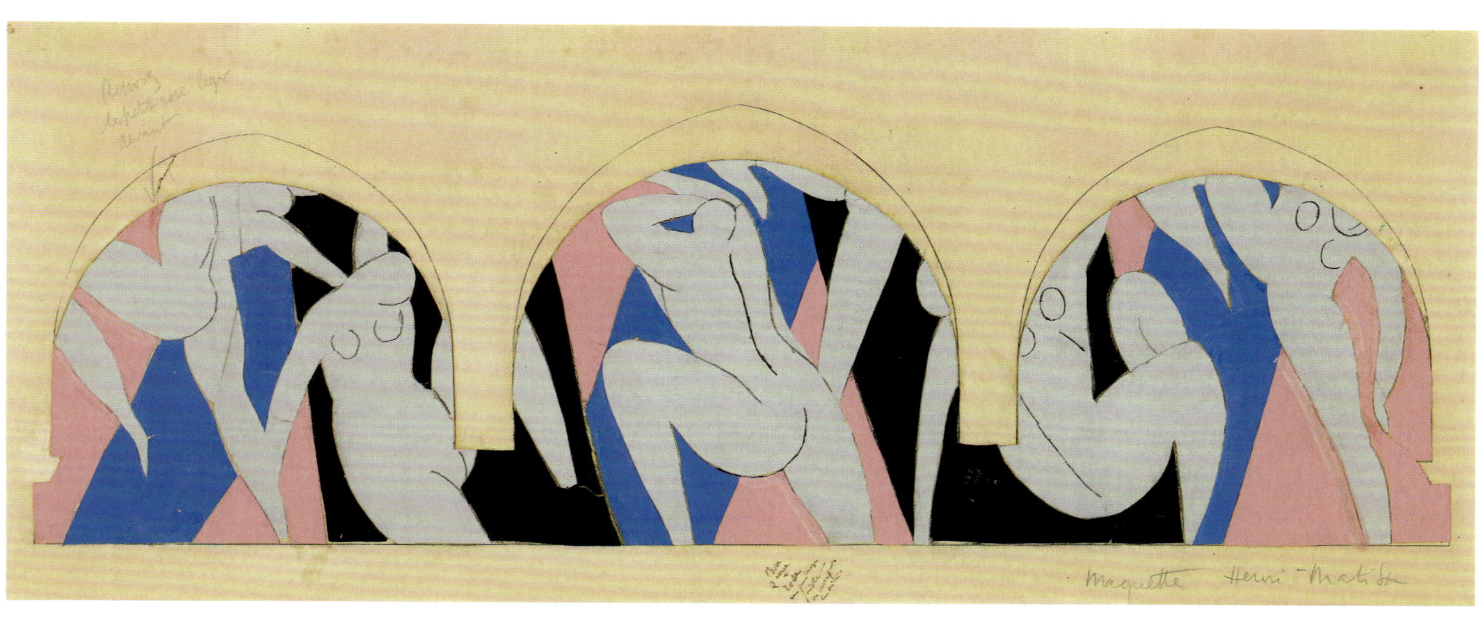
Maquette Henri-Matisse

98
The Dance: Study for the Barnes Mural (Second Version), 1931–32
Gouache and pencil on paper, 11 × 29 ⅞ in. (27.9 × 75.9 cm)
The Metropolitan Museum of Art, New York

99
Dance: After the Paris Version of the Barnes Mural, 1935
Etching and color aquatint on Arches wove paper, 11 ⅞ x 31 ⅝ in. (30.2 × 80.3 cm)
The Metropolitan Museum of Art, New York

100
The Dance, 1930–31
Gouached cut-outs on paper, 9 5/16 × 29 3/16 in. (31 × 77.5 cm)
Musée Matisse Nice

101 (fig.)
Albert Nulty next to the scaffolding for *The Dance*, Barnes Foundation, Merion, May 1933
Barnes Foundation Archives, Philadelphia

102 (fig.)
Christopher Naughton on the scaffolding for *The Dance*, Barnes Foundation, Merion, c. May 15, 1933
Barnes Foundation Archives, Philadelphia

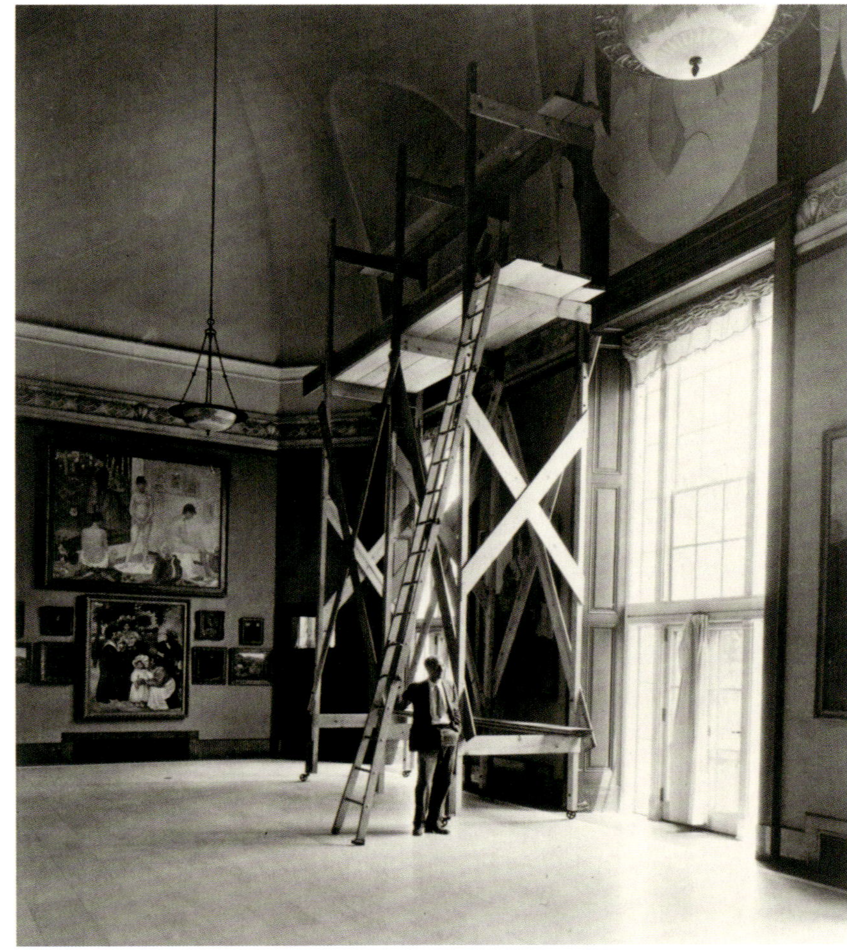

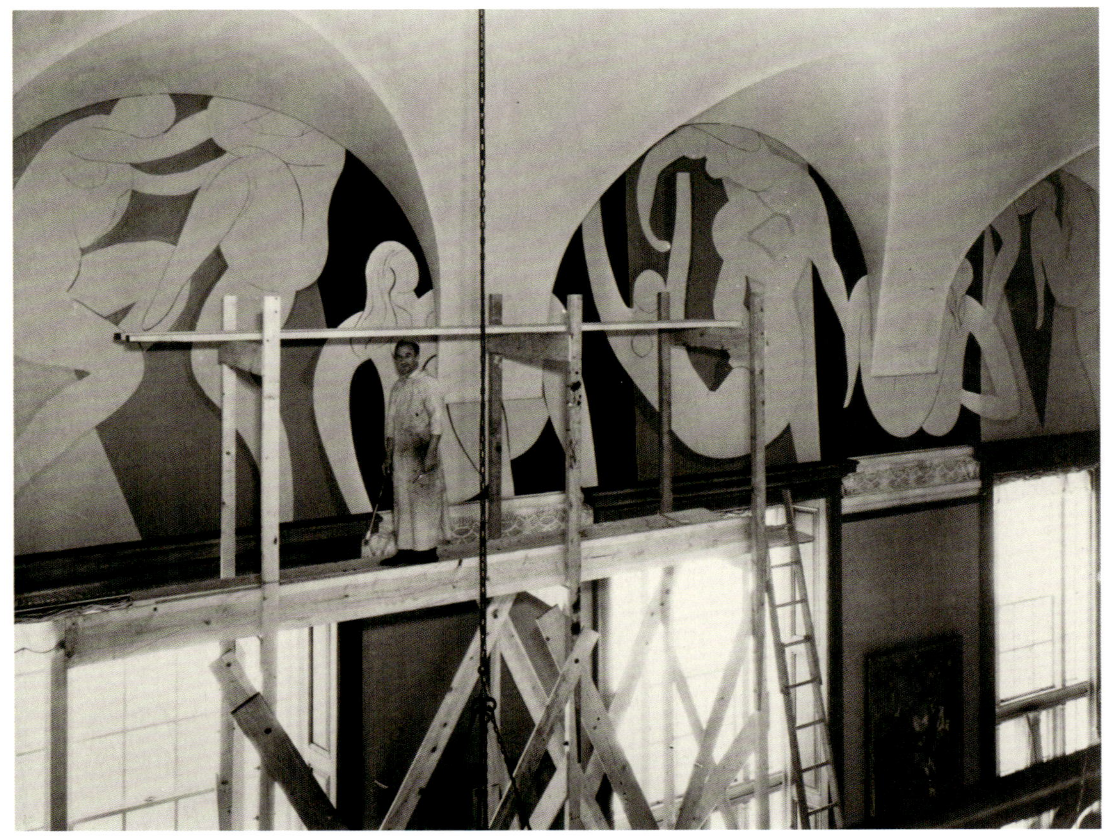

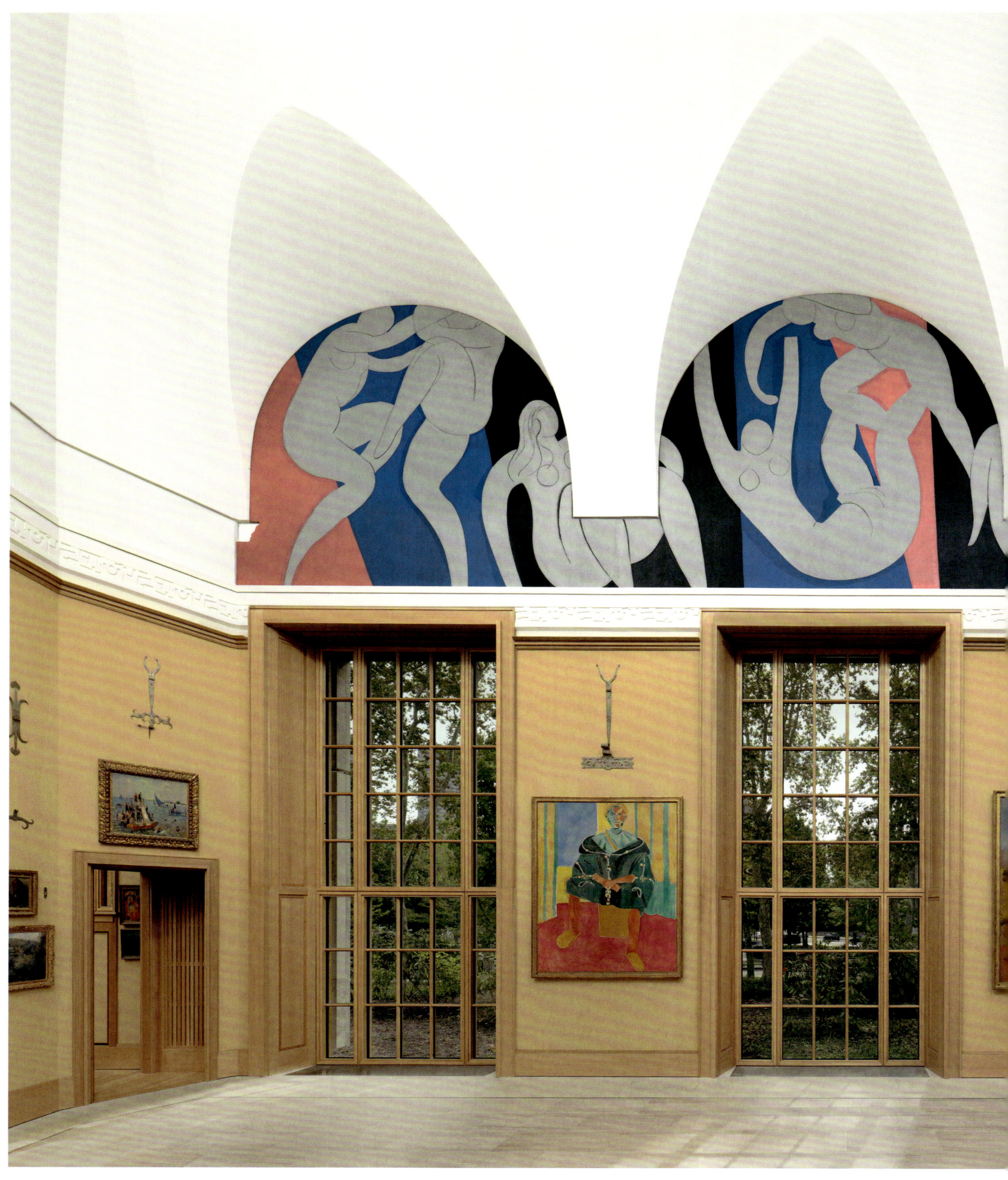

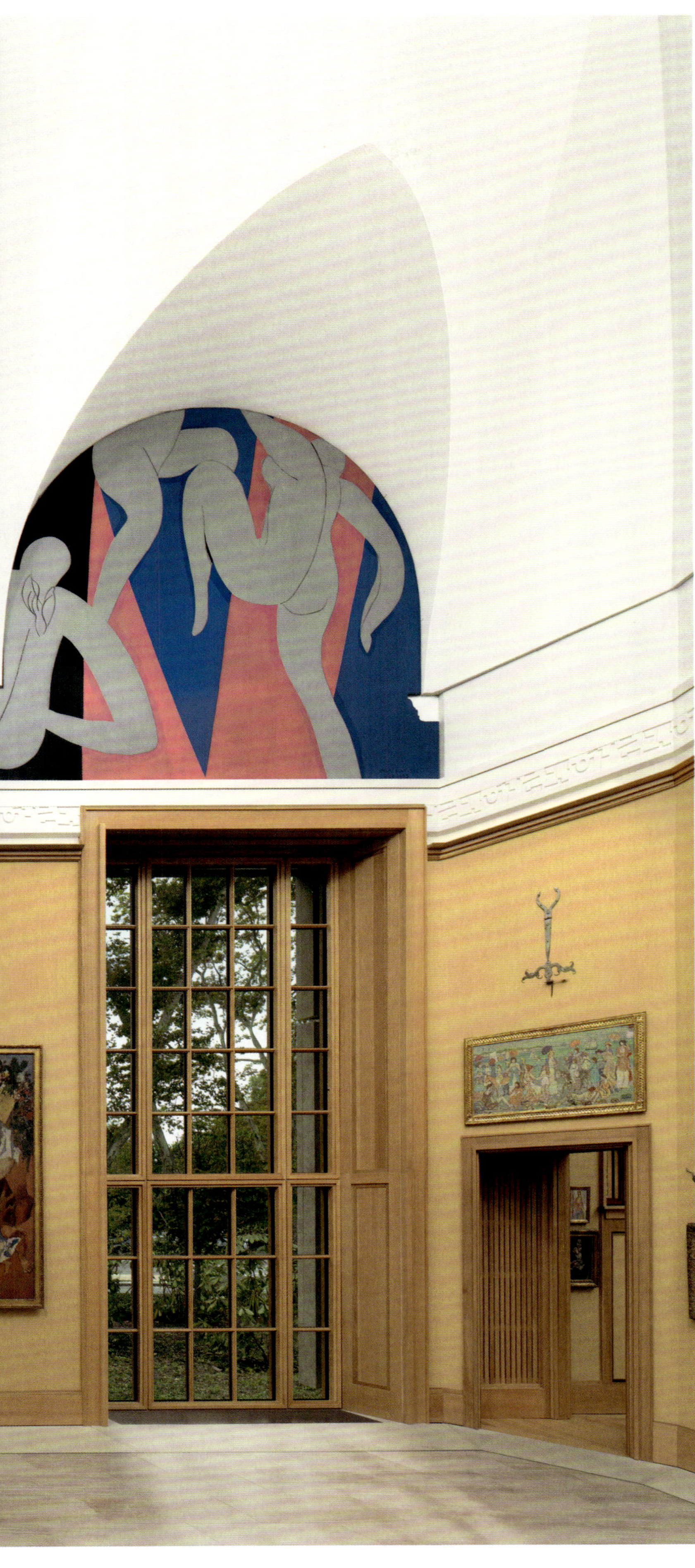

103 (fig.)
The Dance, ensemble view in Room 1 of the south hall, Barnes Foundation, Philadelphia location, 2012
Barnes Foundation, Philadelphia

104
Nude in a Robe, 1933–34
Oil on canvas,
25 9⁄16 × 18 1⁄8 in. (65 × 46 cm)
David and Ezra Nahmad
Collection

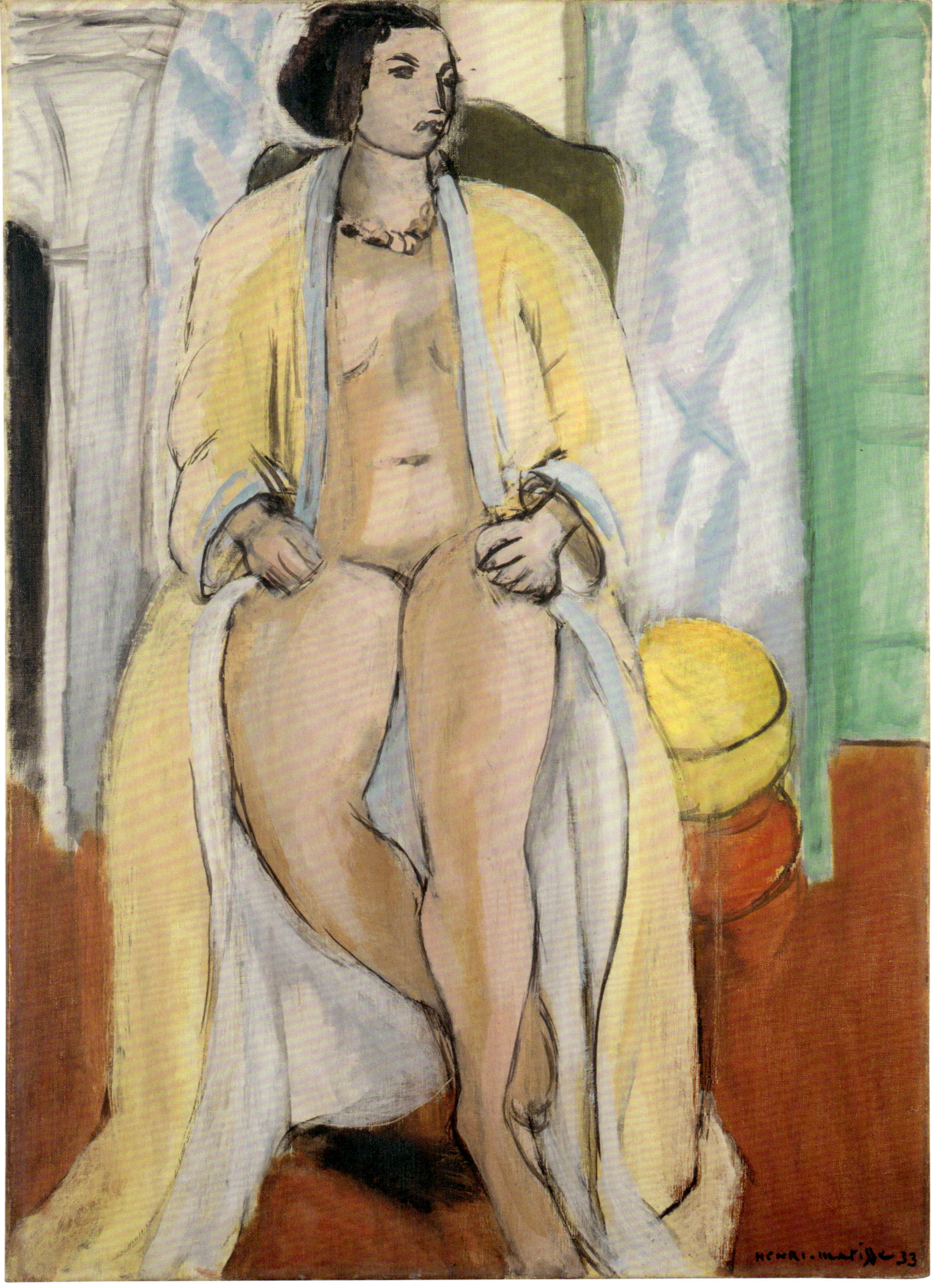
Henri-Matisse 33

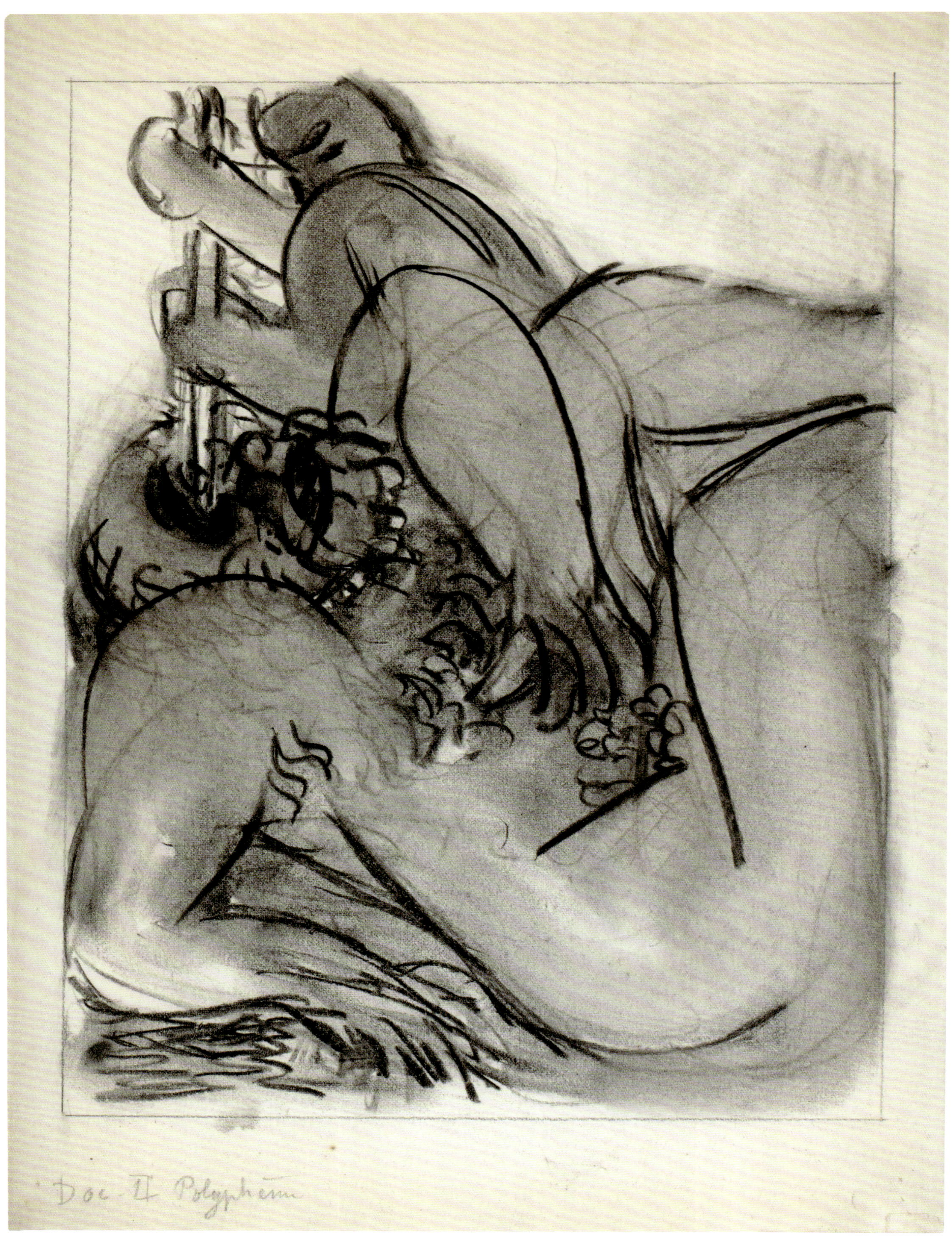

pp. 154–57
Henri Matisse, illustrations for James Joyce's *Ulysses*, 1934

105
Polyphemus
Charcoal on paper, 12 ⅝ × 9 ⅝ in. (32.1 × 24.4 cm)
The William Rubin Collection

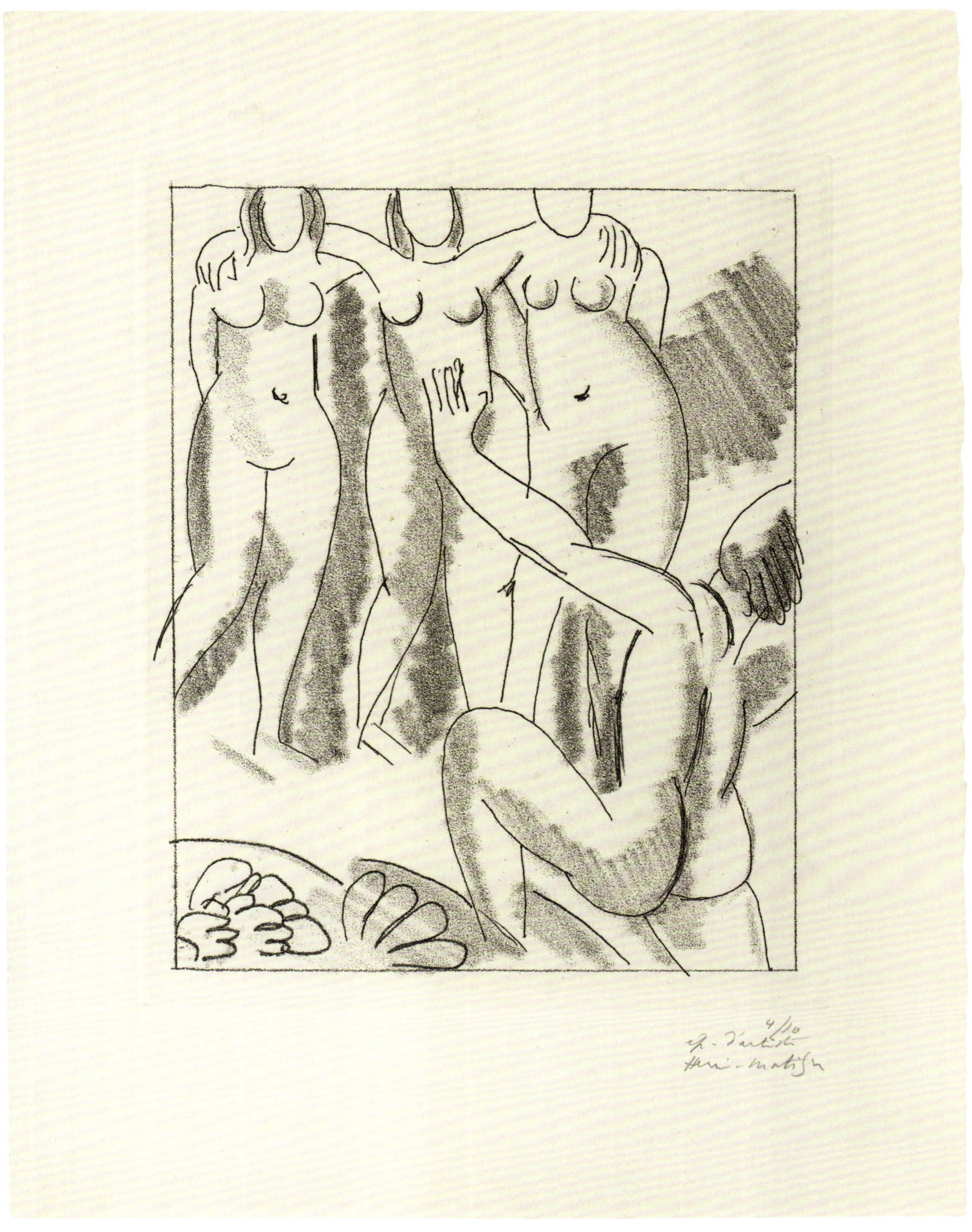

106
Nausicaa
Soft ground etching, 11 ½ × 9 in.
(29.2 × 22.9 cm)
The Pierre and Tana Matisse
Foundation, New York

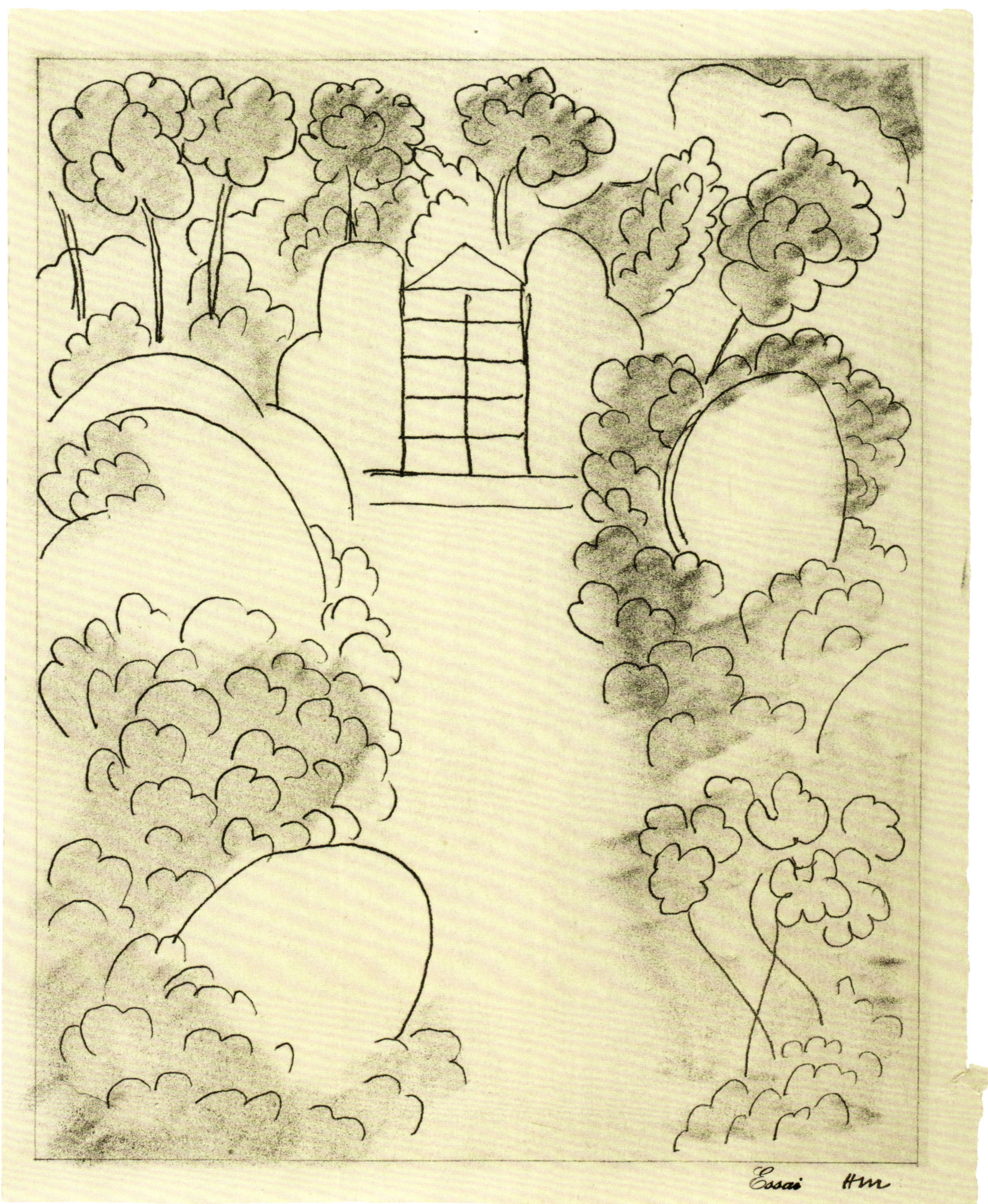

107
Ithaca
Soft ground etching, 11 ¼ × 8 ¾ in.
(28.5 × 22.3 cm)
The Pierre and Tana Matisse
Foundation, New York

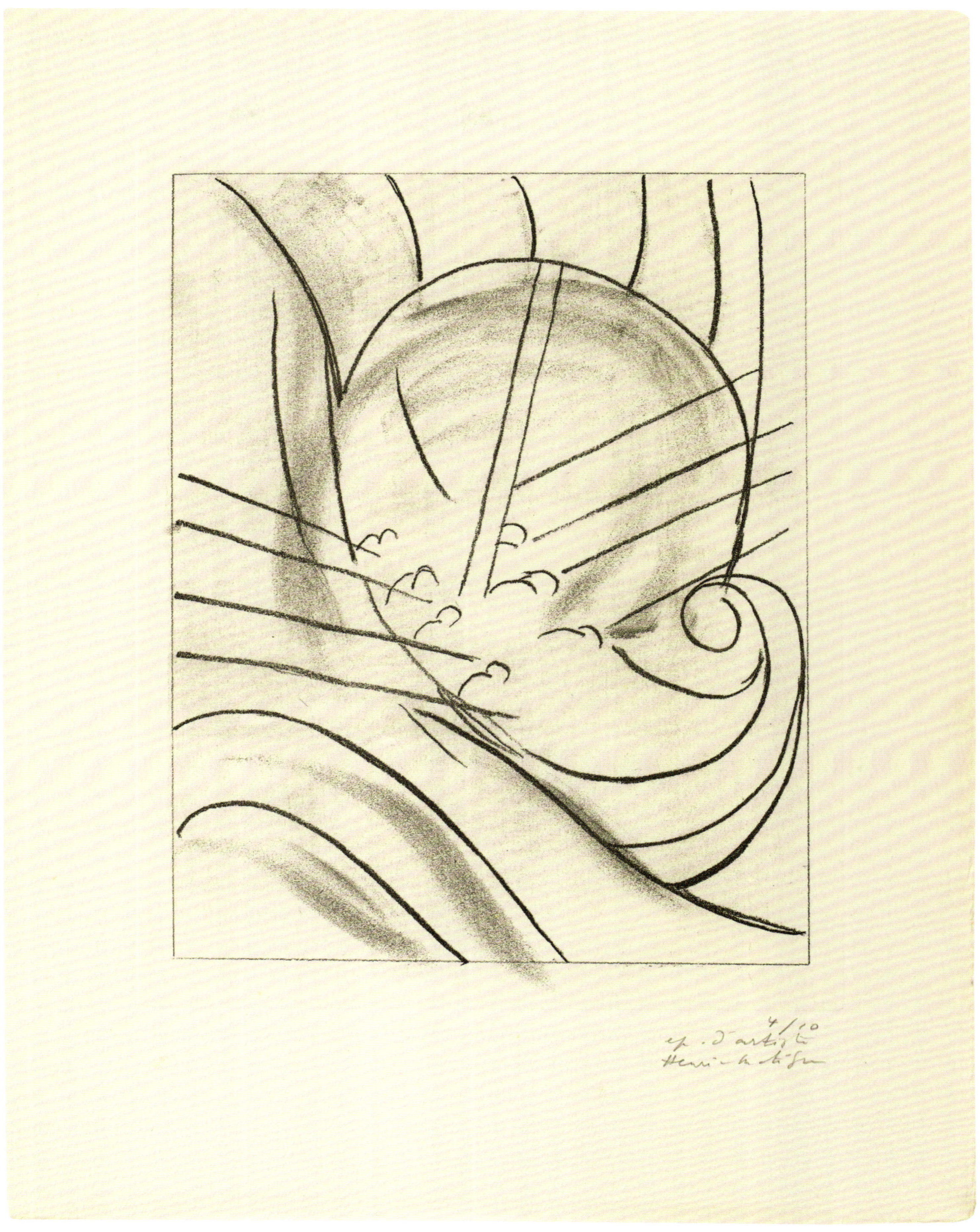

108
Aeolia, 1935
Soft ground etching, 11 5/8 × 9 1/16 in.
(29.5 × 23 cm)
The Pierre and Tana Matisse
Foundation, New York

PIERRE MATISSE GALLERY

1931–39: A DECISIVE DECADE

1 Pierre Matisse [PM]–Henri Matisse [HM], April 3, 1931, Pierre Matisse Gallery Archives, The Morgan Library & Museum, New York [PMGA].

2 As announced in an advertising slogan during the gallery's early days.

3 For example, "Matisse Is Coming," *Art Digest* 4, no. 8 (January 15, 1930): 18.

4 Henri Matisse, *Cinquante dessins*, foreword by Charles Vildrac (Paris: self-published by the artist, 1920).

5 This was the exhibition *Origines et développement de l'art international indépendant*, Musée du Jeu de Paume, Paris, July 30–October 31, 1937.

An art dealer and go-to figure in the modern art world, Matisse's son Pierre moved to New York in 1924 with the help of the artist and consultant Walter Pach and the dealer Joseph Brummer. In 1931 he would open his own art gallery—in the Fuller Building, "on the corner of 57th Street and Madison Avenue"[1]—at a key moment both for the recognition of his father's work in the United States and for its inclusion in major American collections both public and private.

Pierre Matisse initially worked with the Weyhe Gallery, where some of his father's drawings and engravings went on display in 1925, and later joined forces with the art dealer Valentine Dudensing, who opened a gallery in 1926, where he mounted two exhibitions devoted to Matisse in 1927 and 1929. Dudensing tried and failed to obtain a contract with the painter at a time when he was facing competition in the American market from fellow gallery owners Georges Keller and Étienne Bignou.

Pierre never obtained sole rights to sales of his father's work either, but his detailed knowledge of his oeuvre and privileged access to his unpublished works helped him make a name for himself from the early 1930s as a key player just when Matisse was becoming a must-have artist in the international art market. Pierre's gallery, which promised to show the "best modern paintings and sculptures,"[2] built up a solid reputation at a time when a specifically American modern art was taking shape in the United States with the emergence of a New York school, and with the Museum of Modern Art (MoMA) having opened its doors in 1929, followed by the Whitney Museum of American Art in 1931. Pierre developed his strategy while fully apprised of the new climate of cultural nationalism, economic depression, and the rise of fascism in Europe.

During the 1930s, Pierre Matisse devoted four major exhibits to his father, who at that time was only just discovering the United States himself, later staying there on four occasions, notably for the installation of *The Dance* at the Barnes Foundation in Merion, Pennsylvania 103. These meticulously prepared trips earned Matisse some spectacular media coverage,[3] particularly when he sat on the jury for the Carnegie Prize in 1930.

In 1932, after supervising the mounting of the retrospective that Alfred H. Barr Jr. devoted to his father at MoMA, Pierre brought together a set of pen drawings from 1919–20 and helped to get the book of these drawings into many American libraries.[4] Faced with the limited availability of Matisse works at that time, Pierre masterminded some clever hangings by borrowing paintings from outside collections, as was the case early in 1934 on the occasion of the exhibition *Henri Matisse: Paintings* at his gallery, to which hundreds of people flocked in the opening days. In 1936, he showed the first version of *The Dance* (1909; MoMA), which was at that time completely unknown in the United States. This had an immediate effect and helped restore Matisse to his ranking among artists to watch within the international avant-garde. Yvonne Zervos also contributed to elevating his status the following year with the exhibition at the Jeu de Paume museum in Paris.[5] On the eve of World War II, Pierre displayed a series of recent paintings, including *The Romanian Blouse* (1940; Musée National d'Art Moderne–Centre Pompidou, Paris).

Pierre's perceptive programming established the gallery's reputation when times were hard and secured the loyalty of the prestigious collectors who were behind Matisse's entry onto the American art market, such as A. Conger Goodyear, Stephen C. Clark, Samuel A. Lewisohn, James Thrall Soby, and Joseph Pulitzer Jr., whom Pierre accompanied in 1939 to the Grand Hotel in Lucerne for the sale of "degenerate" art, where he purchased *Bathers with a Turtle* (1907–8; Saint Louis Art Museum).

As the driving force behind his father's reception across the Atlantic, Pierre played a decisive role in circulating the artist's works. For his exhibition and catalogue projects he enlisted a network of intellectuals, major collectors, dealers, museum curators, critics, and directors of magazines such as *Cahiers d'art*, in which he purchased many advertising inserts.

On a more personal level, Pierre married Alexina "Teeny" Sattler in 1929, and their three children were born in the following decade: Jacqueline (Jackie for short) in 1931, Paul in 1933, and Pierre-Noël (called Peter) in 1936. At that time, Pierre had an active correspondence with his father, and also with his sister Marguerite. Pierre became a crucial confidant whom Henri would talk to about the ups and downs of his work, and ask for his opinion, which could be very critical, as in this letter from 1935: "The one I like best of all is still the nude you were working on when I left Nice. For me it is more balanced and really seems to be going somewhere. Whereas all the earlier ones strike me as representing research work looking to find a direction and which begins to take off as we see in the nude with a disproportionately long arm against a blue ground, although in my view that canvas is not successful."[6] The entire correspondence between father and son, as well as the gallery's invaluable archives, were gifted by the Pierre and Tana Matisse Foundation to the Pierpont Morgan Library in New York (now the Morgan Library & Museum) and have yielded material for numerous research projects and exhibitions.[7]

To one journalist who interviewed him live on the radio at the time of the opening of the 1948 Matisse retrospective in Philadelphia, asking "who is the flag of French painting . . . I think everyone would say Matisse?" Pierre replied soberly, "Yes, I think so."[8]

AYMERIC JEUDY

6 PM–HM, undated letter [August 13, 1935], PMGA.

7 Claudine Grammont, ed., *Pierre Matisse, un marchand d'art à New York*, exh. cat. (Paris: Bernard Chauveau, 2021).

8 "Archives diverses: Sons des États-Unis," Institut National de l'Audiovisuel, Paris, PHD99101416.

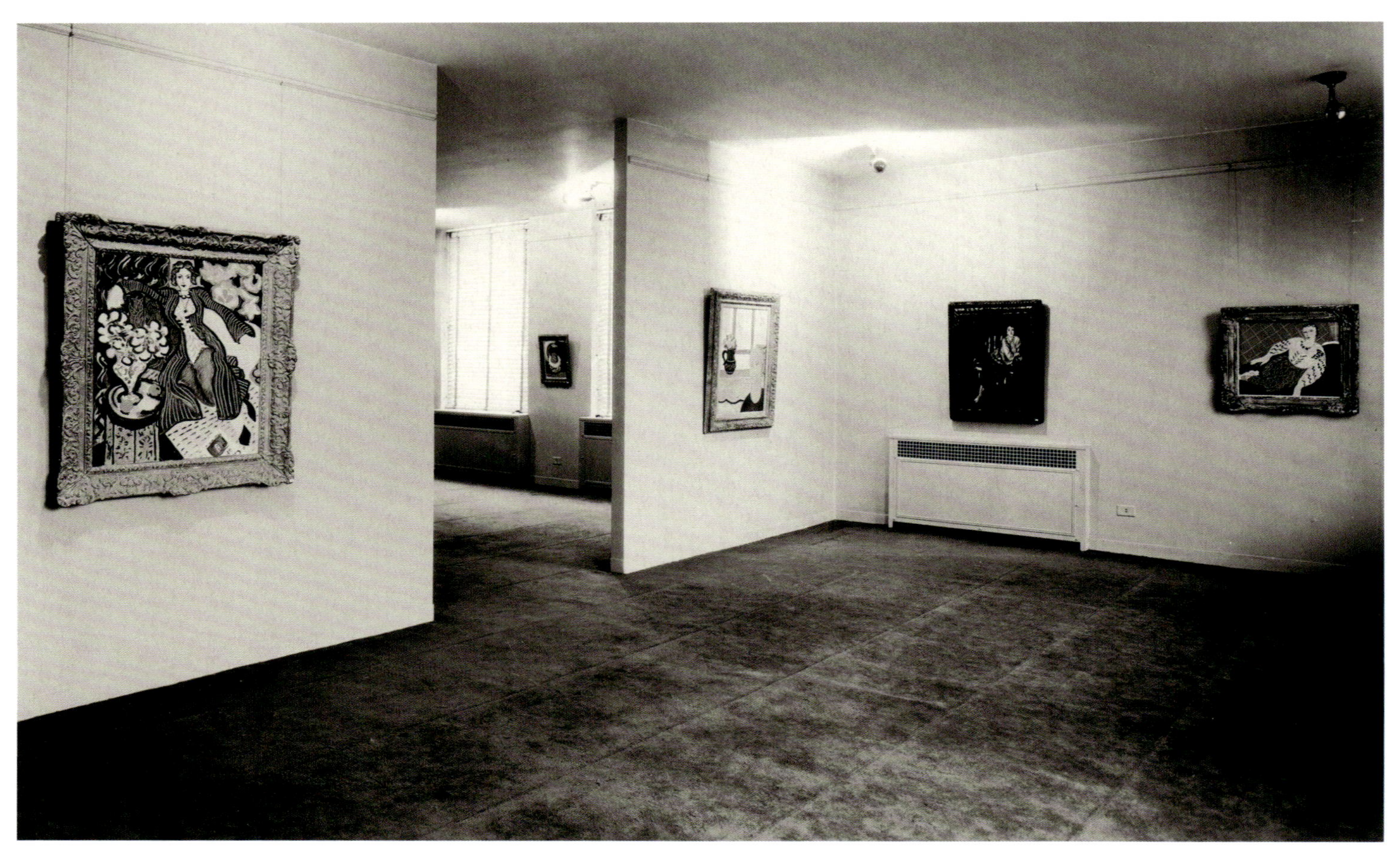

109 a–c (figs.)
Views of the exhibition
Henri Matisse: Paintings and Drawings of 1918 to 1938
at the Pierre Matisse Gallery, New York, November 15–December 10, 1938
Archives Henri Matisse, Issy-les-Moulineaux

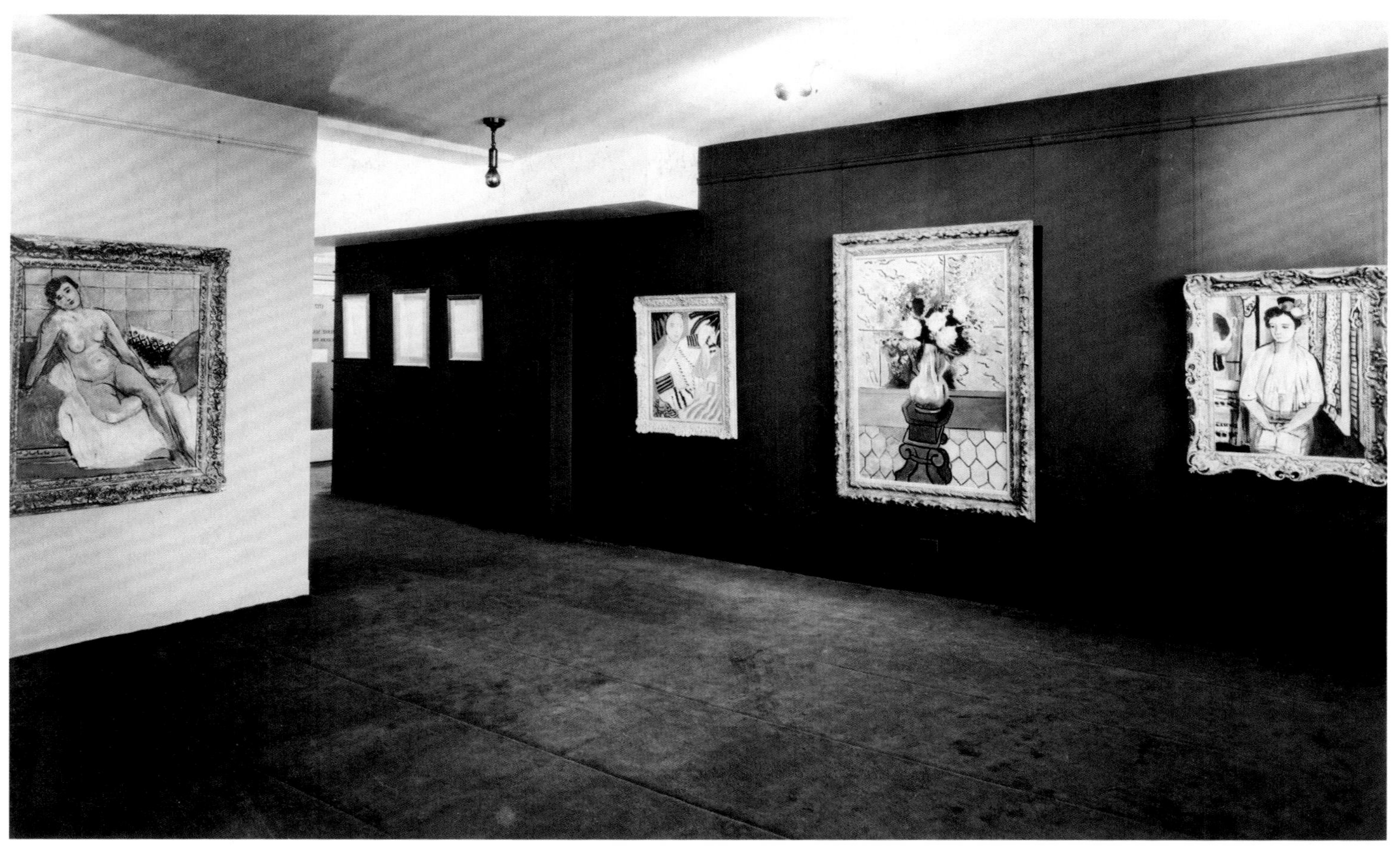

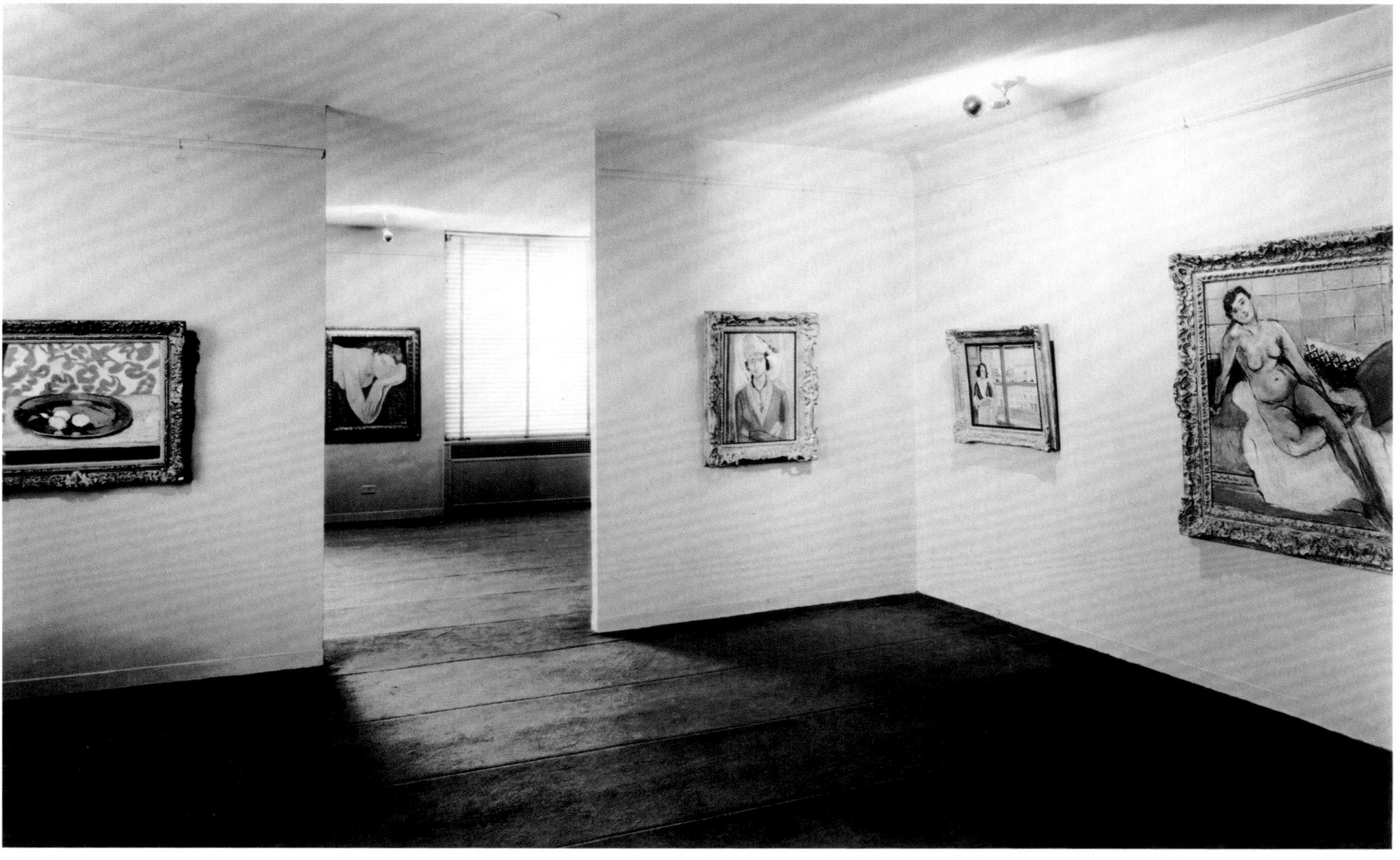

LARGE RECLINING NUDE

A central work in the collection of the Baltimore Museum of Art, Matisse's *Large Reclining Nude* 110 was purchased from the artist by Etta Cone in 1936, after its exhibition that same year at Paul Rosenberg's gallery in Paris. It entered the museum's collections upon Etta Cone's death in 1949, and was presented there for the first time with the title *Pink Nude*.[1] Rarely shown outside the United States, the painting was exhibited in France in 1970 and 2002.[2]

Matisse had only returned to painting in 1934–35, after working with great intensity from 1931 to 1933 on the three versions of *The Dance* for the Barnes Foundation, and having taken to heart the lessons learned from that commission, the "superhuman dimensions" of which marked a turning point in his career.[3] He undertook *Large Reclining Nude* from April to October 1935, before completing *The Dream* 33 and while also working on other paintings, including *Seated Pink Nude* and *Nymph in the Forest (Verdure)* 123 | 116.

Large Reclining Nude perfectly exemplifies the artist's creative process and research methods. It is one of the paintings most documented by means of the in-progress photographs taken systematically at what Matisse regarded as milestone stages in the execution of a canvas. In this instance, the spectacular sequence of twenty-two states dated, numbered, and forwarded to Etta Cone provides valuable insight into this complex and painstaking method introduced by the painter at the beginning of the decade 111. Their juxtaposition offers a flipbook view of the six months of labor devoted to this work and the bodily contortions of the artist's then primary model, Lydia Delectorskaya.

What Matisse describes as a "path" (*route*) is littered with hesitations, pentimenti, erasures, and scratchings-out. His use of gouache-painted paper cut-outs, as for *The Dance*, facilitated a gradual transition from a naturalist nude to a masterpiece of geometric radicality. The purpose of the cut-outs was to allow him to manipulate shapes, colors, and textures until he struck exactly the right chord—the numerous pinholes still visible on the canvas testify to this process. The body lengthens, expands, is amplified in an extreme twist, with the curve and arabesque becoming angular and rigid, as we see, for example, in the model's left elbow. The small bunch of flowers, the Matissian motif par excellence, illustrates the simplification of form as it passes from a seemingly realistic bouquet to an abstract shape comprising a broad swath of flat yellow. Like those Romanesque workers who "distorted their figures out of a need to strike a balance between the architecture and the figures to be set within it,"[4] Matisse places his nude right up to the edges of the canvas on a checkerboard formed by the tiled walls and the square pattern of the blue fabric. The artist transposes into a modest easel-painting format (here 26 ⅛ × 36 ¾ in.) an architectural, monumental experience and his recently acquired views on wall painting by renewing an expansive, decorative approach to the pictorial field. This intense, pure representation of the human body reduced to just a few colors illustrates Matisse's concern for the relationship between things, and constitutes a landmark in his work, its eight states reproduced in Roger Fry's 1935 monograph devoted to the artist.

AYMERIC JEUDY

1 Gertrude Rosenthal, "Selections from the Cone Collection," *Baltimore Museum of Art News*, October–December 1949.

2 Pierre Schneider, ed., *Henri Matisse: Exposition du centenaire*, exh. cat. (Paris: Réunion des Musées Nationaux, 1970); Elizabeth Cowling, Anne Baldassari, and John Elderfield, eds., *Matisse–Picasso*, exh. cat. (London: Tate, 2002).

3 Henri Matisse–Albert C. Barnes, April 18, 1931, cited in Yve-Alain Bois, ed., *Matisse in the Barnes Foundation* (Philadelphia: Barnes Foundation / London: Thames & Hudson, 2015), 3:230.

4 Henri Matisse, *Écrits et propos sur l'art*, ed. Dominique Fourcade (Paris: Hermann, 1972), 39.

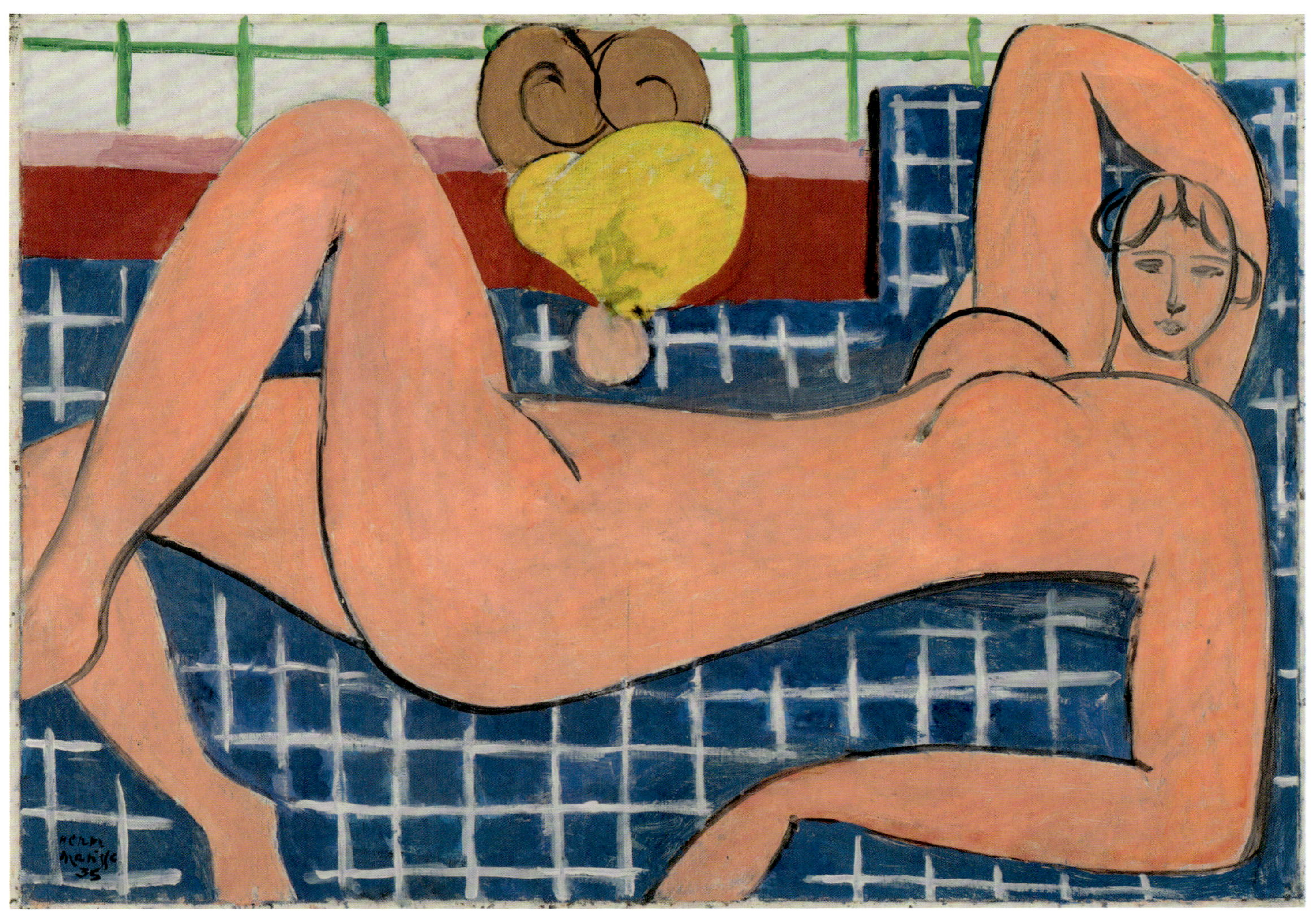

110
Large Reclining Nude, 1935
Oil on canvas, 26 ⅛ × 36 ¾ in.
(66.4 × 93.3 cm)
Baltimore Museum of Art

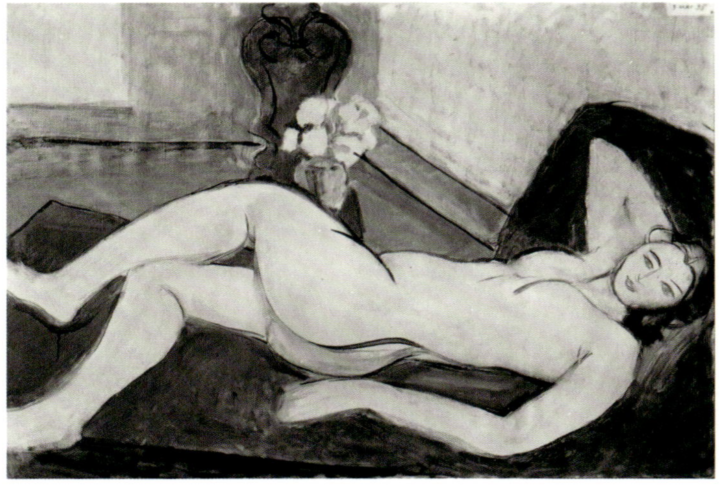

May 3

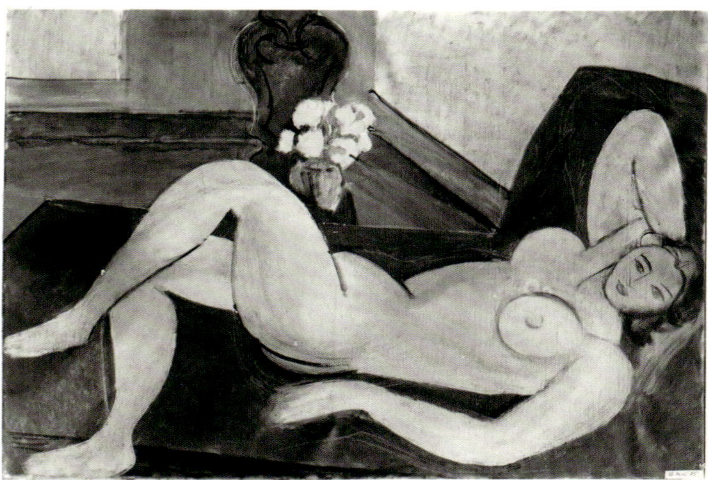

May 16

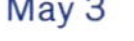

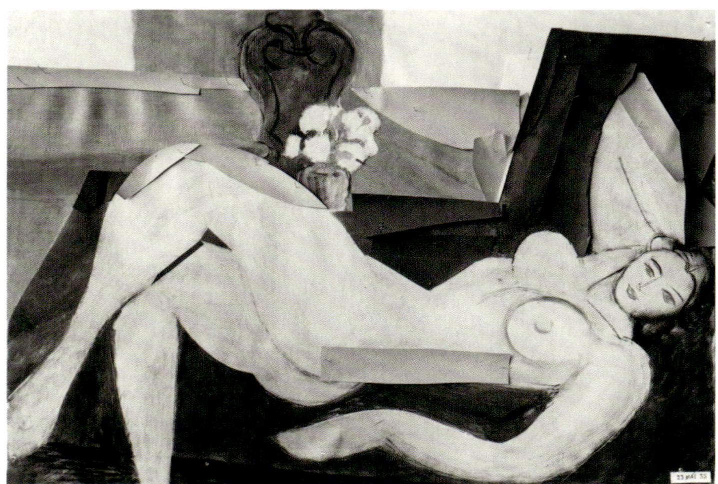

May 23

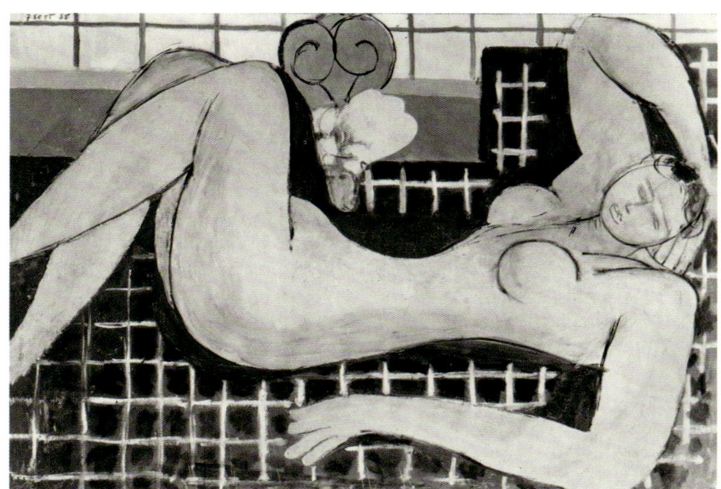

September 7

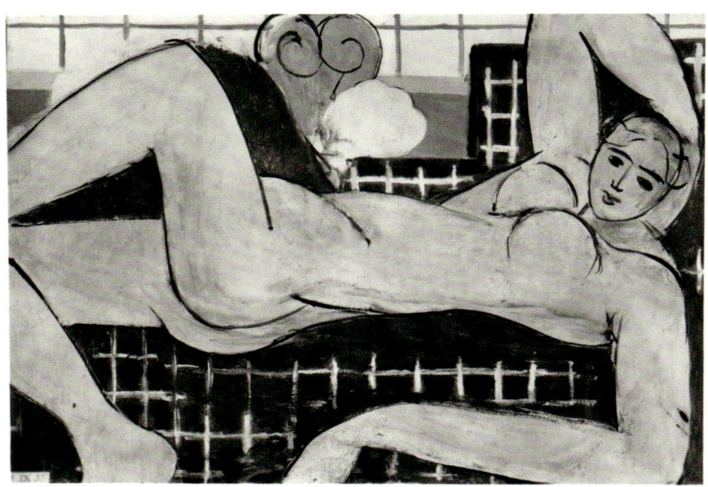

September 15

111 (figs.)
In-progress photographs
of *Large Reclining Nude*, 1935
Archives Henri Matisse,
Issy-les-Moulineaux

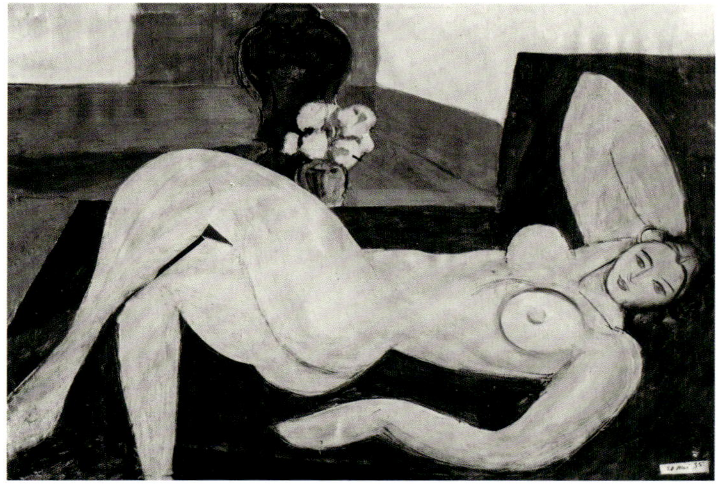

May 20

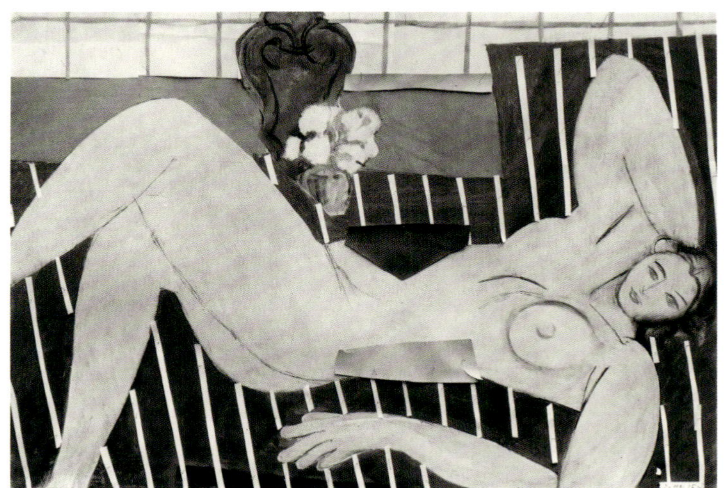

May 29

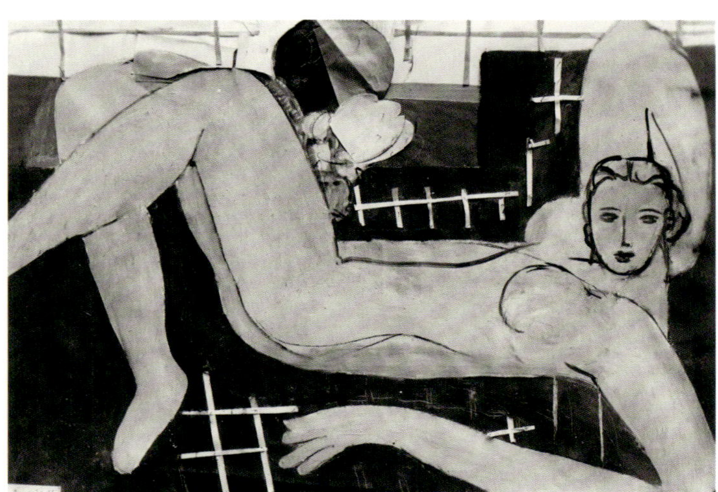

August 20

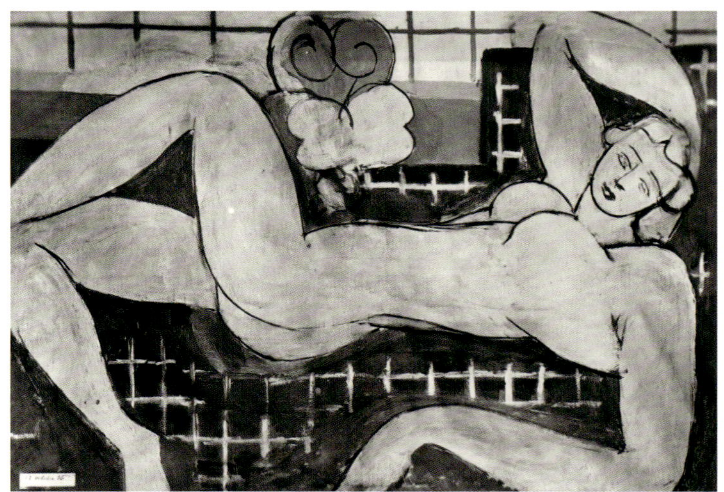

October 13

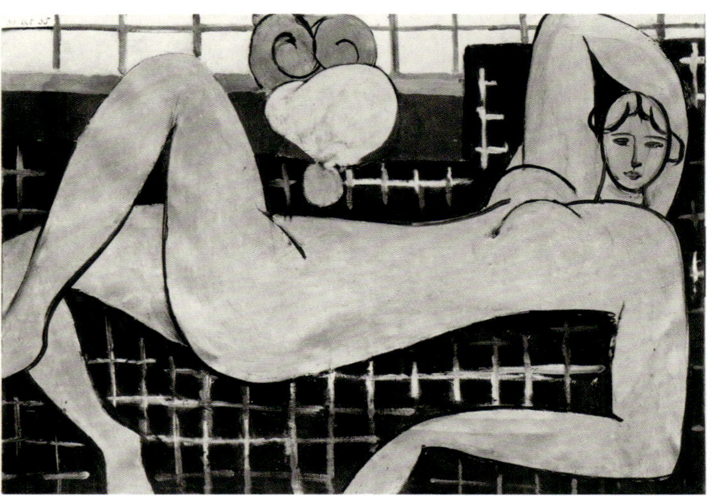

October 15

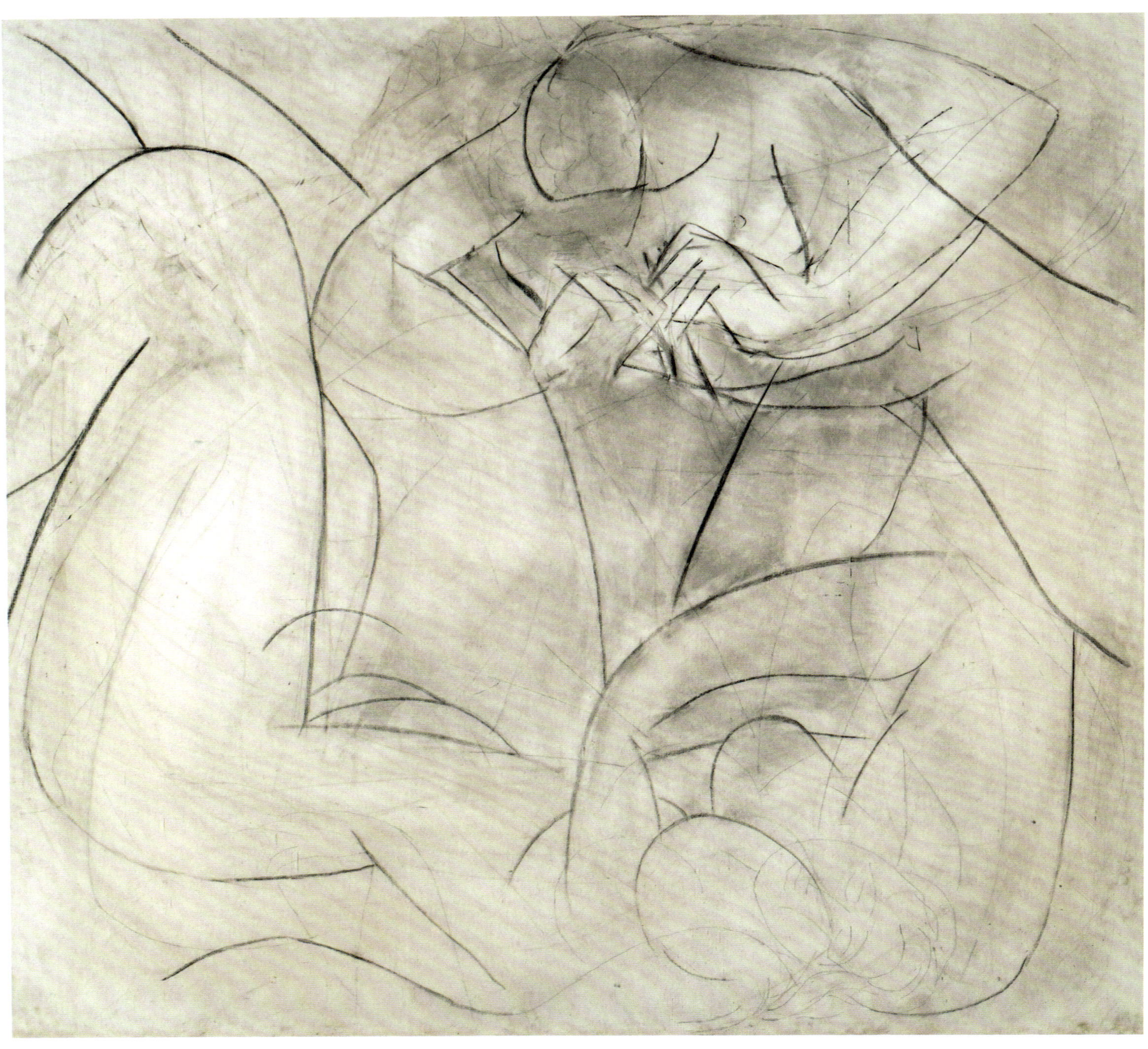

112
Nymph and Faun, April 1935–43
Charcoal and stump on prepared canvas, 60 ⅝ × 65 ¾ in. (154 × 167 cm)
Musée National d'Art Moderne–Centre Pompidou, Paris

NYMPH IN THE FOREST (VERDURE)

Responding in August 1935 to a commission from Marie Cuttoli for a tapestry in Beauvais low warp, Matisse undertook three panels inspired by his illustrations for Stéphane Mallarmé's *Poésies*, the two versions of *Tahiti* 118 | 119 and *Nymph in the Forest (Verdure)* 116. The motif for this last panel synthesizes in a single composition the etching illustrating Mallarmé's "L'Après-midi d'un Faune" (Afternoon of a Faun), for the figures, and that illustrating "Prose pour Des Esseintes" (Prose for Des Esseintes), for the forest. It is also related to the drawings Matisse made as illustrations for James Joyce's *Ulysses*, notably *Calypso* and *Ithaca* 28 | 107. Of these three panels, in the end only one was woven, after *Papeete, Tahiti*. In the case of *Nymph in the Forest*, while its first states address the artist's original intention to create a tapestry, it seems he abandoned this idea fairly quickly on seeing the disappointing outcome of *Papeete, Tahiti*.

After his exhibition in May 1936 at Paul Rosenberg's Paris gallery, where *Nymph in the Forest* was shown along with the two versions of *Tahiti*, the panel was taken back to the studio. He continued to work on it on and off until 1943. In a letter to his daughter, Marguerite, he emphasized the painting's experimental nature: "It is a work that I am working on or that is working on me, and I consider it a very important thing for me, as a result of composition."[1]

In this respect *Nymph in the Forest* pursues the transitory, open character that led to the execution of the panels of *The Dance* between 1930 and 1933. The extended period required to complete the mural, something that did not happen often in Matisse's practice, reminds us of how painting can incorporate a time element and integrate duration within its materiality. As the many surface pentimenti show, *Nymph in the Forest* is not the outcome of a cumulative process of successive applications, but rather of erasures that paradoxically cause the image to appear. This results in a pulsation, a dual movement of contraction and expansion, of the disappearance/appearance of bodies. The unfinished as opposed to the academic finish, which, following Paul Cézanne, had been a crucial resource for Matissian Fauvism, is here combined with an unfinished quality that sets painting apart from its reproducible derivative. This goes some way toward explaining why Matisse did not wish to continue on the path of realizing a tapestry of what quickly became a work in its own right.

For a long time the panel hung on the walls of his studio at the Régina in the hills of Cimiez, overlooking Nice 54. Through its evocation of the forest, it became a part of the luxuriant scenery of the place. As part of the studio setting, it occasionally crops up in other paintings, thereby creating a mise en abyme effect that Matisse was especially fond of, as in *Interior with an Etruscan Vase* and *Still Life with Sleeping Woman* 152 | 155.

CLAUDINE GRAMMONT

1 Henri Matisse–Marguerite Duthuit, March 7, 1936, Archives Henri Matisse, Issy-les-Moulineaux.

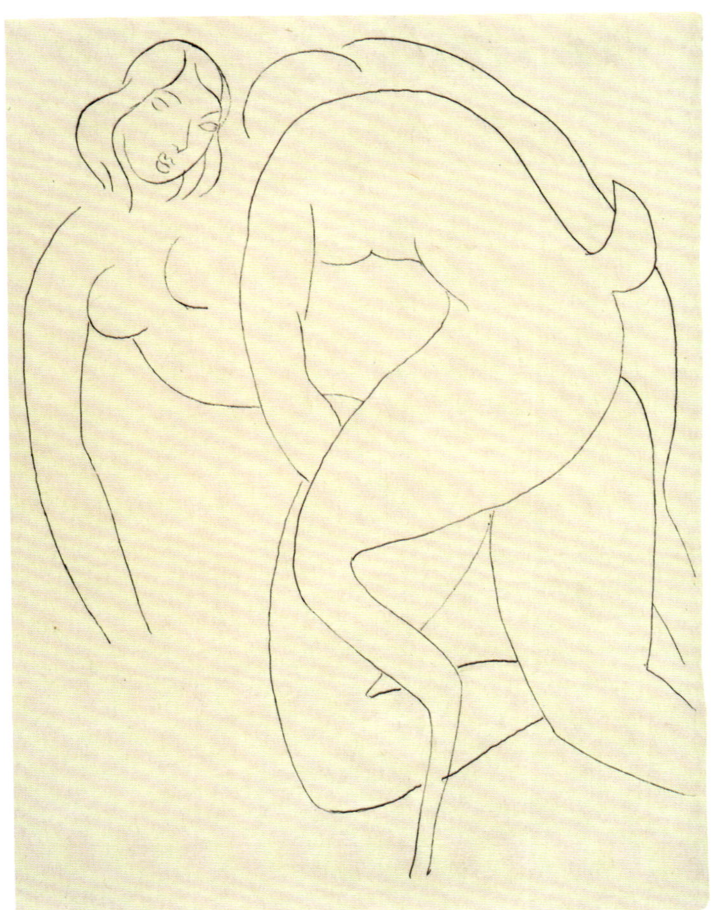
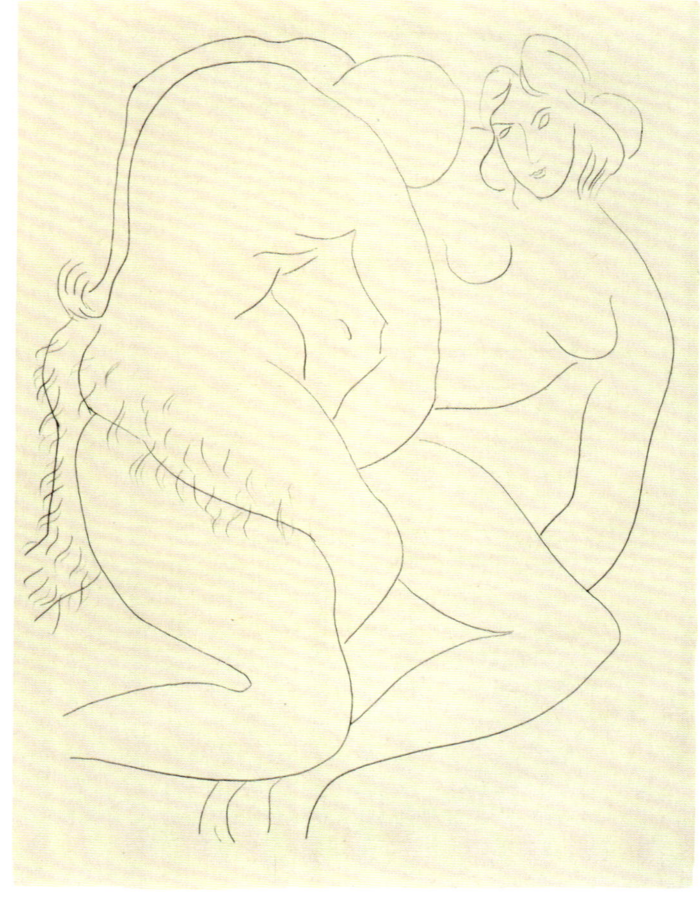

113, **114**
Afternoon of a Faun, 1930–32
Etchings, 13 ⅛ × 9 ⅞ in.
(33.3 × 25.1 cm)
Musée Départemental Matisse,
Le Cateau-Cambrésis

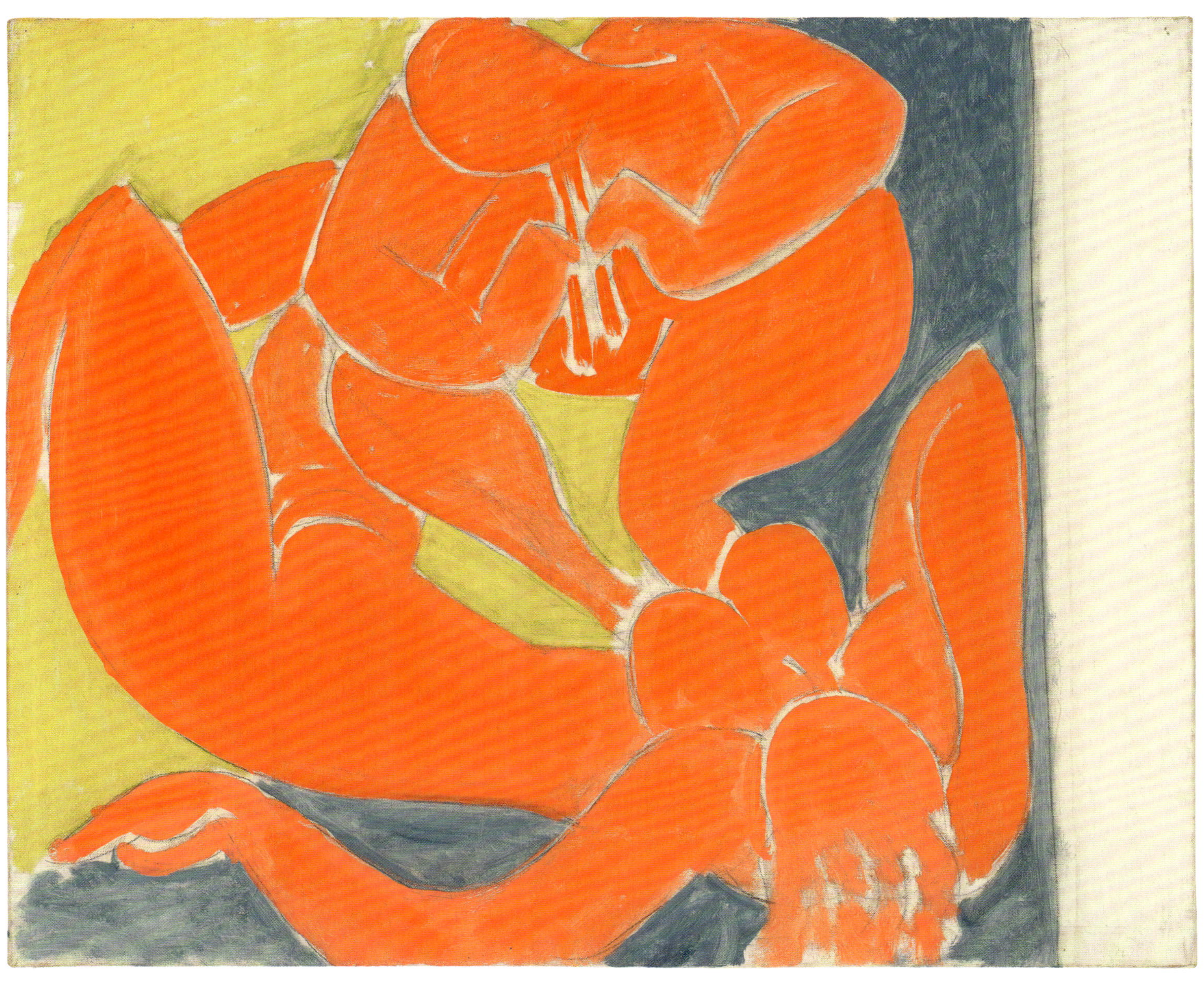

115
Red Nymph and Faun, c. 1935
Oil and Conté crayon on canvas,
19 ¹¹⁄₁₆ × 24 in. (50 × 61 cm)
Private collection

116
Nymph in the Forest (Verdure),
1935–42/43
Oil on canvas, 8 ft. ⅝ in. × 6 ft. 4 ¹⁵⁄₁₆ in.
(245.5 × 195.5 cm)
Musée d'Orsay, Paris, held at the
Musée Matisse Nice, 1978

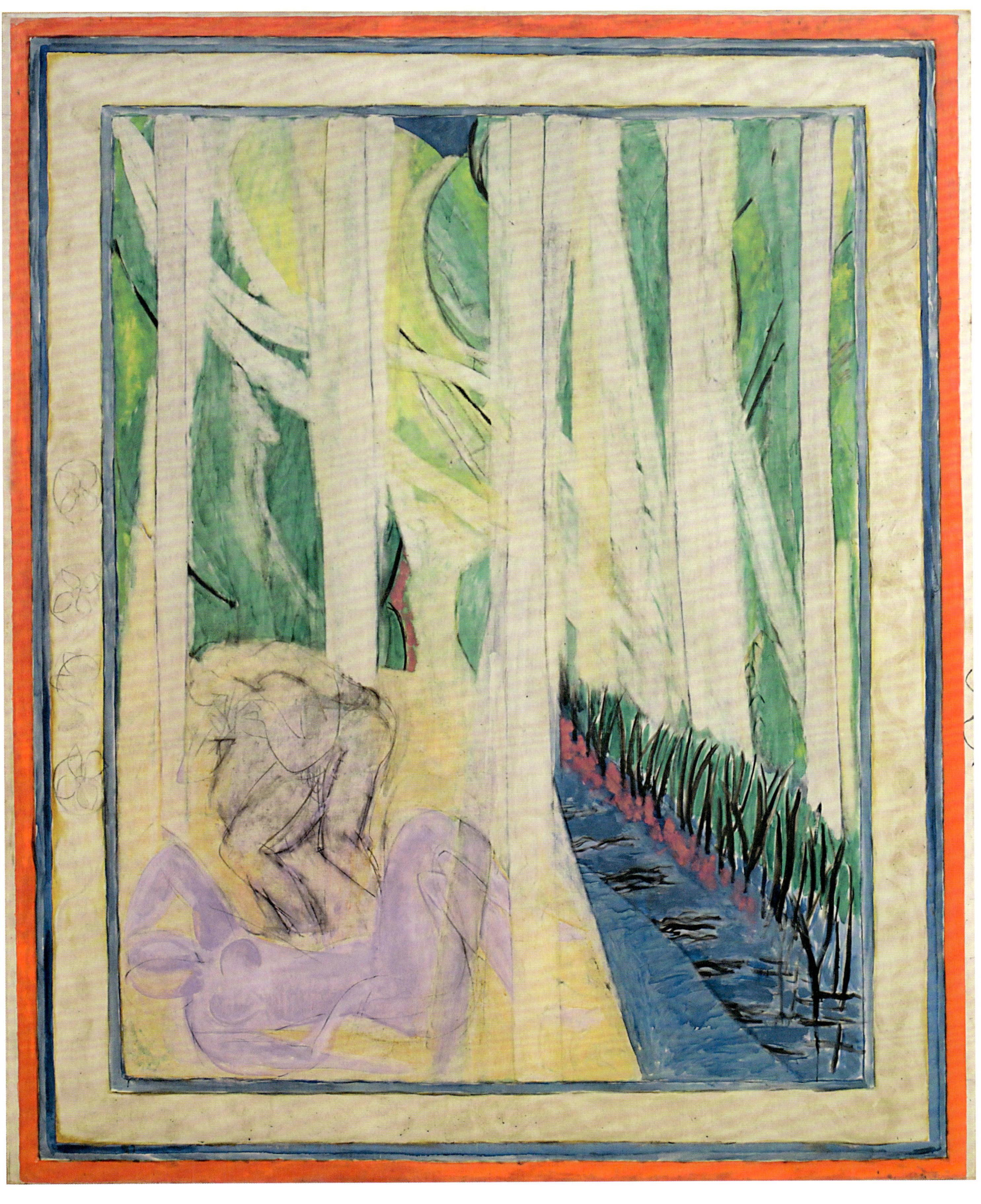

117
Young Girl Seated (La Biche), 1936
Oil on canvas, 24 ⅛ × 19 5/16 in. (61.3 × 49.1 cm)
Allen Memorial Art Museum, Oberlin College, Ohio

118
Papeete, Tahiti (Window at Tahiti; Tahiti I), October 1935
Oil on canvas, 7 ft. 4 9/16 in. × 67 11/16 in. (225 × 172 cm)
Musée Matisse Nice

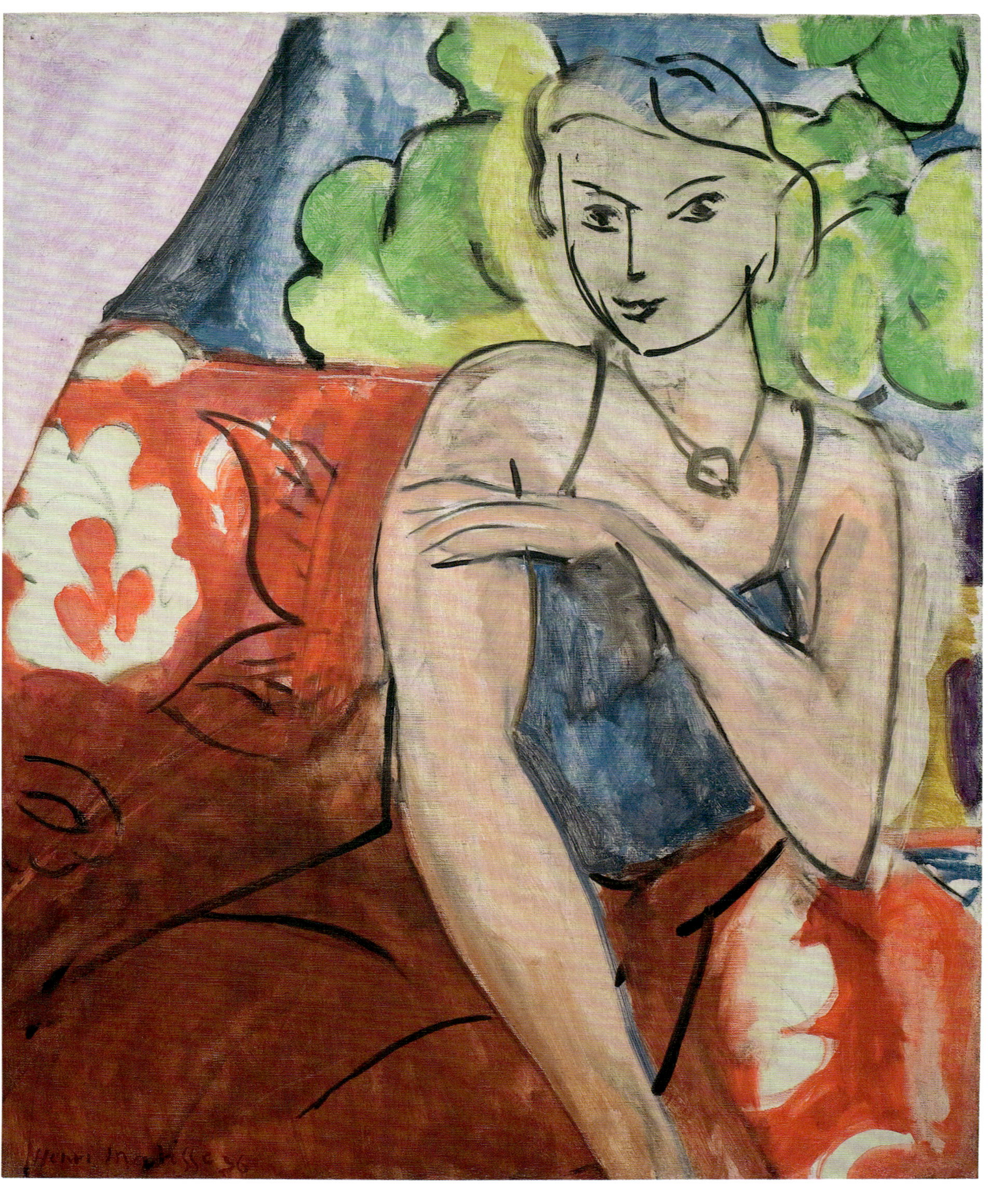

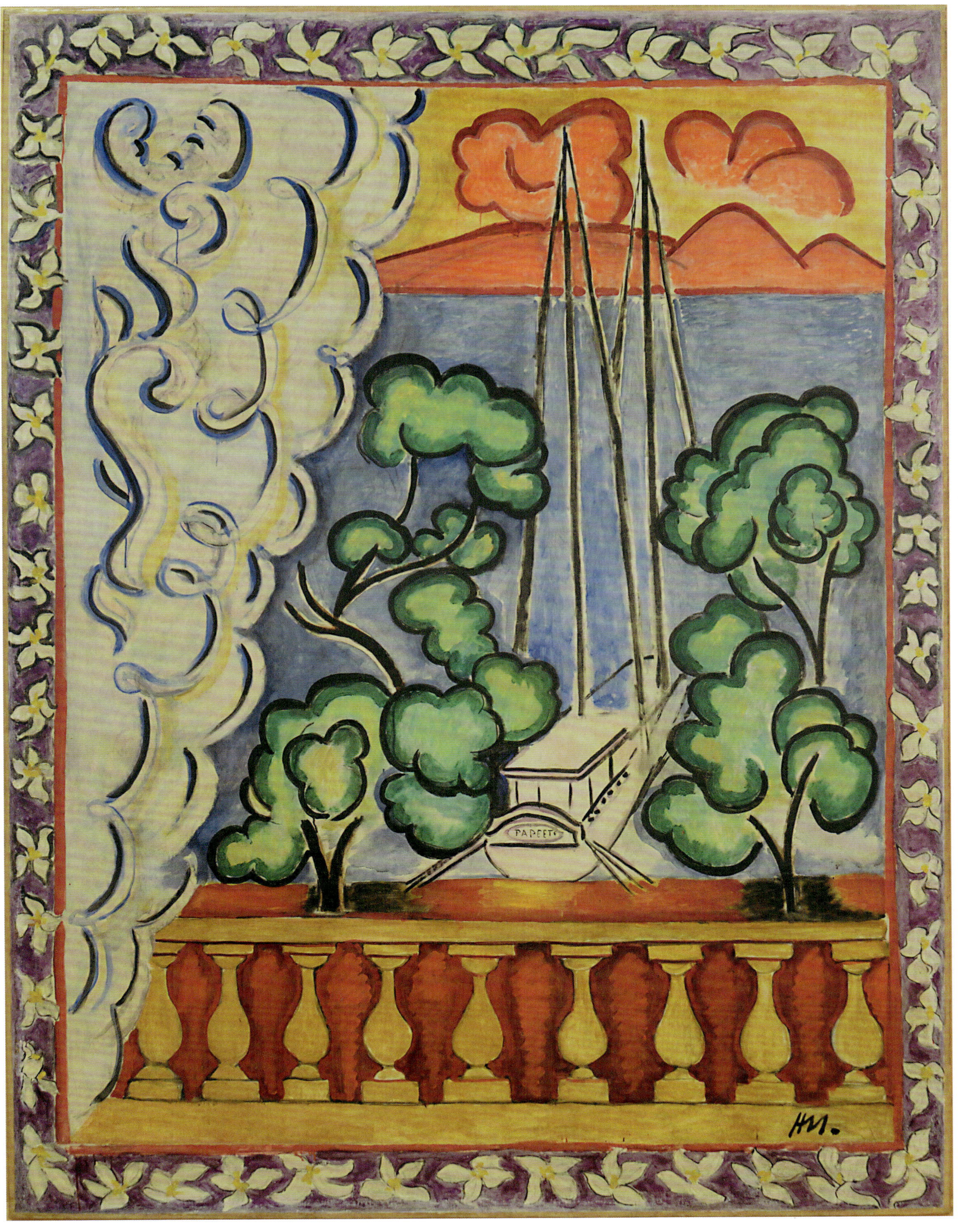
PAPEETE
HM.

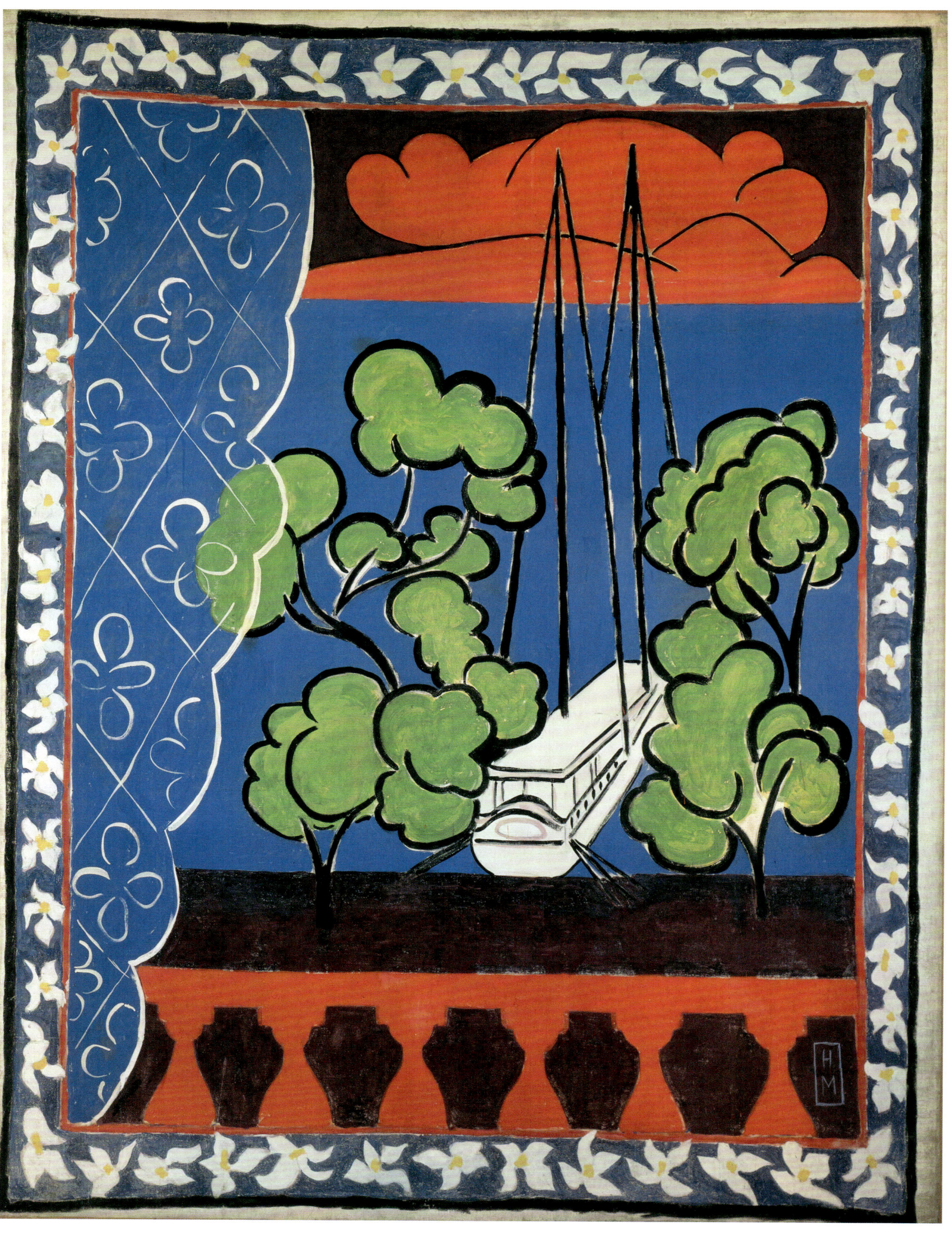

119
Window at Tahiti II,
December 18, 1935–March 15, 1936
Gouache on canvas,
7 ft. $9\frac{11}{16}$ in. × 6 ft. $\frac{1}{16}$ in.
(240 × 195 cm)
Musée Départemental Matisse,
Le Cateau-Cambrésis

120
The Green Blouse,
March 21, 1936
Oil on canvas, $31\frac{7}{8} \times 25\frac{5}{8}$ in.
(81 × 65.1 cm)
Statens Museum for Kunst,
Copenhagen

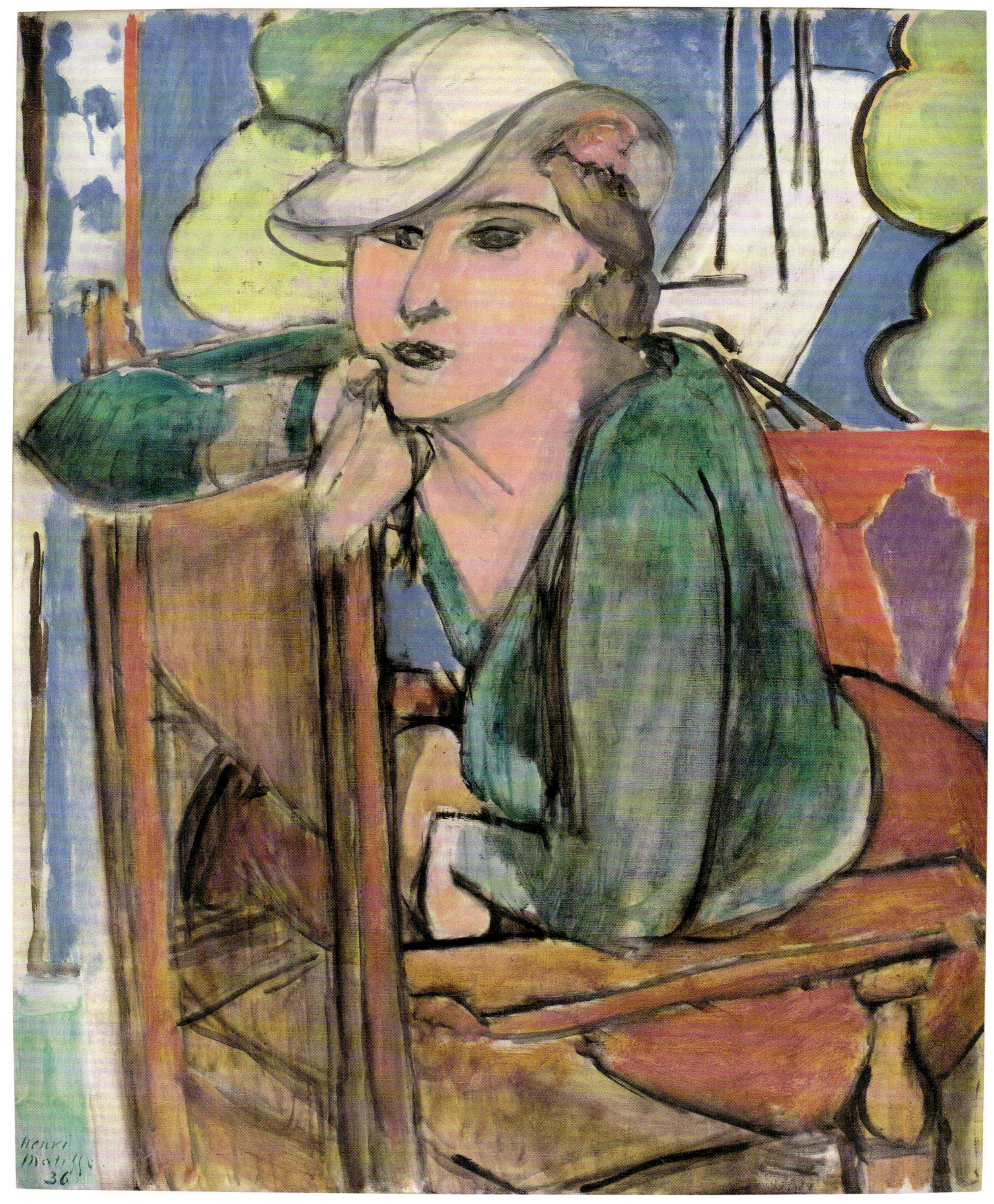

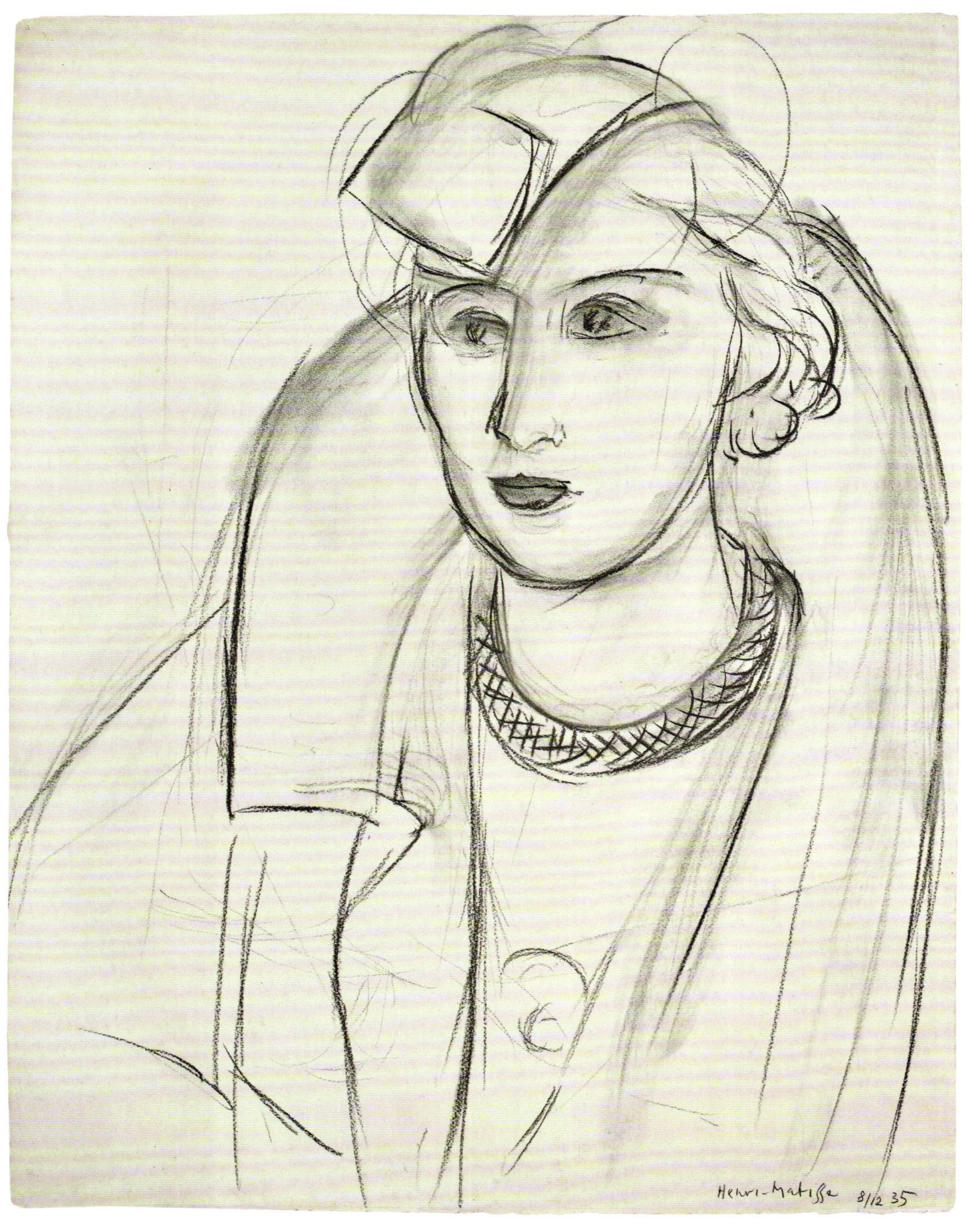

121
Woman with Collar,
December 8, 1935
Charcoal on paper, 23 13⁄16 × 19 7⁄8 in.
(60.5 × 50.5 cm)
Courtesy Galerie de l'Institut, Paris

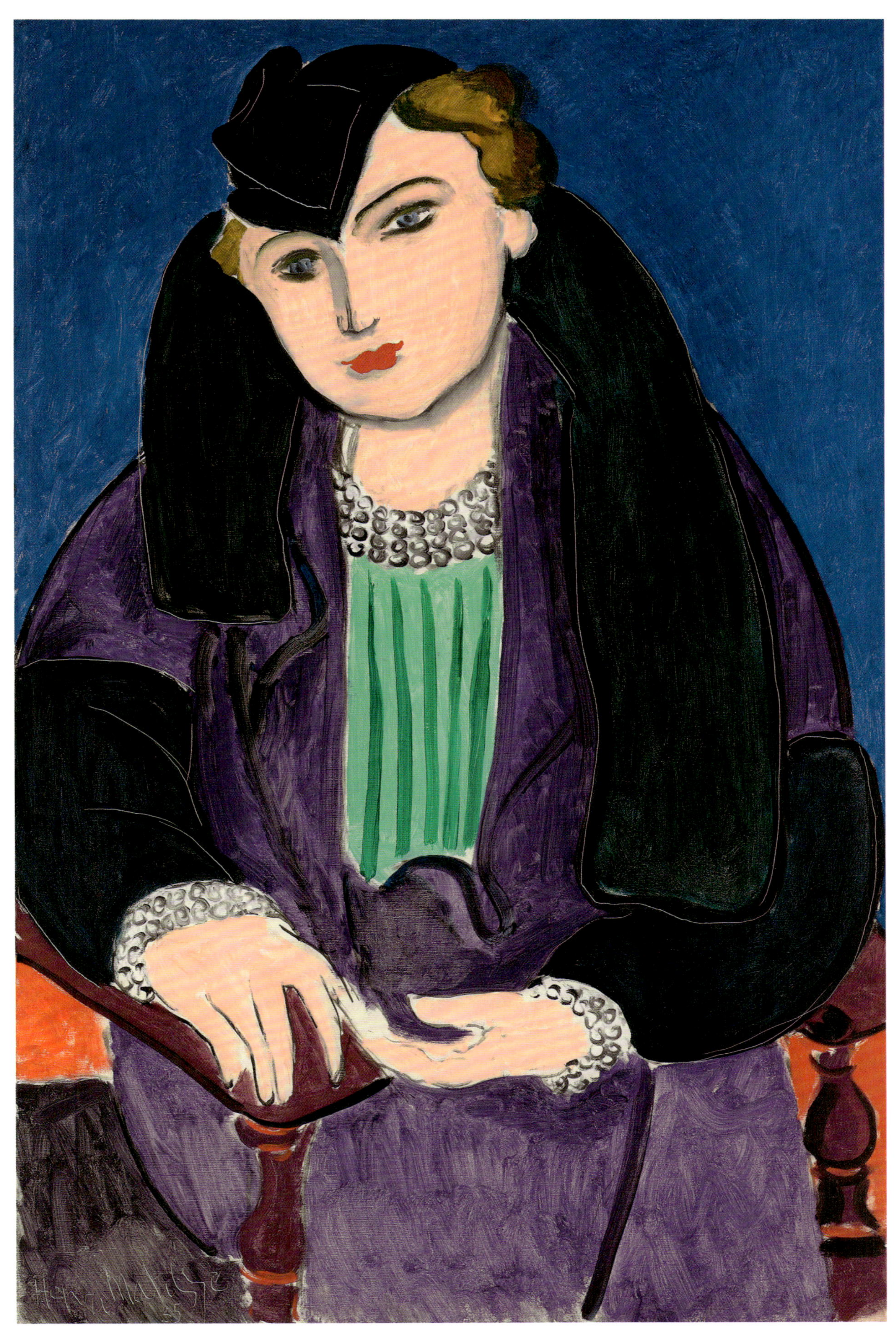

122
Portrait in a Blue Coat, 1935
Oil on canvas, 35 15/16 × 23 9/16 in.
(91.3 × 59.8 cm)
David and Ezra Nahmad Collection

123
Seated Pink Nude, 1935–36
Oil on canvas, 36 ¼ × 28 ¾ in.
(92 × 73 cm)
Musée National d'Art Moderne–
Centre Pompidou, Paris

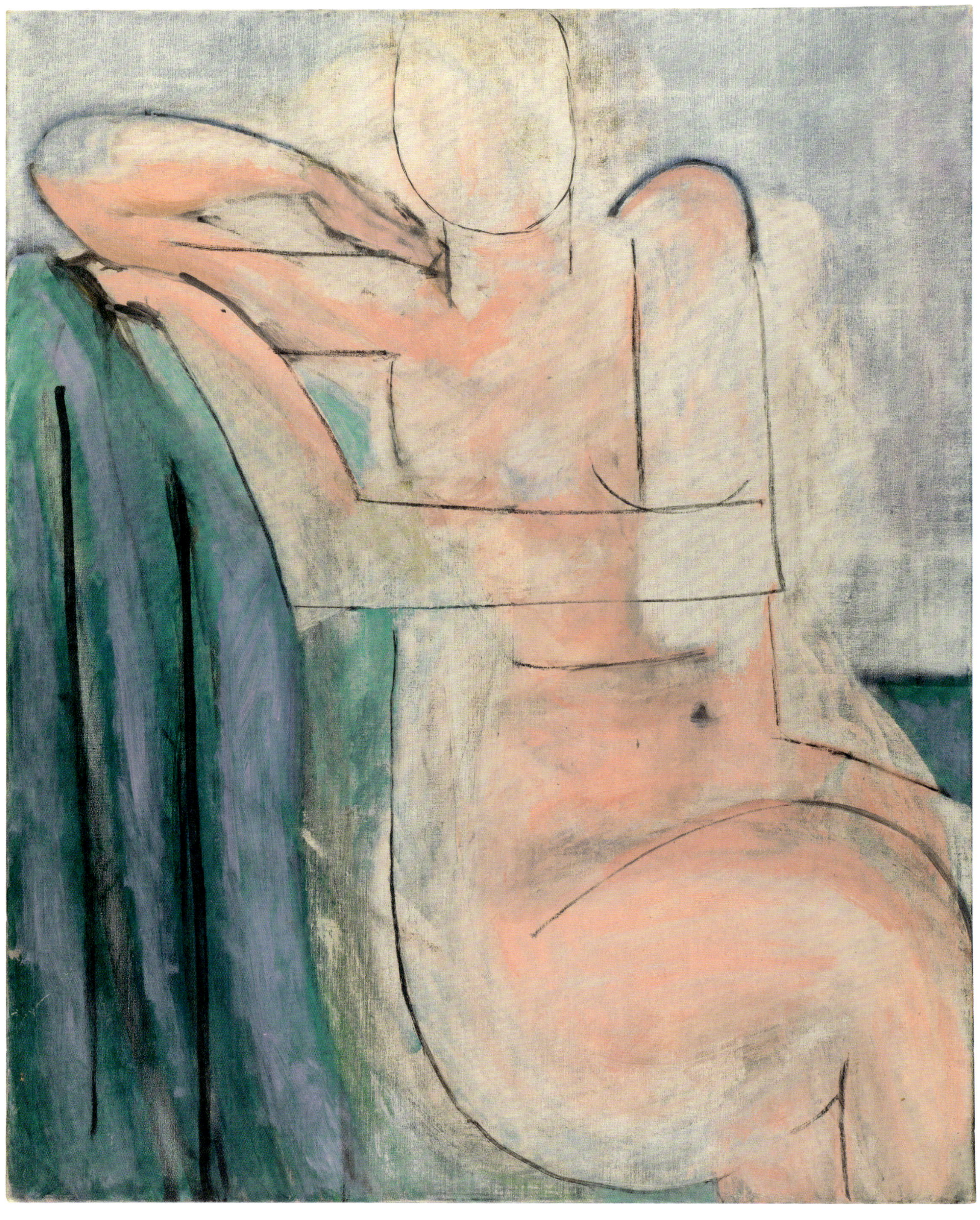

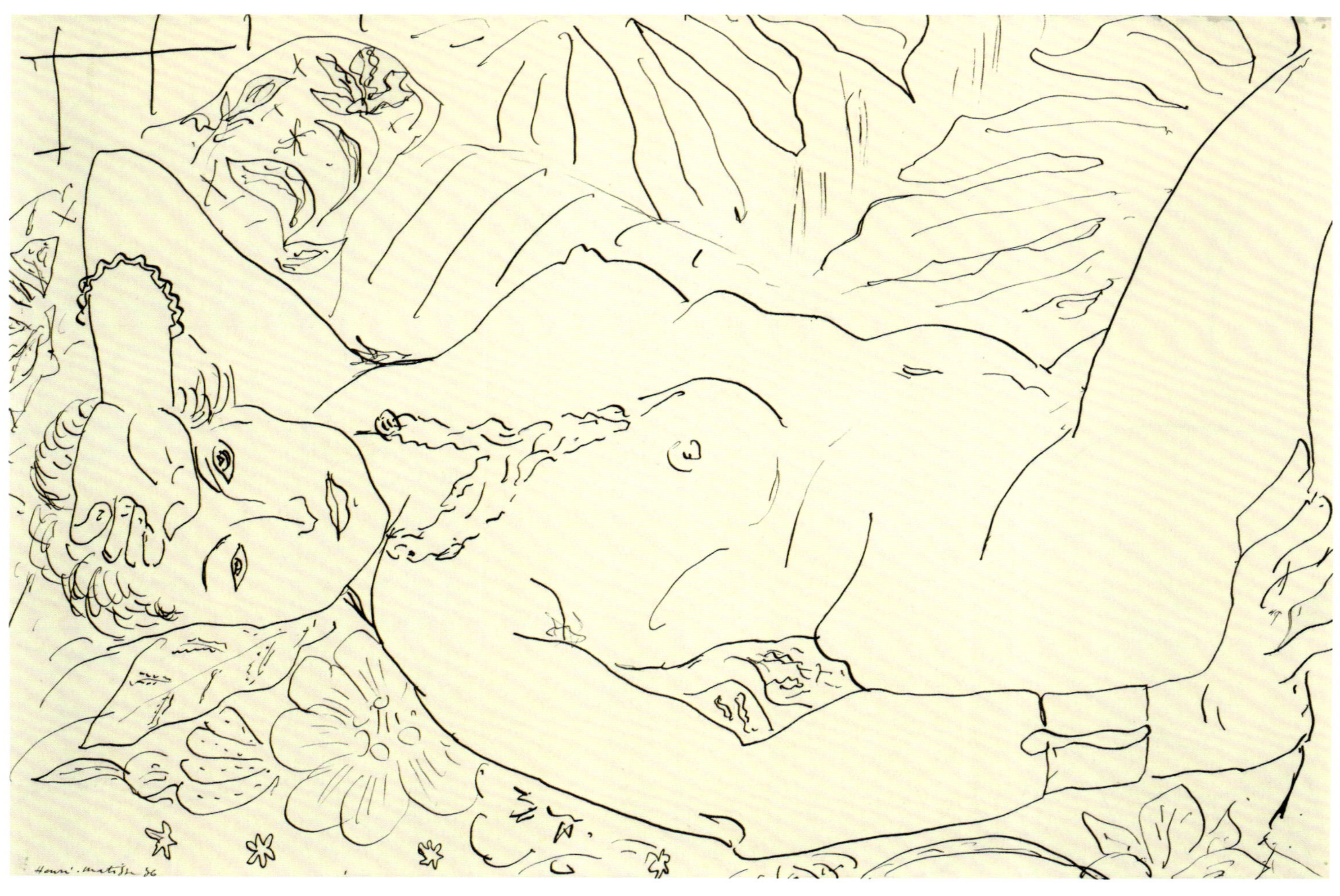

124
Nude Reclining on Flowered Cushions against a Background of Green Plants (Lydia), 1936
India ink on paper, 10 5/16 × 14 15/16 in. (25.6 × 38 cm)
Private collection

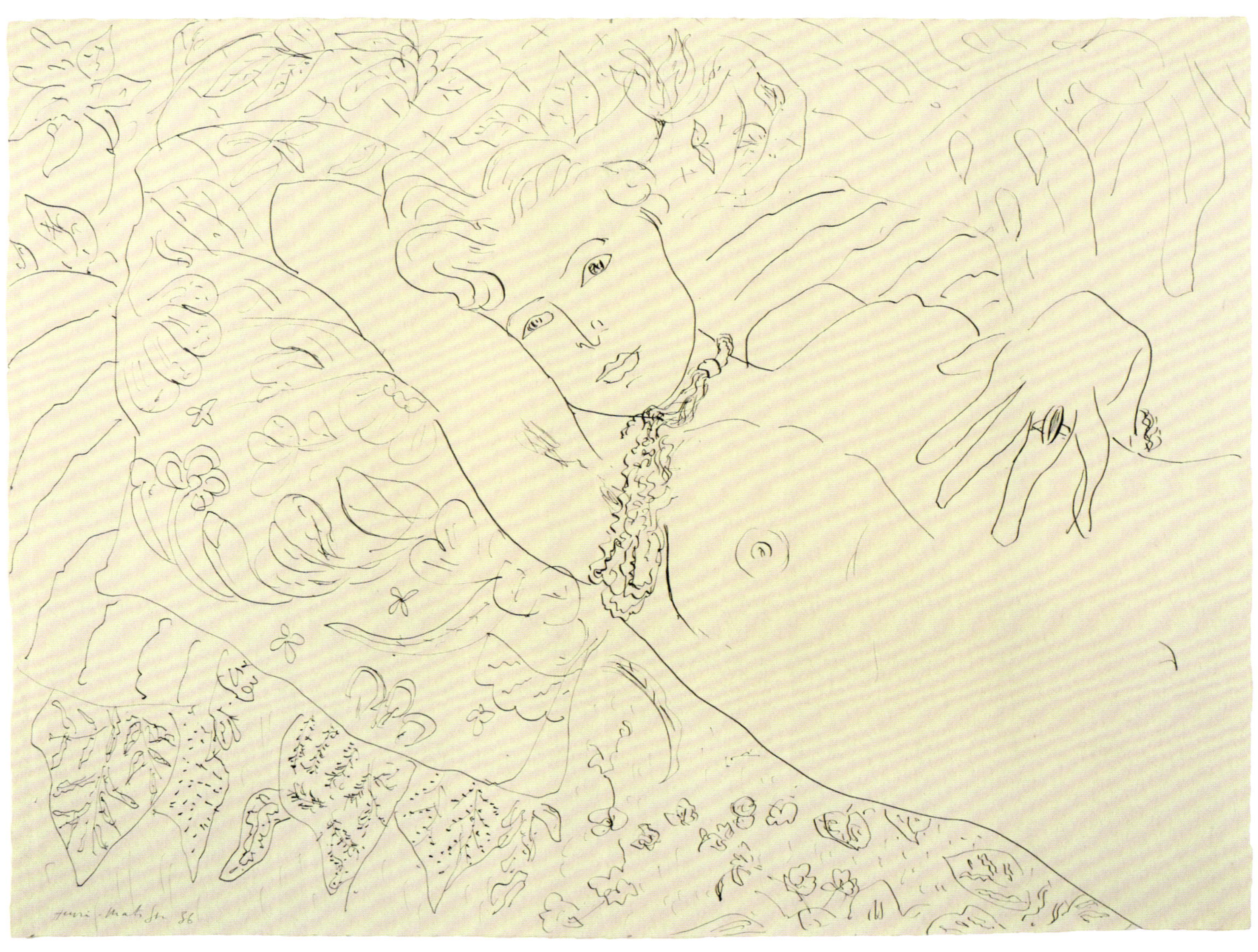

125
Study of a Reclining Nude, 1936
Ink on paper, 15 × 20 ⅛ in.
(38.1 × 51.1 cm)
Hirshhorn Museum and Sculpture Garden, Smithsonian Institution, Washington, DC

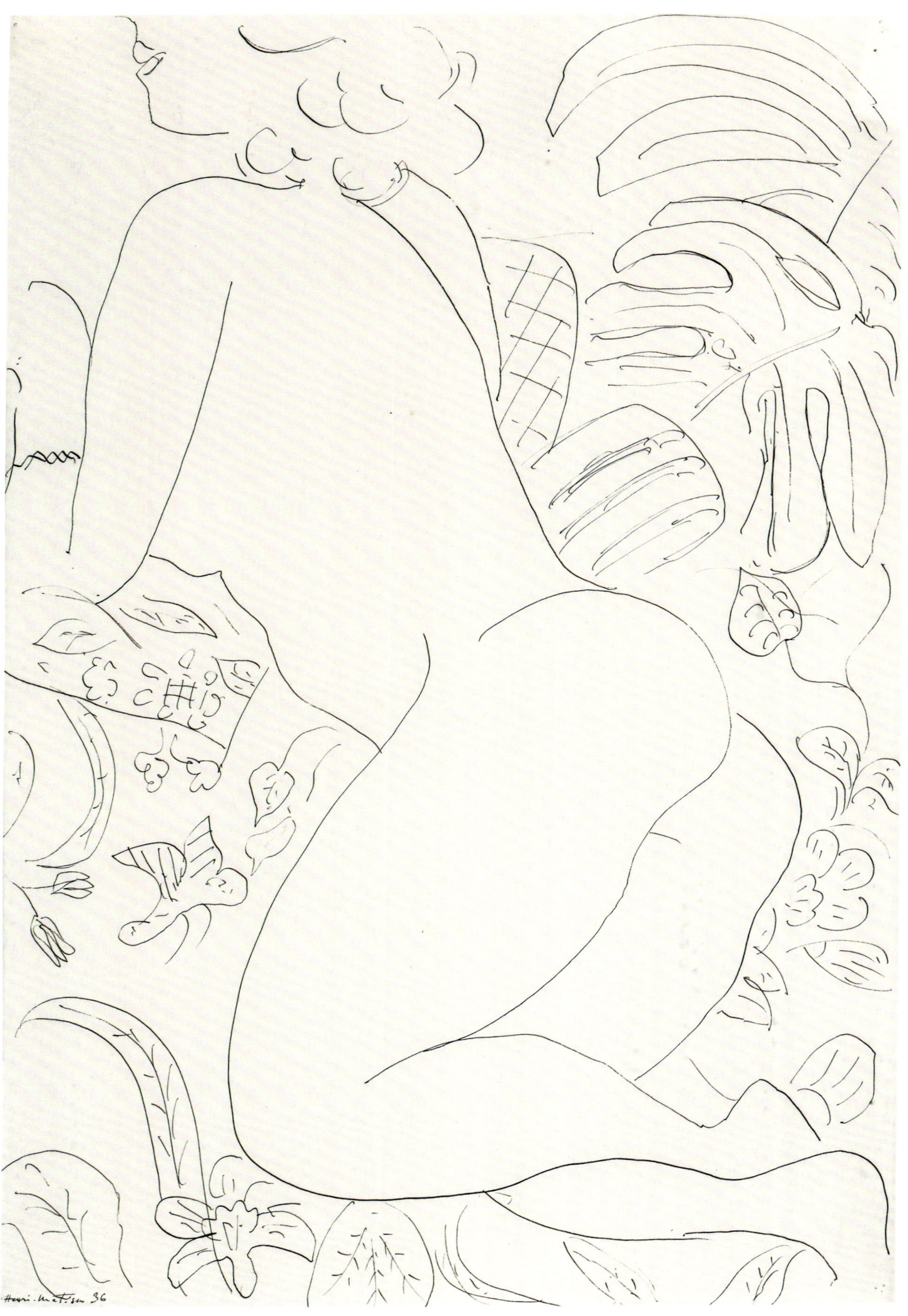

126
Kneeling Nude, 1936
India ink on laid paper,
26 3/16 × 15 1/16 in. (66.5 × 38.2 cm)
Musée d'Art Moderne de Paris

127
Nude with Necklace (Lydia),
1935
Graphite and ink on paper,
17 $\frac{11}{16}$ × 22 ¼ in.
(45 × 56.5 cm)
Private collection

128
Reclining Nude Seen from the Back, May 20, 1935
Charcoal on paper,
14 $\frac{15}{16}$ × 22 ¼ in.
(37.9 × 56.4 cm)
Musée Matisse Nice

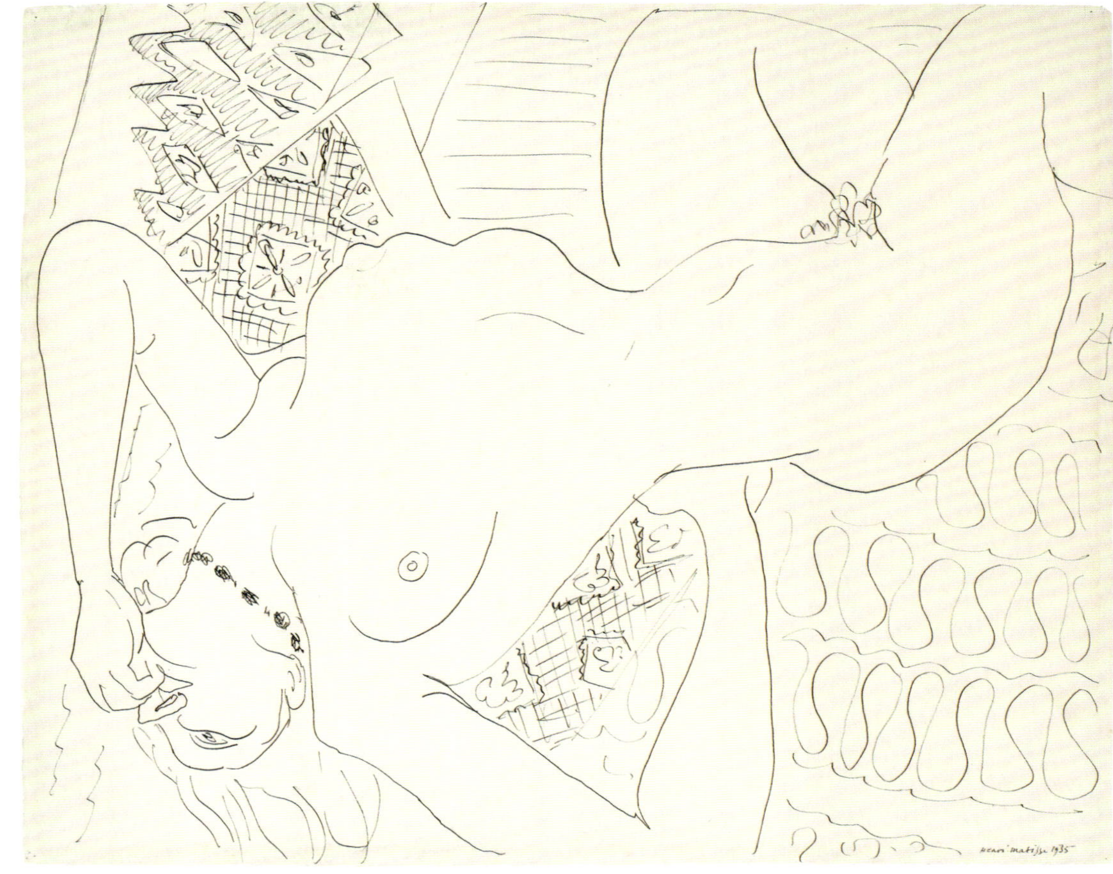

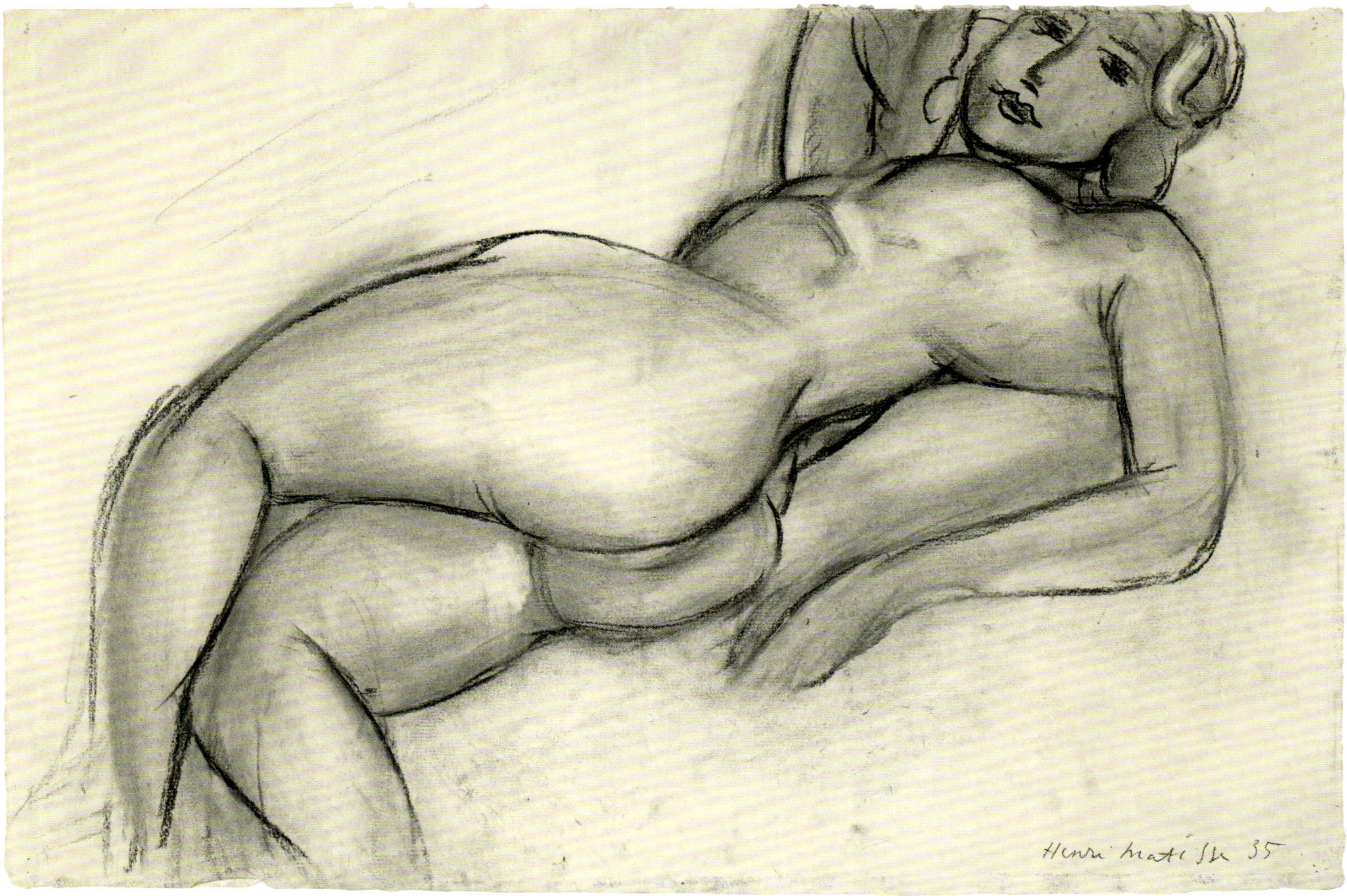

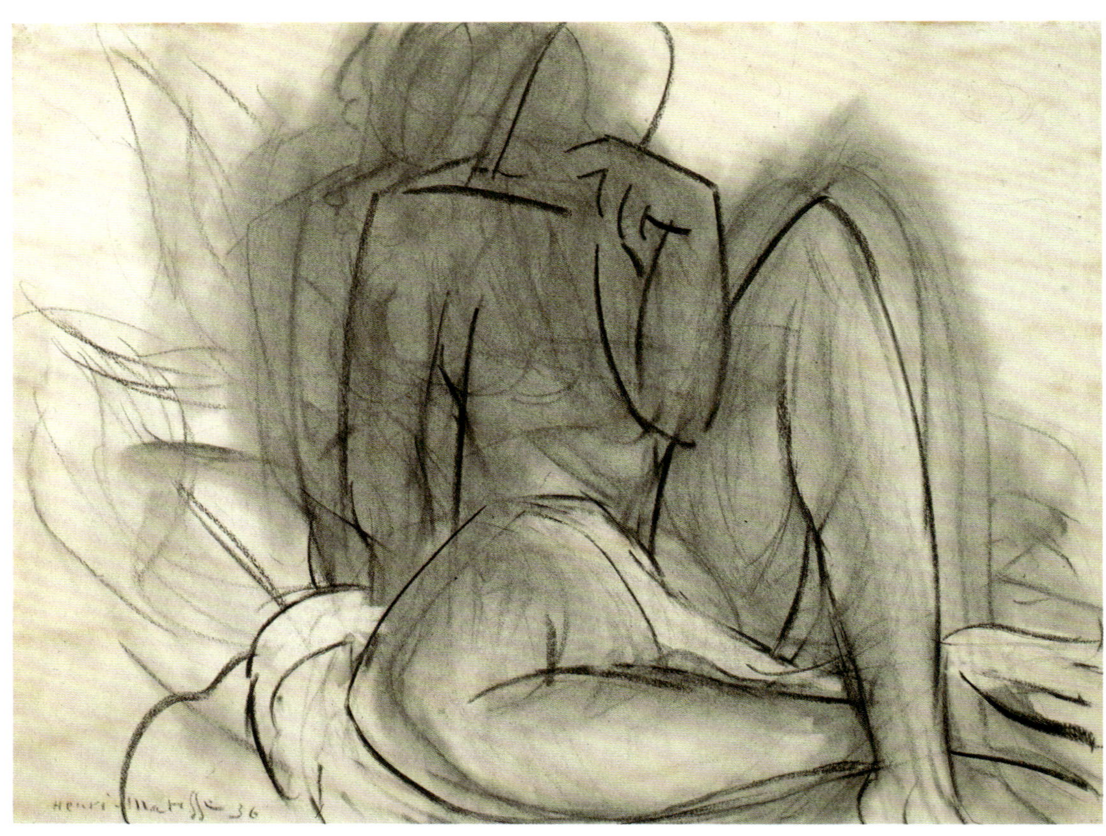

129
Crouching Nude, 1936
Charcoal on paper,
19 11/16 × 26 in. (50 × 66 cm)
Musée Départemental Matisse,
Le Cateau-Cambrésis

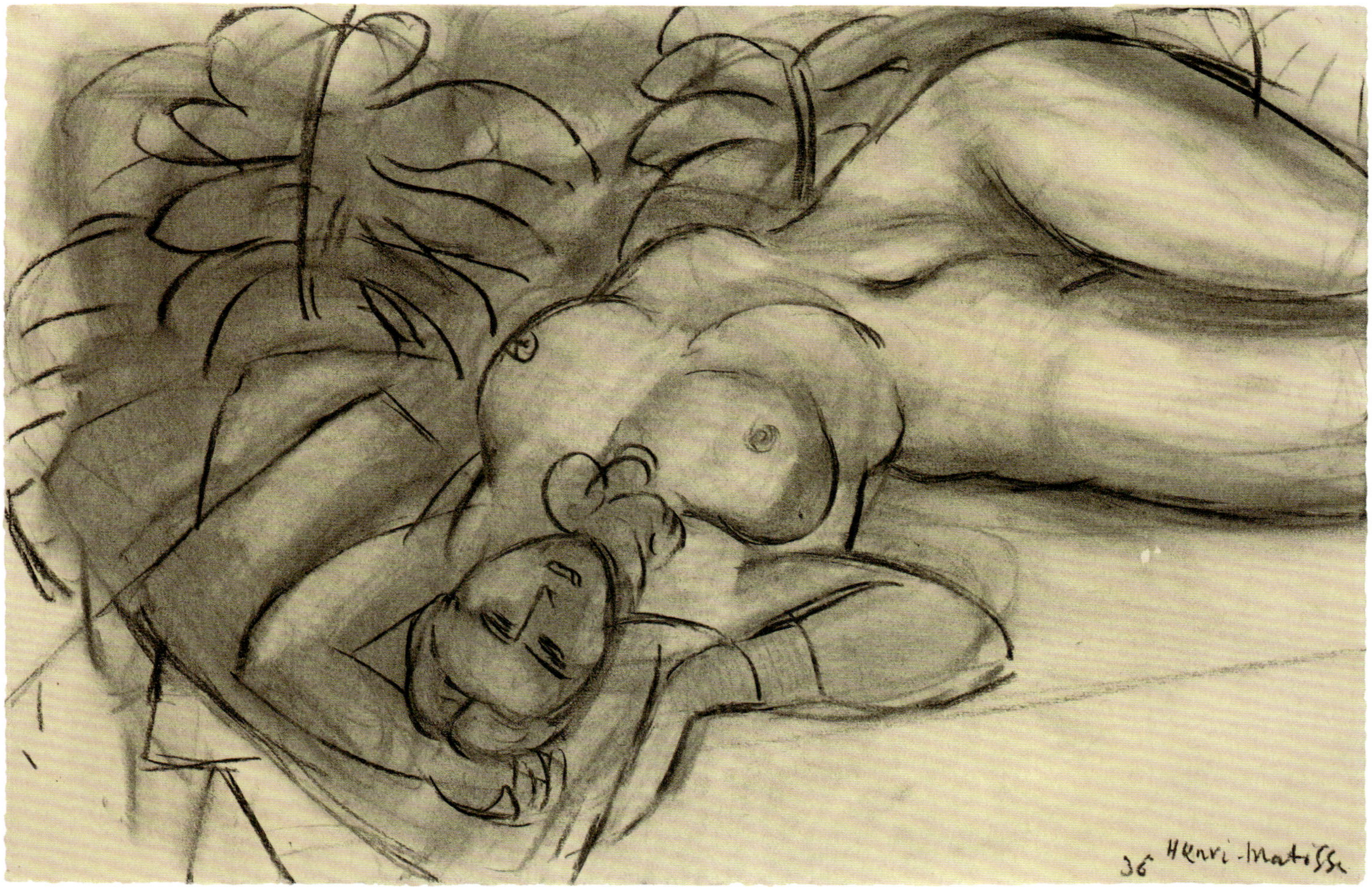

130
Upside-Down Nude and Foliage, February 1936
Charcoal and stump
on Arches watermarked laid
paper, 12 15/16 × 19 3/4 in.
(32.9 × 50.2 cm)
Musée Matisse Nice

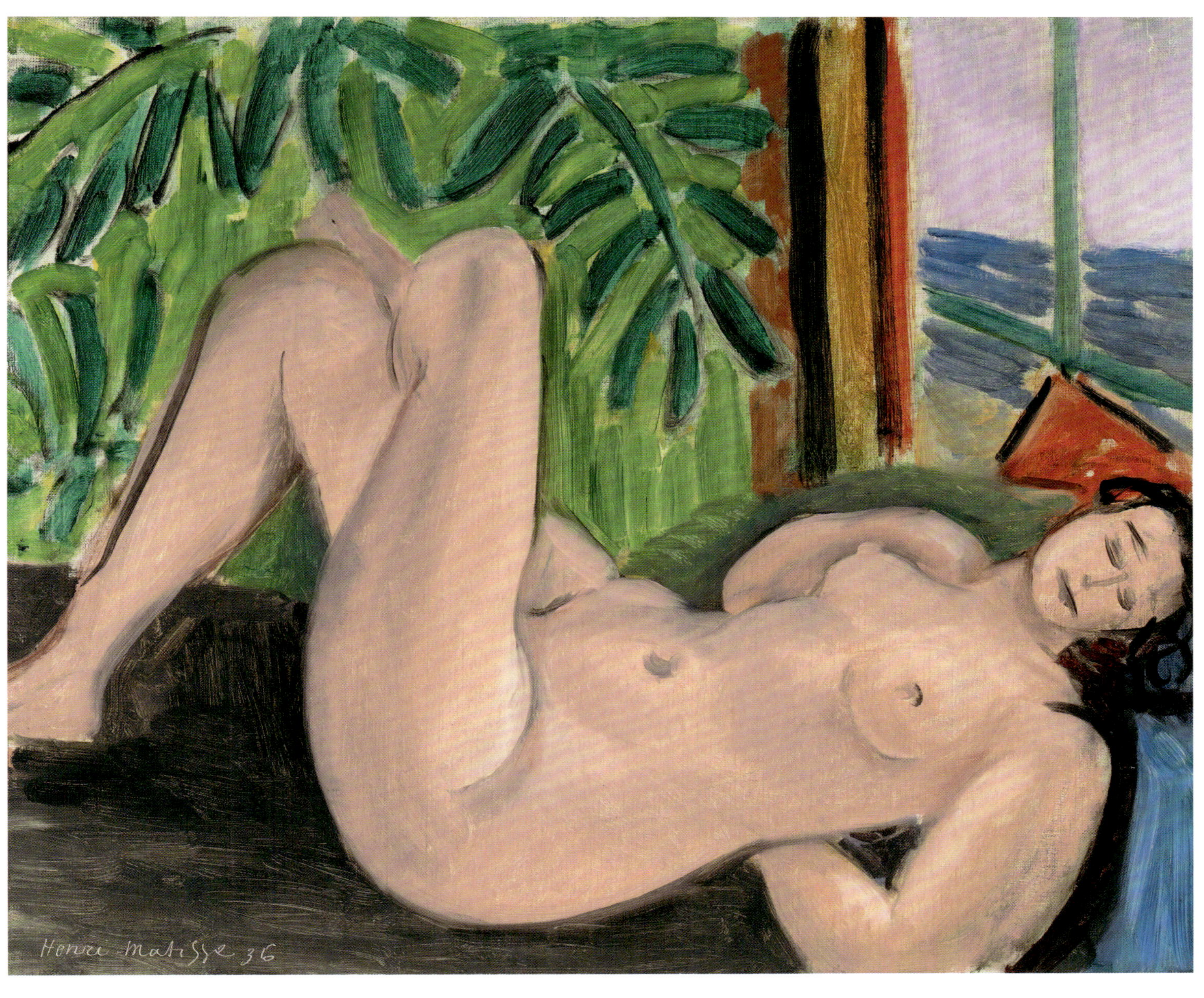

131
Nude with Crossed Legs,
1936
Oil on canvas, 15 × 18 ¼ in.
(38.1 × 46.3 cm)
David and Ezra Nahmad Collection

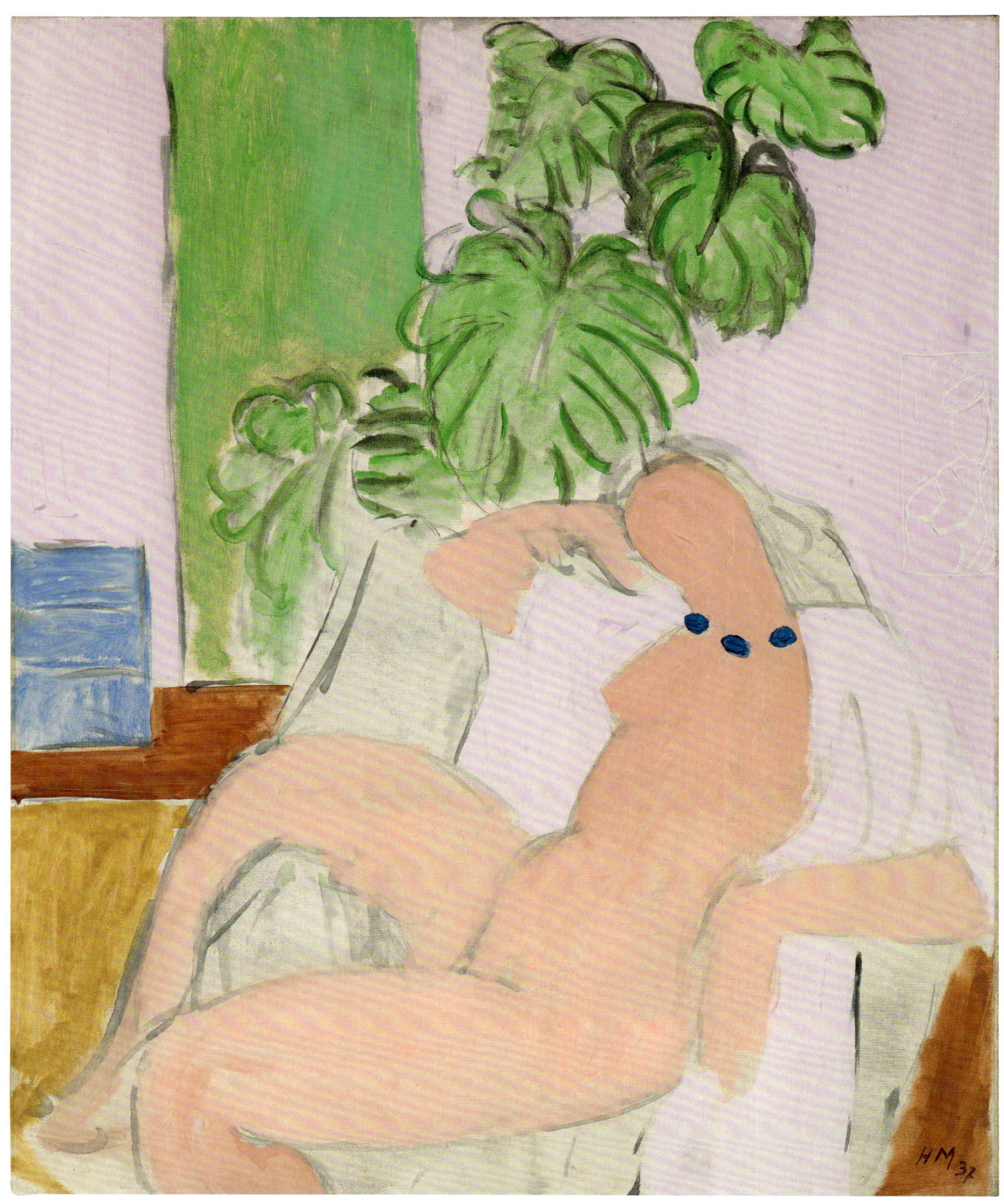

132
Nude in an Armchair, Green Plant,
1937 [November 1936]
Oil on canvas, 28 9/16 × 23 13/16 in.
(72.5 × 60.5 cm)
Musée Matisse Nice

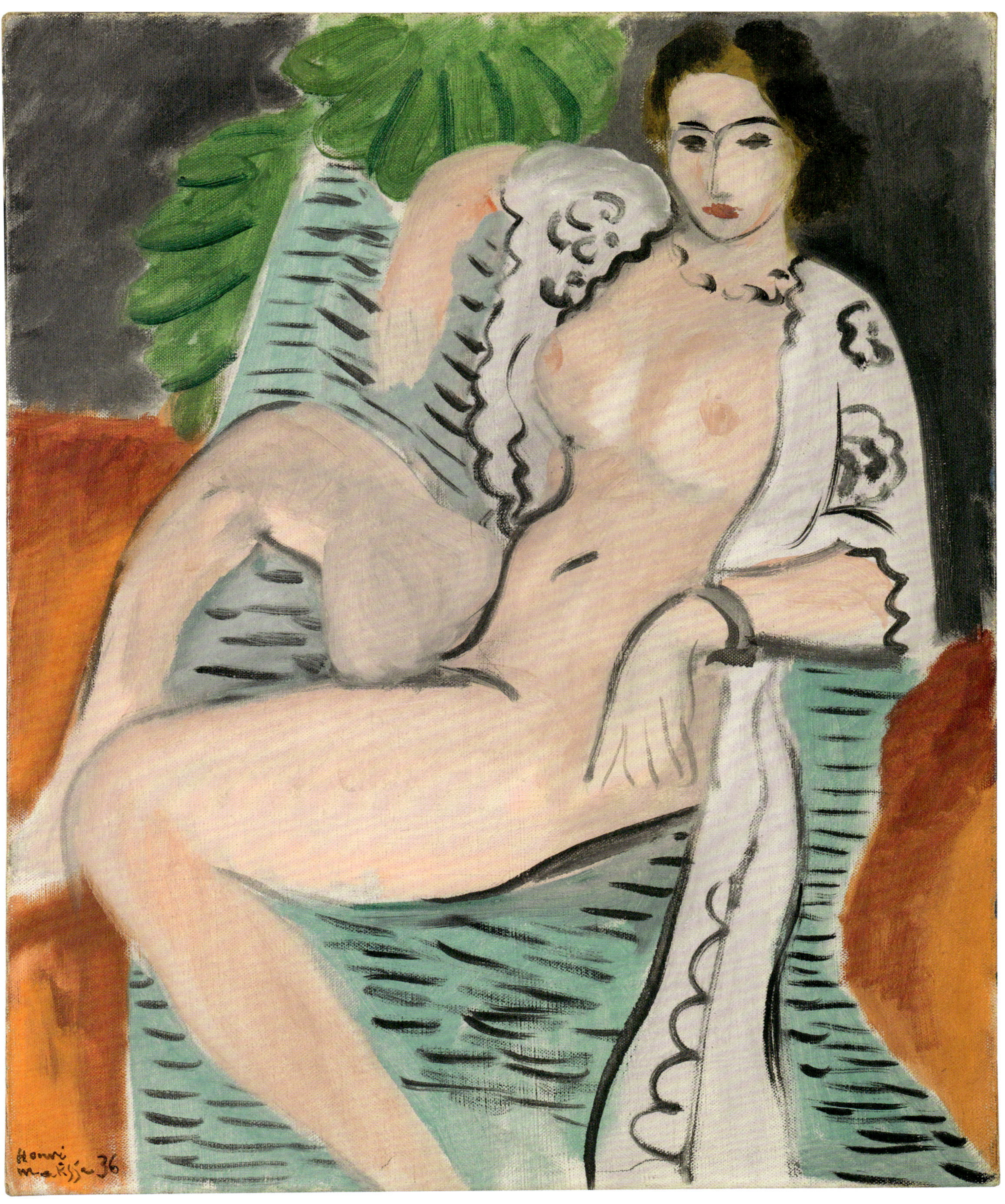

133
Draped Nude, November 6 and 7, 1936
Oil on canvas, 18 × 14 ¾ in. (45.7 × 37.5 cm)
Tate, London

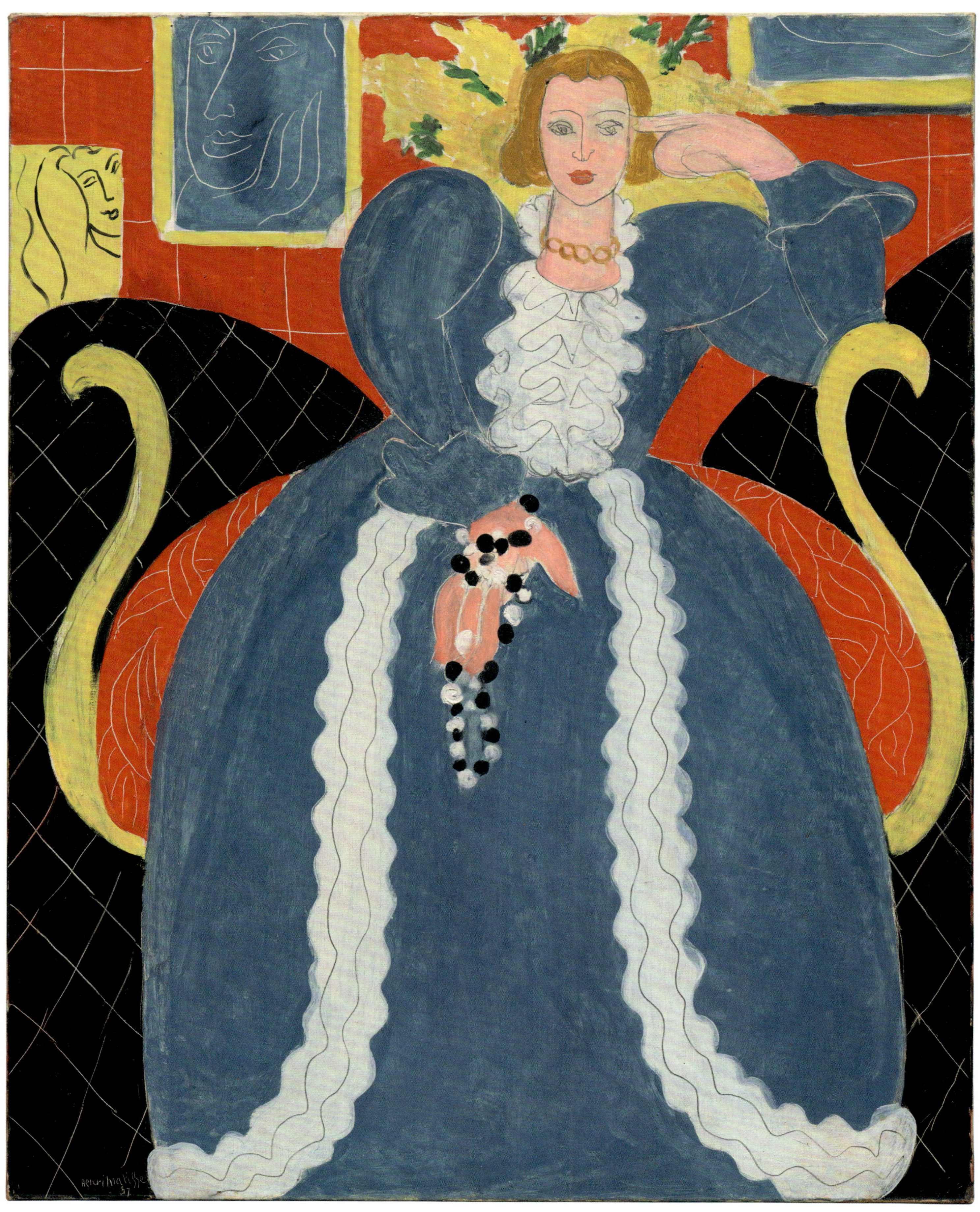

134
Woman in Blue, 1937
Oil on canvas, 36 ½ × 29 in.
(92.7 × 73.7 cm)
Philadelphia Museum of Art

WOMAN IN BLUE

In the 1930s Matisse was accused of paying closer attention to decor and accessories than to the human beings posing for him. One critic described his models as almost soulless objects "charged with decorating the space."[1] Indeed, the exuberant theatricality of the costume in *Woman in Blue* 134 does appear to upstage Lydia Delectorskaya, a somewhat aloof mannequin covered in voluminous puffs of taffeta and white organza ruffles. Black and white beads embellish but also immobilize her right hand, seemingly a metaphor for the suspension of individual agency in favor of rhythmic ornamentation. And yet, as Matisse would insist, his models were never just props. The emotional intensity of their encounter, he explained, was distributed onto the whole of his canvas, and in the invention of "plastic signs [that] probably express their souls."[2] *Woman in Blue* could be said to narrate that process of sublimation. Ten photographs recording its development reveal transformations made to the initially naturalistic pose of Delectorskaya leaning against the arm of a settee. In the final version, she is a hieratic icon hovering upright against her throne, haloed by a golden crown of mimosas. It is difficult to read her as either sitting or standing, thanks in part to the visible reworking of her skirt into a more symmetrical bell shape. Delectorskaya does not decorate the space; rather, it is animated in response to her. The migration of the red wall down into the cushion and the waves of the black floor rising up to meet her leg-of-mutton sleeves flatten three-dimensionality into a jeweled surface to adorn her.

As if to remind us of the depth and duration of the human engagement behind those abstract signs, Matisse includes other images on the wall, like the drawing of Delectorskaya, *Head of a Woman with Chin in Palm* (1937; Pushkin Museum, Moscow), executed a few months earlier. This work on paper belongs to a long series of related images, all variations of her wearing a collar, jabot, and other parts of this complex outfit of her design. *Woman in Blue* is the summation of that history of performance and observation, poetically suggested here in the way the drawing, colored translucent blue, borrows from the world of the painting it inhabits. The interdependence of the two media—the intensity of drawing sessions allowing for the "apparent ease"[3] of painting—is also signaled by the graphite marks of her left eye on raw canvas, peering out from under the colored surface.

After modeling sessions, Delectorskaya usually shifted roles to work on the other side of the easel, scraping down areas of unwanted paint to prepare Matisse for the next day's work. Underlying colors, like the red beneath the blue in the torso under her raised arm, are the still-visible traces of this collaborative process. Delectorskaya's agency is present in almost imperceptible ways, but rarely is it directly portrayed. With earnings from modeling, Delectorskaya soon purchased *Head of a Woman*, the very first work of what would become a vast Matisse collection she donated to museums in her native country.[4] Thus another of her many roles is foreshadowed by *Woman in Blue*: Delectorskaya as an astute patron of the arts, assessing Matisse with a powerful if inscrutable gaze.

ELLEN MCBREEN

1 Claude Roger-Marx, "Les dessins d'Henri Matisse" (1938), trans. in *Matisse: A Retrospective*, ed. Jack Flam (New York: Hugh Lauter Levin Associates, 1988), 324–25.

2 Henri Matisse, "Notes of a Painter on His Drawing" (1939), in *Matisse on Art*, ed. and trans. Jack Flam, rev. ed. (Berkeley: University of California Press, 2015), 130. As Flam proposes, this essay—originally published in *Le Point* in July 1939—was prompted by a desire to refute some of Roger-Marx's charges.

3 Lydia Delectorskaya, *With Apparent Ease. . . Henri Matisse: Paintings from 1935–1939*, trans. Olga Tourkoff (Paris: Adrien Maeght, 1988).

4 Wanda de Guébriant, "Lydia Delectorskaya, biographie," in Dominique Szymusiak et al., *Lydia D.: Lydia Delectorskaya, muse et modèle de Matisse*, exh. cat. (Paris: Réunion des Musées Nationaux, 2010), 204. The drawing is reproduced on p. 25. It would eventually be given to the Pushkin Museum, Moscow.

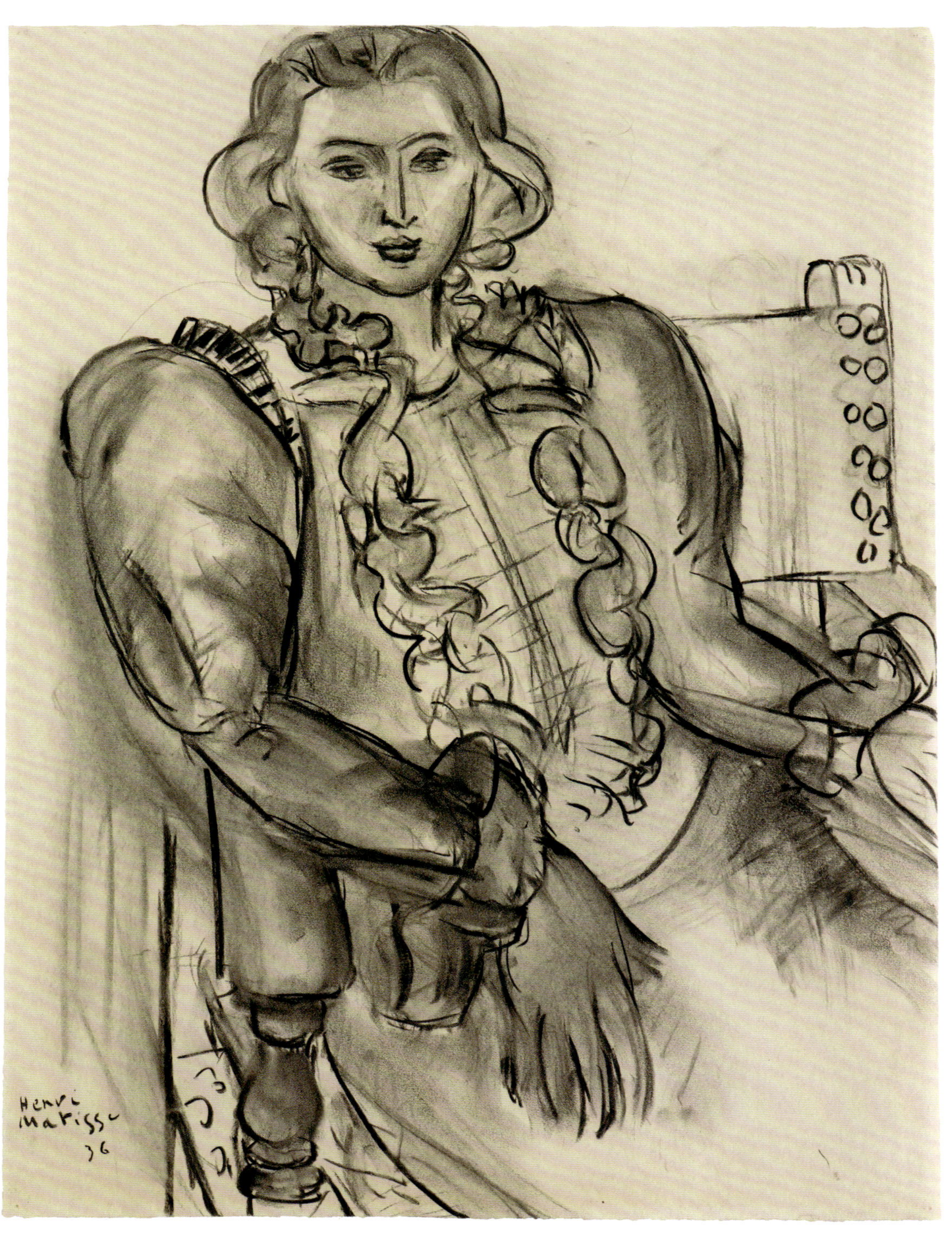

135
Woman in Armchair, 1936
Charcoal on paper, 21 × 16 in.
(53.3 × 40.6 cm)
Saint Louis Art Museum

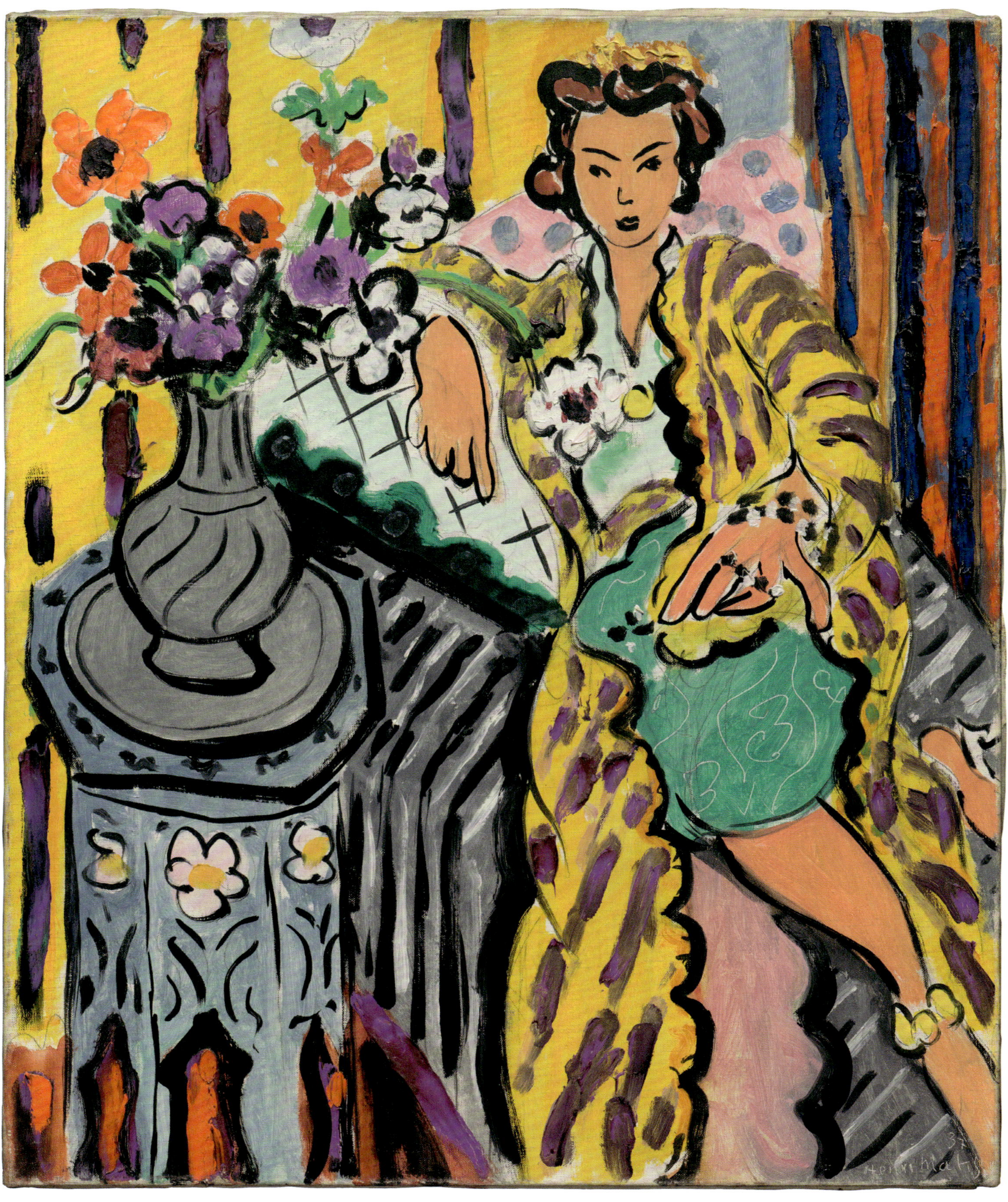

136
Yellow Odalisque, 1937
Oil on canvas, 21 ¾ × 18 ⅛ in.
(55.2 × 46 cm)
Philadelphia Museum of Art

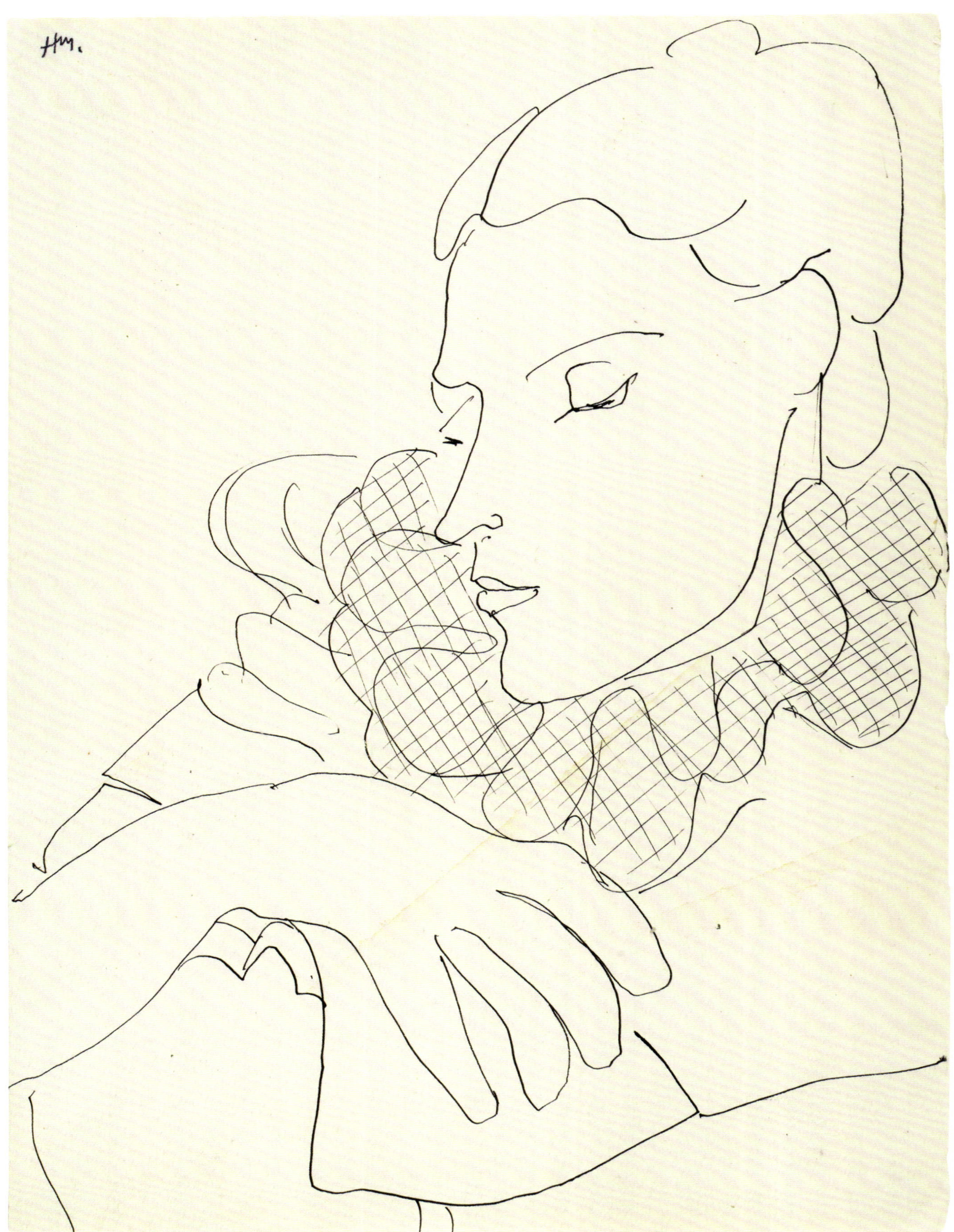

137
Woman with Checked Collar, 1938
Ink on paper, 14 ¾ × 11 in.
(37.5 × 28 cm)
The Pierre and Tana Matisse
Foundation, New York

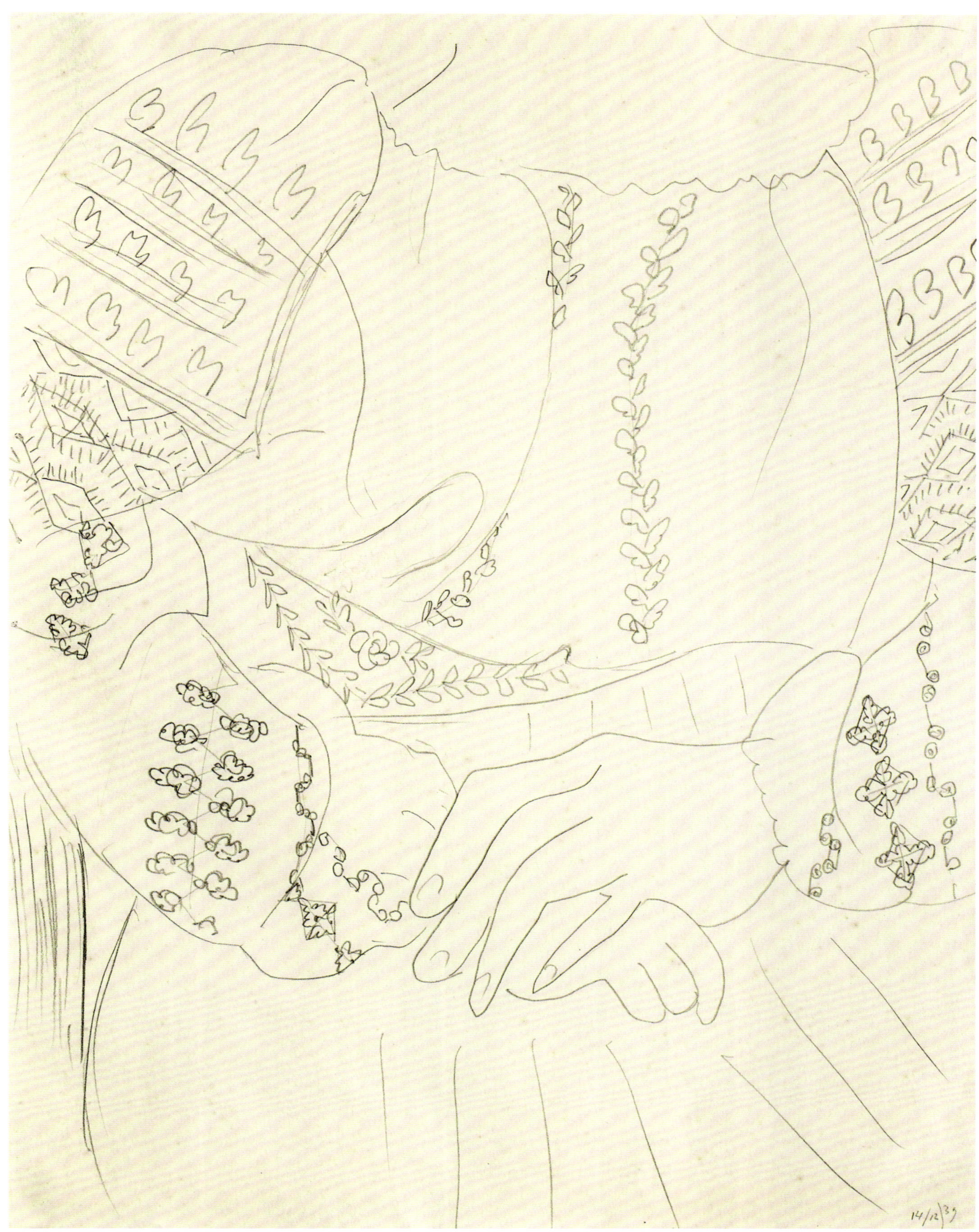

138
Romanian Blouse,
December 14, 1939
Graphite on sketchbook paper,
16 9/16 × 13 in. (42 × 33 cm)
Courtesy Galerie de l'Institut,
Paris

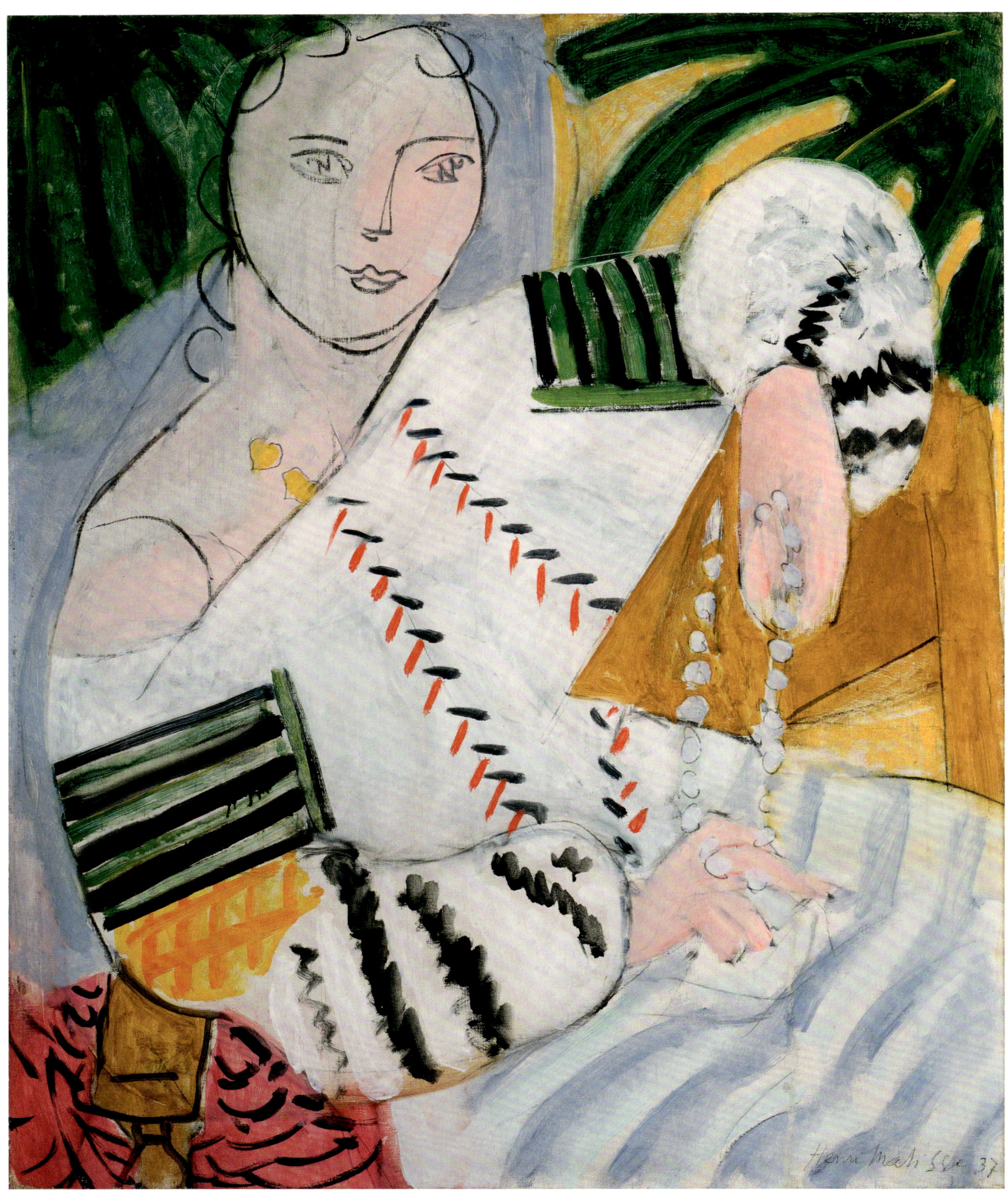

139
Romanian Blouse, late March–
April 1937
Oil on canvas, 28 ¾ × 23 ⅝ in.
(73 × 60 cm)
Cincinnati Art Museum

THE ROMANIAN BLOUSE

In 1936 *Cahiers d'art* published a special issue on Matisse, for which he designed the cover,[1] featuring a gouache cut-out 6.
The issue was richly illustrated with his recent works, including a set of drawings of Romanian blouses. When this motif first appeared in Matisse's work, it was directly connected to the model Lydia Delectorskaya, who had opened up a new period in his practice.
And while other models went on to wear the Romanian blouse, she would remain the symbol of what was for the artist a completely fresh start after the deep inner crisis of 1929.

Fashionable accessories on the French Riviera at the time, these light blouses embroidered with brightly colored stylized flowers became a subject Matisse would return to many times in his work, reflecting his passion for every kind of fabric. The artist grew up in Le Cateau-Cambrésis, a town known for wool-spinning and weaving. Throughout his life he collected carpets and various cloths. Brought home from his travels, they formed not just a textile collection but also a herbarium of motifs from which he could draw inspiration.

Interested in the graphic beauty of these blouses, the embroidery work, and the arrangement of details, which in Romanian tradition carried specific meaning, Matisse would transcribe these aspects in his refined compositions. The geometric organization of the frame lends great sobriety to the series of Romanian blouses. Matisse was looking for voluptuousness in the curves, emphasizing the volumes and arabesques of the loose-fitting sleeves. The model fades into the background, upstaged by the garment, with facial features reduced to the merest suggestion of eyes, nose, and lips. The blouse becomes the central subject of the work.

"Matisse considered the presence of the object to be very important. The imagination cannot find expression without matter.
It needs, in order to operate, to be faced with something delightful to latch onto."[2]
These are the words of Christian Zervos in the article "Automatisme et espace illusoire" (Automatism and illusory space) in the special issue of *Cahiers d'art* of 1936.

That same year, Matisse did four small paintings based on this motif, which from 1937 spawned a host of works, including *Romanian Blouse* 139, painted with his then model, Hélène Mercier-Galitzine.

In this series, line drawing becomes a kind of automatic writing, but it does so through a stylization of the ornaments in the manner of cursive writing, becoming a personal alphabet of forms. By tirelessly returning to the subject of Romanian blouses, and systematically accepting the variations of their patterns born of his hand, Matisse was attempting, based on observation, to create a kind of decorative metaphysics, which was to culminate with two paintings executed during the war years, *The Dream* (1940; private collection) and *The Romanian Blouse* (1940; Musée National d'Art Moderne–Centre Pompidou, Paris).

ALICE MARSAL

1 *Cahiers d'art*, nos. 3–5 (1936).

2 Christian Zervos, "Automatisme et espace illusoire," *Cahiers d'art*, nos. 3–5 (1936): 69.

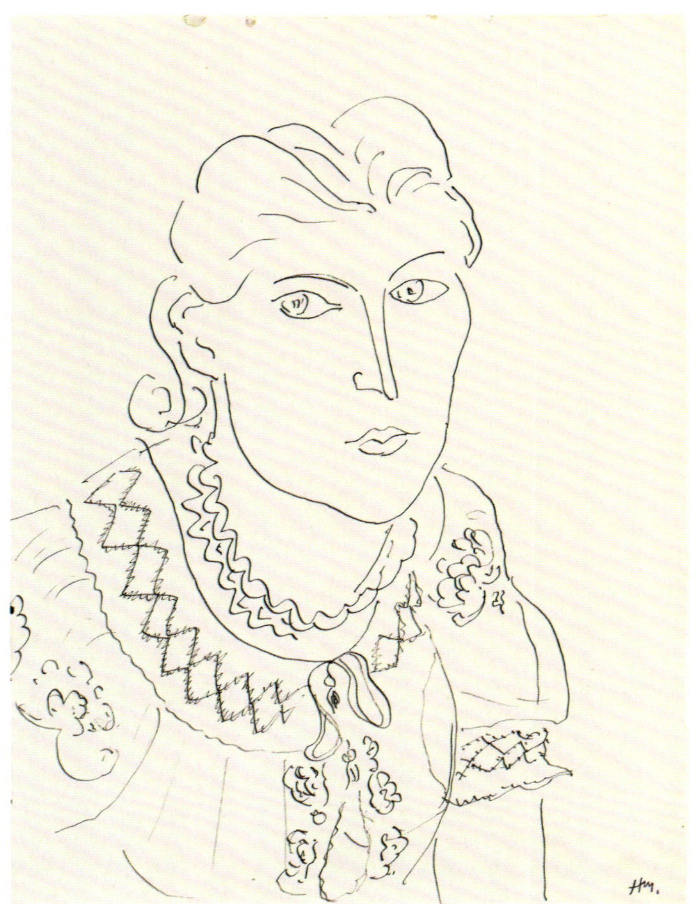

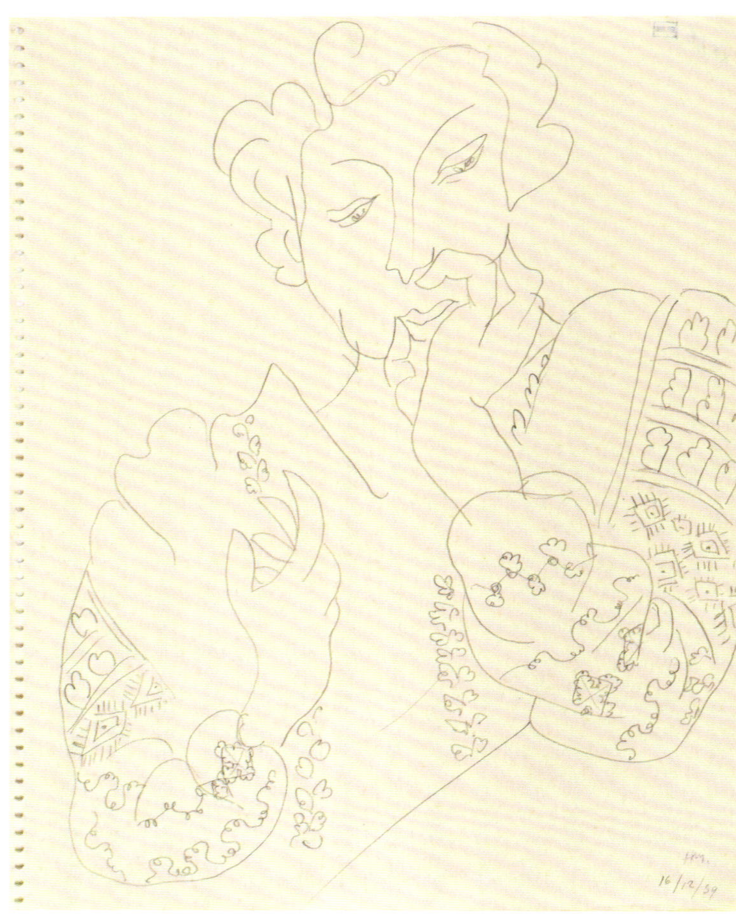

140
The Romanian Blouse, c. 1936
Ink on paper, 14 15/16 × 11 in.
(38 × 28 cm)
The Pierre and Tana Matisse
Foundation, New York

141
The Romanian Blouse,
December 16, 1939
Graphite on paper, 16 9/16 × 13 in.
(42 × 33 cm)
The Pierre and Tana Matisse
Foundation, New York

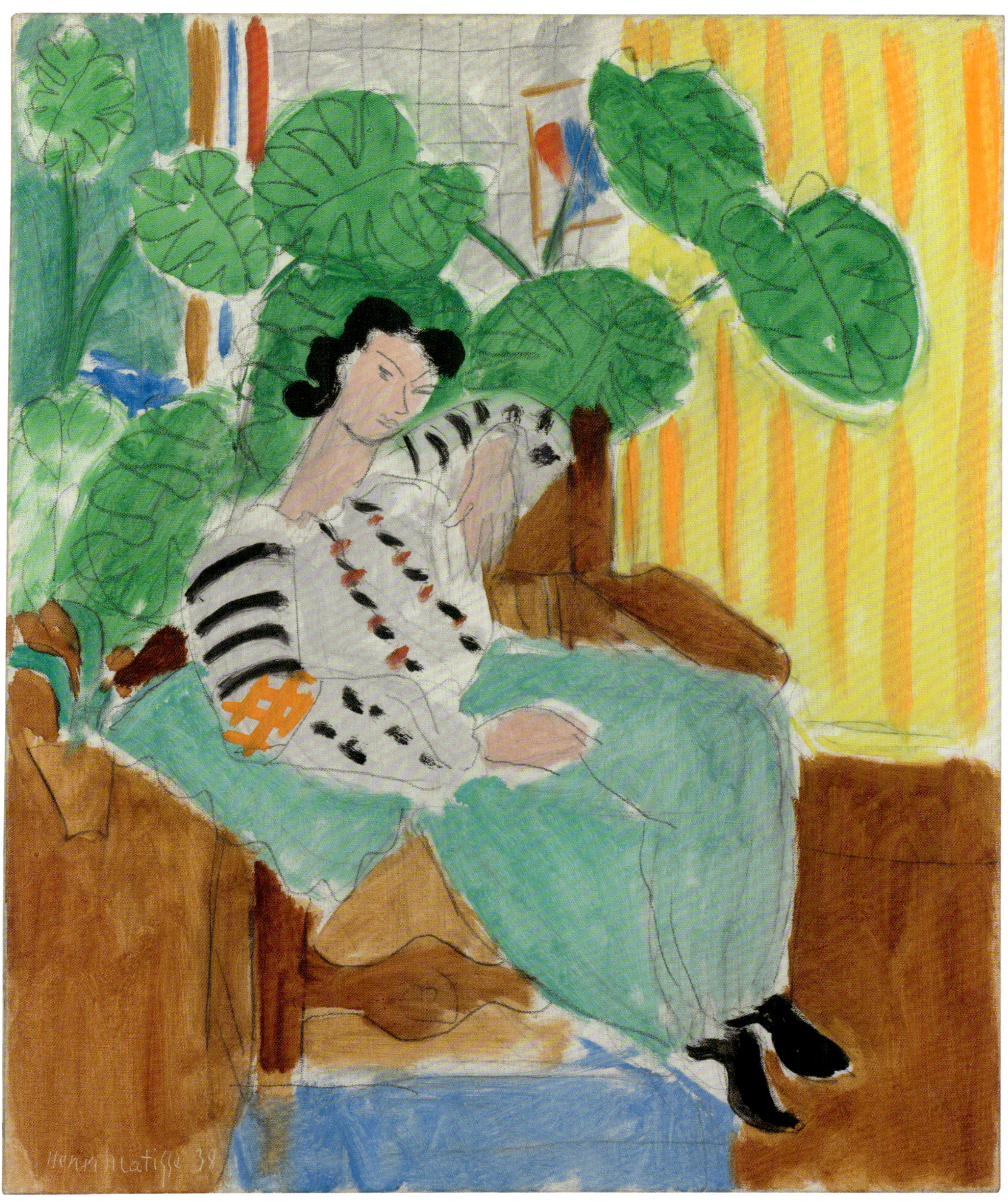

142
Small Romanian Blouse with Foliage,
1938 [November 4, 1937]
Oil and graphite on canvas,
18 ⅛ × 15 in. (46 × 38.1 cm)
Baltimore Museum of Art

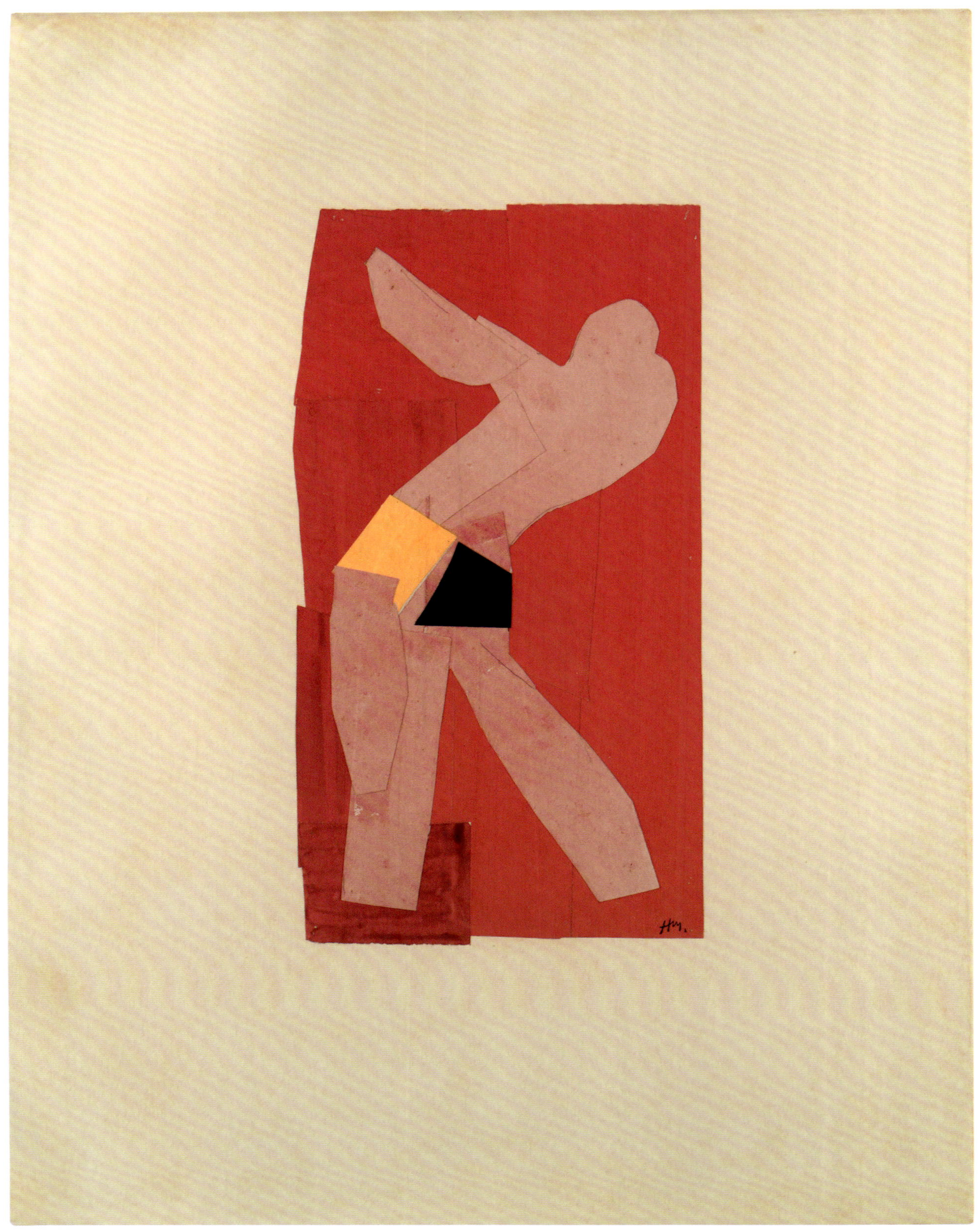

143
Small Dancer on Red Background
(model for the *Rouge et noir* set),
March 1938
Gouache on paper, cut and
pasted, 23 ½ × 18 ¼ in.
(59.7 × 46.4 cm)
Private collection, Houston

ROUGE ET NOIR: A MUSEUM OF SYNTHESIS?

In a letter to his wife, Amélie, written days after his arrival in the Tahitian capital of Papeete, Matisse rhapsodized about the "extraordinary, indescribable costumes" worn by women of the Paumotu Atoll (present-day Tuamotu Archipelago).[1] This panorama—which he compared to a stage decor—prompted a lengthy explanation of the racial biases of European colonists and Tahiti's mixed-race elite against the dark-skinned Paumotu. On his return, Matisse attended the 1931 Exposition Coloniale Internationale in Paris.[2] During his visit, he may have witnessed the "Ballet blanc et noir," a performance specially created for the exposition, danced by classically trained white ballerinas from the Paris Opéra and Black soldiers from French Equatorial Africa.[3] Like the fair as a whole, this spectacle projected an idealized image of *la plus grande France* (greater France) as "an ethnically diverse but politically unified nation-state," even as it reinforced racial hierarchies.[4]

By the time he visited the Exposition Coloniale, Matisse was already immersed in work on his monumental *Dance* mural. In an early oil study 95, he rendered its dancing bodies a deep brown, but eventually opted for a more neutral gray, with the figures set against bands of pink, blue, and black 99 | 100. In 1937, he returned to this composition and, in partnership with the choreographer Léonide Massine, made it the basis for his work on the ballet *L'Étrange Farandole*. Retitled *Rouge et noir* (Red and black) soon after its May 1939 premiere, this production is one of several symphonic ballets—choreographies set to existing concert music—that Massine composed in the 1930s. He envisioned this form as capable of bringing dance, music, and painting together while allowing each art to remain distinct. He invited Matisse to design his first such work, *Les Présages* (Omens; 1933), set to Pyotr Ilych Tchaikovsky's *Fifth Symphony* (1888). (Matisse demurred, recommending André Masson.) Massine interpreted Tchaikovsky's score through "movements and groupings with varying asymmetrical masculine and feminine elements." Visually, this resulted in a changing series of lines, shapes, and patterns formed in counterpoint to Masson's evocative, quasi-abstract backdrop.[5]

The surviving evidence of *Rouge et noir* 145 suggests that it achieved a similar effect.[6] Its scenario was intended to embody the conflict between forces of spirit (white) and matter (black), and to represent themes that Massine associated with the symphony's four movements: aggression, field and city, solitude, and destiny.[7] The action largely centered on two protagonists dressed in white (played by Alicia Markova and Igor Youskevich). In solo, partnered, and group dances, the main characters were tormented by dancers in blue, yellow, red, or black: they were pulled apart, spun around, pushed to the floor, and lifted overhead. When combined with Matisse's designs, this choreography provided a kaleidoscopic spectacle as the dancers massed, dispersed, and mingled. The ballet's movement vocabulary itself alternated between fusion and separation: Massine combined ballet technique with elements of "ethnic" dances, including quick footwork reminiscent of the hornpipe and flamenco-like arm gestures. Through both color and gesture—each of which

1 Henri Matisse–Amélie Matisse, April 2, 1930, Archives Henri Matisse, Issy-les-Moulineaux [AHM].

2 According to his diaries, Matisse visited the Exposition Coloniale on June 23 and 24, 1931.

3 The ballet premiered on June 15, 1931, and was subsequently performed on a regular basis; see Dana Hale, "The 'Ballet blanc et noir': A Study of Racial and Cultural Identity during the 1931 International Colonial Exhibition," in *Empire and Culture: The French Experience, 1830–1940*, ed. Martin Evans (Basingstoke: Palgrave MacMillan, 2004), 103–12.

4 Alice Conklin, Sarah Fishman, and Robert Zaretsky, *France and Its Empire since 1870* (Oxford: Oxford University Press, 2011), 172.

5 Léonide Massine, *My Life in Ballet*, ed. Phyllis Hartnoll and Robert Rubens (London: MacMillan, 1968), 186–87.

6 In addition to preparatory sketches and publicity photographs, two films of the ballet survive. One, in the collection of the Newberry Library, captured part of a performance in Chicago in 1939. The other, now in the New York Public Library for the Performing Arts, recorded a full rehearsal of the ballet, with dancers in practice clothes.

7 Leslie Norton, *Léonide Massine and the Twentieth-Century Ballet* (Jefferson, NC: McFarland, 2004), 226.

correlated with distinct racial and national identities—*Rouge et noir* promised a resolution that it perpetually withheld.

Rouge et noir thus bears out Claudine Grammont's contention that dance in Matisse's oeuvre is more than a mere aesthetic device: it functions as a metaphor for the "integration of the individual into the social body."[8] In 1909, when Matisse first employed the motif of dance in a decorative panel for Sergei Shchukin, this theme facilitated a relatively harmonious integration of painted figures. Ten years later, in his first collaboration with Massine, on the ballet *Le Chant du rossignol* (The song of the nightingale), Matisse aimed—with limited success—to unite bodies on stage through a chinoiserie aesthetic that he associated with both "French" and "Oriental" conceptions of the decorative.[9] By the 1930s, such a synthesis was even more elusive, as reactions to *Rouge et noir* attest. The critic Pierre Michaut, for example, saw the ballet as a "political allegory" evoking "the dramatic crushing of helpless nations" by the army of the Third Reich.[10]

But the ballet's staging of "groups that form, scatter, and reform" (in Michaut's words) resonated equally with internal debates about French nationhood at a moment of political discord and colonial expansion. Its original title, *L'Étrange Farandole*, connected the choreography to unresolved tensions between national and regional identities. The farandole, a dance involving a zigzaging chain of participants, was long identified as a distinctively Provençal form.[11] This was one of many provincial customs reclaimed by the short-lived Popular Front government to "reconcil[e] republican universalism with regional particularism."[12] In 1937, as Matisse and Massine began work on the ballet, the government put those folkloric traditions on display in festivals at the Paris Exposition Internationale and the newly opened Musée National des Arts et Traditions Populaires (ATP). Described by its founder, George-Henri Rivière, as a "museum of synthesis," the ATP was designed to harmonize cultural artifacts from distinct regions in a display that would represent the nation as a whole.[13] The failure of the Popular Front in 1938 may have been a factor in the decision to change the ballet's title. With its reference to Stendhal's famous novel about the social fissures of the post-Napoleonic era, *Rouge et noir* ultimately cast its own political moment as equally divided.

JULIET BELLOW

8 Claudine Grammont, "Danse," in *Tout Matisse*, ed. Grammont (Paris: Robert Laffont, 2018), 221.

9 Juliet Bellow, "Disorienting Decoration: Henri Matisse and *Le Chant du Rossignol*," in *Modernism on Stage: The Ballets Russes and the Parisian Avant-Garde* (Burlington, VT: Ashgate Press, 2013), 167–208.

10 Quoted in Vicente García-Márquez, *Massine: A Biography* (New York: Alfred A. Knopf, 1995), 270.

11 Mark Franko, *The Fascist Turn in the Dance of Serge Lifar: Interwar French Ballet and the German Occupation* (Oxford: Oxford University Press, 2020), 31–32.

12 Conklin, Fishman, and Zaretsky, *France and Its Empire*, 196.

13 Shanny Peer, *France on Display: Peasants, Provincials, and Folklore in the 1937 Paris World's Fair* (Albany: State University of New York Press, 1998), 136, 154. Matisse visited the 1937 Exposition Universelle on August 9, according to records in the AHM.

144
Mademoiselle Roudenko, no. 3 (Dancer of the Ballets Russes), July 1939
Black ink on cream wove paper, 18 ⅞ × 12 ⅜ in. (48 × 31.4 cm)
Harvard Art Museums/ Fogg Museum, Cambridge, Massachusetts

145
Rouge et noir ballet (choreography by Léonide Massine, music by Dmitri Shostakovich, set and costumes by Henri Matisse), 1939
Musée Matisse Nice

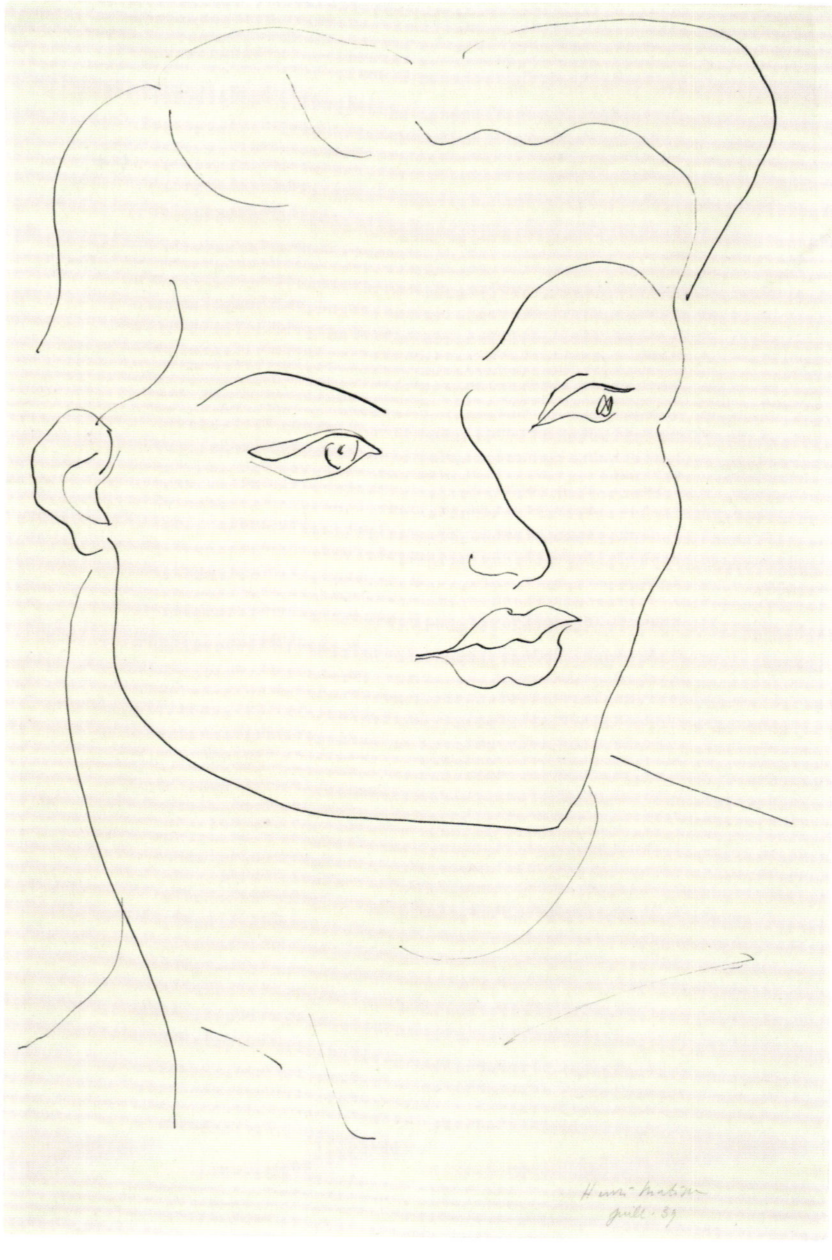

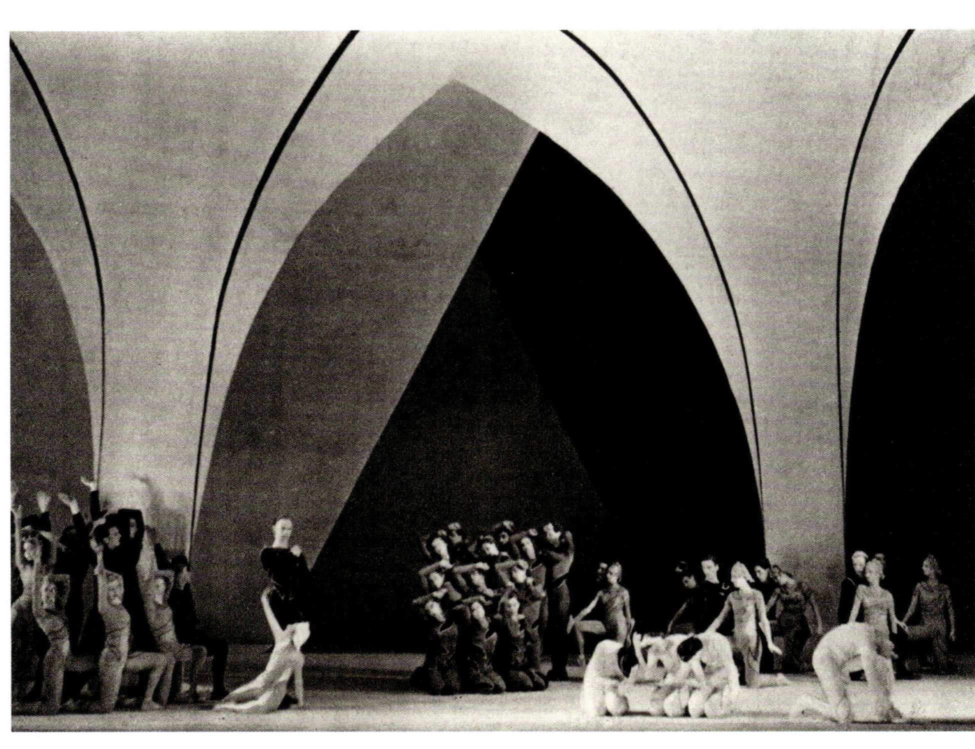

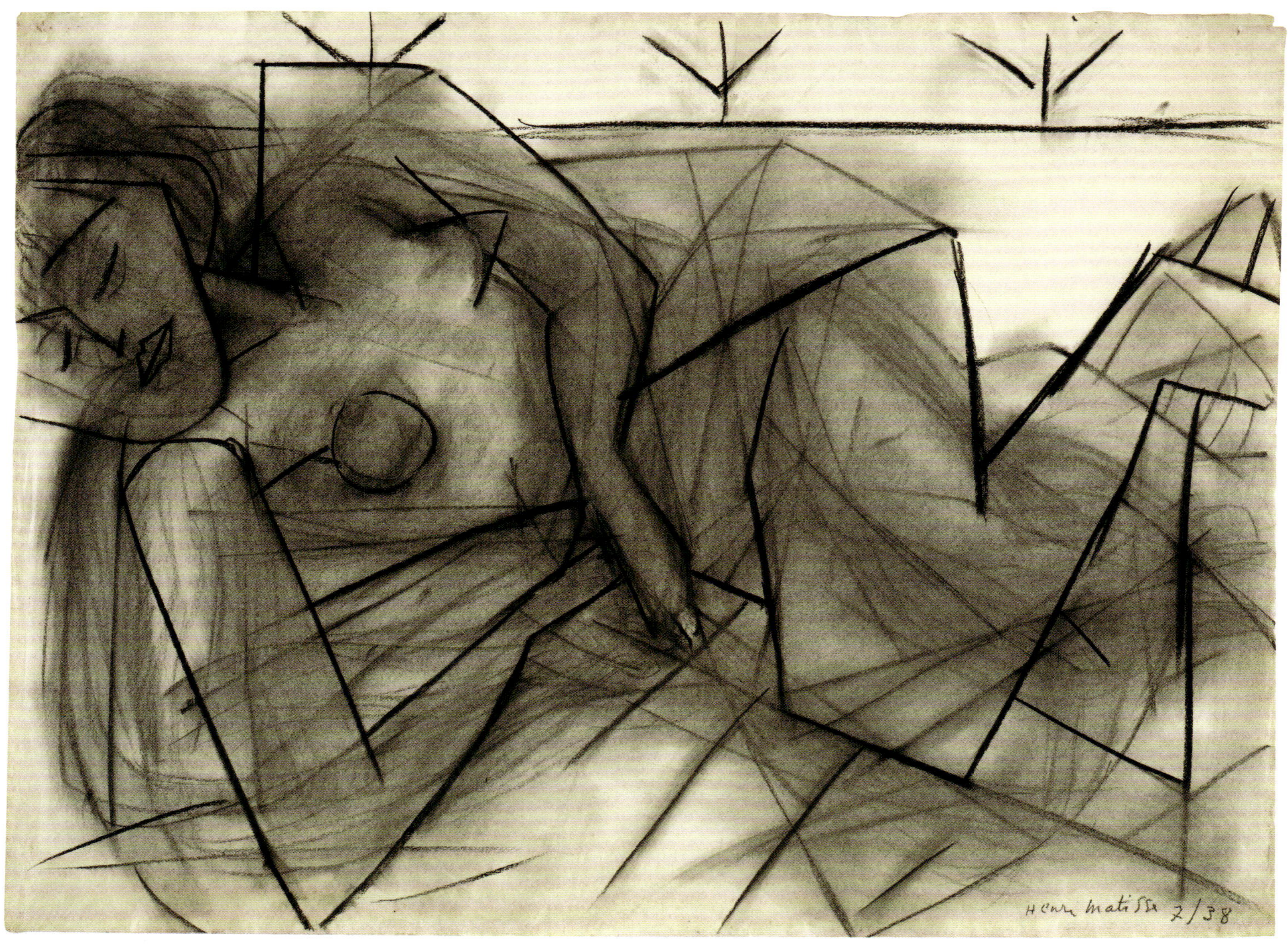

146
Reclining Nude, July 1938
Charcoal on paper, 23 13/16 × 32 in.
(60.5 × 81.3 cm)
The Museum of Modern Art,
New York

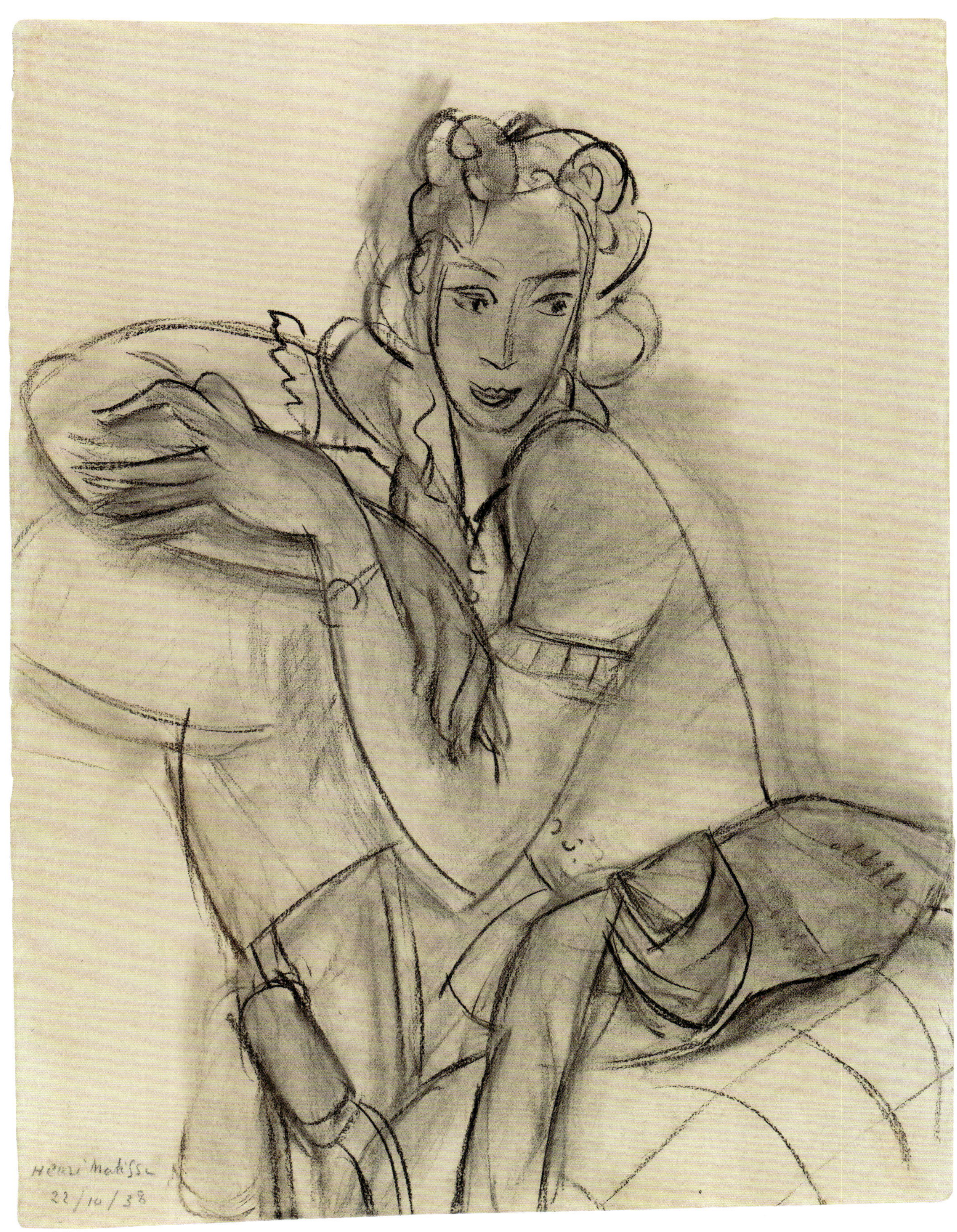

147
Study for "The Song," Portrait of Hélène Mercier, née Princess Galitzine, Seated, October 22, 1938
Charcoal and stump on paper, 25 ¾ × 19 ⅞ in. (65.5 × 50.5 cm)
Private collection

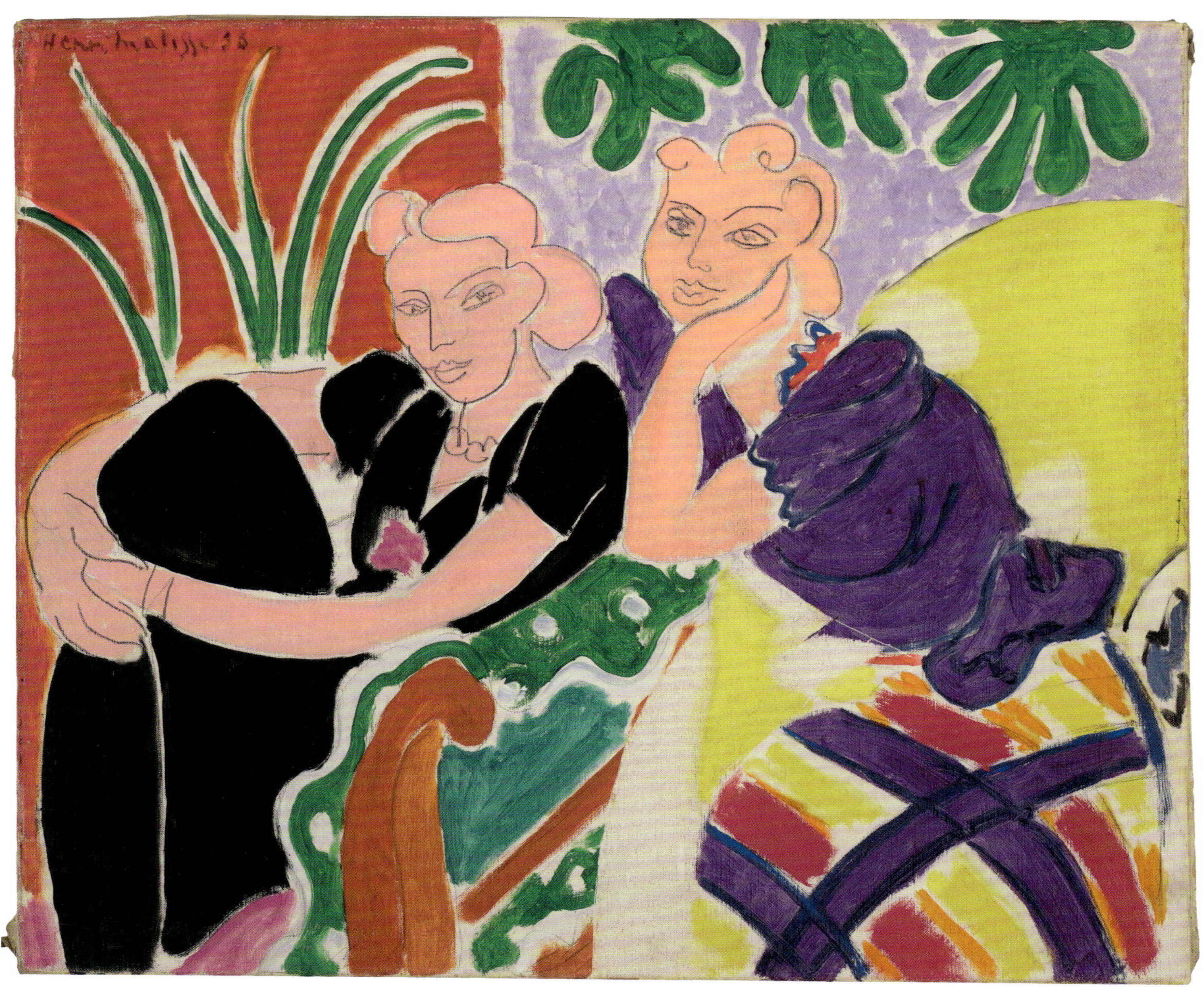

148
The Conversation,
October 1938
Oil on canvas, 18 ⅜ × 21 ¾ in.
(46.7 × 55.2 cm)
San Francisco Museum
of Modern Art

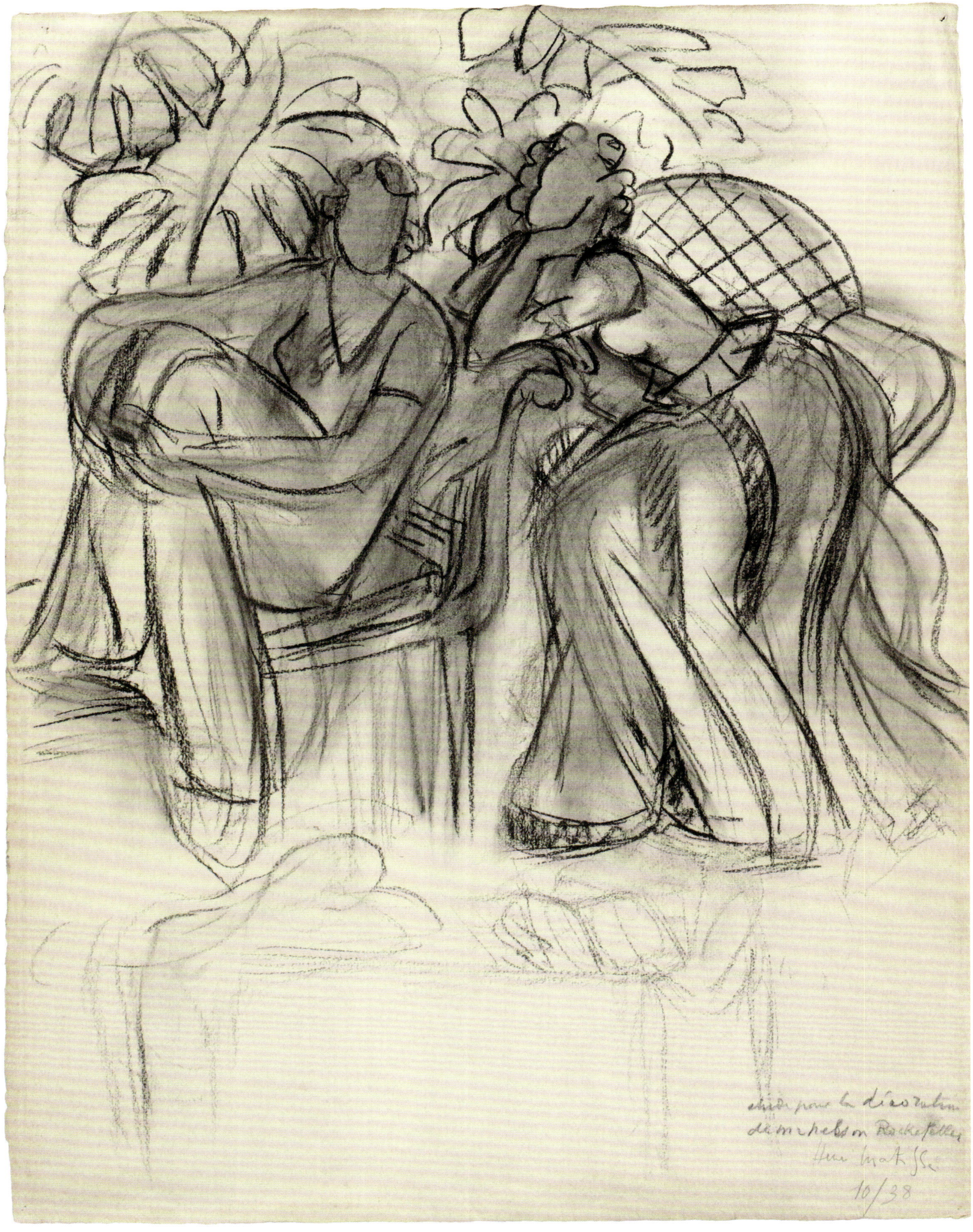

149
Study for "Song," October 1938
Charcoal on paper, 25 ¾ × 20 in.
(65.4 × 50.8 cm)
The Metropolitan Museum of Art,
New York

150
The Striped Dress, January 15 and 26, 1938
Oil on canvas, 18 ⅛ × 14 15/16 in. (46 × 38 cm)
Albertina Museum, Vienna

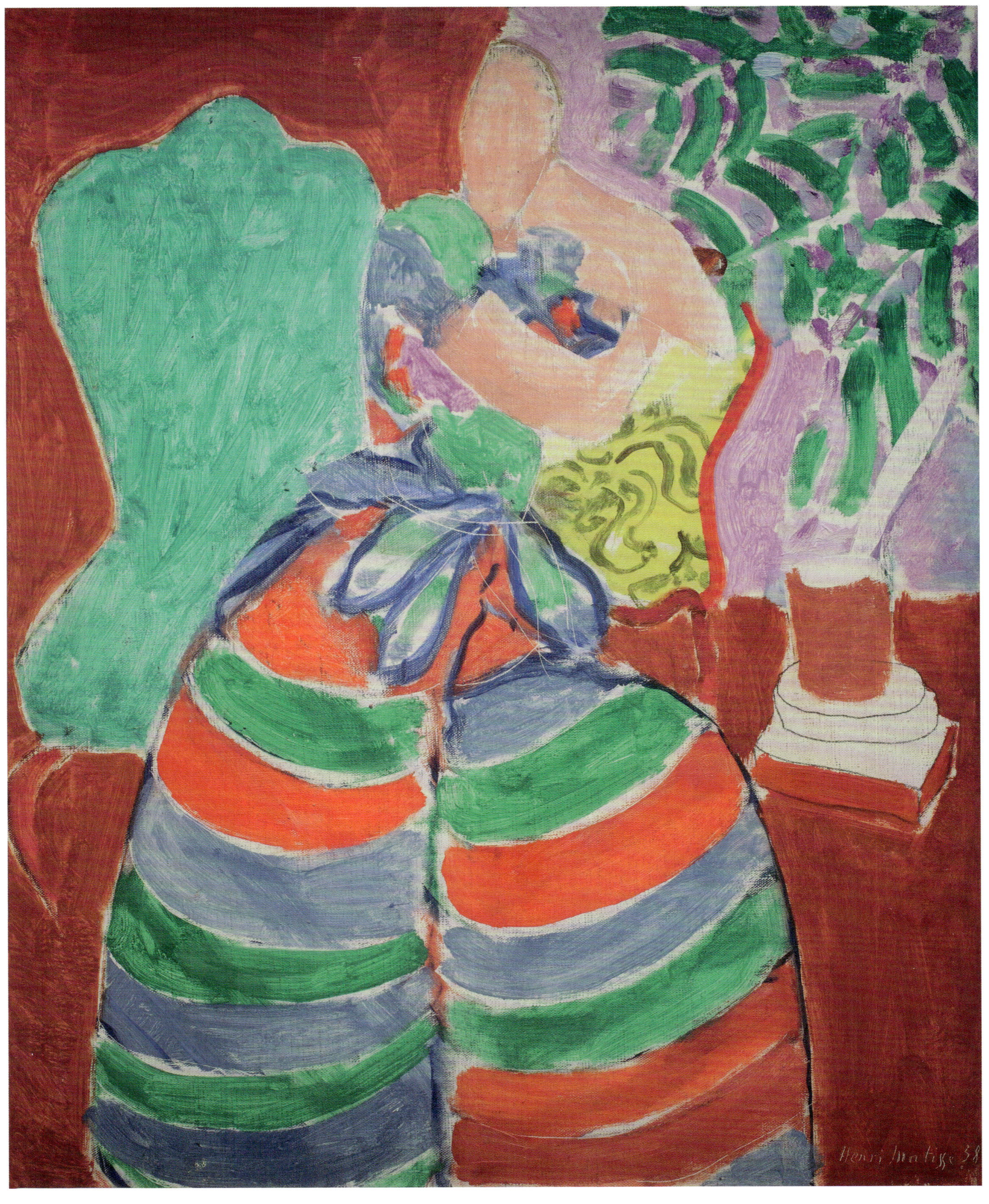
Henri Matisse 38

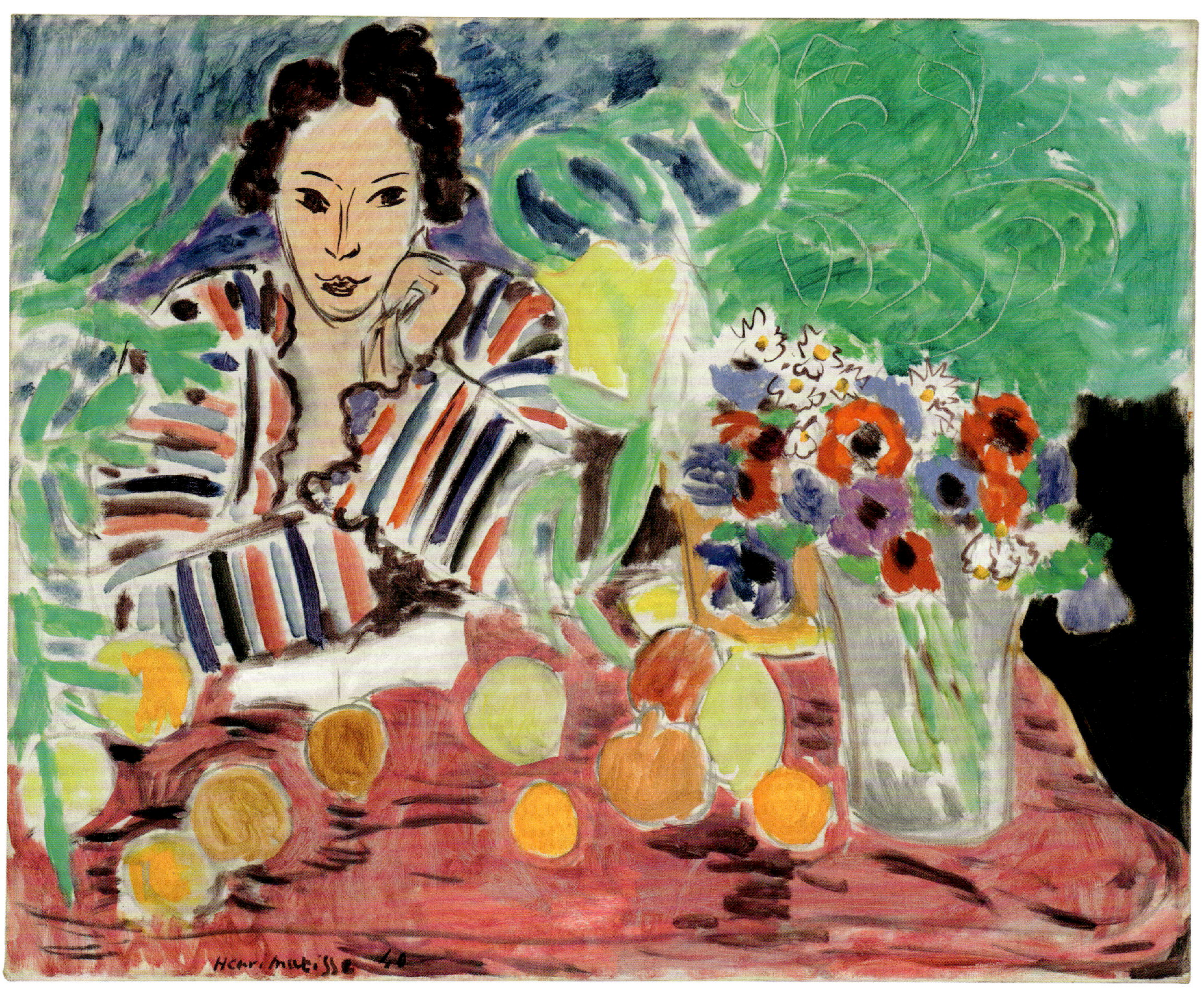

151
Striped Robe, Fruit, and Anemones, 1940
Oil on canvas, 21 5/8 × 25 5/8 in. (54.9 × 64.1 cm)
Baltimore Museum of Art

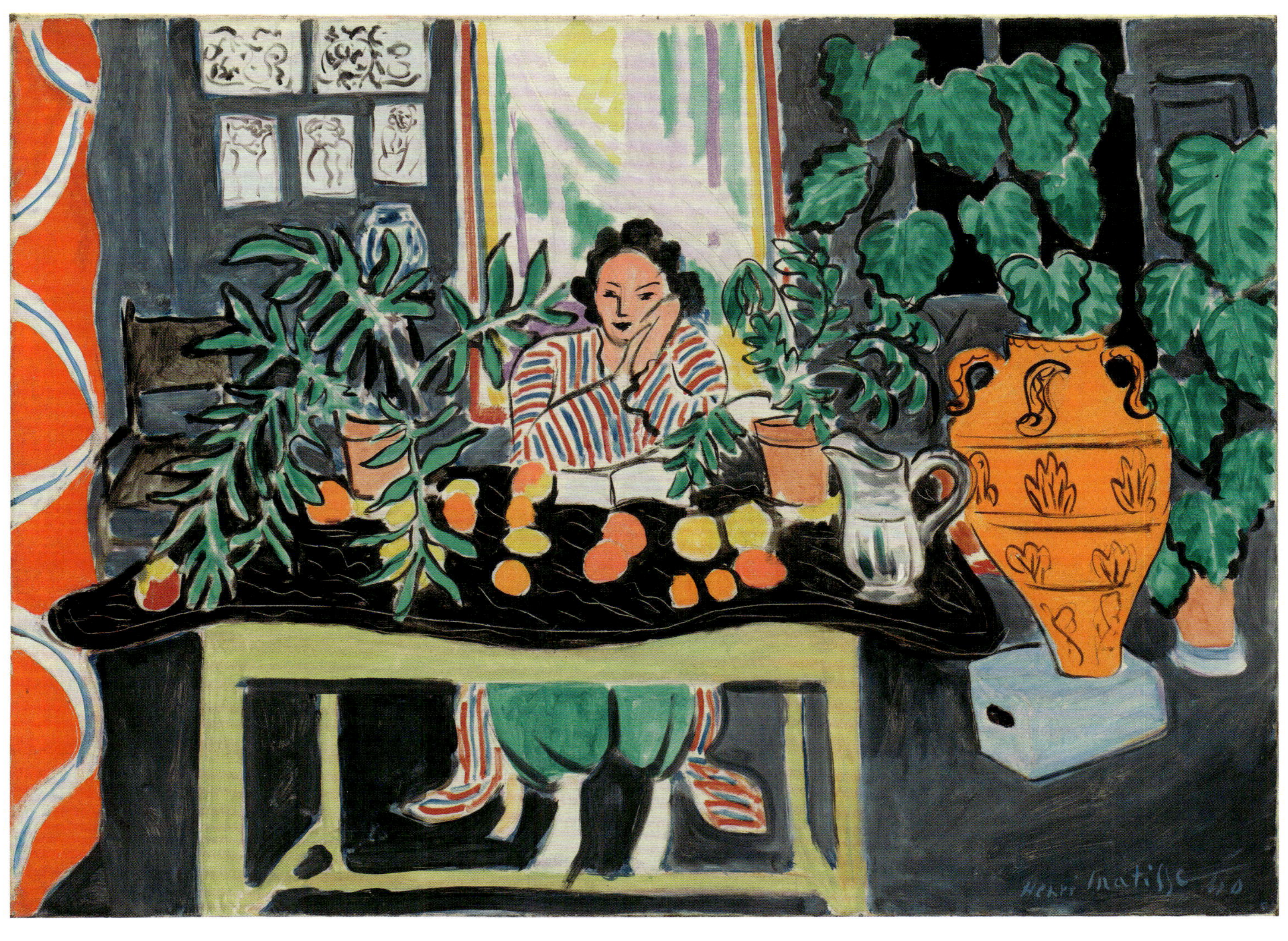

152
Interior with an Etruscan Vase,
1940
Oil on canvas, 29 × 42 ½ in.
(73.7 × 108 cm)
Cleveland Museum of Art

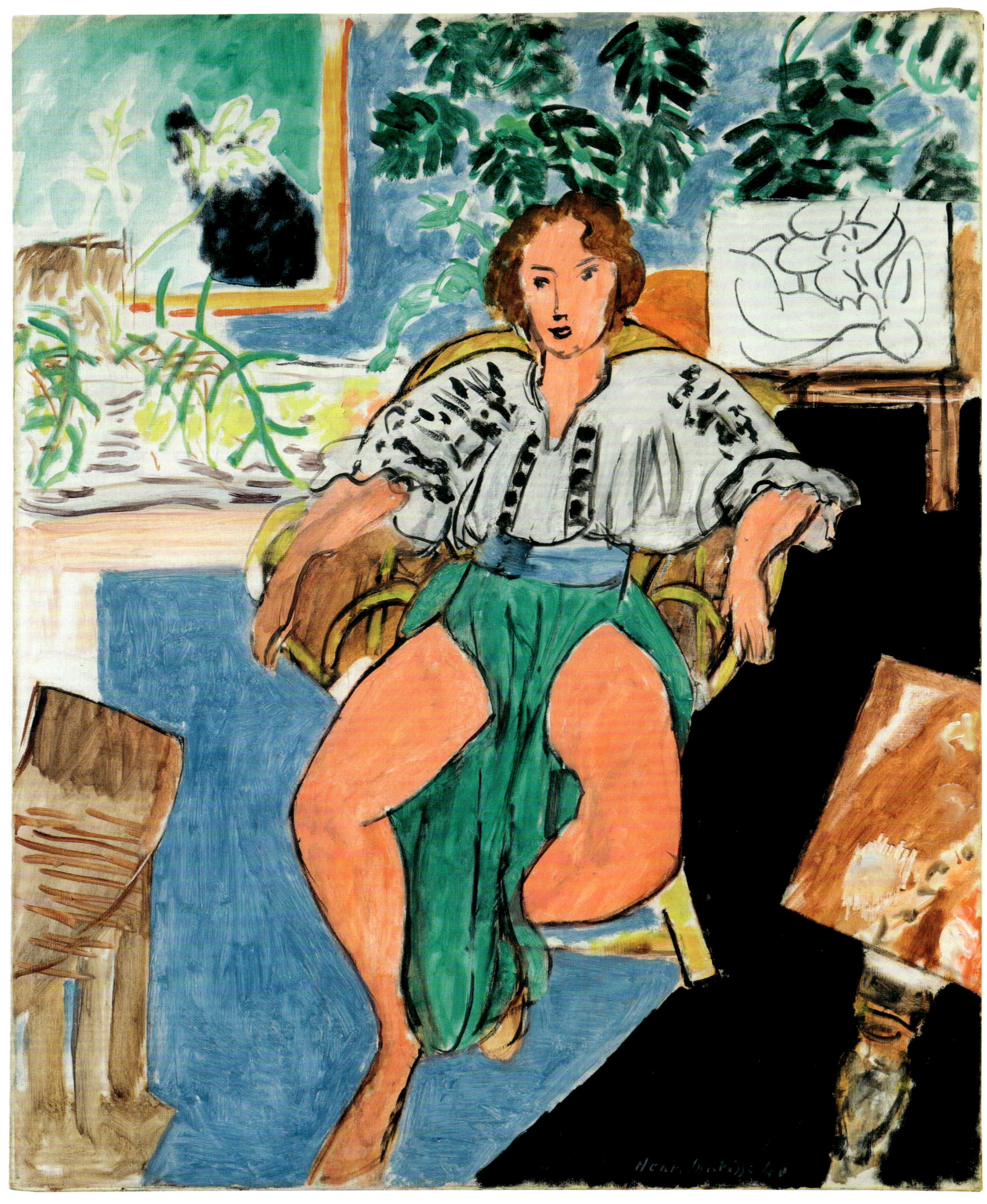

153
Dancer Resting, 1940
Oil on canvas, 32 × 25 ½ in.
(81.3 × 64.8 cm)
Toledo Museum of Art, Ohio

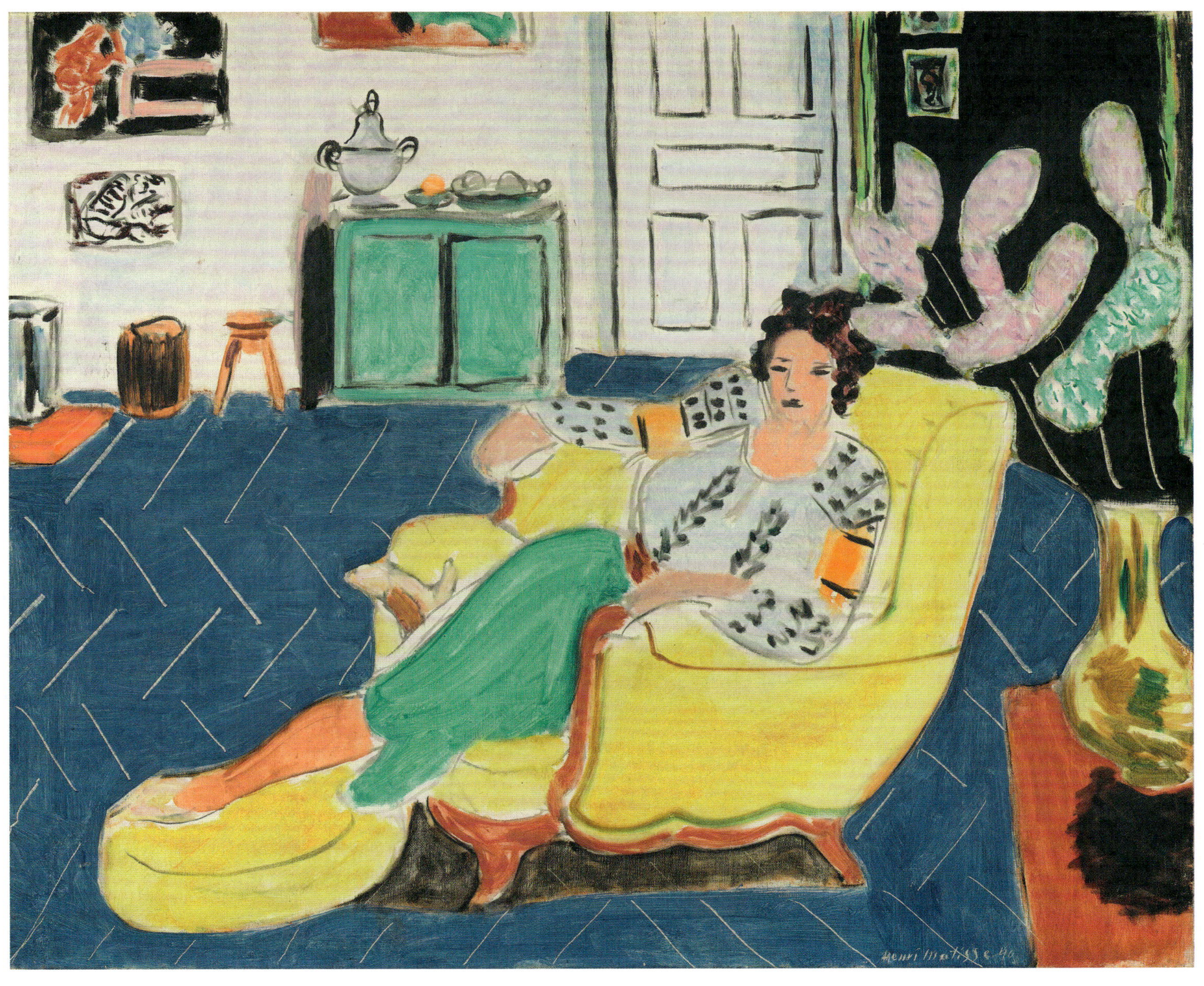

154
Woman Seated in an Armchair, 1940
Oil on canvas, 21 ¼ × 25 ⅝ in.
(54 × 65.1 cm)
National Gallery of Art, Washington

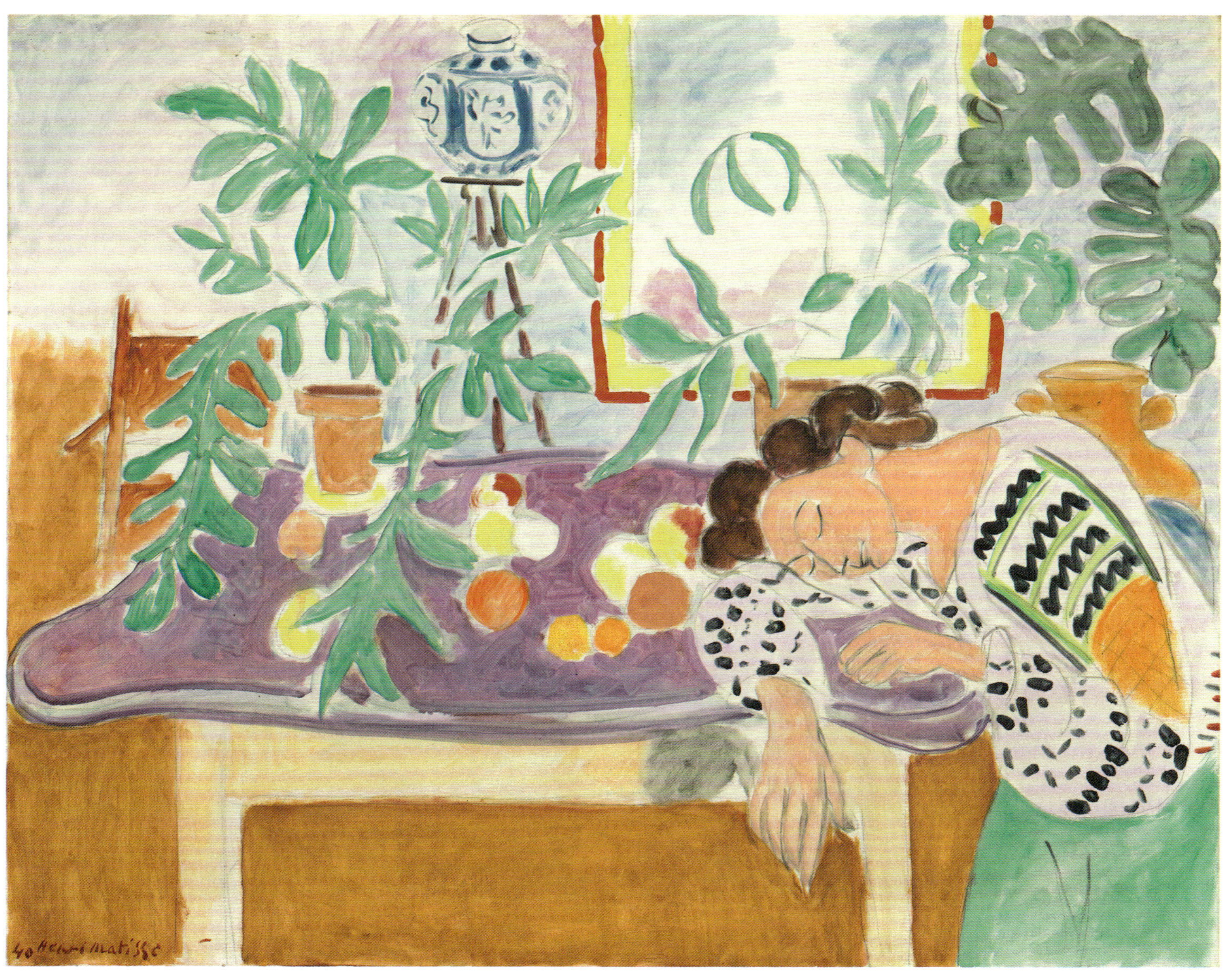

155
Still Life with Sleeping Woman, 1939–40
Oil on canvas, 32 ½ × 39 ⅝ in. (82.5 × 100.7 cm)
National Gallery of Art, Washington

156
Daisies, 1939
Oil on canvas, 36 ¼ × 25 ⁹⁄₁₆ in. (92 × 65 cm)
The Art Institute of Chicago

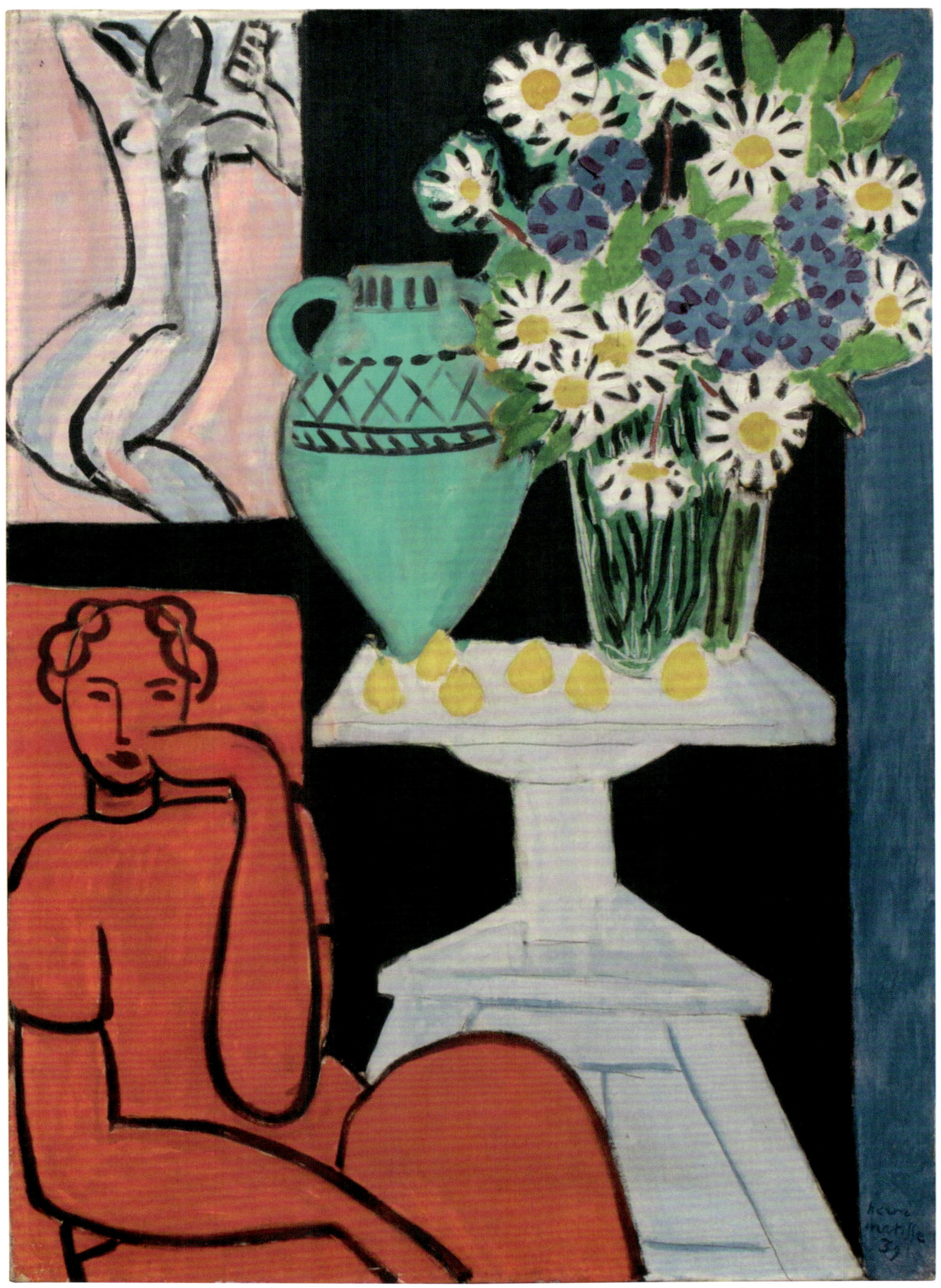

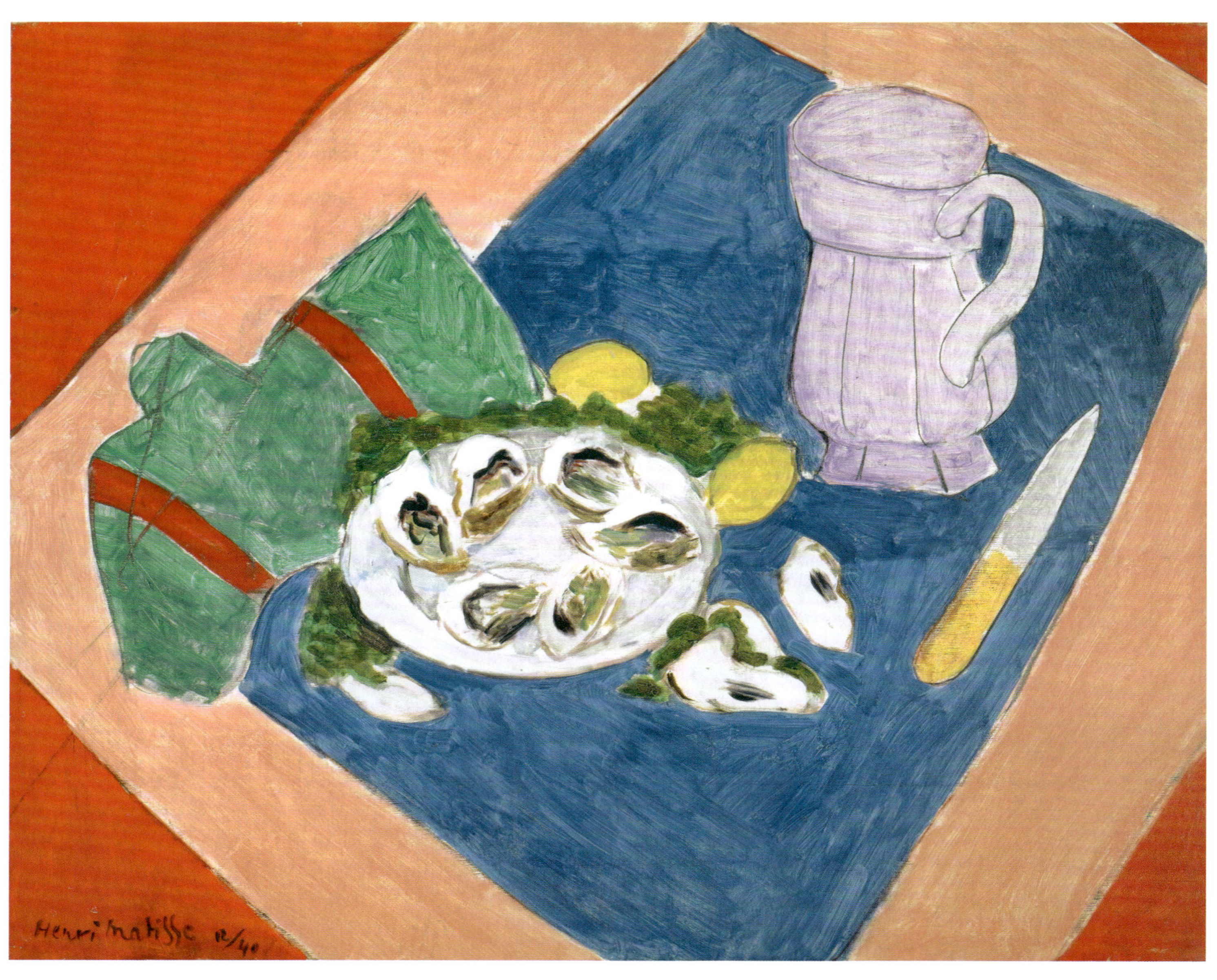

157
Still Life with Oysters, 1940
Oil on canvas, 25 11/16 × 31 7/8 in.
(65.2 × 80.9 cm)
Kunstmuseum Basel

THEMES AND VARIATIONS

Matisse chose to remain in France during World War II. His respite from the reality of the conflict was to focus on work. "My life is between the four walls of my studio," he wrote in a letter to his son, Pierre Matisse, in October 1940.[1] He was also facing a grave personal crisis. In January 1941, the artist underwent a high-risk operation for abdominal cancer in a clinic in Lyon. It was reported that his nurses, observing how close his brush with death had been, dubbed him *le ressuscité* (the resurrected one). Matisse similarly spoke of embarking on a second artistic life, despite his advancing age and ill health, when he finally was able to return to Nice in late May.[2] He painted relatively little but focused on drawing instead, as he would explain in April 1942, in a letter to his daughter, Marguerite Duthuit. "For a year I have made a significant effort, one of the most important of my life. I have perfected my drawing and made surprising progress in terms of ease and sensibility freely expressed, with a great variety of sensations and a minimum of techniques. It's like a blooming. And it's one of the things for which I wanted to continue living."[3]

Matisse was referring to a body of images he had selected from a larger campaign of drawing in 1941 and early 1942. Consisting of 158 sheet drawings divided into seventeen suites lettered *A* through *P* (with two assigned the letter *N*), this corpus comprises a stand-alone work, though its two subjects—female models and still lifes with plants or fruit—were also principal themes in his paintings of the same period **157 | 161**. All but five of the suites started off with expressive charcoal studies. Matisse's procedure—laying down marks, smudging them with a finger or a stump, and then redrawing—produced ghost marks suggesting shadow and texture while also recording his process of internalizing the subject. The initial, or matrix, drawings were followed by between five and nineteen variations (depending on the set), always in either graphite pencil or pen and ink. In these drawings, pure line does the work of defining contours, describing patterns, and positioning the motif in pictorial space without disturbing the ephemeral brightness of the paper support. Matisse hewed to the idea that drawing—pure line drawing most of all—is especially close to improvisation, immediate perception, and the spark of inspiration. By the 1930s, he understood drawing as getting at the essence of his concept of the creative process, which valued the flux of perception and emotion over definitive statements.[4] With their serial and open-ended approach—as in *Theme P*, which depicts a woman in a striped dress in a variety of poses and from a range of viewpoints **158 | 159**—the *Themes and Variations* crystallized that larger trend in Matisse's art.

By early 1942, Matisse was thinking of making an album to bring the *Themes and Variations* to the attention of the public.[5] He was already engaged in a series of conversations with Louis Aragon, the communist poet and member of the French Resistance who had taken refuge in the South of France, resulting in a preface for the publication.[6] The title of Aragon's prologue, "Matisse-en-France," was meant to position Matisse as a personification of authentic national identity in opposition to the Vichy government. Aragon closed his dense, suggestive text with a reference to the *Themes and Variations* as tokens of an artist's quiet resistance to conditions in wartime France: "At the darkest point in our night, they will say, he made those luminous drawings."[7] Martin Fabiani, Matisse's dealer and publisher in Paris, printed *Dessins: Thèmes et variations*, an album of loose-leaf, full-page collotype reproductions, in February 1943, at the height of the war.

MATTHEW AFFRON

1 Henri Matisse [HM]–Pierre Matisse, October 25, 1940, quoted in Lydia Delectorskaya, *Henri Matisse: Contre vents et marées; peintures et livres illustrés de 1939 à 1943* (Paris: Irus et Vincent Hansma, 1996), 118 (author's translation).

2 Claudine Grammont, "Opération de 1941," in *Tout Matisse*, ed. Grammont (Paris: Robert Laffont, 2018), 646–47.

3 HM–Marguerite Duthuit [MD], April 1942, quoted in Marguerite Duthuit-Matisse and Claude Duthuit with Françoise Garnaud, *Henri Matisse: Catalogue raisonné des ouvrages illustrés*, trans. Timothy Bent (Paris: C. Duthuit, 1988), 437 (translation modified).

4 Henri Matisse, "Notes of a Painter on His Drawing" (1939), in *Matisse on Art*, ed. and trans. Jack Flam, rev. ed. (Berkeley: University of California Press, 2015), 130–32.

5 HM–MD, April 1942, in Duthuit-Matisse and Duthuit, *Henri Matisse*, 437 (translation modified).

6 See Hilary Spurling, *Matisse the Master: A Life of Henri Matisse; The Conquest of Colour, 1909–1954* (New York: Alfred A. Knopf, 2005), 405–8. On Matisse's situation during the German occupation, see Laurence Bertrand Dorléac, "Ignoring History," in Henri Matisse with Pierre Courthion, *Chatting with Henri Matisse: The Lost 1941 Interview*, ed. Serge Guilbaut (Los Angeles: Getty Research Institute, 2013), 235–45; and Rémi Labrusse, "Henri Matisse: Guerre et résurrection," in *L'Art en guerre: France, 1938–1947*, ed. Laurence Bertrand Dorléac and Jacqueline Munck (Paris: Paris-Musées, 2012), 385–86.

7 Louis Aragon, *Henri Matisse: A Novel*, trans. Jean Stewart (New York: Harcourt Brace Jovanovich, 1972), 143–44.

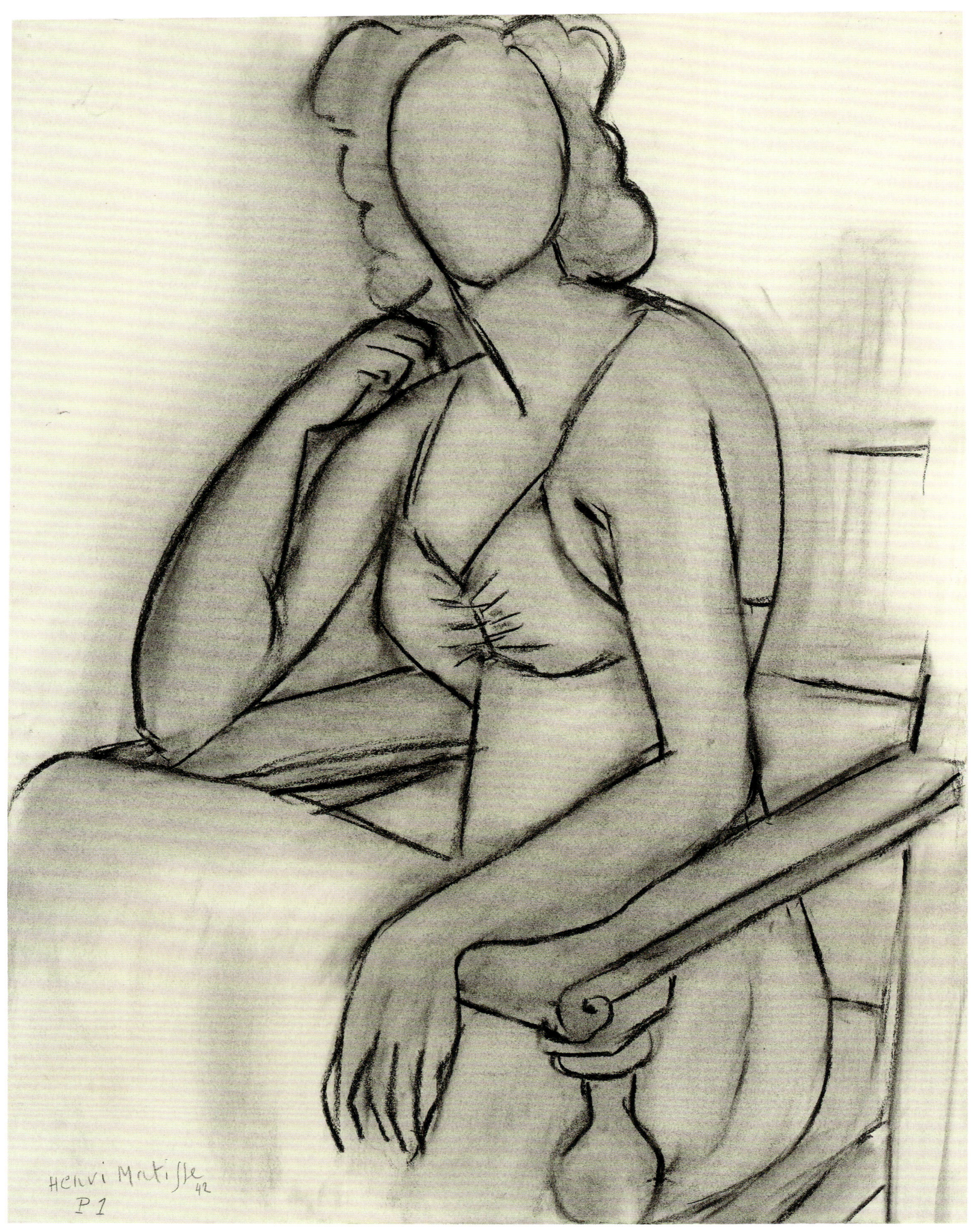

158
Themes and Variations (P1), 1942
Charcoal on paper, 20 9/16 × 15 7/8 in.
(52.3 × 40.3 cm)
Musée des Beaux-Arts, Lyon

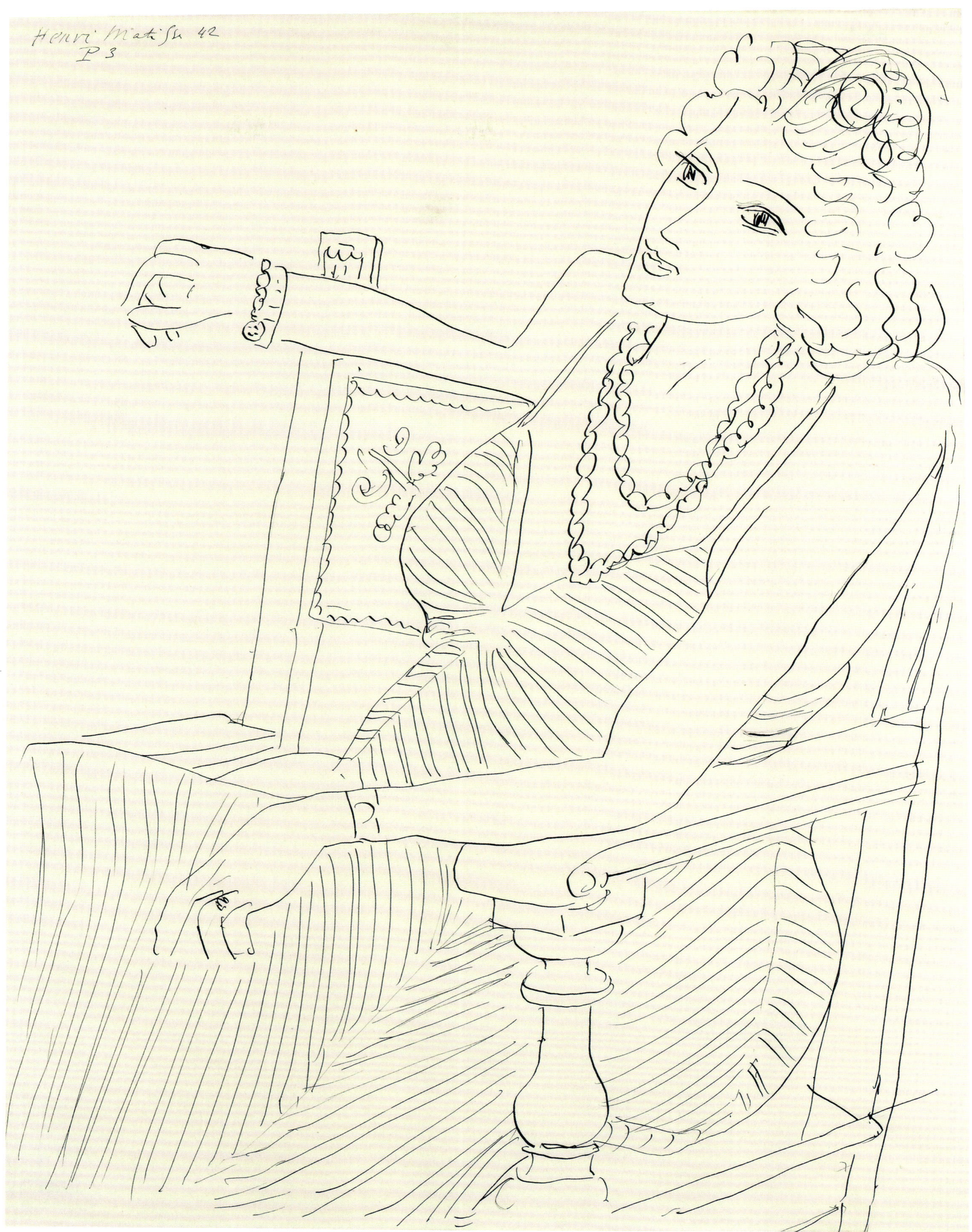

159
Themes and Variations (P3), 1942
Pen and India ink on paper,
20 11⁄16 × 15 15⁄16 in. (52.5 × 40.5 cm)
Musée des Beaux-Arts, Lyon

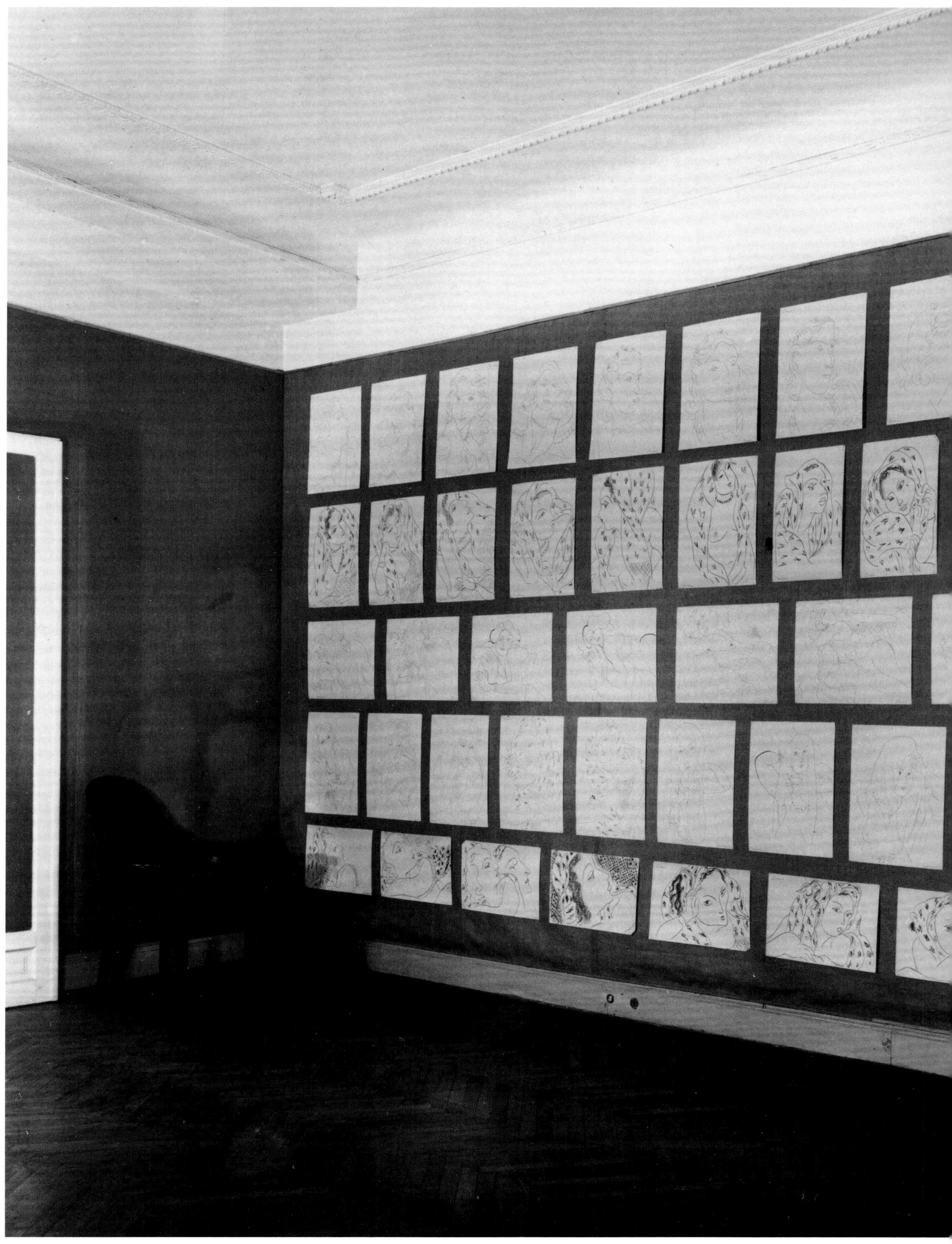

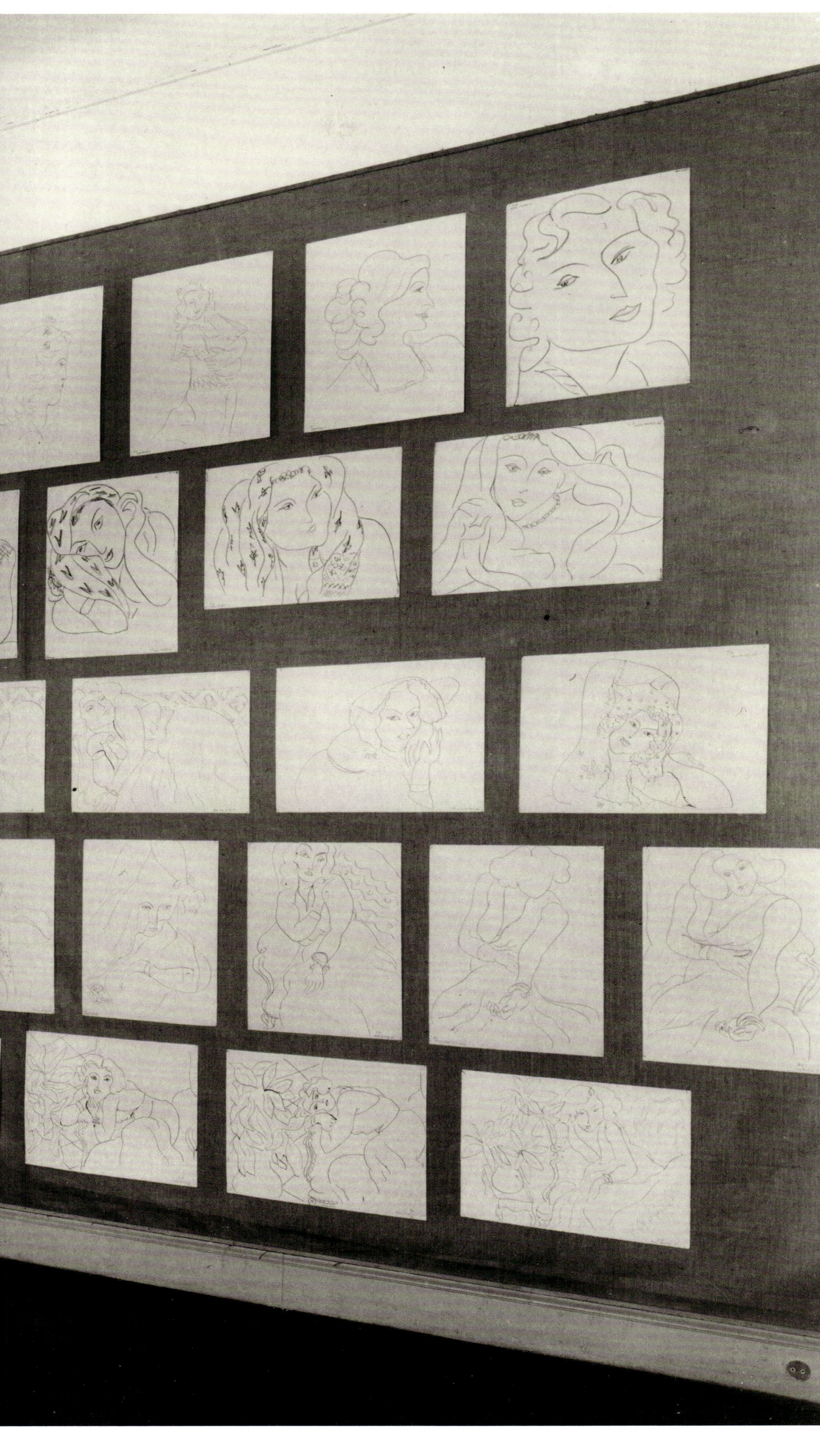

160 (fig.)
The "bright room," studio in the Régina; on the wall:
Themes and Variations, 1942.
Photograph by Maurice Bérard
Archives Henri Matisse, Issy-les-Moulineaux

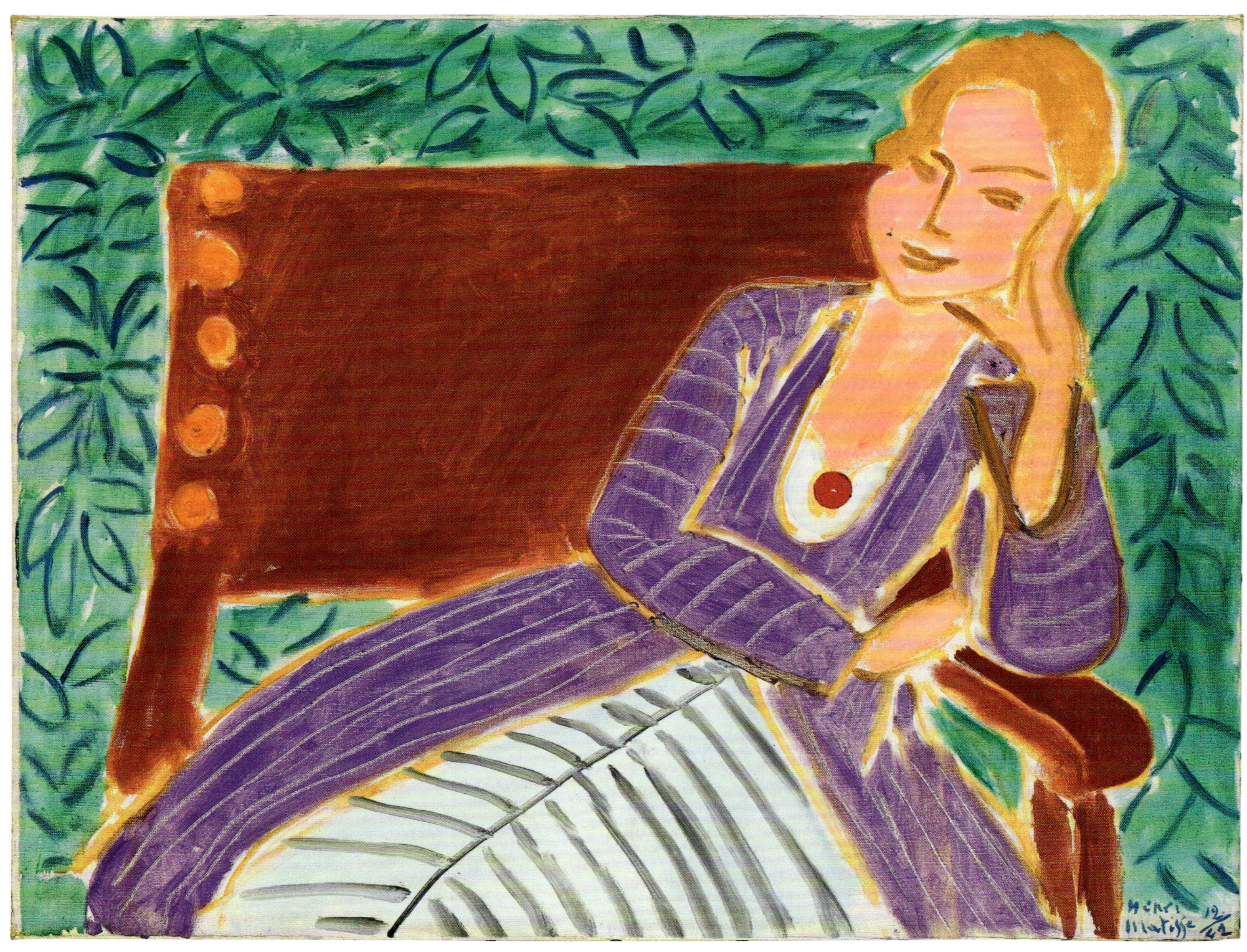

161
Young Woman Seated
in a Persian Dress, 1942
Oil on canvas, 16 15/16 × 22 1/16 in.
(43 × 56 cm)
Musée National Picasso–Paris

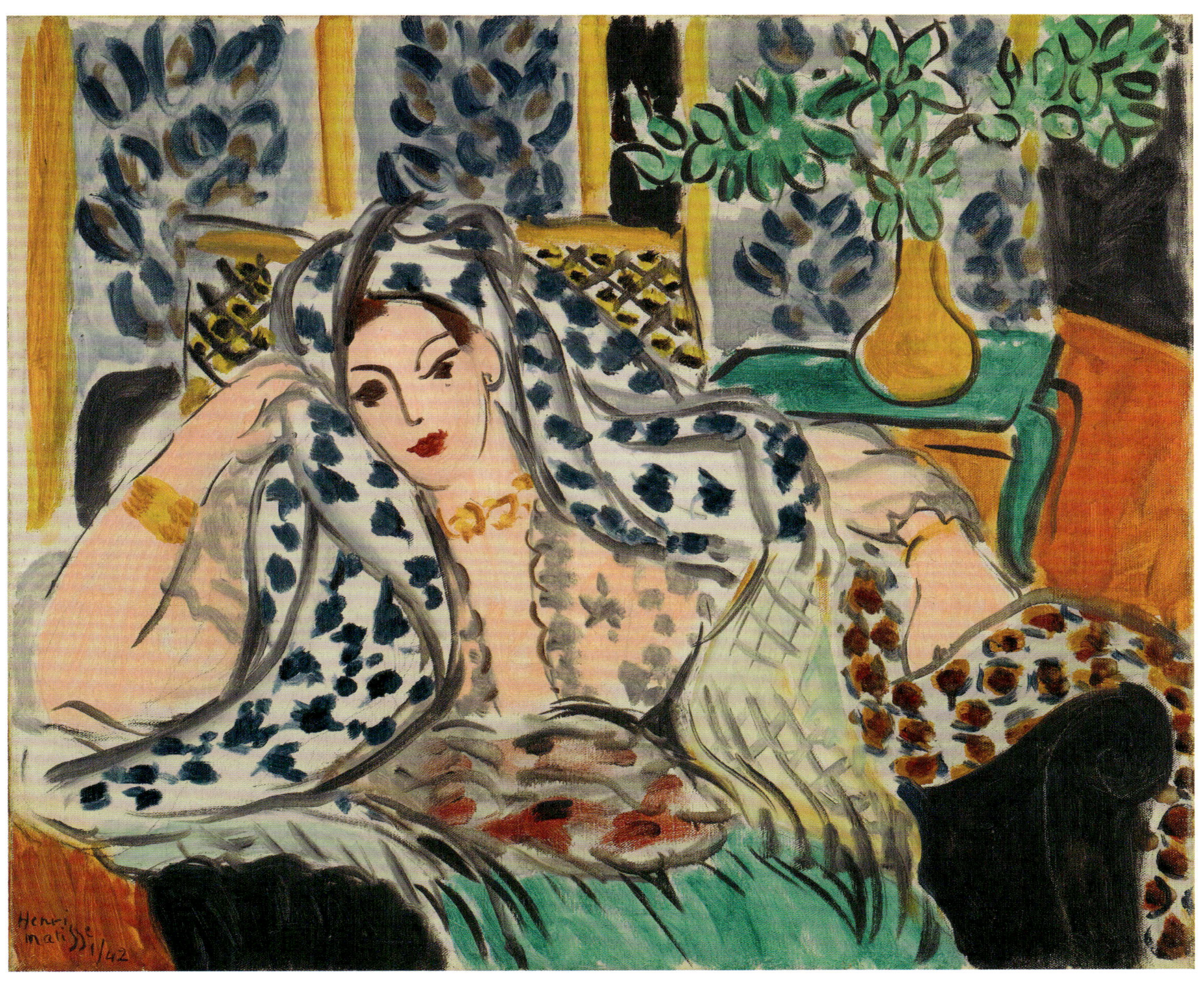

162
Odalisque in a Black Armchair,
January 17 and 18, 1942
Oil on canvas, 14 15/16 × 18 1/8 in.
(38 × 46 cm)
Private collection

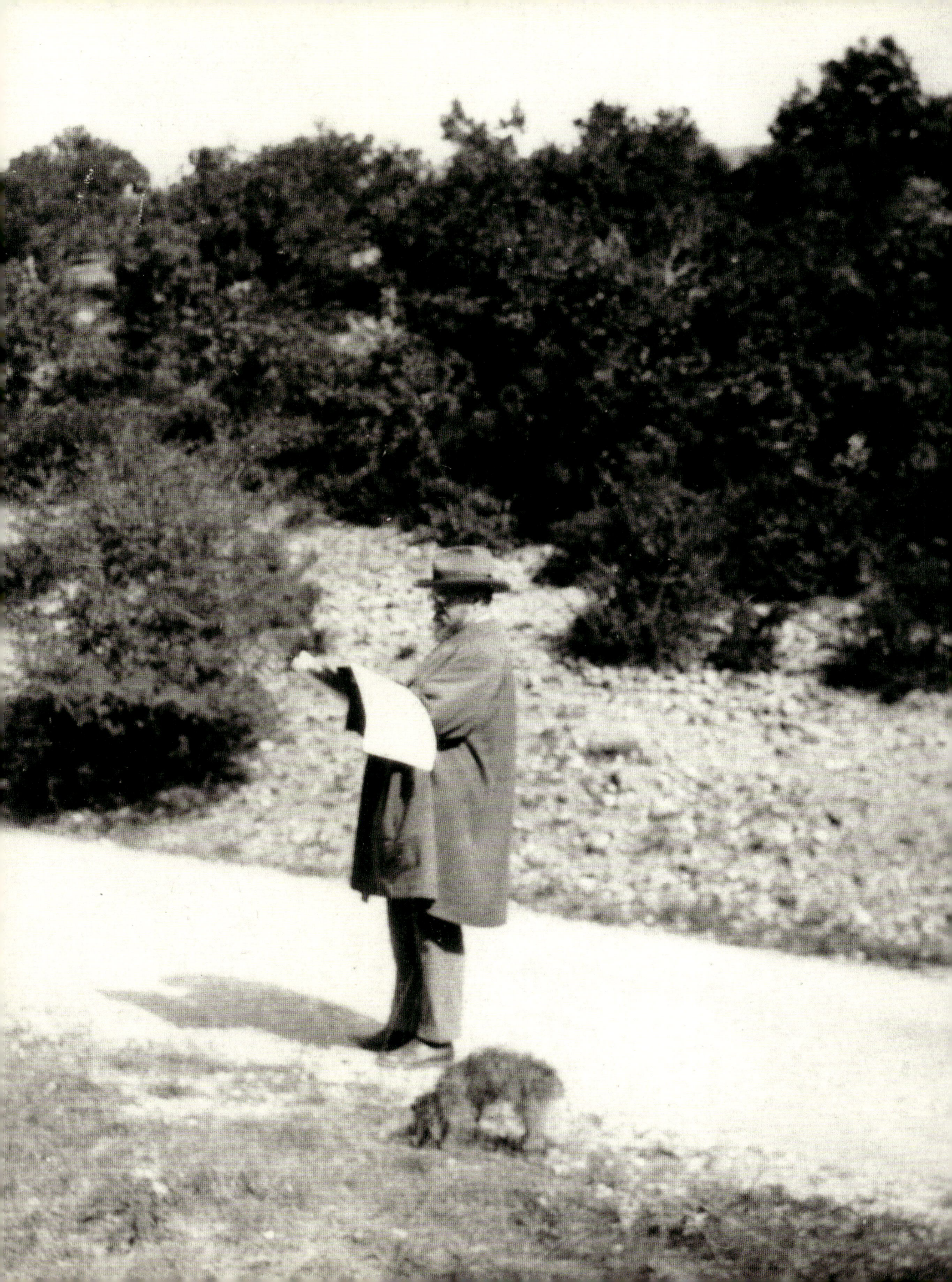

ANNE THÉRY

CHRONOLOGY OF THE ARTIST AT WORK 1926–40

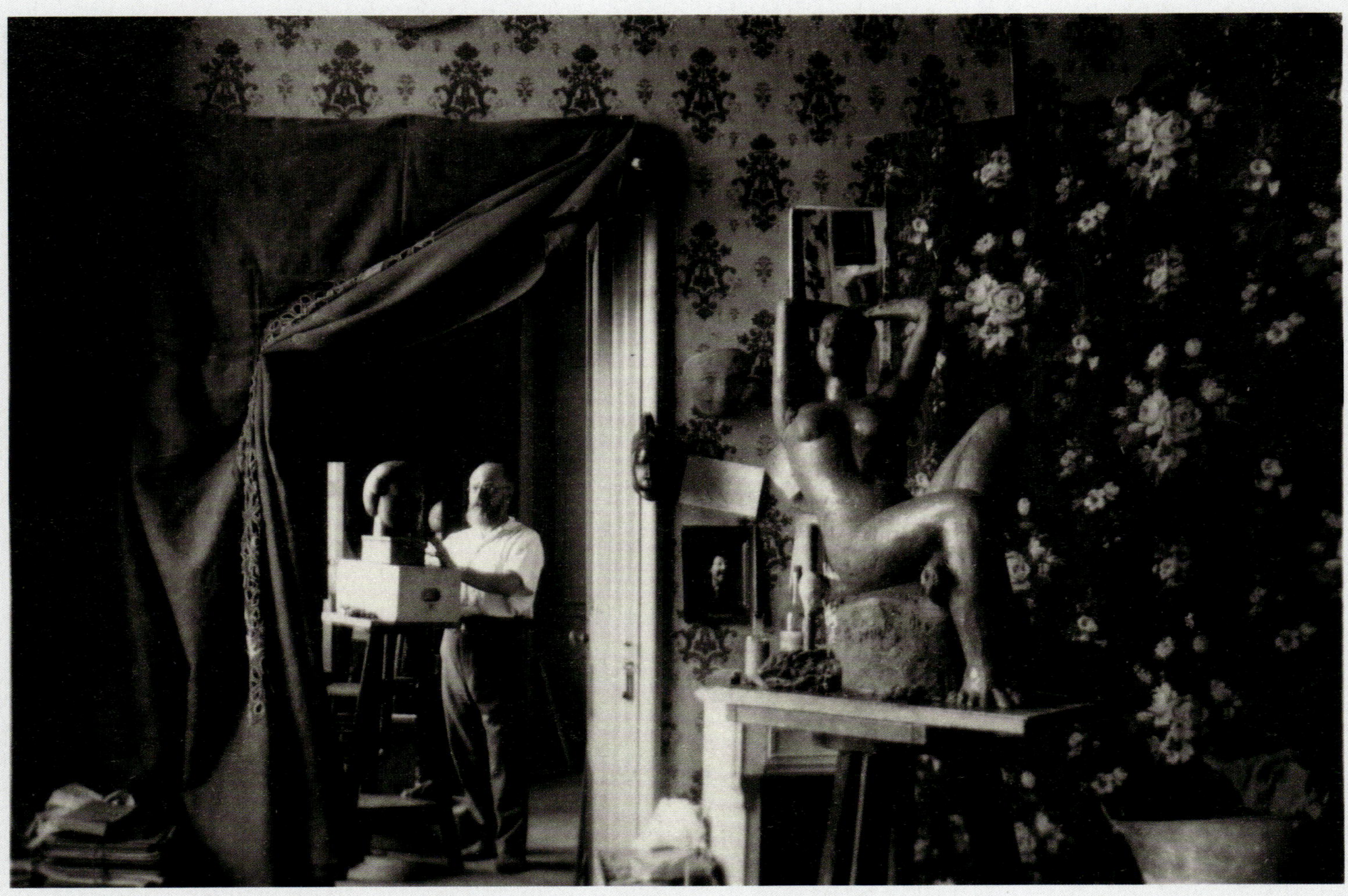

Unless otherwise specified, all the photographs in the chronology are held at the Archives Henri Matisse in Issy-les-Moulineaux.

Previous page
163 (fig.)
Henri Matisse drawing, Antibes, undated

Above
164 (fig.)
Henri Matisse working on *Henriette II*; in the foreground, *Large Seated Nude*, Place Charles-Félix, Nice, c. 1926–27

1926

This chronology is based on Henri Matisse's letters and diaries in the Archives Henri Matisse in Issy-les-Moulineaux. My sincere thanks to Barbara Duthuit and Georges Matisse for allowing me to quote them. The correspondence between Henri and Pierre Matisse is in the collection of the Morgan Library & Museum in New York. For a systematic listing of the artist's individual and group shows during this time, see Catherine Bock-Weiss, *Henri Matisse: A Guide to Research* (New York: Garland Publishing, 1996), 485–509, as well as in the bibliography page 251 in this volume. For a complete summary of the paintings of this period, see Lydia Delectorskaya, *With Apparent Ease . . . Henri Matisse: Paintings from 1935–1939*, trans. Olga Tourkoff (Paris: Adrien Maeght, 1988), and Lydia Delectorskaya, *Henri Matisse: Contre vents et marées; peintures et livres illustrés de 1939 à 1943* (Paris: Irus et Vincent Hansma, 1996).

Matisse was living and working in Nice at 1 place Charles-Félix at the beginning of the year, and his fifth-floor studio offered ample space and light. He wrote to his daughter, Marguerite, that he was grappling with "a no. 60 canvas (it's really big!) . . . begun in fear and trembling, but I finished it quite easily . . . without having to scrape it down as usual and start over every session."[1] The work was *Decorative Figure on an Ornamental Ground* (1925–26; Musée National d'Art Moderne–Centre Pompidou [MNAM–CP], Paris), for which Henriette Darricarrère was the model. It was hung that summer in the fourth Salon des Tuileries in Paris.

In March, Matisse was absorbed in working on two canvases at once—a "dancer" and "a little painting whose primary subject is a white satin dress."[2] He did not leave the studio until the middle of the month, when he made a trip to Toulon to stay with Marguerite and his son-in-law, Georges Duthuit, who were also hosting Juan Gris and his wife. When he returned to Nice, he devoted himself entirely to his work, most notably his sculpture *Large Seated Nude* 81, which he had been working on since 1922.

In April, Matisse agreed to contribute to Christian Zervos's journal, *Cahiers d'art*. One of his lithographs was featured on the cover of the inaugural issue; it was the beginning of an enduring collaboration 55.[3] He spent most of the remainder of the spring working on *Large Seated Nude*. On May 30, Matisse, accompanied by his wife, Amélie, took a cure in the spa town of Dax. On the way, he stopped in Marseille to meet a man named Carli who was responsible for casting his sculpture.[4]

In June, Matisse was working diligently, "standing for two to seven, eight hours, and sometimes eight and a half hours, and then I collapse into bed, exhausted, without dinner,"[5] striving to complete his *Large Seated Nude* by the end of the month. This intense exertion continued throughout the summer. Matisse left Nice only for a few days to sign the property deed for an apartment at 132 boulevard du Montparnasse in Paris.[6]

From October 8 to 14, the Galerie Paul Guillaume presented an exhibition featuring three older works: *Lilacs* (1914; Metropolitan Museum of Art, New York), *The Piano Lesson* (1916; Museum of Modern Art [MoMA], New York), and *Bathers by a River* 20. Duthuit made a presentation on the occasion of the exhibition opening that earned him recognition as one of the foremost authorities on the artist's work.

Matisse spent the month of October in Nice. Forced to live in a hotel (the windows of his studio were blocked by scaffolding) and without the services of a model (Darricarrère was ill at the time), he started work on a still life "without conviction but which [he] managed to complete through sheer force of will."[7] He sent two canvases to the Salon d'Automne:[8] *Odalisque with a Tambourine* (Norton Simon Museum, Pasadena) and *Nude in an Armchair* (MNAM–CP).

In November, Matisse noted, "The work is going slowly, the painting is very difficult, even painful."[9] He had just completed "a still life on a no. 15 canvas" (*Lemons on a Pewter Plate*; Art Institute of Chicago), and he was working on a "no. 20 canvas with a figure." Responding to her anxious and exhausted father, Marguerite wrote that "work is always grueling and tiring early in the season . . . while you can't take pleasure in it, there's nothing to be worried about, and your next paintings will be full of accumulated energy that you'll release into their creation. Perhaps that's what they help us to live for."[10]

---

1 Henri Matisse [HM]–Marguerite Duthuit [MD], January 4, 1926.

2 HM–MD, March 12, 1926.

3 HM–Christian Zervos, April 4, 1926.

4 HM–MD, May 30 and 31, 1926.

5 HM–MD, June 20, 1926.

6 HM–MD, September 30, 1926.

7 HM–MD, October 26, 1926.

8 November 5–December 19, 1926.

9 HM–MD, November 27, 1926. The quotations that follow are from the same source.

10 MD–HM, December 4, 1926.

1927

These were prescient words. In January, Matisse wrote to his son Pierre, "The painting is beginning to take shape."[11] He expected that by the end of the year he would make "something that is more profound and complete." And he continued, "Since returning in October, I've worked from two until seven every day, and I've made real progress in drawing, in-depth progress. One of my drawings has given me an idea for painting a composition. I've already made a cartoon for it." The work was *The Abduction of Europa* (1927–29; National Gallery of Australia, Canberra).

Pierre organized the major show for the Valentine Gallery in New York,[12] which clearly demonstrated this newfound energy. The exhibition was a huge success: "The gallery is packed every day; there's never been recognition like this."[13] Matisse was also represented in a number of individual and group shows in Paris—in the Galerie Bernheim-Jeune,[14] the Salon des Indépendants,[15] the Galerie Bing,[16] and the Salon des Tuileries[17]—and at the Reid & Lefevre Gallery in London.[18]

Matisse worked assiduously until June. His painting sessions—including *Woman with a Veil* 72 and *Reclining Nude Seen from the Back* (private collection)[19]—were added to his exertions in sculpting *Henriette II* 79, but above all the *Large Seated Nude*, which was still a work in progress.[20] Coming to terms with the situation, he wrote to Amélie on June 22, "The sculpture has yet to be either completed or abandoned."[21] After a visit to Paris in July, he continued on to Brittany in August, returning to Nice in September. Darricarrère had created a genuine crisis with her departure during the summer.[22] The artist was drained but forced himself to exercise with frequent rowing outings "to support the huge effort of any fresh impetus."[23] But these efforts lagged: his new models were no more than "fifty percent" satisfactory. "I have a session tomorrow afternoon, and I'll see how that goes. If it doesn't go well, I'll stop for a week."

The *Twenty-Sixth International Exhibition of Paintings* was held at the Carnegie Institute in Pittsburgh from October 13 until December 14. Matisse was represented by five paintings and received first prize for *Flowers and Fruits* (1924; private collection). "It means a great deal to me," the artist wrote to Amélie. "If you don't receive this prize, you tell yourself that so many idiots get it that it doesn't matter in the least, but when you are recognized you change your mind—you convince yourself that, since you've conceded no integrity or platitudes to earn it, it's a triumph, the greatest honor."[24]

This event did not diminish the challenges of finding a model. Matisse had several painting sessions with a "dancer" and "a little thing that Pierre saw in a bath; I've already worked with her twice."[25] But he had to contend with the model's absences and took up still lifes instead. He presented two paintings made with Darricarrère as model in the Salon d'Automne:[26] *Odalisque in Gray Pantaloons* 70 and *Reclining Nude Seen from the Back.*

On December 20, Matisse started work on a painting, *Woman in Oriental Costume, Embroidered Vest* (private collection), with one of his new models, Zita 52. "My drawing is getting lighter and becoming more expressive. It'll be well deserved if it comes to something.[27] Work on the painting continued to occupy him at least until December 27.[28]

11 HM–Pierre Matisse [PM], January 5, 1927. The quotations that follow are from the same source.

12 January 3–31, 1927.

13 PM–HM, February 8, 1927.

14 *Exposition Henri Matisse: Dessins et lithographies*, January 24–February 4, 1927.

15 January 21–February 27, 1927.

16 *Les Fauves, 1904–1908*, April 15–30, 1927.

17 April–June 1927.

18 *Exhibition of Works by Henri Matisse*, June 1927.

19 HM–Amélie Matisse [AM], May 21, 1927.

20 See HM–AM correspondence, June 1927.

21 HM–AM, June 22, 1927.

22 Henriette Darricarrère–MD, undated [1950].

23 HM–AM, October 13, 1927. The quotations that follow are from the same source.

24 HM–AM, October 29, 1927.

25 HM–AM, October 31, 1927.

26 November 4–December 16, 1927.

27 HM–AM, December 21, 1927.

28 Diary.

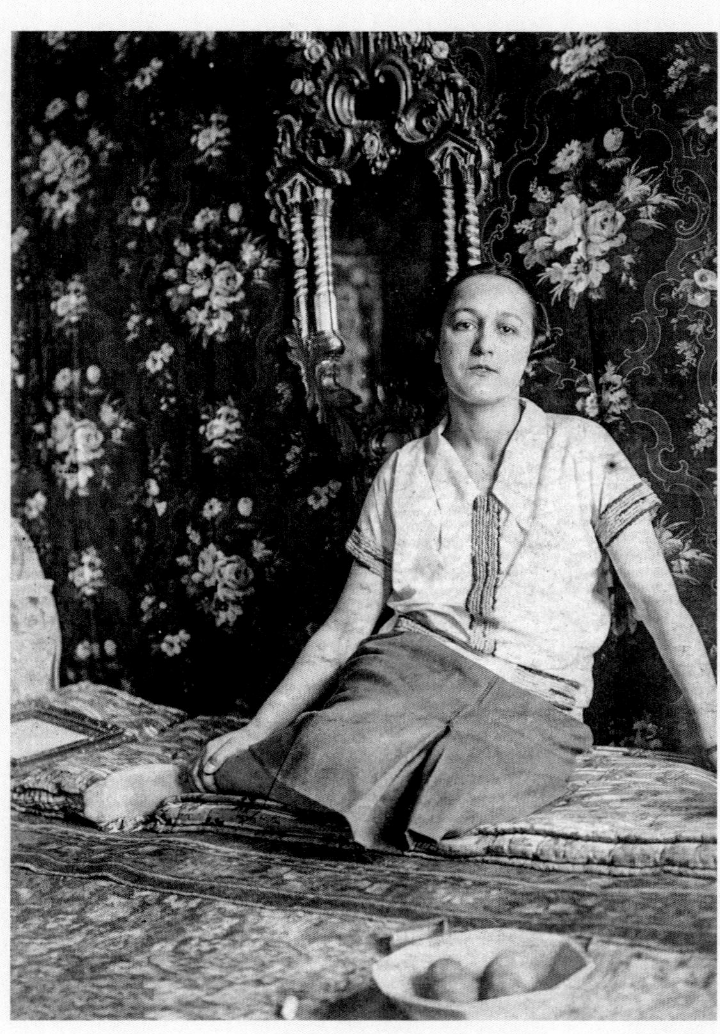

165 (fig.)
Henriette Darricarrère
in the studio,
Place Charles-Félix, Nice,
c. 1926

166 (fig.)
Henri Matisse in the studio,
Place Charles-Félix, Nice,
c. 1926–27

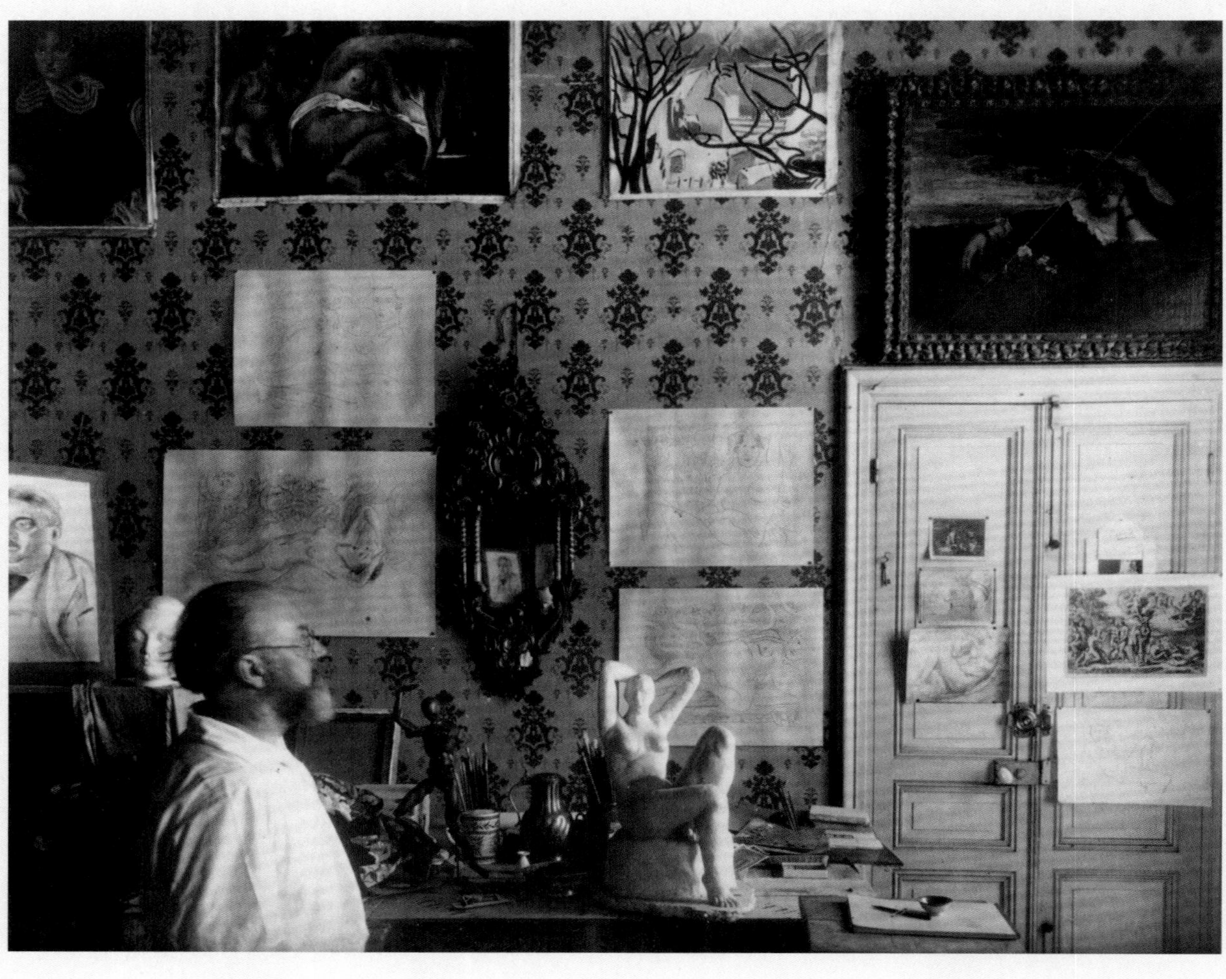

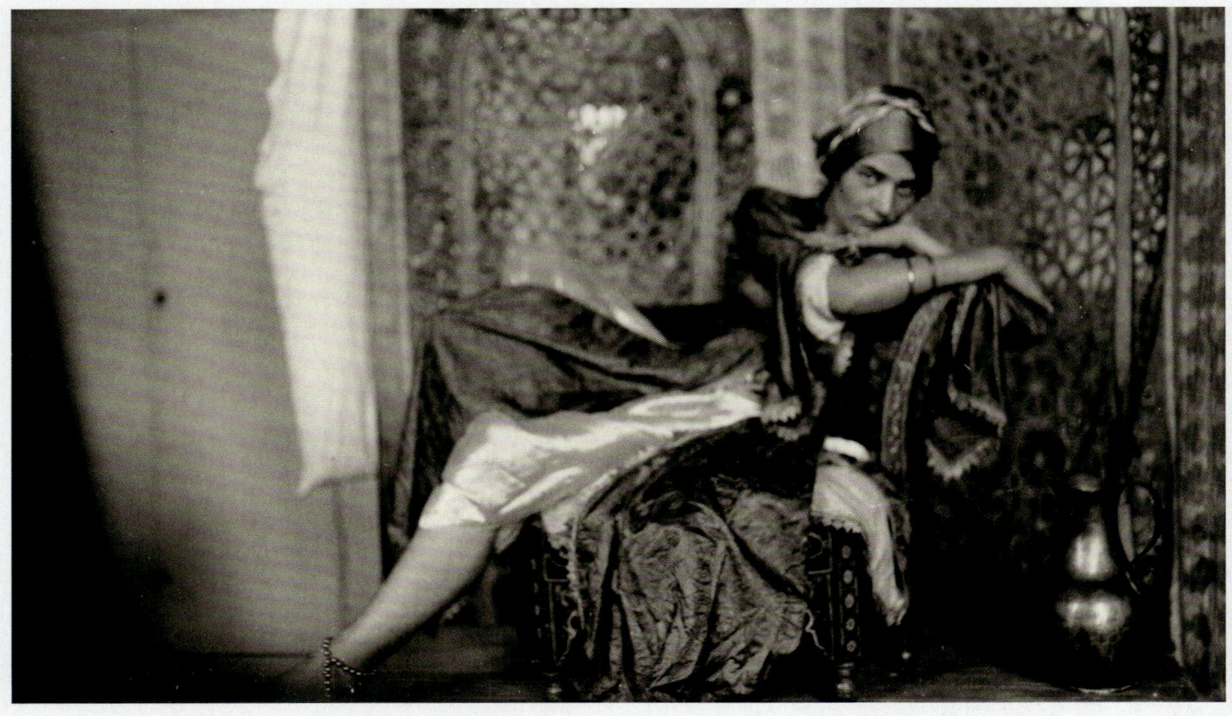

29 Diary, February 21, 1928. The quotations that follow are taken from diary entries of the dates provided.

30 HM–Georges Duthuit [GD], March 14, 1928.

31 Diary. The quotation that follows is from the same source.

32 HM–AM, July 6, 1928. The quotations that follow are taken from letters from Henri to Amélie of the dates provided.

33 HM–MD, September 11, 1928.

34 November 4–December 16, 1928.

35 HM–AM, February 18, 1929. The quotation that follows is from the same source.

36 HM–AM, undated [March 1929].

37 HM–AM, May 7, 1929.

38 HM–MD, November 21, 1929. The quotation that follows is from the same source.

---

167 (fig.)
Lisette Löwengard posing for a series of drawings, Place Charles-Félix, Nice, 1931

168 (fig.)
Henri Matisse on Lake Annecy, summer 1928

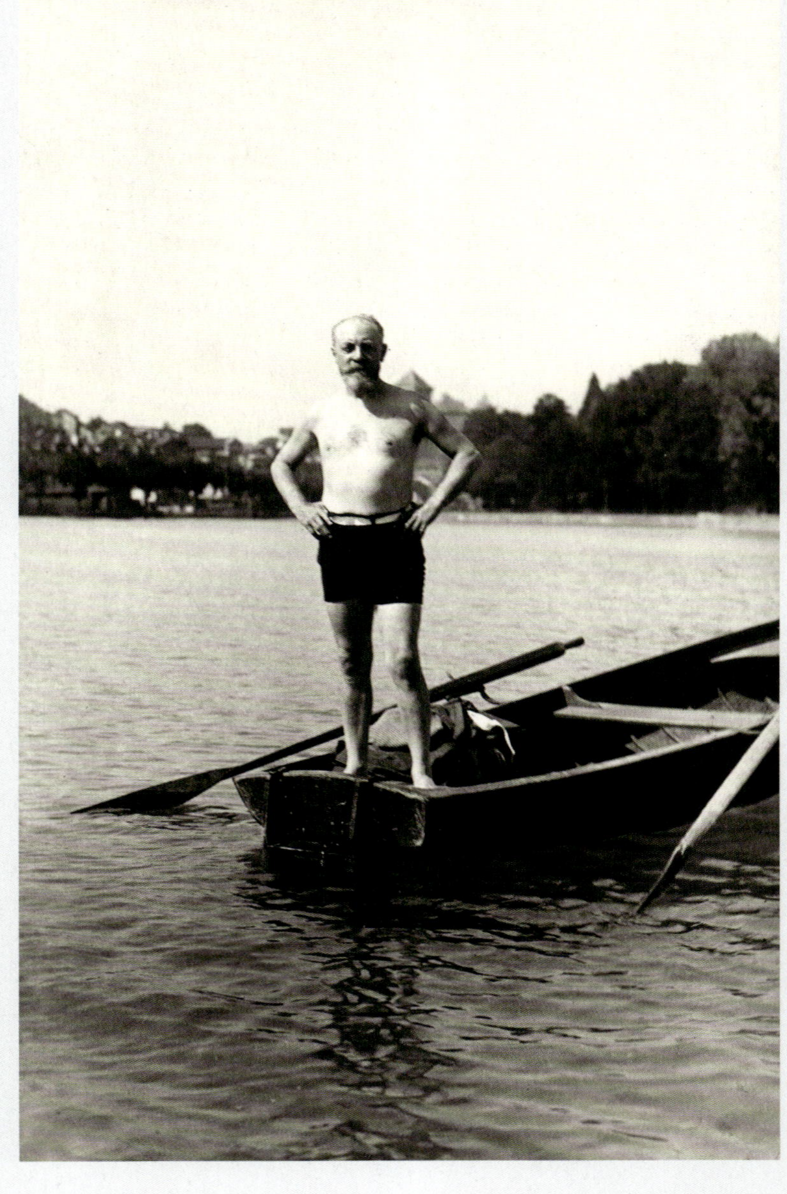

1928

Matisse seems to have settled into a routine. During the month of January, he alternated between rowing exercises and painting and drawing sessions with Zita, who was often accompanied by two other models, Hélène and Lily.

Between February 18 and 26, the artist made several stops during a trip to Dax with Amélie. On February 21, he visited the Musée Bonnat in Bayonne, where he was particularly struck by "three fine Goyas," including a "large full-length portrait of a man reading a letter in the countryside. . . . Contemplating this picture, I had a surge of enthusiasm and felt the urge to paint large canvases in one or two sessions, similar to the style of the three sisters from ten years ago" (*The Three Sisters* 66).[29] On February 25, he visited the Musée de Bordeaux.

Upon his return to Nice on February 27, Matisse devoted his time to *Two Models Resting* (Philadelphia Museum of Art), which he had begun before his departure. It was a laborious process. On February 28, he noted, "Worked on the same painting, which is going better as a whole, but has lost its beauty of color"; on March 3, "Same interminable painting and drawing"; and on March 7, "Afternoon session. Same painting. So tedious."

In March, the artist was putting the same amount of effort into *Two Odalisques* (Moderna Museet, Stockholm): "The challenge for me is to be able to give equal force in the picture to these two differently colored surfaces and subjects, with different sensibilities—a nude woman and a clothed woman. . . . Here's where I am with it—I work from noon until 5:00. I go canoeing every morning and I breakfast at 10:30. . . . Fortunately I've pretty much avoided crises along the way; I wouldn't be strong enough to put up with them considering the intensity of work that I'm obliged to exert to give a bit of clarity to the expression of my paintings."[30] He returned to the work on July 4 and completed it the same day.[31]

On April 19, Matisse was in Monte-Carlo to attend a new performance of Léonide Massine's *Le Chant du rossignol* (The song of the nightingale), to which he had contributed in 1920. "Success. The sets looked faded, as did the costumes. The choreography was awkward. Oh well, everyone liked it except for me." Lily and Hélène left Nice at the end of the month, and Matisse's work refocused on Zita.

On June 14, Matisse began work on *Still Life with Plaster Torso* (private collection), and then, on June 23, *Still Life with Green Buffet* (MNAM–CP). Matisse spent almost the entire summer working on this single canvas. On July 6, he wrote, "It was only today that it assumed its character, or rather my work assumed its character, and I'm very pleased about that. I'd like to have an uninterrupted, sustained period of concentrated painting."[32] On July 7, he went on, "My still life continues. . . . Good or bad as it may be, at least it's forcing me to do things I haven't done before." On the following day, he noted, "I scraped off almost everything and redrew it. I'm very happy with it—it took a lot of courage to do it, but I'm very optimistic about tomorrow, because I expect more joyful color." And on July 15, he continued, "My s.l. [still life] has presence. . . . I think I'll manage to get something accomplished, as well as the personal satisfaction I'll derive from it." Matisse worked several more days on the painting before his departure for Paris on July 25.

After a visit to Savoie at the end of August, and Switzerland in early September, the artist returned to Nice on September 11.[33]

Matisse left Nice again on December 16. After an overnight stop in Marseille, he arrived in Paris the following day. On the 18th he visited the Salon d'Automne.[34] *Still Life with Green Buffet* was exhibited there, and it was purchased by the Association des Amis des Artistes Vivants (Friends of living artists) for the Musée du Luxembourg in early 1929. The artist returned to Nice on December 27.

1929

The first part of the winter was spent on engraving. "It's the kind of work I've never done before," Matisse wrote to Amélie. "I nourish the stone with my pencil, and it stays gray and pale. I hope you'll be amazed. But it's very slow. I work for three hours rubbing the pencil and it barely shows, although the image becomes clearer and clearer. . . . The work is slow and painful on the eyes, but I think it will prove to be very useful for me in this moment."[35] There was also a painting in process, *Woman with a Madras Hat* 84, featuring Lisette Löwengard, who had just begun to pose. "It's a great thing in pure color that I shouldn't drag out for too long, like the large *Riffian*. I decided on it on the spur of the moment, and I'm expecting a lot from it as a point of departure directed toward more emphasis on color."

Suffering from eyestrain, Matisse resumed work on his *Large Seated Nude* sculpture: "So I began on it Monday . . . and right away I got started with a sense of ease and good spirits that I haven't experienced in a long time, except in drawing. All week long I've worked tirelessly for six or seven hours a day. All my efforts in sculpture seem to have converged to make this possible for me. The evening of the first day I was bursting with happiness. I walked all evening, happy and energetic, and that has continued since. I hope very much to regain my equilibrium of mind from this work. I'll return to painting completely transformed, I can feel it."[36]

On May 7, the dealers Siegfried Rosengart and Walther Halvorsen called on the artist. Interested in the *Large Seated Nude*, they led him to understand that "it's a shame to have only this proof, and one can never know what might happen to it."[37] Matisse resolved to finish and have it cast. Within a month, "Le fauvisme," an article by Georges Duthuit, appeared in *Cahiers d'art*, the first of a series that continued until February 1931.

Between June 3 and 14, the Galerie Bernheim-Jeune presented *Quarante lithographies originales de Henri Matisse* (Forty original lithographs by Henri Matisse). The artist continued his work in this medium. Spending the summer in Paris, he was primarily occupied in the printing and refinement of engravings.

Returning at the end of August, Matisse "worked a great deal, but far from the realm of painting."[38] He wrote to his daughter, "I sat down several times to work, but confronted with a canvas I had no idea—whereas in drawing and sculpture, it worked like a dream. This afternoon I made six large plates that will pleasantly surprise you, I hope. These are small works. You have to accept what comes along, glad when anything happens." According to Löwengard, many lithographs date from the period.

The Galerie Le Portique in Paris featured an *Exposition de peintures et dessins de Henri Matisse* (Paintings and drawings by Matisse) from November 7 to 25. This show coincided with the publication of a monograph on the artist by Florent Fels for Éditions des Chroniques du Jour. An English version by Roger Fry, and one in German by Gotthard Jedlicka, were published the following year. The Valentine Gallery in New York presented *Henri Matisse (1927–1929)* from December 9 through January 4.

1930

From February 15 through March 20 or 22, the Thannhauser Gallery in Berlin held a comprehensive retrospective of 250 works by Matisse that inaugurated a series of major exhibitions organized the following year in Paris, Basel, and New York. Marguerite supervised the hanging of these shows.

On February 26, 1930, Matisse embarked for Tahiti from Le Havre. The first port of call was New York, on March 4: "I was amazed at my arrival in the port of N.Y., and in everything that I've seen thus far; the power of the human effort that I sense is reassuring. Now I'm afraid that I'll find the perfumed charms of Oceania rather dull."[39] He proceeded to Chicago, Las Vegas, and Los Angeles. Traveling on a deluxe train, Matisse traversed "farmlands, pastures—cowboy country."[40] On March 15, he left for San Francisco, arriving the following day and departing on March 19.

Matisse arrived in Tahiti on March 29. He was welcomed by Pauline Schyle, who arranged a room for him at the Hôtel Stuart overlooking the port of Papeete. "It is all so new to me despite everything I've read and the photographs I've seen, and Gauguin, I find it all marvelous—the landscapes, trees, flowers, and people—and I haven't seen anything yet, I haven't yet been to the countryside."[41]

Matisse began exploring this unfamiliar territory at once. On May 3, at the invitation of the film director F. W. Murnau, he went to the end of the peninsula in Tautira Bay. On May 15, he embarked for the Tuamotu Islands, where he visited Apataki, Fakarava, and Pakaka. On June 6, he returned to Papeete.

The artist executed only one sketch during his stay, along with a series of drawings and a collection of photographs taken with his Kodak. His creative energy was still focused on his ongoing work in Nice. "I always have my mind turned to the works I left behind—my *Yellow Dress* 73, still to be finished—and my sculptures."[42] Matisse left Papeete on June 15 with a stop in Martinique on July 14 and Guadeloupe on July 16. He arrived back in Nice in early August.

Less than a month after his return, Matisse embarked on a second voyage to New York, on September 8. He arrived on September 19 and left two days later for Pittsburgh. The primary purpose of his trip was to participate in the jury for the Carnegie Prize, which was granted to Pablo Picasso that year. Matisse was in Washington, DC from September 24 to 26. On September 27, he met Albert C. Barnes in Philadelphia; his visit to the Barnes Foundation in Merion, Pennsylvania, was pivotal.[43] The collector gave the artist a commission for a major decorative mural. On September 28, Matisse was back in New York.

Matisse departed on October 3, and docked in Le Havre on October 9. He granted three important interviews with Tériade on October 15, 17, and 20, discussing his travels. The articles were published in *L'Intransigeant* (Uncompromising) from October 27 to 30.

Matisse left on his third transatlantic voyage on December 9. He disembarked in New York on December 15 and traveled immediately to Philadelphia and Merion. The next morning, he and Barnes began to review the wall area he was to decorate. On December 17, he visited the collector Etta Cone in Baltimore. Several additional round trips ensued between New York and Merion, where Matisse stayed the nights of December 19 through 22, and again on December 30 and 31. "I'm very busy and haven't had the time to write you," he scribbled hastily in a note to Amélie. "I am full of optimism and enthusiasm because I've done a sketch for the panel. I've seen the placement of the figures on the panel, three of them, and I've decided on the colors. I think it won't be that difficult for me, because I feel my year of rest has allowed me to make great progress in clarifying my thoughts."[44] Matisse also took advantage of his stay in New York to call on several collectors—the Lewisohns and Clarks among them—and check on his forthcoming exhibition.[45]

39 Diary.

40 HM–AM, March 12, 1930.

41 HM–AM, March 30, 1930.

42 HM–MD, May 10, 1930.

43 Diary.

44 HM–AM, December 26, 1930.

45 *Sculpture by Henri Matisse*, January 5–February 7, 1931, Brummer Gallery, New York. HM–AM, December 30, 1931.

169, **170** (figs.)
New York and Tahiti.
Photographs by Henri Matisse, 1930

171 (fig.)
Henri Matisse in Tahiti, 1930
Photograph by F. W. Murnau [?]

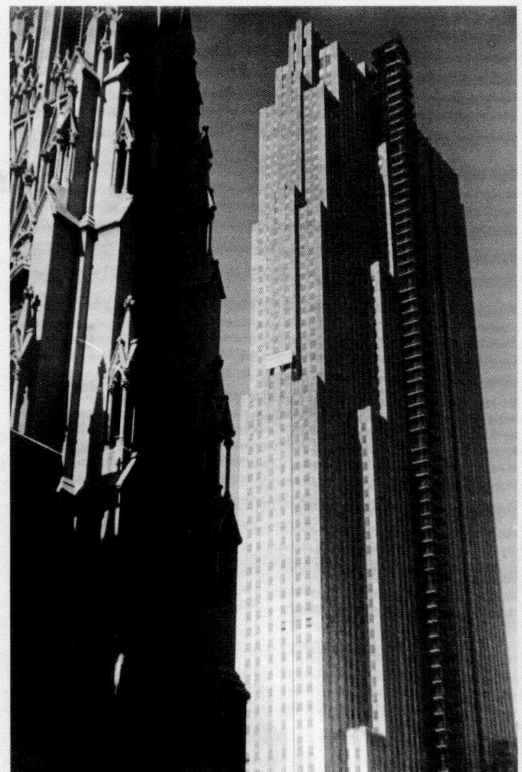

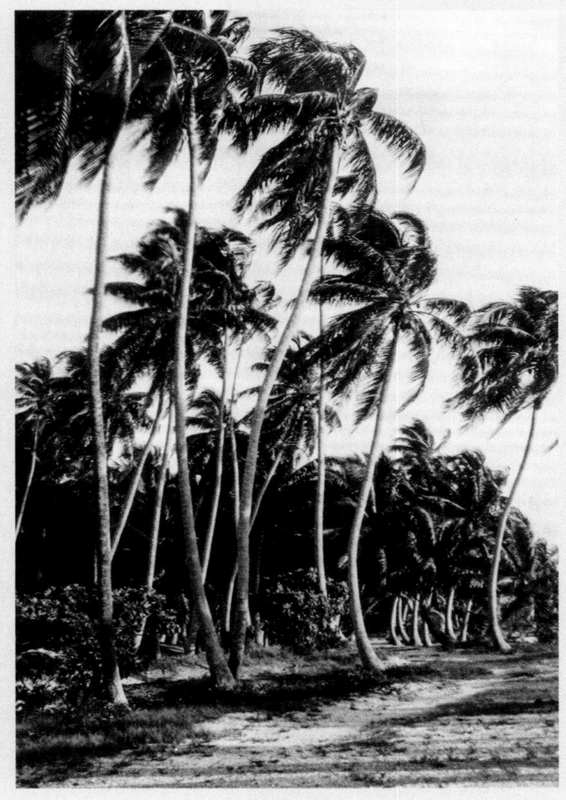

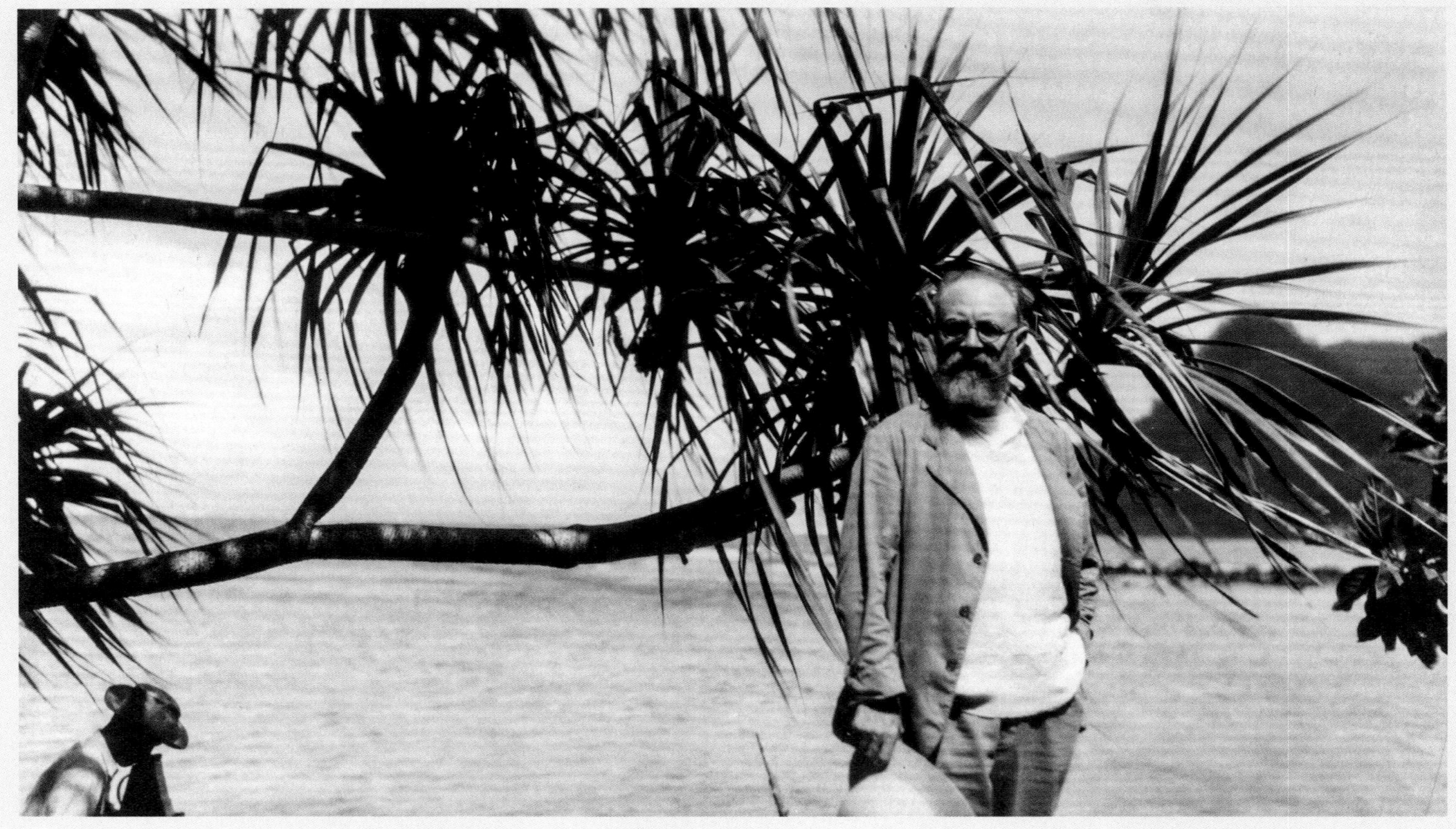

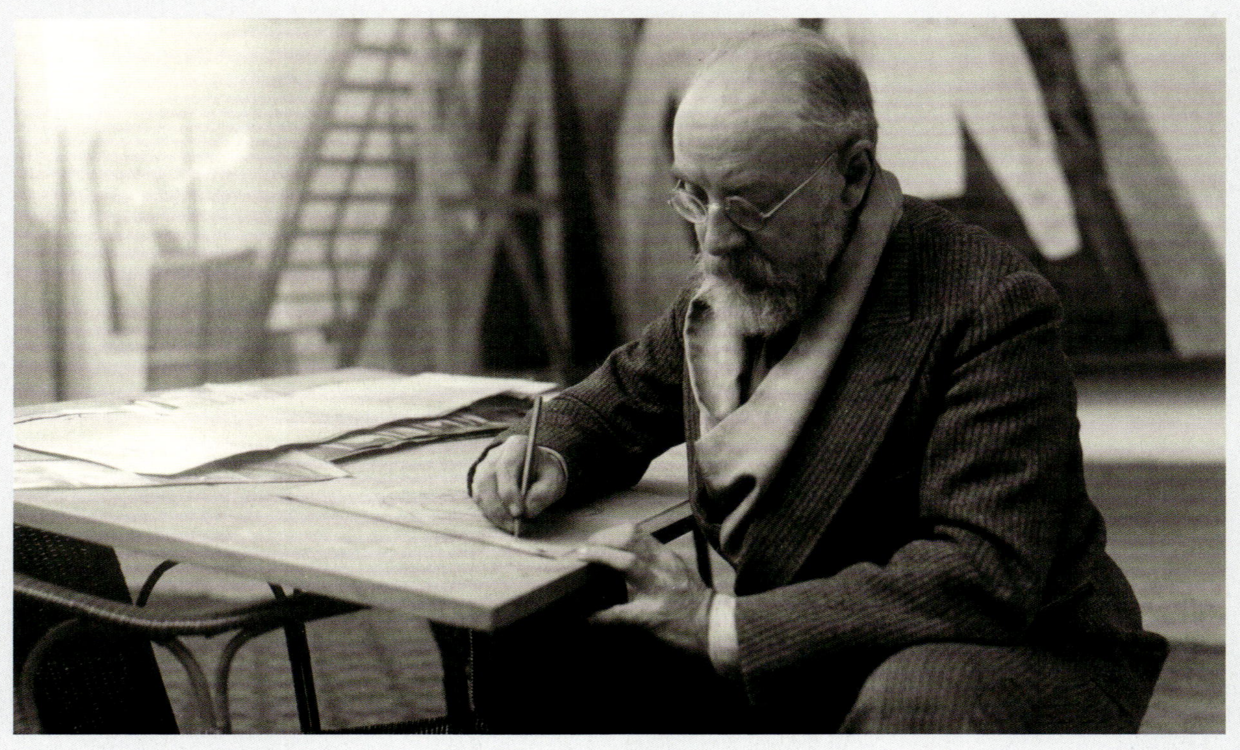

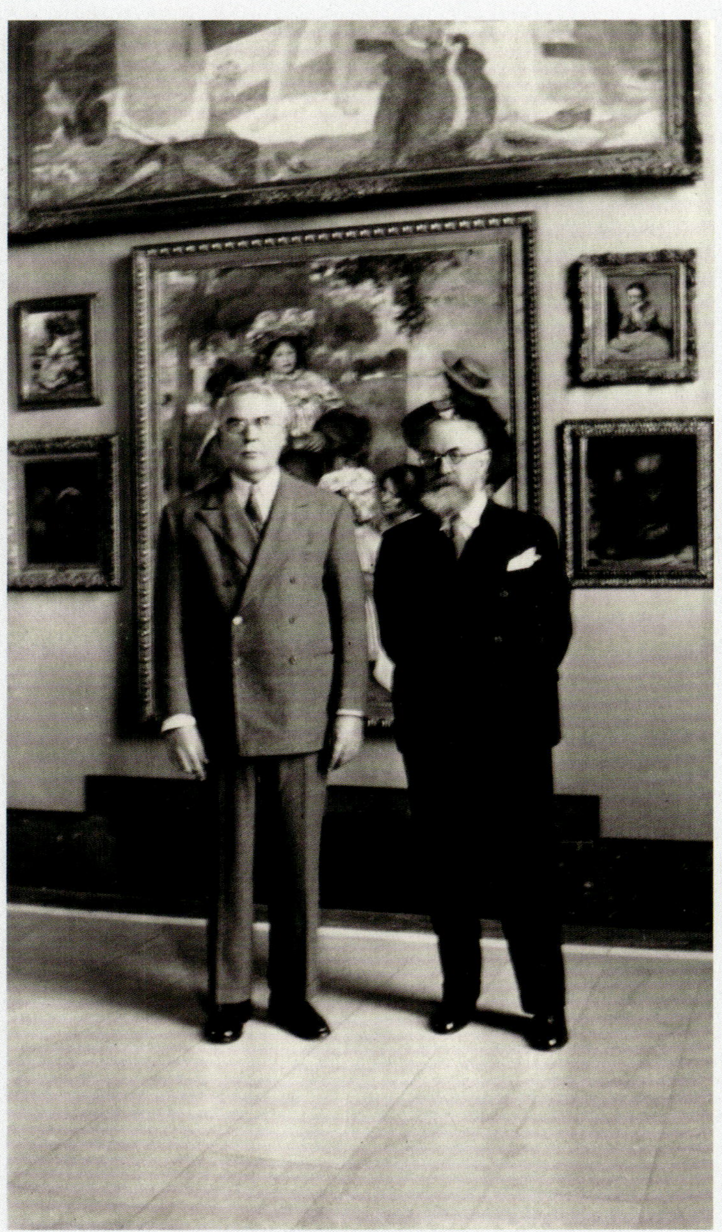

172 (fig.)
Henri Matisse working
on *The Dance*,
8 rue Désiré-Niel, Nice, 1932

173 (fig.)
Henri Matisse and
Albert C. Barnes
at the Barnes Foundation,
Merion, undated

1931

Matisse was back in Paris on January 9 and did not return to Nice for about a week following his arrival. No sooner did he reach Nice than he immediately got going on the mural that Barnes had commissioned, working in a garage he had rented for the purpose at 8 rue Désiré-Niel. The work, which revisited the theme of dance at a new level, was key for him. "I was beginning to tread water, the little pictures didn't get finished any more, I mean to say that I no longer felt the need to do so. I am working on a larger scale now and with a clear objective."[46]

In early April, Matisse set aside a week from his mural project to work with Löwengard in exotic dress. "I put down colors that I am trying to organize. I'm experiencing a crisis that is quite disturbing and a sense of fear is addling my brain."[47] He returned to the project around April 10, all the while continuing to alternate work on the mural and sittings with his model.[48] On April 18, the three canvases for the mural were installed; Matisse saw them as "color studies, because you have to know exactly what you want before you really set to work."[49]

Matisse was in Paris from April 20 until May 5. On April 27 and 28, he met with Albert Skira: a project to illustrate *Poésies* by Stéphane Mallarmé replaced plans for a new edition of *The Loves of Cupid and Psyche* by Jean de La Fontaine. The artist returned to Paris on June 10 for an exhibition organized by Pierre Loeb in his gallery,[50] and for the retrospective displayed by Josse and Gaston Bernheim-Jeune with Étienne Bignou at the Galeries Georges Petit.[51] A smaller version of this exhibition was held at the Kunsthalle in Basel from August 9 through September 15. A special edition of *Cahiers d'art* featuring the artist noted this event. Matisse also visited the Exposition Coloniale during that summer.

In September, Matisse, exhausted by this succession of demands on his time and work on *The Dance*, traveled to Italy for a cure at Abano Terme. On the 5th, he arrived in Milan, where he studied Leonardo da Vinci's frescoes.[52] By September 7, he was in Padua, where he stayed for several days. Every afternoon, he went to see Giotto's frescoes in Santa Maria dell'Arena, which he found "absolutely extraordinary in their clarity of composition."[53]

Upon his return, Matisse abandoned the mural that was in progress—*The Uncompleted Dance* (Musée d'Art Moderne, Paris)—and resumed work on three additional panels, modifying his approach. He used "blue paper for the ground and gray for the figures so they can be painted in when everything is very precisely defined. (But we must not speak of it.)"[54]

From November 3 to December 6, MoMA held its own extensive retrospective of the artist's work under the curatorial supervision of its director, Alfred H. Barr Jr. By the end of that month, Matisse was in Aix visiting André Masson and his wife, who were living in Saint-Jean-de-Grasse.

The year also brought the birth of three grandchildren, whom Matisse doted on and attended to lovingly: Gérard, Jean's son; Jacqueline (Jackie), Pierre's daughter; and Claude, Marguerite's son. Two additional grandsons—Pierre's sons—were born soon afterward: Paul in 1933, and Pierre-Noël (Peter) in 1936.

1932

On February 22, Barnes informed Matisse that there had been an error in measuring the dimensions of the mural that was already in progress.[55] "For me," wrote the artist in a response drafted to his patron, "the tragic thing is that the mural is almost complete—and that it's impossible to add the missing sections. . . . I have no choice but to start over. As I do not want to waste my work, I'm finishing [the ones with] the current dimensions. . . . My spirit survives intact, although this is a heavy blow."[56]

During the summer, Matisse abandoned his first version of *The Dance*, with its erroneous measurements (1931–33; Musée d'Art Moderne, Paris) to launch a second composition, the version that would go to Merion. In October, Lydia Delectorskaya, a young Russian immigrant, was hired as a studio assistant for several weeks. She ended up working in this role for six months, the beginning of a lifetime collaboration.

In early November, Matisse, who had thus far been focusing on "finishing up the book" (Mallarmé's *Poésies*),[57] committed himself to working on the mural full time. "I'm in the drawing phase," he wrote to Pierre. "It's going very well, and I find that I've derived great benefit from the first version and the illustration of Mallarmé. But the challenge (perhaps fortunately), the challenge is a new one—there have to be three compositional focal points. You don't see the entire decorative scheme because of the vaults, except from very far away viewed across several rooms." Successive photographs taken in November and December show *The Dance* in various stages of completion, evidence of Matisse's astoundingly rapid progress 49 | 50.

On December 2, Matisse received a copy of Mallarmé's *Poésies* published by Skira. The presentation was a profound disappointment: "I found all the engravings were flat and empty, bloodless . . . they reminded me of cadavers."[58] The living substance of this work—the preparatory drawings and original etchings—were presented at Marie Harriman's gallery in New York,[59] and the drawings that had been included in the eponymous publication in 1920 were assembled in the exhibition *Fifty Drawings* at the Pierre Matisse Gallery.[60]

46 HM–MD, February–March 1931.

47 HM–MD, April 8, 1931.

48 HM–MD, April 10, 1931.

49 HM– Alfred C. Barnes, unmailed draft, April 18, 1931.

50 June 12–July 31, 1931.

51 June 16–July 25, 1931.

52 HM–AM, September 5, 1931.

53 HM–AM, September 7, 1931, and September 9, 1931.

54 HM–PM, November 25, 1931. (Emphasis in original.)

55 Barnes–HM, February 22, 1932.

56 HM–Barnes, undated [February 1932].

57 HM–PM, November 5, 1932. The quotation that follows is from the same source.

58 HM–Roger Laccourière, December 2, 1932.

59 December 3–30, 1932.

60 November 22–December 17, 1932.

1933

On January 14, Matisse traveled to Palma de Majorca to meet Barnes to discuss the mural. The collector traveled to Nice ten days later to view the work in the studios. *The Dance* was approved and would be featured in a photograph of the artist at work in the book that Barnes produced that year in collaboration with Violette de Mazia, *The Art of Henri-Matisse*.

Between February 21 and 23, Goyo, a housepainter, came to assist Matisse in transposing his paper cut-outs with their flat zones of color. Meanwhile, the artist continued to work on his composition. At the end of March, it seemed finished. Matisse and Goyo were working on painting the panels, but "it's slow work, and it has to dry," Matisse noted to his daughter. "I realized yesterday with your mother that I'm not going to be able to finish before April 13—and then it has to dry for several days."[61] Matisse had to give up on displaying his *Dance* in Paris.

On May 11, Matisse arrived in New York with the painting.[62] On May 17, *The Dance* was hung in Merion [103]. "It's a magnificent thing that cannot be imagined without being seen," he wrote to Simon Bussy, his indefatigable supporter. "I am profoundly exhausted, but very pleased. When I saw the canvas in its place, it detached itself from me to become part of the building. I completely forgot the past, when it had seemed like my personal property."[63]

Matisse returned to Nice at the beginning of June. In July, he received Etta Cone in his studio to show her the first version of *The Dance*. He resumed working on the mural that month "completely from top to bottom for an hour, but fortunately with chalk, so nothing was compromised."[64]

Between August 25 and September 16, the artist took a cure in Vittel. When he returned, the studio was in turmoil. Löwengard had been dismissed, and Delectorskaya was again hired, this time as a companion for Amélie [36].

With Marguerite's help, Matisse restarted work on the mural on October 11 "as it had been abandoned a year ago, with its warlike quality. . . . I had tried to push it further, more space, etc. It wasn't going badly, but after seven or eight sessions, I realized that I was proceeding toward an unreachable goal, I was heading toward the quality of the mural in Merion for the better, but I was now losing the distinctive aspects that it had before being retouched. I courageously resolved to take a step backward and stay there."[65] The work was completed in November.

Matisse continued to work in Nice except for a visit to Paris between November 25 and December 14. He resumed easel painting, including *Nude in a Robe* [104], modeled by Titine Trovato, and *Interior with Dog* (1934; Baltimore Museum of Art).[66] At the end of the year, he executed his first stump portrait drawing of Delectorskaya.

1934

On February 2, Pierre, who was presenting the exhibition *Henri Matisse: Paintings* in his gallery,[67] attempted to persuade his father to embark on the illustration of James Joyce's *Ulysses* for George Macy's Limited Editions Club: "All of the literary circles, snobs, some interesting and others uninteresting, are buying it, and I thought that if the text is not objectionable to you, it would be the perfect book for you to illustrate."[68]

This return to illustration, undertaken in March, was part of a "significant effort in painting for a new start in a territory that is still fresh. . . . If I am to continue, I will have to do other things, resume many challenges I've left aside, and bring them back into play. Imagine afresh with them—in sum, recover former activities with greater awareness. Without that, I wouldn't be able to do anything else, it's a certainty."[69]

Matisse worked wholeheartedly on the illustrations for *Ulysses* [28 | 30 | 32 | 105–8] and the canvas *Interior with Dog*.[70] He made a quick trip to Marseille in May, where he went to the Éden-Théâtre to see "nothing but Mickey Mouse cartoons in color. Very interesting."[71] Matisse resumed drawings for the portraits of the "Cone ladies," his avid collectors in Baltimore, which he worked on every morning for almost a month: "Diminished resources, paper and charcoal. . . . It's hard, but I'm learning a lot."[72]

Matisse left Nice on June 8. Stopping in Marseille, he experienced a moment of introspection, writing, "I don't feel that I'm done. On the contrary, I can still with all due modesty create my finest works."[73] Traveling via Toulouse, he arrived in Paris on June 16. As soon as he got there, Matisse hurried to organize the apartment on Boulevard du Montparnasse with his children to welcome Etta Cone. *Interior with Dog* was presented to her on June 21, and she purchased it shortly thereafter. It was an important turning point for the artist: that autumn, Etta and Claribel Cone published *The Cone Collection: Catalogue of Paintings, Drawings, Sculpture* in conjunction with a major exhibition of works owned by the sisters in the Baltimore Museum of Art.

The artist spent most of July working on *Ulysses* with the printer Duchâtel. On July 17, a worried Matisse wrote in a notebook, "Am I ever going to emerge from all the years I've dedicated to the Barnes panels? Same with the illustrations for Mallarmé. I haven't yet finished the Joyce illustrations that are in progress. These periods devoted to works of the imagination that were completely new to me—never until now have I overstimulated my imagination or worked on nature—have developed an aspect of my mind, but distanced me from the reflex that set in motion the mechanism of my work on nature."[74] On August 15, the artist was back in Nice.[75] After a number of round trips between Paris and Nice in the fall, he definitively returned to the South on December 14.

61 HM–MD, March 30, 1933.

62 HM–AM, May 5, 1933.

63 HM–Simon Bussy, May 17, 1933, Institut National d'Histoire de l'Art, Paris (INHA).

64 HM–Bussy, August 25, 1933, INHA.

65 HM–PM, October 11, 1933.

66 Diary, January 1, 1934.

67 January 23–February 24, 1934.

68 PM–HM, February 2, 1934.

69 HM–PM, March 28, 1934.

70 Ibid., as well as the diary entries for April 27 and May 5, 1934. Also see HM–PM, May 7, 1934.

71 Diary, May 18, 1934.

72 HM–Bussy, May 25, 1934, INHA.

73 Diary, June 8, 1934.

74 Red notebook entry dated July 17, 1934.

75 HM–MD, August 14, 1934.

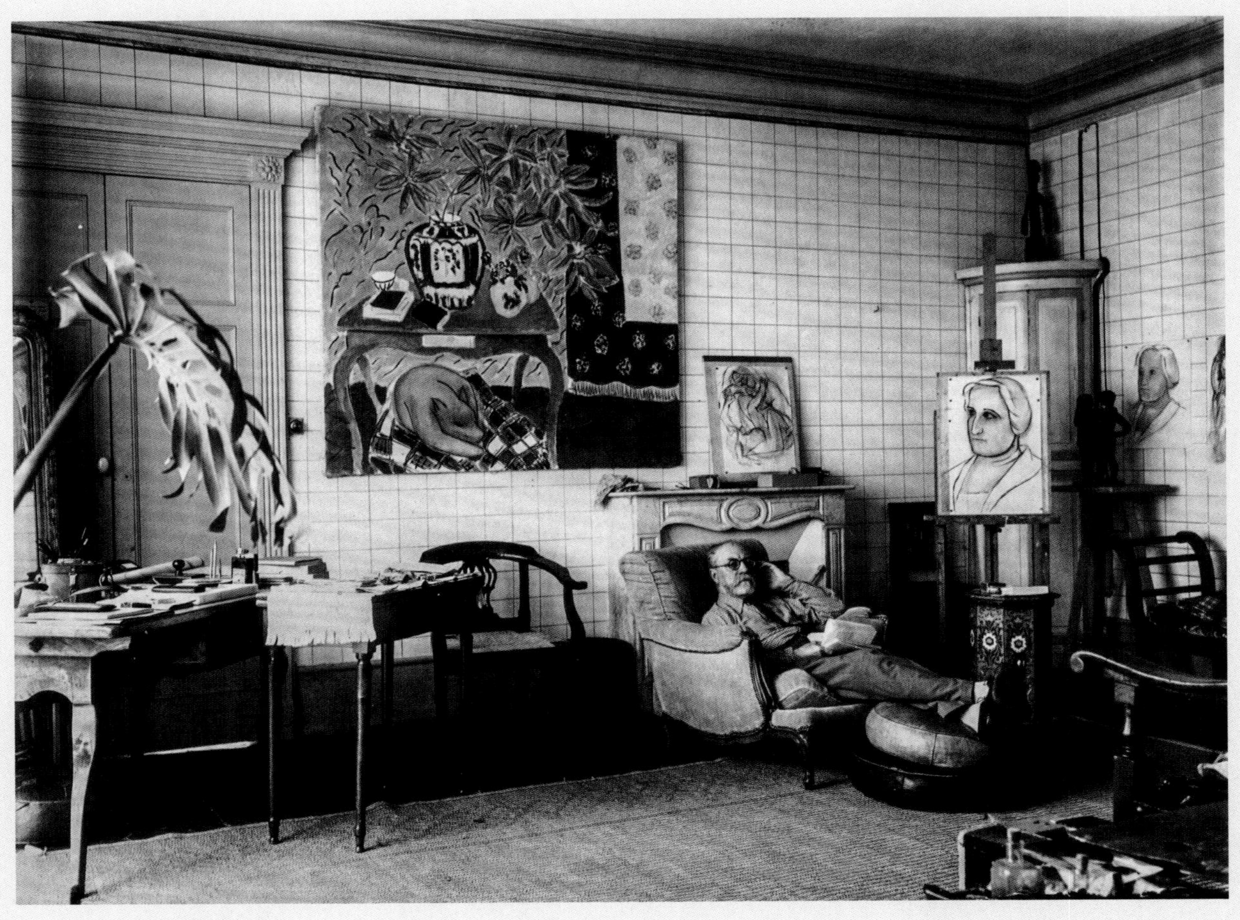

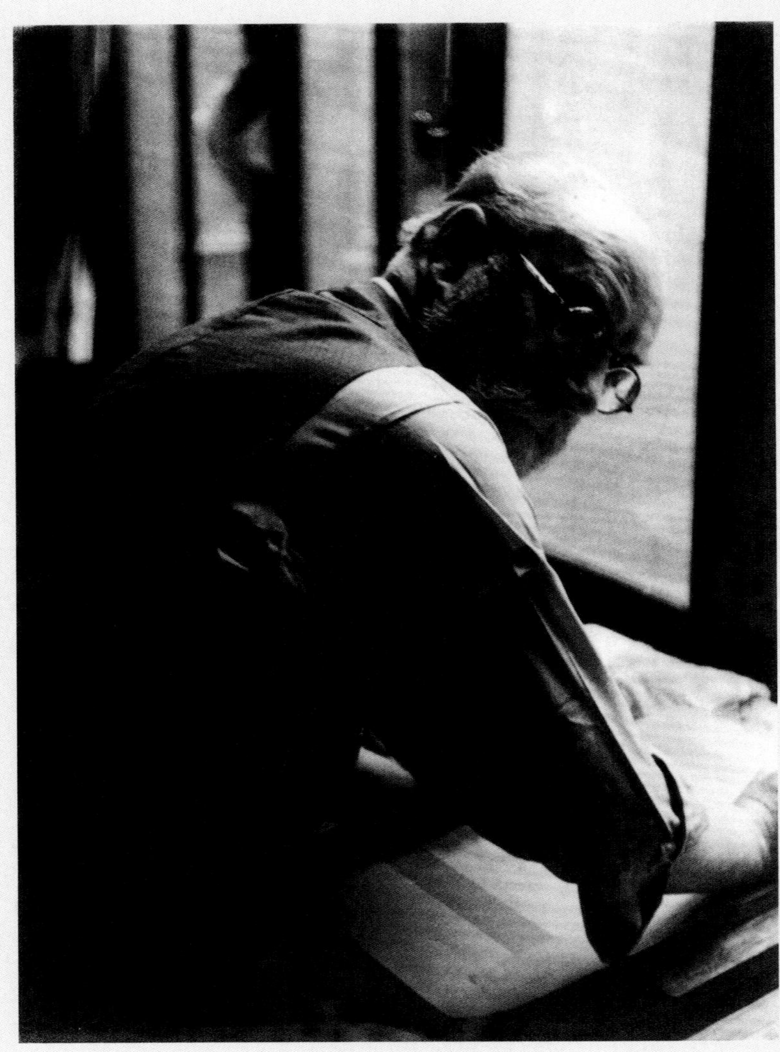

174 (fig.)
Henri Matisse in his studio; on the wall, *Interior with Dog*, Place Charles-Félix, Nice, 1934

175 (fig.)
Henri Matisse in Duchâtel's workshop checking proofs for *Ulysses*, 1934

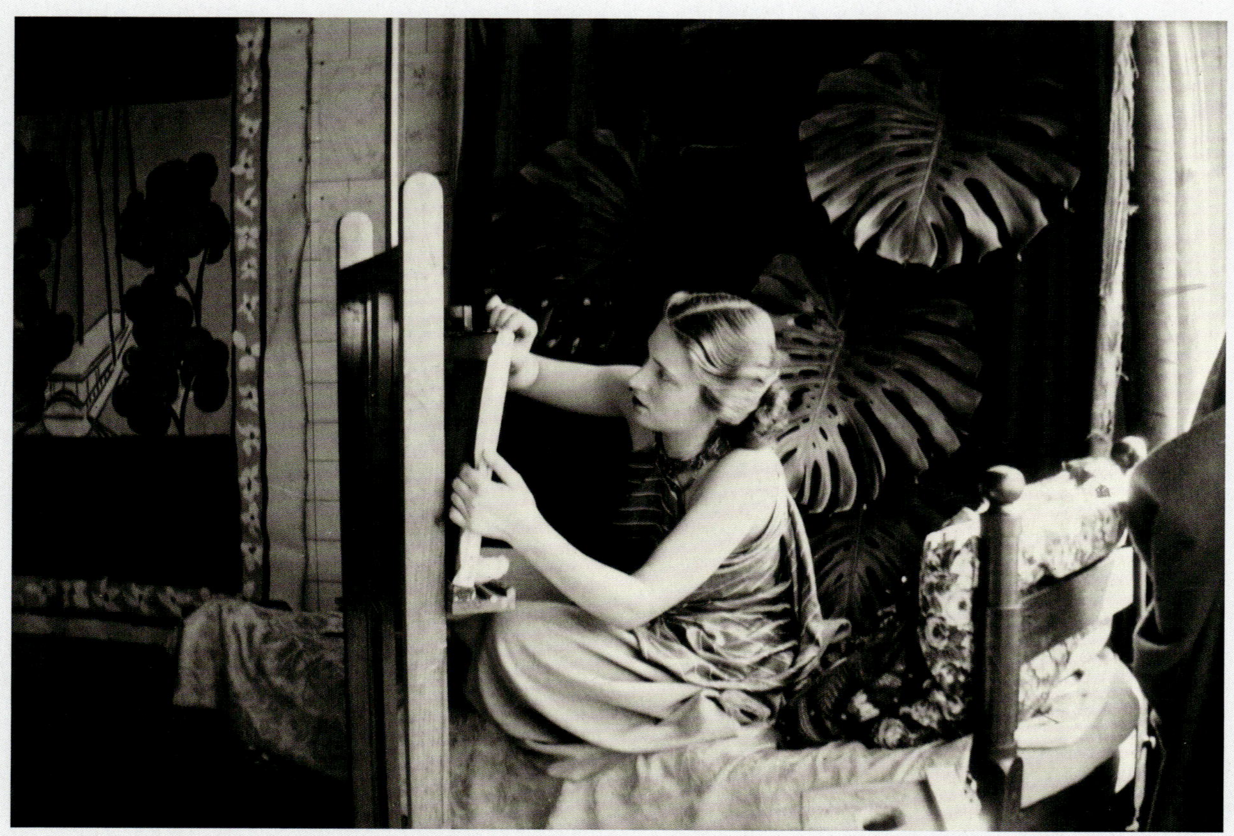

176 (fig.)
Lydia Delectorskaya in the studio; on the wall, *Tahiti II*, Place Charles-Félix, Nice, 1936

177, 178 (figs.)
Lydia Delectorskaya and Henri Matisse in Beauvezer, summer 1935

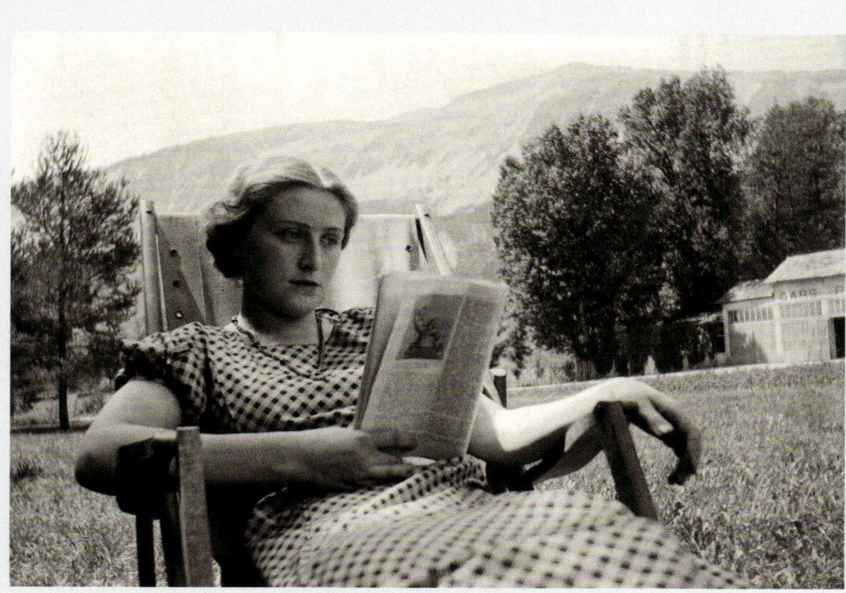

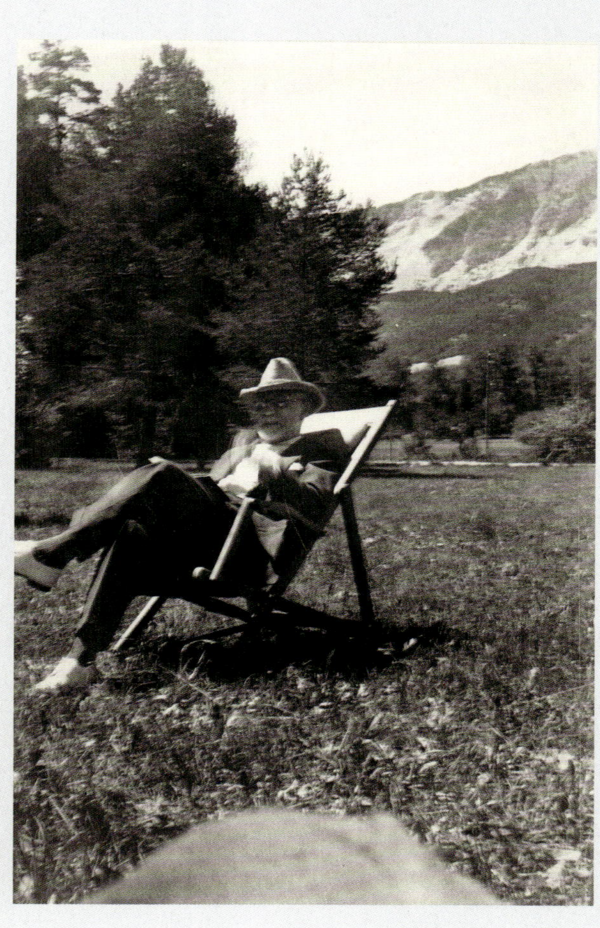

1935

On February 27, Delectorskaya posed with "her head resting on her arms" (*The Blue Eyes* 34).[76] She then modeled for numerous canvases including *Nu rose crevette* (destroyed); *The Scottish Shawl* (March 18; private collection); *The Reflection* 35. She also began to record the dates of her sittings for paintings, facilitating a closer tracking of Matisse's work.

Matisse returned to Paris on April 10. He and Marguerite visited the exhibition *Les Créateurs du cubisme* (Creators of Cubism) at the Galerie Wildenstein. "Negative impression, very old-fashioned, but since I hadn't slept, it should be seen again."[77] They also viewed an exhibition of Goya's work at the Bibliothèque Nationale and the *Peintres et graveurs indépendants* (Independent painters and engravers) show at the Petit Palais. He returned to Nice on April 14.

On April 16, Matisse resumed work on *The Dream* 33, which he had begun with Delectorskaya at the beginning of the month. He began the *Large Reclining Nude* 110 on April 29 and continued to work on it throughout the spring, returning to the use of gouache-painted paper cut-outs in the composition. In May, the English journal *The Studio* published a piece by Matisse titled "On Modernism and Tradition," in which the artist explored the "fermentation" at work in his artistic production.

After a stop in Paris, Matisse arrived at Beauvezer on July 1 with Delectorskaya, Amélie, and his grandson Claude. During this relaxing interlude, the artist worked on drawings and took numerous photographs. It was above all an opportunity for a critical reassessment, particularly by Marguerite: "I think that the work he's done this year is a kind of recapitulation of all his influences, as one does on occasion take stock of oneself. Based on what he's said, it seems that he believes that he has expressed himself fully, whereas I on the contrary have the feeling that there's a dam blocking the release of a rich flow."[78]

Returning to Nice on August 13, Matisse began "on a large torso on a no. 30 canvas" (*Seated Pink Nude* 123),[79] continued the *Large Reclining Nude* "by replacing the papers," and created "a large panel of a satyr and a sleeping nymph in progress" (*Nymph in the Forest [Verdure]* 116). On August 25, an order by Marie Cuttoli for a tapestry cartoon was recorded; the subject was to be "the window in Tahiti that's in the Mallarmé" (*Papeete, Tahiti* 118).[80]

That autumn, Matisse was working on three works simultaneously. The *Large Reclining Nude* demanded the most energy. He had already "changed a lot," as he told his son Pierre on September 16: "I'm killing myself over this. It's odd that for a while it's the color vision that is proving the hardest thing to do. Maybe because having toiled over the work's drawing and composition, I'm a little worn out. It's slow, laborious work that calls for a burst of energy."[81]

Matisse stayed in Paris from September 20 until mid-October.[82] He helped with the launch of *Ulysses* on October 22. When he returned, he finished *Papeete, Tahiti* and the *Large Reclining Nude*; eight of the twenty successive versions of the work were reproduced in Roger Fry's *Henri Matisse*, which was published that year. At the end of November, Matisse visited the exhibition *Matisse, dessins et sculpture* at the Parisian gallery Renou et Colle.[83] During this stay in the capital, Matisse saw the beginning of the weaving of the *Papeete, Tahiti* tapestry in the Beauvais workshops. Disappointed with the results, he began a new version in gouache, *Window at Tahiti II*, on December 18 119.

76 HM–MD, February 27, 1935.
77 Diary.
78 MD–HM, July 16, 1935.
79 HM–PM, August 19, 1935.
80 HM–PM, August 25, 1935.
81 HM–PM, undated [September 16, 1935].
82 Diary.
83 Late November 1935.

1936

84 HM–MD, April 3, 1936.
85 May 2–30, 1936.
86 Diary.
87 Diary. The agreement was signed on July 28, 1936.
88 Diary, September 10, 11, 13–14, and 16, 1936.
89 HM–PM, September 28, 1936.
90 October 27–November 21, 1936.
91 November 23–December 19, 1936.

Hélène Mercier-Galitzine began to pose on January 3. Delectorskaya remained Matisse's favorite model, however, particularly for a series of nudes, among which were numerous drawings done the previous year and presented in February at the Leicester Galleries in London. An exhibition was also displayed in the Marie Harriman Gallery in New York in February.

Matisse created a series of paintings and drawings with Delectorskaya between February and April. But during this time, he dedicated himself primarily to two panels he executed simultaneously, *Window at Tahiti II* and *Nymph in the Forest (Verdure)*. At stake was the upcoming display of his work at Paul Rosenberg's gallery. The artist "wished to make a rather free-form exhibition,"[84] as he told his daughter. And he continued: "There's a wearisome constraint: it's the belief that beyond a certain age one is no longer allowed to exhibit anything but masterpieces. If it were really up to me, I wouldn't have exhibitions despite their real advantages—or else I'd do them exactly as I wish—just show a corner of my studio."

On April 20, the artist was in Paris for the hanging of the *Exposition d'œuvres récentes de Henri-Matisse* (Exhibition of recent works by Henri-Matisse) at the Galerie Rosenberg.[85] Twenty-seven works were displayed, showing "works in progress," including his recent panels, and "lighter subjects" 45.On July 16, he signed a three-year contract with Rosenberg.

This visit also gave the artist an opportunity to maintain his network of contacts. On May 14, he met with Zervos, who had come to select fifty drawings for a special edition of *Cahiers d'art.* Between June 15 and 17, he executed a series of portraits of Mary Hutchinson, one of his collectors. On June 20 and 27, he also met with Joan Miró and Gino Severini.[86] On July 15, Raymond Escholier, the curator of the Petit Palais, visited Matisse's studio to purchase a work for the state.[87] On the recommendation of Gabriel Hanotaux, he chose the first version of *The Dance*.

The historic events that were overtaking France and Europe affected Matisse deeply. On the occasion of the July 14 national holiday, he and Marguerite went to the Théâtre de l'Alhambra to see the performance of Romain Rolland's antifascist play *Le 14 Juillet*. At the exhibition organized by the Maison de la Culture to coincide with the victory of the left-wing Popular Front, Matisse presented a canvas of his choice, *The Moroccans* 43. In response to the outbreak of the Spanish Civil War in August, Matisse, together with many other artists, including Picasso, signed a telegram supporting "the liberty of Spain."

Matisse continued his work with Delectorskaya over the summer. He also resumed work on *Nymph in the Forest (Verdure)* for two sessions and applied himself to a series of drawings of Dorothy Paley. He worked assiduously on drawings and engravings, as well as the special issue of *Cahiers d'art.*[88] On September 28, he wrote to his son that the jacket he had designed from paper cut-outs for the deluxe edition 6 "had created quite an impression in the church of Zervos. . . . The drawings are well presented, and I even made an etching for the deluxe versions. I want this issue to be satisfactory because I have no intention of starting over."[89] In October, the artist created the cover for the ninth issue of the journal *Minotaure*.

Matisse returned to Nice on October 23. He continued working in November, organizing his days with a painting session in the morning and drawing in the afternoon. He completed a painting featuring Mercier-Galitzine, *Woman with a Scarf* (Pola Museum of Art, Hakone). At year-end, he began a series of drawings of Delectorskaya wearing a blue dress with a jabot.

Across the Atlantic, Pierre Matisse's gallery displayed *Henri Matisse, "La Danse": Sketch for the Moscow Decoration*[90] and the Valentine Gallery presented the show *Twenty-One Paintings by Henri Matisse (1912–1936).*[91]

179 (fig.)
Hélène Mercier-Galitzine posing in a Romanian blouse; behind her, *The Abduction of Europa*, Place Charles-Félix, Nice, 1937

180 (fig.)
View of *Exposition d'œuvres récentes de Henri-Matisse*; in the middle, *The Dream*, and on the right, *Portrait in a Blue Coat*, Galerie Rosenberg, Paris, 1936

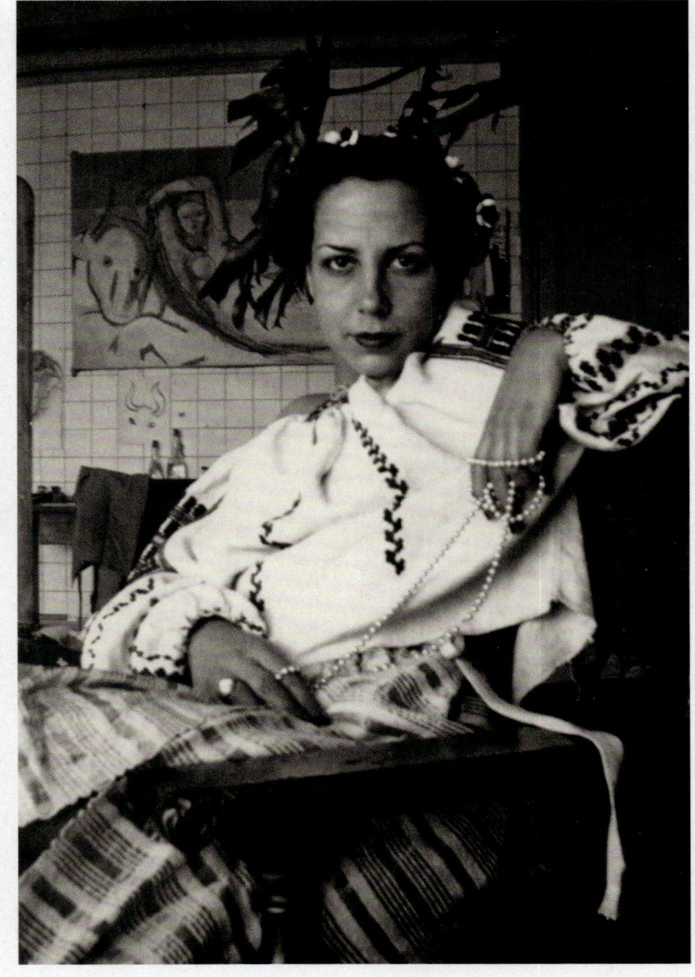

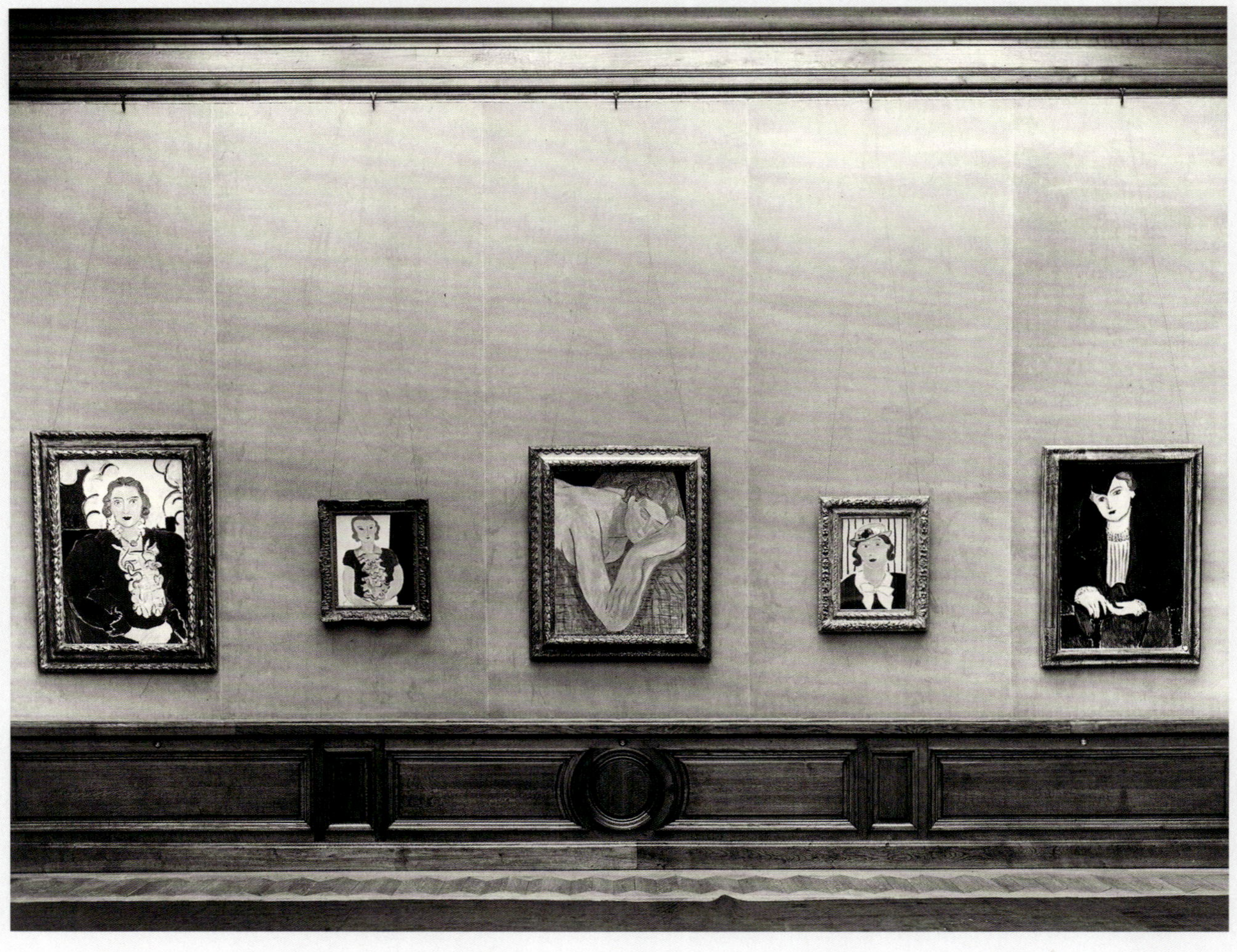

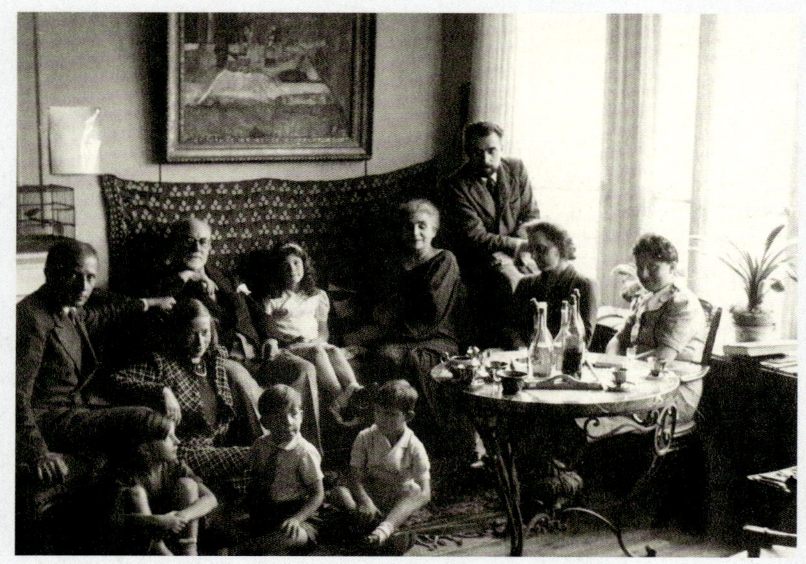

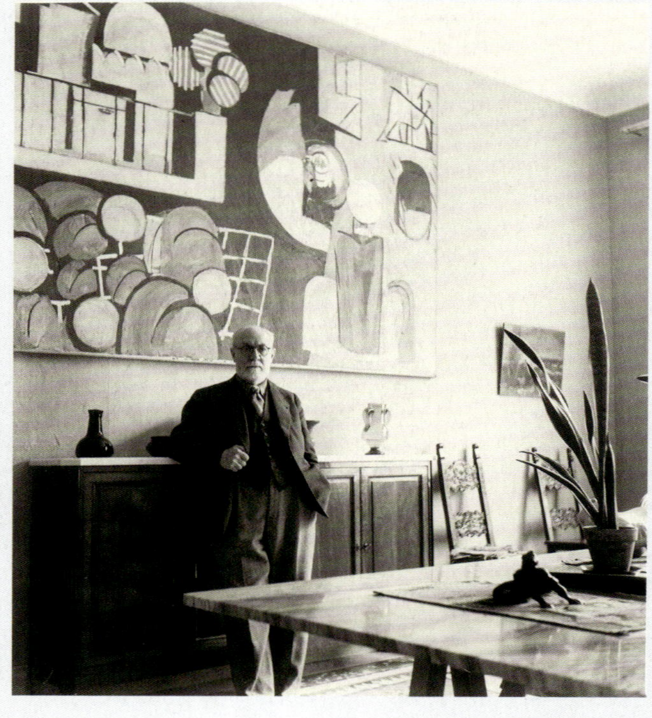

181 (fig.)
The Matisse family in the apartment at 132 boulevard du Montparnasse in Paris, c. 1936. Photograph by Pierre Matisse

182 (fig.)
Henri Matisse in his apartment in the Régina; on the wall, *The Moroccans*, Nice, 1939. Photograph by Pierre Boucher
Photo Library, Musée Matisse Nice

183 (fig.)
Henri Matisse in his apartment in the Régina, Nice, 1939. Photograph by Pierre Boucher
Photo Library, Musée Matisse Nice

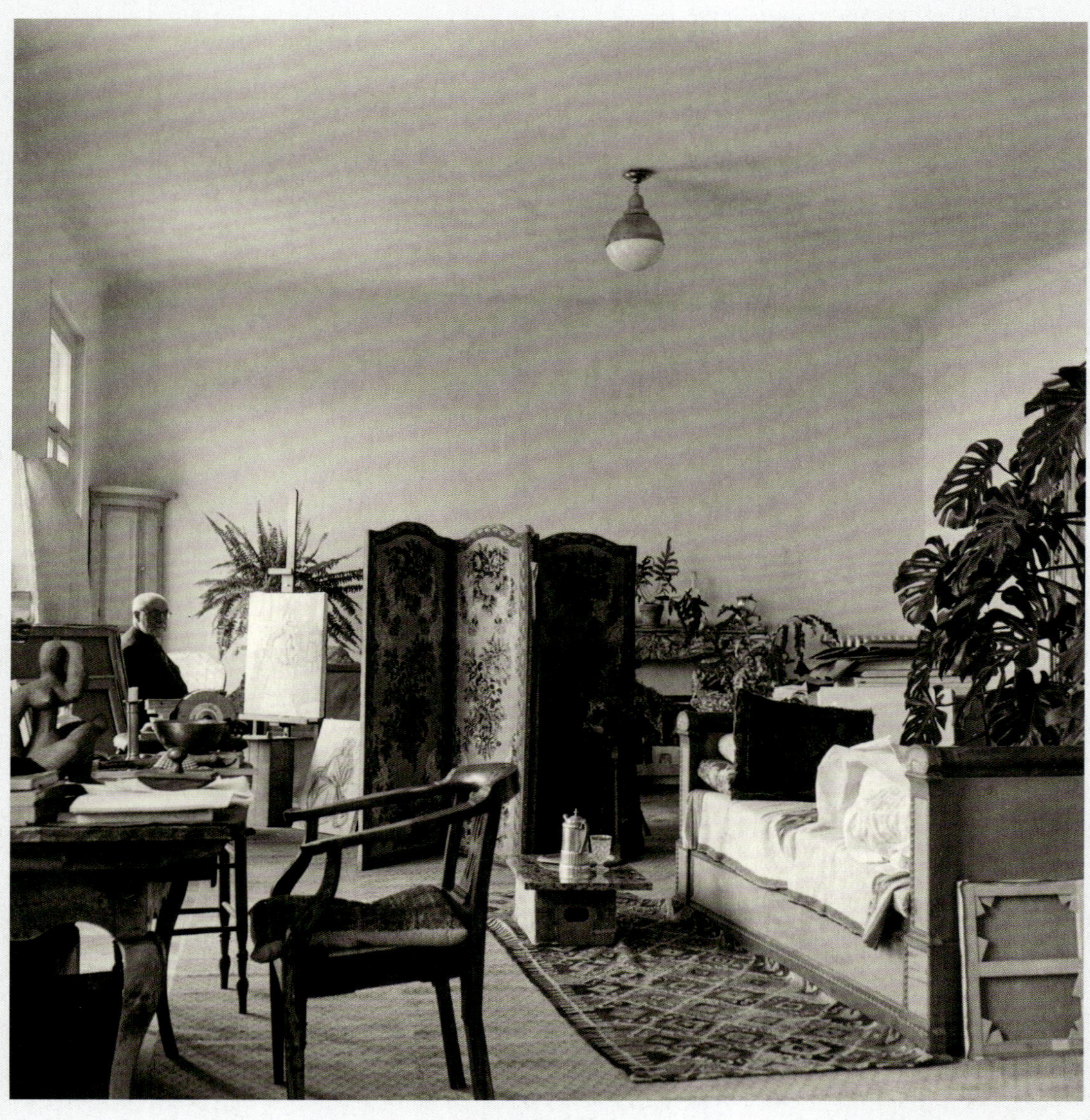

1937

At the beginning of the year, Thomas Whittemore and Henry de Montherlant sat for a series of drawn portraits. Drawing was now assuming a dominant role for Matisse, not only as a medium in its own right, but also as part of his painting process at that time, including *Ochre Head* (private collection), which was completed in several sittings (February 9–12, 17; March 4).

On February 21, the artist began a drawing on canvas for *Woman in Blue* 134. On February 25 and 26, he began to add color to the picture. He worked on the painting during a dozen sittings up until April 2; the major stages in its progress were recorded in photographs.

Matisse was in Paris that spring working on an engraving published by Jean-Gabriel Daragnès for the city of Paris at the Exposition Internationale. He was also busy with two exhibitions that were about to open: *Les Maîtres de l'art indépendant (1895–1937)* (Masters of independent art) at the Petit Palais,[92] curated by Escholier, and *Origines et développement de l'art international indépendant* (Origins and evolution of international independent art) at the Musée du Jeu de Paume,[93] orchestrated by Zervos. Floury's publication of Escholier's monograph, *Henri Matisse*, coincided with these events.

On July 5, Matisse and Rosenberg flew to London to view an exhibition of his recent works at the Rosenberg & Helft Gallery,[94] following one in Paris at the Galerie Rosenberg.[95] Another show of the artist's recent work was held at the Galerie Rosengart in Lucerne.[96] Upon his return to Paris, Matisse undertook a painted portrait of Paley, but on August 7, the project was "dropped."[97] On August 9, Matisse went to view Picasso's *Guernica* (Museo Nacional Centro de Arte Reina Sofía, Madrid) in the Spanish Pavilion at the Exposition Internationale.

Matisse left Paris for Nice on October 21. He resumed working with Mercier-Galitzine, who posed wearing a series of Romanian blouses. Beginning on November 16, Mercier-Galitzine and Delectorskaya modeled together for *The Conservatory* (former Pulitzer collection). The first issue of the journal *Verve*, founded by Tériade, was published in December. Matisse designed the cover and edited a piece entitled "Divagations" (Wanderings).

1938

Matisse, Picasso, Braque, Laurens, a major group show whose first stop was the Kunstnernes Hus in Oslo, marked the beginning of the year.[98] Marguerite supervised the hanging of her father's works, an ensemble of thirty-one pieces dating from 1896 to 1937, assisted by Halvorsen, one of the artist's former students.

On January 12, Matisse signed a purchase agreement for an apartment in the former Excelsior Régina Palace hotel in Cimiez, in the hills overlooking Nice. While waiting to move in, he worked on several canvases in succession, but focused especially on *The Conservatory*, which occupied him throughout February, with several additional sittings in March and May.

After a brief stay in Paris, the artist spent the spring working on the curtain and the costumes for the ballet *Rouge et noir (L'Étrange Farandole)* by Léonide Massine 143 | 145. He designed both using paper cut-outs.

This interlude of decorative projects was short lived. In April and May, Matisse resumed easel painting. He revisited the structural theme of the two models with *Black Dress and Purple Dress*, followed by *The Conversation* 148, for which Delectorskaya and Mercier-Galitzine again posed.

Matisse was in Paris from June 15 until August 25. He attended the People's Celebration marking the opening of the Musée de l'Homme.[99] Upon his return, all his time was given over to supervising the arrangements for the apartment in the Régina. In early October, "the bird room is the only space that's finished," he wrote to Amélie, "but the studio is cluttered and the kitchen, bedroom, and dining room are not yet ready, so it can't be cleared out."[100]

The Régina apartment was finally habitable by the end of October, and the studio was usable. Matisse immediately started work on a panel that Nelson A. Rockefeller had ordered through Pierre in February to decorate the mantel of his New York apartment.[101] The artist first completed a series of charcoal portraits of Delectorskaya and Mercier-Galitzine 147. On November 15, he established the panel's overall composition, and he kept working on it in several sittings (November 16–18, 21–22). He progressed to color on November 23 and continued to work assiduously (November 24–26; November 28–30, December 1–3). *The Song* 42 was dispatched on December 13, 1938. Installed early the following year in the Rockefeller residence, the work "looked very well, astonishingly rich."[102]

A major series of exhibitions in Paris, Cleveland, and New York 109 brought the year to a close.[103]

92 June 17–November 10, 1937.

93 July 30–October 31, 1937.

94 July 5–31, 1937.

95 June 1–19, 1937.

96 July–August 1937.

97 Diary.

98 January 10–February 2, 1938.

99 HM–MD, undated [stamp: June 30, 1938].

100 HM–AM, October 4, 1938.

101 PM–HM, February 28, 1938.

102 PM–HM, January 16, 1939.

103 *Henri-Matisse*, Galerie Rosenberg, October 24–November 12, 1938; *Twenty Oils by Matisse*, Cleveland Museum of Art, November 10–December 18, 1938; and *Henri Matisse: Paintings and Drawings of 1918 to 1938*, Pierre Matisse Gallery, November 15–December 10, 1938.

1939

Matisse faced problems with his eyes in January. “You know, although they say that it’s temporary, it’s still sometimes rather frightening. I’m thinking of an English novel [by Rudyard Kipling] entitled *The Light that Failed*. My light too is turning cloudy.”[104]

The pace slowed in February and March. Matisse nevertheless got going on a major painting, *Music* 48, which he worked on from March 18 until April 8 with Mercier-Galitzine and her cousin. The piece—which the artist called “the finest Matisse”[105]—was sent to New York for fear of “very threatening rumors of war” that were spreading in France. Pierre would later sell the work and exhibit it in his gallery.

Amélie moved out of the family home on March 4, creating an upheaval in Matisse’s private life. The artist embarked on a search for a new Parisian studio during the spring. He was looking for a space with southern exposure, even if it meant he had to “struggle with sunlight, which is so picturesque in its effects.”[106]

Matisse traveled back to Paris, in part to attend the premiere of the ballet *Rouge et noir (L’Étrange Farandole)* on June 5. He stayed at the Lutétia, as the apartment on Boulevard du Montparnasse had been sealed due to the separation from Amélie. During the summer, he began to work in a studio at 37 bis villa d’Alésia, which was made available to him by the American artist Mary Callery. He continued to paint and draw there, “feeling a bit optimistic. . . . It’s more restful, or perhaps it’s cowardice.”[107] Wilma Javor posed in the studio for *Reading Woman on a Black Background* (MNAM–CP). Delectorskaya, who had become available in late 1938, rejoined the studio on July 30.[108]

In the summer of 1939, the art journal *Le Point* published a special issue devoted to Matisse. His essay “Notes d’un peintre sur son dessin” (Notes of a painter on his drawing) was included. When war was declared in September, Matisse left Paris several times. On September 1, he was in Rochefort; on September 4, in La Rochelle; on September 7, in Rambouillet; on September 10, in Clairefontaine; and on September 30, in Rochefort. He executed several drawings of trees while in the forest as an inspirational evocation of renewal. He returned to Paris on October 1 and was once again in Nice on October 17.

He first resumed work on *Nymph in the Forest* (October 20–21, and 23–24). Two models, Tamara and then Micheline Payot, were engaged to pose for a complete series of interior scenes and portraits. Matisse unveiled *Romanian Blouse* (MNAM–CP) on December 13. A few days later, he wrote to his son Pierre “that [he] was stuck in Nice by work,” adding, “I’m stubborn and won’t just flee the battleground like that.”[109]

1940

On January 7, Matisse presented *Sleeping Woman* (private collection), which was executed in several sittings during the month. He finished his *Romanian Blouse* on April 7 and 9; its blue, white, and red color scheme rendered it emblematic of France.

The war dealt a blow to this burst of activity. Matisse was on the point of leaving for Brazil in early May,[110] but canceled his departure at the last moment. “It seemed that to do otherwise would constitute desertion. If everyone who has even a little to offer leaves France, what will be left of her?”[111] He departed from Paris with Delectorskaya for an intense journey:[112] May 20 in Bordeaux, May 23 in Saint-Jean-de-Luz, and May 24 in Ciboure. There he stopped and settled, a few yards from Maurice Ravel’s house. “I don’t pass by it without fond feelings. After so many peregrinations, I’ve found a spot where I can set to work and forget this tragic period we’re all living through.”[113] Two days later, Matisse bought himself an easel and painted *Interior in Ciboure* (Musée Toulouse-Lautrec, Albi).

The artist left Ciboure on June 27 (“penetrating damp . . . gave me pains all over”[114]) and tried to return to Nice. He was forced to stop in Saint-Gaudens, however, unable to find a means of transport.[115] Two days later, he rented an easel and painted *Peaches* (private collection).

Matisse resumed his journey on August 3. After a stop in Carcassonne, he reached Marseille on August 13, where he joined his daughter Marguerite and grandson Claude. The boy was about to sail for the United States, a protective measure by his mother, who had joined the Resistance. The artist executed a series of drawings of her. Returning to Nice at the end of the month, he resumed work almost immediately to occupy his mind. Matisse devoted himself entirely to his *Sleeping Woman*, which he worked on throughout September and into early October.

On October 9, the artist’s son Pierre conveyed, and the artist received, an offer for a professorship at Mills College in Oakland, California. Matisse declined, saying, “As always when I resume work, I experience a great deal of difficulty in getting restarted, because every resumption represents an advance in my understanding. And I am at a particularly important point in my journey and cannot allow any distracting influences. . . . As for the future? I simply await it—whatever happens, I won’t move.”[116]

The artist was then grappling with a painting that demanded all his attention, *Still Life: Seashell on Black Marble* (Pushkin Museum, Moscow). It was painted in about thirty sessions between September 25 and December 4, with the execution of a collage on November 14 (private collection). Exhausted by this endeavor, Matisse altered his methods. Employing “direct vision without transposition,”[117] he embarked on *Still Life with Oysters* 157 on November 22.

Matisse completed several additional paintings, but his health was deteriorating. On December 25, Delectorskaya notified Marguerite that her father was in the hospital.[118] On January 8, 1941, Matisse, accompanied by Delectorskaya, left for Lyon to undergo an operation several days later. The “second life”[119] that ensued was to form a new link in the long continuum of Matisse’s career.

104 HM–PM, January 26, 1939.

105 HM–PM, May 7, 1939. The quotation that follows is from the same source.

106 HM–Zervos, March 18, 1939, private collection.

107 HM–Bussy, August 29, 1939, INHA.

108 Diary.

109 HM–PM, December 17, 1939.

110 HM–Bussy, May 11, 1940, INHA.

111 HM–PM, September 1, 1940.

112 See the corresponding dates in the diary.

113 HM–MD, May 30, 1940.

114 HM–Bussy, June 17, 1940, INHA.

115 HM–Bussy, July 11, 1940, INHA.

116 HM–PM, October 11, 1940.

117 HM–PM, November 28–December 2, 1940.

118 Lydia Delectorskaya–MD, December 25, 1940.

119 HM–Albert Marquet, January 16, 1942, in *Matisse–Marquet: Correspondance (1898–1947)* (Lausanne: La Bibliothèque des Arts, 2008), 143.

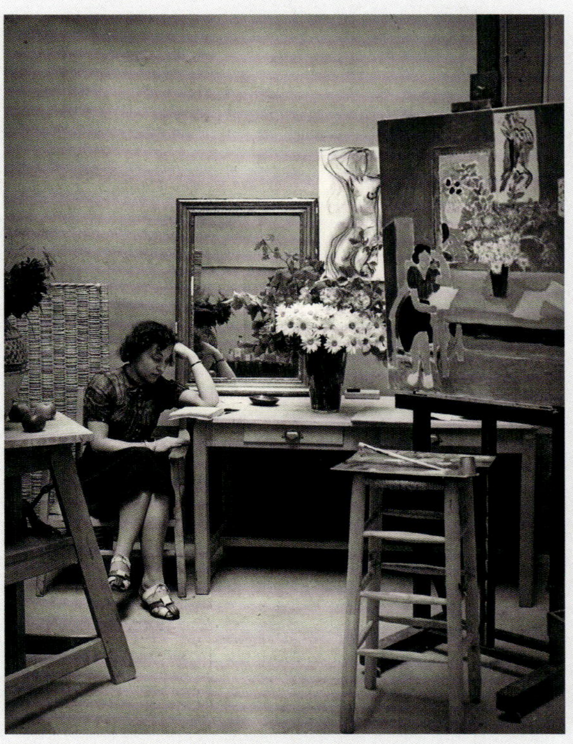

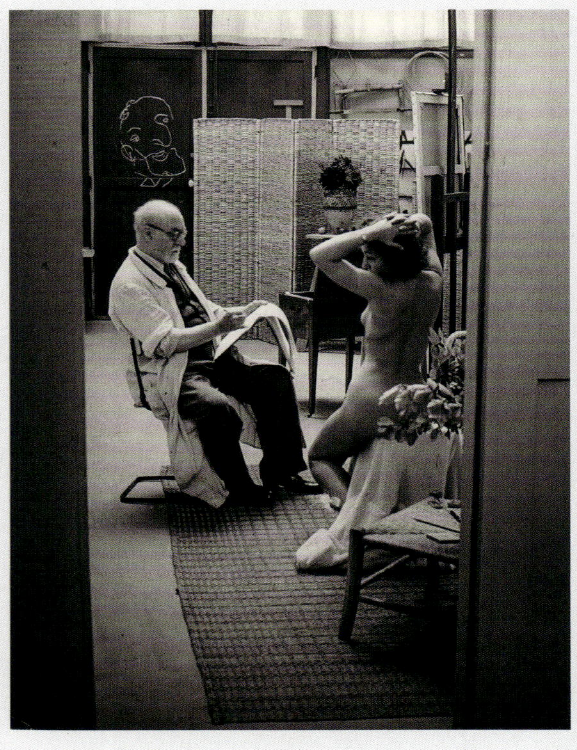

184, **185** (figs.)
Wilma Javor posing and Henri Matisse drawing her, studio in the Villa Alésia, Paris, summer 1939. Photographs by Brassaï

186 (fig.)
Henri Matisse working on *Nymph in the Forest (Verdure)*; on the wall, *Peaches*, studio in the Régina, Nice, summer 1941. Photograph by Varian Fry

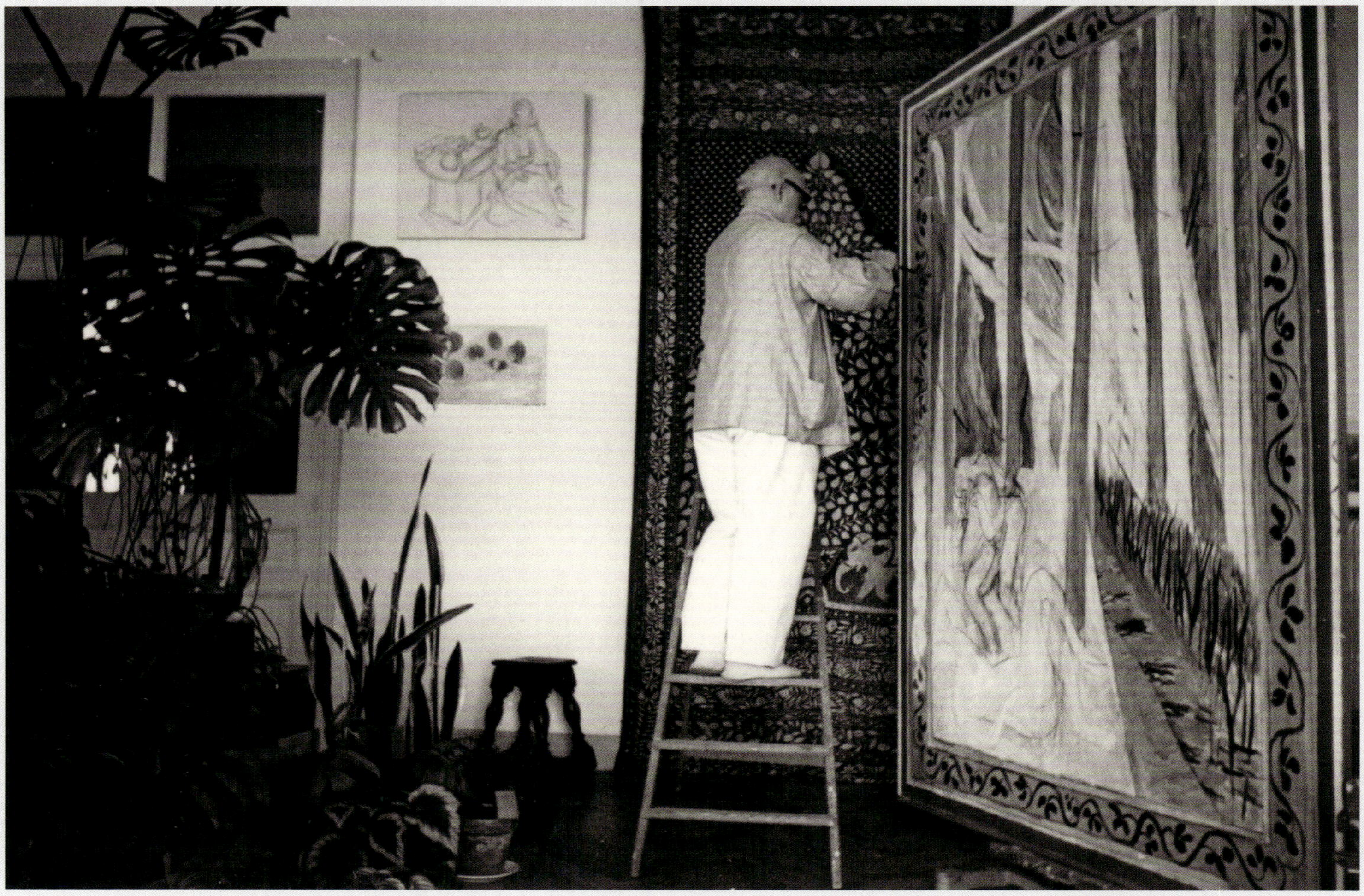

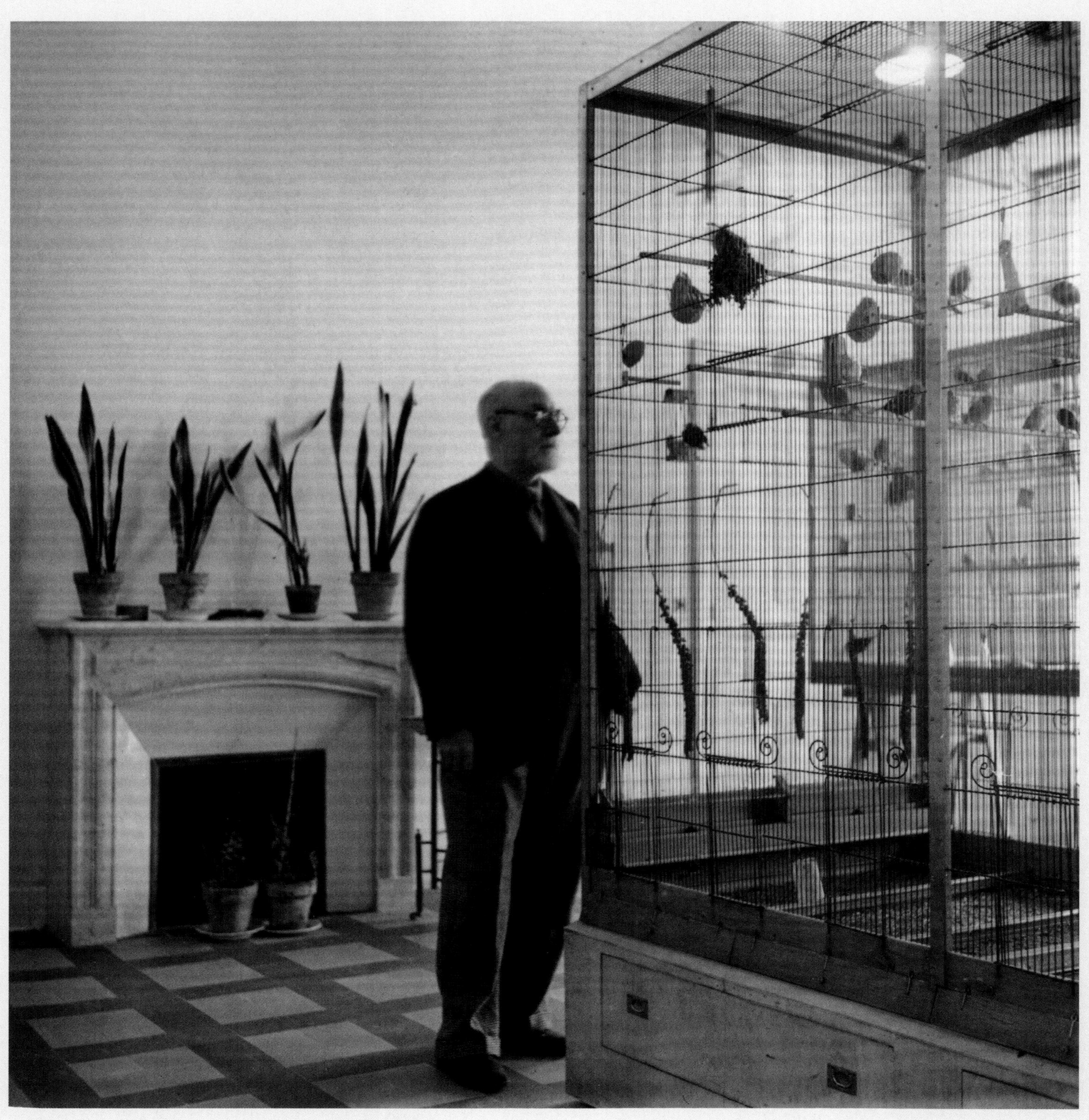

187 (fig.)
Henri Matisse in the bird room, studio in the Régina, Nice, August 1941. Photograph by Varian Fry

CHECKLIST OF THE EXHIBITION

This is a list of the works shown at all three venues of the *Matisse in the 1930s* exhibition. It is divided into two parts: the works by Henri Matisse, grouped by medium, then the works by other artists and documents.

Following each entry, the abbreviations PH (Philadelphia), PA (Paris), and NI (Nice) indicate where the works are being shown. However, this checklist was compiled on the occasion of the first venue of the exhibition in Philadelphia. Changes may occur for the venues in Paris and Nice.

The abbreviation *CDA* (for *Cahiers d'art*) and references indicate the issue, year, and sometimes page number, of the *Cahiers d'art* in which the works are reproduced.

WORKS BY HENRI MATISSE (1869–1954)

PAINTINGS

Breakfast (*Le Petit Déjeuner*), 1920
Oil on canvas, 25 ¼ × 29 ¹/₁₆ in.
(64.1 × 73.8 cm)
Philadelphia Museum of Art: The Samuel S. White 3rd and Vera White Collection, 1967-30-55
PH
Not reproduced

The Conversation (*Robe noire et robe violette, fauteuil tressé*), 1938
Oil on canvas, 18 ⅜ × 21 ¾ in.
(46.7 × 55.2 cm)
San Francisco Museum of Modern Art: Bequest of Mr. James D. Zellerbach, 93.149
PH
148, p. 204

Daisies (*Les Marguerites [Fleurs et figure, pot arabe]*), 1939
Oil on canvas, 36 ¼ × 25 ⁹/₁₆ in.
(92 × 65 cm)
The Art Institute of Chicago: Gift of Helen Pauling Donnelley in memory of her parents, Mary Fredericka and Edward George Pauling, 1983.206
PH
156, p. 213

The Dance, Blue Harmony (*La Danse, harmonie bleue*), 1930–31
Oil on canvas, 13 × 34 ⁹/₁₆ in.
(33 × 87.8 cm)
Musée Matisse Nice, 63.3.3
PH/PA/NI
97, p. 147

The Dance, Gray Harmony (*La Danse, harmonie grise*), 1930–31
Oil on canvas, 13 × 34 ⁹/₁₆ in.
(33 × 87.8 cm)
Musée Matisse Nice, 63.3.1
PH/PA/NI
94, p. 146

The Dance, Ochre Harmony (*La Danse, harmonie ocre*), 1930–31
Oil on canvas, 13 × 34 ⁹/₁₆ in.
(33 × 87.8 cm)
Musée Matisse Nice, 63.3.2
PH/PA/NI
95, p. 146

Dancer Resting (*Danseuse au repos*), 1940
Oil on canvas, 32 × 25 ½ in.
(81.3 × 64.8 cm)
Toledo Museum of Art, Ohio: Gift of Mrs. C. Lockhart McKelvy, 1947.54
PH/PA
153, p. 210

Draped Nude (*Nu au fauteuil, fond rouge*), November 6 and 7, 1936
Oil on canvas, 18 × 14 ¾ in.
(45.7 × 37.5 cm)
Tate, London: Purchased 1959, T00306
PH/PA
133, p. 187

The Dream (*Le Rêve*), 1935
Oil on canvas, 31 ⅞ × 25 ⁹/₁₆ × ⅞ in.
(81 × 65 × 2.2 cm)
Musée National d'Art Moderne–Centre Pompidou, Paris, AM 1979-106
PH
33, p. 56

The Gandoura (Seated Figure and Greek Torso) (*Figure assise et torse grec [La Gandoura]*), January 1939
Oil on canvas, 25 ⁹/₁₆ × 21 ¼ in.
(65 × 54 cm)
David and Ezra Nahmad Collection, HM5415
PH/PA/NI
85, p. 135

The Green Blouse (*La Blouse verte*), March 21, 1936
Oil on canvas, 31 ⅞ × 25 ⅝ in.
(81 × 65.1 cm)
Statens Museum for Kunst, Copenhagen, KMSr 174
PH/PA/NI
120, p. 175

Interior at Nice (Room at the Beau Rivage) (*Ma Chambre au Beau Rivage [La Fenêtre ouverte sur la mer (Nice)]*), 1917–18
Oil on canvas, 29 × 23 ¾ in.
(73.7 × 60.3 cm)
Philadelphia Museum of Art: A. E. Gallatin Collection, 1952-61-79
PH
Not reproduced

Interior with an Etruscan Vase (*Intérieur au vase étrusque*), 1940
Oil on canvas, 29 × 42 ½ in.
(73.7 × 108 cm)
Cleveland Museum of Art: Gift of the Hanna Fund, 1952.153
PH/PA/NI
152, p. 209

Large Reclining Nude (*Grand nu couché*), 1935
Oil on canvas, 26 ⅛ × 36 ¾ in.
(66.4 × 93.3 cm)
Baltimore Museum of Art: The Cone Collection, formed by Dr. Claribel Cone and Miss Etta Cone of Baltimore, Maryland, 1950.258
PH/PA/NI
110, p. 163

The Moorish Screen (*Le Paravent mauresque*), 1921
Oil on canvas, 36 ³/₁₆ × 29 ¼ in.
(91.9 × 74.3 cm)
Philadelphia Museum of Art: Bequest of Lisa Norris Elkins, 1950-92-9
PH
44, p. 72

Nude in an Armchair, Green Plant (*Nu dans un fauteuil, plante verte*), 1937 [November 1936]
Oil on canvas, 28 ⁹/₁₆ × 23 ¹³/₁₆ in.
(72.5 × 60.5 cm)
Musée Matisse Nice, 63.2.3
PH/PA/NI
132, p. 186

Nude in a Robe (*Nu au peignoir*), 1933–34
Oil on canvas, 25 ⁹/₁₆ × 18 ⅛ in.
(65 × 46 cm)
David and Ezra Nahmad Collection, HM76040
PH/NI
CDA, nos. 1–4 (1935): 9
104, p. 153

Nude with Crossed Legs (*Nu aux jambes croisées*), 1936
Oil on canvas, 15 × 18 ¼ in.
(38.1 × 46.3 cm)
David and Ezra Nahmad Collection, HM5538
PH/NI
131, p. 185

Nude with Foliage (*Nu au talon sur le genou [Nu allongé]*), completed on March 14, 1936
Oil on canvas, 14 ¹⁵/₁₆ × 24 in.
(38 × 61 cm)
Private collection
PA
Not reproduced

Nymph in the Forest (Verdure) (*Nymphe dans la forêt [La Verdure]*), 1935–42/43
Oil on canvas, 8 ft. ⅝ in. × 6 ft. 4 ¹⁵/₁₆ in. (245.5 × 195.5 cm)
Musée d'Orsay, Paris, held at the Musée Matisse Nice: Gift of Madame Jean Matisse to the French state, 1978, RF 1978-34; D.78.1.1
PH/PA/NI
116, p. 171

Odalisque in a Black Armchair (*Odalisque au fauteuil noir*), January 17 and 18, 1942
Oil on canvas, 14 ¹⁵/₁₆ × 18 ⅛ in.
(38 × 46 cm)
Private collection
PH
162, p. 221

Odalisque in Gray Pantaloons (*Odalisque à la culotte grise*), 1926–27
Oil on canvas, 21 ¼ × 25 ⁹/₁₆ in.
(54 × 65 cm)
Musée de l'Orangerie, Paris, RF 1963-67
PH/PA/NI
CDA, nos. 7–8 (1927): 270
70, p. 116

Odalisque with a Tambourine (*Odalisque au tambourin*), 1925–26
Oil on canvas, 29 ¼ × 21 ⅞ in.
(74.3 × 55.6 cm)
The Museum of Modern Art, New York: The William S. Paley Collection, SPC21.1990
PH
CDA, no. 7 (1926): 161
68, p. 113

Odalisque with Red Box (*Odalisque au coffret rouge*), 1927
Oil on canvas, 20 ⅛ × 25 ⅝ in.
(50 × 65 cm)
Musée Matisse Nice, 63.2.6
PA/NI
CDA, no. 7 (1926): 155; nos. 8–10 (1932); nos. 1–2 (1933)
71, p. 117

Papeete, Tahiti (Window at Tahiti; Tahiti I) (*Papeete, Tahiti [Fenêtre à Tahiti; Tahiti I]*), October 1935
Oil on canvas, 7 ft. 4 ⁹/₁₆ in. × 67 ¹¹/₁₆ in. (225 × 172 cm)
Musée Matisse Nice, 63.2.15
PH/PA/NI
118, p. 173

Portrait in a Blue Coat (*Portrait au manteau bleu*), 1935
Oil on canvas, 35 ¹⁵/₁₆ × 23 ⁹/₁₆ in.
(91.3 × 59.8 cm)
David and Ezra Nahmad Collection, HM5401
PH/PA/NI
122, p. 177

Red Nymph and Faun (*Nymphe rouge et faune*), c. 1935
Oil and Conté crayon on canvas, 19 ¹¹/₁₆ × 24 in. (50 × 61 cm)
Private collection: Courtesy Connery & Associates
PH
115, p. 169

The Reflection (*Reflet*), 1935
Oil on canvas, 18 ¼ × 21 ⅞ in.
(46.3 × 55.5 cm)
The William Rubin Collection
PH
35, p. 60

Romanian Blouse (*Blouse roumaine aux manches vertes*), late March–April 1937
Oil on canvas, 28 ¾ × 23 ⅝ in.
(73 × 60 cm)
Cincinnati Art Museum: Bequest of Mary E. Johnston, 1967.1427
PH
CDA, nos. 6–7 (1937): 226
139, p. 194

The Romanian Blouse, Red and Blue Background (*La Blouse roumaine, fond rouge et bleu*), November 12, 1937
Oil on canvas, 18 ⅛ × 21 ⅝ in.
(46 × 55 cm)
Private collection
PA
Not reproduced

Seated Pink Nude (*Nu rose assis*), 1935–36
Oil on canvas, 36 ¼ × 28 ¾ in.
(92 × 73 cm)
Musée National d'Art Moderne–Centre Pompidou, Paris, AM 2001-215
PH
123, p. 179

Seated Woman with a Vase of Amaryllis (*Femme assise et vase aux amaryllis*), 1941
Oil on canvas, 13 × 16 ⅛ in.
(33 × 41 cm)
The Museum of Modern Art, New York: The William S. Paley Collection, SPC69.1990
PH
Not reproduced

Small Romanian Blouse with Foliage (*Petite Blouse roumaine au feuillage*), 1938 [November 4, 1937]
Oil and graphite on canvas, 18 ⅛ × 15 in. (46 × 38.1 cm)
Baltimore Museum of Art: The Cone Collection, formed by Dr. Claribel Cone and Miss Etta Cone of Baltimore, Maryland, 1950.262
PH
142, p. 197

The Song (*Le Chant*), 1938
Oil on canvas, 9 ft. 3 in. × 6 ft. ¹/₁₆ in. (282 × 183 cm)
The Lewis Collection TR:380-2014
PH/PA/NI
CDA, nos. 5–10 (1939): 173
42, p. 68

Still Life on a Green Marble Table (*Nature morte à la table de marbre vert*), September 1941
Oil on canvas, 18 ⅛ × 15 ³/₁₆ in.
(46 × 38.5 cm)
Musée National d'Art Moderne–Centre Pompidou, Paris, AM 2591 P
PH
Not reproduced

Still Life on a Table (*Nature morte sur une table*), 1925
Oil on canvas, 31 ¾ × 39 ¼ in. (80.6 × 99.7 cm)
Philadelphia Museum of Art: Gift of Henry P. McIlhenny, 1964-77-1
PH
Not reproduced

Still Life with Oysters (*Nature morte aux huîtres*), 1940
Oil on canvas, 25 ¹¹⁄₁₆ × 31 ⅞ in. (65.2 × 80.9 cm)
Kunstmuseum Basel, Inv. 1881
PH
157, p. 214

Still Life with Sleeping Woman (*Nature morte à la dormeuse*), 1939–40
Oil on canvas, 32 ½ × 39 ⅝ in. (82.5 × 100.7 cm)
National Gallery of Art, Washington: Collection of Mr. and Mrs. Paul Mellon, 1985.64.26
PH/PA/NI
155, p. 212

The Striped Dress (*La Robe rayée*), January 15 and 26, 1938
Oil on canvas, 18 ⅛ × 14 ¹⁵⁄₁₆ in. (46 × 38 cm)
Albertina Museum, Vienna–Sammlung Batliner, GE82DL
PH/PA/NI
CDA, nos. 1–4 (1939): 77
150, p. 207

Striped Robe, Fruit, and Anemones (*Robe rayée, fruits et anémones*), 1940
Oil on canvas, 21 ⅝ × 25 ⅝ in. (54.9 × 64.1 cm)
Baltimore Museum of Art: The Cone Collection, formed by Dr. Claribel Cone and Miss Etta Cone of Baltimore, Maryland, 1950.263
PH/PA/NI
151, p. 208

The Three Sisters (*Les Trois Sœurs*), 1917
Oil on canvas, 36 ¼ × 28 ¾ in. (92 × 73 cm)
Musée de l'Orangerie, Paris, RF 1963-63
PH/PA/NI
CDA, no. 1 (1927): 28; *CDA*, nos. 5–6 (1931): loose leaf 3
66, p. 110

Window at Tahiti II (*Fenêtre à Tahiti II*), December 18, 1935–March 15, 1936
Gouache on canvas, 7 ft. 9 ¹¹⁄₁₆ in. × 6 ft. ¹⁄₁₆ in. (240 × 195 cm)
Musée Départemental Matisse, Le Cateau-Cambrésis, 1952-63
PH/PA/NI
119, p. 174

Woman in Blue (*La Grande Robe bleue et mimosas*), 1937
Oil on canvas, 36 ½ × 29 in. (92.7 × 73.7 cm)
Philadelphia Museum of Art: Gift of Mrs. John Wintersteen, 1956-23-1
PH/PA/NI
134, p. 188

Woman Seated in an Armchair (*Femme assise dans un fauteuil*), 1940
Oil on canvas, 21 ¼ × 25 ⅝ in. (54 × 65.1 cm)
National Gallery of Art, Washington: Given in loving memory of her husband, Taft Schreiber, by Rita Schreiber, 1989.31.1
PH/PA/NI
154, p. 211

Woman with a Veil (*Femme à la voilette*), 1927
Oil on canvas, 24 ¼ × 19 ¾ in. (61.6 × 50.2 cm)
The Museum of Modern Art, New York: The William S. Paley Collection, SPC22.1990
PH/PA/NI
CDA, nos. 5–6 (1931): 314
72, p. 118

The Yellow Dress (*La Robe jaune*), 1929–31
Oil on canvas, 39 ⁹⁄₁₆ × 32 ⅛ in. (100.5 × 81.6 cm)
Baltimore Museum of Art: The Cone Collection, formed by Dr. Claribel Cone and Miss Etta Cone of Baltimore, Maryland, 1950.256
PH
CDA, nos. 1–4 (1935): 17
73, p. 121

Yellow Odalisque (*Odalisque à la robe persane jaune, anémones*), 1937
Oil on canvas, 21 ¾ × 18 ⅛ in. (55.2 × 46 cm)
Philadelphia Museum of Art: The Samuel S. White 3rd and Vera White Collection, 1967, 1967-30-57
PH/PA/NI
CDA, nos. 6–7 (1937): 210
136, p. 191

Young Girl Seated (*La Biche*) (*Corselet sur fond de "Tahiti"*), 1936
Oil on canvas, 24 ⅛ × 19 ⁵⁄₁₆ in. (61.3 × 49.1 cm)
Allen Memorial Art Museum, Oberlin College, Ohio: Gift of Joseph and Enid Bissett, AMAM 1959.120
PH/PA/NI
117, p. 172

Young Woman Seated in a Persian Dress (*Jeune Fille assise, robe persane*), 1942
Oil on canvas, 16 ¹⁵⁄₁₆ × 22 ¹⁄₁₆ in. (43 × 56 cm)
Musée National Picasso–Paris, MP2017-27
PH
161, p. 220

SCULPTURES

Back IV (*Le Dos IV*), 1930–31 (cast 1959–60)
Bronze, 6 ft. 2 ⅜ in. × 45 in. × 6 ¼ in. (188.9 × 114.3 × 15.9 cm)
Hirshhorn Museum and Sculpture Garden, Smithsonian Institution, Washington, DC: Gift of the Joseph H. Hirshhorn Foundation, 1966, 66.3464
PH
82, p. 130

Henriette I, 1925
Bronze, 11 ³⁄₁₆ × 7 ¹⁄₁₆ × 9 ¹⁄₁₆ in. (28.4 × 18 × 23 cm)
Musée d'Orsay, Paris, held at the Musée Matisse Nice: Gift of Madame Jean Matisse to the French state, 1978, RF 3389; D.78.1.45
PH/PA/NI
78, p. 124

Henriette II, 1927
Bronze, 12 ⅝ × 8 ¹¹⁄₁₆ × 10 ⅝ in. (32 × 22 × 27 cm)
Musée d'Orsay, Paris, held at the Musée Matisse Nice: Gift of Madame Jean Matisse to the French state, 1978, RF 3359; D.78.1.16
PH/PA/NI
CDA, no. 7 (1928): 281
79, p. 126

Henriette III, 1929
Bronze, 15 ¾ × 8 ¹¹⁄₁₆ × 9 ¼ in. (40 × 22 × 23.5 cm)
Musée d'Orsay, Paris, held at the Musée Matisse Nice: Gift of Madame Jean Matisse to the French state, 1978, RF 3374; D.78.1.31
PH/PA/NI
80, p. 127

Large Seated Nude (*Grand nu assis*), 1922–29
Bronze, 31 × 33 × 14 in. (78.7 × 83.8 × 35.6 cm)
Philadelphia Museum of Art: Gift of R. Sturgis and Marion B. F. Ingersoll, 1960, 1960-146-1
PH
CDA, no. 7 (1928): 282
81, p. 128–29

Large Seated Nude (*Grand nu assis*), 1922–29
Bronze, 30 ¾ × 33 × 13 ¹³⁄₁₆ in. (78 × 83.8 × 35 cm)
Musée Départemental Matisse, Le Cateau-Cambrésis, 1952–69
PA/NI
Not reproduced

Tiari (*Le Tiaré*), 1930 (cast 1951)
Bronze, 8 ¹⁄₁₆ × 5 ⅞ × 7 ⁵⁄₁₆ in. (20.4 × 15 × 18.5 cm)
Musée d'Orsay, Paris, held at the Musée Matisse Nice: Gift of Madame Jean Matisse to the French state, 1978, RF 3382; D.78.1.39
PH/PA/NI
23, p. 48

Venus in a Shell I (*Vénus à la coquille I*), 1930.
Bronze, 12 ³⁄₁₆ × 6 ¹³⁄₁₆ × 7 ⅞ in. (31 × 17.3 × 20 cm)
Musée d'Orsay, Paris, held at the Musée Matisse Nice: Gift of Madame Jean Matisse to the French state, 1978, RF 3381; D.78.1.38
PH/PA/NI
26, p. 49

Venus in a Shell II (*Vénus à la coquille II*), 1932 (cast 1958)
Bronze, 13 × 6 ¹¹⁄₁₆ × 9 ¹⁄₁₆ in. (33 × 17 × 23 cm)
Musée d'Orsay, Paris, held at the Musée Matisse Nice: Gift of Madame Jean Matisse to the French state, 1978, RF 3387; D.78.1.43
PH/PA/NI
83, p. 131

WORKS ON PAPER

Arabesque, 1924
Transfer lithograph, 19 ⅛ × 12 ¹¹⁄₁₆ in. (48.6 × 32.2 cm)
The Museum of Modern Art, New York: Lillie P. Bliss Collection, 82.1934
PH
67, p. 112

Crouching Nude (*Nu accroupi*), 1936
Charcoal on paper, 19 ¹¹⁄₁₆ × 26 in. (50 × 66 cm)
Musée Départemental Matisse, Le Cateau-Cambrésis, 1952–57
PH/PA/NI
129, p. 184

The Dance (*La Danse*), 1930–31
Gouached cut-outs on paper, 9 ⁵⁄₁₆ × 29 ³⁄₁₆ in. (31 × 77.5 cm)
Musée Matisse Nice, 63.3.92
PA/NI
100, p. 148

The Dance (*La Danse*), created for *Vogue*, June 1938
Watercolor on paper, 20 ⅞ × 29 ⅛ in. (28.5 × 49 cm)
Musée Matisse Nice, 63.3.93
PH/PA/NI
3, p. 15

Dance: After the Paris Version of the Barnes Mural (*La Danse [d'après la version parisienne de la peinture murale de Barnes]*), 1935
Etching and color aquatint on Arches wove paper, 11 ⅞ × 31 ⅝ in. (30.2 × 80.3 cm)
The Metropolitan Museum of Art, New York: The Pierre and Maria-Gaetana Matisse Collection, 2002, 2002.456.86
PH
99, p. 148

The Dance, First Version—Compositional Study (*La Danse, première version. Étude d'ensemble*), 1930–31
Graphite on Arches wove paper, 9 ⅞ × 13 ¹⁄₁₆ in. (25.1 × 33.2 cm)
Musée Matisse Nice, 63.3.94
PH
Not reproduced

The Dance, First Version—Compositional Study (*La Danse, première version. Étude d'ensemble*), 1930–31
Graphite on BFK Rives watermarked laid paper from sketchbook, 10 ¹⁄₁₆ × 26 ⅛ in. (25.6 × 66.4 cm)
Musée Matisse Nice, 63.3.114
PH
Not reproduced

The Dance, First Version—Compositional Study (*La Danse, première version. Étude d'ensemble*), 1930–31
Graphite on MBM watermarked wove paper, 10 ⅞ × 14 ¹³⁄₁₆ in. (27.7 × 37.7 cm)
Musée Matisse Nice, 63.3.111
PH
Not reproduced

The Dance, First Version—Compositional Study (*La Danse, première version. Étude d'ensemble*), 1930-31
Graphite and pencil on paper, 10 × 26 ¹⁄₁₆ in. (25.4 × 66.2 cm)
Musée Matisse Nice 63.3.116
NI
93, p. 146

The Dance, First Version—Compositional Study (*La Danse, première version. Étude d'ensemble*), 1931
Graphite on J. Perrigot Arches watermarked wove paper, 11 ⅛ × 30 in. (28.2 × 76.2 cm)
Musée Matisse Nice, 63.3.117
PH
Not reproduced

The Dance, First Version—Sketch at the Scale of the Central Figure (*La Danse, première version. Étude pour la figure centrale*), 1930–31
India ink and brush on two sheets of transparent paper, joined together and glued on three sheets of Canson paper, mounted on linen with a stretcher, 10 ft. 11 ⅞ in. × 6 ft. 4 ⁹⁄₁₆ in. (335 × 194.5 cm)
Musée d'Orsay, Paris, held at the Musée Matisse Nice: Gift of Monsieur Gérard Matisse to the French state, 1988, RF 41438.BIS, Recto; D.87.2.1
PH/PA/NI
92, p. 144

The Dance, Second Version—Compositional Study (*La Danse, deuxième version. Étude d'ensemble*), 1932
Graphite on wove paper from sketchbook, edition 26/50, 8 ⅛ × 21 in. (20.7 × 53.3 cm)
Musée Matisse Nice, 63.3.110
PH
Not reproduced

The Dance: Study for the Barnes Mural (Second Version) (*La Danse. Étude pour la peinture murale de Barnes [seconde version]*), 1931–32
Gouache and pencil on paper, 11 × 29 ⅞ in. (27.9 × 75.9 cm)
The Metropolitan Museum of Art, New York: The Pierre and Maria-Gaetana Matisse Collection, 2002, 2002.456.43
PH
98, p. 148

The Dance—Study for the Central Figure (*La Danse. Étude pour la figure centrale*), 1931
Graphite on laid paper, 11 13/16 × 10 1/16 in. (30 × 25.5 cm)
Musée Matisse Nice, 63.3.108
PH
Not reproduced

The Dance—Study for Left Panel (*La Danse. Étude pour le panneau de gauche*), January 20–February 25, 1932
Graphite on laid paper, 9 ⅜ × 12 9/16 in. (23.8 × 31.9 cm)
Musée Matisse Nice, 63.3.105
PA/NI
Not reproduced

The Dance—Study for Left Panel (*La Danse. Étude pour le panneau de gauche*), 1931
Graphite on BKF Rives watermarked laid paper, 10 ⅛ × 13 1/16 in. (25.8 × 33.2 cm)
Musée Matisse Nice, 63.3.107
PA/NI
Not reproduced

Faun Charming the Sleeping Nymph (*Faune charmant la nymphe endormie*), 1935
Charcoal and stump on canvas, 60 ⅝ × 65 ¾ in. (154 × 167 cm)
Musée National d'Art Moderne–Centre Pompidou, Paris, AM 2001-216
PH
Not reproduced

Figure, Floral Blouse (*Figure, blouse fleurie*), 1936
White crayon on black paper, 9 13/16 × 7 ⅞ in. (25 × 20 cm)
The Pierre and Tana Matisse Foundation, New York, 301-203014
PH
Not reproduced

Figure in an Armchair (*Figure dans un fauteuil*), December 1939
Pen and India ink on fine wove paper from sketchbook, 16 ½ × 13 in. (41.9 × 33 cm)
Musée Matisse Nice, 63.2.96
PH
Not reproduced

Figure with Face Partly Missing, Seated in an Interior (*Figure au visage coupé assise dans un intérieur*), 1929
Etching printed chine collé, 5 ⅝ × 8 9/16 in. (14.3 × 21.7 cm)
Musée Départemental Matisse, Le Cateau-Cambrésis, 1952-28
PH
77, p. 123

Kneeling Nude (*Nu agenouillé*), 1936
India ink on laid paper, 26 3/16 × 15 1/16 in. (66.5 × 38.2 cm)
Musée d'Art Moderne de Paris, AMD 556
PH
CDA, nos. 3–5 (1936): 142
126, p. 182

Large Odalisque in Striped Pantaloons (*Grande odalisque à la culotte bayadère*), 1925
Transfer lithograph, 28 ⅛ × 22 ⅝ in. (71.4 × 57.5 cm)
Philadelphia Museum of Art: Purchased with the Lisa Norris Elkins Fund, 1950, 1950-129-118
PH
Not reproduced

Large Self-Portrait (*Grand autoportrait*), 1937
Charcoal on paper, 24 3/16 × 15 ¾ in. (61.4 × 40 cm)
The Pierre and Tana Matisse Foundation, New York, 507.206136
PH
Not reproduced

Mademoiselle Roudenko, no. 1 (Dancer of the Ballets Russes) (*Mademoiselle Roudenko n° 1, danseuse des Ballets russes*), 1939
Black ink on cream wove paper, 18 13/16 × 12 ⅜ in. (47.8 × 31.5 cm)
Harvard Art Museums/Fogg Museum, Cambridge, Massachusetts: Bequest from the collection of Maurice Wertheim, Class of 1906, 1951.72
PH
Not reproduced

Mademoiselle Roudenko, no. 2 (Dancer of the Ballets Russes) (*Mademoiselle Roudenko n° 2, danseuse des Ballets russes*), 1939
Black ink on cream wove paper, 18 ⅞ × 12 ⅜ in. (48 × 31.4 cm)
Harvard Art Museums/Fogg Museum, Cambridge, Massachusetts: Bequest from the collection of Maurice Wertheim, Class of 1906, 1951.73A
PH
Not reproduced

Mademoiselle Roudenko, no. 3 (Dancer of the Ballets Russes) (*Mademoiselle Roudenko n° 3, danseuse des Ballets russes*), July 1939
Black ink on cream wove paper, 18 ⅞ × 12 ⅜ in. (48 × 31.4 cm)
Harvard Art Museums/Fogg Museum, Cambridge, Massachusetts: Bequest from the collection of Maurice Wertheim, Class of 1906, 1951.74
PH
144, p. 201

Mademoiselle Roudenko, no. 4 (Dancer of the Ballets Russes) (*Mademoiselle Roudenko n° 4, danseuse des Ballets russes*), 1939
Black ink on cream wove paper, 18 13/16 × 12 ⅜ in. (47.8 × 31.4 cm)
Harvard Art Museums/Fogg Museum, Cambridge, Massachusetts: Bequest from the collection of Maurice Wertheim, Class of 1906, 1951.75
PH
Not reproduced

Nude Reclining on Flowered Cushions against a Background of Green Plants (Lydia) (*Nu couché aux coussins fleuris, sur fond de plantes vertes [Lydia]*), 1936
India Ink on paper, 10 5/16 × 14 15/16 in. (25.6 × 38 cm)
Private collection
PA
124, p. 180

Nude Reclining on Her Stomach, Small African Rug (*Nu allongé sur le ventre, petit tapis africain*), 1935
Ink on paper, 15 ¼ × 19 15/16 in. (38.8 × 50.7 cm)
Musée National d'Art Moderne–Centre Pompidou, Paris, AM 1984-48
PH
Not reproduced

Nude Seated in an Armchair (*Nu assis dans un fauteuil*), 1922
Charcoal on paper, 24 13/16 × 18 13/16 in. (63 × 47.8 cm)
Musée Départemental Matisse, Le Cateau-Cambrésis, 1952-54
PH
Not reproduced

Nude Seated in the Studio (*Nu assis dans l'atelier*), 1929
Etching printed chine collé, 8 ⅛ × 6 in. (20.6 × 15.2 cm)
The Metropolitan Museum of Art, New York: Purchase, Reba and Dave Williams Gift, 1999.267.1
PH
CDA, no. 7 (1929): 286
76, p. 123

Nude Seated on a Banquette in front of a Mirror (*Nu assis sur une banquette devant une glace*), 1937
Ink on paper, 15 ¼ × 11 in. (38.8 × 28 cm)
Musée National d'Art Moderne–Centre Pompidou, Paris, AM 1984-58
PH
41, p. 65

Nude with Blue Cushion beside a Fireplace (*Nu au coussin bleu à côté d'une cheminée*), 1925
Transfer lithograph, 25 1/16 × 18 13/16 in. (63.6 × 47.8 cm)
The Pierre and Tana Matisse Foundation, New York, 1265.101056
PH
Not reproduced

Nude with Necklace (Lydia) (*Nu au collier [Lydia]*), 1935
Graphite and ink on paper, 17 11/16 × 22 ¼ in. (45 × 56.5 cm)
Private collection
PA/NI
CDA, nos. 3–5 (1936): 86
127, p. 183

Nymph and Faun (*Nymphe et faune*), April 1935–43
Charcoal and stump on prepared canvas, 60 ⅝ × 65 ¾ in. (154 × 167 cm)
Musée National d'Art Moderne–Centre Pompidou, Paris, AM 1991-272
NI
112, p. 166

Nymph and Faun (Sketch) (*Nymphe et Faune [esquisse]*), c. 1935
Pencil and charcoal pen on canvas, 19 ½ × 23 13/16 in. (49.5 × 60.5 cm)
Private collection
PH
Not reproduced

Nymph and Faun (Study for "Bataille de femmes") (*Nymphe et faune [étude pour "Bataille de femmes"]*), c. 1934
Pencil on paper, 9 ⅛ × 14 15/16 in. (23.2 × 38 cm)
Bibliothèque Nationale de France, Paris: RES B 16a(8) Boite Ecu_ DESSINS FRANCAIS du XX SIECLE_Matisse
PA
Not reproduced

***Poésies*, by Stéphane Mallarmé, 1932**

Afternoon of a Faun (*L'Après-midi d'un faune*), 1930–32
Etching, 13 ⅛ × 9 ⅞ in. (33.3 × 25.1 cm)
Musée Départemental Matisse, Le Cateau-Cambrésis, 2012-7(13)
PH/PA/NI
113, p. 168

Afternoon of a Faun (*L'Après-midi d'un faune*), 1930–32
Etching, 13 ⅛ × 9 ⅞ in. (33.3 × 25.1 cm)
Musée Départemental Matisse, Le Cateau-Cambrésis, 2012-7(14)
PH/PA/NI
114, p. 168

Fairy in a Luminous Hat—Remembrance of Mallarmé (*Fée au chapeau de clarté. Souvenir du Mallarmé*), 1933
Drypoint printed chine collé, 14 7/16 × 12 ⅝ in. (36.6 × 32 cm)
The Pierre and Tana Matisse Foundation, New York, 1639-106022
PH
91, p. 143

Nude for Cleveland (*Nu pour Cleveland*), 1932
Etching printed chine collé, 14 7/16 × 11 5/16 in. (36.7 × 28.7 cm)
The Metropolitan Museum of Art, New York: Harris Brisbane Dick Fund, 1943, 43.17
PH
90, p. 142

Studies for "The Tomb of Charles Baudelaire" and "The Tomb of Edgar Poe" (*Étude pour "La Tombe de Charles Baudelaire" et "La Tombe d'Edgar Poe"*), 1931–32
Graphite with erasing on paper, 12 ½ × 9 ⅜ in. (31.7 × 23.8 cm)
Baltimore Museum of Art: The Cone Collection, formed by Dr. Claribel Cone and Miss Etta Cone of Baltimore, Maryland, 1950.12.901
PH
Not reproduced

Study for "Apparition" (*Étude pour "Apparition"*), 1931–32
Graphite with erasing and stumping on paper (recto), 13 × 9 ⅞ in. (33 × 25.1 cm)
Baltimore Museum of Art: The Cone Collection, formed by Dr. Claribel Cone and Miss Etta Cone of Baltimore, Maryland, 1950.12.697
PH
Not reproduced

Study for "Prose for Des Esseintes" (*Étude pour "Prose pour Des Esseintes"*), 1931–32
Graphite on paper, 12 ¾ × 9 13/16 in. (32.4 × 25 cm)
Baltimore Museum of Art: Marguerite Matisse Duthuit Collection, 2011.192
PH
Not reproduced

Study for "The Swan" (refused etching) (*Étude pour "Le Cygne" [planche refusée]*), refused etching, 1931–32
Etching, 13 ⅛ × 9 ⅞ in. (33.3 × 25.1 cm)
Baltimore Museum of Art: The Cone Collection, formed by Dr. Claribel Cone and Miss Etta Cone of Baltimore, Maryland, 1950.12.694.24
PH
Not reproduced

Study for "The Swan" (refused etching) (*Étude pour "Le Cygne" [planche refusée]*), 1931–32
Etching, 13 × 9 13/16 in. (33 × 25 cm)
Baltimore Museum of Art: The Cone Collection, formed by Dr. Claribel Cone and Miss Etta Cone of Baltimore, Maryland, 1950.12.694.25
PH
Not reproduced

Study for the 3rd Etching 142 (*Étude pour la 3e eau-forte 142*), c. 1932
10 ⅝ × 8 ¼ in. (27 × 20.9 cm)
Bibliothèque Nationale de France, Paris: RES B 16a(7) Boite Ecu_ DESSINS FRANCAIS du XX SIECLE_Matisse
PA
Not reproduced

Study for the 3rd Etching 143 (*Étude pour la 3e eau-forte 143*), c. 1932
12 13/16 × 9 13/16 in. (32.5 × 25 cm)
Bibliothèque Nationale de France, Paris: RES B 16a(7) Boite Ecu_ DESSINS FRANCAIS du XX SIECLE_Matisse
PA
Not reproduced

Study for the 3rd Etching 145 (*Étude pour la 3e eau-forte 145*), c. 1932
Etching, 12 5/8 × 9 7/8 in. (32.1 × 25.1 cm)
Bibliothèque Nationale de France, Paris: RES B 16a(7) Boite Ecu_ DESSINS FRANCAIS du XX SIECLE_Matisse
PA
Not reproduced

Reclining Nude (*Nu allongé*), July 1938
Charcoal on paper, 23 13/16 × 32 in. (60.5 × 81.3 cm)
The Museum of Modern Art, New York: Purchase, 79.1981
PH
146, p. 202

Reclining Nude Seen from the Back (*Nu allongé, de dos*), May 20, 1935
Charcoal on paper, 14 15/16 × 22 ¼ in. (37.9 × 56.4 cm)
Musée Matisse Nice, 63.2.29
NI
128, p. 183

The Romanian Blouse (*La Blouse roumaine*), c. 1936
Ink on paper, 14 15/16 × 11 in. (38 × 28 cm)
The Pierre and Tana Matisse Foundation, New York, 353.203135
PH
140, p. 196

The Romanian Blouse (*La Blouse roumaine*), December 16, 1939
Graphite on paper, 16 9/16 × 13 in. (42 × 33 cm)
The Pierre and Tana Matisse Foundation, New York, 502.206121
PH
141, p. 196

Romanian Blouse (*Blouse roumaine*), December 14, 1939
Graphite on sketchbook paper, 16 9/16 × 13 in. (42 × 33 cm)
Courtesy Galerie de l'Institut, Paris
NI
138, p. 193

Seated Model with a Guitar (*Femme assise à la guitare*), 1922
Compressed charcoal and charcoal pencil on laid paper, 18 11/16 × 12 3/8 in. (47.5 × 31.5 cm)
Art Gallery of Ontario, Toronto: Gift of Sam and Ayala Zacks, 1970, 71/250
PH
Not reproduced

Seated Nude, Hand on Shoulder (*Nu accroupi, main sur l'épaule*), 1929
Etching, 9 3/8 × 6 9/16 in. (23.8 × 16.7 cm)
Bibliothèque Nationale de France, Paris: RESERVE DC-418 (5)-BOITE FOL_Matisse Henri_D188
PA
Not reproduced

Seated Nude, Hands on Knees (*Nu assis, mains aux genoux*), 1929
Etching, 8 1/16 × 6 in. (20.4 × 15.3 cm)
Bibliothèque Nationale de France, Paris: RESERVE DC-418 (3)-BOITE FOL_Matisse Henri_D135
PA
Not reproduced

Seated Nude, Hands on Knees (*Nu assis, mains aux genoux*), 1929
Etching printed chine collé, 8 1/16 × 6 in. (20.4 × 15.3 cm)
Musée Matisse Nice, 63.4.88
NI
75, p. 122

Seated Nude with Arms Raised (*Nu assis aux bras levés*), c. 1925
Charcoal with stump, with erasing and touches of direct charcoal marks, on ivory wove paper, pieced, 24 1/8 × 19 7/16 in. (61.2 × 49.4 cm)
The Art Institute of Chicago: Wirt D. Walker Fund, 1965.243
PH
Not reproduced

Seated Nude with Star-Patterned Background (*Nu assis, fond de carreaux étoilés*), 1929
Drypoint printed chine collé, 5 13/16 × 4 in. (14.8 × 10.1 cm)
The Pierre and Tana Matisse Foundation, New York, 1542-105031
PH
Not reproduced

Self-Portrait (*Autoportrait*), 1937
Charcoal and stump on laid paper, 13 3/8 × 11 ¼ in. (34 × 28.5 cm)
National Gallery of Art, Washington: Collection of Mr. and Mrs. Paul Mellon, 1985, 1985.64.104
PH
1, p. 6

Sketch for "The Dance" (*Esquisse pour "La Danse"*), 1931
Pencil on tracing paper, pasted on paper, 9 5/8 × 14 3/16 in. (24.5 × 36 cm)
The Pierre and Tana Matisse Foundation, New York, 2311.206240
PH
Not reproduced

Sleeping Figure in front of a Moucharaby Background (*Figure endormie sur fond moucharabieh*), 1929
Etching, 9 13/16 × 7 1/16 in. (25 × 17.9 cm)
Bibliothèque Nationale de France, Paris: RESERVE DC-418 (2)-BOITE FOL_Matisse Henri_D127
PA
Not reproduced

Sleeping Figure in front of a Moucharaby Background (*Figure endormie sur fond moucharabieh*), 1929
Etching printed chine collé, 9 13/16 × 7 1/16 in. (25 × 17.9 cm)
Musée Matisse Nice, 63.4.85
NI
Not reproduced

Sleeping Figure in front of a Moucharaby Background (*Figure endormie sur fond moucharabieh*), 1929
Etching, 9 13/16 × 7 1/16 in. (25 × 17.9 cm)
The Pierre and Tana Matisse Foundation, New York, 1522.105007
PH
Not reproduced

Small Dancer on Red Background (*Petit Danseur sur fond rouge*), March 1938
Gouache on paper, cut and pasted, 23 ½ × 18 ¼ in. (59.7 × 46.4 cm)
Private collection, Houston, MAT,H.LSS.1
PH
143, p. 198

Study for "Song" (*Étude pour "Le Chant"*), October 1938
Charcoal on paper, 25 ¾ × 20 in. (65.4 × 50.8 cm)
The Metropolitan Museum of Art, New York: The Pierre and Maria-Gaetana Matisse Collection, 2002.456.45
PH
149, p. 205

Study for "The Song," Portrait of Hélène Mercier, née Princess Galitzine, Seated (*Étude pour "Le Chant," portrait d'Hélène Mercier, née Galitzine, assise*), October 22, 1938
Charcoal and stump on paper, 25 ¾ × 19 7/8 in. (65.5 × 50.5 cm)
Private collection: with the help of MALINGUE S.A., Paris
NI
CDA, nos. 1–4 (1939): 14
147, p. 203

Study of a Reclining Nude (*Étude de nu allongé*), 1936
Ink on paper, 15 × 20 1/8 in. (38.1 × 51.1 cm)
Hirshhorn Museum and Sculpture Garden, Smithsonian Institution, Washington, DC: Gift of the Joseph H. Hirshhorn Foundation, 1966, 66.3444
PH
CDA, nos. 3–5 (1936): 137
125, p. 181

Study for Upside-Down Nude (*Étude de nu renversé*), 1929
Etching printed chine collé, 6 5/8 × 9 ½ in. (16.8 × 24 cm)
Musée Matisse Nice, 63.4.103
NI
74, p. 122

Tahitian Landscape (*Paysage de Tahiti*), April–May 1930
Pen and India ink on wove paper, 9 7/8 × 12 ¾ in. (25.1 × 32.4 cm)
Musée Matisse Nice, 63.2.93
PA/NI
CDA, nos. 3–5 (1936): 73
89, p. 141

Tahitian Women (*Tahitiennes*), 1930
Pencil and ink on paper, 9 ½ × 13 in. (24 × 33 cm)
Musée du Quai Branly–Jacques Chirac, Paris, 75.15296.1
PA/NI
87, p. 139

Themes and Variations, 1942

Themes and Variations (A1) or Flowers, Fruit, and Cup (*Thèmes et variations [A1] ou Fleurs, fruits et tasse*), 1941
Pen and India ink on paper, 19 ½ × 24 5/8 in. (49.5 × 62.5 cm)
Private Collection, New York: Courtesy of Kasmin Gallery
PH
Not reproduced

Themes and Variations (M) (*Thèmes et variations [M]*), 1942
Musée des Beaux-Arts, Bordeaux: Gift of Henri Matisse, 1943
PH
Not reproduced

M1
Charcoal and stump on Arches paper, 17 11/16 × 20 9/16 in. (45 × 52.3 cm)
Bx M 7973

M2
India ink on Arches paper, 19 11/16 × 24 13/16 in. (50 × 63 cm)
Bx M 601

M3
Black chalk on Arches paper, 19 13/16 × 24 13/16 in. (50.4 × 63 cm)
Bx M 8016

M4
Black chalk on Arches paper, 19 13/16 × 29 ½ in. (50.3 × 75 cm)
Bx M 8015

M5
Black chalk on Arches paper, 19 11/16 × 24 13/16 in. (50 × 63 cm)
Bx M 8014

M6
Black chalk on Arches paper, 19 ¾ × 24 ¾ in. (50.1 × 62.8 cm)
Bx M 8021

M7
Black chalk on Arches paper, 19 ¾ × 24 13/16 in. (50.1 × 63 cm)
Bx M 8017

Themes and Variations (P) (*Thèmes et variations [P]*), 1942
Musée des Beaux-Arts, Lyon

P1
Charcoal on paper, 20 9/16 × 15 7/8 in. (52.3 × 40.3 cm)
1944-4
PH
158, p. 216

P2
Pen and India ink on paper, 20 11/16 × 15 15/16 in. (52.5 × 40.5 cm)
1944-5
PH
Not reproduced

P3
Pen and India ink on paper, 20 11/16 × 15 15/16 in. (52.5 × 40.5 cm)
1944-6
PH
159, p. 217

P4
Pen and India ink on paper, 20 11/16 × 15 15/16 in. (52.5 × 40.5 cm)
1944-7
PH
Not reproduced

P5
Pen and India ink on paper, 20 11/16 × 15 15/16 in. (52.5 × 40.5 cm)
1944-8
PH
Not reproduced

P6
Pen and India ink on paper, 20 ¾ × 15 15/16 in. (52.7 × 40.5 cm)
1944-9
PH
Not reproduced

Ulysses, James Joyce, 1934, published 1935

The Pierre and Tana Matisse Foundation, New York

Soft ground etchings
PH/NI

Aeolia (*Éole*), 11 5/8 × 9 1/16 in. (29.5 × 23 cm)
108, p. 157

Calypso, 11 5/8 × 9 1/16 in. (29.6 × 23 cm)
28, p. 52

Circe (*Circé*), 11 1/8 × 8 9/16 in. (28.3 × 21.8 cm)
30, p. 52

Ithaca (*Ithaque*), 11 ¼ × 8 ¾ in. (28.5 × 22.3 cm)
107, p. 156

Nausicaa, 11 ½ × 9 in. (29.2 × 22.9 cm)
106, p. 155

Polyphemus (*Polyphème*), 11 3/16 × 8 7/8 in. (28.4 × 22.5 cm)
32, p. 53

Polyphemus (*Polyphème*)
Charcoal on paper, 12 5/8 × 9 5/8 in. (32.1 × 24.4 cm)
The William Rubin Collection
PH
105, p. 154

Bibliothèque Nationale de France, Paris
PA
Not reproduced

Aeolia (*Éole*), 2nd plate, 1935
Soft ground etching, 11 3/8 × 8 7/8 in. (28.8 × 22.5 cm)
RESERVE DC-418 (7)-BOITE FOL_ Matisse Henri_D238

Battle of Women (Calypso) (*Bataille de femmes [Calypso]*), 1st plate, 1935
Soft ground etching, trial proof on wove paper with signature stamp, 11 7/16 × 8 ⅞ in. (29 × 22.4 cm)
RESERVE DC-418 (7)-BOITE FOL_ Matisse Henri_D235

Circe (*Circé*), 1934
Soft ground etching, 11 ⅛ × 10 9/16 in. (28.3 × 21.8 cm), RESERVE DC-418 (7)-BOITE FOL_Matisse Henri_ D237

Nausicaa, 4th plate, 1935
Soft ground etching, trial proof on Arches wove paper signed in pencil, 11 ⅝ × 9 1/16 in. (28.1 × 22.1 cm), RESERVE DC-418 (7)-BOITE FOL_ Matisse Henri_D236

Polyphemus (*Polyphème*), 3rd plate, 1935
Soft ground etching, 11 ⅜ × 8 ⅞ in. (28.8 × 22.5 cm)
RESERVE DC-418 (7)-BOITE FOL_ Matisse Henri_D239

Study for "Aeolia" (*Étude pour "Éole"*), 1935
Charcoal and *sanguine*, 15 ⅞ × 10 5/16 in. (40.3 × 26.2 cm)
RES B 16a(8) Boite Ecu_DESSINS FRANCAIS du XX SIECLE_Matisse

Study for "Nausicaa" (*Étude pour "Nausicaa"*), 1934
Sanguine, 12 ¾ × 9 ⅝ in. (32.4 × 24.5 cm)
RES B 16a(8) Boite Ecu_DESSINS FRANCAIS du XX SIECLE _Matisse

Study for "Polyphemus" (*Étude pour "Polyphème"*), c. 1934
Red and blue crayon on tracing paper, 11 ⅝ × 9 1/16 in. (29.5 × 23.5 cm)
RES B 16a(8) Boite Ecu_DESSINS FRANCAIS du XX SIECLE_Matisse Planche XIII

Two Dancers (Deux Danseurs), 1937–38
Gouache on paper, cut and pasted, mounted on board, 24 13/16 × 25 ⅜ in. (63 × 64.5 cm)
Private collection
PH
Not reproduced

Upside-Down Nude and Foliage (*Nu renversé et feuillage*), February 1936
Charcoal and stump on Arches watermarked laid paper, 12 15/16 × 19 ¾ in. (32.9 × 50.2 cm)
Musée Matisse Nice, 63.2.25
PH/PA/NI
130, p. 184

War Drum (*Tambour de guerre*), 1930
India ink on sketchbook paper, 9 ⅞ × 25 ⅝ in. (25 × 65 cm) (recto)
Musée du Quai Branly–Jacques Chirac, Paris, 75.15296.3
PA/NI
88, p. 140

Woman in Armchair (*Femme dans un fauteuil*), 1936
Charcoal on paper, 21 × 16 in. (53.3 × 40.6 cm)
Saint Louis Art Museum, 9:1953
PH
135, p. 190

Woman with a Fishbowl (*Visage de jeune femme et bocal aux trois poissons*), 1929
Etching printed chine collé, 3 ⅝ × 4 ¾ in. (9.2 × 12.1 cm)
The Metropolitan Museum of Art, New York: Purchase, Reba and Dave Williams Gift, 1999.267.2
PH
Not reproduced

Woman with Checked Collar (*Femme à la colerette à carreaux*), 1938
Ink on paper, 14 ¾ × 11 in. (37.5 × 28 cm)
The Pierre and Tana Matisse Foundation, New York, 301.203014
PH
137, p. 192

Woman with Collar (*Femme au col*), December 8, 1935
Charcoal on paper, 23 13/16 × 19 ⅞ in. (60.5 × 50.5 cm)
Courtesy Galerie de l'Institut, Paris
NI
121, p. 176

Woman with Tiered Collar (*Femme au col à volants*), 1938
Ink on paper, 14 15/16 × 11 in. (38 × 28 cm)
The Pierre and Tana Matisse Foundation, New York, 365.203159
PA/NI
Not reproduced

WORKS BY PABLO PICASSO (1881–1973)

SCULPTURES

Bather (*Baigneuse*), unique cast, 1931
Bronze, 27 9/16 × 15 ⅞ × 12 ⅜ in. (70 × 40.2 × 31.5 cm)
Musée National Picasso–Paris MP 289
PA
Not reproduced

Head of a Woman (*Tête de femme*), 1931
Bronze, 33 ⅞ × 12 ⅝ × 19 ⅛ in. (86 × 32 × 48.5 cm)
Musée National Picasso–Paris, MP300
PA
22, p. 48

Metamorphosis II (*Métamorphose II*), 1928
Plaster, 9 ½ × 7 1/16 × 4 ⅜ in. (24 × 18 × 11 cm)
Musée National Picasso–Paris, MP262
PA
24, p. 49

WORKS ON PAPER

***Metamorphoses* by Ovid**

The Combat of Perseus and Phineus for Andromeda (*Combat pour Andromède entre Persée et Phinée*), April 1930
Etching, 12 ¾ × 9 13/16 in. (32.3 × 25 cm)
Musée National Picasso–Paris, MP2126
PA
31, p. 53

Eurydice Stung by a Serpent (*Eurydice piquée par un serpent*), 2nd plate, October 11, 1930
Etching. Second state. Printed in bister on wove paper watermarked "BFK RIVES" with remarques in black by Fort, marked "X," 13 ¼ × 10 ¼ in. (33.7 × 26 cm)
Musée National Picasso–Paris: Acceptance in lieu Pablo Picasso 1979, MP 2137
NI
29, p. 52

Hercules Kills the Centaur Nessus (*Hercule tue le centaure Nessus*), September 20, 1930
Etching. Second state. Printed in bister on wove paper watermarked "BFK RIVES," before the acierage of the plate and bevels, with remarques in black by Fort, marked "IX," 13 ⅜ × 10 ¼ in. (33.9 × 25.9 cm)
Musée National Picasso–Paris: Acceptance in lieu Pablo Picasso 1979, MP2135
PA/NI
Not reproduced

Nude Crowned with Flowers Sitting Cross-Legged (*Femme nue couronnée de fleurs assise en tailleur*), September 16, 1930
Etching printed on Rives wove paper, on varnish by Fort, 15 ¼ × 11 ⅞ in. (38.8 × 30.2 cm)
Musée National Picasso–Paris: Acceptance in lieu Pablo Picasso 1979, MP2169
PA/NI
Not reproduced

Seated Nude Crowned with Flowers (*Femme nue assise couronnée de fleurs*), October 19, 1929
Etching printed by Fort on Simili Japon paper, 17 ¾ × 11 in. (45.2 × 27.8 cm)
Musée National Picasso–Paris: Acceptance in lieu Pablo Picasso 1979, MP2116
PA
Not reproduced

Seated Nude Crowned with Flowers and Holding a Flower Crown (*Femme nue couronnée de fleurs tenant une couronne à la main*), September 16, 1930
Etching printed on Rives wove paper, printed on varnish by Fort, 12 ⅜ × 8 ¾ in. (42.1 × 32.8 cm)
Musée National Picasso–Paris: Acceptance in lieu Pablo Picasso 1979, MP2168
NI
Not reproduced

Seated Nude Crowned with Flowers, Legs Crossed (*Femme nue assise, couronnée de fleurs, aux jambes croisées*), September 16, 1930
Etching. Trial proof by Lacourière in 1937, on Montva laid paper watermarked "M/FRANCE," following the acierage of the plate and bevels, marked "Bon à tirer" and "I," 17 ¾ × 11 in. (45.2 × 27.8 cm)
Musée National Picasso–Paris: Acceptance in lieu Roger and Madeline Lacourière 1982, MP1982-60
PA
Not reproduced

Seated Nude Crowned with Flowers, Legs Crossed (*Femme nue couronnée de fleurs, aux jambes croisées*), September 16, 1930
Etching printed by Fort, on Rives wove paper, before the acierage of the plate and bevels, marked "I" and "M," 15 ⅛ × 10 ⅝ in. (38.4 × 27 cm)
Musée National Picasso–Paris: Acceptance in lieu Pablo Picasso 1979, MP2467
NI
Not reproduced

Struggle between Tereus and His Sister-in-Law Philomela (*Lutte entre Térée et sa belle-soeur Philomèle*), 1st plate, October 18, 1930
Etching printed on "BFK RIVES" watermarked wove paper, in bister with remarques by Fort, marked "II," 13 ⅜ × 10 ¼ in. (33.9 × 25.9 cm)
Musée National Picasso–Paris: Acceptance in lieu Pablo Picasso 1979, MP2155
PA
Not reproduced

Struggle between Tereus and His Sister-in-Law Philomela (*Lutte entre Térée et sa belle-sœur Philomèle*), 2nd plate, October 18, 1930
Etching printed in bister on Rives wove paper, with remarques by Fort, marked "II," 13 ⅜ × 10 ¼ in. (33.9 × 25.9 cm)
Musée National Picasso–Paris: Acceptance in lieu Pablo Picasso 1979, MP2156
NI
27, p. 52

Struggle between Tereus and His Sister-in-Law Philomela (*Lutte entre Térée et sa belle-sœur Philomèle*), 3rd plate, October 18, 1930
Etching. First state. Printed in black by Fort on Arches wove paper, marked "Bon à tirer" in red ink and "VI" in pencil, signed, 12 ¾ × 8 ¾ in. (31.4 × 22.2 cm)
Musée National Picasso–Paris: Acceptance in lieu Pablo Picasso 1979, MP2128
NI
Not reproduced

Struggle between Tereus and His Sister-in-Law Philomela (*Lutte entre Térée et sa belle-soeur Philomèle*), 3rd plate, October 18, 1930
Etching. Second state. Trial proof on Rives "M" watermarked wove paper, printed in bister with remarques in black by Fort, 12 ¾ × 10 in. (32.5 × 25.3 cm)
Musée National Picasso–Paris: Acceptance in lieu Pablo Picasso 1979, MP2129
PA
Not reproduced

HENRI LAURENS (1885–1954)

SCULPTURE

Small Seated Woman (*La Petite Femme assise*), 1932
Grogged earthenware, 12 13/16 × 9 ⅝ × 6 7/16 in. (32.5 × 24.4 × 16.4 cm)
Musée Matisse Nice, 63.2.140
NI
Not reproduced

BOOKS

Dessins: Thèmes et variations, précédés de "Matisse-en-France" par Aragon ([Paris]: Martin Fabiani, 1943)
Volume with letterpress text, illustrated with 3 lithograph ornaments, 158 collotype reproductions of drawings and a linocut frontispiece, 13 9/16 × 10 ⅜ in. (34.5 × 26.4 cm)
The Morgan Library & Museum, New York: Gift of Frances and Michael Baylson, 2010
PH
Not reproduced

Dessins: Thèmes et variations, précédés de "Matisse-en-France" par Aragon ([Paris]: Martin Fabiani, 1943)
Volume with letterpress text, illustrated with 3 lithograph ornaments, 158 collotype reproductions of drawings and a linocut frontispiece, 13 9/16 × 10 ⅜ in. (34.5 × 26.4 cm)
Baltimore Museum of Art: E. Kirkbride Miller Art Reference Library, BMA 2010.41
PH
Not reproduced

Florilège des Amours de Ronsard (Paris: Albert Skira, 1948)
Unbound book with letterpress in black, 127 lithographs in sanguine and one lithograph in black on cream wove paper, tucked in white paperboard cover with purple velvet spine and slipcase with lithograph in dark blue on white wove paper.
The Art Institute of Chicago: Gift of Dorothy Braude Edinburg in memory of Bessie Kisloff Braude, Esq., 2014.498
PH
Not reproduced

Florilège des Amours de Ronsard par Henri Matisse (Paris: Albert Skira, 1948)
Unbound book with letterpress in black, 127 lithographs in sanguine and one lithograph in black on cream wove paper, tucked in white paperboard cover with purple velvet spine and slipcase with lithograph in dark blue on white wove paper
The Morgan Library & Museum, New York: Gift of Frances and Michael Baylson, 2010
PH
Not reproduced

Stéphane Mallarmé (1842–1898), *Poésies. Eaux-fortes originales de Henri Matisse* (Lausanne: Albert Skira et Cie, 1932)
Unbound volume with letterpress text, illustrated with 29 etchings on Japon impériale, and containing a suite of prints with remarques on *papier de Chine*
Philadelphia Museum of Art: Gift of Mrs. W. Averell Harriman, 1952, 1952-87-1a--cc
PH
Not reproduced

Stéphane Mallarmé (1842–1898), *Poésies. Eaux-fortes originales de Henri Matisse* (Lausanne: Albert Skira et Cie, 1932)
Unbound volume with letterpress text, illustrated with 29 etchings on Japon imp.riale, and containing a suite of prints with remarques on *papier de Chine*
LaM, Lille Métropole Musée d'Art Moderne, d'Art Contemporain et d'Art Brut, Villeneuve-d'Ascq, 2003.9.31
PA
Not reproduced

Ulysses by James Joyce; with an introduction by Stuart Gilbert; and illustrations by Henri Matisse (New York: Limited Editions Club, 1935)
Volume with letterpress text, illustrated with 6 soft ground etchings and 20 photogravure reproductions of preliminary drawings
University of Pennsylvania Libraries, Philadelphia: Kislak Center for Special Collections, Rare Books and Manuscripts
PH
Not reproduced

Ulysses by James Joyce; with an introduction by Stuart Gilbert; and illustrations by Henri Matisse (New York: Limited Editions Club, 1935)
Volume with letterpress text, illustrated with 6 Soft ground etchings and 20 photogravure reproductions of preliminary drawings
Temple University Libraries, Philadelphia: Special Collections Research Center
PH
Not reproduced

PERIODICALS

The page numbers in this section refer to those in *Cahiers d'art* compilation volumes; they are different from the page numbers in individual issues.

CAHIERS D'ART

Éditions Cahiers d'Art, Paris

1926, no. 1: Christian Zervos, "Lithographies de Henri Matisse" (Lithographs by Henri Matisse), 7–9, five illustrations
55, p. 93; 56 a–c, p. 94

1926, no. 7: Georges Duthuit, "Œuvres récentes de Henri-Matisse" (Recent works by Henri Matisse), 153–61, thirteen illustrations

1926, no. 9: Sylvain Bonmariage, "Henri Matisse et la peinture pure" (Henri Matisse and pure painting), 239–41, two illustrations
69, p. 114

1927, nos. 7–8: Christian Zervos, "L'art nègre" (African art), 229–46; Georges Salles, "Réflexions sur l'art nègre" (Thoughts on African art), 247–49; G. J. Gros, "Henri Matisse," 268–74, ten illustrations
57, p. 95

1928, no. 4: Christian Zervos, "Idéalisme et naturalisme dans la peinture moderne. – IV: Henri Matisse" (Idealism and naturalism in modern painting), 158–63, six illustrations
58 b, p. 97

1929, no. 5: Georges Duthuit, "Le fauvisme (I)," 177–92, five illustrations

1929, no. 6: Georges Duthuit, "Le fauvisme (II)," 258–68, three illustrations

1929, no. 7: É. Tériade, "L'actualité de Matisse" (Matisse today), 285–98, nineteen illustrations

1929, no. 10: Georges Duthuit, "Le fauvisme," 429–35, four illustrations

1930, no. 3: Christian Zervos, "De l'importance de l'objet dans la peinture aujourd'hui" (On the object's importance in today's painting), 113–20, six illustrations

1931, no. 1: É. Tériade, "Jeunesse!" (Youth), 10–25, ten illustrations

1931, nos. 5–6: "Henri Matisse" special issue, ninety-seven illustrations
60, p. 99; 61 a–d, pp. 100–101

1935, nos. 1–4: Christian Zervos, "Enquête" (Investigation), 5–18, eighteen illustrations
62 a, p. 102

1936, nos. 3–5: "Dessins de Matisse" (Drawings by Matisse) special issue: Christian Zervos, "Automatisme et espace illusoire" (Automatism and illusory space), 69–75; Tristan Tzara, "À Henri-Matisse," 76, thirty-eight illustrations
39, 40, p. 64; 63 a, p. 103

1939, nos. 1–4: Christian Zervos, "Dessins récents de Henri-Matisse" (Recent drawings by Henri-Matisse), 5–24, sixteen illustrations
64 b–d, p. 107

1939, nos. 5–10: Christian Zervos, "2 décorations de Henri-Matisse: Réflexions sur l'art mural" (2 decorations by Henri-Matisse: Thoughts on mural art), 165–78, seventeen illustrations

PHOTOGRAPHS

Unknown photographer, *Paris "Dance" Mural, Early State (Décoration murale "La Danse" de Paris, état primaire)*, October–December 1931
Photograph, 4 ¾ × 15 ½ in. (12.1 × 39.4 cm)
Photograph Collection, Barnes Foundation Archives, Philadelphia
PH
Not reproduced

Unknown photographer, *Paris "Dance" Mural, Early State (Décoration murale "La Danse" de Paris, état primaire)*, October–December 1931
Photograph, 14 ¼ × 30 ½ in. (36.2 × 77.5 cm)
Photograph Collection, Barnes Foundation Archives, Philadelphia
PH
49 a, b, p. 85

Unknown photographer, *Paris "Dance" Mural, Early State (Décoration murale "La Danse" de Paris, état primaire)*, March 8, 1932
Photograph, 4 ¾ × 16 ½ in. (12.1 × 41.9 cm)
Photograph Collection, Barnes Foundation Archives, Philadelphia
PH
Not reproduced

Unknown photographer, *Merion "Dance" Mural, State X*, November 3, 1932
Photograph, 4 ¾ × 17 ½ in. (12.1 × 44.5 cm)
Photograph Collection, Barnes Foundation Archives, Philadelphia
PH
Not reproduced

Unknown photographer, *Merion "Dance" Mural, State XVII*, December 5, 1932
Photograph, 4 ¾ × 17 ½ in. (12.1 × 44.5 cm)
Photograph Collection, Barnes Foundation Archives, Philadelphia
PH
50, p. 85

FILMS

Ann Barzel (1905–2007), *Selections from the Ballets-Russes de Monte Carlo Production of "Rouge et noir" ("Red and Black") at the Auditorium Theater, Chicago*, 1939
Film
The Newberry Library, Chicago: Courtesy of Ann Barzel Film Archive
PH
Not reproduced

Agnes Mitchell Sattler (1877–1956), *Henri Matisse Working on "The Dance" in the Rue Désiré-Niel Studio*, April 16, 1932
Film, 80 seconds
Archives Henri Matisse, Issy-les-Moulineaux
PH/PA/NI
Not reproduced

Friedrich Wilhelm Murnau (1888–1931), Robert Flaherty (1884–1951), *Tabu: A Story of the South Seas*, 1929
Silent film, 82 minutes
Friedrich-Wilhelm-Murnau-Stiftung, Wiesbaden
PA/NI
Not reproduced

ITEMS FROM HENRI MATISSE'S COLLECTION

Bwoom mask, Kuba (Democratic Republic of the Congo), late 19th century–early 20th century
Plant material, textile fibers, cowrie shells, beads, seed husks, copper and ferrous metal plates, 12 ⅝ × 14 ⅝ × 9 ¼ in. (32 × 37 × 23.5 cm)
Musée Matisse Nice, 63.2.137
PA/NI
Not reproduced

Garment fragment, Kuba (Democratic Republic of the Congo), late 19th century–early 20th century
Woven raffia fabric, embroidered with cut threads, 10 13/16 × 29 ⅛ in. (27.5 × 74 cm)
Musée Matisse Nice, 63.2.189
PA/NI
Not reproduced

Offering bowl on a lotus flower-shaped stand, Chinese, Song period (960–1279)
Bronze, 5 5/16 × 6 ⅛ in. (13.5 × 15.5 cm)
Musée Matisse Nice, 63.2.178
PA/NI
Not reproduced

Sculpture, Malagan, New Ireland, 20th century
Sculpted hardwood, painted decoration, vegetable fiber, shells, 51 9/16 × 9 7/16 × 8 11/16 in. (131 × 24 × 22 cm) without base
Musée Matisse Nice, 63.2.136
NI
Not reproduced

Shell necklace, Tahitian
Yellow and white shells, 9 7/16 × 8 11/16 × 13/16 in. (24 × 22 × 2.1 cm)
Musée Matisse Nice, 63.2.161
NI
Not reproduced

Shell necklace, Tasmanian
Shells in three gathered strands, 28 15/16 in. (73.5 cm)
Musée Matisse Nice, 63.2.168
NI
Not reproduced

Stool, 19th century
Hardwood, sculpted decoration, 24 7/16 × 19 ⅛ × 10 13/16 in. (62 × 48.6 × 27.5 cm)
Musée Matisse Nice, 63.2.124
NI
Not reproduced

Woman's skirt depicted in *Woman in Blue* made and modeled by Lydia Delectorskaya, 1937
Silk plain weave, cotton lace edging, 51 in. (length), 29 in. (waist)
Philadelphia Museum of Art: Gift of Mrs. Barbara Duthuit, 2013-15-1
PH
Not reproduced

SELECT BIBLIOGRAPHY

PRINCIPAL WORKS (1925–39)

Barnes, Albert C., and Violette de Mazia. *The Art of Henri-Matisse*. New York: Charles Scribner's Sons, 1933.

Bertram, Anthony. *Henri Matisse*. World's Masters 10. London: Galerie Paul Guillaume and The Studio, 1930.

Cassou, Jean. *Matisse*. Paris: Braun, 1939.

Courthion, Pierre. *Henri-Matisse*. Paris: Rieder, 1934.

Eglinton, Guy. "L'histoire d'un fauve." In *Reaching for Art*, 37–66. London: Morley & Mitchell; Boston: May, 1931.

Einstein, Carl. "Henri Matisse." In *Die Kunst des 20. Jahrhunderts*, 24–34. Berlin: Propyläen-Verlag, 1926.

Escholier, Raymond. *Henri Matisse*. Paris: Floury, 1937.

Fels, Florent. *Henri-Matisse*. Paris: Chroniques du Jour, 1929.

Fry, Roger. *Henri-Matisse*. Paris: Chroniques du Jour; London: A. Zwemmer; New York: E. Weyhe, 1930.

———. *Henri-Matisse*. London: A. Zwemmer; New York: E. Weyhe, 1935.

George, Waldemar. *Dessins de Henri-Matisse*. Paris: Quatre Chemins, 1925.

Guenne, Jacques. "Henri Matisse." In *Portraits d'artistes*. Paris: Michel Seheur, 1927.

Hoppe, Ragnar. "På visit hos Matisse [My visit with Matisse]." In *Städer och Konstnärer: Resebrev och Essäer om Konst*, 200–225. Stockholm: Albert Bonniers Förlag, 1931.

Huddleston, Sisley. *Back to Montparnasse*. London: G. Harrap, 1931.

Jedlicka, Gotthard. *Henri-Matisse*. Paris: Chroniques du Jour, 1930.

———. "Begegnungen mit Matisse." In *Begegnungen: Künstlernovellen*, 102–26. Basel: Benno Schwabe, 1933.

Kawashima, Riichiro. *Matisse*. Tokyo: Atelier-Sha, 1936.

Kunstler, Charles, and Adolphe Basler. *La Peinture indépendante en France*. Vol. 2, *De Matisse à Segonzac*. Paris: G. Crès, 1929.

McBride, Henry. *Matisse*. New York: Alfred A. Knopf, 1930.

Moholy-Nagy, Laszlo. *The New Vision: Fundamentals of Design, Painting, Sculpture, Architecture*. London: Faber & Faber, 1939.

Pach, Walter. *Queer Thing, Painting: Forty Years in the World of Art*. New York: Harper & Brothers, 1938.

Palmer, Mildred. "A Note on Henri Matisse." In *Henri Matisse*. The Arts: Portfolio Series. New York: Arts Publishing, 1929.

Romm, Alexander. *Henri-Matisse*. Translated by Chen I-Wan. Moscow: Ogiz-Isogiz, 1937 (first published 1935).

Scheiwiller, Giovanni. *Henri Matisse*. Milan: Ulrico Hoepli, 1947 (first published 1930).

Svrček, J. B. *Henri Matisse*. Prague: Melantrich, 1937.

Zervos, Christian. *Histoire de l'art contemporain*. Paris: Cahiers d'Art, 1938.

GENERAL WORKS

Bois, Yve-Alain. *Matisse and Picasso*. Paris: Flammarion, 1999.

———, ed. *Matisse in the Barnes Foundation*. Philadelphia: Barnes Foundation; London: Thames & Hudson, 2015.

Butler, Karen K. "Henri Matisse according to Dr. Barnes." In *Matisse in the Barnes Foundation*, edited by Yve-Alain Bois, 170–99. Philadelphia: Barnes Foundation; London: Thames & Hudson, 2015.

Cauman, John. "Matisse and America (1905–1933)." PhD diss., City University of New York, 2000.

Derouet, Christian, ed. *"Cahiers d'art": Musée Zervos à Vézelay*. Paris: Hazan, 2006.

———, ed. *Zervos et "Cahiers d'art."* Paris: Centre Pompidou, 2011.

Flam, Jack, ed. *Henri Matisse (1869–1954)*. Cologne: Könemann, 1994.

———, ed. *Matisse on Art*. Berkeley: University of California Press, 2015 (first published 1995).

———. *Matisse in the Cone Collection: The Poetics of Vision*. Baltimore: Baltimore Museum of Art, 2001.

Grammont, Claudine. "Matisse in the Laboratory of Dr. Barnes: How and Why Barnes Collected Matisse." In *Matisse in the Barnes Foundation*, edited by Yve-Alain Bois, 28–60. Philadelphia: Barnes Foundation; London: Thames & Hudson, 2015.

———, ed. *Tout Matisse*. Paris: Robert Laffont, "Bouquins" coll., 2018.

Jaume Adrover, Magdalena. "Sobre el proceso. 'La Verdure' (1935–1943). Un cuadro de Henri Matisse." PhD diss., University of Barcelona, 2013.

Klein, John. "Matisse après Tahiti: La maturation d'une expérience exotique." In *Matisse et l'Océanie: Le voyage à Tahiti*, edited by Dominique Szymusiak, 177–220. Exh. cat. Le Cateau-Cambrésis: Musée Matisse, 1998.

———. *Matisse and Decoration*. New Haven: Yale University Press, 2018.

Matisse, Henri. *Écrits et propos sur l'art*. Edited by Dominique Fourcade. Paris: Hermann, 2014 (first published 1972).

Schneider, Pierre. *Henri Matisse*. Paris: Flammarion, 2020 (first published 1992).

Spurling, Hilary. *Matisse the Master: A Life of Henri Matisse; The Conquest of Colour, 1909–1954*. London: Hamish Hamilton; New York: Alfred A. Knopf, 2005.

PERIODICALS (1925–41)

1925

Allard, Roger. "Henri Matisse." *L'Art vivant*, no. 4 (February 15, 1925): 1–3.

Cortissoz, Royal. "A Matisse Exhibition." *New York Times*, March 22, 1925.

Guenne, Jacques. "Entretien avec Henri Matisse." *L'Art vivant*, no. 18 (September 15, 1925): 1–6.

1926

Charensol, Georges. "Le Salon des Tuileries." *L'Amour de l'art*, no. 37 (June 6, 1926): 204–12.

1927

Charensol, Georges. "Le Salon des Tuileries." *L'Art vivant*, no. 57 (May 1, 1927): 333–38.

George, Waldemar. "Le mouvement fauve." *L'Art vivant*, no. 54 (March 15, 1927): 208.

Gillet, Louis. "Le Salon d'automne." *Le Gaulois*, November 3, 1927, 5.

Guillaume, Paul. "La vie intense de la fondation Barnes." *Les Arts à Paris*, no. 13 (May 1, 1927): 19.

Jewell, Edward Alden. "Matisse Treads the High Road to Fame." *New York Times*, November 17, 1927.

Le Triangle Rouge. "La presse devant deux tableaux de Matisse." *Les Arts à Paris*, no. 13 (May 1, 1927): 19–22.

Roger-Marx, Claude. "Le Salon d'automne." *Art et décoration* 52 (October 1927): 161–80.

Watson, Forbes. "Henri Matisse." *Arts* 11 (January 1927): 29–40.

1928

Guenne, Jacques. "Le Salon d'automne." *L'Art vivant*, no. 69 (November 5, 1928): 869, 884.

1929

Fels, Florent. "L'exemple de Matisse." *L'Art vivant*, no. 116 (October 15, 1929): 792–95.

Manson, J. B. "Mr. Frank Stoop's Modern Pictures." *Apollo* 10, no. 57 (September 1929): 126–33.

Neugass, Fritz. "Henri-Matisse (1869–1929)." *Deutsche Kunst und Dekoration* 32, no. 6 (March 1929): 373–80; translated as "Henri Matisse pour son soixantième anniversaire" in *Cahiers de Belgique*, no. 3 (March 1930): 100.

———. "Henri Matisse." *Die Kunst für alle*, no. 61 (October 1, 1929): 12–21; translated in *L'Art et les artistes* 20, no. 106 (April 1930): 235–40.

Scheffler, Karl. "Der sechzigjährige Henri Matisse in der Galerie Thannhauser, Berlin." *Kunst und Künstler*, no. 28 (1929–30): 287–90.

Tériade, Émile. "Visite à Henri Matisse." *L'Intransigeant*, January 14 and 22, 1929.

1930

Gauthier, Maximilien. "Notice bibliographique des peintres figurant à l'exposition de L'Art vivant. Henri Matisse." *L'Art vivant*, no. 6 (May 15, 1930): 409.

George, Waldemar. "La collection Fukushima." *La Renaissance de l'art français* 13, no. 3 (March 1930): 102–8.

Huyghe, René. "Matisse et la couleur." *Formes*, no. 1 (January 1930): 5–10.

Levinson, André. "Les soixante ans de Henri Matisse." *L'Art vivant*, no. 121 (January 1, 1930): 24–28.

Matisse, Henri. "Interview on Rembrandt and Modern Art." *Minneapolis Institute of Art Bulletin*, no. 19 (March 29, 1930): 62.

———. "Study Art in America." *Literary Digest* 107, no. 3 (October 18, 1930): 21.

"Matisse Is Coming." *Art Digest* 4, no. 8 (January 15, 1930): 18.

Tériade, Émile. "Henri Matisse en Amérique." *L'Intransigeant*, October 20 and 27, 1930.

Terkel-Deri, Flora. "Exhibition, Thannhauser Galerie." *Art News* 28 (March 8, 1930): 6.

Watson, Forbes. "The Carnegie International." *Arts*, no. 17 (November 1930): 65–72, and no. 18 (December 1930): 167–71.

1931

Courthion, Pierre. "Rencontre avec Matisse." *Les Nouvelles littéraires*, June 27, 1931, 1.

Fierens, Paul. "For and against Henri Matisse." *Les Chroniques du jour*, no. 9 (April 1931): 275–76.

Flint, Ralph. "Interview on the Eve of Sailing." *Art News* 29 (January 3, 1931): 3.

George, Waldemar. "Psychanalyse de Matisse. Lettre à Raymond Cogniat." *Les Chroniques du jour*, no. 9 (April 1931): 6–8.

Nirdlinger, Virginia. "The Matisse Way: Forty Years in the Evolution of an Individualist." *Parnassus* 3, no. 7 (November 1931): 4–6, 37.

Rey, Robert. "Souvenirs d'un étudiant." *Les Chroniques du jour*, no. 9 (April 1931): 4–5.

Rouault, Georges. "Évocations." *Les Chroniques du jour*, no. 9 (April 1931): 8–9.

Tériade, Émile. "Autour d'une rétrospective, Henri Matisse parle . . ." *L'Intransigeant*, June 16, 1931.

1932

Heilmaier, Hans. "Bei Henri Matisse." *Die Kunst für alle* 47, no. 7 (April 1932): 206–9.

Jedlicka, Gotthard. "Persons and Personages: Meeting Matisse." *Living Age*, February 1932, 341.

Jewell, Edward Alden. "Mr. and Mrs. S.C. Clark Open Benefit Exhibition of Their Collection of Matisse Canvases." *New York Times*, November 16, 1932.

Schapiro, Meyer. "Matisse and Impressionism." *Androcles* 1, no. 1 (February 1932): 21–36.

Tériade, Émile. "Édouard Manet vu par Henri Matisse." *L'Intransigeant*, January 25, 1932.

1933

Bell, Clive. "Matisse and Picasso." *Europa*, no. 88 (May–June 1933): 294–95.

Cassou, Jean. "L'histoire de l'art contemporain. Henri Matisse." *L'Amour de l'art* 14, no. 5 (May 1933): 108–10.

Charlot, Jean. "Pinning Butterflies." *Creative Art* 12 (May 1933): 354–59.

Lhote, André. "Dessins de Matisse (galerie Pierre Colle)." *La Nouvelle Revue française*, no. 235 (April 1, 1933): 693–95.

Matisse, Henri. "Matisse Speaks." *Art News* 31, no. 36 (June 3, 1933): 8.

———. "Suite de dessins préparatoires pour 'L'après-midi d'un faune' de Stéphane Mallarmé." *Minotaure* 1, no. 1 (1933): 72.

Morse, C. R. "Matisse's Palette." *Art Digest*, no. 7 (February 1933): 26.

Peyrollaz, Lys. "Position de Matisse dans la peinture d'aujourd'hui." *La Revue française*, January 25, 1933, 102–11.

Raynal, Maurice. "Mallarmé continué par Henri Matisse." *L'Intransigeant*, June 6, 1933.

Tériade, Émile. "Émancipation de la peinture." *Minotaure* 1, nos. 3–4 (1933): 9–20.

1934

Dudley, Dorothy. "Notes on Painting: The Matisse Fresco in Merion, Pennsylvania." *Hound and Horn* 7, no. 2 (January–March 1934): 298–303.

Lipman, Jean H. "Matisse Paintings in the Stephen C. Clark Collection." *Art in America* 22, no. 4 (October 1934): 134–44.

Morsell, Mary. "Finely Arranged Matisse Exhibit Now on Display." *Art News* 32, no. 17 (January 27, 1934): 3–4.

1935

Matisse, Henri. "Testimony against Gertrude Stein." *Transition*, no. 23, supplement, pamphlet no. 1 (February 1935): 3.

———. "On Modernism and Tradition." *Studio* 9, no. 50 (May 1935).

1936

Bazin, Germain. "Œuvres récentes de Matisse, galerie Paul Rosenberg." *L'Amour de l'art*, no. 6 (June 1936): 228–29.

Guenne, Jacques. "Les expositions Matisse–Gromaire." *L'Art vivant*, no. 204 (July 1936): 158.

Morley, G. L. M. "Museum Events: Exhibition San Francisco Museum of Art." *Parnassus* 8, no. 3 (March 1936): 17.

Pach, Walter. "The Outlook for Modern Art." *Parnassus* 8, no. 4 (April 1936): 5–8 and 43.

Roger-Marx, Claude. "Œuvres récentes d'Henri Matisse." *Le Jour*, May 9, 1936.

Tériade, Émile. "Constance d u fauvisme." *Minotaure* 2, no. 9 (October 15, 1936): 1–9.

1937

Brassaï. "Henri Matisse et ses oiseaux dans son atelier à Paris." *Verve*, no. 1, December 1937, 13–15.

Cantatore, Domenico. "Vita di artisti a Parigi. Incontro con Matisse." *L'Ambrosiano*, October 19, 1937.

Gillet, Louis. "L'atelier de Gustave Moreau.

M. Henri Matisse." *Revue des Deux Mondes*, no. 107 (July 15, 1937): 330–37.

Huppert, Janine. "Montherlant vu par Matisse." *Beaux-Arts*, no. 243 (August 27, 1937): 1.

Matisse, Henri. "Divagations." *Verve* 1, no. 1, December 1937, 80–84.

1938

Fierens, Paul. "Matisse e il Fauvismo." *Emporium* 88 (October 1938): 195–208.

Matisse, Henri. *Verve*, no. 3, June 1938 (ill.).

———. *Verve*, no. 4, November 1938 (ill.).

Montherlant, Henri de. "En écoutant Matisse." *L'Art et les artistes* 33, no. 189 (July 1938): 336–39.

1939

Besson, George. "Arrivée de Matisse à Nice. Matisse et quelques personnages." *Le Point*, no. 21 (July 1939): 39–44.

"Evolution of a Painting." *Magazine of Art* 32, no. 7 (July 1939): 414–15.

Matisse, Henri. "Notes d'un peintre sur son dessin." *Le Point*, no. 21 (July 1939): 8–14.

Puy, Jean. "Souvenirs." *Le Point*, no. 21 (July 1939): 16–37.

CAHIERS D'ART (1926–54)

Italicized items indicate issues of Cahiers d'art *that include reproductions of works by Matisse that are not in themselves the subject of an article.*

1926

Bonmariage, Sylvain. "Henri Matisse et la peinture pure." No. 9 (1926): 239–41.

Duthuit, Georges. "Œuvres récentes de Henri-Matisse." No. 7 (1926): 153–61.

Matisse, Henri. No. 6 (1926): 128.

Tériade, Émile. "Propos sur le salon des Tuileries." No. 5 (1926): 109–13.

Zervos, Christian. "Lithographies de Henri Matisse." No. 1 (1926): 7–9.

1927

"Exposition de Glasgow." *Feuilles volantes*, supplement. Nos. 3–4 (1927): 7.

Gros, Gabriel-Joseph. "Henri Matisse." Nos. 7–8 (1927): 268–74.

Matisse, Henri. No. 1 (1927): 28.

Matisse, Henri. No. 3 (1927): 95.

Matisse, Henri. Nos. 7–8 (1927): 257, 258, 279.

Matisse, Henri. Feuilles volantes, supplement. No. 10 (1927): 7.

Zervos, Christian. "Entretien avec Monsieur Jos. Hessel." *Feuilles volantes*, supplement. Nos. 4–5 (1927): 189–90.

———. "Entretien avec M. Léonce Rosenberg." *Feuilles volantes*, supplement. No. 6 (1927): 29–30.

———. "L'art nègre." Nos. 7–8 (1927): 229–47.

———. "Entretien avec Alfred Flechtheim." *Feuilles volantes*, supplement. No. 10 (1927): 369–70.

1928

Matisse, Henri. No. 8 (1928): 359.

Zervos, Christian. "Idéalisme et naturalisme dans la peinture moderne. – IV: Henri Matisse." No. 4 (1928): 158–63.

———. "Sculpture des peintres d'aujourd'hui." No. 7 (1928): 276–89.

1929

Duthuit, Georges. "Le fauvisme (I)." No. 5 (1929): 177–92.

———. "Le fauvisme (II)." No. 6 (1929): 258–68.

———. "Le fauvisme (III)." No. 10 (1929): 429–35.

Tériade, Émile. "L'actualité de Matisse." No. 7 (1929): 285–98.

———. "Documentaire sur la jeune peinture. – II: L'avènement classique du cubisme." No. 10 (1929): 447–55.

1930

"Les expositions (galerie Thannhauser)." No. 2 (1930): 107–8.

"Les expositions." No. 5 (1930): 276.

"Les expositions (galerie Flechtheim)." No. 7 (1930): 387.

Tériade, Émile. "Documentaire sur la jeune peinture. – IV: La réaction littéraire." No. 2 (1930): 69–84.

Zervos, Christian. "De l'importance de l'objet dans la peinture d'aujourd'hui." No. 3 (1930): 113–20.

1931

Duthuit, Georges. "Le fauvisme (fin)." No. 2 (1931): 78–82.

"Henri Matisse" special issue. Nos. 5–6 (1931): 229–316. [An English-language edition of this issue was also published.]

McBride, Henry. "Matisse in America." Nos. 5–6 (1931): 291–96.

Salles, Georges. "Henri Matisse." Nos. 5–6 (1931): 281–82.

Tériade, Émile. "Jeunesse!" No. 1 (1931): 10–25.

Zervos, Christian. "Notes sur la formation et le développement de l'œuvre de Henri Matisse." Nos. 5–6 (1931): 229–52.

1932

Sweeney, James Johnson. "La peinture française moderne à l'Institut des beaux-arts de Chicago." Nos. 8–10 (1932): 334–36.

1933

"Vente de la collection des Cahiers d'art." *Nos. 1–2 (1933).*

1935

Zervos, Christian, "Enquête." Nos. 1–4 (1935): 9–18.

1936

"Les ventes." Nos. 8–10 (1936): 276.

Tzara, Tristan. "À Henri-Matisse." "Dessins de Matisse" special issue. Nos. 3–5 (1936): 76.

Zervos, Christian. "Automatisme et espace illusoire." "Dessins de Matisse" special issue. Nos. 3–5 (1936): 69–75.

1937

Duthuit, Georges. "Henri Laurens. À propos de l'exposition Braque, Laurens, Matisse, Picasso à Oslo, Stockholm, Copenhague." Nos. 6–7 (1937): 222–30.

Halvorsen, M. Walther. "Exposition Braque, Laurens, Matisse à Oslo, Stockholm, Copenhague." Nos. 6–7 (1937): 221.

Matisse, Henri. Nos. 6–7 (1937): 215–18.

1939

Matisse, Henri. Nos. 1–4 (1939): 76–78.

Zervos, Christian. "Dessins récents de Henri-Matisse." Nos. 1–4 (1939): 5–24.

———. "2 décorations de Henri-Matisse: Réflexions sur l'art mural." Nos. 5–10, 1939: 165–78.

1940

Matisse, Henri. Nos. 3–4 (1940): 68–69.

1944

Matisse, Henri. 1940–44 issue (1944): 123–46.

1946

Char, René. *"Le requin et la mouette." 1945–46 issue (1946): 77.*

Matisse, Henri. 1945–46 issue (1946): 428.

Zervos, Christian. "Peines d'esprit et joies de Matisse." 1945–46 issue (1946): 162–96.

1949

Matisse, Henri. 1949, 352 (ill.).

Zervos, Christian. "À propos de l'exposition Matisse au musée d'Art moderne de Paris." No. 1 (1949): 159–70.

1950

Zervos, Christian. "Le musée d'Art moderne occidental de Moscou." No. 2 (1950): 342–43.

———. "À propos de l'exposition Matisse à la Maison de la pensée française." No. 2 (1950): 387–88.

1951

"Les expositions." 1951, 209.

1952

"À propos de l'exposition du Fauvisme au musée national d'Art moderne." No. 1 (1952): 83, 252.

"Faux tableaux de Matisse." No. 1 (1952): 94.

Matisse, Henri. No. 1 (1952): 55–66.

1953

"Numéro consacré au dessin contemporain." No. 2 (1953): 195 and cover.

1954

Zervos, Christian. "Jeune peinture et critique: À propos du Xe Salon de mai." No. 1 (1954): 5–6.

EXHIBITIONS (1926–41)

1926

Deux toiles de Henri Matisse. Galerie Paul Guillaume, Paris, October 8–14.

IVe Salon des Tuileries. Palais des Bois, Paris.

1927

A Retrospective Exhibition of Paintings by Henri-Matisse, the First Painting 1890, the Latest Painting 1926. Valentine Dudensing Gallery, New York, January 3–31, and The Arts Club of Chicago, February 17–27.

Exposition Henri Matisse: Dessins et lithographies. Galerie Bernheim-Jeune, Paris, January 24–February 4.

Exhibition of Works by Henri Matisse. Alex Reid & Lefevre, London, June.

1929

Exposition de peintures et dessins de Henri Matisse. Galerie Le Portique, Paris, November 7–25.

Henri-Matisse (1927–1929). Valentine Gallery, New York, December 9, 1929–January 4, 1930.

1930

Henri Matisse. Galerie Thannhauser, Berlin, February 15–March 20 or 22. Catalogue with preface by Hans Purrmann.

1931

Sculpture by Henri Matisse. Brummer Gallery, New York, January 5–February 7.

Henri-Matisse: Exposition organisée au profit de l'Orphelinat des arts. Galeries Georges Petit, Paris, June 16–July 25.

Henri Matisse. Kunsthalle, Basel, August 9–September 15.

Henri Matisse: Retrospective. Museum of Modern Art, New York, November 3–December 6.

1932

Henri Matisse: Exhibition of Fifty Drawings. Pierre Matisse Gallery, New York, November 22–December 17.

1934

Henri Matisse Paintings. Pierre Matisse Gallery, New York, January 23–February 24.

Les Fauves: L'atelier Gustave Moreau. Galerie des Beaux-Arts, Paris, November–December. Catalogue by Raymond Cogniat, preface by Louis Vauxcelles.

1936

Exposition d'œuvres récentes de Henri-Matisse. Galerie Paul Rosenberg, Paris, May 2–30.

Matisse: "Dance" and Other Works on the Theme by Matisse and Others. Pierre Matisse Gallery, New York, October 27–November 21.

1937

Œuvres récentes de Henri-Matisse. Galerie Paul Rosenberg, Paris, June 1–29.

Les Maîtres de l'art indépendant (1895–1937). Petit Palais, Paris, June 17–November 10. Catalogue with preface by Raymond Escholier.

Origines et développement de l'art international indépendant. Musée du Jeu de Paume, Paris, July 20–October 31.

1938

Matisse, Picasso, Braque, Laurens. Kunstnernes Hus, Oslo, January 10–February 2.

Henri Matisse: Paintings and Drawings of 1918 to 1938. Pierre Matisse Gallery, New York, November 15–December 10.

1941

Henri Matisse: Drawings. Pierre Matisse Gallery, New York, April 15–May 3.

Henri Matisse: Dessins à l'encre de chine, fusains, œuvres récentes. Galerie Louis Carré, Paris, November 10–30.

RECENT EXHIBITION CATALOGUES

Girard, Xavier, ed. *Matisse et Tahiti*. Cahiers Henri Matisse 1. Exh. cat. Galerie des Ponchettes, Nice. Nice: Musée Matisse, 1986.

Cowart, Jack, and Dominique Fourcade, eds. *Henri Matisse: The Early Years in Nice (1916–1930)*. Exh. cat. Washington: National Gallery of Art; New York: Abrams, 1986.

Autour d'un chef-d'œuvre de Matisse: Les trois versions de "La Danse Barnes" (1930–1933). Exh. cat. Musée d'Art Moderne, Paris. Paris: Paris-Musées; Réunion des Musées Nationaux, 1993.

Szymusiak, Dominique, ed. *Matisse et l'Océanie: Le voyage à Tahiti*. Exh. cat. Le Cateau-Cambrésis: Musée Matisse, 1998.

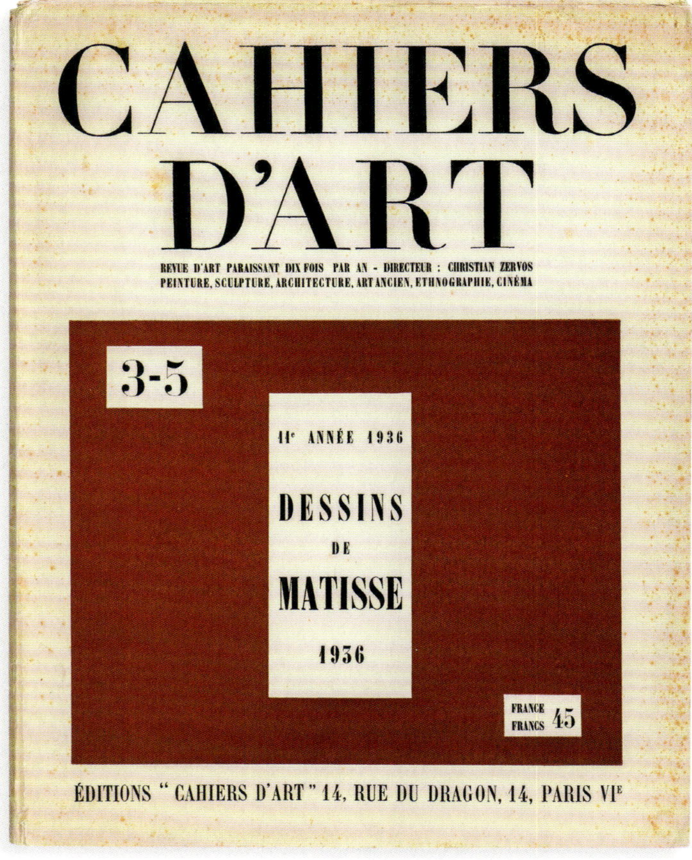

188 (fig.)
Cahiers d'art, 1936, nos. 3–5, front cover
Éditions Cahiers d'Art, Paris

A

B

C

D

E

F

G

H

I

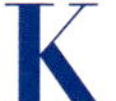

K

L

Front cover: Photo San Francisco Museum of Modern Art / Ben Blackwell
Back cover: Photo Morgan Library & Museum, New York / Wolfgang Wenneman

1 National Gallery of Art, Washington • **2** Photo Morgan Library & Museum, New York / Wolfgang Wenneman • **3** Photo Musée Matisse, Nice / François Fernandez • **4** Archives Henri Matisse • **5–9** Courtesy Éditions Cahiers d'Art, Paris 2022 • **10** Private collection • **11–17** Archives Henri Matisse • **18** Photo 2022, Digital image, Museum of Modern Art, New York / Scala, Florence • **19** © Estate Brassaï – RMN-Grand Palais / RMN-Grand Palais (Musée National Picasso–Paris) / Franck Raux • **20** Photo Art Institute of Chicago, dist. RMN-Grand Palais / image Art Institute of Chicago • **21** © Succession Picasso 2022 / Photo 2022, Digital image, Museum of Modern Art, New York / Scala, Florence • **22** © Succession Picasso 2022 / Photo RMN-Grand Palais (Musée National Picasso–Paris) / Mathieu Rabeau • **23** Photo Musée Matisse, Nice / François Fernandez • **24**, **25**, **27** © Succession Picasso 2022 / Photo RMN-Grand Palais (Musée National Picasso–Paris) / Adrien Didierjean • **26** Photo RMN-Grand Palais / Adrien Didierjean • **28**, **30**, **32** Photo Pierre and Tana Matisse Foundation / Christopher Burke Studios • **29**, **31** © Succession Picasso 2022 / Photo RMN-Grand Palais (Musée National Picasso–Paris) / Thierry Le Mage • **33** Photo Centre Pompidou, MNAM–CCI, dist. RMN-Grand Palais / Bertrand Prévost • **34** Photo Baltimore Museum of Art / Mitro Hood • **35** Photo William Rubin Collection • **36**, **37** Archives Henri Matisse • **38** © Hélène Adant – All rights reserved / Photo Centre Pompidou, MNAM–CCI Bibliothèque Kandinsky, dist. RMN-Grand Palais / Hélène Adant • **39**, **40** Courtesy Éditions Cahiers d'Art, Paris 2022 • **41** Photo Centre Pompidou, MNAM–CCI, dist. RMN-Grand Palais / Georges Meguerditchian • **42** Photo Museum of Fine Arts, Houston / Will Michels • **43** Photo 2022, Digital image, Museum of Modern Art, New York / Scala, Florence • **44** Photo Philadelphia Museum of Art • **45** Photo Centre Pompidou, MNAM–CCI Bibliothèque Kandinsky, dist. RMN-Grand Palais / Fonds Rosenberg • **46**, **47** Courtesy Éditions Cahiers d'Art, Paris 2022 • **48** Photo Albright-Knox Art Gallery, Buffalo / Tom Loonan and Brenda Bieger • **49**, **50** Photo 2022 Barnes Foundation • **51** Private collection • **52** Archives Henri Matisse • **53** © Agnes Mitchell Sattler / Photo Archives Henri Matisse • **54** © Varian Fry – By permission of James and Sylvia Fry / Photo Archives Henri Matisse • **55**, **58a**, **60**, **62a**, **64a** Courtesy Éditions Cahiers d'Art, Paris 2022 / Photo Musée d'Orsay, Paris / Sophie Crépy • **56**, **57**, **58b**, **59**, **61**, **62b**, **63**, **64b–d** Courtesy Éditions Cahiers d'Art, Paris 2022 • **65** Archives Henri Matisse • **66** Photo RMN-Grand Palais (musée de l'Orangerie) / Michel Urtado / Benoit Touchard • **67**, **68** Photo 2022, Digital image, Museum of Modern Art, New York / Scala, Florence • **69** Courtesy Éditions Cahiers d'Art, Paris 2022 • **70** Photo RMN-Grand Palais (musée de l'Orangerie) / Michel Urtado / Benoit Touchard • **71** Photo Musée Matisse, Nice / François Fernandez • **72** Photo 2022, Digital image, Museum of Modern Art, New York / Scala, Florence • **73** Photo Baltimore Museum of Art / Mitro Hood • **74**, **75** Photo Musée Matisse, Nice / François Fernandez • **76** Photo Metropolitan Museum of Art, dist. RMN-Grand Palais / image of the MMA • **77** Photo Musée Départemental Matisse, Le Cateau-Cambrésis • **78–80** Photo Musée Matisse, Nice / François Fernandez • **81** Photo Philadelphia Museum of Art • **82** Photo Hirshhorn Museum and Sculpture Garden, Washington / Lee Stalsworth • **83** Photo RMN-Grand Palais / Adrien Didierjean • **84** Photo Bridgeman Images • **85** David and Ezra Nahmad Collection • **86** Archives Henri Matisse • **87** Photo RMN-Grand Palais (Musée du Quai Branly – Jacques Chirac) / Daniel Arnaudet • **88** Photo Musée du Quai Branly – Jacques Chirac, dist. RMN-Grand Palais / Michel Urtado / Thierry Ollivier • **89** Photo Musée Matisse, Nice / François Fernandez • **90** Photo Metropolitan Museum of Art, dist. RMN-Grand Palais / image of the MMA • **91** Photo Pierre and Tana Matisse Foundation / Christopher Burke Studios • **92** Photo Musée Matisse, Nice / CICRP – Odile Guillon • **93–95**, **97**, **100** Photo Musée Matisse, Nice / François Fernandez • **96** Archives Henri Matisse • **98**, **99** Photo Metropolitan Museum of Art, dist. RMN-Grand Palais / image of the MMA • **101–3** Photo 2022, Barnes Foundation • **104** David and Ezra Nahmad Collection • **105** Photo Visko Hatfield • **106–8** Photo Pierre and Tana Matisse Foundation / Christopher Burke Studios • **109** Estate of Soichi Sunami / photo Archives Matisse • **110** Photo Baltimore Museum of Art / Mitro Hood • **111** Archives Henri Matisse • **112** Photo Centre Pompidou, MNAM–CCI, dist. RMN-Grand Palais / Philippe Migeat • **113**, **114** Photo Musée Départemental Matisse, Le Cateau-Cambrésis / Philip Bernard • **115** Photo Christie's Images Limited 2022 / Bridgeman Images • **116** Photo Musée Matisse, Nice / François Fernandez • **117** Allen Memorial Art Museum, Oberlin • **118** Photo Musée Matisse, Nice / François Fernandez • **119** Photo Musée Départemental Matisse, Le Cateau-Cambrésis / Philip Bernard • **120** Photo Statens Museum for Kunst, Copenhagen • **121** Photo courtesy Galerie de l'Institut, Paris / Thomas Hennocque • **122** David and Ezra Nahmad Collection • **123** Photo Centre Pompidou, MNAM–CCI, dist. RMN-Grand Palais / Philippe Migeat • **124** Photo Fondation Dina Vierny – Musée Maillol / Jean-Louis Losi © Adagp, Paris, 2022 • **125** Photo Hirshhorn Museum and Sculpture Garden / Lee Stalsworth • **126** Photo Paris Musées, Musée d'Art Moderne, dist. RMN-Grand Palais / image ville de Paris • **127** Photo Fondation Dina Vierny – Musée Maillol / Jean-Louis Losi © Adagp, Paris, 2022 • **128** Photo Musée Matisse, Nice / François Fernandez • **129** Photo Musée Départemental Matisse, Le Cateau-Cambrésis • **130** Photo Musée Matisse, Nice / François Fernandez • **131** David and Ezra Nahmad Collection • **132** Photo Musée Matisse, Nice / François Fernandez • **133** Photo Tate, London / Tate Images • **134** Photo Philadelphia Museum of Art • **135** Photo Saint Louis Art Museum, Saint Louis • **136** Photo Philadelphia Museum of Art • **137** Photo Pierre and Tana Matisse Foundation / Christopher Burke Studios • **138** Photo courtesy Galerie de l'Institut, Paris • **139** Photo Bridgeman Images • **140**, **141** Photo Pierre and Tana Matisse Foundation / Christopher Burke Studios • **142** Photo Baltimore Museum of Art / Mitro Hood • **143** Photo private collection, Houston / Paul Hester • **144** Photo President and Fellows of Harvard College, Cambridge • **145** Photo Musée Matisse, Nice / All rights reserved • **146** Photo 2022, Digital image, Museum of Modern Art, New York / Scala, Florence • **147** Photo private collection, courtesy Galerie Malingue, Paris • **148** Photo San Francisco Museum of Modern Art, San Francisco / Ben Blackwell • **149** Photo Metropolitan Museum of Art, dist. RMN-Grand Palais / image of the MMA • **150** Photo Albertina Museum, Vienna • **151** Photo Baltimore Museum of Art / Mitro Hood • **152** Photo Cleveland Museum of Art, Cleveland • **153** Photo Toledo Museum of Art • **154**, **155** Photo National Gallery of Art, Washington • **156** Photo Art Institute of Chicago, dist. RMN-Grand Palais / image Art Institute of Chicago • **157** Photo Bridgeman Images • **158**, **159** Photo Musée des Beaux-Arts, Lyon / Alain Basset • **160** Archives Henri Matisse • **161** Photo RMN-Grand Palais (Musée National Picasso–Paris) / Mathieu Rabeau • **162** Photo Boltin Picture Library / Bridgeman Images • **163–72**, **174–81** Archives Henri Matisse • **173** Photo 2022 Barnes Foundation • **182** © Fonds Pierre Boucher / Photo Musée Matisse, Nice / François Fernandez • **183** © Fonds Pierre Boucher / Photo Archives Henri Matisse • **184**, **185** © Estate Brassaï – RMN-Grand Palais / Photo Archives Henri Matisse • **186** © Varian Fry – By permission of James and Sylvia Fry / Photo Archives Henri Matisse • **187** © Fonds Pierre Boucher / Photo Archives Henri Matisse • **188** Courtesy Éditions Cahiers d'Art, Paris 2022 / Photo Musée d'Orsay, Paris / Sophie Crépy

Colophon

Musées d'Orsay et de l'Orangerie
Head of Publications
Marie-Caroline Dufayet

Editors
Colette Taylor-Jones
Jean-Benoit Ormal-Grenon
With the help of Thomas Bari Garnier

Translation from the French
Elizabeth Heard (É. de Chassey, A. Théry)
John Lee (A. Agret, C. Debray, C. Girardeau, C. Grammont, A. Jeudy, A. Marsal, L. Schlosser)

Copy-editing and Proofreading
Sarah Kane

Philadelphia Museum of Art
Interim Head of Publishing, Editorial
Kathleen Krattenmaker

Interim Head of Publishing, Production
Richard Bonk

Proofreading
Nadia Balzani Zamir, Katie Brennan, and Laura Lesswing

Réunion des musées nationaux– Grand Palais
Head of Publications
Sophie Laporte

Head of Book Department
Claire Bonnevie

Production Manager
Isabelle Loric, with the help of Marine Stephan and Manon Pellerano

Picture Research
Elise Vanhaecke

Design and Layout
Léo Grunstein

Color Separation
Les Artisans du Regard

The editors wish to address special thanks to Anne Théry of the Archives Henri Matisse for her invaluable help.

62, rue de Lille
75007 Paris
ISBN 978-2-35433-3454

2525 Pennsylvania Avenue
Philadelphia, PA 19130-2440
philamuseum.org

Published in association with
Yale University Press
302 Temple Street
P.O. Box 209040
New Haven, CT 06520-9040
yalebooks.com/art

Library of Congress Control Number: 2022940209
ISBN 978-0-87633-299-3

254–256, rue de Bercy
75577 Paris Cedex 12
ISBN 978-2-7118-7928-1
EK 197928

Printed and bound by Graphicom in Vicenza, Italy
Legal deposit: June 2022

Front cover:
The Conversation, 1938
Oil on canvas, 18 ⅜ × 21 ¾ in. (46.7 × 55.2 cm)
San Francisco Museum of Modern Art

Back cover:
Henri Matisse, Nice, April 1933.
Photograph by Wolfgang Vennemann
Pierre Matisse Gallery Archives, The Morgan Library & Museum, New York